D1598642

Spanish Women Writers

SPANISH WOMEN WRITERS

A Bio-Bibliographical Source Book

Edited by
LINDA GOULD LEVINE,
ELLEN ENGELSON MARSON,
and GLORIA FEIMAN WALDMAN

GREENWOOD PRESS
WESTPORT, CONNECTICUT
LONDON

Copyright Acknowledgments

The editors and publisher gratefully acknowledge the following sources for permission to reproduce copyrighted material:

Colección de Libros ''Álamo''

Ediciones Cátedra

Ediciones Hiperión

Editorial Ayuso

Promociones y Publicaciones Universitarias

Visor Libros

Library of Congress Cataloging-in-Publication Data

Spanish women writers : a bio-bibliographical source book / edited by
  Linda Gould Levine, Ellen Engelson Marson, and Gloria Feiman
  Waldman.
      p.   cm.
    Includes bibliographical references and indexes.
    ISBN 0–313–26823–1 (alk. paper)
    1. Spanish literature—Women authors—Biography.   2. Spanish
  literature—Women authors—Bibliography.   3. Spanish literature—Bio-
  bibliography.   I. Levine, Linda Gould.   II. Marson, Ellen
  Engelson.   III. Waldman, Gloria.
  PQ6055.S63   1993
  860.9'9287—dc20
  [B]   92–42432

British Library Cataloguing in Publication Data is available.

Library of Congress Catalog Card Number: 92–42432

ISBN: 0–313–26823–1

First published in 1993

Greenwood Press, 88 Post Road West, Westport, CT 06881
An imprint of Greenwood Publishing Group, Inc.

Printed in the United States of America

The paper used in this book complies with the
Permanent Paper Standard issued by the National
Information Standards Organization (Z39.48–1984).

10 9 8 7 6 5 4 3 2 1

For our parents, who raised their daughters to value
womanhood and to bequeath this legacy to future generations.

CONTENTS

Contents

PREFACE AND
ACKNOWLEDGMENTS

Often at the conclusion of a lengthy academic endeavor, there is the pressing need to re-create all the steps involved in the process. It is almost as if the sense of disbelief were so great that one needed to be convinced that the job had actually been done, that one's waking and sleeping hours would no longer be filled with and consumed by piles of manuscripts begging to be read and words requiring thoughtful assimilation. Certainly for us, the completion of this three-year project is an occasion that calls for a healthy dose of celebration, reflection, and acknowledgment, as well as a joyous and hearty cry of relief.

When Marilyn Brownstein of Greenwood Press first approached us in 1989 with the proposal to edit a biobibliographical source book on Spanish women writers, we were immediately tantalized by the idea. Committed to the field of feminist literary criticism and convinced of the need for a text that would elaborate upon Carolyn Galerstein's biobibliographical guide to women writers of Spain (Greenwood, 1986), we eagerly accepted the challenge and began the painstaking process of selecting the authors to include in our study. Galerstein's list of 289 writers, enhanced by Kathleen McNerney's addition of 129 non-Castilian authors, served as an invaluable beginning for our selection. The annotations provided by their contributors spoke to us of names both familiar and unknown, of texts canonized and forgotten; more important, theirs was a volume whose sum total of 468 authors was so great that it made our projected figure of fifty seem both limited and problematic. Had it not been for the skillful guidance of the many persons who responded to our call for papers and suggestions concerning the scope of the book, it would have been extremely difficult to proceed beyond the initial phase.

We have tried to provide a balance of many different aspects in our selection of the fifty writers. Among our concerns was the inclusion of authors from the fourteenth to the early twentieth centuries whose writings have received little acknowledgment and study among Hispanists. Also of importance was our desire to diffuse the works of Spain's young writers. Clearly, we could not neglect the best-known women writers, but where they have been revisited, the readings provided by our contributors—strongly oriented toward feminist theory—offer new insights into the complex relationships among gender, creativity, and social mores. We have also attempted to balance the various genres cultivated by our authors, assuring that poets, novelists, essayists, short story writers, and dramatists find representation in this volume. We regret the exclusion of many fine writers, in some cases simply because of lack of space and in others because their works were not sufficiently accessible.

In our desire to move beyond descriptive analyses of each author's biography, major themes, and critical reception, we have also focused on issues of thematic and stylistic subversion, revisions of the canon, the critique of patriarchy, and the struggle between tradition and personal and literary autonomy. In this sense, *Spanish Women Writers* extends the confines of a traditional source book and contributes to the growing and exciting field of feminist criticism in Spanish literature. Together with the selected bibliography we include at the end of the volume, the bibliographical data provided for each author is a veritable mine for those either unfamiliar with the literature or previously unsuccessful in tracking down original texts or critical studies. Our contributors have been assiduous and relentless in their search for modern editions, their scrutiny of different editions, their listings of complete works, and their compilation of papers presented at conferences. Original works are organized chronologically within genres, when applicable, including a section of translations if available; critical studies are listed alphabetically by author. Primary and secondary sources that became available after the preparation of this volume have been added to the appropriate bibliographies.

While conforming to Greenwood's standard of providing quotations in English, we have at times—especially with regard to poetry—deemed it necessary to include the original Spanish as well as the English translation. Unless otherwise indicated, all translations were provided by the contributors themselves. We have included two appendixes to highlight certain information contained in this volume: List of Authors by Date of Birth and Works Available in English Translation. A Title Index and a Subject Index have been included to provide easy access to major subjects, titles, and critics cited throughout the articles.

Finally, the words of gratitude and acknowledgment that are part of the obligatory rite of passage of any publication are truly a pleasure for us to express. The memory of Carolyn Galerstein is with us today as we salute her monumental efforts in her 1986 Greenwood volume. Without her detailed and thorough work and the concerted collaboration of editor Kathleen McNerney, this project would no doubt have taken more than three years to complete. The memory of Montserrat Roig and Maria Aurèlia Capmany, writers whose deaths occurred during the production of this volume, is also a continual presence in our lives as we bring forth a book that pays tribute to the cause they so passionately advocated.

We also acknowledge our colleagues whose assistance in providing information about possible authors to include in the volume, as well as suggestions concerning contributors and experts in the field, was invaluable throughout the editing of this volume. In particular, we wish to thank Maryellen Bieder, José Olivio Jiménez, Susan Kirkpatrick, Kathleen McNerney, Patricia O'Connor, Dolores Santos, Elizabeth Starčević, Marcia Welles, and Phyllis Zatlin. Without Diane Marting's guidance and fine-tuned experience in editing Greenwood's *Spanish American Women Writers* (1990), our attempts to organize such a vast array of material would have been all the more cumbersome. Our contributors have been an editor's dream. Their welcome words of support and encouragement, as well as their good humor in the face of frequent letters and phone calls, were truly extraordinary. We are also grateful to Marilyn Brownstein, Maureen Melino, and Sally Scott of Greenwood Press for their assistance and generous support throughout. The staffs of the Harry S. Sprague Library of Montclair State College (especially Kevin Prendergast), the New York Public Library, and the York College Library deserve special mention for their assistance in locating difficult texts and facilitating interlibrary loan orders, and for demonstrating good nature in the process.

Sabbaticals, the most joyful of paroles offered to college professors, were a veritable lifesaver for each of us. We acknowledge Montclair State College, John Jay College of Criminal Justice, and York College for contributing to the completion of this volume, and the Alumni Association, the Career Development Fund, and the College Research Committee of Montclair State College for financial support and released time for research.

Finally, each one of us has been attended by certain fairy godmothers and godfathers, and even little elves, during the completion of this book. All of them warrant individual expressions of love and gratitude.

From Linda:

My parents, Edna and Ben Gould, who years ago instilled in me a passion for literature and encouraged me to follow my dream of studying Spanish, and whose support and love, as well as vitality and pride in my accomplishments, will be with me always.

My dear friend and colleague, Alice Freed, whose wisdom, empathy, continual willingness to listen, concrete suggestions, and involvement in this project made her an invaluable sounding board who was treasured throughout.

My wonderful children, Daniel and Andrew, whose boisterous laughter brought me joy and respite from the job at hand, whose diligence in looking up words in the dictionary saved me time, whose understanding of my frequent absences from family outings lightened my spirit, and whose sensitivity toward issues of sexism brings me hope for the future.

And finally, my husband and special friend, Barry, who has endured with characteristic generosity and love the frenzy of yet another book in our household, and whose delightful sense of humor, infinite patience, unswerving loyalty, practical advice, and invaluable computer expertise saved me from being hopelessly overwhelmed and enabled me to laugh at myself and continue onward.

From Ellen:

My mother, Lillian, who understood my passion for Spanish before I did, and who encouraged and loved me all the way.

My father, Paul, with sadness, who died before we finished; to his belief in the strength of women and his extraordinary love and enthusiasm I dedicate these pages.

Aunt Marion and Evelyn, whose almost daily doses of support and love helped keep me going.

Uncle Bobbie, who would have been so proud.

My husband, Bernie—my staunchest supporter—for his humor, his selfless devotion to child care, his urgent trips home as computer technician, his encouraging belief in my talents, and his unconditional love for us all.

My son, Alexander, my beloved sounding board, who not only introduced me to the computer but then so generously relinquished his own to hasten the production of this volume.

My darling daughter, Eve, who never complained about her often-absent Mommy and who already delights me with signs of the creativity and energy of the writers included in our book.

From Gloria:

My beloved friend Elizabeth Starčević, for three years of debriefings.

My Dad, who eagerly awaits and appreciates every new publication of mine and especially this one, which he lived through telephonically from New York and Puerto Rico to Florida.

My brother, Jules, and sister, Rhonda, for their great advice and loving encouragement.

Jack Cooper, Bibliography Maven, without whom . . .

Bonnie Grossman, secretary extraordinaire, with magic hands and a generous heart.

Steven Beltzer, Petra Hall, Leonelli Rampersad, and Carmen Saavedra, guardian angels all.

My friends, colleagues, and relatives, who actively listened, commiserated, and spurred me on to complete this monumental undertaking.

INTRODUCTION
View from a Tightrope: Six Centuries of Spanish Women Writers

*Linda Gould Levine
and Ellen Engelson Marson*

The genesis of artistic creation is a concept that has long captivated the minds of humanists and scholars. Envisioned as a richly textured tapestry, its design is carefully woven with multiple threads of biography, language, literature, social environment, personal demons, national constructs, and political forces. Yet even when all the pieces are neatly ordered in this strange puzzle of life and artistry, the final composition is often more elusive than the individual parts. The mastery of the great writers seems to escape definition, resist synthesis, and mockingly cast back those clues we have worked so hard to assemble. Yet the need to explain and understand is ever compelling, even in the face of the irreducibility of the subject.

Confronted with the lives and works of fifty women writers from Spain spanning six centuries, our task of creating patterns from diversity, of seeking those common experiences that led from silence to expression and from submission to subversion is one that carries us on a journey through the regions of Spain. We move from the Castile of religious strife and dissension of the sixteenth and seventeenth centuries to the cause of Galician nationalism in the nineteenth and the suppression of Catalan culture in the twentieth. The contributors to this volume—aided by documents, letters, self-portraits, testimonies, and literary criticism—have constructed, reconstructed, rescued, and disinterred a lineage of female artistry consistently ignored or relegated to the margins, glorified only to be forgotten, critiqued and mythified in the annals of Spanish literature. As we begin our own reconstruction of their words, we acknowledge their Amazonian labor and bear tribute to their noble subjects of study.

The mark of economic privilege clearly characterizes the majority of the writers of this volume born prior to, and in some cases shortly after, the beginning of the twentieth century. A glance at the circumstances of their birth and family background speaks of a dynasty of voices joined together either by wealth or by a rich cultural heritage. They were the daughters of distinguished families of converts, royalty, aristocracy, Renaissance writers, Golden Age playwrights, physicians, attorneys, noted actors and directors, landowners, influential politicians, and the Catalan bourgeoisie; the external trappings of their lives indeed seem propitious for the cultivation of the arts. With family libraries at their disposal, private tutors in their homes, and the possibility of an unorthodox education that would free them from the obligatory world of needlepoint and social etiquette, it is not surprising that many among them—Josefa Amar y Borbón, Emilia Pardo Bazán, Rosario de Acuña, Margarita Nelken, Maria Aurèlia Capmany—would argue for women's right to education and the end to the tyranny of female socialization.

Others, however, most notably Julia Maura, who were brought up in the same environment of travel, literature, and private instruction, would deny their female characters the benefits of such a tutelage and would summon instead the "angel of the house" as a role model for women. And still others, such as Rosalía de Castro, deprived of a legitimate birth, would nonetheless be given a solid academic formation that would quickly dispel the equivocal relationship between patrimony and culture. Indeed, as one penetrates further into the lives of the fifty women of this volume, it becomes increasingly clear that notions of privilege cannot be condensed into simple truths. Behind the closed doors of nobility and abundance often lurks the somber figure of "starvation," as Carolyn Heilbrun forcefully argues in her essay on "privileged women" (63, 76). The deprivation of the soul longing for acknowledgment and self-esteem, so poignantly expressed in the biography of Lope de Vega's daughter, Sor Marcela; the starvation of the creative mind, ridiculed for its hunger and subject to abuse as in the case of Faustina Sáez de Melgar, daughter of an aristocrat; the frustration of the poetic muse unable to express itself on paper for want of time and space, as seen in Carolina Coronado's adolescence in a landowning family—these examples bespeak the chasms and caverns in the hollow notion of privilege and the inner battles of those seemingly endowed with wealth or title.

Others, of course, were not privy to such cultural entitlement. Rather, in the tradition of Cervantes, the Golden Age *genio lego* (lay genius), they recognized that we are all heirs and children of our own works. Centuries later, Caterina Albert, Mercè Rodoreda, and Teresa Pàmies come before us as examples of women who educated themselves or learned to write on their own, seeking empowerment in the concept of self and knowledge. The example of Pàmies is particularly compelling because she enjoyed the support of a working-class father committed to social justice and world change. This intense filial bond would prove, however, a source of conflict for Cecilia Böhl de Faber, caught between the creativity and autonomy of her mother and the aristocratic traditions of her father. Yet the very model of maternal intellectuality rejected by this author, the future Fernán Caballero, served as a source of inspiration for Montserrat Roig many decades later, thus revealing the individual permutations that each life history contains.

As we contemplate other writers, our musings become more tentative and speculative. We have yet to discover how María de Zayas acquired the culture and knowledge that propelled her to center stage in Spain's Golden Age, or the exact nature of the conditions that led to Ana Caro's role as the "Tenth Muse of Seville." Too many stories lie buried in documents that might further clarify the ability of the female spirit to transcend historical circumstance and leave its mark on the culture of the time. The testimonies in prose and poetry that do exist, however, speak of more than just childhood or the formative years; they also bear witness to the crucial passages in female reality when property rights are duly transferred from the father to the husband, when the dowry of female intellectuality and creativity is handed over to the new owner to be used or misused, treasured or pilfered, as circumstance dictates.

The refuge of the convent, a compelling choice for the early writers of this volume—Teresa de Cartagena, Saint Teresa, María de San José, and Sor Marcela—who realized within institutional walls a body of writing that derived its strength precisely from the personal interpretation of religion that each one envisioned, slowly disappears as a vital option for later writers. And there were those who, even as early as the seventeenth century, sought to express themselves from within other walls less isolated from society and often more formidable— the massive fortifications of patriarchy itself. The prominent writers María de Zayas and Ana Caro are notable in this regard. Literary history is yet to clarify the correlation between their critique of society and their disappearance from sight at midcentury.

Despite notable gaps in the reconstruction of some of our writers' lives, the bond between past and present looms before us as the model of seventeenth-century poet and playwright Leonor de la Cueva, who seemingly rejected marriage and the convent, is re-created in the figure of twentieth-century Rosa Montero, who vowed never to marry. For the vast majority of the writers in this volume, however, marriage was part of the obligatory rite of passage. In the best of instances, it involved choice and free will, as with Emilia Pardo Bazán and Carmen de Burgos; in the worst, enclosure and entrapment, as painfully experienced by Mercè Rodoreda, forced to marry her uncle at age twenty. From the critic's point of view, the professional profiles of our authors' husbands, as well as their histories of marital infidelity and separation, offer fertile terrain for a fascinating study of the relationship between female artistry and domestic discord in Spain.

If for the North American literary imagination the destructive yet symbiotic union between Zelda and Scott Fitzgerald has a certain fascination that conjures up images of male jealousy, gender stereotypes, madness, and insecurity, within the realm of Spanish letters the scenario unfolds somewhat differently. While the list of professions cultivated by the husbands is clearly impressive and includes such diverse livelihoods as writer, lawyer, journalist, diplomat, playwright, engineer, poet, editor, actor, painter, physician, architect, physicist, and university professor, the internal fusion of male drive and female creativity has often been an explosive one resulting in tension and estrangement.

Unwilling or unable to mold their literary genius or personal psychology to the dictates of husbands who were unfaithful, demanding, uncommunicative, or conventional in their gender expectations, many of our writers—Cecilia Böhl de Faber, Faustina Sáez de Melgar, María del Pilar Sinués, Emilia Pardo Bazán, Rosario de Acuña, María Martínez Sierra, Mercè Rodoreda, Carmen Laforet, Ana María Matute, Montserrat Roig, Paloma Pedrero—chose separation as a means of reclaiming their autonomy. While the case of Pardo Bazán is clearly the most dramatic of all and powerfully reveals the transformation of the once-supportive husband who folds under public pressure and demands unsuccessfully that his wife stop writing, other stories suggest similarly disturbing examples of male domination as well as still undeciphered domestic intrigues. Why did Rosalía de Castro instruct her daughter to burn her papers upon her death? Is there any relationship between this somber request for "texticide" and her husband's statement that Rosalía's personal life was not a matter of public concern? How can we make sense of the grievous case of Ana María Matute, who was unable to claim an international literary prize in the 1950s for want of authorization to leave the country from her writer-husband, from whom she was separated at the time (Pérez 8)? This disquieting example of the husband as metonym for the oppressive mechanism of the state blatantly highlights the insidious misuse and abuse of legislation in the private sphere that affected countless other women until the revision of the Civil Code following Franco's death in 1975.

The patterns of rupture and disruption thus appear glaringly clear, although recast in a different light when María del Pilar Sinués triumphantly drops her husband's last name upon their separation and Carmen de Burgos, in turn, drops her husband and leaves for Madrid with her baby in her arms. Yet there are other protagonists, most notably the younger writers of this volume (among them Soledad Puértolas), who emphasize the balance that children and husband provide and the support they derive from such caring. The specter of infant mortality, which also helped to configure domestic reality for many of our writers and which produced such anguish in the lives of nineteenth- and early-twentieth-century authors Arenal, Coronado, Sáez de Melgar, Castro, Pàmies, and Figuera, has clearly receded from prominence, creating the possibility of strong maternal links unthreatened by early death.

If medical advances have eased the traumas of premodern existence, however, the harsh reality of exile and civil war—not only inner and domestic but also geographical and political—has been a pressing force of disjunction in women's personal and professional lives. Much has been written about the tragic effects of Spain's Civil War on generations of male writers uprooted from their homeland. The early and brutal death of Federico García Lorca, the imprisonment of Miguel Hernández, the painful journey on foot of Antonio Machado and his mother to the French border, and the exile of Pedro Salinas, Jorge Guillén, Ramón Sender, Francisco Ayala, Rafael Alberti, and countless others have provided models of resistance and artistic freedom for those who have studied or experienced this painful period in Spanish history. Unfortunately, until recently the records have been notably silent with regard to the exile of the female protagonists of the times. Doubly exiled because of gender and politics, and subject to the mechanisms of both official censorship and male privilege—even in leftist circles—the odysseys of writers such as Margarita Nelken, Rosa Chacel, María Teresa León, Ernestina de Champourcin, Mercè Rodoreda, and Teresa Pàmies have been acknowledged only as brief footnotes in literary studies.

We know that the need to relocate in other countries not only ruptured family ties but also interrupted literary careers. Some were forced to take jobs as seamstresses and translators in order to survive or to provide income while their husbands continued their own literary endeavors. Exile also had the predictable effect of rendering invisible writers of note who had achieved literary stature prior to the war. Ana María Moix tells how she discovered, at age sixteen, Rosa Chacel's novel *Teresa* in the backroom of a Barcelona bookstore (Nichols 104). Soon after, she initiated a correspondence with the author, who was living in Brazil at the time, thus acknowledging her artistry two full decades before Chacel was awarded the National Prize for Letters in 1987.

The circumstances that provoked the massive exile of the 1930s provide testimony of a wave of political and ideological activism among women that also applies to many of the writers of this volume born prior to the twentieth century. From the religious activism of Saint Teresa and María de San José, who were respectively denounced and imprisoned in solitary confinement in the sixteenth century for their attempts to make the church more responsive to nuns, to the political and feminist activism of Lidia Falcón, who was incarcerated during the Franco regime, the lifelines among women stretch across the centuries, as each takes up the banner of freedom in her time and bequeaths it to her daughters and grandchildren centuries later.

Although barely mentioned in the annals of nineteenth-century history, where the struggle between liberals and conservatives occupies center stage in a national panorama of blighted attempts at change, the "herstory" of the authors included in this volume speaks with passion of the sustained efforts of so many women in so many different aspects of Spanish life: Arenal's monumental effort on behalf of prison reform and legal justice for women; Coronado's position as mentor for a generation of "lyrical sisters"; Sáez de Melgar's participation in the women's committee of the Spanish Abolitionist Society and the cause of female education, also advocated in the eighteenth century by Amar y Borbón, one of the main protagonists in the "woman question" debate; Castro's personal and political commitment to her Galician homeland; Pardo Bazán's directorship of the Biblioteca de la Mujer; Acuña's leading role in the freethinking movement; Gimeno de Flaquer's tireless efforts to promote women's issues in her own periodical.

This continual willingness to swim against the current not only defied gender stereotypes of woman's passive nature but also provided the basis for a political activism among women that would become even more pronounced in the twentieth century as the consolidation of leftist forces created a space for their intervention in national affairs. Among the major contributions to the Spanish Republic and the defeat of fascism, there are the active participation of María Martínez Sierra and Margarita Nelken in the Socialist Workers' Party and their election as delegates to the Spanish Parliament, the central role of María Teresa León in the Alliance of Antifascist Intellectuals, and the countless foreign travels and speeches of Teresa Pàmies to solicit support for the republic. Their labors, in many instances, were not only directed toward the general cause of freedom but also specifically oriented toward women's rights. Martínez Sierra's activism in the International Woman's Suffrage Alliance and Nelken's repeated and ultimately successful attempts to have divorce legalized in Spain, thus vindicating the earlier efforts on this behalf of Carmen de Burgos, are indicative of their broad-based political commitment that successfully incorporated issues of gender and democratic change.

For the radical feminists who follow in their footsteps in the second half of the twentieth century, heirs of the Francoist suppression of major legislative victories of the Republic—legalization of abortion, female suffrage, civil marriage, divorce, shared *patria potestad* (custody), female autonomy in administering property—the struggle for women's rights assumes a pressing urgency. Disenchanted with the Left's subordination of the feminist cause to other issues, activists such as Lidia Falcón conclude that the demand for sexual equality must be voiced from within a feminist political party. While Maria Aurèlia Capmany has sought to create parity between the feminist issue and the general issue of social revolution from within the rank and file of the Catalan Communist Party and her role as a committed Catalanist, Falcón has initiated the unprecedented move of creating the first feminist political party in Spain devoted to the struggle of women as a distinct social class. The road from convent to Parliament, from relegation to the kitchen to participation in a delegation, is a five-century-long stretch of land filled with mine fields and potholes. That the writers included in this volume have been able to skirt the fields of resistance and restructure the terrain constitutes a noble chapter in the history of international women's rights voiced from the cradle of machismo itself.

While all fifty writers profiled here obviously did not share the same passion for political and social activism, the extraordinary level of ideological commitment shown by some is joined by the equally noteworthy accomplishments of others. The list of honors and accolades is indeed impressive, and in many cases signals a first or landmark achievement for women in Spanish letters. If Teresa de Jesús was posthumously declared the first female Doctor of the Church, during their lifetimes Josefa Amar y Borbón was the first woman to be admitted to the prestigious Aragonese Economic Society, and Emilia Pardo Bazán was the first female professor of Romance languages at the University of Madrid. Rosario de Acuña was the first woman to lecture at the Ateneo of Madrid, Carmen de Burgos was the first female editor of a daily newspaper, and Margarita Nelken was the only woman to be elected to all three sessions of Parliament during the Republic.

Within the competitive world of letters, Mercè Rodoreda was the first and only woman to date to receive the most prestigious award granted to a Catalan writer, the Premi d'Honor de les Lletres Catalanes. Similarly, Carmen Laforet was the first winner of the well-known Nadal Prize for Literature, a recognition that served as an inspiration for other aspiring women writers, among them Carmen Martín Gaite, awarded such prestigious honors as the National Prize for Literature (1979), the Prince of Asturias Prize (1988), and the Castile and León Prize (1992). Finally, although she is not included in this volume, it is imperative to mention that in 1978 Carmen Conde was the first woman named to the Real Academia Española, thus further eroding the fortified chambers of the male canon.

One cannot underestimate the achievement of such honors from a culture that has historically ridiculed women for their intellectuality, cast ''thorns'' in their path instead of ''flowers'' (Pardo Bazán), prevented them from studying at the university without assuming male disguise, labeled them morally inferior and unfit for the public sphere, accused them of inauthenticity of authorship, slandered them for their dress and conduct, and schizophrenically converted them into ''romantically idealized'' muses and ''victimized outcast[s]'' (Eagleton 190). Their success, while clearly a tribute to personal strength of character as well as the individual circumstances of their lives, also results from the ''contradictory, fragmentary nature of patriarchal ideology,'' as Toril Moi persuasively argues in *Sexual/Textual Politics* (64). Indeed, one might argue that the strategies of subversion and survival utilized by Spanish women writers over the centuries were designed precisely to navigate the uneven waters of patriarchy and provide life jackets for those who ventured into the deceptively tranquil currents only to encounter torrential floods along the way. In some cases our authors, cast in the role of skillful military tacticians, devised strategies consisting of elaborate camouflages that enabled them to penetrate the ''enemy lines'' (Levine 97) and issue messages in prose and verse from the center of the war zone itself.

Conscious of the fact that their act of writing constituted an intrusion into the sealed-off territory of male authorship and paternity, many of the early writers— Leonor López de Córdova, Teresa de Cartagena, Saint Teresa, María de San José, Sor Marcela—sought to conceal their ''unfeminine'' assertiveness and pride beneath the mask of humility, ambivalent or stereotypical feminine wordings, proclamations of obedience, and invocations of higher authorities. Disguise and subterfuge had indeed become common and necessary practices for those who deviated from orthodoxy and convention, and writers of both sexes were acutely aware of the dangers of self-expression. It is not coincidental that Fernando de Rojas, the Renaissance writer and converted Jew who entered a literary arena dominated by Christians, felt compelled to hide his marginal identity in the subtly crafted acrostic verses that introduce *La Celestina*. Yet although he did not feel similarly compelled to mollify his harsh indictment of Spanish society within his text itself, this was not the case with our women writers of the same period and later centuries. Confronted with a limited choice of acceptable female expression, they engaged in calculated stylistic efforts designed to reduce the subversive content of their writings that posited women as protagonists in the domestic and historical intrigues of the fifteenth century, the recording of the first-generation Discalced Carmelite women's movement, the rendition of religious plays, and narratives depicting religious experience.

Their need to juggle all the elements of style, content, and identity acutely demonstrates the intense and problematic split between the literary woman's private and public lives, and the pressure to mold the inner self to the expectations of the public sphere. Indeed, the history of women's writing in Spain from the fourteenth century to the present time may be viewed as a constant tightrope act as each author tests the strength of the wire that extends from one gendered world to the other. Continual questions surge before us as we contemplate our writers cautiously balanced on this unstable perch. Did the fifteenth-century Teresa de Cartagena really believe that her "female intellect" was "weak," thus manifesting the "confession of inadequacy" that Patricia Spacks has observed in eighteenth-century female autobiographical writing (59)? Or was she merely assuaging or outwitting her male readers, who would be told that God had inspired her to write much as Judith had been inspired to pick up the sword? Is Cartagena's mixed message of frailty and strength re-created more than four centuries later when Caterina Albert, veiled behind the name Víctor Català, urges a delicate female public not to read her harsh writings at the same time that she provokes them to do just the opposite? Has the woman writer become a new Janus figure, with one face supporting gender conventions and the other undermining and subverting them in an uncomfortable coexistence mandated by society?

These thorny issues of double identity, undercover identity, and subterfuge that convert the process of writing into a complex literary espionage unfold in countless ways as our brilliant strategists transform men and masculine symbols into unwitting pawns of their newly forged plots. Recognizing the value of the male voice as a source of authority, they consciously appropriate that voice only to use it against patriarchy itself. Ana Caro's skillful creation of a male character who comically undermines the male-gendered world of values and codes in the seventeenth century is echoed anew more than two centuries later when Emilia Pardo Bazán, María Martínez Sierra, and Ana Diosdado similarly express their critique of patriarchy through characters whose values are antithetical to those of their own gender. Self-conscious parody and humor have given way to serious discourse, yet the mask persists and brings forth new renditions of searching identities in the twentieth century as the male narrator becomes the male transvestite in Ana Rossetti's prose and the virile facade conceals a female discourse in the writings of Rosa Chacel.

"No more masks! No more mythologies!" the poet Muriel Rukeyser proclaims (Howes and Bass 1). Through these words, Rukeyser expresses a cry for freedom from the subterfuge that has marked the life of the female creator and that is manifested still further in the Spanish peninsula as the male voice becomes male garb for a youthful Concepción Arenal desirous of university study, and the female name quietly cedes its place of authority to the male pseudonym. The camouflage is thus complete: assertiveness, body, and name have been neatly concealed in packages acceptable to the dominant culture. Yet the combined sense of entrapment and empowerment within a foreign form—that profound sense of literary schizophrenia—cannot be understated. Hispanists and critics of the Generation of 1898 have taken great care to document the process by which José Martínez Ruiz becomes Azorín, the diminutive philosopher who consciously molds his new identity to the small wonders of life he exalts. But the hermaphrodites of Spain, those who felt compelled to authorize their use of pen instead of distaff with a name of privilege, are still for the most part shrouded in mystery, equally camouflaged today as they were during their lifetimes.

Beyond the well-known case of Cecilia Böhl de Faber/Fernán Caballero and the lesser-known dichotomy of Caterina Albert/Víctor Català, little has been written about Carmen de Burgos's appropriation of "Colombine" as her nom de plume, Concepción Arenal's utilization of her ten-year-old son's name for one of her essays, Rosario de Acuña's convenient guise of Remigio Andrés Delafón for the opening of one of her plays, Caterina Albert's first experimentation with the pseudonym "Virgili Alacseal," María Teresa León's adolescent mask of León de Lara, and María Martínez Sierra's total fusion and confusion of self and husband through her "baptism" as Gregorio Martínez Sierra. Also warranting further study are the authors who do not appear in our volume but whose use of pseudonyms, both male and female, has been carefully documented by Janet Pérez and Kathleen McNerney—Mercedes Fórmica, Mercedes Ballesteros, and Maria Domènech, to mention just a few.

The careful recuperation of this forgotten chapter of Spanish literature by feminist scholars confirms and adds new insights to the theories of "anxiety of influence" and authorship discussed by Harold Bloom, Sandra Gilbert and Susan Gubar (*Madwoman* 46–53), and Edward Said. If male writers have often waged a battle with the phantoms of their literary past in order to forge a style of their own, at times engaging in acts of literary "parricide" (Said 209), the woman writer, instead, has been obliged to extinguish part of her very being. Much as Dr. Frankenstein and his monster, as well as Dr. Jeckyll and Mr. Hyde, are carefully separated in the confines of the split mind and body, some of our writers reveal a dissociation of such intensity between the author and the person that one can only speculate as to the inner battle that must have raged within them as they contemplated their transgression and deviation from acceptable gender expectations. Fernán would not receive letters about her work directed to Cecilia; Víctor only once spoke of herself in a literary vein as Caterina; Gregorio succumbed to silence rather than authorize her own voice as María; and Carolina Coronado, who did not resort at any time to a male pseudonym, nonetheless negated at the end of her life the feminist content of her writing and advocated, instead, a return to the very principles of femininity she had once passionately opposed.

This calculated assassination of the female self as a strategy for both literary and personal survival not only impinges on the authors' private worlds but also haunts their writings, creating countless ambiguities and mixed messages of failure and strength that bear witness to the difficulties of combining the private and the public in a literary work. If the pressures against writing and supporting a debt-ridden husband were indeed as great as some critics have suggested, it is not surprising that Fernán Caballero would attempt to atone for her double transgression by creating a character whose talent as a singer led to suffering and marital unhappiness. If Pardo Bazán chose creativity over marriage to an unsupportive husband, it is understandable that she would enact in her fiction a different scenario, in which her protagonist succumbs to her husband's demands and gives up her theatrical career. The female Janus is clearly a soul in conflict who simultaneously exacts commitment to truth and acquiescence to convention.

For the other writers who avoided or rejected humility and obedience, male narrator and male garb, male authority and male pseudonym, there were still further tactics of subversion and diversion that allowed them to voice the conflicting realities of their gendered condition. Evoking the classical model of the brave Penelope, María del Pilar Sinués assiduously assumed the pose of the avid sewer as she received visitors into her home, thus carefully obfuscating beneath the cozy demeanor of homespun domesticity her jarring image of novelist and essayist, creator of sensationalist themes and taboo topics. Yet the shadow of the other, the angel of discord, the creative woman entrapped behind the yellow wallpaper lurked within her own home and the private spheres of other nineteenth-century women writers. Unwilling or unable to mute their anger or frustration, their creative muses bring forth homicidal rebels who defile the system with one swift blow, as in Rosalía de Castro's poetry; dark doubles whose power exceeds that allotted to acquiescent females, as in Julia Maura's works; and countless negative female characters penned by Sinués and María Martínez Sierra, "whose power to do evil is a direct function of their powerlessness to do anything else" (Ostriker 322). The ultimate defeat of such negative stereotypes by virtuous heroines and the forces of good, while clearly predictable and reminiscent of the short stories of María de Zayas, is perhaps less significant than the fact that their authors subversively cast them to center stage to grant their readers, and perhaps themselves, a vicarious escape from the merciless dictates of social conventions.

If the nineteenth-century authors' defiance of convention was thus primarily expressed at the level of content and characterization, transgression is translated into more complex narrative strategies for such twentieth-century authors as

Gloria Fuertes, Ana María Matute, María Victoria Atencia, and Adelaida García Morales. Their selective use of such devices as double-voiced discourse, third-person allusions to famous women in art, unexpected poetic reversals, and intertextual references skillfully enables them to affirm or conceal their own voice within a chorus of other textual and artistic voices. While the need for elaborate constructions of literary survival has decreased consistently as we near the end of the twentieth century, women writers have yet to cast aside their disguises. The continued existence of stylistic and thematic camouflages provides a persuasive argument in the literary sphere for a further restructuring of patriarchy that may facilitate the harmonious coexistence of female and male without masks and without mythologies.

In part because of the conflictive nature of the relationship between the two sexes, women writers have successfully created a buffer zone and resting ground far from the dominant culture where they have replenished their resources and gathered strength for their impending endeavors. Sandra Gilbert and Susan Gubar have described in *No Man's Land* the process by which "literary matrilineage has been repeatedly erased, obscured and fragmented," making it difficult to establish a logical sense of "female genealogy" (199). Despite the many lagoons and hollow caverns that appear before us in Spanish women's writings, research by the contributors to this volume has unearthed a vast and detailed genealogy of roots and relationships between authors of different periods—a newly defined buffer zone inhabited by grandmothers, mothers, and daughters conscious of the need to recuperate a rich literary tradition.

The search for the consolidation of their own identity as women and writers is, in some sense, not very different from the quest in which selected male authors have engaged to vindicate voices from the past that also have "disappeared" from official Spanish literary histories. Much as Juan Goytisolo has rediscovered his dissidence in the pages of the forgotten José María Blanco White, and José Ángel Valente's poetry has been enriched through his careful study of the enigmatic verses of San Juan de la Cruz, the authors of this volume have re-created, resurrected, redefined, and found strength in a literary past filled with models of creativity and defiance. From the sixteenth-century María de San José, who wanted to record women's history, to the eighteenth-century Josefa Amar y Borbón, who commented on famous women authors of Spain's past, to the nineteenth-century Carolina Coronado, María del Pilar Sinués, Emilia Pardo Bazán, María Martínez Sierra, and Concepción Gimeno de Flaquer, who returned in their works to Spain's Golden Age and the compelling figures of Luisa Sigea, María de Zayas, and Saint Teresa—their words clearly tell us that they will not forget their ancestors.

Twentieth-century authors similarly continue this dialogue with the past as they seek bonds with women of their own regions or of oppressed national minorities as a means of elucidating a complex history in which gender, language, and ethnicity struggle and blend together to inform the process of creativity.

Marina Mayoral's critical works on sister Galicians Rosalía de Castro and Emilia Pardo Bazán, and Teresa Pàmies's passionate sense of identification with Rosalía de Castro despite regional and family differences bear witness to the diversity of their quests and their connection to the past. There is a comforting sense of literary justice in these encounters as well as the bequeathal of a female lineage to future generations as Margarita Nelken writes about Ana Caro and Pardo Bazán, and Maria Aurèlia Capmany, in turn, writes about Nelken. One wonders who will be the author of the twenty-first century who will capture the originality of Carmen Martín Gaite with the same respect, wit, and intelligence that she has brought forth in her essays on Saint Teresa, María de Zayas, Fernán Caballero, Rosalía de Castro, and Carmen Laforet, as well as on the subcultures that women inhabited in the eighteenth century and the post–Civil War era.

Clearly, literary "herstory" is in the making as the implicit bonds between women of different centuries are reproduced among contemporaries who acknowledge the role that other writers have had on their lives, and who support and encourage one another's creativity. Of foremost importance in this regard is the tremendous impact of the nineteenth-century periodicals founded by women, whether oriented toward a specific female readership or dedicated to publishing works by women or espousing feminist causes. The contribution of Sáez de Melgar's *La Violeta*, Pardo Bazán's *Nuevo Teatro Crítico*, and Gimeno de Flaquer's *El Album de la Mujer* as vehicles for serializing novels by women, providing literary outlets for unknown writers, and familiarizing the public with gender-related issues is of a magnitude we have yet to fully understand. In more recent times, Lidia Falcón has carefully described the monumental financial and political difficulties involved in sustaining a feminist publication; it is indeed telling that her first magazine, *Vindicación Feminista*, founded in 1976, closed down after three years of publication, but was resurrected in 1979 as *Poder y Libertad*. The intrusion onto male turf and the radical content of the aforementioned publications have undoubtedly varied tremendously and been affected by the ideology of each of their founders. Despite differences in content and format, the autonomy they have provided to women in the last two centuries and the opportunity they have made available for fostering female solidarity clearly warrant a separate chapter in the history of Spain's notable periodicals.

Also significant in this multifaceted bonding among women is the rarely discussed concept of female mentorship. The articles in this volume continually attest to the tribute women offer to those who have influenced them and given them the courage to write. Carolina Coronado's role as mentor to Concepción Gimeno de Flaquer, Carmen de Burgos's debt to Rosario de Acuña, María Teresa León's acknowledgment of Emilia Pardo Bazán, and Montserrat Roig's re-creation of both Maria Aurèlia Capmany and Mercè Rodoreda in her fiction provide a marked contrast to the "anxiety of influence" experienced by male writers (Bloom). Potential acts of literary matricide are replaced by support and solidarity as nineteenth- and twentieth-century women authors write prologues for one another's books, introduce each other at the Ateneo, and quote from one another's writings in their own body of work. These intense bonds of community and respect suggest a spirit of nurturing reminiscent of the "white ink" of creativity referred to by Hélène Cixous ("Medusa" 251) and that is bequeathed from mother to daughter and from sister to sister in this new genealogy forged by women.

The generation of such a consciousness has been strong enough to blur the face reflected in the looking glass of patriarchy. Instead of the countenance of the competitor and the voice of the rival that set woman against woman, as noted by Gilbert and Gubar (*Madwoman* 38), the image projected by our authors is that of the ally and companion. From the warm relationships of the sixteenth and seventeenth centuries between María de San José and Saint Teresa, and between Ana Caro and María de Zayas, to the nineteenth-century bonds between Carolina Coronado and Ángela Grassi, and between María Martínez Sierra and María de Maeztu, to the many twentieth-century friendships documented in this volume, the lifelines are there for the taking, assuring that few will sink in the uneven waters of patriarchy. The bonds of solidarity among women also extend beyond the Spanish peninsula as María Teresa León writes about the abuses suffered by Chinese women, Teresa Pàmies reflects on the fate of French women in refugee camps, and Lidia Falcón takes on the cause of female oppression worldwide in her magazine.

If our authors' support of one another seems for the most part uncontaminated by the murky concept of rivalry, their celebration of their creativity and status as writer has been fraught with a tension they have documented in their texts and attempted to exorcise from their souls. Nowhere has their consciousness of swimming against the current been more palpably expressed than in Rosalía de Castro's sarcastic and angry "Carta a Eduarda" (in *Las literatas*), in which she rails against a male economy that has marginalized creative women and converted them into perpetual outcasts scorned by society. Her implicit plea for recognition and respect is echoed throughout the nineteenth and twentieth centuries as Coronado and Gimeno de Flaquer defend woman's right to self-expression, Fuertes critiques a society that impedes women from writing, Atencia seeks to free the "voice" that "they" have "walled up," and Martín Gaite unabashedly posits herself as woman writer and protagonist of her award-winning *Cuarto de atrás*. The impact of Castro's words has not been lost upon Martín Gaite. By rejecting the status of manly woman, the "Eduarda" whom Castro satirically invents to reveal the confines of female creativity in patriarchy, Martín Gaite brings us back full circle to the notion of female literary autonomy devoid of subterfuge and camouflage.

The walls of patriarchal thought are crumbling, slowly eroded over time by the hit-and-run attacks launched against their massive structure by six centuries of writers whose works seek to revise and redefine the status of women in society as well as to offer new models and possibilities that extend far beyond the limits of acceptable behavior for their time and gender. Inserting themselves at the forefront of debates that have raged for centuries concerning woman's nature, questions of equality, sex-role stereotyping, and the search for identity and autonomy, our writers provide a consistently feminist critique of the institution of patriarchy and the psychological and physical violence it perpetrates against women. Their persuasive arguments serve to unravel basic premises of the "great" thinkers of the Western world whose writings have formed the basis of an evolving theory of phallologocentric ideology. They categorically reject Aristotle's postulation of woman as an "inferior" or "misbegotten male." They point to the fallacies in Thomas Aquinas's view of men as the sex endowed with "intellectual" prowess and women as the "helpers" needed for procreation. And they conflictively confront and accommodate in the space of their own lives Freud's dictate that "anatomy is destiny." The example of their writings and experiences forcefully argues that woman's identity is shaped less by nature than by nurture, and that the traditional process of socialization can be reversed and restructured.

From the seventeenth-century writings of María de Zayas, which denounce women's legacy of "distaff" and "sewing cushion," devoid of the "sword" and "books" that would radically reframe their existence and give them better arms for self-defense, to the twentieth-century fiction of Carme Riera, which portrays women struggling to redefine the construction of gender roles, their words seek to deconstruct the male/female binary opposition bequeathed by their Spanish patrimony. Main currents in feminist thought are echoed or anticipated by decades in such arguments brought forth by our writers as Arenal's premise that women are not weak, but weakened; Pardo Bazán's critique of woman's identity defined in terms of relationships; Martínez Sierra and Diosdado's respective observations that woman's concept of self is produced and exploited by male values and a capitalist consumer society; Fuertes's and Romero's belief that men deny women the right of self-expression; and Falcón's condemnation of reproduction as the material source of female oppression.

Although this critique of patriarchy finds similar expression in the writings of Mary Wollstonecraft, Simone de Beauvoir, Shulamith Firestone, and Julia Kristeva, the link between women of different nationalities should not be viewed merely in a global context of female victimization that obfuscates the particulars of Spanish reality. Writers as diverse as Saint Teresa, María de Zayas, Teresa Pàmies, Lidia Falcón, and Montserrat Roig introduce within their respective periods the radical concept that there is indeed a relationship between the devaluation or silencing of women and Spain's political status, and that the latter cannot be changed without a serious restructuring of gender roles. Alternatives to patriarchal patterns are amply provided in their works. As one examines the varied texts of the fifty authors included in this volume, one senses the formulation of a Spanish version of the *Vindication of the Rights of Women*, complete with specific suggestions for the transformation of patterns of male dominance. Their disavowal of patriarchy is, in some cases, not only visionary but also reminiscent of the platform for social reform advocated by Spain's Instituto de la Mujer and the Plan for Equal Opportunities for Women adopted by Felipe González's government in 1988.

  Decades before such ideas would be included in a national debate, these authors had the wisdom to foresee and the courage to express the need for such radical options as the abolition of the traditional double standard in morality and role assignments (Amar y Borbón, Martínez Sierra, Rodoreda, Pàmies, Romero, Moix), the elimination of sex-role stereotyping in domestic matters (Acuña, Martínez Sierra, Romero), and the end to the multiple types of violence daily inflicted upon women in the form of wife-beating (Zayas, Coronado, Puértolas), rape (Maura), homicide (Català), and incest (Rodoreda). They passionately argued for woman's access to education and learning (María de San José, Amar y Borbón, Arenal, Sáez de Melgar, Gimeno de Flaquer, de Burgos, Martín Gaite), and they further proposed implementation of equal pay and economic independence for women (Arenal, Martínez Sierra, Nelken), and equality before the law (Gimeno de Flaquer, Martínez Sierra, Nelken, Alós, Falcón). The institution of marriage as an impediment to female intellectual development, as well as a form of prostitution founded on the inferior status of women, did not escape their concerted critique (Pardo Bazán, de Burgos, Nelken, Rodoreda, Alós, Diosdado, Roig, Pedrero). Finally, cognizant of the fact that change cannot occur without a radical restructuring of language, they have rejected male discourse, male textual authority, male reasoning, and male bureaucratic formulas (Capmany, Fuertes, Falcón, Tusquets, Diosdado, Romero, Moix, García Morales, Montero, Pedrero).

  As they seek to break the asphyxiating cycles of entrapment, these extraordinary women subversively rewrite traditional gender roles and claim a space of difference and defiance from which to reconstruct a new female identity. Banished from the pages of Leonor de la Cueva is the stereotype of the beautiful woman, recast in her poetry as a homely type afflicted with mange and other defects. Absent is the lyrical image of woman as flower, a delicate incarnation of the world of natural beauty. Her petals are now withered and faded, replaced by the ''chained eagle'' and ''captured insect'' of Carolina Coronado's verses, which seek freedom from the enclosure of the male text and imagination. When the flower does bloom again, however, as in Angela Figuera's poetry, it is not due to patriarchal design but because woman herself does the flowering, a bold appropriation of the birthright of generative power reserved for the male creator. The solitary voice looking inward is enriched by a chorus of other voices and derives strength from the awareness of every woman's experience as part of a cycle that can be used not just to ensnare but also to raise the consciousness of those who subscribe to its rituals, as María Teresa León and Concha Alós suggest in their fiction.

  The leap out of the ''looking glass'' of the patriarchal plot (Gilbert and Gubar, *Madwoman*) is indeed an odyssey of great magnitude as, one by one, our authors further take on the mythologies that have formed and deformed their existence, and join hands with the sibyls and sirens awaiting them on the other shore. The angelic Beatrice cedes her place of honor to the rebellious muse in Rosalía de

Castro's fiction. An androgynous God is humanized and likened in his or her compassion to the woman poet in Fuertes's verses. Woman as Nature returns to the earth to make room for woman as inhabitant of the imaginary or the symbolic in Clara Janés's poetry. The sexually repressed Sleeping Beauty becomes a caffeine addict determined not to sleep for one hundred years in Ana María Moix's debunking of the fairy tale canon. The seduced virgin becomes the sensual seducer in Ana Rossetti's world. And the ultimate metamorphosis of male into female and female into male is dramatized in Paloma Pedrero's theater, in a fascinating rendition of role reversals and gender-constructed identities.

The silenced voice of the female body, entrapped in the complex religious and moral codes of centuries, seeks to break the walls of muteness and reclaim for itself a register and tonality unique to women. Rewriting patriarchy's practice, which alternately "denies woman access to her own pleasure," as Luce Irigaray has noted (qtd. in Moi 143), or grants her pleasure "provided it isn't discussed" (Kristeva 165–66), our authors posit the body as the site of "resistance to an authority already . . . in place" (Smith 1–2) and fill their pages with the longings and desires of their female protagonists. Accepting the fact that sexual desire can be "dangerous and destructive" (Kirkpatrick 289), writers such as Pardo Bazán and Carmen de Burgos nonetheless brandish the scarlet letter with conviction and explore their characters' need for sexual fulfillment. Sister writers from different centuries merge in a commonality of subversion, as María de Zayas's suggestion of lesbian attractions among her characters is re-created in the works of Tusquets, Moix, Riera, Rossetti, and Pedrero. The power of Lilith is thus slowly rescued from the confines of damnation as the walls of taboo that have suppressed female desire are deconstructed, also making room for the articulation of the hidden realms of menstruation, masturbation, bisexuality, homosexuality, and incestuous desire in the writings of Alós, Janés, Mayoral, Moix, Rossetti, and others.

Not all of the authors included here ventured to swim against the current in this way, nor were there accolades and honors for those who did. If Ana Rossetti was able to win the Sonrisa Vertical Prize for erotic writing in the 1990s, one of Paloma Pedrero's plays was labeled "obscene" in the 1980s, and Ana María Moix's daring fiction was subject to forty-five cuts by the censors in the 1970s. Decades and centuries earlier, the guardians of the faith were of course equally vigilant, branding María de Zayas's writing pornographic and scrutinizing Pardo Bazán's texts for signs of immorality. While in some sense the harshness of these attacks—particularly the most recent ones—attests to the subversive and threatening nature of the articulation of female desire, it is also a caveat against complacency and premature cries of victory. If woman's sexuality is no longer considered a "dark continent" or "holy vessel," it is nonetheless still subject to political and literary ploys, and applauded or condemned as suits the ideology or commercial market of the times.

Given this context, it is not surprising that the safer routes of limited maneuvering around mine fields of tradition, compliance, and plain old resignation were paths selected by still other writers whose search for autonomy was too circumscribed by society to allow radically iconoclastic gestures. Ana Caro had the daring to recast the Golden Age concept of honor from a female point of view, but she could not conceive of the abolition of the institution of marriage. Nineteenth-century authors struggled with the conflict between creativity and motherhood but nonetheless affirmed in most instances the importance of ''moral motherhood.'' Carmen Laforet posed the problem of the quest for female identity in artistic and psychological terms, but still offered marriage and church as ultimate solutions for the majority of her protagonists. Do these scenarios imply a lack of vision or an inability to dream about faraway utopias conceptualized by Charlotte Perkins Gilman, Monique Wittig, and others? Or, rather, do they reveal, as Nancy K. Miller has observed, the ''constraints the maxim places on rendering a female life in fiction'' (356)?

Certainly one notes, in some cases, the difficulties in silencing the male voice within and the subsequent assimilation to a male economy. Concepción Arenal's passionate work on behalf of social reform for women is suddenly belied by a gender bias that considers members of her sex unsuitable to be surgeons or judges. Rosa Chacel's discomfort at belonging to the old boy's network is obfuscated in favor of her denial of the significance of women's exclusion from the canon. Ernestina de Champourcin's stature in 1934 as one of the two women anthologized in Gerardo Diego's *Poesía española (Contemporáneos)* precludes her ability to cast herself center stage when lauded or to highlight her own literary techniques rather than those of her mentor, Juan Ramón Jiménez. And Soledad Puértolas's rejection of gender as a determining factor in human experience not only contradicts the scenarios of wife beating found in her own works but also ignores the fact that rape, limited abortion rights, job segregation, and lack of female representation in Parliament and the higher levels of government are pressing realities still operative in Spain in the 1990s.

In the face of these barriers to women's full participation in Spanish life and the ensuing lack of communication between the sexes documented in the fiction of Chacel, Capmany, Martín Gaite, Falcón, Tusquets, Moix, Montero, Pedrero, and countless others, our authors exercise the ultimate right of literary autonomy as a means of staking claim to a territory still not fully theirs. The diversity of their artistry, which makes full use of a wide range of literary techniques encompassing irony, mythical patterns, metafictional and metatheatrical structures, intellectual wordplay, hybrid forms of narrative and drama, re-creation of historical interludes, feminist and woman-centered revisions of biblical tales, and surrealistic images, attests to the impossibility of enclosing women's writings in neat categories of ''feminine'' sensitivity. Sophisticated literary experimentation and intellectual abstraction thus coexist with powerful attempts ''to redefine the social order'' (Tompkins xi), creating a multidimensional tapestry. Indeed, the versatility of our authors' texts and lives decries the continual attempts that have been made to mythify their persons and cast their complex realities into easily consumed stereotypical molds for the male palate.

Nowhere is this appropriation of the woman writer by the male establishment more palpable than in the case of Rosalía de Castro. Much as the Mexican culture has seized upon the conflicted figure of Rosario Castellanos and converted her into the "second Virgin of Guadalupe" (Poniatowska 46), Spanish critics have assiduously reshaped the contours of Castro's life and work. The Galician nationalist, feminist, and dissident critic of her times has been eradicated from their pages and cast as martyr into the sanctified slot of the eternal dichotomy—virgin/whore—with all its ensuing implications that have haunted women's lives. Only in recent times, with the surge of feminist and politically oriented literary criticism, has the demythification of her person begun along with the reconstruction of the complexities of her work.

Firmly nestled alongside the saints of the literary world—Santa Teresa as well as Rosalía de Castro—one finds an assortment of muses (María de Zayas, the "Tenth Muse of Madrid"; Ana Caro, the "Tenth Muse of Seville"), dutiful daughters (Sor Marcela), and paradigms of feminine sensitivity (Coronado) so dismembered and disfigured by their critics that they are barely recognizable to those familiar with their works and biographies. In a characteristically patriarchal fashion, when these authors are not canonized or placed on angelic pedestals, they are pitted against one another in the name of the highest accolade bestowed upon a woman writer: the comparison of her artistry to the force of the virile pen. If nineteenth-century authors Pardo Bazán, Acuña, and Gimeno de Flaquer were considered serious writers of intellect with a "manly" prose, they were obviously superior to the feminine (that is, frivolous) *literatas*. If Angela Figuera was praised as a great "poeta" of her time, the label was carefully designed to differentiate her verses from those of the majority of the "poetisas," a stereotype that Gloria Fuertes in particular categorically rejects in her poetry.

Together with these mythifications, skewed compliments reflecting patriarchal values, and subversive attempts to divide and conquer, one finds in the literary establishment an attitude toward women writers that suddenly reveals the other side in this dualistic conceptualization of female reality. The saint gives way to the whore, the delicate flower is replaced by the crude iconoclast whose ink sullies the purity of the sacred stereotype. Converted into targets of a deadly literary inquisition, our authors' dissidence, affirmation of self, critique of society, and attempts at proposing new models of being are branded unorthodox, irregular, scandalous, immodest, and inappropriate.

Certainly the guardians of the faith have not only turned their watchdogs against women writers daringly balanced on the tightrope. The testimonies and lives of Fernando de Rojas, Fernando Delicado, San Juan de la Cruz, José María Blanco White, Luis Cernuda, and Juan Goytisolo, among others, bear witness to the nullification process that Spaniards have perfected over the centuries. Yet as we ponder the disappearance of certain women writers from literary and historical accounts, the lost manuscripts that have not been located, the biographies yet to be written, the legacies still unacknowledged, the lives shrouded in mystery and ambiguity, the scarcity of critical studies, and the lack of recent editions, we become convinced that the Cerberuses of the literary canon clearly howl most ferociously at those who seek access to their female chambers.

Nonetheless, in the tradition of the sibyl who granted Aeneas safe keeping in his odyssey through the underworld, the fifty contributors to this volume offer those who follow their journey into both uncharted and familiar territory a thoughtful guide, a knowledge of intimate passageways, and a delightful sense of defiance and resistance toward the stumbling blocks they encounter in their path. Newly created Demeters, they rescue the forgotten or misinterpreted daughters of Spanish literary history from the grasps of those who have appropriated their writings for themselves. Utilizing a felicitous blend of contemporary feminist criticism and detailed attention to the particulars of the Spanish peninsula, their articles serve to fill in those hollow spaces and spacious caverns of women's writings as well as to erode structures massively fortified by years of tradition. With such an array of demythicizing strategies, it is not surprising that the newly created muses chuckle with laughter as they pick up the broken pieces of their age-old pedestals and head for home.

WORKS CITED

Bloom, Harold. *The Anxiety of Influence: A Theory of Poetry*. New York: Oxford UP, 1973.

Cixous, Hélène. "The Laugh of the Medusa." Trans. Keith Cohen and Paula Cohen. Marks and de Courtivron 245–64.

Eagleton, Terry. *Literary Theory: An Introduction*. Minneapolis: U of Minnesota P, 1983.

Gilbert, Sandra M., and Susan Gubar. *The Madwoman in the Attic: The Woman Writer and the Nineteenth-Century Literary Imagination*. New Haven: Yale UP, 1979.

———. *No Man's Land: The Place of the Woman Writer in the Twentieth Century*. Vol. I. *The War of the Worlds*. New Haven: Yale UP, 1988.

Heilbrun, Carolyn. "Non-Autobiographies of 'Privileged' Women: England and America." *Life/Lines: Theorizing Women's Autobiography*. Ed. Bella Brodzki and Celeste Schenck. Ithaca, NY: Cornell UP, 1988. 62–76.

Kirkpatrick, Susan. *Las Románticas: Women Writers and Subjectivity in Spain, 1835–1850*. Berkeley: U of California P, 1989.

Kristeva, Julia. "Oscillation Between Power and Denial." Interview with Xavière Gauthier. Trans. Marilyn A. August. Marks and de Courtivron 165–67.

Levine, Linda Gould. "Behind the 'Enemy Lines': Strategies for Interpreting *Las virtudes peligrosas* of Ana María Moix." *Nuevos y novísimos: Algunas perspectivas críticas sobre la narrativa española de los sesenta*. Ed. Ricardo Landeira and Luis González-del-Valle. Boulder, CO: Society of Spanish and Spanish-American Studies, 1987. 97–111.

Marks, Elaine, and Isabel de Courtivron, eds. *New French Feminism: An Anthology*. Amherst: U of Massachusetts P, 1980.

McNerney, Kathleen, ed. "Non-Castilian Materials." *Women Writers of Spain: An Annotated Bio-Bibliographical Guide*. Ed. Carolyn L. Galerstein. Westport, CT: Greenwood Press, 1986.

Miller, Nancy K. "Emphasis Added: Plot and Plausibilities in Women's Fiction." Showalter 339–60.

Moi, Toril. *Sexual/Textual Politics: Feminist Literary Theory*. London: Methuen, 1985.

Nichols, Geraldine C. *Escribir, espacio propio: Laforet, Matute, Moix, Tusquets, Riera y Roig por sí mismas*. Minneapolis: Institute for the Study of Ideologies and Literature, 1989.

Olsen, Tillie. *Silences*. New York: Delacorte Press, 1978.

Ostriker, Alicia. "The Thieves of Language: Women Poets and Revisionist Mythmaking." Showalter 314–38.

Pérez, Janet. *Contemporary Women Writers of Spain*. Boston: Twayne, 1988.

Poniatowska, Elena. *¡Ay vida, no me mereces!* Mexico City: Joaquín Mortiz, 1985.

Rukeyser, Muriel. "The Poem as Mask." *No More Masks!: An Anthology of Poems by Women*. Ed. Florence Howe and Ellen Bass. Garden City, NY: Anchor Press, 1973. 1.

Said, Edward. *Beginnings: Intention and Method*. New York: Basic Books, 1975.

Showalter, Elaine, ed. *The New Feminist Criticism: Essays on Women, Literature, and Theory*. New York: Pantheon Books, 1985.

Smith, Paul Julian. *The Body Hispanic: Gender and Sexuality in Spanish and Spanish American Literature*. Oxford: Clarendon Press, 1989.

Spacks, Patricia Meyer. *Imagining a Self*. Cambridge: Harvard UP, 1976.

Tompkins, Jane. *Sensational Designs: The Cultural World of American Fiction 1790–1860*. New York: Oxford UP, 1985.

Spanish
Women
Writers

ROSARIO DE ACUÑA (1851–1923)

María del Carmen Simón Palmer
Translated by Myrsa Landrón

BIOGRAPHY

Rosario de Acuña was born in Madrid in 1851 to Felipe de Acuña and Dolores Villanueva, both of aristocratic lineage. Her father could trace his descent from the family of Bishop Acuña, a prominent participant in the sixteenth-century insurrection of the Castilian communities. Acuña, who, like many of her colleagues, experienced severe vision problems in early childhood, was taken out of school by her parents and educated at home. She later recommended such unorthodox education, which set her apart from the majority of the women of her day, to her female readers. Trips abroad were an important part of this education. She spent some time in Rome with her uncle, the historian Antonio Benavides, while he served there as ambassador. In 1867 she visited the Paris Exposition as well as Portugal, the country that welcomed her years later. While her father was alive, she enjoyed his staunch support. In fact, so great was her identification with him that even after his death in 1883 she continued to dedicate many of her works to him and to address him in her prologues. His death affected her so deeply that she briefly stopped writing for *El Correo de la Moda*, a publication to which she had begun to contribute in 1882.

At age twenty-five, having already had her first play, *Rienzi el Tribuno* (1876; "Rienzi the Tribune"), performed, Acuña married Commander Rafael de la Iglesia. Everything seemed to point to an orderly existence similar to that of her female contemporaries, but shortly afterward she discovered her husband's infidelity. Instead of bearing up and suffering in silence, as advised by other nineteenth-century authors such as Pilar Sinués, she left him. Since she refers to herself as a widow in her will, written many years later, it is almost certain that her separation was never legalized. From the time she decided to go her own way, she began a vital and ideological evolution that led her to join the movement of the *Librepensadores* (Freethinkers), with whom she made close friends. Although until that time she had maintained in her writings that it was useless to fight for female emancipation, she now viewed this struggle as the only hope for young women.

On April 20, 1884, Acuña became the first woman to lecture at the Ateneo in Madrid. She read several poems, among them selections from *Sentir y pensar* (1884; "Feeling and Thinking"). The novelty of seeing a woman on the stage of an auditorium filled with elegantly dressed women was a great shock to the exclusively male membership, who viewed the occasion as a dangerous precedent. The dearth of enthusiasm was reflected in the press, which took note only of the large audience and the author's mastery in reciting. Even José Ortega Munilla, writing in *Los Lunes de El Imparcial* immediately following the lecture, remarked on the success of authors who can recite well even though their poetry may be mediocre and on the failure of others with talent who cannot read. Years later, Andrés Borrego commented that the conservative element of the Ateneo had to listen to her attacks upon the vices and weaknesses of the morality of the day (*Rosario de Acuña en la Escuela* 16).

Acuña's literary production encompasses diverse genres. She began her career with a poem dedicated to Queen Isabel II, "Un ramo de violetas" (1873; "A Bouquet of Violets"), and then focused on the theater. Her early plays belong to the school of José Echegaray, the dramatist of the moment, and manifest all the typical characteristics of the historical theater of the "new romanticism": grand heroes, unbridled passions, and terrible finales. As Acuña became more interested in content, she gradually moved into a more socially critical literature, influenced by authors such as Benito Pérez Galdós.

In early 1885 Acuña started writing for *Las Dominicales del Libre Pensamiento*, the publication of the Spanish freethinkers edited by Antonio Zozaya. It is important to remember that freethought maintains that reason is the only force that can guide human beings toward good; as such, it rejects morality that is based on religious ideas. Acuña's acute awareness of the low esteem in which this movement was held by the general public is revealed in a letter to a female friend in which she confesses: "for Spaniards, a freethinker is an evil person, a good-for-nothing, . . . at the very least, mentally unstable. And if she's a woman, she can't even be a good prostitute. The only thing that awaits the woman who seeks her own redemption is calvary, with all of its attendant consequences; and when she cares to seek the redemption of others, then it's truly a miracle that she reach the age of sixty alive."[1]

The freethinkers incorporated diverse associations, such as Freemasonry and spiritism. Acuña's desire to be independent of any particular movement put her at odds with female colleagues, especially with followers of spiritism, who were insistent that she join their sect. Of special interest is the insistence of Amalia Domingo Soler, the principal spiritual writer of the period, to link Acuña with this school.[2] In the correspondence between these two women, Acuña's anger is apparent as she declares herself a "freethinker, ever respectful of the thoughts of others, provided they flow along the great current of life guided by the unassailable motto: 'love thy neighbor' '' (Domingo 353–75).

Acuña gradually distanced herself from a Madrid society that in turn rejected this rather unorthodox writer. Her frequent rides to the country afforded her the opportunity to become familiar with rural life, about which she wrote extensively in later years. The novel idea of touring the mountainous zones of Asturias and Galicia for five months on horseback, accompanied only by a manservant, was not, however, problem free. Local authorities, who viewed Acuña's ecological motives with suspicion, detained her in the belief that she was a conspirator trying to encourage social uprisings.

Although freethinking and Freemasonry are not synonymous and should not be confused, the aspects they have in common—anticlericalism, the search for human progress, and the respect for freedom and tolerance—made it possible for many Freemasons to collaborate in the publications of freethinkers. Freemasonry, the secret society that aspired to universality, revealed its political character by fighting against the institutions hostile to progress and freedom. It included among its basic tenets freedom of conscience and freedom of thought, principles that Acuña supported. A year after Acuña began to write for *Las Dominicales*, the writer Mercedes Vargas de Chambó succeeded in persuading her to join the ranks of the Freemasons.

Acuña's initiation ceremony into the Constante Alona lodge of the Freemasons took place in Alicante on February 20, 1886, at which time she took the symbolic name of Hypatia, the eminent Roman scholar and philosopher of fourth-century Alexandria. She was received at the train station by a great number of admirers; committees of the Constante Alona and Alona Freemason lodges and the Echegaray Dramatic Society; and representatives of the local press. From that time on, although averse to social gatherings, Acuña attended functions held in the provinces by various lodges. Her friends Fernando Lozano, Ramón Chíes, José Francos Rodríguez, and the writer Angeles López de Ayala were also Freemasons. Acuña's passion for rural life led to long stays at her family's country house in Pinto. There she met with fellow Freemasons who included several members of the Lamo family. Regina Lamo—who mysteriously refers to herself as Acuña's "niece"—founded a publishing house to issue the work left by Acuña after her death.

Just as in the male sector of the freethinking movement there was diversity of opinion, there was a similar opposition in the female sector. Some writers, such as Acuña and Ángeles López de Ayala, defined themselves as apart from Catholicism, while others, such as Amalia Domingo Soler, leaned toward a spiritist philosophy. Amalia Domingo Soler, in the publication of her organization, *La Humanidad*, acknowledges Acuña as the ultimate authority among female freethinkers in the struggle between ignorance and superstition, and praises her effort to regenerate women.

In March 1888, Acuña gave two lectures, titled "Social Conventions" and the "Consequences of Female Degeneration," at the Fomento de las Artes in Madrid.[3] She expressed her hope that women would be regenerated and that in the future, Spanish women, by that time peers of rationalist men, would remember the women who had sacrificed themselves to achieve that status. In 1891, after the controversial opening of her play *El Padre Juan* ("Father John"), Acuña returned to her Pinto property, no doubt concerned about the great scandal she had created with that play. By that time, her writings were already known in France, Germany, Portugal, and Latin America. She traveled throughout the 1890s and for a time lived in Cueto, Santander, where she put into practice what she had been advocating in her books: the founding of an experimental poultry farm near her mother's house. In 1909 she went to live in Gijón, where she maintained contact with the Jovellanos lodge and participated in the inauguration of a nonsectarian graduate school funded by lodge affiliates. She continued to write for Latin American journals and for *Hojas Libres,* published in Paris and London by Luis Bonafoux, who, paradoxically, had ridiculed self-proclaimed freethinkers such as Carmen de Burgos for being scandalized by Parisian life.[4]

Nevertheless, her trust in Bonafoux led Acuña to share with him, in a letter dated November 1911, her indignation at the attack that two female North American students had apparently suffered while leaving the University of Barcelona. She did not hesitate to call the male Spanish students "a group of young effeminates." Bonafoux decided to publish this letter with the title "La Chanza de la Universidad" in *El Internacional*, the paper he was then running in Paris. It was also carried in Barcelona, in Lerroux's newspaper *El Progreso*, edited by Emiliano Iglesias. Students, angered by the letter, gathered at the Hospital Clínico in Barcelona and began their demonstrations with the cry "For the honor of our mothers, and to show that we are men, be there."

Once again, Acuña's pen caused a controversy that went beyond her own persona. Her letter gave rise to a scandal of such magnitude that it led to the closing of all Spanish universities. The enmities, more or less covert, from the "feminine element" were then manifested in allegations against her, published in the press by "ladies" of the aristocracy, the class to which Acuña belonged and from which she had broken, and also by Catholic women. Some students asked for the resignation of the chancellor of the University of Salamanca, Miguel de Unamuno, whom they believed to be in solidarity with the Acuña text. Unamuno wrote a letter to *La Correspondencia de España* stating that not only had he not read the text but that his two sons had protested against it. He denounced the strong political bent of the student movement in trying to create problems for the liberal government. Once again, Acuña's work was manipulated to serve shadowy interests. Although her friends tried to convince her that she was not in danger, her fear of imprisonment made her opt for self-exile in Portugal, where she remained for four years. In her absence, she was ruled in contempt of court and sentenced to prison. She had to wait until the count of Romanones came to power (1912) to obtain a pardon from the government.

Upon her return to Spain, Acuña retired to a large old house (now demolished) at the end of the beach at Gijón, close to El Cervigón cliff, where she lived a modest life. During these years, she became a respected and symbolic figure for the Asturian workers' movement, whose representatives used to visit her every May 1 after the usual festivities. Rosario de Acuña died from a brain clot on May 5, 1923, and in accordance with her wishes was buried in the civil cemetery. Her will, published by Luciano Castañón, is an accurate portrait of her personality:

> Let it be known, then, that I lived and died completely divorced from the Catholic Church (and from any other religious sect) and should I in my last moments of life state otherwise, let it be known that I, in good physical and mental health, object to such a statement, which should be considered as a product of my illness or as the product of a more or less hypocritical clerical intrigue while I lay dying. . . . I absolutely forbid any type of social funeral arrangement, any invitation, any obituary, announcement or notice, whether public or private, printed or oral that will let society know about my passing ("Aportación" 167–69)

In July 1923, the Workers' Athenaeum in Gijón presented Acuña's play *El Padre Juan* at the Robledo Theater, in tribute to her memory. It was not until 1933, however, after the coming of the Spanish Republic, that Madrid named a school unit after her at the request of Andrés Saborit, who published a volume entitled *Rosario de Acuña en la escuela*, in which authors such as J. Francos Rodríguez, Benito Pérez Galdós, Ramón de Campoamor, and Andrés Borrego praised Acuña to the residents of the Latina district, where the school is located.

MAJOR THEMES

Although history expressed in poetry was her earliest literary pursuit, Rosario de Acuña's later interests centered around the theater. Drama is the genre least cultivated by women writers, who seem daunted not only by the difficulties of staging a play but even more by the public's reaction. Acuña, however, became the first woman, after Gertrudis Gómez de Avellaneda, to premiere a play at the Teatro Español of Madrid, a feat repeated by Sofía Casanova quite a few years later. On March 13, 1913, a critic for *El Liberal*, one of the major dailies in Madrid, commented on the occasion of Casanova's opening: "Feminism has not succeeded in banishing certain concerns sufficiently so that a woman may decide to assume the arduous task of writing for the theater. Here in Spain regrettably we lag far behind the rest of Europe with regard to the feminist issue" (n. pag.).

Acuña's first play, *Rienzi el Tribuno*, opened at the Circo de Madrid on the evening of February 12, 1876, to a triumphant reception. It ran for eighteen consecutive evenings, and there was even a benefit gala in honor of the playwright. Her concern for social issues was already evident in the plot, which, set in the Palace of the Capitol in Rome, deals with the struggle between the people and the Roman nobility from 1347 to 1354. The protagonist is the last patrician,

Rienzi, who is fighting for the freedom and salvation of a decadent Rome and for the unification of Italy. Although he achieves the unity of the nobles for a fleeting moment, they eventually turn the people against their leader. The argument was not new; it could be found in Edward George Bulwer Lytton's novel, which had been translated into Spanish in 1843 by Antonio Ferrer del Río. Coincidentally, just a few days before Acuña's play opened, the first opera by Richard Wagner was presented in Madrid with Rienzi as its protagonist. During the 1870s there was a romantic renaissance on the Spanish stage and a return to period pieces. In *Rienzi*, the public is moved by the qualities of valor, honor, and loyalty. Like Avellaneda, Acuña received the highest accolade of her time when her talent was described as "virile." An explanation followed, however, to the effect that she was really very "feminine" because she had a fiancé and was soon to be married; furthermore, she devoted her life to her mother and her home.

In her second dramatic venture, Acuña decided for the first and only time to hide behind a pseudonym, Remigio Andrés Delafón, for the opening of her play *Amor a la Patria* (1877; "Love for the Fatherland") on November 27, 1878, in Zaragoza. She again addressed the patriotic theme in *Tribunales de venganza* (1880; "Tribunals of Vengeance"), a play about Valencian guilds in the sixteenth century that opened at the Teatro Español on April 6, 1880. Not until years later, following her ideological evolution, did Acuña turn to recent history for dramatic material, continuing her interest in patriotic themes. The tableau *La voz de la Patria* (1893; "The Voice of the Fatherland"), also staged at the Teatro Español, presented women's opposition to their men marching off to the war in Africa and the final triumph of patriotism.

Women, although seldom portrayed as protagonists, are always present in Acuña's works. In the early years of her writing career, she maintained the pointlessness of female emancipation since women first had to have been enslaved in order to be freed. To the contrary, Acuña believed that women did have certain powers, since judges, physicians, and other professionals were clearly influenced by their wives. Men, for their part, needed to be trained to see that education would not lead women astray ("Algo sobre la mujer" ["A Few Words About Women"], in her *Tiempo perdido* [1881; "Lost Time"]).

In 1882 Acuña began writing for *El Correo de la Moda*, the only women's magazine to which she contributed; it is in its pages that she began to make public some ideas that did not coincide with those of her colleagues. She divided her readers into three categories: the aristocrats who lived for the latest fashions from Paris and did not read, those who bought magazines because everyone did, and, finally, those with common sense who read them. It is for this last group that Acuña tried to be of some use with her advice about country life.

A regular contributor to several newspapers and magazines, Acuña later collected these writings in two volumes: *Tiempo perdido* and *La siesta. Colección de artículos* (1882; "The Nap. A Collection of Articles"). Her love of nature is evident in all her works, from her articles on country life to her stories for children, *Lecturas instructivas para los niños. Páginas de la naturaleza* (1888;

"Instructive Readings for Children. Pages from Nature"). In *Influencia de la vida del campo en la familia* (1882; "The Influence of Country Life on the Family") and *El lujo en los pueblos rurales* (1882; "Luxury in Rural Villages"), Acuña comes across as a pioneer in her support of life close to nature as opposed to life in the city, where family members barely have time to communicate with one another and an unhealthy environment contributes to nervous disorders that have a negative impact on communal life. However Acuña considered life in the village almost as detrimental; there the small population, obsessed with reproducing an urban model, fomented a "keep one step ahead of the Joneses" attitude. Acuña found the solution to the country/city dilemma in life in an isolated country house with enough land to provide sustenance and, if possible, a livelihood. With great vision, Acuña foresaw the day when access to the cities and to public utilities would afford city dwellers the opportunity to acquire houses close to nature for weekend sojourns. She viewed nature as an ideal medium for the informal education of women through observation.

Acuña dramatically transformed her perspective on women, coming to view them as slaves: "their *rational* and *intelligent* spirit is tainted by a disgusting slavery that turns them into instruments of co-opted pleasures, into *incubators* of men's children, or into decorative figures for devastating ambitions. . . . Yes! they are in need of liberation. . . . We have to awaken these sleeping servants who kiss the chains that bind them, be they pearls or glass beads or the false and empty adulation of being queen for a day" (Domingo 357–58). This strong passion for the emancipation of women, along with an insistence on clean living, led Acuña to offer detailed practical advice that was rather surprising for her times; she considered whiteness basic for walls and clothing, along with simple furniture, marble floors, and even rounded rooms to avoid the accumulation of dirt in the corners. Her radically advanced ideas heralded the equality of the sexes and the need for both men and women to learn domestic skills in light of women's impending freedom from enslavement.

Acuña also wrote about progress and freedom as an indissoluble unit. Her play *El Padre Juan* crystallizes her ideas about the society of her time and is one of the first examples of rural theater of a social nature. It is intended as propaganda for freethinking ideas and shows possible influences of Galdós's *Doña Perfecta*, which dramatically portrayed the intransigence of Catholic Church representatives toward all those harboring other ideas. In her clearly anticlerical play, Acuña develops the principle that progress implies the need to tear down, to leave the field free of rubble and mud before building anew. She presents the confrontation between believers (superstition) and freethinkers (reason) and between the country (healthy living) and the city (unconventionalism). The intentions of the leading couple, Ramón and Isabel, could not be more revolutionary. They want to have a civil marriage and buy the spring next to the holy shrine, which they intend to demolish. They plan to erect a spa, a hospital, a school, and an asylum in front of the monastery to underscore the monks' uselessness. The anticlerical spirit of this play is specifically grounded in the portrayal of the title character. Padre Juan, while appearing only as a shadow, has actually "fathered" the entire conflict; it is revealed that he is in fact Ramón's natural father and the instigator of his son's murder.

Unable to find a producer willing to stage such a controversial play, Acuña had to rent the Teatro de la Alhambra from Count Michelena and execute all the staging herself, including the costumes. The play was presented for the first and only time on April 3, 1891. The thorny nature of the subject and of the denouement unleashed a great scandal that led the governor to ban further performances. The two thousand copies of the printed edition sold out, as did the somewhat moderated second edition. The press split in two groups, with *El Globo* and *La Justicia* favorably disposed toward the play and the conservative newspapers pitiless in their attacks.

It would be logical to think that after this controversy Acuña would not be inclined to pursue another theatrical venture, but she came back to the Spanish theater two years later with the opening of her play *La voz de la Patria*. In addition, on her initiative, an Ateneo Familiar made up of a group of freethinkers including Acuña, Regina Lamo, and Anselmo Lamo was organized. In her final years Acuña returned to Gijón and devoted herself to writing articles of a social nature as a means of achieving her goal of regenerating Spain.

SURVEY OF CRITICISM

The work of a female author who evolves from the monarchic ideal to free thought finds different receptions according to the times and the ideological background of the critics. Initially Acuña received nothing but praise when her life and ideas resembled those of other women writers. Concepción Jimeno de Flaquer acclaimed the opening of Acuña's *Rienzi el Tribuno*. To her, it was proof that intelligence had no sex. "The spontaneous and enthusiastic applause echoed in our hearts because any glory won by a woman is a glory for the entire sex" (*La mujer española* 234).

The highest praise for a woman writer in Spain was that her talent was considered "virile." Even José Echegaray commented after attending one of Acuña's opening nights: "A marvel. She does not resemble any of the Sapphos of this century; she sounds the virile notes of patriotism, and yearns for freedom as if she were a colleague of Manuel Ruiz de Zorrilla. Not a very feminine woman" (qtd. in *Rosario de Acuña en la Escuela* 21–22).

Being from a distinguished family (she was actually a countess, although she never used her title), Acuña's heterodoxy seemed even more scandalous. She became the focus of attacks by the conservative press, and often served as a pretext for political skirmishes, which were of no interest to her. For example, she was unfairly assailed by the poet José Martí, who, believing her to be Cuban, wrote a long poem entitled "Rosario de Acuña" in which he accused her of being a traitor to her country. José Gutiérrez Abascal ("Kasabal") was equally as critical of Acuña and her ideology. He wrote: "Señora Acuña is viewed by men as a woman of letters, and as a freethinker by women, but she garners little sympathy from either group" (*El Salón de la Moda* n. pag.) The Augustinian priest Francisco Blanco García, in his book *Literatura española del siglo XIX*, arrived at the negative conclusion that her talent had "ended in a point, like the pyramids. . . . Yearning for immortality above all else, she aligned herself with the posturing heretics of *Las Dominicales*, she wrote incendiary poetry, and announced an ultrainane melodrama which eloquently reveals the unfortunate mental condition of its author" (429–30). While writing Acuña's biography in 1896, Ramón de la Huerta Posada expressed his hope that her talent and her erudition would "make her see the way of truth and . . . return . . . to the fold of the Catholic Church where the affection of men and women await her" (355–56).

Through all this, Acuña's female colleagues were noticeably silent before her controversial figure; only Angeles López de Ayala and Carmen de Burgos acknowledged her as a role model. Interestingly, Acuña had some male defenders. J. Francos Rodríguez called her a "great mystic" (*Rosario de Acuña* 26); Enrique D. Madrazo, a "martyr for freedom in the XIX century" (*Rosario de Acuña* 26–28); and Roberto Castrovido, "the Spanish writer who most resembled Teresa de Cepeda" (*Rosario de Acuña* 15–16). There is no denying that the steadfastness and integrity with which Acuña espoused her ideas until she died turned her into a model for struggling sectors of that time. Then, like other controversial writers, her work was completely forgotten. Whether or not one agrees with Rosario de Acuña, it cannot be denied that her accurate forecast for the future of society and her espousal of female emancipation are already in great part a reality.

NOTES

1. "Carta a una amiga sobre la senda a seguir para la emancipación," *El Gladiador*, 17 Mar. 1917: n. pag.

2. Amalia Domingo Soler was born in Seville in 1835 and died in Barcelona in 1912. For twenty years she directed *La Luz del Porvenir* and *Semanario Espiritista*, and she wrote numerous books. See María del Carmen Simón Palmer, *Escritoras españolas del siglo XIX* (Madrid: Castalia, 1991).

3. These lectures were published as supplements to *Las Domincales del Libre Pensamiento* 21 and 25 Apr. 1988.

4. Luis Bonafoux, virulently anticlerical, was a polemic writer and satirical journalist who lived in Puerto Rico for several years. He founded the weekly newspapers *El Español*, *El Intransigente*, and *El Progreso* and was a reporter for *El Globo* and *El Resumen*. In Paris he founded *La Campaña* and directed *El Internacional*.

BIBLIOGRAPHY

Works by Rosario de Acuña

Poetry

A S. M la Reina Doña Isabel II. Un ramo de violetas. Bayona: Imprenta de Lamaignère, 1873.

La vuelta de una golondrina. Madrid: Imprenta Sociedad Tipográfica, 1875.
Ecos del alma. Madrid: Imprenta A. Gómez Fuentenebro, 1876.
Morirse a tiempo. Zaragoza: Manuel Ventura, 1879. [Short poem in the style of Cam-
poamor]
Sentir y pensar. Madrid: Imprenta de Tello, 1884. [Comic poem]

Theater

Rienzi el Tribuno. Madrid: Imprenta José Rodríguez, 1876. [Tragedy in two acts and an
epilogue]
Amor a la Patria. Madrid: Imprenta José Rodríguez, 1877. [Verse tragedy in one act]
Tribunales de venganza. Madrid: Imprenta José Rodríguez, 1880. [Historical tragedy in
two acts and an epilogue]
El Padre Juan. Madrid: R. Velasco, 1891. [Prose play in three acts]
La voz de la Patria. Madrid: R. Velasco, 1893. [Verse drama in one act]
Rienzi el Tribuno. El Padre Juan. Ed. María del Carmen Simón Palmer. Madrid: Castalia,
1990.

Short Stories, Articles, and Lectures

Tiempo perdido (Cuentos y bocetos). Madrid: Imprenta de Manuel Minuesa de los Ríos,
1881.
Influencia de la vida del campo en la familia. Madrid: Tipografía Montegrifo, 1882.
El lujo en los pueblos rurales. Madrid: Tipografía Montegrifo, 1882.
La siesta. Colección de artículos. Madrid: G. Estrada, 1882.
Lecturas instructivas para los niños. Páginas de la naturaleza. La casa de muñecas.
Madrid: Ramón Angulo, 1888.
Lecturas instructivas para los niños. Páginas de la naturaleza. Certamen de insectos.
Madrid: Romero, 1888.
Cosas mías. Tortosa; Spain: Monclús, 1917.

Works about Rosario de Acuña

Blanco García, Francisco. *La literatura española del siglo XIX*. Vol. II. Madrid: Sáenz
Jubera Hermanos, 1910. 429–30.
Castañón, Luciano. ''Aportación a la biografía de Rosario de Acuña.'' *Boletín del Instituto
de Estudios Asturianos* 40 (1986): 151–71.
Criado y Domínguez, Juan Pedro. *Literatas españolas del siglo XIX. Apuntes biblio-
gráficos*. Madrid: Imprenta de Antonio Pérez Dubrull, 1889.
Domingo Soler, Amalia. *Sus más hermosos escritos*. Barcelona: Maucci, n.d.
Gutiérrez Abascal, José. *El Salón de la Moda* 28 Apr. 1884: n. pag.
Huerta Posada, Ramón de la. *El Album Ibero-Americano* (1896): 355–56.
Jimeno de Flaquer, María de la Concepción. *La mujer española*. Madrid: Imprenta Miguel
Guijarro, 1877.
Martí, José. *Obras completas*. Ed. and intro. Alberto Ghiraldo. Vol. I. Madrid: Atlántida,
n.d. 105–13.
Ortega Munilla, José. *Los Lunes de El Imparcial*. 20, 27 Apr. 1884: n. pag.
¿Quién fué Rosario de Acuña? Madrid: Artes Gráficas Municipales, 1933.
Rosario de Acuña en la Escuela. Madrid: De Lamo Hermanos, 1933. This volume was

coordinated by Andrés Saborit and includes personal comments on Rosario de Acuña by Nora Avanti, 9–10; Claudia García y Luz García, 10; Eladio de Lezama, 10; Luis de Zulueta, 11; Fernando Dicenta, 11; José Nakens, 11; Luis Bonafoux, 12; Odón de Buén, 12; Calixto Ballesteros, 12; Fernando Lozano, 12; Manuel Pedregal, 12; Ricardo León, 13; José Diéz Fernández, 13–14; Torralba Beci, 14; Virginia González, 15; Roberto Castrovido, 15–16; Benito Pérez Galdós, 16; Ramón de Campoamor, 16; Andrés Borrego, 16–17; Santos Agero, 17; Joaquín Dicenta, 18; Luis Huerta, 18–19; Regina Lamo O'Neill, 20; Amalia Domingo Soler, 20; Manuel Tamayo y Baus, 20–21; Emilio Gutiérrez Gamero, 21–22; Manuel de la Revilla, 22; Carmen de Burgos "Colombine," 23–24; Victoriano Tamayo, 24–25; Angeles López de Ayala, 25–26; J. Francos Rodríguez, 26; Augusto G. de Linares, 26; Enrique D. Madrazo, 26–28. The volume also includes a group of unpublished poems dedicated to Acuña on the occasion of an homage organized by her contemporaries in 1876.

Simón Palmer, María del Carmen. *Escritoras españolas del siglo XIX. Manual bio-bibliográfico*. Madrid: Castalia, 1991. 3–9.

———. *Rosario de Acuña. Teatro. Rienzi el Tribuno. El Padre Juan*. Madrid: Castalia, 1990.

Unamuno, Miguel de. "Carta." *La Correspondencia de España* 6 Dec. 1911: n. pag.

CATERINA ALBERT I PARADÍS ("VÍCTOR CATALÀ") (1869–1966)

Teresa M. Vilarós

BIOGRAPHY

Caterina Albert i Paradís was born on September 11, 1869, in the little seaside town of L'Escala, in northeast Catalonia. Her father, Lluís Albert i Paradeda, a well-known and respected lawyer of the village, was involved in local politics. Her mother, Dolors Paradís i Farrés, was an occasional writer and poet, although she never attempted to publish any of her work.

Caterina Albert spent her youth in her native village, leading a quiet family life. She attended school only occasionally due to a rebellious attitude. Basically an autodidact, she learned her impressive and extensive Catalan vocabulary mainly from her maternal grandmother and godmother, Caterina Farrés i Sureda, who was very influential during the first years of her life (Oller 14). After her father's death in 1890, her family continued to live in the house that belonged to Caterina's grandmother in L'Escala. Following Caterina Farrés's death in 1899, the family periodically spent time in Barcelona and finally moved there in 1904.

Attracted to painting and drawing from an early age, Albert was encouraged by her family in both endeavors. Around 1901 she gravitated toward writing, and it was not until 1955 that her pictorial work received some attention. Joaquim Folch i Camarassa promoted a limited, deluxe edition of a book with reproductions of Albert's paintings, drawings, and sculptures (1955; *Els dibuixos de Víctor Català*), one of the few public recognitions of her artistic talent. There was also an exhibition of her work at the Circle Artístic de Sant Lluc in Barcelona from December 1955 to January 1956. Her complete works (1972) include a selection of her artwork.

Soon after she began writing, Caterina Albert adopted the pseudonym ''Virgili

Alacseal.'' Under that name she submitted some of her literary work to the Jocs Florals, a highly respected Catalan literary competition. In 1898 she was awarded the Jocs Florals Prize of the city of Olot for the monologue *La infanticida* (''The Infanticide'') and the poem ''El llibre nou'' (''The New Book''). *La infanticida* was published in 1901, along with three other short pieces for the theater, in the volume *Quatre monòlegs* (''Four Monologues'') and signed ''Víctor Català.'' Despite Albert's success in publishing these early works, staging them was a different matter. *La infanticida* was not performed until 1967, a year after her death, along with the three short pieces *Les cartes* (''Letters''), *Verbagàlia* (''Talkativeness''), and *L'Alcavota* (''The Go-between''). These theater pieces were published in 1967 under the title *Teatre inèdit* (''Unpublished Theater''). *La infanticida* was performed in 1991 in Granollers (Barcelona Province), and in 1992 in Barcelona.

Also in 1901, before the publication of *Quatre monòlegs*, Albert published a collection of poems, *El cant dels messos* (''Song of the Months''), the first of her works signed as ''Víctor Català,'' the pen name she subsequently kept. She took this pseudonym from the main character of the novel she was in the process of writing, ''Càlzer d'amargor'' (''Bitter Chalice''). After her appropriation of the name, the novel remained unfinished, with only two chapters written. Considered by the critics to have been penned by a man, *El cant dels messos* was favorably reviewed in Barcelona by the poet Joan Maragall in 1901. Maragall, probably the most respected poet at the time, corresponded with Albert as ''Víctor Català.'' At that time she chose not to reveal her identity to him.

Albert's next literary work, *Drames rurals* (1902; *Dramas rurales. Novelas breves* 1921; ''Rural Dramas''), a collection of short stories, was also published under the signature ''Víctor Català''; again, it was received as the work of a man. Maragall's review, although basically positive, criticized Català's harsh style on the basis that it was somehow too *carregat* (loaded). His remarks inspired a new set of correspondence between them. In a letter dated December 1902, rumors already having spread as to the true identity of the author of *Drames rurals*, Caterina Albert finally revealed to him that she was a woman. In reply, Maragall expressed his highest regard for her and his respect for her not only as a woman but as a woman ''full of genius'' (Serrahima 230). He graciously accepted Albert's use of the male pen name, feeling that it was through ''Víctor Català'' that the writer could express herself: ''Above all, I want to thank you for the great consideration you show toward me, revealing yourself to me . . . through Víctor Català'' (230).

The year 1904 saw publication of *Ombrívoles* (''Shady Places''), a collection of short stories thematically similar to those in *Drames*. It was also the year Albert started writing her most celebrated work, the novel *Solitud* (1905; *Soledad* 1986; *Solitude* 1993) published in forty-six segments by the journal *Joventut*, whose editors had asked her to submit a novel in chapters. The first segment appeared in 1904 and the last in 1905. The immediate success of the novel was followed by excellent reviews. Albert was virtually unanimously acknowledged as one of the best writers in Catalan. In 1905, she published a new book of poems, *Llibre blanc* ("The White Book"), the only collection of poetry she wrote after *El cant dels messos*. Two years later she wrote *Caires vius* ("Lively Attitudes"), a collection of short stories. In 1909 she was awarded the prestigious Premi Fastenrath, and in 1917 she was designated president and keynote speaker of the 1917 Jocs Florals of the City of Barcelona, the most important of all Jocs. In 1920 Albert published *La mare-balena* (*La madre ballena* 1921; "Mother Whale"), another collection of short stories.

These collections prompted Albert to write her second and last novel, an experimental text titled *Un film (3.000 mètres)* ("A Film [3,000 Meters]"). Published by the periodical *Catalan* between 1918 and 1920, it was later issued in one volume by the publishing house Catalonia (1926). With *Un film*, Albert departed from the harsh writing with which she had been (and still is) strongly associated. *Un film* does not deal with the peasantry and lower-class atmosphere and characters presented in most of her earlier works. In spite of that, or perhaps because of that, the book was not favorably received. Critics and public alike seemed to expect Albert to return to the stern themes of her earlier works. After *Un film*, she never produced another experimental novel, but neither did she completely return to her former style and themes.

Why Albert's second novel was unsuccessful is still a subject of analysis. Maria Aurèlia Capmany addressed this issue in her article "Epíleg: els silencis de Caterina Albert." She refers to the new literary modes and attitudes introduced by the *noucentistes*, the twentieth-century Catalan literary generation that rejected many of the premises of their predecessors, whom they characterized as mere "narrators." Carles Riba—one of its leaders and husband of the much less known but excellent poet Clementina Arderiu—titled his classic article on the subject "Una generació sense novel.la?" Víctor Català was a member of the generation dismissed by Riba, and although not directly attacked by him, the literary reviews of *Un film* were consonant with the changing literary tastes.

The year 1928 saw publication of *Marines* ("Sea Sights"), a book with two short narratives that had already been published in the 1903 volume of the Jocs Florals. They were originally planned as chapters in a novel that was never finished. Nor did Caterina Albert write another novel that she had previously announced, "La tragèdia de Dama Nisa" ("The Tragedy of Lady Nisa"). The foreword, published in *Catalan* in 1926, and included in her complete works, was the only part of this novel to be written. Nor do we know if Albert wrote the following works, announced at different times: "La pena negra" ("Dark Pain"), "Vegetar" ("Vegetate"), "Intimitats" ("Intimacies"), and "Les sis nits de Llorenç Moré" ("The Six Nights of Llorenç Moré") (Alvarado, "Víctor Català" 24). The explanations for her silence—partially studied by Capmany—constitute an area of further investigation for modern scholars.

After the Spanish Civil War, Albert returned to L'Escala, where she stayed until her death in 1966. She led a quiet, private life, with occasional visits to Barcelona. During these years she published three volumes of short narratives:

Contrallums (1930; "Chiaroscuros"); *Vida mòlta* (1950; "Hard Life"); and *Jubileu* (1951; "Jubilation"). Several other short works were later collected in *Narracions disperses* ("Random Stories") and published in her *Obres completes* ("Complete Works"). She also wrote short, impressionistic articles on everyday life, collected in 1946 under the title *Mosaic* ("Mosaic"), as well as introductions, speeches, and several translations.

Albert, a very elusive woman, never revealed anything about her private life. Maurici Serrahima mentions how perplexed all those who interviewed her were. He says that when the writer and journalist Baltasar Porcel interviewed Albert shortly before her death, he could not even elicit which authors had interested her the most (234). Years before, the writer Josep Plà had had the same experience (Serrahima 235).

The stern themes of her writings, the use of a masculine pen name, and the fact that Albert, who never married, had always been very secretive have provoked "whispered speculation about Albert's homosexuality, the word lesbian never being mentioned" (Alvarado, "Víctor Català" 22-23). To know about her private life would require intensive study of her correspondence, unfortunately of very difficult access nowadays. The reserved and evasive Albert always wore the mask of Víctor Català in public because "Víctor Català" was a dual persona, a woman in man's drag, an androgynous voice consciously at work in Caterina Albert/Víctor Català's writings. Serrahima notes that only once—in the foreword of *Ombrívoles*—did she speak briefly about herself; even then, however, it was as a male writer (235).

Albert was not, however, a radical, political feminist. In the best-known of her speeches, her January 14, 1923, address given when she became a full member of the Real Academia de Bones Lletres de Barcelona, she speaks to the audience as Víctor Català, as her grammatical choice of the masculine form indicates: "[H]ow is it that such a House full of eminent scholars . . . could open its doors to a mere aficionado?" (*OC* 1658). Only once does she use a feminine adjective for herself—*sabedora* (wise) (*OC* 1658)—either a Freudian slip or a conscious recognition of self. The topic of her/his talk is not a feminist one. Close attention should be paid, however, to certain subversions in this address, such as her statement that we "all are what we are and not what we would like to be" (*OC* 1659). Why should we all be what we "are" when Albert herself is not? She is never "one," as Luce Irigaray proposes—neither exclusively Albert nor Català, neither Caterina nor Víctor. It is this resistance to being "one" that is central for a feminist reading of Albert/Català's works.

MAJOR THEMES

In her novel *Solitud*, as well as in her *Drames rurals* and many of her short stories, "Víctor Català" fuels a textual masquerade where violence is often perpetuated by women. A young woman kills her infant in *La infanticida*; in "La pua de rampí" ("The Prong of the Rake"), a short story included in the volume *Contrallums*, a young girl kills a man who attempted to rape her; a four-year-old girl kills her baby brother out of jealousy in "Temptació" ("Temptation"), one of the short stories of the collection *La mare-balena*.

The authorial persona submerges herself/himself in a thematic pool that centers on the most helpless and marginal human beings (Alvarado, "Víctor Català" 30). For Català/Albert, women form a sizable group in this marginal social spectrum. Their isolation is evident in most of her works, death or violence being the common narrative irruption in their lives.

There is no joy in Albert's writings, no relief, no hope. Love stories and happy endings are almost impossible in Català/Albert's somber world. "Carnestoltes" ("Carnival") in *Caires vius*, the only story that deals with the theme of love between women—a marquise and her chamber maid—begins on the symbolic day of the start of Carnival and ends with the death of the marquise. *Solitud*, Albert's most praised novel, shows the physical and psychic isolation and degradation of a young bride, Mila, taken by her husband to a remote hermitage in the mountains, where they are to be the churchkeepers. Her husband does not give Mila affection, love, or companionship. Gradually he becomes a gambler and a drunkard, spending less and less time with her. Most of the time, the young woman is left alone at the church, where she experiences extreme solitude with occasional visits from an old shepherd who becomes her only friend. Mila is sexually assaulted by a brutal and degrading trapper, who first murders the old shepherd. After the rape, Mila leaves her husband and walks away from the church and the mountain to an uncertain future.

La infanticida offers no solution to the mad young woman who kills her baby out of misery, desperation, and social pressure. As Català/Albert writes in her foreword to *Ombrívoles*: "Something inside prompts me to talk about somber sadnesses; it does not ask me to tell you about them, but to retell them to myself" (*OC* 559). We could add: to retell, or rather to rewrite as a "disguised male." This relocation is perhaps the only possibility for Albert, in search of a psychological understanding of the brutal "wants" of most of her male characters, and their consequences for women.

Josep Miquel Sobré emphasizes that Albert's descriptions deliberately avoid sentimentality. He suggests that "her stern themes and style may have prompted the early pen name she kept throughout her career" (13). Helena Alvarado has offered a similar explanation, and further reasons that Albert's desire to protect herself a priori from sexist criticism may have been another factor in her choice ("Víctor Català" 23). Núria Nardi has said that the fact that Albert belonged to the upper middle class was also a factor in choosing a male pseudonym, since for Albert the task of writing seems to have been a task for men, one that women could perform only through masquerade or dissimulation (Vilarós, Interview). For Vilarós, and without disregarding the former explanations, Albert's use of a masculine pen name should be viewed as an authorial androgynous personification within the text, a reading that can be supported by the ambiguous and rhetorical *prec*, her well-known foreword to *Drames rurals*.

This *prec* provides an authoritarian male warning addressed to women, specifically to urban women. It is supposedly written to warn "delicate," "fragile,"
and "graceful damsels" *not* to read this book because of its nature. Its themes,
we are told, are "rocks . . . with sharp and tough angles" that cannot please
them; its stories are "wild flowers . . . of such a strong odor that it makes people
not used to it turn their faces away" (*OC* 431). The kind of harsh writing Català/
Albert presents in *Drames rurals* belongs, supposedly, to a man's world. Since
almost all the short stories are written in a "naturalist" and realist style that
vividly shows the misery, pains, and violence of rural life, the author warns
women readers against pursuing such reading. Not everybody can enter this
territory, not even every man. *Drames rurals*, Víctor Català claims, "is not
intended for you [urban women] . . . it is intended for more courageous hands
and more masculine taste" (*OC* 431). The warning could not be more unequivocal. But it is a rhetorical warning, a request (*prec*) that unveils, by means of
its own rhetoric, precisely that which it claims to veil: the author's desire that
women—urban, fragile, and delicate women—in fact read the book. The ad-
monition that "this book is not intended for you women" underlines that it is
precisely to women that it is directed.

The introduction is an offering of wisdom and knowledge to women. Men
are absent from the scene; they are made explicit only on the margins, as outsiders
who already possess the "taste" that is needed to be able to read the book. The
disguised voice of the author presents the forbidden fruit to women, and only
to women, who "lack taste." It exhorts them not to read the text while it
simultaneously piques their curiosity and entices them to read. The *prec* in
Drames proposes a breaking of the rules, a subversive act of trespassing gender
distinctions. This call for disguise asks women readers to do what Caterina
Albert, the writer, had already done through her use of the name "Víctor Català":
to wear a masculine mask.

How conscious Caterina Albert's motives were in using her pen name as a
mask can be seen in her letter of December 1902 to Joan Maragall: "I take off
for the first time the mask of Víctor Català" (*OC* 1787). She does not really
pretend to be a man but, rather, as a woman, to pose as a man. Under the
"Català" signature, she bitterly complains to Maragall in January 1903: "Why
is it that, referring to *that thing* [her writing] that is almost a stranger to me,
there is a need to disclose the sex, the name, and all these particularities that
have nothing to do with the thing [writing] itself?" (*OC* 1787).

From 1902 on, Albert did not hide the fact that she was a woman. *Drames
rurals*, as well as her other works, include her picture and pen name together
in early editions, and both her name and her pseudonym are printed in later
editions. Joan Oller tells the readers of his biography of Albert that people in
the street would point at her and affectionately say, "There she goes *la* Víctor
Català" (33). Caterina Albert is openly *la* Víctor Català. The gender mark of
the feminine article is always present in the mind of the reader, who would never
mistake her for a man. Disguise and masquerade cannot be dismissed in the

course of reading her work. As Joan Maragall wrote, she reveals and writes herself through Víctor Català, and it is exactly that which she keeps asking her readers to consider in her *precs*, thus illustrating the complexity of the creative process for a woman writing in Spain during her lifetime.

SURVEY OF CRITICISM

The literary criticism on Víctor Català/Caterina Albert is difficult to obtain in the United States and has appeared mainly in various Catalan journals, some of them no longer in circulation. The common trend is to place Caterina Albert/ Víctor Català's literary work in a canonical and safe drawer under the label of "harsh" or "naturalistic." Maria Aurèlia Capmany and Helena Alvarado rightly and strongly disagree with this view, and point out the urgent necessity for a new reading of Català/Albert.

That Caterina Albert was alert and in tune with her time can be easily seen in her urban novel *Un film*, where she displays an innovative narrative structural technique that reveals a deep knowledge of film and theater. Maria Aurèlia Capmany attempts to clarify the poor reception accorded this work in her article "Epíleg: els silencis de Caterina Albert." Among other explanations, Capmany reasons that the novel's failure was related to the fact that experimental cinema was not well understood in Catalonia at that time. Films were simply considered popular entertainment. The possibility of developing literary narrative techniques based on cinematic ones, which is precisely what Albert was trying to do with her novel, was not considered a viable one. After *Un film*, Albert produced no other major work.

Capmany not only tries to relate Albert's disappointment with the reception of *Un film* to her subsequent literary silence, but she also notes that close attention should be paid to the interviews given by Albert, as well as to her forewords and *precs*, as they can shed light on the life and opinions of this very defensive and evasive writer. Of special interest is the rare interview given to Tomàs Garcès in 1926. There she offers her opinions on literary topics and tries to explain her position as a writer. Baltasar Porcel was less successful in his interview with her late in her life.

Of social importance is the impressionistic biography by Joan Oller, *Víctor Català*. Since Joan Oller is the son of Narcís Oller—who, with the poet Joan Maragall, was a central figure in Albert's life—his comments are representative of the kind of reception that Víctor Català experienced among the Catalan intelligentsia of the time, although they display a very paternalistic tone. The biography by Josep Miracle—like Oller's, but without its "glamour"—is a typical example of a traditional and patriarchal approach.

Also of great interest are the scholarly articles in the proceedings of the April 1992 meeting at L'Escala commemorating the twenty-fifth anniversary of Albert's death. Close attention should be paid to the new edition by Núria Nardi of the novel *Solitud*, as well as to the articles of Lola Badia, G. Bloomquist, and Jordi Castellanos on that novel. Nardi's article for the series on the history of Catalan literature published in the newspaper *Aviu* offers a broad historical approach rather than a critical view, since it was written as a more general essay.

Of major interest for feminist scholars are the essays by Alvarado, Nardi, and Otero in *Primeres jornades d'estudi*, to be published in 1993, as well as the introduction by Helena Alvarado to the edition of *La infanticida i altres contes*, and the epilogue by Maria Aurèlia Capmany to the *Obres completes*. Alvarado, Otero, and Capmany underline some of the important questions that any feminist study on Albert/Català should address today. Unfortunately, they are not extensive studies. A reinterpretation of the nature of Albert's work and her subversive approach to writing has only just begun.

BIBLIOGRAPHY

Works by Caterina Albert/Víctor Català

Obres completes de Víctor Català. 1948, 1951. Prologue. Manuel de Montoliu. Epilogue. Maria Aurèlia Capmany. Barcelona: Selecta, 1972. [Cited in text as *OC*, this volume includes letters, addresses, drawings, and miscellanea]

Novels

Solitud. 1905. Rpt. Barcelona: Edicions 62, 1990.
Un film (3.000 metres). Barcelona: Catalonia, 1926. Barcelona: Edicions 62, 1985.

Short Stories and Narratives

Drames rurals. 1904. Barcelona: Selecta, 1948. With *Caires vius*, Barcelona: Edicions 62, 1982.
Ombrívoles. Barcelona: n.p. 1904.
Caires vius. 1907. Intro. Carme Arnau. Barcelona: Edicions 62, 1982.
La mare-balena. Barcelona: n.p. 1920.
Marines. Barcelona: n.p. 1928. [Literary impressions on the sea]
Contrallums. Barcelona: n.p. 1930. [Short narratives on everyday life]
Vida mòlta. Barcelona: n.p. 1950. [Short narratives on everyday life]
Jubileu. Novíssims contes inèdits. Barcelona: Selecta, 1951.
Contes diversos. Ed. Núria Nardi. Barcelona: Laia, 1981.

Poetry

El cant dels messos. Barcelona: n.p. 1901.
Llibre blanc. Barcelona: L'il.lustació Catalana. 1905.

Theater

Quatre monòlegs. Barcelona: L'avenç, 1901.
Teatre inèdit. Barcelona: P. Camps Calmet, 1967.
La infanticida i altres textos. Intro. Helena Alvarado. Barcelona: La Sal, 1984.

Miscellaneous

Mosaic. Barcelona: Dalmau 1946. [Literary impressions on domestic themes]
Els dibuixos de Víctor Català. Intro. Josep María Folch i Torres. Barcelona: Josep Porter,
     1955. [Paintings, drawings and sculptures]

Film

Adversidad. Adaptation of *Solitud*. Dir. Miquel Iglésias. 1944. [Lost]
Idil.li xorc. Dir. Romà Guardiet. 1983.
Solitud. Dir. Romà Guardiet. With Omero Antonutti and Nuria Cano. Quasar, 1992.

Translations

Sankt Pons; Roman. Trans. unknown. Berlin: Fisher, 1909. [Trans. of short story "Sant
     Ponç"]
Dramas rurales. Novelas breves. Trans. Rafael Marquina. Madrid: Espasa-Calpe, 1921.
La madre ballena. Trans. Rafael Marquina. Madrid: La Pluma, 1921. [Trans. of *La
     mare-balena*]
Solitud. Roman. Trans. Marcel Robin. Paris: del Noël, 1938.
Soledad. Trans. Basilio Losada. Madrid: Alianza, 1986. [Trans. of *Solitud*]
Solitude. Trans. David H. Rosenthal. Columbia, LA: Reader's International, 1993.

Works about Caterina Albert

Albert, Lluís. "Aspectes inèdits de Víctor Català." *Primeres jornades d'estudi*. [Forth-
     coming]
Albó, Núria. "Victor Català. Vigencia i enigma." *Primeres jornades d'estudi*. [Forth-
     coming]
Alvarado, Helena. "La adaptació cinematogràfica de *Solitud*." *Cultura* (Jan. 1991): 47.
———. "Caterina Albert/Víctor Català: una autora motriu-matriu dins la literatura ca-
     talana de dones." *Literatura catalana de dones: una visió del món*. Barcelona:
     La Sal, 1988. 25–40.
———. "Caterina Albert/Víctor Català: la modernitat d'una clàssica de la literatura
     catalana." *Cultura* (Jan. 1991): 43–46.
———. "*Solitud*: Somnis, signes i símbols. Una mirada des de l'altre angle." *Primeres
     jornades d'estudi*. [Forthcoming]
———. "Víctor Català/Caterina Albert o l'apassionament per l'escriptura." *La infan-
     ticida i altres textos*. By Víctor Català. Barcelona: La Sal, 1984. 9–35.
Badia, Lola. " 'Solitud,' novel.la." *Quaderns crema* 8 (1984): 27–35.
Belliu, Carme, et al. "L'expressió plàstica en Caterina Albert." *Primeres jornades
     d'estudi*. [Forthcoming]
Bloomquist, G. "Notes per a una lectura de *Solitud*." *El marges* 3 (1975): 104–07.
Bofarull, Benjamí. "Víctor Català i Empúries." *Primeres jornades d'estudi*. [Forthcom-
     ing]
Capmany, Maria Aurèlia. "Epíleg: els silencis de Caterina Albert." *Obres completes de
     Víctor Català*. Barcelona: Selecta, 1972. 1851–68.
Castellanos, Jordi. "Dotze cartes de Víctor Català a Tomas Roig i Llop." *Els marges*
     11 (1977): 73–89.

————. " 'Solitud,' novel.la modernista." *Els Marges* 25 (1983): 45–70.

————. "Víctor Català i el modernisme." *Primeres jornades d'estudi.* [Forthcoming]

Centelles, Aurora. "*Solitud* de Víctor Català: Un texto para una experimentación comparatista." *Primeres jornades d'estudi.* [Forthcoming]

Cerdà, Mariàngela. "*Solitud*, més enllà de l'imaginari." *Primeres jornades d'estudi.* [Forthcoming]

Ciurana, Montserrat. "Aportacions a l'estudi de Víctor Català: unes cartes inèdites." Diss. U of Barcelona, 1972.

Esteban, Sofía, and Carme Mas. "Caterina Albert—Dolors Monserdà: 10 anys de relació epistolar." *Primeres jornades d'estudi.* [Forthcoming]

Ferrer, Araceli. "Presencia de naturalismo y modernismo en las narraciones de Víctor Català." Diss. U of Barcelona, 1973.

Font, Rosa. "*Un film (3.000 metres)*: La resposta de Víctor Català als models noucentistes." *Primeres jornades d'estudi.* [Forthcoming]

Garcès, Tomàs. "Conversa amb Víctor Català." *Revista de Catalunya* 3. 26 (1926): 126–34. Rpt. *Obres completes de Víctor Català.* Barcelona: Selecta, 1972. 1747–55.

Gómez, Laura. "El símil en *Solitud.* Estudio semántico." *Primeres jornades d'estudi.* [Forthcoming]

Julià, Lluïsa. "Les imatges de la dona en la narrativa de Víctor Català." *Primeres jornades d'estudi.* [Forthcoming]

Madrenas, Dolors, and Joan M. Ribera, "Modernisme i modernistes, (I): Perfil estètic de les idees de Víctor Català (II): Estudi contrastiu entre *Solitud* de V. Català i 'Sonata de primavera' de Ramón M. del Valle-Inclán." *Primeres jornades d'estudi.* [Forthcoming]

Miracle, Josep. *Caterina Albert i Paradís, "Víctor Català."* Barcelona: Dopesa, 1978.

Montoliu, Manuel de. "L'obra de Víctor Català." *Obres completes de Víctor Català.* Barcelona: Selecta, 1972. ix–lxiii.

Nardi, Núria. "A propòsit d'Encunys'." *Primeres jornades d'estudi.* [Forthcoming]

————. "Caterina Albert/Víctor Català" la llengua propia com a propia llengua." *Primeres jornades d'estudi.* [Forthcoming]

————. "Els *Drames rurals* de Víctor Català." Diss. Bellaterra, 1973.

————. "Entorn a la segona edició de les *Obres Completes* de Víctor Català." *El marges* 1 (1974): 108–10.

————. "Pròleg a Víctor Català." *Contes diversos.* Barcelona: Laia, 1981. 7–21.

————. "Víctor Català." *Història de la literatura catalana. Fascicles de L' Avui* 2. 59 (1990): 93–104. Rpt. *Història de la literatura catalana.* Barcelona: Edicions 62, 1991. 93–104.

————. "Víctor Català." Intro. to *Solitud.* Barcelona: Edicions 62, 1990. 5–30.

Oller i Rabassa, Joan. *Biografía de Víctor Català.* Barcelona: Dalmau, 1967.

Ortega, Juan José. "Posibles modelos estructurales en las secuencias narrativas de *Solitud* de Víctor Català." *Primeres jornades d'estudi.* [Forthcoming]

Otero, Mercè. " 'Com ho havia de fer tota soleta. . . .?' " *Primeres jornades d'estudi.* [Forthcoming]

Plà, Josep. "Caterina Albert-Víctor Català." *Retrats de passaport.* Barcelona: Destino, 1970. 448–55.

Porcel, Baltasar. "Víctor Català a contrallum." *Serra d'Or* (Oct. 1966): 769–73.

Primeres jornades d'estudi. Vida i obra de Caterina Albert i Paradís (Víctor Català). 1869–1966. Montserrat, Spain: Publicacions de l'Abadía, 1993.

Serrahima, Maurici. "Víctor Català." *Dotze mestres.* Barcelona: Destino, 1973. 227–50.

Sobré, Josep Miquel. "Víctor Català." *Women Writers of Spain. An Annotated Bio-Bibliographical Guide.* Carolyn L. Galerstein, ed. Westport, CT: Greenwood Press, 1986. 13–15.

Triadú, Joan. "Viatge de retorn a Víctor Català." *Serra d'Or* 120 (Sept. 1969): 51–53.

Tubert, Enric. "Víctor Català i les arts plastiques." *Primeres jornades d'estudi.* [Forthcoming]

Vidal Alcover, Jaume. "Víctor Català, autenticitat i eficàcia." *Serra d'Or* 120 (Sept. 1969): 57–59.

Vilarós, Teresa M. Interview with Núria Nardi. June 1992.

Yates, Alan. "*Solitud* i els *Drames rurals.*" *Serra d'Or* 120 (Sept. 1969): 54–56.

CONCHA ALÓS
(b. 1922)

Ada Ortúzar-Young

BIOGRAPHY

María Concepción ("Concha") Alós Domingo was born in Valencia into a working-class family in 1922. When she was three months old, her adoptive father, Francisco Alós Tárrega, and her mother, Pilar Domingo Pardo, took her to Castellón de la Plana, where she spent her childhood and adolescence (Ortúzar-Young, Letter). An only child, solitary and shy, Alós spent most of her time at home playing with dolls in a world where she became the protagonist of imaginary stories and movies. She liked to draw and was an insatiable reader. Her mother had very traditional ideas about her upbringing. In fact, Alós believes that her mother's ambition was for her to become a good dressmaker (Ortúzar-Young, Letter). One of her teachers convinced her parents to send her to a private school for girls. Unfortunately for Alós, this school was directed by a woman whose curriculum centered on praying, sewing, needlework, and singing. Consequently, Alós was inadequately prepared for high school and failed her first entrance exam. When she was finally admitted, she found in high school the freedom that she had not been able to enjoy until then.

During the Spanish Civil War, which broke out when Alós was thirteen, heavy Nationalist air attacks were launched against the city of Castellón. As a result of the war and the difficulties her family suffered, Alós's mother began to experience mental disorders that were aggravated when her father, a Republican sympathizer, decided to take the family to Lorca (Murcia) before the Francoist armies took Castellón. In Lorca the family endured hunger and further difficulties. In 1939, after the war was over, the family returned to Castellón. Their house had been destroyed, and they were forced to live with relatives.

As with many of her contemporaries, the precarious conditions that prevailed after the Civil War left a lasting impression on Alós. These events haunted her for many years and would provide the setting for two of her novels, *El caballo rojo* (1966; "The Red Horse Inn") and *La madama* (1969; "The Madam"). Shortly after the Civil War, Alós's mother died and her father remarried. Her relations with her stepmother were not very cordial, and Alós, feeling hopeless, dreamed of escape.

In 1943 Alós married the journalist Eliseo Feijóo. Shortly afterward, he was transferred to Palma de Mallorca, where, away from friends and relatives, she felt displaced. Years later, Alós indicated in a letter that her husband was "not a bad man, but . . . not very communicative" (Ortúzar-Young). As a means of dealing with her isolation, she decided to enroll in the local teachers college, an experience that changed the course of her life. There she found an excellent, well-prepared faculty who espoused liberal ideas. She studied and wrote with enthusiasm, and contributed to local newspapers and magazines. In 1953 she completed her training and began her teaching career in Santa María and C'an Picafort, two small towns in the northeast part of Mallorca, which she describes in *Las hogueras* (1964; "The Bonfires"). Alós wrote short stories and was a finalist for the Sésamo Literary Prize for her story "El agosto" ("August"). She wrote a novel, "Cuando la luna cambia de color" ("When the Moon Changes Color"), which, although never published, was selected as a finalist for the Ciudad de Palma Prize. These early successes encouraged her to continue writing.

In 1959 Alós separated from her husband and moved to Barcelona, where she earned a living taking care of children and giving private lessons; in her free time she continued to write. She lived in the Pensión María Luisa, a boarding-house in the Ramblas section of the city. This house provided the setting and numerous characters for her first Barcelona novel, *Los enanos* (1962; "The Dwarfs"). In 1962 Alós entered this work in a Plaza y Janés competition, Selecciones de Lengua Española. Some time later, the publishing house's director, Tomás Salvador, told her that he did not intend to publish the novel because he considered that it had "socialist tendencies" (Ortúzar-Young). She then entered it in the competition for the prestigious Planeta Prize, which she won. Salvador, who was present at the awards banquet, created a literary scandal when he claimed to have a contract to publish the novel. Eventually, *Los enanos* was published by Plaza y Janés and was well received. In 1964 Alós was again awarded the Planeta Prize for her second novel, *Las hogueras*. This series of successes marked the beginning of a fruitful career. Alós lectures frequently and contributes to newspapers and magazines, and she has also written scripts for Spanish television. She is a prolific writer and one of Spain's most prominent feminist authors. Today Alós resides in Barcelona and lives exclusively on the income from her writing.

MAJOR THEMES

When asked about the themes that most attract her, Alós replied that her main concern is to give expression to her world (Rodríguez 106). Like many of her contemporaries, she draws heavily upon her social surroundings. Throughout her work, which spans the period from 1938 to the present, the reader finds numerous autobiographical references. In every one of her novels there is a character who corresponds to some aspects of the author's life or intellectual concerns.

Alós has dedicated her career as a novelist almost exclusively to a single theme: the portrayal of women in contemporary Spain, the limitations placed on them by society, and their reactions to their social and cultural surroundings. Seven of her nine major works focus on women. The other two, her Civil War novels, *El caballo rojo* and *La madama*, present important female characters and reflect the same concerns seen throughout the rest of her writings. With the exception of Clemente in *La madama*, male figures remain in the background and are poorly developed. As is often the case in traditional women's fiction, Alós has a preference for enclosed spaces and for those aspects of life that reflect the collective female experience. Although her novels portray women of all ages and social conditions, she seems less interested in the individual than in the forces that dominate Spain's patriarchal society, a society that she succinctly says presents women with two options: "honor, duty, sacrifice . . . lover, mistress, whore" (*Los enanos* 237).

In *Los enanos*, her first major novel, Alós introduces two themes that reappear in her writing: prostitution and love outside the bonds of marriage. She does this through the depiction of the lives of Sabina and María. Sabina is Alós's most successful treatment of the prostitute. She comes to Barcelona to work and earns a living ironing clothing, a job she leaves to work as a prostitute because she can no longer stand the intense heat of the iron and the meager pay. Although prostitution solves her economic situation, it does not provide happiness or a place in society. Sabina ultimately opts for societal acceptance when she marries Don Benito, a man she dislikes but who will provide her with a home and a name. She thus becomes "Doña Sabina." While this relationship is sanctioned by society, it is merely another form of prostitution; she trades her body for economic security.

As a feminist, Alós approaches this subject with understanding and compassion as she juxtaposes the lives of her female characters to demonstrate the reasons for their choices. In contrast to Sabina, she presents María, a woman who follows the married man she loves. While Sabina clearly has a pragmatic outlook on life, María is guilt ridden and feels haunted by the voices of society that serve as a constant reminder of her "sin." Sabina adjusts to her environment and survives; María, like the rat the children drown in a bucket of water at the end of the novel, is suffocated by society and dies. Marriage in Alós's novels brings stability and social respectability, but not happiness.

Limited by their education and restricted by moral and legal considerations, women have few options. They must offer the commodity most in demand by men. Alós illustrates the exploitation of women through Cecilia, an important character in *La madama*, who is forced to accept the sexual advances of a married man in order to support herself and her small children while her husband remains a prisoner after the Civil War. The prostitute reappears in *Los cien pájaros* (1963; "A Hundred Birds"), *Os habla Electra* (1975; "Electra Speaking"), and *El asesino de los sueños* (1986; "The Assassin of Dreams"). These women eventually marry and succeed in establishing a home, although their past haunts both them and their illegitimate daughters, who suffer from the stigma of their mothers' former lives.

Love or sex outside the bonds of marriage appears in most of Alós's works and is treated in a variety of ways. For Cristina, the young protagonist of *Los cien pájaros*, the loss of her virginity and the resultant pregnancy constitute an awakening as well as a liberation. She rejects the security provided by traditional patriarchal society in favor of independence. She departs for Barcelona to start a new life alone. Instead of a bird in hand, her future unfolds as a hundred birds in flight. As with the protagonist of *Los cien pájaros*, love for Jano in *Argeo ha muerto, supongo* (1982; "Argeo Is Dead, I Suppose") is painful and short-lived, and leads to a rude awakening. When her love relationship with Argeo, her foundling brother, is discovered, Jano, ostracized by her family, friends, and priest, is placed in complete isolation in a convent cell. Social acceptance comes only after a slow and painful atonement for her sin. Argeo, although as guilty as Jano, is nevertheless spared the rigorous punishment, a clear indication of the double standard applied to men and women. Aware of the need to survive, Jano becomes cautious and astute, and eventually marries a wealthy and distinguished man who mistakenly believes she is a virgin. Having become part of the institution of marriage, Jano assumes the place patriarchal society has reserved for her, and thus brings honor and pride to her family. Order is reestablished.

Alós explores the issue of female sexuality even further in *Las hogueras*, where she focuses alternately on two women: Sibila, a former Parisian model who turns to a brutal day laborer (Daniel el Monegro) when her husband becomes impotent, and the schoolteacher Asunción, the stereotypical spinster. Sibila, vain and devoid of any intellectual interests, is the product of her father's dream: His only desire was to raise his daughter to be a beauty queen who would never work. Sibila, however, expresses the idea that there should be brothels for women. After taking the initiative and visiting Daniel el Monegro in his hut, she buys him a watch, an act that can be interpreted as payment for his services. Asunción, on the other hand, relieves her sexual frustration by placing a bag of warm water in her bed, thus creating the illusion of a human presence. Society is clearly unable to repress women's sexual needs.

Sibila and Asunción are atypical, however. For the most part, women in Alós's novels are a product of their culture and shun sexual experiences. They often feel physically sick at the first contact with men. It is significant that Sibila, the only woman who seeks sexual relations for pleasure, is a foreigner. Like the *suecas* (Swedish women) who appear in the works of some of Alós's contemporaries, foreign women are considered to be sexually freer. Likewise, the only two husbands who take back their adulterous wives, in *Las hogueras* and in *El asesino de los sueños,* are foreigners. This behavior would be unthinkable for Spaniards, who in the truest Hispanic tradition must avenge their wives' acts for the sake of their honor. The reader cannot help but remember the limitations faced by women writers in Franco's Spain and both the subtle and overt self-censorship that took place so as not to offend official morality.

Since society provides no remedy for her female protagonists, Alós begins to explore alternatives in her more experimental works. In a hallucinatory atmosphere reminiscent of Kafka, her story "La coraza" ("Armor"), in *Rey de gatos. Narraciones antropófagas* (1972; "King of Cats. Cannibalistic Tales"), serves as a reminder that in the animal kingdom the male is not always dominant. Unable to cope with the rejection of the man she loves, the female narrator consults a psychiatrist, who advises her to depersonalize the sexual act. When she complies, an unexpected metamorphosis takes place in her body. Transformed into an insect covered with armor and endowed with two long and powerful claws, she at last becomes convinced of her strength. Taking advantage of the fact that the male is still in ecstasy and therefore not in a position to fight back, she devours him. This symbolic act avenges her against all men and brings her happiness.

Patriarchy restricts women's choice of sexual expression and monitors their reproductive functions while encouraging the continuance of patriarchy itself. In sharp contrast to the freethinking and often rebellious women who occupy the center of Alós's fiction, the figure of the self-effacing and sacrificing mother, fulfilling her biological and cultural functions, remains in the background of most of her works. There is a lack of communication—although not a lack of affection—among mothers and daughters. Ironically, the mother in charge of raising her children is instrumental in transmitting those values that perpetuate the system that ultimately thwarts her sense of wholeness and personal identity. The mother who, in Alós's first novel, *Los enanos,* advises her daugher to be prudent and to build a home is no different from the mother in her latest novel, *El asesino de los sueños,* who on two occasions destroys her daughter's love relationships so that she will marry an elderly man who can provide her with security.

Alós's last three novels—*Os habla Electra, Argeo ha muerto, supongo,* and *El asesino de los sueños*—continue to reflect her preoccupation with woman's marginal position in a patriarchal society, but they depart from her previous works in terms of style and technique. The main character in each novel is a mature and disillusioned woman who reflects on her condition as woman, lover, and wife, and examines other women's lives, in particular that of her own mother. Characters and themes reappear, thus establishing important links among the three novels. In *El asesino de los sueños,* Teodora Pardo, the narrator who remarkably resembles Concha Alós, is presented as the author of *Os habla Electra.* Teodora explains, "I had invented a character—Electra—whom I would have liked to resemble . . . a free and courageous woman" (114). This search for an understanding of the female condition begins as a personal journey in which the main character of *Os habla Electra* rummages through her memory for the distant past, often confusing the boundaries of the real and the imaginary. The figure of the mother, previously relegated to the background, assumes a prominent and active role in these last novels. Electra-mother, in an oneiric voyage, withdraws to an ancestral "green world" that closely resembles the one described by Annis Pratt in *Archetypal Patterns in Women's Fiction.*[1] Outside patriarchal boundaries, she is able to establish a matrifocal society. She enjoys great erotic expression and the ability to control her own destiny, an autonomy that would be impossible to sustain in contemporary Spanish society. In the end, however, she loses her powers and must capitulate to patriarchal values, incarnated by Madame la Baronne, who is instrumental in the destruction of Electra's green world.

It is through the mother–daughter confrontation that the daughter/protagonist reaches an understanding of her own female condition. At the end of *Os habla Electra*, Electra-daughter fully identifies with Electra-mother: "At times my mother's papers become confused with my own recollections . . . I could have written them" (79–80). This search leads Electra-daughter to understand the commonality of the collective female experience, "because Electra, then, was not Electra, but a symbol. She was I and my daughters and my daughter's daughters and all the young women who will one day be born . . . I locked myself in my room and cried helplessly, but lucidly" (183).

Unlike Alós's other works, *Os habla Electra* takes place outside contemporary Spanish society. Without set boundaries of time and place that render "considerations of chronology problematic, if not impossible" (Lee-Bonanno 108), this ambitious and experimental novel traces the creation of matriarchy, and its subsequent annihilation by the establishment of patriarchal laws. Alós returns to myths, archetypes, and classical Greek drama, as well as to the Freudian concept of the Electra complex, to capture this process. For example, the quarrels and hatred between Electra and her mother, and her devotion to her father's memory, remind the reader of similar conflicts and characters in Sophocles' tragedy. Scenes surrounding the birth of Electra-daughter's illegitimate child also bring to mind Euripides' version of the myth and his portrayal of Clytemnestra. However, while the integration of mythological and Freudian references frames her characters' traits, it does not constitute per se a rewriting or modern-day version of the Electra myth. Alós also skillfully combines the recurring myths and archetypes of the text with numerous elements that ground the action of her novel in contemporary times.

In *Argeo ha muerto, supongo*, Jano looks back at her past from the vantage point of the present, where she is a respectable mother and wife. Her first memories are of growing up with a double handicap, being a girl and having a deformed foot, both summed up in the popular Spanish proverb, "La mujer en casa con la pata rota" ("The woman at home, with a broken leg"). Jano is painfully aware of the disadvantages of being female, and she compares the privileges her mother reserves for her brother Argeo, the man of the family, with her own restrictive and traditional upbringing. When her mother discovers Jano's illicit love relationship with Argeo, her fate is similar to that suffered by the protagonist of *El asesino de los sueños*. She is confined again to the strictures of patriarchal norms. Thus the rebellious daughters, as they mature, often come to accept reluctantly the roles assigned to them by their mothers and society in general. A capitulation, one might think, or, as Concha Alós has indicated, an act of love and wisdom; that is, the sad realization on the part of the mothers that the price of freedom is too high and that their daughters' ambitions are unattainable in contemporary Spanish society (Ortúzar-Young, Letter).

SURVEY OF CRITICISM

Alós's work, widely read in Spain, has not received similar attention in the United States. This is reflected in the paucity of both literary criticism and translations into English of her works. Most often she is included in histories of contemporary Spanish literature and among "lesser-known writers" in broad studies such as Janet W. Pérez's *Contemporary Women Writers of Spain*. While this type of panoramic view fails to provide an in-depth analysis of her work, it does succeed in properly placing her among her contemporaries and can be useful for those approaching her writing for the first time.

Fermín Rodríguez's *Mujer y sociedad: La novelística de Concha Alós* is the only book-length study available to date. Although published in 1985, it seems to have been written more than ten years earlier and does not include her last works, for Alós's writing since *Rey de gatos* departs radically in terms of style and technique from the social realism that characterized her first five novels. Rodríguez provides a general discussion of themes and values he finds in Alós's early novels. He also includes biographical and bibliographical information and, perhaps more important, summarizes male critical responses to her fiction, which are found for the most part in publications not readily available outside Spain. The acerbic reaction by some of these critics gives the reader a sense of the difficulties encountered by female writers during the Franco era. In reference to *La madama*, Iglesia Laguna asserts that it is "written in a language unnecessarily crude. I say unnecessarily—and abstain from adding quotes—because coarseness does not fit in a cultured and refined woman like Concha Alós. It does not matter that the disgusting terms are put in the mouths of vulgar individuals at the appropriate moment" (qtd. in *Mujer y sociedad* 20). Another critic, unnamed by Rodríguez, provides a clear indication of what is expected from women writers: "Concha Alós with coarse words, filth, and smelly physiology, but with accuracy and style, has given us one more proof of her skills. She is already good; she can feel sure of herself. Now she should enrich her palette with other colors and she should make us laugh" (qtd. in *Mujer y sociedad* 22). At issue here is not Concha Alós herself but the fact that a woman has invaded an exclusively male territory. Alós defends women's rights to artistic expression in her literary creations and in her essay, "El sexo de las artes" (1970; "The Sex of the Arts"), where she responds with an indictment of patriarchy to a male writer who claims that "no woman has been capable of painting the execution scenes that Goya did." She concludes that "because of . . . restrictive social structures, the female member of the species has not yet painted any painting that could be compared to Goya's executions. But . . . perhaps she is painting it now, or will paint it tomorrow" (27).

Recent literary criticism has concentrated exclusively on *Os habla Electra*. This is unfortunate because, although an important work, it is not Alós's most representative one. Both Elizabeth Ordóñez and Lucy Lee-Bonanno provide insightful studies of this novel, applying the latest theories of feminist literary criticism. For Ordóñez, *Os habla Electra* is an archetypal study reinterpreted and recombined to tell of the quest and struggle of Electra—mother and daughter—who is emblematic of Everywoman. Ordóñez specifically relates two modes of being, matriarchal and patriarchal, to the characterization of Electra-mother and Madame la Baronne. Lee-Bonanno, adding to Ordóñez's study, traces Electra's movement from a world of freedom to one of confinement and reveals the consequences of such a trajectory for women. Following Pratt's *Archetypal Patterns in Women's Fiction*, she finds two mythological frameworks in *Os habla Electra*: the Greek legend of Electra and the Demeter/Kore archetype. Her detailed and well-supported study traces Electra's downfall under the powers of patriarchy, and her subsequent confinement in the city of the Gargoyles.

Although the Ordóñez and Lee-Bonanno studies are well written and documented, they treat *Os habla Electra* in isolation, and fail to recognize the continuity of characters and situations in Alós's works. For example, the city (sometimes the street) of Gargoyles appears in several of her novels, sometimes associated with the red light district where a number of the protagonists' mothers worked as prostitutes. A study tracing the figure of the mother within contemporary Spanish patriarchy could prove most revealing. There is a need for more revisionist studies on the complete body of Alós's work, which to date remains virtually unexplored by critics.

NOTE

1. Annis Pratt, *Archetypal Patterns in Women's Fiction* (Bloomington: Indiana UP; 1981).

BIBLIOGRAPHY

Works by Concha Alós

Published Works

Los enanos. Barcelona: Plaza y Janés, 1962.
Los cien pájaros. Barcelona: Plaza y Janés, 1963.

Las hogueras. Barcelona: Editorial Planeta, 1964.
El caballo rojo. Barcelona: Editorial Planeta, 1966.
La madama. Barcelona: Plaza y Janés, 1969.
"El sexo de las artes." *Destino* 16 May 1970: 25, 27.
Rey de gatos. Narraciones antropófogas. Barcelona: Barral Editores, 1972.
Os habla Electra. Barcelona: Plaza y Janés, 1975.
Argeo ha muerto, supongo. Barcelona: Plaza y Janés, 1982.
El asesino de los sueños. Barcelona: Plaza y Janés, 1986.

Unpublished Works

"El agosto." [Short story]
"Cuando la luna cambia de color." [Novel]

Translation

"Armor." Trans. Doris Rolfe. *Aphra: The Feminist Literary Magazine* 5.1 (Winter 1983–
    84): 2–8.

Works about Concha Alós

Lee-Bonanno, Lucy. "Concha Alós' *Os habla Electra*: The Matriarchy Revisited."
    Anales de la Literatura Española Contemporánea 12.1-2 (1987): 95–109.
Ordóñez, Elizabeth. "The Barcelona Group: The Fiction of Alós, Moix, and Tusquets."
    Letras Femeninas 6 (Spring 1980): 38–49.
———. "The Female Quest Pattern in Concha Alós' *Os habla Electra*." *Revista de
    Estudios Hispánicos* 14 (1980): 51–56.
Ortúzar-Young, Ada. Letter to Concha Alós. 22 Jan. 1990.
Rodríguez, Fermín. *Mujer y sociedad: la novelística de Concha Alós.* Madrid: Orígenes,
    1985.
Valis, Noël M. "Concha Alós." *Women Writers of Spain. An Annotated Bio-Biblio-
    graphical Guide.* Ed. Carolyn Galerstein. Westport, CT: Greenwood Press, 1986.
    19–21.

JOSEFA AMAR Y BORBÓN
(1749–1833)

Constance A. Sullivan

BIOGRAPHY

Considering the degree to which Josefa Amar y Borbón's contemporaries in the late eighteenth century acknowledged her literary efforts and erudition, details of her life remain vague for scholars of the late twentieth century. Her date of birth has been put variously as 1743, 1749, 1752, or 1753, and despite Melchor Poza Rodríguez's 1884 assertion that he had seen her gravestone listing 1743–1833 as the ninety years of her life, most commentators have been uncertain as to when she died, especially because Poza Rodríguez's bibliographical data on Amar are so inaccurate that one must distrust the dates he provides. In effect, what we know about Josefa Amar is something of her public life and literary activities up to the turn of the nineteenth century, and very little of her private life.

Through careful research, this critic has been able to verify the birth and death dates of Josefa Amar y Borbón. She was born in Zaragoza in February 1749, the fifth of sixteen children born to José Amar Arguedas and Ignacia Borbón y Vallejo de Santa Cruz. José Amar was a well-known doctor of medicine and Ignacia Borbón was the daughter of a famous Aragonese physician, Miguel Borbón, and his first wife. The Borbón family had deep roots as members of the lower nobility in Zaragoza; they were not directly related to the Franco-Spanish Borbón monarchical line. José Amar became one of Fernando VI's (and later, Carlos III's) chamber physicians in 1755 and took his family with him to Madrid. There Josefa was tutored by the king's librarian, Rafael Casalbón, in Latin, French, and literature. She was also taught Greek by the curate Antonio Berdejo. With these beginnings Amar continued her education, apparently teaching herself Italian and English, and reading assiduously in the royal and private libraries accessible to her. She was married in 1764 to Joaquín Fuertes Piquer, a lawyer born in Valbona (Teruel) and perhaps a relative of Andrés Piquer, a prominent Aragonese doctor who was a physician of the king's chamber at the time. Amar returned to Zaragoza in 1772 when her husband was appointed a judge in the Criminal Court of the Royal Tribunal in that city. She lived there for the rest of her life except for occasional trips to Madrid, at least in the last two decades of the eighteenth century. The couple had at least one child, a son named Felipe.

As a member of the educated professional and governmental elite, Joaquín Fuertes Piquer joined the Aragonese Economic Society in 1776, when it was established. He participated in the Society's activities, such as the doomed 1783 effort to implement the new Guild Plan, and served as its vice director in 1785 and 1786. Josefa Amar no doubt encouraged by Carlos III's appreciation of the exiled Jesuit Xavier Lampillas's spirited defense of Spanish literature, began translating Lampillas's six-volume text from the Italian as soon as it appeared in 1778–1781 (*Ensayo histórico-apologético de la Literatura española*). The Aragonese Economic Society rewarded her literary efforts by electing her to regular membership, for her merits (*socia de mérito*), in October 1782. She was the first woman to be admitted; four others were accepted in 1792, 1801, and 1805.

In the decade following her admission to the Aragonese Economic Society, Amar was an active supporter of, and participant in, its efforts for enlightened reform, using its library and occasionally attending its meetings. To further its projects for the improvement of agriculture, the Economic Society asked her to translate from the Italian Francesco Griselini's book on how village priests could instruct farmers in better agricultural methods. After her translation was published in 1784, the Economic Society used the book as one of the texts read to male farm workers at free agricultural seminars held in Zaragoza on Sunday afternoons.

Another project sponsored by the Economic Society was a school to teach new spinning techniques to poor young women. In 1783, and again in 1785, the leader of the society, Juan Antonio Hernández de Larrea, spearheaded an attempt to find some highly ranked women to take over the management of the school from eight men. Two noblewomen demurred, but Amar and Eulalia Terán offered to assume that responsibility if two more women would join them. None did, and the men continued to run the school. In the meantime, Amar continued to translate the polemical Lampillas text, publishing in 1786 his one-volume answer to the Italian scholar Girolamo Tiraboschi, who had attacked Lampillas's literary history. A seven-volume second edition of the entire translation, with Amar's indexed, annotated bibliography, was issued in 1789.

Having spent her adolescence at the Madrid court, Amar y Borbón had friends among the aristocratic women there, particularly the countess of Montijo. Through those contacts, and the frequent formal and informal contacts among the various economic societies in Spain, she learned in early 1786 that the Madrid Economic Society was debating whether to admit women as regular members (*socias*). Two prominent figures of the King's Council in Madrid, Gaspar Melchor de Jovellanos and Francisco Cabarrús, contributed opposing opinions to that debate on admitting women: Jovellanos was mildly in favor for practical reasons, Cabarrús was heatedly against. Their essays were published in the *Memorial literario*, in April and May 1786, respectively; Amar entered the public debate in July 1786 by sending the Madrid Economic Society a long essay, "Discurso en defensa del talento de las mugeres, y de su aptitud para el gobierno, y otros cargos en que se emplean los hombres" ("Discourse in Defense of the Talent of Women, and of Their Aptitude for Government, and Other Positions Occupied by Men"), in which she argued in favor of the admission of qualified women. Amar's essay was published in an Italian translation by the exiled Catalan Jesuit abbot Juan Francisco Masdeu. We can infer from the essay's quick publication in the *Memorial literario*, the Italian translation, and the Madrid Economic Society's September 1786 agreement to admit women members that her statement on the issue had been admired and had some impact. However, in early 1787 Carlos III decreed the establishment of a separate and subordinate Junta de Damas (Ladies' Group) for the Madrid Economic Society. Women were never to become full, regular members; they met apart from the men, who of course reviewed everything the women's group did. The male officers of the Economic Society selected the first thirteen women members of the Junta de Damas. Josefa Amar y Borbón was not among them, but the women's first act was to elect her to their membership.

Recognizing that Carlos III's decree officially precluded women's equal participation in the public sphere, and despite her irritation at the gender prescriptions of the decree, Amar was an active member of the Madrid Junta de Damas. She attended its weekly meeting whenever she made a trip to Madrid in the late 1780s and early 1790s, and submitted an essay on the moral education of women for one of its projects in 1795. That essay was not reviewed by the Madrid Economic Society's censor until 1801, however, and the manuscript has since been lost. In 1790 Amar's major book, *Discurso sobre la educación física y moral de las mugeres* ("Discourse on the Physical and Moral Education of Women"), was published in Madrid; in recognition of the medical information contained in Part I of the book she was named a member of the Medical Society of Barcelona. Thus, by 1791 Amar y Borbón had the most impressive curriculum vitae of public affiliations and respected publications of any woman in Spain in the entire eighteenth century.

She never published again. Félix de Latassa y Ortin's 1802 discussion indicates that Amar had other translations in manuscript, but no one, with the possible exception of family members, has ever seen them (the Bibliography Department at the University of Madrid has declared them either lost or imaginary). Her husband suffered a stroke in 1786 that left him paralyzed, and that illness and his death in 1798 must have affected her life in practical, if not intellectual, ways. The last known, but unpublished, piece of Amar's writing is a first-person account of the French siege of Zaragoza in a manuscript signed and dated October

23, 1809, when she was the senior female member of a charitable group of lay people who assisted the sick at the General Hospital of Our Lady of Grace in that city. Amar outlived her entire family, dying in February 1833, at the age of eighty-four. Thus, major biographical questions remain concerning this intelligent, erudite woman writer of the Spanish Enlightenment who published extensively from 1782 to 1790, and then lived forty-three years longer in near-complete silence and apparent anonymity.

MAJOR THEMES

Josefa Amar y Borbón's self-perception as the intellectual equal of any man in Spain is palpable in all that she wrote. Never apologizing for being a woman who dares to write, her tone is always assured, and she brandishes an impressive erudition. But she also knew that her education had been exceptional for a woman of her time, even for a woman of her privileged social and economic class. A permeating theme in Amar's work is her desire to share with other women what she calls the "advantages" of learning by encouraging them to aspire to, and work at, the acquisition of knowledge that goes beyond simple handiwork, social graces, and homemaking skills. Through education, women themselves would contradict the negative stereotyped view Spanish society held of their sex.

Amar's translation of Griselini's treatise on agriculture was a purely utilitarian patriotic exercise for her, its subject being far from her literary and feminist interests and warranting no elaboration of her own. The translation of Lampillas's defense of Spanish literature, on the other hand, was a double act of love: for literature and for her country. Amar's confidence in her familiarity with Spanish literature, especially of the sixteenth and seventeenth centuries, led her to add her own notes to the translated text; in them she provided explanations, amplifications, even corrections and new bibliographical information. Lampillas's work defends Spain's literary prestige and, as befitted a member of the enlightened elite, Amar's patriotic sentiments played a part in inspiring her to this massive task of translating and editing. Even here, however, Amar included a note to women readers in her prologue, pointing out that volume IV contained a section on famous Spanish women writers of the past. That small note concerning women's literary accomplishments links her translation with the woman-centered essays she wrote in 1786, 1787, and 1790.

The "Discurso en defensa del talento de las mugeres" of 1786 is divided into two related arguments: that the intelligence of women is equal to that of men, and that educated, dedicated women are qualified to take part in activities in the public sphere, like those of the economic societies, and thus should be admitted as equals in those patriotically inspired groups. Amar refuses to accept any gender-specific characteristics, stressing the diversity among men and women that responds to differences of class, education, and incentives. She thus argues that nurture, rather than nature, is responsible for many of the differences between people, positing that if the social environment causes inequalities and vices, changing that environment will diminish or eliminate those social deficiencies. Generally, her argumentative techniques fall within the model set by Spain's early Enlightenment essayist, the Benedictine friar Benito Jerónimo Feijóo: reason, logic, historical evidence, and observed fact. In this essay, Amar does not argue on the basis of past authorities' statements, and she frequently adduces a woman's perspective on the world that had not been present in the male-authored eighteenth-century debate on women in Spain. Cognizant throughout that it is men who control how society is structured, she challenges men to change that structure and their own attitudes and behavior toward women. While Amar does not hesitate to recognize the vanity, frivolity, or licentiousness of many women of her time and class, she refuses to blame women for those behaviors.

The second section of the essay attacks the arguments that claimed that the presence of females in deliberations on public policy would inhibit decorum or the seriousness of discussion; Amar again challenges men to change their insistently reductive view of women as mere erotically attractive or repulsive bodies. She speaks here from a sense of solidarity with other women who wanted, and deserved, a formally recognized role in the reforms being devised by the economic societies and other public groups of Spain's absolutist regime.

If no one else recognized in Carlos III's creation of the Junta de Damas the exclusion of women from the public sphere and their reenclosure within a domestic space firmly gendered as feminine, Amar did. The disillusionment and frustration she felt are evident in her 1787 "Oración gratulatoria" ("Letter of Appreciation") to the newly established, and separate, Ladies' Group associated with the Madrid Economic Society that had just elected her to their membership. Amar here converts what was to be a pro forma letter of praise of the group and its plans into a subtle satire of the gender prescriptions in the king's decree, a deprecation of the insignificant mechanical devices invented by the Madrid Economic Society's male members who were impatient for quick solutions to Spain's agricultural and economic backwardness, and a fierce rhetorical questioning of the capability of Spain and its kings to appreciate the constructive volunteer efforts of its patriotic citizens, particularly its dedicated and hardworking women, whose patient labor, she claims, would bring real change to the country.

It seems to have been very difficult for Amar to accept that intelligent, educated women had been newly relegated to secondary and dependent status, and confined to home and marriage. In the prologue to her 1790 *Discurso sobre la educación*, after musing on alternative ways of organizing the gender specificity of public and domestic space (where women might go out to work and men would take care of the home), she concludes that such alternatives are still impossible: "Let's not devise a fantastic plan: let's only try to correct where possible the one that is already established" (xxxii). Later, Amar contrasts a bachelor's freedom to move in society and have a career with society's denial of those possibilities to unmarried women, thus explaining why young women have only two life options: marriage or the convent (265). The intended readership of this book, which is in great part a "conduct book" like those written in the nineteenth century, based on models proposed in the Spanish Renaissance by Luis Vives and Fray Luis de León, is explicitly female: women of the comfortable middle class and the nobility. Its purpose is to help those women bring up their daughters in ways that will increase the happiness of their lives, their marriages, and their solitude. But Amar goes beyond the Renaissance model in her text, which walks a fine line between what men decreed was possible in late-eighteenth-century Spanish society for "decent" women and her yearning for something more.

Part I discusses the best experimental medical opinion of the European eighteenth century on conception, pregnancy, childbirth, lactation, and the care of new mothers and infants. Comprising one-third of the book, this section gives advice drawn from contemporary medical texts in several languages and is concerned with how women can ensure that their children are born healthy and survive early childhood. Part II is more properly called a conduct book, in that it advises mothers on how best to raise their daughters for the limited marriage or convent options available to them. Still, Amar's emphasis is on educating women's minds: paying mere lip service to the necessity of learning good manners, handiwork, and how to run a household, she states that organizing one's time permits a woman to fulfill her domestic responsibilities and still be able to study and challenge her intellect despite her forced retirement from the larger world. She provides a curriculum, complete with recommended texts in areas of study that range from literature in the native language, to mathematics, history, geography, and classical languages, and she encourages the brightest women to aspire to read biblical and philosophical texts in Greek and Latin.

Amar's admonitions frequently make explicit room for the different class and financial circumstances women face, and she stresses how difficult marriage is for any woman, pointing out the problems of day-to-day intimacy, arguments, a husband's bad temper or infidelity, his possible failure to provide an income sufficient to maintain the household, and the excruciating boredom women face if they stay at home as society expects respectable women to do. Amar, at times rather desperately, it seems, proposes that reading and study can alleviate some of these problems, especially as a woman ages and loses her physical attractiveness and perhaps her husband's companionship. She encourages mothers to forge strong links of mutual trust and understanding with their daughters, and to protect them from making rash decisions that have the potential to destroy their happiness for a lifetime, such as choosing to enter a convent without true religious vocation or choosing the wrong husband.

Throughout this book Amar suggests ways for Spanish women of the middle and upper classes to acquire an internal sense of self-worth that depends on intelligence, education, organization of time, and the development of long-lasting personal attributes that go beyond physical beauty, dress, and adornment.

SURVEY OF CRITICISM

Josefa Amar y Borbón's publications received reviews, brief summaries, and praise throughout the decade from 1782 to 1791. Her translation of Lampillas's multivolume historical defense of Spanish literature sold well and had an enlarged second edition, but no one has yet analyzed Amar's contributions to it. Another Amar text that has received no commentary is the fascinatingly complex and impassioned 1787 letter of appreciation she sent to the Madrid Junta de Damas when that group elected her to membership.

In the time between the 1802 study by Latassa y Ortín and the rediscovery of Josefa Amar y Borbón by feminist scholars in the 1970s, critics and historians of Spanish literature generally ignored her. If her work was mentioned at all outside of bibliographies, it was in a footnote reference to her 1790 book on the education of women or to the fact that she translated Lampillas and Griselini. Some of that long ignoring of Amar carried traces of attempts to silence her as an educated and outspoken feminist. For example, Miguel de Gómez Uriel, in his 1884 recasting of Latassa's bibliographies of Aragonese writers, removed much of the information Félix de Latassa had provided about Amar's education, her undisputed erudition, her ranking among other illustrious Spanish and European women writers, and the esteem in which she was held by Spanish Enlightenment figures. Melchor Poza Rodríguez did likewise in the same year.

Jean Sarrailh's ground-breaking study of Spain's Enlightenment began to reassert Amar y Borbón's former prestige, and the work of other archival historians of the 1970s—Carmen Martín Gaite, Paula de Demerson, Lucienne Domergue, Eloy Fernández Clemente, Paloma Fernández-Quintanilla, Manuel López Torrijo—highlighted her intellectual and reformist activities, including for the first time an appreciation of her aggressively feminist "Discurso sobre el talento" as well as her *Discurso sobre la educación*. It is still these social and cultural historians, rather than literary Hispanists, who must be credited with resituating Amar as a feminist and an active patriot within the small enlightened elite of Spain's late eighteenth century. And, although they do not analyze her discursive style or thematics, the historical studies of the circumstances and problematics of eighteenth-century women's lives by Carmen Martín Gaite and María Victoria López-Cordón Cortezo provide the contextualization of Amar's works necessary to their being examined carefully.

The socialist activist Margarita Nelken, in her 1930 *Las escritoras españolas*, looked askance at all the published complaints by eighteenth-century women of privilege that they were oppressed by men. Nelken limited her assessment of Amar y Borbón to a claim that the feminism of the writer's essay in defense of women's talent was contradicted by the more traditional conservatism of her book on the education of women (175–76). María del Pilar Oñate's 1938 chapter on eighteenth-century feminism in Spanish literature mentions Amar y Borbón only briefly in a discussion that focuses on Benito Jerónimo Feijóo's 1726 essay "Defensa de las mugeres." The editors of the 1980 *Los orígenes del feminismo en España* were more appreciative of Amar's feminist sympathies, but by omitting their source for the Amar text that they anthologized they obscured the fact that it was really—with about seven pages cut and one paragraph added—the prologue to her 1790 book on the education of women. That book, frequently cited by many critics, has never been reprinted and therefore remains relatively inaccessible to modern scholars. None of Amar's work has been translated into English.

Overall, and despite their excellent historical contextualization of her written work, historians of Spain's eighteenth century have tended to provide paraphrasings of Amar's original writings, interspersed with brief quotations of a paragraph or less. The first literary scholars to go beyond that kind of presentation were Eva Rudat in 1976 and Carmen McClendon in 1978. Both these Hispanists initiated analyses of Amar's feminism and her essayistic style, studying the *Discurso sobre la educación* and the greatly ignored "Discurso en defensa del talento de las mugeres." McClendon reprinted the latter in 1980, as did Olegario Negrín Fajardo in 1984.

Rudat has highlighted Amar y Borbón's contributions to the Spanish polemic on women and her place in the general European debates on the essence, rights, and roles of women. Rudat suggests a parallel, as yet unexamined, between Amar y Borbón's spirited 1786 defense of women and those of French and British feminists of the 1790s: Olympe de Gouges, Theodore de Hippel, and Mary Wollstonecraft. After briefly summarizing the essay's feminist goals, Rudat encapsulates major features of the author's book on the education of women. Here she, like McClendon after her, points to elements of the apparent conservatism of Amar's views of women's proper roles in marriage and motherhood, although Amar insisted throughout that intelligent and motivated girls be permitted and encouraged to devote themselves seriously to sustained studies beyond the severely limited female education of the time. Rudat's sensitive essays center on Amar's erudition, her moralistic and didactic tone, and her rigid ethical and religious principles; Rudat is always firmly aware of the feminist views that run through all of Amar's writing and of her desire to improve the situation of women in the limited roles their society defined for them.

McClendon's articles are also descriptive summaries of Amar y Borbón's book on women's education and 1786 essay in defense of women, and several constitute brief introductions of this Spanish woman writer to audiences totally unfamiliar with her life and work—or, indeed, with Spain's Enlightenment. It is unfortunate that her studies of Amar contain biographical and bibliographical inaccuracies. Those who have read all of Amar's publications and are familiar as well with Spain's Enlightenment might argue with McClendon's assertions that Amar's translations were mere mental exercises and that her ideas on education were based on those of Rousseau ("Josefa Amar y Borbón y la educación femenina" 7).

McClendon's "Josefa Amar y Borbón: Essayist" mistakenly lumps together Amar's two major works as if they were similar in tone, style, occasion, or argumentative technique, and compounds that mistake by looking at them through the lens of definitions and models of the essay as genre that have been proposed or written by men of later periods. This article comes to some startling conclusions in its characterizations of Amar's method of argumentation, among them that the writer digresses frequently and avoids drawing conclusions to her arguments, leaving them open ended. A seriously misleading use of analytical and descriptive terminology here confuses Spanish Enlightenment writers' utilization of historical example and direct or experimental observation with a dependence on "tradition" and "authority" in argument. In fact, only Part II of Amar's book on women's education can be said to argue from traditional authorities of classical Greece and Rome or the Spanish Renaissance. Her essay on the talent of women argues from historical example and logic, while Part I of her book, which deals with how to assure the physical health of mothers and babies, is replete with the results of the most up-to-date experimental medicine of her time, a fact that only Rudat and López Torrijo have observed in print. Elizabeth Franklin's more recent article, "Feijóo, Josefa Amar y Borbón, and the Feminist Debate in Eighteenth-Century Spain," is derivative of McClendon's discussion of Amar's "Defensa del talento" but shows appreciation for the author's feminism.

There is need for a more searching and theoretically informed analysis of the works of Josefa Amar y Borbón, in terms of her sustained feminism and the relationships between her writing, her public activities, and significant historical events that influenced her evolving perspectives on women's situation in late-eighteenth-century society. Furthermore, it is quite possible that a closer examination of her book on the education of women will reveal its intensely autobiographical content, in particular with regard to her own education. We look forward as well to new editions of her original works and to comparative studies of her feminism and that of her contemporaries in other parts of Europe. Recently reintroduced to the scholarly community, Amar y Borbón deserves the recognition that would allow her to reclaim the place she seems to have had in Spanish literary history at the end of the eighteenth century.

BIBLIOGRAPHY

Works by Josefa Amar y Borbón

Translations

Ensayo histórico-apologético de la Literatura española, contra las opiniones preocupadas de algunos escritores modernos italianos. Disertaciones del Abate Don Xavier Lampillas. Translated from the Italian by Doña Josepha Amar y Borbón. 6 vols. Zaragoza: Blas Miedes, 1782–1784.
————. 2nd ed. corrected, enlarged, and illustrated with notes, by the translator herself, 7 vols. Madrid: Pedro Marín, 1789.
Discurso sobre el problema de si corresponde a los Párrocos y Curas de las aldeas el instruir a los labradores en los buenos elementos de la economía campestre: al qual va adjunto un plan que debe seguirse en la formación de una obra dirigida a la mencionada instrucción del Señor Francisco Griselini, miembro de las principales Academias de Europa, y Secretario de la Sociedad Patriótica de

Milán. . . . Translated from the Italian, at the request of the Aragonese Society of Friends of the Country, by Doña Josepha Amar y Borbón, Member for Her Merits of that Society. Zaragoza: Blas Miedes, 1784.

Respuesta del Señor Abate Don Xavier Lampillas a los cargos recopilados por el Señor Abate Tiraboschi en su carta al Señor Abate N. N. sobre el Ensayo histórico-apologético de la Literatura Española. Translated from the Italian by Doña Josepha Amar y Borbón. Including an alphabetical index of the principal authors and topics compiled by the translator. Zaragoza: Blas Miedes, 1786.

Nonfiction

"Discurso en defensa del talento de las mugeres, y de su aptitud para el gobierno, y otros cargos en que se emplean los hombres." *Memorial literario, instructivo y curioso de la Corte de Madrid* 8.3 (Aug. 1786): 399–430.

————. Ed. Carmen Chaves McClendon. *Dieciocho* 3.2 (1980): 144–61.

————. Ed. Olegario Negrín Fajardo. *Ilustración y educación. La Sociedad Económica Matritense.* Madrid: Editora Nacional, 1984. 162–76.

"Oración gratulatoria . . . a la junta de Señoras de la Real Sociedad Económica de Madrid." *Memorial literario, instructivo y curioso de la Corte de Madrid* 12 (Dec. 1787): 588–92.

Oración gratulatoria que la Señora Doña Josepha Amar y Borbón, elegida Socia de mérito, dirigió a la junta de Señoras en 1787. Madrid: Sancha, n.d.

Discurso sobre la educación física y moral de las mugeres. Madrid: Benito Cano, 1790.

————. Ed. Constance A. Sullivan. Madrid: Siglo XXI. [Forthcoming]

"(Prólogo): Importancia de la instrucción que conviene dar a las mugeres (1784)." *Los orígenes del feminismo en España.* Ed. Anabel González, Amalia López, Ana Mendoza, and Isabel Uruena. Madrid: Zero, 1980. 158–64.

Translation

"*Discurso sobre la educación física y moral de las mugeres* by Josefa Amar y Borbón: A Translation with Introduction and Notes." Trans. Carmen Chaves McClendon. Diss. U of Mississippi, 1976.

Works about Josefa Amar y Borbón

Aguilar Piñal, Francisco. "Josefa Amar y Borbón." *Bibliografía de autores españoles del siglo XVIII.* Vol. I. Madrid: C.S.I.C., 1981. 228–29.

Aldaraca, Bridget A. "The Perfect Wife." "*El Angel del Hogar.*" *Galdós and the Ideology of Domesticity in Spain.* Chapel Hill: Dept. of Romance Languages, U of North Carolina, 1991. 33–54, esp. 45–53.

Asún Escartín, Raquel. "Josefa Amar y Borbón." *Gran Enciclopedia Aragonesa.* Vol. 1. Zaragoza: Unión Aragonesa del Libro, 1980. 178–79.

Demerson, Paula de. *María Francisca de Sales Portocarrero, Condesa del Montijo: Una figura de la Ilustración.* Madrid: Editora Nacional, 1975. 127–39, 172–77.

Departamento de Bibliografía de la Universidad Complutense de Madrid. "Josefa Amar y Borbón." *Repertorio de impresos españoles perdidos o imaginarios.* Vol. I. Madrid: Instituto Bibliográfico Hispánico/Ministerio de Cultura, 1982. 31.

Domergue, Lucienne. "Jovellanos et l'admission des femmes à la *Matritense.*" *Jove-*

llanos à la Société Économique des Amis du Pays de Madrid (1778–1795). Toulouse: Université de Toulouse-Le Mirail, 1971. 233–66.

Fernández Clemente, Eloy. "Filosofía, utopía y pedagogía. Sobre un cúmulo de buenos maestros, tres figuras de proyección nacional: Andrés Piquer, Nipho y Josefa Amar." *La Ilustración aragonesa (Una obsesión pedagógica)*. Zaragoza: Caja de Ahorros y Monte de Piedad de Zaragoza, 1973. 70–100.

Fernández-Quintanilla, Paloma. *La mujer ilustrada en la España del siglo XVIII*. Madrid: Ministerio de Cultura, 1981. 55–65, 130–32.

Forniés Casals, José Francisco. "La estructura social de los Amigos del país en Aragón." *Boletín de Documentación del Fondo para la Investigación Económica y Social* 9.2 (1977): 285–307.

Franklin, Elizabeth M. "Feijóo, Josefa Amar y Borbón, and the Feminist Debate in Eighteenth-Century Spain." *Dieciocho* 12.2 (Fall 1989): 188–99.

Gómez Uriel, Miguel, ed. *Bibliotecas antigua y nueva de escritores aragoneses de Latassa, aumentadas y refundidas en forma de diccionario bibliográfico-biográfico*. Vol I. Zaragoza: Calisto Ariño, 1884. 52–53.

González, Anabel, Amalia López, Ana Mendoza, and Isabel Urueña, eds. "La situación de la mujer en el Siglo de las Luces." *Los orígenes del feminismo en España*. Madrid: Zero, 1980. 73–107.

Latassa y Ortín, Félix de. "Doña Josefa Amar y Borbón." *Biblioteca nueva de los escritores aragoneses*. Vol. 6. Pamplona: Joaquín de Domingo, 1802. 231–35.

López-Cordón Cortezo, María Victoria. "La situación de la mujer a finales del Antiguo Régimen (1760–1860)." *Mujer y sociedad en España (1700–1975)*. Ed. Rosa María Capel Martínez. Madrid: Ministerio de Cultura, 1982. 47–107.

López Torrijo, Manuel. "El pensamiento pedagógico ilustrado sobre la mujer en Josefa Amar y Borbón." *Educación e Ilustración en España. III. Coloquio de Historia de la Educación*. Departamento de Educación Comparada e Historia de la Educación. Barcelona: Universidad de Barcelona, 1984. 114–29.

Martín Gaite, Carmen. *Usos amorosos del dieciocho en España*. Madrid: Siglo XXI, 1972.

McClendon, Carmen Chaves. "Josefa Amar y Borbón: Essayist." *Dieciocho* 3.2 (1980): 138–42.

———. "Josefa Amar y Borbón, Forgotten Figure of the Spanish Enlightenment." *Seven Essays in Medieval English Literature and Other Essays*. Ed. Richard H. Bowers. Jackson: UP of Mississippi, 1983. 133–39.

———. "Josefa Amar y Borbón y la educación femenina." *Letras Femeninas* 4.2 (1978): 3–11.

———. "Neojansenist Elements in the Work of Josefa Amar y Borbón." *Letras Femeninas* 7 (1981): 41–48.

Negrín Fajardo, Olegario, ed. "Introducción." *Ilustración y educación. La Sociedad Económica Matritense*. Madrid: Editora Nacional, 1984. 9–39, esp. 33–38.

Nelken, Margarita. "Las cultas y las cultalatiniparlas." *Las escritoras españolas*. Barcelona: Labor, 1930. 169–84, esp. 175–76.

Oñate, María del Pilar. *El feminismo en la literatura española*. Madrid: Espasa-Calpe, 1938. 157–98.

Ortega López, Margarita. " 'La Defensa de las Mujeres' en la sociedad del Antiguo Régimen." *El feminismo en España: Dos siglos de historia*. Ed. Pilar Folguera. Madrid: Pablo Iglesias, 1988. 3–28, esp. 26–28.

Poza Rodríguez, Melchor. "Josefa Amar y Borbón." *Mujeres célebres aragonesas*. Zaragoza: Mariano Salas, 1884. 189–92.

Roig, Mercedes. "España. El Despotismo Ilustrado." *A través de la Prensa. La Mujer en la Historia: Francia, Italia, España S. XVIII-XX*. Madrid: Ministerio de Asuntos Sociales, Instituto de la Mujer, 1989. 52–64, esp. 58–59.

Rudat, Eva Kahiluoto. "La mujer ilustrada." *Letras Femeninas* 2.1 (1976): 2–32.

———. "The View from Spain: Rococo Finesse and Esprit Versus Plebeian Manners." *French Women and the Age of Enlightenment*. Ed. Samia Spencer. Bloomington: Indiana UP, 1984. 395–406, esp. 404–06.

Sarrailh, Jean. *La España ilustrada de la segunda mitad del siglo XVIII*. Trans. Antonio Alatorre. Mexico: Fondo de Cultura Económica, 1957. 215–16, 259, 685, 695.

Sempere y Guarinos, Juan. *Ensayo de una biblioteca de los mejores escritores del reynado de Carlos III*. Vol. 3. Madrid: Imprenta Real, 1786. 137–39, 166.

Serrano y Sanz, Manuel. "Josefa Amar y Borbón." *Apuntes para una biblioteca de escritoras españolas desde el año 1401 al 1833*. Madrid: Atlas, 1975. Biblioteca de Autores Españoles. Vol. 268. 27–30. Rpt. of 1903 ed. Madrid: Sucesores de Rivadeneyra.

Sullivan, Constance A. "Josefa Amar y Borbón and the Royal Aragonese Economic Society (with documents)." *Dieciocho* 15.1 (1992). [Forthcoming]

Villota, Paloma. "El siglo de la Ilustración y la capacidad intelectual de la mujer." *Mujeres y hombres en la formación del pensamiento occidental, II. Actas de las VII Jornadas de Investigación Interdisciplinaria*. Ed. Virginia Maquieira D'Angelo, Guadalupe Gómez-Ferrer Morant, and Margarita Ortega López. Madrid: Universidad Autónoma, 1989. 185–96, esp. 191–93.

CONCEPCIÓN ARENAL (1820–1893)

Estelle Irizarry

BIOGRAPHY

Born in El Ferrol, Galicia, on January 30, 1820, Concepción Arenal was the first of three children in a family of distinguished and once-affluent lineage. Her father abandoned his law studies to join the military when the French invaded Spain in 1808, and he later became a fugitive for his part as a liberal in a rebellion against the repressive Fernando VII. According to several biographers, he died in prison when Concepción was nine years old. The family moved to the ancestral home of Concepción's paternal grandmother in Armaño, Liábana, in the mountains of Asturias. During the five years she spent there, Concepción read every book she could find, from her father's law books to *Don Quijote*.

In 1835 Concepción began her studies in Madrid at a school for girls of distinguished families—an education for women that she later described in *La mujer del porvenir* (1861; "The Woman of the Future") as "the art of wasting time" (in *Emancipación* 175). Her biographers Elvira Martín and Maria Campo Alange say she learned Italian and French on her own, at the same time that she acquired extraordinary proficiency in the "feminine labors" of sewing and embroidery. Her intention to attend the university and become a lawyer met with the consternation of her mother, who viewed her daughter's career aspirations as a threat to the family's honor and the possibility of marriage.

Arenal subsequently became the first woman to attend classes, as an auditor, at the Central University of Madrid, in the fall semester of 1842 (Campo Alange). Biographers speculate that she continued to attend law courses for three years. Several sources attest that Arenal came to classes dressed as a man, the only way she could study at an institution that prohibited women. Male disguise also freed her from the social convention of having to be accompanied by a family member or servant in public.

Arenal's activities while at the university are largely a matter of conjecture among her biographers. Martín offers the romantic account that the discovery of her female identity by a curious fellow student who followed her home led to a melée and that Fernando García Carrasco, a law student whom she later married, came to her defense. Martín adds that the rector of the university agreed to give Arenal a test to evaluate her intellectual capacity and subsequently allowed her to continue attending classes, on the condition that she not dress as a woman. In 1848 she and Fernando, who at the time was forty, twelve years her senior, decided to marry. This in itself was extraordinary in an era in which parental authority rather than love determined most marriages.

Arenal abandoned male garb and her outside activities to have her first child, a girl, who died of hydrocephalus at the age of two. In 1848, she followed her husband to Asturias, where he sought refuge from persecution for his liberal ideas. He was subsequently named editor of the liberal newspaper *La Iberia*. In 1850 Arenal gave birth in Madrid to a son, Fernando. The birth of another son, Ramón, two years later, left her in frail health. In 1851, Arenal began writing poems for a series called "Anales de la virtud" ("Annals of Virtue"), for which she was honored by several civic associations (Alarcón, *Celebridad* 90). During this period, she also penned several plays (unpublished) and *Fábulas en verso* (1854; "Fables in Verse").

When Fernando became ill with tuberculosis, Arenal continued his work by writing articles under his name for his column in *La Iberia*. In 1855, his death left her a thirty-five-year-old widow with two children. She continued to write for the newspaper anonymously, at half the salary her husband had received. Then a new law requiring that articles be signed brought an end to her editorials in *La Iberia*. The newspaper announced her retirement, thus at last acknowledging her collaboration.

In 1856, Arenal returned to the mountains of Asturias and two years later wrote the essays "¡Dios y la Libertad!" ("God and Freedom!" [unpublished]) and "¿De dónde venimos, adónde vamos?" ("Where Do We Come From, Where Are We Going?" [lost]). After three years of self-imposed mourning and confinement, she began to visit and minister to the poor while continuing to write, often into the early morning hours. In Potes she created a women's branch of the Conferencias de San Vicente de Paul, a charitable organization.

Arenal's essay *Beneficencia, filantropía y caridad* (1861; "Beneficence, Philanthropy, and Charity"), which she initially signed with the name of her ten-year-old son, Fernando, won a competition sponsored by the Academy of Moral and Political Science in 1860. The academy decided to allow the prize to stand, despite the revelation that the author was a woman. Later that year she published *El Visitador del pobre* (1860; "The Visitor to the Poor"), which appeared throughout Europe in six languages.

In 1863 Arenal became inspector of women's prisons in Galicia and moved to La Coruña, where the widowed countess of Espoz y Mina, a well-known philanthropist, funded the publication of many of her works. In 1864 she founded

Las Magdalenas, a group that visited women prisoners, read to them, and helped them upon their release. During this time Arenal wrote *Cartas a los delincuentes* (1865; "Letters to Delinquents").

In spite of failing health, Arenal began a campaign for prison reform and was inspector of the women's houses of correction until 1873, when the position was terminated. In 1867, she published *El reo, el pueblo y el verdugo* ("The Criminal, the People, and the Executioner"), and four years later published *Cartas a un obrero* (1871; "Letters to a Worker"). She cofounded a magazine called *La Voz de la Caridad* (1870), in which she published 474 articles during a period of fifteen years (Mañach 43). Although the proliferation of her charitable endeavors and publication of books brought her fame, Arenal always shunned publicity.

In 1872, after the death of her friend the countess of Espoz y Mina, Arenal fell seriously ill. The next year, the short-lived Republic, guided in large measure by Krausist ideas, brought a wave of liberalism with respect to the education of women. Arenal was named a member of the commission for prison reform.

With the outbreak of the last Carlist war in 1872, Arenal organized the Red Cross services and military health service, served for five months in a military hospital, and wrote *Cuadros de la guerra* (1874; "War Stories"). In 1875 she moved to Gijón with her son Fernando and two years later published *Estudios penitenciarios* (1877; "Prison Studies"), followed by *Derecho de gentes* (1879; "People's Rights"). She sent papers to several international conferences, and she contributed to the establishment of the Model Prison in Madrid.

In 1884 *La Voz de la Caridad*, the magazine Arenal had cofounded in 1870, closed due to financial problems. That same year her younger son, Ramón, died. Arenal devoted herself to writing and to social projects and, in 1889, moved to Vigo, where four years later she died of chronic bronchitis. The year before her death, she revised her complete works for publication, and sent essays on the education of workers and women to a Luso-Spanish-American conference on education.

Arenal, always a very private person, burned all but one photograph as well as all her personal correspondence, leaving behind only her published works. This has created many gaps in the reconstruction of her biography, and the critic must rely largely on correspondence from friends like Jesús Monasterio and the countess of Espoz y Mina for information about her life.

MAJOR THEMES

Many of Arenal's "literary" writings are unpublished or lost. Her first extant work is *Fábulas en verso*, poems with allegorical characters whose dialogues lead to maxims about human behavior. In it Alarcón reproduces several of her poetic "Anales de la virtud," written in the early 1850s, which are uplifting *romances* (ballads celebrating the heroism of humble folk). She also wrote religious poetry and the powerful *Oda a la abolición de la esclavitud* (1866; "Ode to the Abolition of Slavery").

Arenal's major contribution, however, is as an essayist. Her essays, which date from the early 1860s, earn her the distinction in Spanish literary history as the country's first woman essayist to address public issues. Indeed, she achieved eminence in the genre two full decades before the publication of the well-known essays of *La cuestión palpitante* (1882–1883) by her sister Galician Emilia Pardo Bazán, whose focus was intellectual rather than social. A precedent may be found in the reformist spirit of some of Saint Teresa's seventeenth-century autobiographical and doctrinal prose, but Arenal's essays avoid both autobiography and religion, traditionally acceptable subjects for "women's writing."

Arenal's fame rests mainly on her social writings, which she began several years after her husband's death with *Beneficencia, filantropía y caridad*. This work includes a thoroughly researched history of charity in Spain. Arenal's astonishing relevance and psychological acumen are evident in one of the most outstanding nineteenth-century books on social problems, *El visitador del pobre*. It was intended as a manual for both the San Vicente de Paul visitors and all who would answer her call: "God help the poor man who sins and the rich man who doesn't try to turn him from sin" (27). Today, more than ever, it is a fascinating text that proposes practical approaches to the problems of poverty, child abuse, and vice. Arenal views laziness, alcoholism, profligacy, and slovenliness not as the *cause* of the poor man's misfortunes but as the *results* of his poverty. She details how to help the poor, on a one-to-one basis, and how to help them to recover their self-respect and break the cycle of poverty. Treatment includes education, friendship, role models, guidance, removal from an unhealthy environment, and redirection. Arenal is realistic in her aims and hopes; she recommends patience and perseverance in working toward the gradual regeneration of an individual and the breaking of the vicious cycles of indigence and child abuse.

In her essays on justice and prison reform, the cornerstone of Arenal's thought is justice tempered by compassion, as expressed in her famous exhortation: "Hate the crime and pity the criminal" (Campo Alange, *Estudio* 27). She sees criminals not as incorrigible but as uncorrected, and recognizes the influence of family, friends, economic situation, and pure luck. She has faith that those who visit prisoners can help them to correct their moral weakness and to return to society. This was indeed surprising in the 1880s, in view of the growing influence of French naturalism, with its emphasis on determinism dictated by heredity and environment. Just as Emilia Pardo Bazán distilled naturalism into a more acceptable Catholic version in *La cuestión palpitante* and in her novels, Arenal advocated objectivity but rejected determinism.

Arenal directs some of her essays to the criminals themselves, as in *Cartas a los delincuentes*, and others to society and concerned citizens, as in *El derecho de gracia* (1880; "The Right to Pardon") and *El reo, el pueblo y el verdugo*. In the latter, she stands up for the principle of equality in the treatment of criminals, decries granting "grace" or pardon on an arbitrary and capricious basis, condemns public executions, and recommends humane methods of execution. In several of her writings she claims that the criminality of men is more frequent and serious than that of women, who might be expected to resort more often to crime because of their exclusion from education and honorable, well-paying employment.

What most distinguishes Arenal's work from that of other authors of her time, however, is her forceful writing about women. She reiterates in several works the idea that women are superior to men with regard to sensitivity, compassion, and patience. She asks: "Who suffers *with* those who suffer and is as compassionate as a woman?" (*La mujer del porvenir*; in *Emancipación* 114). Arenal's major "feminist" works are *La mujer del porvenir*, written in 1861 and published seven years later, and *La mujer de su casa* (1881; "The Woman in Her Home"). Mauro Armiño's compilation of these fundamental essays, together with two shorter ones, in *Emancipación* brings to the modern reader one of the most extraordinary books of Spanish writing on "the woman question."

In *La mujer del porvenir*, Arenal addresses allegations concerning the supposed physical and moral inferiority of women. She laments their exclusion from intellectual history as well as their ill treatment by both civilized and uncivilized societies. She examines the ways in which lack of education harms women, men, and society in general; the effect of education on women's character; and the benefits for the family of professional and intellectual training for women. Arenal defends a forgotten and much-maligned member of society—the single woman—and points out her role and value in the community. The book concludes with a forceful declaration of demands for women, among them civil rights, dignity, economic opportunity, and moral independence.

The title of *La mujer de su casa* echoes the popular saying that maintains that women's place is in the home. Arenal characterizes this as an erroneous male ideal designed to foster male progress and female immobility. She proposes the cooperation of both men and women to achieve the eradication of social and moral ills. She denies that women are weak, claiming they have only been weakened. She suggests that the same voice that asked Cain what he had done to his brother should resound in the conscience of man, obliging him to examine what he has done to the strength of woman.

In her 1891 article "El trabajo de las mujeres" ("Women's Work" in *Emancipación*) Arenal advocates greater opportunities for women to work outside the home, equal pay, and special arrangements to allow them to be workers, wives, and mothers at the same time. In *La educación de la mujer* ("The Education of Women"), first presented at a pedagogical conference in 1892, she contrasts the education of males and females and affirms that, since education is a means of perfecting the human being socially and morally, it is even more vital for women, who have been disadvantaged by law and custom. "It is a grave error," she says, "to inculcate in a woman that her only mission is to be wife and mother; it is equivalent to telling her that on her own she cannot be anything, and to annihilating her moral and intellectual self'' (in *Emancipación* 67). Arenal calls for the rights of women to a job that dignifies, citing their aptitude for professions and the absurdity of a society that considers the most inept man superior to the most intelligent woman (74). She defends both professional and physical education for women against masculine ideals of beauty for women that glorify weakness and intellectual inactivity. She reveals her own gender bias, however, when she alleges that certain occupations, notably the professions of judge and surgeon, endanger women's special sensitivity and compassion.

Shortly before her death in 1893, Arenal wrote ''Estado actual de la mujer en España'' (''The Present State of Women in Spain'' in *Emancipación*), an updated version of an essay that originally appeared in English in a volume called *The Woman Question in Europe*, edited and translated by Theodore Stanton in 1884. Arenal attributes to woman's ''muscular feebleness'' the origin of ''man's view of himself as superior in everything'' (''Spain'' 340). She deplores men's oppression of women as workers, thinkers, lovers, and wives, and considers women's economic dependency to be equivalent to slavery. She further decries the notion held by foreigners that Spanish women are extremely religious; according to Arenal, their devoutness is superficial, ritualistic, and marked by submission to the authority of the church. She scrutinizes the injustice of unequal education, prejudicial administration of punishment for crimes, political laws that exclude women from public office and professions, contradictory civil laws that give married women no more rights than those of minor children, and double standards for reputation and morality. The later, revised essay registers modest advances in all areas. Undoubtedly these advances would have been impossible without Arenal's contributions as an indefatigable promulgator of women's rights.

Arenal's concern for women permeates even those works that do not focus on them. In *Beneficencia, filantropía y caridad* she recommends that women, being naturally more disposed toward altruism and gentleness, take charge of charitable projects (*Obras completas* 2:215–19). She devotes a chapter of *Estudios penitenciarios* to protesting against preventive custody—prolonged incarceration in appalling conditions—as an abominable practice that inflicts unusually cruel punishment upon nursing mothers, mostly among the poor, and their infants. She further censures the ''monstrous injustice'' of a society that does not allow women to pursue professions and dispenses punishment with extreme severity.

She directs several of her *Cartas a los delincuentes* to women, noting that criminality in women goes against their nature and exhorting women prisoners to learn from her book. She writes to women prisoners about such ''taboo'' subjects as prostitution, venereal disease, infanticide, and abortion. Her persistent interest in how women fare before the law opens up a new branch of law that today might be called ''female law.''

Education was also one of Arenal's prime concerns, which she expressed in essays on educating workers, women, prisoners, and orphans. She corresponded with Don Francisco Giner de los Ríos, founder of the famous Institución Libre de Enseñanza and promoter of the education of women, who published some of her articles in the bulletin of the institution.

The moving force, however, behind all of Arenal's works is undoubtedly her often-repeated conviction that "the moral element is the most important in all society" ("Estado actual de la mujer en España" in *Emancipación* 27). The idea of free will permeates her work in all genres and fields, as does its corollary, faith in the human ability to reform.

A constant in Arenal's essays is the idea that injustice harms not only the victims but also those who inflict it. Thus she maintains that cruel and arbitrary punishment does as much harm to society and the executioner as to the criminal. Similarly, she compares this concept to the relationship between men and women and warns: "In the measure that men diminish women, they themselves are diminished materially, morally, and intellectually" (*La mujer de su casa*; in *Emancipación* 204).

SURVEY OF CRITICISM

Arenal's reputation confirms a much-proved truth about women writers: Even when they gain recognition, they are soon relegated to oblivion. As recently as 1975, the countess of Campo Alange observed that Arenal "is a name rarely heard of, although many Spaniards know it." She adds that it remains almost forgotten in the attics of history (5). Clearly, this neglect is not due to a lack of information. In 1907, Mañach edited a volume of tribute to Arenal consisting of over two hundred expressions of encomiastic praise, including anecdotes and poems, from four continents. A dozen women joined in this tribute, among them Emilia Pardo Bazán. Mañach laments the fact that Father Blanco (Francisco Blanco García), author of an important history of Spanish literature at that time, omitted Arenal's name. Mañach's volume is designed to compensate for that omission and to acknowledge Arenal's many contributions.

The author of one of the first critical volumes on Arenal, Julio Alarcón y Meléndez, S.J., reproaches her for not being Catholic enough to make her feminism acceptable. His assessment of Arenal obviously is strongly biased. He attempts to refute the claim of Spanish liberals that Arenal was one of their own by demonstrating her Catholicism while at the same time observing that her orthodoxy falls short of making her a model woman writer of great stature. He is one of the few critics who discusses Arenal's poetry, but his praise is limited to verses of a personal and religious nature.

Lamentably, Arenal has not been the subject of much serious criticism, although her life has attracted much attention. The publication of Maria Campo Alange's "documentary biographical study" in 1973 filled a great need for a reliable recounting of Arenal's life, since the biographer had access to the author's letters and other unpublished material. Other biographers have tended to employ more fervor than fact, to disagree on dates, to fictionalize and mythologize some events, and to indulge in a good deal of empty hyperbole. Even Campo Alange, who had access to an impressive array of letters and documents by people who were in direct contact with Arenal, recognizes the difficulty of separating fact from myth.

Arenal's writings have mainly attracted the attention of biographers and sociologists. To date, the most comprehensive study of her works is René Vaillant's 1926 book, *Concepción Arenal*, which treats themes, influences (Gaspar Jovellanos, Mme. de Staël, François Guizot, and Herbert Spencer), and style. Arenal's works in all genres await further serious study and analysis, not only of their content but also of their style. Perhaps this critical neglect is due in part to the scarcity of available texts. Nevertheless, the publication of compilations and new editions of several of Arenal's major works since the 1970s has made some of her writings more accessible to the public.

As a forceful essayist, a staunch defender of women's rights, and a sociologist of international reputation, Arenal was an outstanding figure in her time. All her writings are essentially speech acts of a persuasive woman of intense social conscience, designed to influence attitudes toward women and other disadvantaged people in nineteenth-century Spain. They merit not only renewed attention but also the type of substantive criticism that is needed to confirm Concepción Arenal's stature in Spain's intellectual and literary history.

BIBLIOGRAPHY

Works by Concepción Arenal

Obras completas. 23 vols. Vol. 1. Madrid: Sucesores de Rivadeneyra, 1894. Subsequent volumes, Madrid: V. Suárez, 1895–1898, 1913. Included are the following works:
El visitador del pobre (1860).
Beneficencia, filantropía y caridad (1861).
La mujer del porvenir (1861).
La igualdad social y política (1862).
Cartas a los delincuentes (1865).
Oda a la abolición de la esclavitud (1866).
El reo, el pueblo y el verdugo (1867).
A todos (1869).
Examen de las bases aprobadas por las cortes para la reforma de prisiones (1869).
Cartas a un obrero (1871).
Cuadros de la guerra (1874).
La cárcel llamada Modelo (1875).
Cartas a un señor (1875).
La pena de deportación (1875).
Estudios penitenciarios (1877).
Congresos penitenciarios (1878, 1890).
La instrucción del pueblo (1878).
Derecho de gentes (1879).
El derecho de gracia ante la justicia (1880).

La mujer de su casa (1881).
Observaciones sobre la educación física, intelectual y moral de Herbert Spencer (1882).
El visitador del preso (1891).
El delito colectivo (1892).
La educación de la mujer (1892).
La instrucción del obrero (1892).
El pauperismo (1895).
Beneficencia y prisiones. [Collected articles]

Early Editions (of individual titles not included in *Obras completas* or other compilations)

Fábulas en verso. Madrid: 1854.
Apelación al público de un fallo de la Real Academia Española. Madrid: Imprenta de Anoz, 1861.
A los vencedores y a los vencidos. Madrid: Las Novedades, 1869.

Modern Editions and Compilations

El pensamiento vivo de Concepción Arenal. Ed. Clara Campoamor. Buenos Aires: Editorial Losada, 1939, 1943.
El visitador del pobre. Buenos Aires: Emecé, 1941.
Cuadros de la guerra. Buenos Aires: Nova, 1942.
La cuestión social. Cartas a un obrero. Buenos Aires: Tato, 1945.
El visitador del preso. Madrid: V. Suárez, 1946.
El delito colectivo. Buenos Aires: Atalaya, 1947.
Breviario humano (Antología de pensamientos). Ed. María Barbeio y Cerviño. Madrid: Aguilar, 1949.
Fábulas. Ed. María de Pina. Mexico City: Porrúa, 1963.
Antología popular. Buenos Aires: Centro Gallego, 1966.
La emancipación de la mujer en España. Ed. Mauro Armiño. Madrid: Júcar, 1974. [A compilation of Arenal's books *La educación de la mujer*, *La mujer de su casa*, and *La mujer del porvenir*, and her articles "Estado actual de la mujer en España" and "El trabajo de las mujeres"; cited in text as *Emancipación*]
Cartas inéditas de Concepción Arenal. La Coruña: Excelentísima. Diputación Provincial, 1984.

Translations

"Spain." *The Woman Question in Europe*. Ed. and trans. Theodore Stanton. New York: G. P. Putnam, 1884. 330–53.
Manuel du visiteur du prisonnier. Trans. unknown. Paris: Secrétariat de l'Oeuvre des libérées de Saint-Lazare, 1893.

Works about Concepción Arenal

Alarcón y Meléndez, S. J. Julio. *Una celebridad desconocida*. Madrid: Razón y Fe, 1914.
———. *Un feminismo aceptable*. Madrid: Razón y Fe, 1908.

Armengol y Cornet, Pedro. *Bosquejo necrológico de Doña Concepción Arenal*. Barcelona: J. Jepsus, 1893.

Bayardo Bengoa, Fernando. *Concepción Arenal: vigencia de su humanismo en la hora presente*. Montevideo: n.p., 1973.

Cabezas, Juan Antonio. *Concepción Arenal, o el sentido romántico de la justicia*. Madrid: Espasa-Calpe, 1942.

Campo Alange, Maria. *Concepción Arenal en el origen de unos cambios sociales*. Madrid: Fundación Universitaria Española, 1975.

———. *Concepción Arenal 1820–1893. Estudio biográfico documental*. Madrid: Revista de Occidente, 1973.

Casas Fernández, Manuel. *Concepción Arenal. Su vida y su obra*. Madrid: Victoriano Suárez, 1936.

Correal y Freyre de Andrade, Narciso. *Concepción Arenal y los problemas sociales contemporáneos*. Madrid: n.p., 1923.

Dorado y Montero, Pedro. *Concepción. Estudio biográfico*. Madrid: La España Moderna, 1892.

Gómez Bustillo, Miguel R. *Concepción Arenal, su vida y obra*. Buenos Aires: Ediciones Depalma, 1981.

Landín Carrasco, Rafael. "Concepción Arenal." Supplemento dominical [Sunday supp.] *Faro de Vigo*. 19 Mar. 1981: 25.

Mañach, Francisco. *Concepción Arenal, la mujer más grande del siglo XIX*. Buenos Aires: J. A. Alsina, 1907.

Marsa Vancells, Plutarco. *Actualidad permanente del pensamiento de Concepción Arenal*. Madrid: El Fragua, 1983.

Martín, Elvira. *Tres mujeres gallegas del siglo XIX*. 2nd ed. Barcelona: Aedos, 1977.

Martínez Ruiz, José ("Azorín"). "Concepción Arenal. Ideario." *ABC* 15 Oct. 1929: n. pag.

Romero Maroto, Martín. *El Hospital del siglo XIX en la obra de Concepción Arenal*. La Coruña, Spain: Diputación Provincial, 1988.

Salgado Toimil, Ramón. *Concepción Arenal en el aspecto pedagógico*. Lugo, Spain: n.p., 1925.

Salillas, Rafael. *Inspiradores de doña Concepción Arenal*. Madrid: Reus, 1920.

Tarifa Guillén, Milagros. *La promoción humana de la mujer en Concepción Arenal*. Diss. abstract. Salamanca: Universidad Pontífica, 1982.

Tobío Fernández, Jesús. *Las ideas sociales de Concepción Arenal*. Monografías Histórico-Sociales, 5. Madrid: Instituto "Balmes" de Sociología, 1960.

Vaillant, René E. G. *Concepción Arenal*. New York: Instituto de las Españas en los Estados Unidos, 1926.

Vientós Gastón, Nilita. "Concepción Arenal." *Sin Nombre* 7.3 (1976): 46–61.

MARÍA VICTORIA ATENCIA
(b. 1931)

Sharon Keefe Ugalde

BIOGRAPHY

Born in Málaga, Spain, in 1931, María Victoria Atencia has resided in that southern coastal city all of her life, with the exception of short periods in the nearby countryside. The picturesque Paseo de la Farola is home to the poet today, and from the terrace of the family apartment it is possible to view not only the docks of Málaga, the lighthouse, and the sea but also the Glorieta de Guillén, whose official dedication the late poet Jorge Guillén viewed from the balcony of her home.

During Atencia's formative years, it was not customary for young women to leave home to pursue a university degree. Thus she enrolled in the Conservatory, the only institution of higher learning in Málaga at the time (Ugalde, *Conversaciones* 4). In addition to music, she was interested in painting, but after meeting the poet and editor Rafael León, her future husband, she decided to write. In the early days of her poetic career, Atencia met members of the Málaga literary community, some of whom were to become lifelong friends. Her acquaintance with Bernabí Fernández-Canivell, director of the literary journal *Caracola*, was especially significant. He acted as her literary mentor, as did Rafael León, suggesting names of poets she should read and introducing her to other writers from Málaga and beyond, including Dámaso Alonso, Vicente Aleixandre, and Jorge Guillén. Atencia also established contact with Pablo García Baena, the director of *Cántico*, a journal published in Córdoba, as well as with the women poets Rosa Chacel, María Zambrano, Elena Martín Vivaldi, and Clara Janés.

Atencia began writing when she was about twenty years old and published her first poems and chapbooks, including *Cañada de los Ingleses* (1961; ''The English Glen''), locally. *Arte y parte* (1961; ''Art and Part'') is a milestone because it appeared in the respected Adonais poetry collection in Madrid. During her early years as a writer, Atencia was occupied with other activities as well. She was the mother of four young children and an aviator with a private pilot's license, flying routes that spanned distances from Stockholm to Tangier and from New York City to Cologne.

A fifteen-year suspension of poetic activity followed the 1961 publications, a silence that has not been clearly explained. Atencia has commented that it was a period of human enrichment and continuous reading (Espada Sánchez, Interview 394). She has also suggested that her style was not compatible with the social poetry popular in Spain during the 1960s (*Thesaurus*, Interview 22). *Marta & María* (1976; "Martha & Mary") broke the long silence; the poet confessed that the book was written in a moment of "tension and anguish in the face of a possible breakdown" (Ugalde, *Conversaciones* 6). Since her return to poetry, Atencia has written and published prolifically. *Los sueños* (1976; "Dreams") and *El mundo de M.V.* (1978; "The World of M.V.") closed her period of renewal. Almost immediately afterward, a new phase began that shares certain characteristics with the *culturalismo* trend in Spanish poetry during the 1970s, a trend that José Olivio Jiménez describes as "the oblique or direct mention of characters, situations, phrases that the poet takes from the history of culture and re-creates in order to—in most cases—transform them into a transmitter of his or her own intuitions."[1] *El coleccionista* (1979; "The Collector") is the first major book of this third period; the brief *Paseo de la Farola* (1978; "Lighthouse Boulevard") had appeared a year earlier. Other books of the period are *Paulina o el libro de las aguas* (1984; "Paulina or the Book of the Waters"), *Compás binario* (1984; "Binary Time"), and *Trances de Nuestra Señora* (1986; "Perils of Our Lady"). *De la llama en que arde* (1988; "The Flame in Which One Burns") and *La Pared contigua* (1989; "Adjacent Wall") initiated a fourth period, in which the autobiographical "I," now less veiled and less distanced, reclaims a greater space for itself.[2]

In addition to these books, four collections of Atencia's poetry have appeared: *Ex Libris* (1984), which contains nearly all of her poetry up to the year of its publication; *La Glorieta de Guillén* (1986; "Guillén Circle"), a selection of poems associated with Málaga; *Nave de piedra* (1990; "Stone Nave"), a collection of fourteen previously published poems preceded by a rare statement by Atencia of her poetics; and *Antología poética* (1990; "Poetic Anthology"), an extensive selection with an introduction by José Luis García Martín. Most recently published is a volume entitled *La señal* (1990; "The Sign"), containing, with a few exceptions, the complete poetic work of Atencia and a prologue by Clara Janés.

MAJOR THEMES

In many ways, Atencia's books form a unified text. With respect to formal qualities, there is a preference for brevity, poems ranging from as few as three verses to nearly twenty. A predilection for blank Alexandrine verse, and occasionally for seven- and eleven-syllable verse, imposes further constraints. Each poem is an enclosed space that challenges the poet's artistry of synthesis and conciseness. The poem "El coleccionista" (*Ex Libris*), for example, likens the delicate precision with which the poet fashions her texts to that required to preserve a butterfly specimen in perfect condition:

> Sujétala con leves alfileres, abierta
> rotulada en su caja, y quedará preciosa.
> Procura no paplar el polvo de sus alas:
> has de ser delicado, como mandan los libros. (109)

The Collector

> Fasten it with pins, spread open.
> Labeled in a box, it will be precious.
> Touch not the dust on the wings:
> Be delicate, as ordained in books.

Certain objective referents, often associated with women's writing, are consistently chosen by Atencia to sustain her poetic insights: everyday items and activities; enclosed spaces, such as houses and boats; and elements of nature, especially the sea. In a substantial portion of her poetry, Atencia selects aspects characteristic of *culturalista* poetry: statues, paintings, architectural monuments, literary characters, authors, and historical figures. The topical material is perfectly formed into an object of beauty. Masterpieces such as Auguste Rodin's *Eve* (*La Pared*) and Andrew Wyeth's *"Christina's World* (*Compás*), as well as domestic items such as English marmalade, (*La llama*), are presented with such descriptive skill and sensual presence that a first reading might lead to the conclusion that Atencia's talents lie exclusively in preciosity and neo-Parnassian formalism. But, as Ortiz has emphasized, Atencia offers the reader more than the exquisite chill of a masterfully carved gem ("Leer"). Truth about the human condition, the hidden beauty of the poem, lies subtly beneath the surface. The understanding gained within the confines of the text at times surpasses the poet's conscious knowledge of herself. Atencia recognizes the power of the poem to reach deep levels of insight: "And we can even write about things that we don't know have happened to us, or that we don't know have affected us in a certain way, but that nevertheless constitute a part of us" (Janés, Interview).

Throughout Atencia's poetry, conceptual discoveries are characteristically enveloped in emotions that range from despair to the serene delight of transcendence. Feelings never explode into strident exclamations but form a softly burning flame within the boundaries of a classic notion of beauty. Each poem represents a fragile equilibrium that harmoniously balances affective-conceptual insights and sensual referents, re-created impressionistically.

The poet's struggle for knowledge most often centers on time and female identity and the relationship of the poetic process to both. The subtle evolution of Atencia's poetry is apparent in the way in which she treats these two major themes. Shaken by the deaths of two friends—one an instructor from the flying school, the other, Blancanieves, the daughter of Fernández-Canivell—and by the death of her parents, Atencia ended her lengthy silence to search for a deeper understanding of human morality. In *Marta & María* and *El mundo de M.V.*, the poet struggles with the fleetingness of her own personal existence. For example, the hopelessness of an irretrievable past is expressed in "Sueño de Churriana" ("Dream of Churriana," *El mundo*); the despair caused by the death of a loved one in "Casa de Blanca" ("House of Blanca," *Marta & María*); and the poignant longing to stop time in "Muñecas" ("Dolls," *Marta & María*).

The poet's relationship to time changes dramatically in *Paseo de la farola* and *El coleccionista*. The hopelessness of never recovering the child she once was and the anguish of approaching death are replaced with the splendor of a present moment of transcendence, achieved through the contemplation of natural and artistic beauty. Clara Janés describes the change in this way: "Finally . . . she takes one more step and decisively reveals the positive side of the coin; the poem emerges like a rose in the fog of a chaotic world, leaving behind, for other poets, the phase of being seduced by death" ("María Victoria" 38). In the style of Juan Ramón Jiménez, the poet contemplates beauty—for example, a painting by William Turner ("I. Rain"), the city of Venice ("Vigilia de Venecia"), and the port of Málaga at dawn ("Amanece")—and reaches an overwhelming sense of plenitude and light that stills time. In "Jardín de Intra" ("Garden of Intra"), the passage of time, symbolized by autumn, dissolves into a splash of color so spectacular that the approach of winter is forgotten:

> En medio de la plaza
> el otoño derrama
> rojos, carmines, ocres. (*Ex Libris* 102)

> In the center of the plaza
> autumn cascades
> reds, crimsons, ochers.

Paulina o el libro de las aguas reveals that the triumph over time is related not only to beauty but also to the poet's creative power, which eternalizes the lucid instants within the boundaries of the text. "That Light" (*Selected Poems*), for example, explores the complex relationship between timelessness and the poetic process. An atmosphere of solitude, night, and silence transposes the poet to the realm of creation, where she can both perceive transcendent light and confront death, through the act of writing.

The interwoven themes of memory and time, which in *Marta & María* convey a sense of loss, are again a central focus in *De la llama en que arde*, but with an astonishing difference. Atencia has discovered a place—the brief enclosure of her poetic text—where she has the power to triumph over time. This victory is even more striking than that achieved through the contemplation of beauty

because it is linked more directly to her personal existence. It is not a moment
of plenitude she gains but fragments of her own self, recovered from the rubble
by her poetic ability to fuse the past and the present. The poem "Escalera"
("Staircase") expresses this form of salvation:

> La noche me ofrendaba el tramo de silencio
> de una angosta escalera que mi fiebre mullía.
> En el rellano estabas—niña yo en ti—mirándome,
> resistiéndote al sueño en tus ojos perplejos.
> Me detuve un instante para besar tus sienes.
> Seguí subiendo luego, y entré en el cuarto, cómplice.
>
> (*De la llama en que arde* 36)

> The night offered me a parcel of silence
> from the narrow staircase that my fever fluffed up.
> You on the landing—little girl I in you—looking at me,
> resisting the sleep of your perplexed eyes.
> I stopped an instant to kiss your forehead.
> Then continued up, and entered the room, accomplice.

The words "night" and "silence," when read in the context of Atencia's
idiolect, have a symbolic significance seen above in "That Light." Both allude
to the poet's creative writing. "Fever" is added to the same paradigm, connoting
inspiration that can enhance ("fluff up") reality. Within the context of women's
writing, the word "room" is the most significant addition. Since the mid-nineteenth century, when Emily Dickinson transformed the limits of her room—
logically a symbol of women's imprisonment within the bounds of servile domesticity—into a space for self-realization through the power of her poetry,
"room" has come to symbolize a form of liberation, the hope that women
writing can (re)create an authentic identity for themselves. It is in this context
that Emily Dickinson said to her niece, "Matty: here's freedom," when they
entered her second-floor bedroom.[3] The title of Virginia Woolf's work *A Room
of One's Own* greatly enhances the connotative richness of the term, which
gradually has been transformed into an expressive gift that women writers give
to one another.

The upward movement of the speaker in "Staircase" also has symbolic value:
the possibility of spiritual transcendence. On an anecdotal level, the child the
speaker encounters could be a young daughter, perplexed by bumping into her
mother at such a late hour. But the poetic truth of the poem is found in another
identity that can be attributed to the child, the speaker when she was a little girl.
The poem serenely rescues childhood by transforming it into a present moment
("I stopped *an instant*"). The final verse is the victorious revelation, forceful
precisely because of its understated tone, that the speaker recognizes the power
of her word to overcome time. Almost with a wink, she acknowledges her part
("accomplice") in erasing the years that separate her from those days in the old
family house.

When read from a feminist perspective, the meaning of the text multiplies. It is significant that what the speaker retrieves from the past is her femaleness in its still uninscribed state. The words "little girl," in a central position in the text, are even more visible because of their enclosure in dashes. The highlighting of "little girl" in this way suggests that the poet can also be an accomplice in the inscription of an authentic female identity.

Female identity is, in fact, a frequent theme in much of Atencia's work. The poetic text provides a space in which an obedient daughter of patriarchy is free to search for her authentic self. Poems of the second period suggest an awakening to the pain of a self divided, a common theme in contemporary women's poetry.[4] There is muddled recognition by the poet-speaker that she is not that passive individual who relinquished her self to patriarchy. The opening lines of "What to Do if Suddenly . . . " (*Selected* 9), for example, capture this awareness: "What to do if suddenly you discover you are lived in/And utterly engulfed by someone alien to you/who bewilders your tongue with a different word." In "Marta & María" (*Marta y María*) the poet expresses a conflict between the practical woman who bears the responsibilities of everyday reality and the dreamer, whose creativity empowers her with a world all her own.

Other poems of this period suggest a vague longing for a prelinguistic bonding with the mother ("Dejadme," "Let Me Be") or with other female figures from the speaker's childhood ("Las mujeres de la casa," "Women of the House").[5] Some texts, "El duro pan" ("Dry Bread"), for example, convey the intuition, still not clearly formulated, that the despair that destroys the poet-speaker is in some way related to her female role of serving "el egoísmo ajeno" ("another's egoism"; 53).

In the third period, represented by *Paulina* and *Compás*, the poet intensifies the exploration of her female condition and gains clearer insight into woman's entrapment and absence of self. The poet resolves the dilemma between a publicly acceptable persona and the poetically invented truth about her female self by turning to a more veiled and indirect form of expression. Third-person descriptions of female figures portrayed in works of art replace the intimacy of the first-person-singular voice characteristic of the previous period. Guillermo Carnero attributes this indirection to the stylistic preferences of contemporary poetry, in place since T. S. Eliot called for the extinction of personality (63), but it may well be that the turn to concealment is related to gender. Sandra Gilbert has analyzed women writers' tendency to employ even extreme forms of indirection and arrives at the following conclusion: "Women as a rule, even sophisticated women writers, haven't until quite recently been brought to think of themselves as conscious subjects in the world . . . they have disguised the stories of their own psychic growth, even from themselves, in a multitude of extravagant, apparently irrelevant forms and images."[6]

Objects of art, which initially, in *El coleccionista*, enabled the poet to transcend temporality, are expressed in a duplicitous language that simultaneously conveys the beauty of the object and the desperation of female entrapment. This doubleness resembles that found by Alicia Ostriker in the poetry of Emily Dickinson (40–41). Poems such as "Paulina Borghese," which refers to Antonio Canova's sculpture, and "Retrato de una joven dormida" ("Portrait of a Young Woman Asleep"), cited below, exemplify this duplicitous form of expression:

Si por la oculta noche retenida
me pudiese llegar a tu lienzo y velarte,
tan cándida y cercana y tan ausente,
                        acaso
la luz que se detiene en tu pecho y lo alza
alcanzara a decirme si duermes a la vida,
si vives en la muerte, si puedo ser contigo
Ofelia de tu légamo, Desdémona en tu almohada. (*Paulina* 16)

If through the hidden, suspended night
I could reach your canvas and keep vigil,
so candid and near and so absent,
                        perhaps
the light that tarries on your breast and lifts it up
might reach me and tell if you sleep in life,
if you live in death, if I can be together with you
Ophelia of your mire, Desdemona of your pillow.

The Goya canvas referred to in the text covers the painful acknowledgment of nonexistence as an autonomous subject. As in many of Atencia's ekphrastic poems, those in which there is a verbal description of a work of art, the focus on a painting implies spatial limits, reiterated in the brevity of the text itself (Ugalde, "Time" 8).[7] Immobility is also paramount because the figure is trapped in a fixed position by the painter's brush. The anguish of being locked in a mummified existence ("sleep in life," "live in death") intensifies with allusions to two Shakespearean female characters: Ophelia, the fragile, passive woman who drowns in the tragic events that surround her and over which she has no control, and Desdemona, victim of male hegemony that makes a wife vulnerable to her husband's jealous rage. The poem's carefully structured equilibrium rests on the line "the light that tarries on your breast and lifts it up" (16), which integrates the objective referent (the canvas) and the insights that its contemplation reveals. The "light" symbolizes the poet's power (also conveyed by "suspended night," which denotes the moment of writing) to reveal the profound beauty of the painting, which is truth about womanhood. There is a suggestion here (Metzler), as in other Atencia poems, that the power of self-discovery is closely bound to the female body ("tarries on your *breast*" 16).

In her two most recent volumes, particularly in *La pared*, Atencia continues to explore the nature of femaleness, but with a new boldness. Insights about womanhood are now more precise, and although she does not abandon candid indirection her expression is less veiled. In some poems the tone is notably more emphatic than in previous works. "La Gran Muralla" ("The Great Wall"), for example, recognizes that a patriarchally constructed society silences women and concludes with "they [men] walled up my voice" (*La pared* 36); "Flores de cera" ("Wax Flowers"), using elderly nuns as a referent, reveals the deception and falsehood of a cloistered existence. Not only is the protest more audible; there are also poems that move away from what Elaine Showalter has termed the "Feminist" or protest phase of women's writing, to the "Female" phase of self-discovery.[8] Atencia learns that the power of her words not only conquers time but also reconquers her "self," so long held captive by male hegemony. The poem "La noche" ("Night") is an excellent example of this rediscovery. The title immediately suggests the act of writing because of the significance of "noche" in Atencia's poetry. The power of the female body in the process of self-discovery is also embedded in the title, which refers to a sculpture by Aristides Maillol of a nude woman in a sitting position, head down, as if contemplating her center. Uncertainty and confusion have dissipated; the female-poet persona recognizes and embraces her power to name herself: "en mi paisaje solo, yo, mi causa y destino" (*La pared* 45; "in my solitary landscape, I, my cause and my destiny").

SURVEY OF CRITICISM

Feminist studies of Atencia's work, which could enhance the understanding of her contribution to the inscription of female identity, are almost nonexistent. The critical climate in Spain, where most studies have appeared, is still resistant to feminist perspectives. Another factor that has affected the poet's treatment by critics is provincial isolation. Essays on Atencia's poetry began to appear in the 1980s, coinciding with the broader distribution and greater publicity afforded by the major poetry presses of Madrid. Prior to 1984, Atencia had published only two volumes in Madrid; since that year all of her works have appeared there. It should also be pointed out that the status of women poets shifted substantially in Spain in the 1980s, with a boom in women's poetry fomented by the general climate of change produced by the democratization of the country after Franco's death in 1975. Thus, several factors came together to draw attention to Atencia's work. Besides brief reviews and notes, there are now a substantial number of essays on her poetry, published principally in literary journals, and the pace of their appearance is rapidly accelerating. In addition, the notes, prologues, and epilogues in several of Atencia's books provide important insights.

María Victoria's fifteen-year silence has influenced the treatment of her poetry by literary critics and historians. She is a generational misfit, in part because during the 1960s she did not publish, and because after her return to poetry in the 1970s, she wrote in a manner similar to the next younger group of *culturalista* poets. Chronologically, Atencia belongs to the second wave of Postwar Poetry, but she was never mentioned in the numerous anthologies and book-length studies of that generation until recently. She was included for the first time in José Luis

García Martín's *La segunda generación poética de posguerra* (1986), a more inclusive study than earlier ones that were often limited to a focus on "social poetry." Gender undoubtedly also played a role in Atencia's early exclusion, because, as Roberta Quance documents, in Spain women's poetry was viewed as inferior and inappropriate for mainstream generational anthologies.[9]

Some relatively recent articles serve as useful introductions to Atencia's poetry. José Luis Cano (1980) characterizes each book through *El coleccionista*, emphasizing the exploration of time and childhood. In his analysis of *Marta & María* and *El mundo de M.V.*, he points out the presence of everyday referents and the house as the predominant poetic space. Cano finds the brevity of the poems of *El coleccionista* very unusual within the context of Spanish women's poetry. Emilio Miró (1985) adds to Cano's descriptions by focusing on metric preferences and the poet's insistence on polishing and perfecting her texts. The latter is substantiated through his comparison of the poems of *Ex Libris* with their earlier published versions. The closing mention of female onomastics in Atencia's work is an invitation to further study. In his review of *De la llama en que arde*, Miró (1990) dedicates a paragraph to *Trances de Nuestra Señora*, which largely slipped through the crevices of the usual review process because of its publication as a special Christmas edition. He views the volume as a major contribution to Mariology poetry, not because of its verbal exuberance but because of its naked purity. With respect to *De la llama en que arde*, Miró again underscores Atencia's formal perfection and her gift for transcending the patches of reality—objects, memories, places, especially those of southern Spain—she brings to her poems.

Biruté Ciplijauskaité also emphasizes Atencia's ability to move beyond temporal and geographic limits, and the presence of an internal tension of opposites through which true plenitude is achieved. The critic stresses that Atencia's work defies the confines of any particular poetic tendency or group, and underscores how the poet objectifies experience and consistently affirms her female condition. José Luis García Martín's (1990) introduction to *Antología poética* offers an important overview of the four periods of Atencia's poetry. García Martín frequently relates aspects of Atencia's work to a broader poetic tradition but seems purposely to avoid attributing any aspects, such as early marginality or long silence, to the fact that she is a woman. Especially useful is the emphasis on intertexts, both in the introductory article and in the annotations of the poems included in the anthology.

That there is as yet no book-length study of Atencia's poetry can be viewed as an opportunity, especially for feminist critics. The author of those unwritten pages will have the privilege of inscribing in history the place of a poet who one day may be recognized as the twentieth-century Emily Dickinson of Spain.

NOTES

1. José Olivio Jiménez, *Diez años de poesía española* (Madrid: Insula, 1972) 378. See García Martín, *La segunda generación poética de posguerra* 205–40 for a more extensive discussion of *culturalismo*.

2. Biruté Ciplijauskaité suggests that this change may reflect the most recent development in the evolution of Spanish poetry, a move in the direction of "poetry of experience" (9).

3. Adrienne Rich, "Vesuvius at Home: The Power of Emily Dickinson," *Shakespeare's Sisters. Feminist Essays on Women Poets,* ed. Sandra M. Gilbert and Susan
Gubar (Bloomington: Indiana UP, 1979) 99, recounts this anecdote about Dickinson.

4. Alicia Ostriker, *Stealing the Language. The Emergence of Women's Poetry in
America* (Boston: Beacon Press, 1986) 59–90.

5. Alicia Ostriker, *Stealing the Language* 166–67, describes contemporary women
poets' insights into female bonding and the mother-daughter relationship. See also, Nancy
Chodorow, *The Reproduction of Motherhood* (Berkeley: U of California P, 1978).

6. Sandra M. Gilbert, "A Fine, White Flying Myth: The Life/Work of Sylvia Plath,"
Shakespeare's Sisters 245–60.

7. See also Diane Chaffe, "Visual Art in Literature: The Role of Time and Space in
Ekphrastic Creation," *Revista Canadiense de Estudios Hispánicos* 8.3 (1984): 312.

8. Elaine Showalter, *A Literature of Their Own. British Women Novelists from Brontë
to Lessing* (Princeton: Princeton UP, 1977) 13.

9. See Roberta Quance, "Entre líneas: Postura crítica ante la poesía escrita por mujeres," *La Balsa de la Medusa* (Madrid) 4 (1987): 73–84.

BIBLIOGRAPHY

Major Works by María Victoria Atencia

Arte y parte. Madrid: Adonais, 1961.
Cañada de los Ingleses. Málaga: Cuadernos de María Cristina, 1961.
Marta & María. Málaga: n.p., 1976. 2nd ed. Madrid: Caballo Griego para la Poesía,
    1984.
Los sueños. Málaga: n.p., 1976.
El mundo de M.V. Madrid: Insula, 1978.
Paseo de la Farola. Málaga: Nuevos Cuadernos de Poesía, 1978.
El coleccionista. Sevilla: Calle del Aire, 1979.
Compás binario. Madrid: Hiperión, 1984.
Ex Libris. Madrid: Visor, 1984.
Paulina o el libro de las aguas. Madrid: Trieste, 1984.
La Glorieta de Guillén. Málaga: Puerta del Mar, 1986.
Trances de Nuestra Señora. Madrid: Hiperión, 1986.
De la llama en que arde. Madrid: Visor, 1988.
La pared contigua. Madrid: Hiperión, 1989.
Nave de Piedra (Antología). Málaga: I. B. Sierra Bermeja, 1990.
Antología poética. Madrid: Castalia/Instituto de la Mujer, 1990.
La señal. Málaga: Excelentísimo Ayuntamiento de Málaga, 1990.

Translations

Epitaffo di una faniculla. Trans. Margherita Guidacci. Bilingual ed. Málaga: Cuadernos
    de Europa 5, 1964.
Vilceaua anglezilor. Trans. Comnita Dumitrescu. Málaga: n.p., 1970.

Capelle Medicee. Trans. Margherita Guidacci. Bilingual ed. Málaga: Torre de las Palomas, 1979.

Exilio. Trans. José Bento. Lisbon: Assírio e Alvim, 1986.

Fragile. Trans. Emilio Coco. Málaga: Sur, 1987.

Os gestos usuais. Trans. José Bento. Lisbon: Assírio e Alvim, 1987.

Selected Poems. Trans. Louis Bourne. Fredericksburg, MD: Mainstay Press, 1987.

L'Occhio di Mercurio. Trans. Emilio Coco. Bari, Italy: Levante Editori, 1988.

Svenciausios Karalienés Ekstazés. Trans. Biruté Ciplijauskaité. Málaga: n.p., 1989.

Vybrané Básne. Trans. Josef Forbelsky. Málaga: n.p., 1990.

Works about María Victoria Atencia

Aleixandre, Vicente. "Unas palabras." *Ex Libris.* By María Victoria Atencia. Madrid: Visor, 1984. 7–8. [Preliminary note]

Cano, José Luis. "La poesía de María Victoria Atencia." *Insula* 398 (1980): 8–9.

Carnero, Guillermo. Afterword. *Marta & María.* By María Victoria Atencia. 2nd ed. Madrid: Caballo Griego de la Poesía, 1984. 61–65.

Ciplijauskaité, Biruté. "La serena plenitud de MVA." *Alaluz* 22.1 (1990): 7–12.

Espada Sánchez, José. Interview. *Poetas del sur.* Madrid: Espasa-Calpe, 1989. 387–405.

García Martín, José Luis. Introduction. *Antología poética.* By María Victoria Atencia. Madrid: Castalia/Instituto de la Mujer, 1990. 7–38.

———. *La segunda generación poética de posguerra.* Badajoz; Spain: Dept. de Publicaciones de la Exca. Diputación, 1986.

Interview. *Revista Universitaria de Poesía* (Barcelona) 3 (1988): 21–22.

Janés, Clara. Interview with María Victoria Atencia. [Unpublished]

———. "María Victoria Atencia o el triunfo de la belleza." *Los Cuadernos del Norte* 3.16 (1982): 38–39.

León, Rafael. Preliminary note. *Glorieta de Guillén.* By María Victoria Atencia. Málaga: Puerta del Mar, 1986. 11–13.

Morales Zaragoza, María Luisa. "La poética de dos polaridades de femenino." *Marta & María.* By María Victoria Atencia. 2nd ed. Madrid: Caballo Griego de la Poesía, 1984. 9–14. [Preliminary note]

Metzler, Linda. "The Images of the Body in the Poetry of María Victoria Atencia." International Symposium on "Literatura Femenina Contemporánea de España." U of California, Northridge, 23 Feb. 1990.

Miró, Emilio. "*De la llama en que arde* de María Victoria Atencia." *Insula* 517 (1990): 11.

———. "El mundo lírico de María Victoria Atencia." *Insula* 462 (1985): 6.

Ortiz, Fernando. "La difícil serenidad de María Victoria Atencia." *La estirpe de Bécquer.* 2nd ed. Seville: Editoriales Andaluzas Unidas, 1985. 258–63.

———. "Leer a María Victoria Atencia." 422 *El Ciervo* (1986): 23–26.

Rodríguez Padrón, Jorge. "María Victoria Atencia: Indagando en la soledad." *Insula* 458–59 (1985): 30.

Romero Márquez, Antonio. "María Victoria Atencia: *Paulina o el libro de las aguas.*" *Insula* 474 (1986): 17.

Ugalde, Sharon Keefe. *Conversaciones y poemas. La nueva poesía femenina española en castellano.* Madrid: Siglo XXI, 1991.

———. "La sujetividad desde 'lo otro' en la poesía de María Sanz, María Victoria

Atencia y Clara Janés." *Revista Canadiense de Estudios Hispánicos* 14.3 (1990): 511–23.

———. "Time and Ekphrasis in the Poetry of María Victoria Atencia." *Confluencia* 3.1 (1987): 7–12.

Zambrano, María. "El reposo de la luz." *Trances de Nuestra Señora*. By María Victoria Atencia. Madrid: Hiperión, 1986. 9–12. [Preliminary note]

CECILIA BÖHL DE FABER Y LARREA ("FERNÁN CABALLERO") (1796–1877)

Martha J. Manier

BIOGRAPHY

The first years of Cecilia Böhl's life give little indication that, writing under the pseudonym Fernán Caballero, she would restore the novel to a place of prominence in Spain during the 1850s. Cecilia spent her formative years in Germany with her father and brother, far from the Andalusia she came to love and describe. Her father, Juan Nicolás Böhl, had returned to his homeland after suffering business setbacks in Cádiz. Unable to adjust to the move to Germany, his wife, Francisca Larrea, returned to Spain with her younger children to pursue intellectual endeavors, especially as an advocate for women's rights. With her mother's departure, the young Cecilia lost her Spanish-language teacher and soon her skills in that language lagged, replaced by those in German and French. In 1823 a consular appointment reestablished father and children in Spain. This reunited the Böhl family for a three-year period before Cecilia's departure to marry.

If anything from this period influenced Fernán's fiction, it was her interest in family, the problems it confronted, the values it preserved, and the roles of its women. In addition, her mother's independence prejudiced the person Cecilia and the writer Fernán against women who strayed from the norm, causing others to suffer. In spite of this attitude, or perhaps because of it, Cecilia followed her mother's path. She became a prolific writer who, by advocating tradition and its inherent religious and moral values, earned enough to support herself and her debt-ridden third husband. She enjoyed the respect of readers and critics, was befriended by the Spanish royal family, and received international acclaim.

In 1816 Cecilia Böhl married for the first time. The marriage indicated both a stable and a promising future, for her husband, Captain Antonio Planels Bardají, was from a rich Ibizan family and he had, by the age of twenty-six, a promising military career. Unfortunately, that future did not materialize. Nothing in Planels's background prepared Cecilia for her life with him the following year in Puerto Rico. Planels's debaucheries led to his sudden death and her return to Spain, a widow. Critics such as E. Herman Hespelt and Javier Herrero have traced how this marriage experience influenced her novel *Clemencia*, published in 1852. Perhaps it also colored her views on military life in general: the changes it effects in the soldier's personality, the safe haven it offers rogues and cheats, and the hollow glories it continuously exalts. These views were vented in several works, including *La familia de Alvareda* (1849; *The Alvareda Family* 1872), *Lucas García* (1852), and *La farisea* (1863; "The Woman Pharisee").

If this one-year period affected Fernán Caballero's writing to some extent, then the next period, her thirteen-year marriage to Francisco Ruiz del Arco, the marquis of Arco Hermoso, would affect it even more. During this time she lived happily in Seville and the nearby town of Dos Hermanas. In the former, she knew and observed the nobility and its habits, morals, pastimes, and discussions. In the latter, she met farmers, laborers, and their families. She listened to the stories they told, the songs they sang, and the local lore, and then recorded it all on her "little scraps of paper." When categorized, her collection provided enough material for three volumes of folklore: *Colección de artículos religiosos y morales* (1862; "A Collection of Religious and Moral Stories"), *Cuentos, oraciones, adivinas, y refranes populares e infantiles* (1877; "Popular and Children's Stories, Prayers, Riddles, and Sayings"), and *Cuentos y poesías populares andaluzas* (1859; "Popular Andalusian Poems and Stories"). It also provided her with scenes within works (*La gaviota* 1849; *The Sea Gull* 1867, 1965) or with the basic premise for an entire work (*La familia de Alvareda*).

During this period Cecilia came to know the American writer Washington Irving. Much has been written of Irving's meeting with her in 1828, his praise of her early draft of *La familia de Alvareda,* and his encouragement of her writing. At the same time, it can be argued that she introduced him to *costumbrismo* (local color writing), which, according to Williams, would influence his style in *The Alhambra, The Sketch Book, Bracebridge Hall,* and *Tales of a Traveller.*

That Cecilia Böhl wrote during her second marriage cannot be disputed. Besides the draft of *La familia de Alvareda*, she completed *Elia* (Hespelt and Williams) and "La madre, o el combatiente de Trafalgar" ("The Mother or the Soldier of Trafalgar"). Although the first two of these works were not published until 1849, her mother sent "La madre" to the journal *El Artista*, which published it in 1835. The fact that this story was printed without her consent angered Cecilia and furthered the resentment she felt toward her mother. She wrote to the editors requesting that no other example of her works be published, because she did not write for the public; it was not a women's prerogative to do so. She believed, or at least seemed to believe, that women should dedicate themselves to domestic occupations and maintain the domestic peace. Women were quiet and complacent, obedient and long-suffering.

Yet Cecilia's very act of writing, whether for private expression or public consideration, removed her from the domestic sphere and contradicted her feminine ideal. She composed sketches, stories, and novels based on accounts that her neighbors and acquaintances of Dos Hermanas had offered her, seemingly to preserve the oral history that she found so interesting. The fact that she expanded upon the same material, adding her own touches from observations, personal insight, and imagination, indicates that writing had become for her a carefully studied form. This personal struggle between the artistic and the ideal is fictionalized in *La gaviota*. There the resolution returns the protagonist, Marisalada, to the domestic sphere, her talent diminished by circumstance and illness. In contrast, Cecilia, deviating from this ideal, continued to write. The fact that her fiction extols the traditionally domestic may indicate her compromise with a social reality she could not reject.

Cecilia's reluctance to publish in 1835 had roots in other personal factors: her own social standing, her relationship with her father, and his attitude toward women. As a member of the nobility by marriage, Cecilia had to protect her position in Seville's social circles, where the conservative view prevailed. Women were simply not expected to develop intellectually. If they read and thought, their ideas and reflections were limited to stimulating conversation during private receptions and evening social gatherings and were not intended for distribution. Cecilia may have wanted to avoid her father's displeasure, since she knew he had little regard for women intellectuals. Böhl himself admitted he had never read anything Cecilia wrote while she was single, since "women's things" were not to his liking (Heinerman 97; Fox-Lockert 38). Their father–daughter relationship was, in any case, a close one; she adored him and he exhibited pride in her, especially with her announced intent to depict the Spanish people and their customs (Herrero 330). Böhl's attitude, however, corresponds more to his own romantic philosophy and interest in folklore than to an acceptance of his daughter's nascent narrative talent.

Cecilia's second husband died in 1835, and her father the next year. This sudden loss of the two men she most loved led Cecilia into unwise relationships. In 1836 she had an affair with an Englishman whose name, Federico Cuthbert, comes to us through her letters. She was fond of him, but he had greater interest in seduction than a lasting relationship. The following year, she surprised many people by marrying Antonio Arrom de Ayala, a man nineteen years her junior. Lengthy separations and his miscalculations in business characterized their marriage, which ended with his suicide in London in 1859.

Cecilia continued to write during this period. Moved by economic necessity and changing attitudes (society's and her own), she began to publish. Nine works appeared in 1849, and another six the following year. Her stories, novels, and sketches first appeared serialized in the Madrid newspaper *El Heraldo*. They later appeared in book form through the efforts of the Madrid publisher Mellado. Cecilia's publication rate proved prodigious for the next decade, as did her popularity in Spain and abroad. Translations abounded in French, German, and English. When she published, however, Cecilia masked her identity with the pseudonym Fernán Caballero. According to legend, she had seen the name in a newspaper account relating a Manchegan murder and had taken it for her own. Such an ominous baptism disguises the symbolic nature of the name used in this case and in other examples of her fiction as well. The reference to noble and knight recalls past glories and traditional values. The same can be said of a second pseudonym used when she published in the newspaper *La España*: León de Lara.

Whether or not readers and critics surmised Böhl's true identity before 1853 is unknown. In that year Vicente Barrantes, after analyzing *Clemencia*, determined its author to be "a woman of the most tender, kind and passionate of hearts" (qtd. in Sánchez 403). It soon proved impossible for her to continue to conceal her identity. Nonetheless she insisted on the separate nature of her private and literary lives, to the point that correspondence about her work had to be addressed to Fernán.

What Fernán Caballero achieved by writing is remarkable. When she first put pen to paper, the novel had all but disappeared in Spain. Writers preferred other genres. In addition, the prevailing political situation forced intellectuals, writers included, into exile. Lacking adequate native fiction, the reading public turned to translations of French and English works given to fantasy, sentimentality, and historical invention. Fernán changed this trend. In an original fashion, she wrote about what she knew and loved: Andalusia and its people, their thoughts, values, and customs. Blending disparate elements, concentrating on what E. Allison Peers calls the "living present" (157) and copying the morphology, syntax, and content of everyday speech, she created a new novel of truthful discourse.

When Fernán wrote "the novel is not invented, it is observed" (qtd. in Peers 158), she revealed the secret of her narrative success. She also established the method and style that later realists such as Benito Pérez Galdós and Juan Valera followed. Unfortunately, these writers and others rejected Fernán Caballero's contributions to narration because of her gender and her neo-Catholicism, which influenced the moral didacticism and religiosity found in her fiction. Furthermore, the novelists did not acknowledge her role as a precursor of Spanish realism. Fernán herself may have contributed to this lack of interest in her work by appearing to downplay her accomplishments, referring to certain writings as *obrillas* (little works). In addition, her insistence that she did nothing more than compile and copy implies a lack of creativity. Feminist criticism by Susan Kirkpatrick has radically altered this interpretation. Kirkpatrick proposes that the "modesty" exhibited in these statements holds a double significance, "for modesty can be read inversely as claiming an authenticity not found in contemporary Spanish novels" ("Genre" 327). She finds Fernán's statement on copying a clever assertion of her literary technique because it places her within the realm of European realist discourse, and it underscores the fact that she has succeeded in presenting an authentic version of Andalusian society through faithfulness to detail. Fernán's carefully couched words mask her awareness of skill and refinement of craft.

Today's reader may consider Fernán Caballero's fiction trite because it incorporates quaint folk elements, formula narration, melodrama, allegory, and moralizing; yet it was these very traits that appealed to her readers, many of whom were women. Unfortunately, when the public taste changed, Fernán Caballero was unable or unwilling to comply. During her later years she continued to write local color sketches; for the most part, however, she lived in obscurity until her death in 1877, at the age of eighty-one.

MAJOR THEMES

Fernán Caballero writes, above all, of the family. In doing so, she also writes about women and their place in society, for family and the home were women's domain, separated and protected from the political and economic reality of the male-dominated world. While the sentimental discourse of female contemporaries such as María del Pilar Sinués de Marco exalts family as a paradisiacal refuge and women as the domestic angels, Fernán presents a vision that is truer to life: her families are beseiged by the forces of social disorder; her women sin and suffer, the happiness of domesticity eluding them for the most part. There are exceptions, of course, but these are few.

La gaviota, Fernán's first published novel, is a moral tale of selfish ambitions of the protagonist. Marisalada rejects family and women's duty in the hope of becoming a successful opera singer. She triumphs thanks to her talent and the aid afforded her by both husband and benefactor, but her growing pride, as well as theirs, wreaks destruction on everyone. Widowed and alone, her talent destroyed by illness, she returns to Villamar and marries the town's barber, a mediocre singer. Far from happy and no longer beautiful, she serves her penance with two small children clinging to her skirts.

This image is far from the innocent woman Fernán depicts in the novel's opening chapters—a long-legged girl who lives by the sea and whose voice complements the sounds of the waves and the birds. Her innocence is corrupted by the institutions of family, community, and church, which fail her by not teaching her traditional principles. Not instructed in moral values, she is unprepared for the men she meets and the success of her career.

La familia de Alvareda stresses the importance of faith in maintaining the family intact. Through her narrative Fernán shows how a generation raised in the Christian faith turns from it, in the process destroying themselves and the family nucleus. The novel's protagonist, Pedro Alvareda, realizes his error on the day of his execution for murder and thievery. He confesses: "I preferred a vain thing men call honor, which at times is bought with suffering and blood, over the Gospel teachings, which turn suffering into virtue and pardon into duty" (Ed. Rodríguez Luis 187). Pedro forgets he has broken another commandment.

His fall from grace begins when he fails to honor his mother and her warning of the ills befalling those who commit incest. He marries his cousin Rita, who enters into an adulterous relation with his friend Ventura. Rita, like Marisalada, suffers from pride. Ventura introduces another of Fernán Caballero's themes, the corrupting influences of military life.

In other works Fernán rails against both military policy and military officers for their antifamily stance. In *Deudas pagadas* (1857; "Debts Repaid") she details how the government's conscription of peasants to fight the African wars caused family hardship and a mother's anguish. The end result of those wars is reduced to the hollow trappings of victory parades in *La hija del sol* (1849; "The Daughter of the Sun"). Through the double example of an aging general who neglects his young wife to achieve public acclaim and a young major who attempts to destroy a family through his adulterous relationship with the same woman, Fernán indicates that even in glory, family suffers.

Any discussion of the military as antifamily would not be complete without the example of a family's debasement found in *Clemencia*. In this novel, an army captain marries the girl of the title to win a bet made with fellow officers. If we accept, as critics have suggested, that the novel is founded upon Cecilia Böhl's own first marriage, Fernán's disillusionment with military men and the institution they represent becomes clear. The patterns of family presented in the above discussion repeat themselves in the remainder of Fernán Caballero's fiction, as a foundation of her work.

SURVEY OF CRITICISM

Considering the popularity of Fernán Caballero in her epoch and her noted contributions to Spanish letters, relatively little has been written about her or her work. This can be attributed to the readership that abandoned and continues to abandon her, as well as to the scholarly community that has just recently begun to study her work from a feminist perspective. Fernán Caballero is a difficult writer to address because of the contradictions found in both her life and her fiction. José Montesinos treats other problems one encounters when writing about Fernán: the lack of suitable editions of her work, the early studies written by "pobres diablos" (poor devils; *Ensayo de justificación* viii) who could not maintain critical impartiality, and Fernán's own unwillingness or inability to reveal herself even to herself. Montesinos's study is the most thorough to date and the most perceptive. Delving into author and epoch, he provides valuable insights into her poetic reality and narrative truth, defines her particular style of *costumbrismo*, and explores her indebtedness to folklore.

Prior to Montesinos's book (1961) the first serious investigations regarding Fernán and her work date from the 1930s. Herman Hespelt and Stanley T. Williams examine the influence of Washington Irving on Fernán Caballero and hers on him. Their case may be overstated, since Caballero and Irving met once, in December 1828, and there is no other known communication between the two. Nevertheless, Hespelt's and Williams's studies are important in that they show something of Fernán's creative process and establish the time frame in which her fiction evolved.

The question of influences also emerges in later studies. Javier Herrero explores the influence of Juan Nicolás Böhl and Francisca Larrea on their daughter, especially with regard to her love for Andalusia. José F. Montesinos and Lawrence Klibbe theorize that Fernán derived the formula for her novel of customs from Balzac, her favorite French writer, just as she copied from him, though not as masterfully, his mode of characterization. Fernán copied from other French authors as well, notably Madame de Staël and George Sand, whose successes preceded her own. Biruté Ciplijauskaité details how certain scenes of *La gaviota* closely parallel those found in de Staël's *Corinne* and Sand's *Consuelo*: the opening sea adventure and the singing debut, respectively. She also points out striking similarities between Fernán's Stein and de Staël's Oswald, Fernán's Marisalada and Sand's Consuelo. Furthermore, Fernán and de Staël both tend to make generalizations about other nationalities, thus revealing their distinct cultural biases.

In an overlooked article, "*La gaviota* One Hundred Years After," Charles Qualia speaks of Fernán as a powerful influence on the Spanish novel of the second half of her century. By introducing a writing style based on direct observation, she made it possible for others—Pedro Antonio de Alarcón, Juan Valera, Benito Pérez Galdós, José María de Pereda, Antonio de Trueba, and Armando Palacio Valdés—to evolve their own realism based upon this same observational skill. In the case of the latter three, Fernán's influence on the art of the novel is greatest even in its didacticism (66). As Qualia further points out, Fernán provided these writers not only with an example but also with a theory of the novel. It is unfortunate that these authors, as well as critics, have failed to recognize her contributions—ideologies and moral stance aside. Qualia's 1951 study ended with a call for reappraising Fernán and her influence. His challenge still stands.

Qualia's emphasis on Fernán as a realist, or at the very least a precursor of the realists, raises a problem that has stirred a great deal of critical debate. How can one classify Fernán's literary style as romantic, *costumbrista*, or realist when her works contain aspects of each genre but conform to none? Portraying daily life with exactitude, explaining actions instead of sentimentalizing them, adhering to truth (albeit her own version of that truth), and concentrating on the history of the locale are characteristics that certainly ally her with realism. But can she be a realist if, as Rafael Castillo has written, "the society she paint[ed] was not yet real; it was not an active society, but an object to be contemplated with the paternalistic look of writer of customs" (193). It is true that Fernán regarded herself a writer of customs, but her work differs greatly from that of other writers associated with the style: Mariano José de Larra, Serafín Estébanez Calderón, Ramón de Mesonero Romanos. While they produced sketches of character types, entertainments, and customs in order to record life or to satirize it, Fernán combined sketches with plot and moral didacticism to protest social change and teach traditional ways. Her stated intent of painting the *pueblo* (with *pueblo* meaning at the same time the town, its inhabitants, the nation, and the race) was not a descriptive exercise but a treatise. At times she resorted to enhancing her message through symbol, superficiality, and the picturesque (Montesinos, *Ensayo de justificación* 38, 53). This, coupled with optimism, didactic subjectivity, idealization of Spain, and the fact that "she never escapes from herself" (Peers 159), places her with the romantics.

With such scope to her work, it is no wonder that Fernán Caballero is often referred to, perhaps disparagingly, as a transitional writer. What makes her unique to her generation? For Susan Kirkpatrick the answer lies in Fernán's unresolved conflict over the established roles of gender and her own reality, which results in her split self. As the product of a conservative family and society, she was faced with the choice of staying within the "boundaries" of traditional female behavior or following her needs and talents into the male realm of writing. She chose the latter but strove to justify the former. The moral didacticism she incorporated into her works "shielded her from charges of having stepped out of the place assigned her in that old order of society" ("Gender" 328). The justifications, concealments, and contradictions woven into her work are to that same end and, as Kirkpatrick argues, give rise to her "innovative yet inhibited treatment of the distinctions among literary discourses" ("Gender" 324).

Assessment of Fernán Caballero is far from finished. Along with the question of gender that Kirkpatrick has raised, other issues concerning Fernán Caballero and her work wait to be addressed: the structure of her work, her indebtedness to folklore, her theories of the novel, and her influence on the realists. The task is great, but Fernán's task was greater. She combined and reformulated aspects of style and society belonging to the first half of her century. Further, Fernán Caballero paved the way for the resurgence of novelistic fiction that matured in the second half of the nineteenth century and beyond.

BIBLIOGRAPHY

Major Works by Fernán Caballero

Since few of Fernán Caballero's works, especially the lesser ones, have received new separate editions, the following indicate their places in the *Obras de Fernán Caballero* published in the series Biblioteca de Autores Españoles, the most accessible edition of her fiction. All were published in Madrid by Atlas in 1961 and appear in vols. 136–40 of the series. Indicated below in chronological order are the original dates of publication, the volume of the Biblioteca de Autores Españoles, and the pages. Where a modern edition is available, that information is provided together with the original date of publication.

Los dos amigos. 1849. Vol. 137. 287–91.

Elia; o España treinta años ha. 1849. Ed. Julio Rodríguez Luis. Madrid: Alianza, 1968.

La familia de Alvareda. 1849. Ed. Julio Rodríguez Luis. Madrid: Castalia, 1979.

La gaviota. 1849. Ed. Carmen Bravo Villasante. Madrid: Castalia, 1979.

La hija del sol. 1849. Vol. 137. 295–300.

Una en otra. 1849. Vol. 138. 231–93.

Callar en vida y perdonar en muerte. 1850. Vol. 137. 237–49.

El ex-voto. 1850. Vol. 139. 267–82.

Lágrimas. 1850. Vol. 137. 107–232.

No transige la conciencia. 1850. Vol. 137. 253–71.

Con mal o con bien a los tuyos te ten. 1851. Vol. 138. 297–322.

Clemencia. 1852. Ed. Julio Rodríguez Luis. Madrid: Cátedra, 1982.

Lucas García. 1852. Vol. 139. 196–226.

Pobre Dolores. 1852. Vol. 137. 389–425.

Un verano en Bornos. 1852. Vol. 138. 145–205.

Más largo es el tiempo que la fortuna. 1853. Vol. 137. 325–45.

Simón Verde. 1853. Vol. 139. 81–115.

Las dos Gracias o la expiación. 1855. Vol. 138. 349–92.

La estrella de Vandalia: cuadro de costumbres. 1855. Vol. 138. 93–141.

La flor de las ruinas. 1855. Vol 137. 276–83.

Justa y Rufina. 1855. Vol. 137. 305–22.

Un servilón y un liberalito; o tres almas de Dios. Original title *Tres almas de Dios.*
    1855. Puerto Santa María, Spain: Casa de Cultura, 1975.

Deudas pagadas. 1857. Vol. 139. 331–49.

El día de Reyes. 1857. Vol. 139. 257–64.

El dolor es una agonía sin muerte. 1857. Vol. 139. 237–41.

Lady Virginia. 1857. Vol. 138. 209–28.

Más vale honor que honores. 1857. Vol. 139. 159–92.

La noche de Navidad. 1857. Vol. 139. 248–53.

Obrar bien . . . que Dios es Dios. 1857. Vol. 139. 229–34.

El último consuelo. 1857. Vol. 139. 121–55.

Cuentos y poesías populares andaluzas. 1859. Vol. 140. 64–191.

Vulgaridad y nobleza. 1860. Vol. 138. 395–420.

Cosa cumplida . . . sólo en la otra vida. 1861. Vol. 139. 7–76.

Dicha y suerte. 1861. Vol. 139. 139–55.

Colección de artículos religiosos y morales. 1862. Vol. 140. 354–361.

La farisea. 1863. Vol. 138. 325–46.

Cuentos, oraciones, adivinas, y refranes populares e infantiles. 1877. Vol. 140. 195–
    287.

Estar de más. 1878. Vol. 137. 346–71.

Magdalena. 1878. Vol. 137. 375–83.

Translations

The Castle and the Cottage in Spain. Trans. Lady Wallace. London: Saunders, Otley &
    Co., 1861. [Trans. of *Elia, Callar en vida y perdonar en muerte, La familia de
    Alvareda,* and *Pobre Dolores*]

The Sea Gull. Trans. J. Leander Starr. NY: Bradburn, 1864.

The Sea Gull. Trans. Augusta Bethell. London: R. Bentley, 1867.

Elia, or Spain Fifty Years Ago. Trans. unknown. New York: D. Appleton, 1868.

The Alvareda Family. Trans. Viscount Pollington. London: Newby, 1872.

The Bird of Truth and Other Fairy Tales. Trans. John H. Ingram. London: Sonnenschein
	& Allen, 1881.

"The Old and the New; or Three Souls Too Good for This World." Trans. Helen and
	Alice Zimmern. In *Half-Hours with Foreign Novelists.* London: Chatto and Win-
	dus, 1882.

Silence in Life and Forgiveness in Death. Trans. J. J. Kelly. London: Richardson, 1883.

Air Built Castles: Stories from the Spanish of F. Caballero. Trans. Mrs. Pauli. London:
	London Literary Society, 1887.

The Seagull. Trans. Joan Maclean. Woodbury, NY: Barrons, 1965.

Works about Fernán Caballero

Asensio, José María. "Fernán Caballero y la novela contemporánea." *Obras completas.*
	By Fernán Caballero. Vol. I. Madrid: Colección de Escritores Castellanos, 1893.
	[Prologue]

Caldera, Ermanno. "Poetizar la verdad en Fernán Caballero." *Romanticismo 3–4: Atti
	del IV Congresso sul romanticismo spagnolo e ispanoamericano (Bordighere, 9–
	11 April 1987): La narrativa romántica.* Ed. Ermanno Caldera. Genoa: Biblioteca
	de Lett., 1988. 17–22.

Caseda Teresa, Jesús. "Costumbrismo y estética literaria de Fernán Caballero." *Cua-
	dernos de Investigación Filológica* 69. 12–13 (May–Dec. 1987): 82.

Castillo, Rafael. "Los prólogos a las novelas de Fernán Caballero y los problemas del
	realismo." *Letras de Deusto* 8.25 (1977): 185–93.

Castro y Calvo, José María. Prologue. *Obras de Fernán Caballero.* Biblioteca de Autores
	Españoles. Vol. 137. Madrid: Atlas, 1961.

Charnon Deutsch, Lou. "Godfather Death: A European Folktale and Its Spanish Var-
	iants." *Inti* 12 (Autumn 1980): 2–19.

———. "On Desire and Domesticity in Spanish Nineteenth Century Women's Novels."
	Revista Canadiense de Estudios Hispánicos 14.3 (Spring 1990): 395–414.

Ciplijauskaité, Biruté. "*La gaviota* y la novela femenina en Francia." *La Chispa 1983.*
	Ed. Gilbert Paolini. New Orleans: Tulane UP, 1983. 61–65.

Corti, Valentina, and Monica Di Martino. "La función adjetival en *La gaviota.*" Caldera
	17–22.

Croce, Benedetto. "Fernán Caballero." *Poesía e non poesía.* Bari: Guis, Laterza & Figli,
	1923. 207–25.

Fox Lockert, Lucía. *Women Novelists in Spain and Spanish America.* Metuchen, NJ:
	Scarecrow Press, 1979.

Heinerman, Theodore, ed. *Cecilia Böhl de Faber y Juan Eugenio Hartzenbusch.* Madrid:
	Espasa-Calpe, 1944.

Herrero, Javier. *Fernán Caballero: un nuevo planteamiento.* Madrid: Gredos, 1963.

———. "El 'Schlosser' de Fernán Caballero." *Romanische Forschungen* 74 (1962):
	404–12.

Hespelt, E. Herman. "The Genesis of *La familia de Alvareda.*" *Hispanic Review* 2
	(1934): 179–201.

———. "The Porto Rican Episode in the Life of Fernán Caballero." *Revista de Estudios
	Hispánicos* 1 (1928): 62–67.

———. "A Second Pseudonym of Cecilia Böhl de Arrom." *Modern Language Notes* 41.2 (Feb. 1926): 123–25.

———. "Washington Irving's Notes on Fernán Caballero's Stories." *PMLA* 49 (1935): 1129–39.

———, and Stanley T. Williams. "Two Unpublished Anecdotes by Fernán Caballero Preserved by Washington Irving." *Modern Language Notes* 49 (1934): 25–31.

Horrent, J. "Sur *La gaviota* de Fernán Caballero." *Revue des Langues Vivantes* 32 (1966): 227–37.

Kirkpatrick, Susan. "Denying the Self." *Las Románticas: Women Writers and Subjectivity in Spain 1835–1850.* Berkeley: U of California P, 1989. 244–78.

———. "On the Threshold of the Realist Novel: Gender and Genre in *La gaviota.*" *PMLA* 98 (1983): 323–40.

Klibbe, Lawrence H. *Fernán Caballero.* New York: Twayne, 1973.

Manier, Martha J. "El mito de Rodrigo el último godo y *La familia de Alvareda.*" *Revista de Feria* (Dos Hermanas, Spain, 1985): 31–33.

Montesinos, José F. "Un esbozo de Fernán Caballero." *Volkstum und Kultur der Romanen* 3 (1930): 232–57.

———. *Fernán Caballero: Ensayo de justificación.* Berkeley: U of California P, 1961.

Olson, Paul R. "Reacción y subversión en *La gaviota* de Fernán Caballero." *Actas del VIII Congreso de la Asociación Internacional de Hispanistas, II.* Ed. A. David Kossoff, José Amor Vásquez, Ruth H. Kossoff, and Geoffrey W. Ribbans. Madrid: Istmo, 1986. 375–81.

Peers, E. Allison. *A History of the Romantic Movement in Spain.* Vol. 2. New York and London: Hafner, 1964.

Pitollet, Camille. "A Propos de Fernán Caballero et de M. Montesinos." *Bulletin Hispanique* 33 (1931): 335–40.

———. "Deux mots encore sur Fernán Caballero." *Bulletin Hispanique* 34 (1932): 153–60.

———. "Les premiers essais littéraires de Fernán Caballero." *Bulletin Hispanique* 9 (1907): 67–86, 286–302; 10 (1908): 286–305, 378–96.

Qualia, Charles B. "*La gaviota* One Hundred Years After." *Hispania* 34 (1951): 63–67.

Rodríguez Luis, Julio. "*La gaviota*: Fernán Caballero entre romanticismo y realismo." *Anales Galdosianos* 8 (1973): 123–36.

Sánchez, José. "Fernán Caballero–Barrantes Correspondence." *Hispanic Review* 9 (1941): 402–404.

Valis, Noël. "Eden and the Tree of Knowledge in Fernán Caballero's *Clemencia.*" *Kentucky Romance Quarterly* 29.3 (1982): 251–61.

Varela, José Luis. "Fernán Caballero y El Volkgeist." *Arbor* 379–380 (1975): 22–28.

Williams, Stanley T. "Washington Irving and Fernán Caballero." *Journal of English and Germanic Philology* 29 (1931): 352–56.

MARIA AURÈLIA CAPMANY
(1918–1991)

Barbara Dale May

BIOGRAPHY

A major intellectual figure and architect of modern Spanish feminism, Maria Aurèlia Capmany was, from early childhood, exposed to cultural and political activism. The daughter of liberal bourgeois parents, she was born in Barcelona in 1918, during an era of intense pro-Catalan agitation marked by a richness of cultural activity and aggressive political vanguardism. Fascinated by books, which she recalled as her family's greatest luxury, Capmany was a precocious student of literature, history, and philosophy. She completed her early education in one of the most progressive schools in the country, the Institut-Escola de la Generalitat. When the Spanish Civil War began in 1936, she was eighteen years old and a student of philosophy at the Universidad Autónoma de Barcelona. With the collapse of the Spanish Republic at the end of the Civil War in 1939, Capmany's world changed drastically. Educated during an era that saw the birth of the Spanish Republic and with it a flourishing of Catalan culture, she was now witness to the deliberate suppression of the Catalan language, both written and spoken.

Immediately after the war, massive book burnings took place, and all periodicals in Catalan were suppressed, as were radio broadcasts in the language. On the losing side in the war, Catalans were long forbidden to speak their language outside the home. Relaxation of these and other restrictions was piecemeal and punishingly slow.

By the time Capmany finished her studies at the Universidad Autónoma in 1942, her spirit as a committed Catalanist was far from extinguished. At the same time that she was teaching at the university, in itself an extraordinary feat, she was moving in literary and political circles vaguely identified as the Catalan underground. By the time she was in her early thirties, she was considered a leader of "Els Grans" (The Elders), a generation of gifted Catalan writers who, during the years from 1939 to 1951, published not a word. Making a conscious decision not to publish at all rather than abandon Catalan as a written language, Capmany, like other members of the group, continued to write during the years of official intolerance.

Even when policies regarding use of regional languages relaxed—and only as a pragmatic sign of the Franco regime's growing awareness of its isolation as a fascist nation in postwar Europe—Capmany and her colleagues still had to contend with the limitations of censorship. The fact that in 1948 she was awarded the prestigious Joanot Martorell Prize for her unpublished manuscript "El cel no és transparent" ("The Sky Is Not Clear"), is evidence of ongoing Catalanist literary activity during the years of restriction of regional identity. Suppressed at the time of its writing by official censors, the novel was published nearly fifteen years later, during a period of relative modulation of policies regarding publication in regional languages, under the title *La pluja als vidres* (1963; "Rain on the Windowpanes"). The first novel that Capmany published, *Necessitem morir* (1952; "We Must Die"), was therefore not the first book she wrote but the first to find a willing publishing house upon clearing the censor. With the publication of this novel, Capmany's long career as a skilled dancer through the mine field of Spanish censorship began.

Necessitem morir was followed by many other novels, among them *L'altra ciutat* (1955; "The Other City"); *Betulia* (1956); *Tana, o La felicitat* (1956; "Tana, or Happiness"); *Traduit de L'americá* (1959; "Translated from the American"); *El gust de la pols* (1962; "The Taste of Dust"); *La pluja als vidres*; *Un lloc entre els morts* (1969; *Un lugar entre los muertos* 1970; "A Place Among the Dead"); *Felicment, io soc una dona* (1969; "Fortunately, I'm a Woman"); *Vitrines d'Amsterdam* (1970; "Showcases of Amsterdam"); *Quim/ Quima* (1971); *El jaquè de la democracia* (1972; "Democracy's Dinner Jacket"); and most recently, *Lo color mès blau* (1982; *La color más azul* 1984; "The Bluest One").

Also an actor and theater director, Capmany, with Ricard Salvat, founded the Escola d'Art Dramàtic Adriá Gual. She also wrote a number of plays, including *Tu i l'hipòcrita* (1960; *Tú y el hipócrita* 1960; "You and the Hypocrite"); *El desert dels dies* (1966; "The Desert of the Days"); *Vent de Garbi i una mica de por* (1968; "Southwest Wind and a Little Fear"), in collaboration with the historian Xavier Romeu; *Preguntes i repostes sobre la vida i la mort de Francesc Layret, advocat dels obrers de Catalunya* (1971; "Questions and Answers on the Life and Death of Francesc Layret, Defender of the Workers of Catalonia"); and *L'alt rei en Jaume* (1977; "Old King James"). In addition, she authored several collections of cabaret acts composed of monologues and songs, primarily with political or social commentary, and, in collaboration with Jaume Vidal Alcover, *Ca, barret!* (1984; "Ca-baret!").

In the late 1960s, when Capmany left academia and devoted her efforts to writing and political activity, she established herself as a feminist and consummate political essayist. Her first collection, *La Dona a Catalunya* ("Woman in Catalonia"), was published in 1966. Other volumes include *Dia si, dia no* (1968; "Every Other Day"); *La joventut, es una nova classe?* (1969; "Are the Young a New Class?"), in collaboration with Carmen Alcalde; *El feminismo ibérico* (1970; "Iberian Feminism"); *De profesión, Mujer* (1970; "Profession: Woman"); *Cartes impertinents* (1971; "Impertinent Letters"); *El feminisme a Catalunya* (1973; "Feminism in Catalonia"); *Carta abierta al macho ibérico* (1973; "Open Letter to the Iberian Macho"); *El comportamiento amoroso de la mujer* (1974; "Woman's Affective Behavior"); *Dona, doneta, donota* (1975; "Woman, Little Woman, Big Woman"); and *Dietari de prudències* (1982; "Diary of Relevant Happenings").

Although most of Capmany's works originally appeared in her native language, most notably those written during the period of greatest suppression of Catalan language and culture, she wrote a number of books in Castilian and many of her novels and essays have been translated into Castilian. A tireless writer and activist associated with the Catalan Communist Party, Capmany continued to write and lecture. She was for some time cultural council member for the city of Barcelona until her death in 1991.

MAJOR THEMES

Although overt autobiographical reference is infrequent in Capmany's writing, there exists an intimate correspondence between her works and her personal evolution: Indeed, all of her production, regardless of genre or period, may be considered political. Ever aware of the constraints of censorship in postwar Spain, yet defiantly committed to free expression, Capmany found the historical novel to be an appropriately oblique medium. *Un lloc entre els morts* is a masterfully crafted novel that well represents her creative response to the problem of censorship. The novel traces the life of a fictional poet, Jeroni Campdepadròs, a bourgeois intellectual of the nineteenth century. A fascinating and convincing account of an invented life, the book leaves the reader wondering if perhaps Campdepadròs, whose poetry and journal entries occasionally find their way into the novel, really existed. On another level the novel is a powerful and subtle examination of the Catalan national identity in an era preceding the "Renaixença" of Catalan letters. It is also a critical examination of a number of themes found throughout Capmany's work: the power of language and its relationship to individual and national identity, the relationship of materialism to pleasure and decadence, the conditional aspect of reality. Throughout the book, Capmany's narrator questions the story that would have been told if Campdepadròs's widow had not burned the poet's memoirs. She also questions what would have happened had historical events been rearranged, deleted, or replaced by other accidents of history. Capmany's fascination with conditional reality, in this novel and in many others, such as *L'altra ciutat, Betulia, El jaquè de la democracia*, and *Lo color mès blau*, mirrors a preoccupation with the tension between literature and history, fiction and reportage, resulting in the ambiguity that marks her work.

Un lloc entre els morts is of particular interest in that it may be read on yet another level, as a feminist critique of one man's life. Campdepadròs, not quite an antihero, is at best an unsympathetic protagonist, a self-absorbed revolutionary at odds with his bourgeois appetite for luxury and frivolous pleasure. He has nothing but contempt for the women in his life. Each woman—the empty-headed stepmother, the conventional and devoted wife, the little girl he seduces and later hires as nurse in his last days—is a muted witness to his self-destruction. Each in turn is mistreated and rejected by Campdepadròs. Capmany plays with the reader through the novel's biographer/narrator, who, in sympathizing with Campdepadròs, reveals his own sexism and bias, thus exposing the dubious credibility of male-defined historical "objectivity."

A frequent target of Capmany's criticism is the bourgeoisie, whom she targets for its materialism, hypocrisy, and dependence on convention. This is clearly seen in her plays, particularly in *Tu i l' hipòcrita*, one of a few plays by Capmany to be translated into Castilian. Utilizing a tense, insistent monologue presented by the hypocrite, a middle-class man in his forties, Capmany elicits uncomfortably close participation on the part of the audience, identified as the "tu" in the title. In such a way, the dramatist forcefully requires the bourgeois audience to engage in self-criticism.

Few contemporary Spanish writers can claim as early and as intense a commitment to feminism as Capmany, who once named Virginia Woolf's *Three Guineas* and Maria Campo Alange's *La secreta guerra dels sexes* as two works closest to her own intellectual and moral commitment. Capmany's style parallels these writers' use of intelligent irony in examining woman's lot in society. An apt example of her preoccupation with feminism, as well as with class and conditional reality, is *Lo color mès blau*, published in Catalan in 1982 and translated into Castilian in 1984. The novel's protagonists, Oliva and Delia, are both fifteen when the story begins in 1939. Good friends, they are separated at the end of the war when Delia, the daughter of militant Communists, goes into exile with her parents. Oliva remains in Barcelona with her bourgeois parents, who are relieved at the outcome of the war and not at all unhappy to see Delia's influence over their daughter removed. The action spans twenty-nine years in the lives of the two women, tracing Delia's experience as an exile living in various places around the world and Oliva's adolescence and adulthood in Franco's postwar Spain. The novel ends with a disappointing reunion of the two in Paris in 1968. Sadly, neither woman can really communicate with the other because Oliva, although from a privileged family, has opted to reject the bourgeois values that led to her oppression in the first place, whereas Delia has willingly traded the values of her working-class parents for those of the class that has exploited both women.

A gifted essayist, Capmany treats the question of class and the women's movement in a number of collections, among them *El feminismo ibérico*, *Cartes impertinents*, and *Dona, doneta, donota*. A key problem in Spanish feminism, as Capmany sees it, is that it had its historical origin within the bourgeoisie rather than the proletariat, resulting in a brand of feminism that is blandly reformist and opportunist. For a radical change of society, the bourgeois feminist will have to control her means of production, and the proletarian woman will have to reject the bourgeois values that provide the infrastructure to her dream of getting ahead in society. At the heart of the problem are the passivity and conventionality of the bourgeois woman and the imitative spirit of the working-class woman.

In an insightful examination of feminism's repetitious rise-and-fall cycle, Capmany, in *El feminismo ibérico*, indicts a sexist society that, when threatened by the women's movement, seeks to digest, co-opt, and assimilate. The writer's historical analysis of a feminist polemic of the 1920s between Maria Cambrils, author of *Feminismo socialista*, and Celsia Regis, editor of the feminist magazine *La Voz de la Mujer*, serves as a pretext for Capmany's questioning of whether women should align themselves with other political movements or remain unaffiliated, unified only as an oppressed class struggling for equality. Written in 1970, *El feminismo ibérico* was Capmany's second in a series of essays concerning Spanish feminism, the first being *Dia si, dia no*, published two years earlier. In both works, Capmany underscores the insidious nature of women's oppression and the primary urgency of women's liberation.

Much like her younger colleague, the feminist writer and activist Lidia Falcón, Capmany questions the basic unit of society: the family. In *El comportamiento amoroso de la mujer* she challenges women to examine their behavior within a compulsorily heterosexual society. From her early years as a member of the defiant "Els Grans," through the period of censorship, to the era of political reawakening following Franco's death, Capmany remained, with Lidia Falcón, Carmen Alcalde, and Victoria Sau Sànchez, one of a small constellation of outspoken radical feminists in Spain. In spite of her association with the Catalan Communist Party, she rejects the notion that feminist objectives should be secondary to the greater social revolution, and throughout her writing she expresses impatience with women from any class who remain uncommitted to the struggle for sexual equality.

SURVEY OF CRITICISM

Arthur Terry, in his renowned study of Spanish literature, *A Literary History of Spain: Catalan Literature* (1972), identifies the Catalan novel of the postwar period as the literary genre showing the most variety and originality. He evaluates Capmany as a serious, mature novelist "of achievement rather than mere promise," whose name should appear on even the most exclusive list of distinguished Catalan writers (117).

Echoing Terry is Joan Fuster, who places Capmany at the head of this elite:

"Maria Aurèlia Capmany is, without a doubt, a key figure of the movement which during the postwar era represents the spirited and willful tradition of the Catalan novel" (389). Furthermore, he underscores the importance of Capmany's feminist consciousness and political commitment. Her literary work, relentlessly militant, acquires special meaning by the fact that it is the work of a woman and, moreover, the work of a woman energetically conscious of being a woman. Alienated by superficial feminism, Capmany refuses to translate women's issues into mere rhetoric or facile explanations. Her work is clearly based on frank and "irrefutable objectivity" (389). Fuster examines in some detail Capmany's study of androgynous identity in her novel *Quim/Quima*, which was inspired by Virginia Woolf's *Orlando*.

A useful analysis of Capmany's impressionist perspectives in the novel is Manuel de Pedrolo's "Impressions-Expressions sobre tres novel.les de la Maria Aurèlia," in which Pedrolo reveals a close tie between Capmany's use of multiple perspectives and her dissatisfaction with any unilaterally presented reality. Pedrolo's essay, much like the novels it studies, is a fine example of the oblique political criticism that surfaced in the mid-1970s, when the Franco era was nearing an end.

Barbara Dale May's "Power Dynamics of Woman's Anger in Maria Aurèlia Capmany's *La color más azul*" is a feminist analysis of empowerment and activism viewed within the context of class in Capmany's novel. Also treated is Capmany's use of epistolary structure in this novel and earlier works.

Capmany's dramatic productions and her work as a theater director, actor, and teacher have been recognized by a number of critics. Arthur Terry, noting the special problems faced by dramatists of the Franco years, wrote, "though all kinds of writing have suffered from the hazards of official censorship, the difficulties of establishing a serious professional theatre in Catalan are still enormous. . . . All too often, the production of new plays has been limited to a single performance, and opportunities of seeing plays in Catalan outside Barcelona are still very restricted" (118). Terry considers Capmany's work with EADAG (Escola d'Art Dramàtic Adriá Gual) to be of major importance in the development of Catalan theater.

Maria Lourdes Möller-Soler, in an article in *Estreno: Cuadernos del Teatro Español Contemporáneo*, traces the pioneering work of dramatist Carme Montoriol during the 1930s, noting the abundance and complexity of her female protagonists. She sees a striking contrast between Montoriol's prewar drama and Capmany's theater of the postwar years: "The theater of Montoriol is based on mutual love, faithful and solid, between men and women. The women, although immersed in the interior space of the home, occupy, in fact, the center of the stage as well as the action" (7). Unlike Montoriol's women, however, Capmany's fail to connect emotionally or intellectually with men. "In all of her works, Capmany denies the possibility of intelligible communication between men and women and, particularly on the part of women, denies the possibility of love between the two" (7). Möller-Soler indicts Capmany's infrequent use of female protagonists in her plays and describes her women characters as secondary and inferior, concluding that Capmany "sees them through the eyes of the male protagonist with whom she identifies, directing herself primarily to a male audience" (8).

Given Capmany's radical questioning of the dynamics of heterosexual communication, most apparent in *El comportamiento amoroso de la mujer*, it seems more likely that her objective is the ironic demythification of heterosexual models such as those proposed by Montoriol. Far from validating the male perspective in works like *Tu i l'hipòcrita*, where only the male has a voice, she is more likely revealing the poverty of a reality in which woman is muted. Capmany's unsympathetic female characters, at odds with each other as well as with men, are usually unconscious accomplices in their own oppression, their emotional deformation a predictable symptom of a pathological society. Can women ever be equals within the conventional paradigm? Capmany repeats the question throughout her plays, novels, and essays.

Although Janet Pérez's discussion of Capmany in *Contemporary Women Writers of Spain* is in part a distillation of Miquela Misiego's comments in Carolyn Galerstein's *Women Writers of Spain: An Annotated Bio-Bibliographical Guide* and May's "Power Dynamics of Woman's Anger," her analysis is useful in situating Capmany among others of her literary generation in Catalonia and within the greater context of contemporary Spanish literature. Pérez correctly asserts that Capmany, like her Catalan contemporaries and younger colleagues, is "more radically feminist, more aggressively activist, and more to the left on the political continuum than those writing in Castilian" (200).

BIBLIOGRAPHY

Major Works by Maria Aurèlia Capmany

Novels

Necessitem morir. Barcelona: Nova Terra, 1952.
L'altra ciutat. Barcelona: Biblioteca Selecta, 1955.
Betulia. Barcelona: Biblioteca Selecta, 1956.
Tana, o la felicitat. Palma de Mallorca: Francesc de B. Moll, 1956.
Traduit de L'americà. Palma de Mallorca: Francesc de B. Moll, 1959.
El gust de la pols. Barcelona: Destino, 1962.
La pluja als vidres. Barcelona: Club Editor, 1963.
Felicment, io soc una dona. Barcelona: Nova Terra, 1969.
Un lloc entre els morts. Barcelona: Nova Terra, 1969.
Vitrines d'Amsterdam. Barcelona: Club Editor, 1970.
Quim/Quima. Barcelona: Estela, 1971.
El jaquè de la democracia. Barcelona: Nova Terra, 1972.
Lo color mès blau. Barcelona: Planeta, 1982.

Plays

Tu i l'hipòcrita. Palma de Mallorca: Francesc de B. Moll, 1960.
El desert dels dies. Barcelona: Occitánia, 1966.
Vent de Garbi i una mica de por. Palma de Mallorca: Francesc de B. Moll, 1968. [Written with Xavier Romeu]
Preguntes i repostes sobre la vida i la mort de Francesc Layret, Advocat dels obrers de Catalunya. Paris: Edicions Catalanes, 1971.
L'alt rei en Jaume. Barcelona: Aymá, 1977.
Ca, barret! Palma de Mallorca: Francesc de B. Moll, 1984. [In collaboration with Jaume Vidal Alcover]

Essays

La dona a Catalunya. Conciencia i situacio. Barcelona: Ediciones 62, 1966.
Dia si, dia no. Barcelona: Llibres Siera, 1968.
La joventut, es una nova classe? Barcelona: Edición 62, 1969. [With Carmen Alcalde]
De profesión, mujer. Barcelona: Plaza y Janés, 1970.
El feminismo ibérico. Barcelona: Oikos-Tau, 1970.
Cartes impertinents. Palma de Mallorca: Francesc de B. Moll, 1971.
Carta abierta al macho ibérico. Madrid: Ediciones 99, 1973.
El feminisme a Catalunya. Barcelona: Nova Terra, 1973.
El comportamiento amoroso de la mujer. Barcelona: Dopesa, 1974.
Dona, doneta, donota. Barcelona: Dopesa, 1975.
Dietari de prudències. Barcelona: Nova Terra, 1982.

Translations

Tú y el hipócrita. Trans. María-Lourdes Möller-Soler. Palma de Mallorca: Francesc de B. Moll, 1960.
Un lugar entre los muertos. Trans. Jaume Vidal Alcover. Barcelona: Nova Terra, 1970.
La color más azul. Trans. Carolina Rosés. Barcelona: Planeta, 1984.

Works about Maria Aurèlia Capmany

Fuster, Joan. *Literatura catalana contemporánea*. Barcelona: Curial, 1980. 348, passim.
May, Barbara Dale. "The Power Dynamics of Woman's Anger in Maria Aurèlia Capmany's *La color más azul*." *Letras Femeninas* 12.1-2 (1986): 103–13.
Meliá Josep. Introduction. *Un lugar entre los muertos*. By Maria Aurèlia Capmany. Barcelona: Nova Terra, 1970. 9–12.
Misiego, Miquela. "Maria Aurèlia Capmany Farnès." *Women Writers of Spain: An Annotated Bio-Bibliographical Guide*. Ed. Carolyn L. Galerstein. Westport, CT: Greenwood Press, 1986. 59–65.
Möller-Soler, Maria Lourdes. "La mujer en la pre- y postguerra civil española en las obras teatrales de Carme Montoriol y Maria Aurèlia Capmany." *Estreno: Cuadernos del Teatro Español Contemporáneo* 12 (Spring 1986): 6–8.
Pedrolo, Manuel de. "Impressions-Expressions sobre tres novel.les de la Maria Aurèlia. *Betulia, El gust de la pols, Un lloc entre els morts*." By Maria Aurèlia Capmany. Barcelona: Nova Terra, 1974. 9–23.
Pérez, Janet. *Contemporary Women Writers of Spain*. Boston: Twayne, 1988. 140–48.

Terry, Arthur. *A Literary History of Spain: Catalan Literature.* London: Ernest Benn, 1972. 117–18.

Valdivieso, L. Teresa. "A propósito de la versión castellana de *Tu i l'hipócrita.*" *Estreno: Cuadernos del Teatro Español Contemporáneo* 12 (Spring 1986): 9–10.

ANA CARO MALLÉN DE SOTO
(Seventeenth Century)

Amy Kaminsky

BIOGRAPHY

Though Ana Caro Mallén was a public figure whose plays and poetry were well known in seventeenth-century Seville and Madrid, there is virtually no historical documentation on Caro herself. We know that Juan Caro was her brother, that he was born in Granada, and that when he died in 1655 he was old enough to have left a grandson. From this information, as well as from the dates of her poems and plays, Manuel Serrano y Sanz assumes that Ana Caro was born in the early part of the century in Granada. She spent much of her life in Seville, and Luis Vélez de Guevara called her that city's tenth muse.

Caro was a professional author who cultivated several genres. Rodrigo Caro, who may have been a distant relative of hers, reports that she wrote many plays performed in Seville and Madrid. He also celebrates the numerous poems that won Caro prizes in the literary academies of the day. Only two of Caro's secular plays survive: *El Conde de Partinuplés* (1653; "The Count of Partinuplés") and *Valor, agravio y mujer* (n.d.; "Valor, Affront and Woman"). We do not know the titles of any of the others, nor how many more she wrote, but we do know that Caro earned money as a playwright. She was paid 300 reales for an *auto sacramental*, or religious play, "La puerta de la Macarena" ("The Door of the Macarena"), performed in 1641, and the same amount for another play, whose title has been lost, performed in 1645. Though her *autos sacramentales* do not survive, we know the titles of two: the aforementioned "La puerta de la Macarena" and "La cuesta de Castilleja" (1642; "The Hill of Castilleja"), both written for the festival of Corpus Christi in Seville.

One intriguing contemporaneous reference to Ana Caro can be found in Alonso de Castillo Solórzano's *La garduña de Sevilla*, which documents her close friendship with María de Zayas. Castillo Solórzano's observation that in Madrid they were frequently in each other's company is borne out by Zayas's mention of Caro's work in one of her novellas and by Caro's laudatory sonnet that prefaces Zayas's *Novelas amorosas y ejemplares*. Curiously, both authors disappear from literary and historical records within a six-year period, Zayas in 1647 and Caro in 1653.

MAJOR THEMES

Caro's work is remarkably free of the feminine humility topoi that are so common in the work of women writers who followed her. Her few gestures of humility rarely refer to her gender, and they are offset by her self-assured heroic verses. Yet Caro was certainly aware of her anomalous position as a woman writer. The servant, Ribete, in *Valor, agravio y mujer*, tells his incredulous provincial counterpart, Tomillo, that the latest thing in Madrid is women writing for the stage. When Tomillo comments that women should be home doing needlework, Ribete gives him a short lesson on women poets. In this wonderfully self-conscious moment, Caro shows that she is keenly aware of her society's objections to women's writing; she deftly undermines these objections by placing them in the mouth of the most foolish of all the characters of the play.

While gender politics is a major theme in Caro's plays, her heroic poems are thoroughly assimilated to a masculine economy. The values of heroism, empire, nobility, and courage are cast in conventional ways, and the personages who emerge from these texts are fully masculine, in the most traditional sense of the term. The "Grandiosa victoria" (1633; "Grandiose Victory") is a late example of the *romance noticiero*, which had had the function of recounting, in ballad form, battles between Christians and Moors in the wars of the Reconquest. Caro's *romance* celebrates an event that seems to be nothing more than an episode of glorified cattle rustling. A group of Christian soldiers in the North African colony of Ceuta chases after a large number of cows, goats, and sheep, and steals them from the enemy Moors who own them. Caro describes the general who leads them in heroic terms and catalogs all the men who went with him on this mission. The poetic tension rises as the hardy band is at first foiled by the enemy, only to triumph in the end, to their eternal glory, when they capture the livestock.

Three of Ana Caro's surviving poems are examples of a now largely ignored genre, the *relaciones de fiestas*, reports of public celebrations in verse. These poems honor the aristocrats who underwrote the feasts, briefly describe the event that occasioned the festivities, and document the celebration itself, from the floats and fireworks displays to the men who preached sermons during the days-long events. The *Relación, en que se da cuenta de las grandiosas fiestas, que en el convento de N.P.S. Francisco de la Ciudad de Sevilla se han hecho a los Santos Mártires del Japón* (1628; "Report of the Great Celebrations in the Convent of Saint Francis in the City of Seville for the Holy Martyrs of Japan") recounts the celebration in honor of a group of Franciscan missionaries and their Japanese converts, beatified in 1627 after their crucifixion by a shogun who was no doubt enraged by the Christian attempt to undermine both his culture and his power.

The *Relación de la grandiosa fiesta, y octava, que en la Iglesia paroquial de el glorioso san Miguel de la Ciudad de Sevilla, hizo don García Sarmiento de Sotomayor, conde de Salvatierra* . . . (1635; "Report on the Great Feast and Eight-Day Festival that don García Sarmiento de Sotomayor, Count of Salvatierra, Gave . . . in the Church of Saint Michael in the City of Seville") tells of the festivities commemorating the death of the Catholic faithful killed by Huguenots in 1635 in the Flemish town of Trillemont. In these two *relaciones* by Caro, the events commemorated are instances of religious suffering, hardly the subject for merrymaking. It is Spanish Catholicism, not the painful events, that is being celebrated here. The poems, like the festivals, are part of the project of the Counter-Reformation, and they reflect a desire to bring together all social classes in a celebration of religious and patriotic unity. Caro pays relatively little attention in her *relaciones* to the tragic and dramatic events that occasion the feasts. These poems are about the celebrations, and like the *romance* commemorating the victory at Tetuán, it is important that all the major players in the celebration be named and praised.

The third of these *relaciones*, *Contexto de las reales fiestas que se hicieron en el Palacio del Buen Retiro* . . . (1637; "Context of the Royal Festivities That Were Held in the Buen Retiro Palace . . . ''), tells of the festivities surrounding the arrival in Madrid of the princess of Cariñan and the coronation of Fernando III as Holy Roman Emperor. The *Contexto* consists of three poems, the second of which begins by recounting the speaker's departure from Seville and her arrival in Madrid. The lines describing her excitement in anticipation of seeing the king are the closest thing to a personal voice in all of Caro's surviving poetry.

Religion and politics are intertwined in Caro's long poems, as they are in her "Loa sacramental" of 1639. The *loa* is traditionally a dramatic monologue that precedes a full-length play. It is not necessarily written by the play's author, and in fact is most often anonymous. Caro's *loa* is unusual in that it is signed, another indication of her renown as a poet and her sense of importance as such. This *loa* is a multilingual panegyric to the sacrament of the mass. The speaker begins in Portuguese, then goes on to quote a Frenchman, a Morisco (Christianized Arab), and a West African, imitating their peculiar dialects of Spanish. Standard Castilian is the spectral language of Caro's *loa*—all the speakers refer to it, just as they all celebrate Spanish Catholic values. Racial and religious differences are contained in this poem, in that they are both present and kept under control by the speaker, who is European and Catholic. Though the Frenchman, the African, and the Arab are imperfectly united, each speaking a Spanish filtered through his own language and then through Portuguese, Caro's inclusion of them under the rubric of the Catholic faith and the sign of empire, gestures again toward a desire for social, political, and religious unity.

These poems demonstrate Caro's participation in the conventional poetic life of the era; and a sonnet to whose title José Simón refers, "Estilo nuevo de escrituras públicas" ("A New Style of Public Writing"), also suggests that she theorized about this mode of writing. Furthermore, her poems attest to the participation of women in the literary patronage system as both writers and patrons. Caro dedicated her poem for the Church of San Miguel to Doña Leonor de Luna Enríquez, countess of Salvatierra, from whom she no doubt sought patronage. In addition, her one surviving piece of intimate occasional verse—a get-well sonnet—is also dedicated to a woman, Doña Inés Jacinta Manrique de Lara.

In their overt support of the power structure and reinforcement of the norms of imperial Catholic Spain, Caro's poems champion traditional values. Her two surviving plays, however, question one of the underpinnings of both empire and church: traditional gender relations, specifically focused on issues of power, marriage, and women's sexuality. Rosaura, the heroine of *El Conde de Parti-nuplés*, is a queen who has refused marriage in order to protect her kingdom and her life, but finally must marry in order to produce an heir. The solution she finds is to control the marriage process to the fullest extent possible. Leonor, the protagonist of *Valor, agravio y mujer*, has been deceived by her lover, and though she frequently states that she intends to kill him, she ultimately contrives to marry him on her own terms. Leonor initiates the primary action of the play by disguising herself as the noble Don Leonardo and sets off with her servant, Ribete, to seek vengeance against her unfaithful lover, Don Juan. She finds him at the court of Prince Ludovico, in the company of her brother, Don Fernando. Also in the household are the cousins Estela and Lisarda. When Leonor arrives, all the men are in love with Estela, but Don Juan is her favorite. In the guise of Leonardo, Leonor woos Estela and easily wins her away from the inconstant Don Juan. Leonor orchestrates a series of meetings under cover of night, during which she tricks Don Juan into revealing to Estela his love affair with her. She also complicates the men's friendships with each other, and in all ways furthers her own goals. Leonor is determined to kill Don Juan to satisfy her lost honor, but she settles for his repentance in the end.

Valor, agravio y mujer is immediately recognizable as an honor play, and its protagonist is a familiar figure on the Golden Age stage, the woman disguised as a man. In this play, however, honor is seen from a woman's point of view. Since the male honor code excludes women, an honor code that includes them must be constituted in a different manner. While the traditional remedy for sexual transgression is the death of the woman and lover (Fernando is chagrined at the thought of having to kill the sister he has not seen in so many years), Leonor seeks not her own death but that of her seducer. His broken promise of marriage, not her lost virginity, is the cause of her dishonor. Leonor stakes claim to her own sexuality; the story she invents to justify her actions is that Don Leonardo is Leonor's lover and has promised to avenge her honor by killing Don Juan, although he, too, has slept with her. Leonor thoroughly enjoys the farce and Don Juan's discomfort and jealousy.

Leonor's brother, Fernando, has become fast friends with Don Juan and is amused by his exploits until he finds out that his friend's victim is his sister. In a fine parody of honor repair, Don Juan and Don Fernando despair because each must kill the other, as well as the fictional Leonardo, to avenge the various affronts resulting from Leonor's real and imagined sexual activity. Fernando says in Act 3: "We all have to kill each other; I see no other solution" (210). Leonor, of course, does see another solution. Extracting a declaration of love and contrition from Don Juan, she reveals her identity and agrees to marry him. The play quickly resolves itself with the marriage of all the aristocratic characters.

El conde de Partinuplés concerns Rosaura, queen of Constantinople, who is told by her advisers that if she does not marry and produce an heir, they will choose a new ruler. Though she appreciates their concern for the stability of the kingdom, Rosaura also knows that, according to the horoscope her father had drawn for her, her future husband is destined to kill her and put her kingdom in jeopardy. Forced to choose between her crown and her freedom to wield the power it affords her (as well as, perhaps, her life), Rosaura turns to her confidante and cousin, Aldora. Adept in magic, Aldora conjures up each of Rosaura's royal suitors to give her a preview that will enable her to choose wisely. Rosaura's choice, the count of Partinuplés, is already engaged to his cousin, Lisbella, daughter of the king of France. Aldora uses her magic to make the count fall in love with Rosaura and to bring him to Constantinople. Once there, he meets his beloved, but she literally keeps him in the dark about who she is, permitting him to meet her only at night and not revealing her identity. Shortly after his arrival, Rosaura proves her love by informing the count that France is in danger and needs his services. She sends him away to save France, and when he returns, she asks to hear of his victory. Rosaura falls asleep during the telling, however, and the count allows his servant, Gaulín, to persuade him to use a nearby torch to light Rosaura's sleeping face. She awakens and, furious at his disobedience— the first sign of betrayal foretold by the astrologer—condemns him to death. Aldora contrives to save him: He will be the unknown knight with whom Rosaura's suitors do mock battle in a tourney set to decide which of them will marry her.

Partinuplés will win, of course, but before he has the chance, Lisbella arrives, armed for battle, to claim her cousin. She no longer loves him, but her father has died and Partinuplés has inherited the throne. Faced with few options, she has no choice but to marry him and plans to lay siege to Rosaura's kingdom if the queen does not let him go. Rosaura reassures her that Partinuplés is not among the candidates for her future husband. Triumphant in the tourney, Partinuplés solves Lisbella's dilemma by handing France over to her, and suggests she marry one of Rosaura's other suitors. Lisbella agrees to this plan, Aldora marries another of the suitors, and Partinuplés and Rosaura wed. Only the servant, Gaulín, is left without a wife, but he comments that he is better off single.

Written during the full flower of the Golden Age *comedia*, *El conde de Partinuplés* is evidence of Caro's ability to manipulate the conventions of the genre. As one of Caro's later works, it reflects her maturity as a writer who participates fully in the literary life of her era. Based on a twelfth-century French romance, *El Conde de Partinuplés* is, as well, in dialogue with Pedro Calderón de la Barca's *La vida es sueño*. Caro's protagonist is named Rosaura, one of her suitors is Segismundo's son, and both plays depend on a dire horoscope prediction to set the plot in motion. Caro also refers both directly and indirectly to classical texts, particularly in her reworking of the Psyche and Cupid myth. The mortal Psyche, like Rosaura destined to marry a monstrous husband, temporarily loses her beloved. In defiance of traditional gender stereotypes, it is Caro's Partinuplés who, in the role of Psyche, grows curious and shines the light on Rosaura/Cupid.

The play's strongest characters are three women: Rosaura, Aldora, and Lisbella. Rosaura and Lisbella derive their primary power from their royal status, but once Rosaura can no longer sustain her refusal to marry by that means she relies on another source of female power, magic. So-called white magic was a pastime of the ladies of the court during Caro's era, though it was frowned upon by the church. In the play, Aldora's skill at magic is condoned. Only Gaulín questions the conjuring; in the end magic brings about the conventional ending.

For her part, Lisbella, in her final scene, is determined, powerful, and motivated not by love but by the demands of state and the desire to maintain her status as queen of France. The actions of the count, on the other hand, are all functions of the needs and desires of others. He is brave and noble, but those characteristics are beside the point. Unlike Othello, who woos Desdemona with tales of his military exploits, Partinuplés puts Rosaura to sleep when he recounts his feats of war. The count is, ultimately, a token who moves among the female characters. This is an extraordinary reversal of the typical plot in which female characters fulfill such a role between men.

As in *El Conde*, women's power is central to *Valor, agravio y mujer*. Like Rosaura and Aldora, Leonor puts virtually all the play's action into motion. She is the author of love entanglements and altercations among men. She is clever and handy with a sword, and until the end she is determined to kill her wayward lover. And while Estela and Lisarda are in no way as valiant as Leonor, they are first depicted in the forest hunting deer by themselves. Further, Estela claims her right to love whomever she wants and to enjoy her sexuality. Nor is she particularly distressed to learn that she has declared her love for someone who turns out to be a woman. Similarly, Leonor is a confident lover who, far from being distressed by another woman's passion for her, actively encourages it.

Particularly worthy of note is Caro's attitude toward heterosexual love and marriage. Her plays are about the conflictual relationships between men and women and the stretching of gender constraints before the requisite ending. Love and marriage in these plays are inevitable though demonstrably not in women's best interest. In response to this double bind, Caro focuses on the action women take to control the courtship and marriage process to the greatest extent possible. *Valor*'s Estela is willing to marry, but she does insist on her right to choose her mate and to change her mind about her choice. In *El Conde*, Rosaura first uses her status as queen to avoid marriage, and when that fails, she turns to Aldora's skill at magic to control her future. If she wishes to retain power, Rosaura's only recourse is to mitigate the dangers of wedlock by knowing as much as possible about her future husband.

Caro's friend María de Zayas also wrote about the perils of marriage for women and the ways in which even the most cautious woman can be destroyed by a husband. The protagonist in her novella *Mal presagio casar lejos* sees her sisters murdered by their husbands, and therefore insists on a lengthy courtship to assure herself that her husband will not harm her. Once she marries and goes off to a foreign land to live with him, he reverts to type and kills her. Caro's play ends with Rosaura's marriage to Partinuplés; though nothing happens to undermine this happy ending, the play comes to a close before the prophecy of the horoscope can be wholly fulfilled, leaving any seventeenth-century audience with a sense of foreboding.

In *Valor*, Leonor repeatedly states her intention and demonstrates her capacity to kill her fickle lover, but she knows that her only viable option is to keep Don Juan alive and marry him. To make this at all palatable, she must first make him recognize his continuing love for her and his desire to marry her. In an ideal world, Caro suggests, it would be best for Rosaura to remain single and for Leonor to kill Don Juan in a duel, but the real world they inhabit, be it the *comedia*'s or history's, makes those outcomes untenable.

Ultimately, the critique of marriage in these plays must be transferred to the lower classes. If the conventions of the *comedia* require restoration of order via the stabilization of traditional gender relations through marriage of the upper-class characters, the critique of marriage and traditional gender relations that drives the play can be sustained in the end only if it is redirected to and enunciated by the lower classes. Thus, the final warning about marriage comes not from the noble women, who have a class-derived stake in maintaining the social order, but from the male servants. In an ironic inversion, they see themselves as the potential victims of marriage. *Valor*'s Ribete hopes to escape marriage to the deceitful, thieving Flora, since, as he notes, there is only one woman for the two serving men. Ribete tells Flora that neither of the men wants her; but her mistress, Estela, gives her to him along with a considerable sum of money. Ribete accepts, but makes it clear that he does so for the cash, ending the play with the idea that marriage is less about love, or even stability, than about economic necessity. Gaulín, in *El Conde*, does escape marriage. In the middle of the play he tells the audience that Caro made a mistake and left him without a prospective mate. This single break in the play's illusion calls attention to the anomaly and indicates that the author has deliberately ruled out marriage for Gaulín. The best the protagonists can do is reform marriage, not repeal it; and the best the playwright can do is make the pairings-off as perfunctory as possible.

It is not only in the attitude toward marriage that Caro's plays recast intimate relationships. They also portray homosocial relationships differently, skewing the conventions of the *comedia* without breaking them. The close friendship between women, in this case Rosaura and Aldora, is not uncommon in plays of the period; what is uncommon is the ability of these women, together, to make decisions and exercise power. In the one moment when they are not working in concert, Aldora is still plotting in Rosaura's best interests to restore Partinuplés's love. Likewise, the rivalry between Lisbella and Rosaura is truly remarkable. Both women want to marry the same man, but in both cases it is ultimately the pressing needs of state and their desire to maintain their thrones that determine their desire for him. The confrontation between the two queens is awesome in its noble grandeur. They treat each other with respect and courtesy, and though they prefer peace, they are willing to wage war.

In *Valor*, men's friendships, as well as their rivalries, are dependent, both personally and structurally, on the actions of women. In a severe breach of hospitality, Ludovico is ready to murder his house guest, Don Juan, who is his rival for Estela. And Fernando, who is willing to sacrifice his love for Estela to his friendship with Don Juan, is faced with the necessity of killing him once he learns that Don Juan was his sister's lover.

Caro also disturbs conventional class relations in *Valor* when Leonor declares that she considers Ribete not her servant but rather her friend, and that she respects him as an equal. Such demonstrations of interclass equality are indeed unusual in the period. Ribete himself complains that people believe servants must always be fools, ignoring the possibility of self-improvement. As previously noted, it is this character whom Caro ultimately entrusts to defend women's right to the pen, citing the past models of Argentaria, Sappho, Areta, and Blesilla as justifications for the boldness of contemporary female writers.

SURVEY OF CRITICISM

Ana Caro was well thought of, or at least written about admiringly, in her day; the greater part of her work has been lost, however, and she is now barely remembered. She is rarely named in histories of Golden Age literature, unless they deal specifically with issues relating to women. Thus, it is impossible to make sense of the critical reception to Caro's work without taking note of the unavailability of her texts. Melveena McKendrick and Carmen Bravo-Villasante, for example, were unaware of the existence of *Valor, agravio y mujer* when they wrote their books on women in Golden Age theater, though they mention Caro with reference to *El Conde de Partinuplés*. That play was reprinted in 1951 in the Biblioteca de Autores Españoles. Manuel Serrano y Sanz's *Apuntes para una biblioteca de escritoras españolas* (1903), in which *Valor, agravio y mujer* was published in its first modern edition, was not regularly consulted by scholars until feminist Hispanists rediscovered it. In 1977 Luisa F. Foley completed an edition of *Valor* as a master's thesis but never published it. In addition, the play has been translated as *Valor, Affront and Woman* and will appear in Amy Kaminsky's anthology of Spanish women writers.

Thanks to the painstaking archival work of Francisco López Estrada, modern readers have access to four of Caro's poems. López Estrada writes of Caro with affection, reserve, and respect, and his sturdy philological work provides solid ground for future Caro scholars. López Estrada located the rare *pliegos sueltos* (loose sheets) of Caro's poems in such far-flung places as New York City; Madison, Wisconsin; Seville; and Madrid. He is, to date, the only contemporary scholar to have paid attention to Caro's poetry, and his contribution to Caro scholarship cannot be overestimated. Until López Estrada began to edit Caro's work in 1976, the only example of the author's major poems available to twentieth-century readers was Antonio Pérez Gómez's 1951 facsimile edition of the *Contexto de las reales fiestas.*

Caro's work has received some critical attention in the last few years, with the growth of feminist scholarship in Hispanic studies. Historian Mary Elizabeth Perry, for example, mentions Caro briefly in *Gender and Disorder in Early Modern Seville.* Matthew D. Stroud raises some interesting questions about Caro and feminism. But, starting from a rather unsophisticated notion of feminism and a perfunctory knowledge of feminist literary theory, he simply decides that Caro does not cut it as a feminist, first because Leonor agrees to marriage at the end of *Valor, agravio y mujer*, and second because Caro herself acquiesced to writing in a man-made genre. Stroud's work contrasts with Elizabeth Ordóñez's subtle reading of Caro's plays. Ordóñez analyzes the ways in which Caro subverts the man-made forms of her culture and era. In Ordóñez's reading, Caro's heroines are analogous to the woman playwright who manipulates the cultural plot to fulfill her own goals. Though Ordóñez's discussion of Caro occupies only part of a journal article, it is the most lucid published analysis of Caro's plays to date.

Frederick A. de Armas reads *El Conde de Partinuplés* as an example of what he calls the "invisible mistress" plot. His discussion is useful for showing where Caro diverges from the original Partinuplés story, adding the *gracioso* (comic figure), strengthening the character of Rosaura, and eliminating many of the count's heroic deeds. The two latter changes shift the emphasis toward the woman and her plot, though de Armas does not draw this conclusion. He contends that the marriage at the play's end represents a recognition of reality, in which the protagonists accept each other's imperfections. He also argues that the play turns on the problem of the man's treachery, foreseen in the horoscope, and that finally the predictions are fulfilled. De Armas implicitly disagrees with Melveena McKendrick, who dismisses this play as very poor indeed, and for whom the horoscope device serves only to get the action going. For Amy Kaminsky, the horoscope is a representation of both the rule and the forecast of patriarchal power. She also suggests that the prediction that marriage will harm both the woman and her kingdom creates a double bind from which no escape is possible. Only women's magic, which functions outside the patriarchal pact, can mitigate the inevitable.

A certain amount of women's magic, in the form of feminist literary studies (which can be performed by men as well as women), has begun to make Caro's work reappear after so many years of oblivion. Her work is deserving of more study, and if we are lucky some enterprising scholar will discover more of her lost manuscripts.

BIBLIOGRAPHY

Works by Ana Caro

Short Poems

"A Doña Inés Jacinta Manrique de Lara, estando enferma." In Manuel Serrano y Sanz. *Apuntes para una biblioteca de escritoras españolas desde el año 1401 al 1833.* Madrid: Atlas, 1975. Biblioteca de Autores Españoles. Vol. 268. 216. Rpt. of 1903 ed. Madrid: Sucesores de Rivadeneyra.

"A Doña María de Zayas y Sotomayor. Décimas." In María de Zayas y Sotomayor. *Novelas ejemplares y amorosas.* Zaragoza, 1638. Preliminary pages. Rpt. in Manuel Serrano y Sanz. *Antología de poetisas líricas.* Madrid: Tipografía de Archivos, Bibliotecas y Museos, 1915. 306–07.

Long Poems

The first three poems listed here, as well as the fifth, have been edited and reprinted by Francisco López Estrada. See "Works about Ana Caro" for bibliographic details.

Relación, en que se da cuenta de las grandiosas fiestas, que en el Convento de N.P.S. Francisco de la Ciudad de Sevilla se han hecho a los Santos Mártires del Japón (1628).

Grandiosa victoria que alcanzó de los Moros de Tetuán Jorge de Mendoza y Picaña, General de Ceuta, quitándoles gran suma de ganados cerca de las mesmas puertas de Tetuán (1633).

Relación de la grandiosa fiesta, y octava, que en la Iglesia parroquial de el glorioso san Miguel de la Ciudad de Sevilla, hizo don García Sarmiento de Sotomayor, Conde de Salvatierra . . . (1635).

Contexto de las reales fiestas que se hicieron en el Palacio del Buen Retiro a la coronación de Rey de Romanos, y entrada en Madrid de la señora Princesa de Cariñán en tres descursos (1637). Rpt. under the direction of Antonio Pérez Gómez. Valencia: Talleres de Tipografía Moderna, 1951.

"Loa sacramental, que se representó en el Carro de Antonio de Prado, en las fiestas del Corpus de Sevilla" (1639).

Plays

El Conde de Partinuplés. Madrid. 1653. Rpt. in Biblioteca de Autores Españoles. Vol. 49. Madrid, 1951. 125–38.

Valor, agravio, y mujer. N.d. Rpt. in Manuel Serrano y Sanz. *Apuntes para una biblioteca de escritoras desde el año 1401 al 1833.* Madrid: Atlas, 1975. Biblioteca de Autores Españoles. Vol. 268. 179–212. Rpt. of 1903 ed. Madrid: Sucesores de Rivadeneyra.

"Valor, agravio, y mujer." Ed. Luisa F. Foley. Master's thesis, 1977.

Valor, agravio y mujer. Rpt. in *Flores del agua/Waterlilies: Anthology of Spanish Women Writers.* Ed. Amy Kaminsky. Minneapolis: U of Minnesota P. [Forthcoming]

Lost or Unpublished Works

"Estilo nuevo de escrituras públicas" (1635).
"Elogio de D. Francisco Garces y Ribera" (1640).
"La puerta de la Macarena" (1641).
"La cuesta de Castilleja" (1642).
"Elogio de Tomás de Palomares" (1645).

Translation

"Valor, Affront, and Woman." Trans. Amy Kaminsky and Donna Lazarus. *Flores del Agua/Waterlilies*. Ed. Amy Kaminsky. Minneapolis: U of Minnesota P. [Forthcoming]

Works about Ana Caro

Bravo Villasante, Carmen. *La mujer vestida de hombre en el teatro español (Siglos XVI-XVII)*. Madrid: Sociedad General Española de Librería, 1976.

Caro, Rodrigo. *Varones insignes en letras naturales de la ilustrísima ciudad de Sevilla. Epistolario*. Ed. Santiago Montoto. Seville: Real Academia Sevillana de Buenas Letras, 1915.

Castillo Solórzano, Alonso de. *La garduña de Sevilla*. 1642. Rpt. Madrid: Espasa-Calpe, 1957.

de Armas, Frederick A. "Ana Caro Mallén de Soto." *Women Writers in Spain: An Annotated Bio-Bibliographical Guide*. Ed. Carolyn Galerstein. Westport: Greenwood Press, 1986. 66–67.

———. "Princess Rosaura." *The Invisible Mistress: Aspects of Feminism and Fantasy in the Golden Age*. Charlottesville, VA: Biblioteca Siglo de Oro, 1976. 174–86.

Kaminsky, Amy. "María de Zayas y Sotomayor and the Creation of a (Fictional) Women's Writing Community." [In circulation]

López Estrada, Francisco. "Costumbres sevillanas: El poema sobre la fiesta y octava celebradas con motivo de los sucesos de Flandes en la Iglesia de San Miguel (1635) por Ana Caro Mallén." *Archivo Hispalense* 203 (1984): 109–50.

———. "La frontera allende el mar: El romance por la victoria de Tetuán (1633) de Ana Caro de Mallén." *Homenaje a José Manuel Blecua. Ofrecido por sus discípulos, colegas, y amigos*. Madrid: Gredos, 1983.

———. "Una loa del Santísimo Sacramento de Ana Caro Mallén, en cuatro lenguas." *Revista de Dialectología y Tradiciones Populares* 32 (1976): 263–74.

———. "La relación de las fiestas por los mártires del Japón, de Doña Ana Caro Mallén (Sevilla), 1628." *Libro-Homenaje a Antonio Pérez Gómez*. Cieza: " . . . la fonte que mana y corre . . . ," 1978. 51–69.

McKendrick, Melveena. "The 'Mujer Esquiva'—A Measure of the Feminist Sympathies of Seventeenth-Century Spanish Dramatists." *Hispanic Review* 40 (Spring 1972): 162–97.

———. *Woman and Society in the Spanish Drama of the Golden Age*. London: Cambridge UP, 1974.

Ordóñez, Elizabeth. "Woman and Her Text in the Works of María de Zayas and Ana Caro." *Revista de Estudios Hispánicos* 19.1 (Jan. 1985): 3–15.

Perry, Mary Elizabeth. *Gender and Disorder in Early Modern Seville*. Princeton: Princeton UP, 1990.

Sánchez Arjona, José. *Anales del teatro en Sevilla*. Sevilla: Imprenta de E. Rasco, 1898.

―――. *El teatro en Sevilla en los siglos XVI y XVII*. Madrid: A. Alonso, 1887.

Serrano y Sanz, Manuel. *Apuntes para una biblioteca de escritoras españolas desde el año 1401 al 1833*. Madrid: Atlas, 1975. Biblioteca de Autores Españoles. Vol. 271. 584, 587, 629–30. Rpt. of 1903 ed. Madrid: Sucesores de Rivadeneyra.

Simón, José. "Caro de Mallén, Ana." *Bibliografía de la literatura hispánica*. Vol 7. Madrid, 1967. 494–96.

Stroud, Matthew D. "La literatura y la mujer en el barroco: *Valor, agravio y mujer* de Ana Caro." Actas del VII Congreso de Hispanistas. II. Ed. A. David Kossoff and José Amor y Vázquez. Madrid: Istmo, 1986.

Vélez de Guevara, Luis. *El diablo cojuelo*. Madrid: n.p., 1641. Rpt. New York: Ediciones Ebro, 1975.

TERESA DE CARTAGENA
(1420/25?–after 1460?)

Ronald E. Surtz

BIOGRAPHY

Teresa de Cartagena was born, probably between 1420 and 1425, into a distinguished family of converts from Judaism. Her grandfather, Salomon Halevy, was chief rabbi of Burgos. After his conversion in 1390, he adopted the name Pablo de Santa María and became bishop of Burgos. He was both a poet and a celebrated writer of exegetical treatises. Teresa's great-uncle was the chronicler Alvar García de Santa María. Her uncle, Alfonso de Cartagena, was a translator of Cicero and Seneca as well as the author of didactic treatises in both Latin and Castilian. Her family was thus both socially and intellectually prominent. Teresa herself, in *Arboleda de los enfermos* (1453–60?; ''The Grove of the Afflicted''), claimed to have studied at the University of Salamanca, although it is not clear what she meant by that declaration (103).

Teresa went deaf at an early age, an experience she describes in the *Arboleda* as a ''cloud of human and earthly sadness that cloaked my entire life and carried me off in a dense whirlwind of suffering to an island called 'The Reproach of Men and the Outcast of the People' '' (37; cf. Psalm 22:7). She eventually became a nun, probably in the Franciscan order. Lewis J. Hutton conjectures that her family may have placed her in the convent in order to relieve themselves of her care (480); Teresa herself observes that relatives not only scorn those afflicted with illness but also try to dispatch them from their homes (*Arboleda* 63, 76–77).

In her writings Teresa reveals how her sense of isolation was increased when she was in the company of other people because she could not hear their speech. The act of writing became a means both of self-consolation and of communication. According to Francisco Cantera Burgos (546), Teresa's principal work, the *Arboleda de los enfermos*, was probably composed between 1453 and 1460. Sometime after the *Arboleda* began to circulate in manuscript, Teresa was criticized for writing a spiritual treatise, an activity deemed appropriate only for men. In response, she penned a spirited defense of her right to literary expression, the *Admiraçión operum Dey* (n.d.?; "Wonderment at the Works of God"). The *Admiraçión* is not only what we might now call a feminist text but also, as Alan Deyermond observes, a rare example in medieval Spanish literature of "a writer's reflections on the creative process, an indication of how it feels to be a writer" (25).

Both the *Arboleda* and the *Admiraçión* are addressed to a female dedicatee who is explicitly identified in the *Admiraçión* as the noblewoman Juana de Mendoza, the wife of the poet and political figure, Gómez Manrique. Teresa justifies the writing of the *Arboleda* by using a strategy employed by other female authors of devotional treatises, the claim that God inspired her to write. In the dedication of the *Admiraçión* to Juana de Mendoza, Teresa likewise asserts that God will inspire her to compose the subsequent treatise, but she adds the claim that her patroness asked her to write the work. Teresa thereby not only shields her work with the authority of Juana de Mendoza's aristocratic social status but also implies that her self-defense is not written of her own free will but rather out of obedience to her patroness.

MAJOR THEMES

The *Arboleda de los enfermos* is intended to demonstrate the spiritual benefits of bodily infirmities. The motif of illness, which is used as a metaphor by other writers, is both literal and figurative for Teresa, since she uses her own deafness as an example for her readers or listeners. The *Arboleda* is thus notable for its conjugation of personal experience and devotional commonplaces, for the nun supports her observations by invoking the authority of both her own experience and written sources, largely biblical and patristic.

The main idea of the *Arboleda* is that the suffering born of sickness is in reality beneficial because, through the cultivation of the virtue of patience, bodily illness can lead to spiritual health and thereby to salvation. Thus, Teresa considers her deafness a blessing because it has prevented her from hearing worldly noises that were drowning out the healthy doctrines of the Lord. In her allegorical introduction, she says that for a long time she has lived in exile on a desert island, but with the help of the Lord she has been led to understand that her isolation is actually a blessing. By planting the island with groves of solid doctrine and spiritual consolations, she has transformed the painful solitude of earthly chatter into the company of virtuous behavior. Alone on her island, Teresa will write the *Arboleda* in order to combat idleness.

The treatise proper is fundamentally a commentary on Psalm 45:10 ("Hearken, O daughter, and see, and incline thy ear; and forget thy people and thy father's house") and Psalm 32:9 ("Do not become like the horse and the mule, who have no understanding. With bit and bridle bind fast their jaws, that they may not come near unto thee''). Thus, Teresa must listen with the ear of her soul and abandon both her father's house (sinfulness) and her people (earthly desires). Further, the ''bit'' (reason) and the ''bridle'' (temperance) must constrain the ''jaws'' (vain desires). More specifically, it is Teresa's illness that has served as both bit and bridle by preventing her from eating foods harmful to her spiritual health.

Continuing with the alimentary imagery and re-creating the biblical parable of the great supper (Luke 14:16–24), Teresa observes that while God has invited everyone to His heavenly banquet, the sick and suffering are in a sense forcibly dragged to the feast by their afflictions. Here she rejects traditional allegorical expositions of the parable, which usually identified those compelled to attend the supper with the heathen, the Jews, and the heretics. Instead, she personalizes her source by interpreting the parable literally: She associates her own physical affliction with the crippled, the blind, and the lame mentioned in the Bible. Teresa goes on to mix architectonic and alimentary images, comparing her deafness to God's cloistering her hearing. Those who are ill can be said to have professed in the convent of the suffering, whose abbess is the virtue of patience. The convent of the suffering is blessed, for it enables those who profess in it to join in the Lord's banquet. Next, Teresa defines two degrees of patience. Suffering with prudence characterizes the first degree of patience, but when suffering leads to spiritual blessings, it makes for an even more perfect form of patience. Drawing on her own experience and re-creating the biblical parable of the talents (Matthew 25:14–30), Teresa asserts that those who suffer receive five coins from God and then go on to earn five more through their suffering. She discusses each of the allegorical coins, giving special attention to the second, suffering itself, which she expounds by means of a medical image: Christ the physician gives the spiritually ill the bitter medicine of suffering, which paradoxically makes the body sick and the soul healthy. Concretely, suffering is a medicine that cures the seven fevers (the seven deadly sins) that afflict the soul.

Seeking an appropriate authority to support her assertions, Teresa recalls hearing a sermon in which the preacher invoked the authority of Peter Lombard, the Master of the Sentences. She, however, will invoke Job, whom she dubs the ''Master of the Patiences.'' In so doing, Teresa rejects the standard patriarchal form of authority based on the writings of learned men in order to invoke the authority of experience, personified in the sufferings of Job. She ends her treatise by observing how perfect patience entails not only the virtue of prudence but all the other cardinal and theological virtues as well.

The negative reception accorded the *Arboleda* motivated the writing of an apology, the *Admiración operum Dey*. In her introduction, Teresa highlights the theme of divine grace, for it was only with the help of God that her otherwise weak female intellect was able to compose the *Arboleda*. Her treatise, she observes, caused great wonderment, not because of its contents but because it was written by a woman.

As the *Admiración* proper begins, Teresa asks why some things cause more amazement than others, if everything the Creator has done is worthy of our admiration. The answer, she believes, lies in the fact that the things wrought by God, which we see every day, seem so natural to us that they do not cause us to marvel. Applying this observation to her own situation as a writer, Teresa postulates that men were amazed by a woman's writing such a treatise precisely because erudite activities are normally performed by men, not by women. Nonetheless, she argues, God is omnipotent and can just as well grant wisdom to a woman as to a man.

Men's intellectual abilities, she reminds her readers, are not inherent in their male status but are, rather, a divine gift. If God granted certain gifts to the male sex, it was not because He wished to favor that sex with greater grace but for His own secret purposes. Although God made the male sex strong, brave, and daring, and the female sex weak and cowardly, human nature is one. In fact, the differences between the sexes are divinely ordained in such a way that each one complements the other. To illustrate the complementarity of the sexes, Teresa uses a simile taken from nature; she compares the strong male and the weak female to the tough bark (*corteza*) that covers the soft pith (*meollo*) of certain plants. Just as both bark and pith are necessary for the preservation of the plant, so the strong male and the weaker female are necessary for the preservation of the human species.

The use of the botanical image is a good example of the limits of Teresa's feminism. She accepts traditional gender roles for men and women, and nowhere does she advocate education for women, preferring to emphasize the miraculous nature of her own empowerment to write a book. Teresa is nonetheless capable of moments of subversion, however ambiguous, in her acceptance of the status quo. Thus, it is worth noting in passing that the *corteza/meollo* simile is often used in medieval Spanish literature to contrast the surface meaning of a text with its hidden didactic content. Would it have been lost on Teresa's readers that the essential part, the *meollo*, corresponds to the female element in her natural simile, while the superficial interpretation corresponds to the male?

Teresa proceeds to reiterate that man and woman form a sort of team, and that neither sex should be considered better than the other. God inspires notable works in both men and women, and His marvelous deeds include inspiring a woman to compose a learned treatise. Teresa admits that such an erudite activity is not normal for women; it is as uncommon as for a woman to take up a sword to defend her country. Nonetheless, the biblical Judith, empowered by divine grace, wielded a sword. If God could inspire Judith to take up the sword, would it not be even easier for Him to inspire a woman to take up the pen? Teresa thus defends her act of writing, making explicit the comparison between herself and Judith, for both were divinely empowered to wield typically masculine—dare one say phallic?—instruments.

If Teresa's treatise occasioned astonishment, she argues, it was because that which is out of the ordinary causes wonderment. Nonetheless, Teresa cautions that there are two kinds of amazement, one good, the other bad. The gift of grace, she reminds her readers, comes from God. "Good" amazement is that which is properly directed at the source of all grace, God Himself. "Bad" admiration occurs when we express wonderment at the human recipient of divine grace instead of at its source. Teresa thus attempts to control the reception of her treatise through a sort of blackmail: readers who do not wish to be guilty of "bad" admiration should not focus on the nun herself (should not criticize her?) and should concentrate instead on God's manifestation through her.

Next, Teresa asserts that the learned contents of her treatise are considerably less remarkable than the fact that it was written by a woman. Indeed, what is the value of learning if many wise men have been damned and many ignorant men saved? True wisdom, she says, is that learned in the school of the constant recollection of the blessings of God. Her own work is not really a philosophical or theological tract but, rather, a record of God's gifts and hidden favors. Thus, in one stroke, Teresa assails the potential vanity of male erudition and extols the divine origin of her own empowerment to compose a learned treatise. Moreover, she feels compelled to respond to one specific criticism that was leveled against her by denying that her treatise was copied from other books. As Deyermond points out, Teresa's detractors were guilty of applying a double standard, for such intertextuality was the rule in medieval literature (25).

Teresa then compares her intellect, which God inspired to write the *Arboleda*, to the blind man whom Christ met on the road to Jericho (Luke 18:35–43). At first she relates in the third person how her intellect called upon the Son of David to have mercy; then she suddenly injects herself into the biblical narrative, shifting to the first person and imagining herself calling out to Christ from the side of the road to Jericho. In the allegorical interpretation that follows, Teresa explains that just as He cured the blind man, Christ the true physician cured her and permitted her to see the light. Therefore, let those who doubt that she wrote the *Arboleda* abandon their disbelief and instead marvel at the power of the Lord.

Teresa's feminism is at best reticent, for she is more inclined to hide behind such typical responses as the assertion of divine inspiration and to emphasize the exceptional nature of her empowerment to carry out a "male" task than to imply that all women should be so empowered. Nonetheless, the fact that she directs her apology to a female authority suggests a careful balance of the notion of male and female power, at the same time that it introduces the possibility of what a contemporary reader might view as female bonding.

SURVEY OF CRITICISM

Aside from the biographical data and the brief overview of Teresa's works provided by Cantera Burgos, the first critic to give serious attention to Teresa de Cartagena was Juan Marichal in the few but illuminating pages he devotes to her in his book on the history of the essay in Spain. Marichal sees Teresa's deafness and her status as a woman and a descendant of converted Jews as factors that isolated her. Therefore the act of writing became not a means of communication with those around her but a means of communicating with herself, that is, a medium for self-knowledge. Lewis Joseph Hutton's doctoral dissertation, published in 1967, provides a reliable edition of Teresa's works. His introduction calls attention to, among other topics, Teresa's principal sources, the Bible and the *Libro de las consolaciones de la vida humana* (ca. 1420), written by the antipope Pedro de Luna. More recently, Deyermond and Ronald Surtz have considered the literary aspects of Teresa's writings, especially her imagery.

Further critical studies on the works of Teresa de Cartagena are clearly needed, for her significance goes beyond her status as one of a handful of female authors in medieval Spain. She is remarkable not only for writing a spiritual treatise at a time when that activity was not considered appropriate to her gender but also for having the courage to defend that action.

BIBLIOGRAPHY

Works by Teresa de Cartagena

Arboleda de los enfermos. Admiraçión operum Dey. 1453–1460[?]. Ed. Lewis Joseph Hutton. Madrid: Anejos del Boletín de la Real Academia Española XVI, 1967.

Works about Teresa de Cartagena

Cantera Burgos, Francisco. *Alvar García de Santa María y su familia de conversos. Historia de la judería de Burgos y de sus conversos más egregios.* Madrid: Instituto Arias Montano, 1952. 536–58.

Deyermond, Alan. " 'El convento de dolençias': The Works of Teresa de Cartagena." *Journal of Hispanic Philology* 1 (1976): 19–29.

Hutton, Lewis J. "Teresa de Cartagena: A Study in Castilian Spirituality." *Theology Today* 12 (1955–56): 477–83.

Marichal, Juan. *La voluntad de estilo.* 2nd ed. Madrid: Revista de Occidente, 1971. 42–45.

Surtz, Ronald E. "Image Patterns in Teresa de Cartagena's *Arboleda de los enfermos.*" *La Chispa '87: Selected Proceedings of the Eighth Louisiana Conference on Hispanic Languages and Literatures.* New Orleans: Tulane U, 1987. 297–304.

ROSALÍA DE CASTRO
(1837–1885)

Kathleen N. March

BIOGRAPHY

Rosalía de Castro was born on February 25, 1837, in Santiago de Compostela to Teresa Castro and a priest named José Martínez Viojo. She was raised in secret by her father's relatives until her mother claimed her several years later. Her origin as a child born out of wedlock has been overly emphasized as a partial explanation for the anguished nature of her poetry; indeed, statistics provided by the critic Francisco Rodríguez Sánchez (39) show that natural children were relatively common in this area. The high rate of emigration left many women alone as "widows of the living," and others were unable to find husbands. Whatever the details of her personal situation, Rosalía nonetheless received a strong academic education, studying music, French, and other subjects in the Liceo de San Agustín and the Sociedad Económica de los Amigos del País in Santiago. This institution is known to have had a good library, and there the young writer-to-be must have been introduced to a wide variety of works, both fictional and historical.

Before leaving for Madrid in 1856, Rosalía starred in a play and may have considered an acting career (Carballo Calero, *Estudos* 53–56). While in the capital, she is thought to have moved in cultural circles. There she met and on October 10, 1858, married an established Galician writer, Manuel Martínez Murguía. They had seven children, two of whom died at an early age and are mentioned in her poetry (Bouza Álvarez, *Cantares*). Their oldest child, Alejandra, was born during the initial year of marriage; the next was born more than ten years later. During this interval, Castro and Murguía traveled together but also were separated often, as he was forced to accept employment as an archivist wherever it was available. Even after all the children were born, Rosalía's household responsibilities did not prevent her from writing with some regularity. Between 1857 and 1884, she published five books of poetry, five novels, and several essays. A short story was published posthumously in 1946. We also know that at least one novel manuscript and a biography of her grandfather have disappeared, and that she instructed Alejandra to burn her papers, including abundant correspondence, at her death.

The amount of extant material must be noted, for it is considerable if we take into account the presence of a large family, steadily declining health (mentioned indirectly in her letters to her husband; cf. *Obras completas*), and economic difficulties that may be attributed to ways in which the political activities of the couple ran contrary to the dominant social structures, particularly those controlled by Madrid (Rodríguez Sánchez). Castro's social concern has always been noted by critics, although they have mainly referred to her "feminine concern" for human suffering (Piñeiro; Rof Carballo et al.) rather than her awareness of political events. Yet it was this powerful political persona who befriended many writers and who led the process of promoting Galician nationalism and rights. One of the writers whom Castro befriended, the Romantic poet Aurelio Aguirre, has been linked to her sentimentally (Kulp). Recently, it has been shown that Castro strongly supported the Revolution of 1868 and opposed the subsequent restoration of the Bourbon monarchy in 1874, which coincided with the consolidation of conservative politics. Shortly before her death, she went to Carral, the site where twelve martyrs had been killed in 1846 during a popular uprising that protested Madrid's colonialist treatment of Galicia. This was perhaps a final testimony to her social commitment.

Castro frequently uses the term "regeneration" in her novels; this seems to be a reference to the liberal Galicians who were seeking equality with the rest of Spain after generations of economic exploitation. Rosalía's participation in these political activities was directly related to the difficulty she faced when trying to publish her books. *Follas Novas* (*New Leaves* 1991), which was first announced in 1874 on the inside flap of the second edition of *Cantares Gallegos* (1863; *Galician Songs* 1991), did not appear until 1880, in Havana, where it was financed by Galician immigrants. On March 28, 1881, the first of Castro's local color stories, "Costumbres gallegas" ("Galician Customs"), appeared in the newspaper *Los lunes de El Imparcial* of Madrid. Another story, which appeared on April 4, 1881, was seen by critics writing in *El Anunciador* and *La Concordia* as too revealing of the coastal population's practice of showing hospitality by allowing daughters to spend the night with sailors who had been long at sea. When her story "El Codio" ("The Crust of Bread"), critical of seminarians, was scheduled to appear, Castro's candor was once again criticized and the window of the press in Lugo, Soto Freire, was stoned, resulting in the loss of this text. She was so hurt by the incident, which underscored local misunderstanding of her intention to portray reality, that she refused to publish again in Galician.

After a long bout with uterine cancer, during which time she completed and published *En las orillas del Sar* (1884; *Beside the River Sar* 1937, *By the River Sar* 1991), Rosalía de Castro died in Padrón, Galicia, on July 15, 1885, saying "Abrídeme a xanela, que quero ver a mar" (qtd. in García Martí 123; Open the window for me, I want to see the sea). She was first buried, as she had wished, in the small nearby cemetery of Adina, but in 1891 her remains were moved to the Pantheon of Illustrious Galicians at Santo Domingo de Bonaval in Santiago. Her husband did not attend the exhumation or the reinterment.

Only recently has the process of molding the writer's life and work to a specified image by traditional critics been brought to the forefront (Rodríguez Sánchez). The "adaptation" of this image has aimed to facilitate Castro's identification as a major figure of Spanish literature, and includes ignoring her controversial novels while concentrating most specifically on her last work, *En las orillas del Sar*. As Rosalía de Castro had written extensively in Galician and often made her native land a part of her prose, she was suspected of anti-Spanish sentiment. The fate of the author and the fate of Galicia were so closely intertwined that her first burial site, the unkempt grave in Adina, was seen by area leaders as a symbol of the treatment of Galicia by the Spanish government. Castro was also considered suspect because of her strong temperament.

After her death, critics of diverse nationalities felt it necessary to reinterpret or silence Castro's life and writing in such a way as to nullify indications of nonconformity. Many critics even dropped her last name, preferring to use Rosalía and gradually transformed her into "santa" and "mártir"—nonthreatening symbols of an oppressed Galicia. The implication was that as a woman, her natural destiny was to face hardships, just as her motherland Galicia hoped to shelter and recover her children, many of whom were forced to leave for economic reasons. Other critics have not been sensitive to the essentially paternalistic and centralist perspective they have promoted. The emphasis has long been on the painful state this existence signified, rather than on the constructive and denunciatory activities in which author and nation were involved. These conflicted visions form the basis for a dual feminist/nationalist rereading of Rosalía de Castro today.

Rosalía's husband, Murguía, provided a most interesting evaluation of the author shortly after her death in his essay "Rosalía de Castro," included in *Los precursores* (1885). He consciously silenced personal information about her, insisting that a woman's life is centered within the home and that her personal affairs are of no interest to anyone but her immediate family. This is the man who, it has been said, "helped" his wife to write. In fact, there are manuscripts of hers with changes made by her husband, but there is no indication that these were made with her approval. We should also recall that Castro was an assiduous collaborator in her husband's historical research, for which he is better known than for his creative writing.

MAJOR THEMES

The major themes in Castro's writings—motherland, love, existential anguish, and resignation in the face of a selfish, false, and cruel humankind—are frequently repeated and cross genre lines. They are certainly present in her books of poetry: *La flor* (1857; ''The Flower''); *Cantares Gallegos; A mi madre* (1863; ''To My Mother''); *Follas Novas*; and *En las orillas del Sar*. *La flor* is a traditional book of romantic love poetry, reminiscent of the style of José de Espronceda; it is also where Aurelio Aguirre's influence is most evident. It is thought that Murguía's review of the brief volume in *La Ilustración Gallega y Asturiana* (May 12, 1857) was the beginning of their relationship. The poems reflect the escapism through fantasy and the disillusionment of many writers of the time as well as with the fleeting nature of happiness. *A mi madre*, written immediately after Doña Teresa's death, is a personal testimony to a mother who faced adverse circumstances in order to raise her daughter. These two volumes are the least original of her works, and although the poetic technique indicates skill, they alone would not have been likely to establish Castro as a widely recognized literary figure.

Cantares Gallegos was written with the encouragement of Murguía, who was unable or afraid to write in the Galician language in spite of his nationalistic sentiment. Many verses were gleaned from Castro's experiences as a girl in the country and were thus more naturally expressed in the Galician language. This volume reveals not only a boldness in using the hitherto stigmatized Galician— for which Castro had no written model—but also a great sensitivity for poetic creation. Castro used forms such as the *versos da gaita galega* (Galician bagpipe verses), which were important because they had helped to preserve the language during centuries of banishment from official usage. These *versos* were an integral part of many popular celebrations. Castro's use of the peasants' language immersed her in the themes related to their life: pre-Christian beliefs, romantic encounters, religious and other customs, poverty, hard work, death. There is humor in her verses, but never an attitude of superiority. Rosalía felt great compassion for those whose daily life was a struggle to survive, as it was for so many in nineteenth century Galicia, ravaged by plague and famine. She states in her introduction to *Cantares Gallegos*:

> I am so sorry about the injustices of the French toward us, but at this time I am almost thankful, for they give me a means to make the injustice Spain inflicts upon us more obvious.
>
>   This was the main reason that led me to publish this book . . . to pardon [its] defects I was very careful to reproduce the true spirit of our people. . . . May someone more talented than I some day describe . . . the beautiful scenes found there, even in the most hidden and forgotten corner, so that, at least in fame, if not in fortune, Galicia will receive and be seen with the respect and admiration it deserves! (266–67)

In the prologue, Castro clearly affirms her intention to vindicate her people. Yet the economic deprivation portrayed in the *Cantares* never signifies intellectual deficiency; her subjects are spontaneous, resourceful, and realistic, and have a strength that comes only from authorial respect. The concern for the hostile conditions of life in Galicia led to themes such as emigration, solitude, and separation from the homeland. The latter, called *morriña* or *saudade* (nostalgia), is treated by other Galician-Portuguese writers, and its presence in the landmark *Cantares Gallegos* is fundamental for its later development within the national literature.

In her Galician poetry, Castro portrays her people as victims of exploitation by other groups, such as the Castilians, and expresses her deep love for the natural world, its well-watered fertile hills in vehement contrast with the desertlike regions of much of Spain. This love of the land, present in popular verses, is still an important aspect of Galician identity, and is one of the reasons why Castro's poetry has remained as alive as it was over a century ago. Thus, while non-Galician critics, with the exception of Catherine Davies, Elena Sánchez Mora, and Kathleen March, have tended to pay more attention to the Rosalía of *En las orillas del Sar*, in her homeland, *Cantares Gallegos* is credited with initiating the Galician *Rexurdimento* (Renaissance). On the centennial of its date of publication, May 17, 1963, the first Día das Letras Galegas, now celebrated annually, was dedicated to Rosalía de Castro.

Follas Novas appears in a sense to continue the line of solidarity with the rural world, and in it Castro portrays her love for the people, the land, and the language with unabashed passion and simplicity. She is not afraid to defend or accuse, as the case warrants, and she revels in nature's sensuality. Yet her political ideals are clearly defined, and prevent today's critics from reducing her to either of two distinct roles attributed to her by critics of the past: the promoter of the superficially popular or the creator of such motifs as the *negra sombra* (dark shadow) or madness. This madness was seen as a function of the author's "delicate, excitable" mind as well as of her gender or state of "illegitimacy." It is incorrect to categorize the whole of her poetic creation, however, as a spontaneous corpus arising from moments of irrational or emotional inspiration. As seen in her choice of the Galician language and of oral verse form, there is a clear commitment to her society.

Rosalía de Castro's Galician poems, such as "A xusticia pol-a man" ("Justice by My Own Hands") and "Xan," are examples of a harsh and continuous diatribe against an unjust society and a special concern for women's rights. This haunting dark shadow is not that of a hypersensitive soul alienated from its surroundings but, rather, a codified statement of the distorting, violent effects of social structure on its victims and dissidents. Under these circumstances, women's rebellion can be forceful, even leading them to take the law into their own hands, declaring the death sentence for the exploiting masters responsible for the starvation of peasant children and their mothers' shame. Although the law condemned her, the woman in "A xusticia pol-a man" killed the masters as they slept in their soft, warm beds:

> Aqués que ten fama d'honrados n'a vila
> roubáronme tanta brancura qu'eu tiña,
> botáronme estrume n'as galas d'un día

a roupa de cote puñéronme en tiras.
. . .

Estonces cal loba doente ou ferida,
d'un salto con rabia pilley a fouciña,
rondei paseniño. . . . ¡Ni-as herbas sentían!
Y-a lua escondíase, y á fera dormía
cos seus compañeiros en cama mullida.
Mireinos con calma, y as mans extendidas,
d'un golpe, ¡d'un soyo!, deixeinos sin vida. (*Follas Novas* 231)

Those who are known as honorable in the village,
stole all my purity,
stained my fine dress one day,
tore my clothing to shreds.
. . .

Then like a she-wolf, ill or wounded,
in a flash I madly grabbed the sickle,
slowly circled. . . . Not even the grass heard me!
And the moon hid, and the beast slept
with its companions in a soft bed.
I looked at them coolly, and hands outstretched,
with one blow—just one!—I left them dead.

In her final book of poetry, *En las orillas del Sar*, Rosalía's perspective becomes more somber. Perhaps her failing health contributed to this change, but some of the compositions had been written years earlier and are closer to the political events that so disillusioned her. In a context where openly denunciatory writing would not have been published, especially coming from the pen of a woman, she masked her dissidence behind an existential resignation to life's destiny or to the maladjustment of the self.

In this volume, Castro criticized the well-known Galician author Emilia Pardo Bazán, who had won more than one prize in the Floral Games that were overseen by the church after the Bourbon Restoration of 1874. The relationship between the two women seems to have been fraught with tension, and each was openly critical of the other. In Rosalía's untitled poem (*En las orillas del Sar* 649), the Countess is portrayed as haughty and arrogant. Pardo Bazán, for her part, included a derogatory comment in *De mi tierra* (1888) regarding the political commitment of Castro's poetry. The reason for the mutual dislike is not completely clear, but it would seem that although both were feminists, their differences with regard to class and interpretation of Galician identity were great. Pardo Bazán, unlike Castro, never used the national language. In addition, she belonged to a higher social class and frequently lived outside of Galicia. It should also be noted that Castro initially expressed fondness for the writer Fernán Caballero. Although she admired the pages Caballero had devoted to Galicia, this relationship later cooled, perhaps because of the conservative Caballero's strong support of the church and the monarchy.

En las orillas del Sar is ultimately the result of a life filled with the desire to love and a sense of persecution, isolation, nostalgia, and pride in the poet's ideals. It bears the mark of approaching death, but only in part. It may be more accurately assessed as a summary of Castro's vital experiences, intimate as well as patriotic and ideological. In support of Galicia's language, culture, and people against centralism, in support of peasants and especially peasant women, Castro angrily etched their difficult lives, poverty, and loneliness in all of her literary creations.

Castro published five novels: *La hija del mar* (1859; "The Daughter of the Sea"), *Flavio* (1861), *Ruinas* (1866; "Ruins"), *El caballero de las botas azules* (1867; "The Gentleman in the Blue Boots"), and *El primer loco* (1881; "The First Madman"). Long overlooked, they have been termed out-of-date, sentimental, poorly written, almost anything but the fine, lucid portrayals of society that they are. Importantly, all five works reveal a concern for women; that this aspect was scarcely noticed in its own right until a century later may have two explanations. First, the notion of a feminist writer went against the "safer" image of a simple provincial woman who had been officially cultivated, whose first loyalty was supposed to be to husband and family, and whose writing was intuitive—that is, due to spontaneous inspiration rather than rational analysis. This resulted in a far greater preference for her poetry, a more "feminine" genre. Castro's outstanding feature was "determined" to be her sentimentality; her technique, to be simple. It was easy to overlook the numerous quotes, some in French, and intertextual references in the novels, many from sources other than Spanish writers. The careful cross-references of *El caballero de las botas azules*, for example, went without comment. Second, the impetus to reread her novels has its roots in the general growth of feminist criticism as well as the evolution of Galician nationalism since the death of Franco in 1975. The large international conference held on the centennial of Castro's death in Santiago de Compostela in 1985 played a major role in bringing together both traditional and innovative scholars within the Galician context.

Among the matters debated at the conference was Castro's political awareness and its reflection in her works. *El caballero de las botas azules* was shown to be a portrayal not only of the effects of bad literature on social mores but also of the state of Spanish culture and politics as a whole, with Madrid signifying the degradation to which the country had fallen prey. In turn, this society was viewed by Castro as being detrimental to the development of women, for it encouraged them to accept roles that made them slaves to men. In the prologue entitled "Un hombre y una musa," the rebellious Muse refuses to obey the male writer's orders. She resists being his passive source of inspiration and instead insists on dictating what she considers appropriate. She criticizes his desire for immortality, his audacity, ambition, vanity, his belief that he is a "self-made man," his use of others for supposed philanthropic activities. In addition, she scoffs at his desire to surprise Europe and write an original book that will bring him glory. She accuses the writer of calling her when he realizes nothing new is left; in so doing, he reveals his need for her. She discloses her origin only so that he will respect her, saying she is "perhaps" born from a relative of Revolution, Liberty, Order, Honor, meant to lead people along the paths of the world (not the glorious heavens); that she is Other, and thus can show him what is worthwhile in life, literature, and society. This complex novel, a profound interpretation and denunciation of the author's times, continues a theme of an earlier novel, *Flavio*, in which a woman refuses to accept her suitor's demands and is therefore "misread" by society and by many critics.

Among the contextualizing studies of recent times are those that point to regional mythology of a Celtic nature, but even more important are those that provide data on the Galician press of the period, particularly the debates concerning the "nature of women" (Barreiro). A writer such as Rosalía de Castro, who read works by other women and who gave major importance to her female characters, could hardly have been unaware of the exchanges on this topic. Women in general, and women writers in particular, were frequently a focus of her work; for a long time, however, the critics did not perceive a clear intent to condemn patriarchal patterns, which she saw as supported by economic control by one sex, along with attempts to control the participation of women in such areas as literary creation. When Castro is recognized as a victim of the relegation of "regional writing" to secondary importance, it immediately becomes obvious that she employed female protagonists to delineate and reject accepted social patterns: Teresa and Esperanza of *La hija del mar* refuse to be imprisoned by the pirate Ansot in his patriarchal house, where rape and incest are threatened, and Mara of *Flavio* denies Flavio the privilege of writing his romantic text by not conforming to his definition of her role. Thus, in these two novels, and even in *El primer loco*, the discourse of heightened passion was not an outmoded technique but, rather, an intentional parody of superficial, oppressive behavior, in which madness is clearly the result of male attempts to dominate.

SURVEY OF CRITICISM

The critical approaches to Rosalía de Castro's poetry may be arranged in four categories. The first is that of her contemporaries and other nineteenth-century studies through the early twentieth century. The relatively few available documents, generally book reviews, appeared in journals that were among the most respected of the Iberian Peninsula. Many of the authors had been acquainted with Castro; even her husband may be counted among her critics. By the beginning of the twentieth century, Castro was already the symbol of a maternal Galicia—"primitive child" of the Spanish state—for writers such as Azorín and Miguel de Unamuno.

Without chronological categorizing, the second group of Rosalía scholars consists of the traditional ones, and includes some present-day critics. They focus on linguistic/stylistic features; thematic studies (Nogales, Piñeiro, Ruiz Silva); comparative criticism, especially with reference to Gustavo Adolfo Bécquer, Heinrich Heine (Machado da Rosa), and José de Espronceda (Poullain); historical content; and structural features (Otero Pedrayo, Varela Jácome). There are publications of posthumous texts, usually with introductory commentary (Naya Pérez), and annotated bibliographies (Carré Aldao, Carballo Calero). Few in this group have given serious attention to the novels, which they generally consider inferior to her poetry (Mayoral). Important personal information has been provided by Fermín Bouza Brey and Xosé Filgueira Valverde.

The third group of critics initiates a transitional stage. While not rejecting previous critical works, they emphasize Castro as a woman writer (Albert Robatto, Stevens), as a Galician, and as a product of a specific sociopolitical context rather than as an isolated case of poetic genius (Poullain). In one early study, Xesús Alonso Montero emphasizes the contextual factors, and in another, Nidia Díaz clearly identifies the author as a nonconformist.

The fourth critical approach consciously tries to break with the traditional view of the sorrowful, suffering "poetess." As of 1985, the break is more obvious and definitive. Rosalía is explored as a feminist (Sánchez Mora, García Negro, Rodríguez Sánchez, March), a nationalist (Rodríguez Sánchez), and a *literata*. The slender collective volume, *Rosalía de Castro: Unha obra non asumida* (1985), followed by the excellent studies of Catherine Davies (1987) and Francisco Rodríguez Sánchez (1988), have revolutionized critical approaches to Castro. Studies of her influence on later Galician women poets, among them Luz Pozo Garza, Pura Vázquez Iglesias, María do Carmo Kruckenberg, Xohana Torres (March, *Actas*), require a double focus on both the reading that these poets have done and the (in)accuracy of that reading. Studies of the historical context such as Davies's provide data that make new interpretations possible and point toward new possibilities for understanding Rosalía's life and work. The latest perspectives shed an entirely new light on the life and work of this woman writer from the "provinces." Such critical approaches are beginning to convince the public of the need to reevaluate Rosalía de Castro's position as a Galician writer within her time and context.

BIBLIOGRAPHY

Works by Rosalía de Castro

Obras completas. Ed. Victoriano García Martí. Madrid: Aguilar, 1952.

Poetry

La flor. Madrid: Imprenta de M. González, 1857.
A mi madre. Vigo, Spain: Juan Compañel, 1863.
Cantares Gallegos. Vigo, Spain: Juan Compañel, 1863. 2nd ed., corrected and with additions. Madrid: Rivadeneyra, 1872.
Follas Novas. Havana: La Propaganda Literaria, 1880. Madrid: Aurelio J. Allaría, 1880.
En las orillas del Sar. Madrid: Est. Tip. de Fernando Fé, 1884.
En las orillas del Sar. Ed. Xesús Alonso Montero. Madrid: Cátedra, 1990.

Prose

Lieders. Vigo, Spain: El Album del Miño, 1858.
La hija del mar. Vigo, Spain: Juan Compañel, 1859.
Flavio (ensayo de novela). Madrid: La Crónica de Ambos Mundos, 1861.
El cadiceño. Lugo, Spain: El Almanaque de Galicia, 1866.
Las literatas. Lugo, Spain: Almanaque de Galicia, Soto Freire, 1866.
Ruinas. Desdichas de tres vidas ejemplares. Phantom ed. given for Madrid in 1866.
   Published in Vigo, Spain: Juan Compañel, 1864.
El caballero de las botas azules. Cuento extraño. Lugo, Spain: Manuel Soto Freire,
   1867.
Padrón y las inundaciones. La Ilustración Gallega y Asturiana, 28 Feb., 8, 18, 28 Mar.
   1881: n. pag.
El primer loco. Cuento extraño. Madrid: Moya y Plaza, 1881.
"Conto galego." Published by Fermín Bouza Brey in *Cuadernos de Estudios Gallegos*
   fasc. 6 (1946): n. pag. [Title provided by Bouza Brey]

Translations

Beside the River Sar. Trans. Griswold S. Morley. Berkeley: U of Cal. P, 1937.
Poems by Rosalía de Castro. Trans. Charles David Ley. Madrid: Ministry of Foreign
   Affairs, 1964.
*The Defiant Muse. Hispanic Feminist Poems From the Middle Ages to the Present. A
   Bilingual Anthology*. Trans. Kate Flores. Ed. and intro. Ángel Flores and Kate
   Flores. New York: The Feminist Press of the City of NY, 1986. Included in this
   volume are the following poems: "Feeling Her End Would Come with Summer's
   End," 43; "From the Cadenced Roar of the Waves," 41; "Justice of Men! I
   Look for You." 41; "Lieder" (Trans. Ángel Flores and Kate Flores), 39; "This
   One Goes and That One Goes," 39; "Today Black Hair," 39.
Poems. Ed. and trans. Anna-Marie Aldaz, Barbara N. Gantt, and Anne C. Bromley.
   Albany: State U of New York P, 1991. [Selections from *Galician Songs*, *New
   Leaves* and *By the River Sar*]

Works about Rosalía de Castro

Actas do congreso internacional de estudios sobre Rosalía de Castro e o seu tempo. 3
   vols. Santiago de Compostela: Consello da Cultura Galega e Universidade de
   Santiago de Compostela, 1986. [Hereafter cited as *Actas*]
Aguiar e Silva, Víctor Manuel. "Para una leitura desconstrutivista da poesia de Rosalia
   de Castro." *Actas* 2: 184–91.
Albert Robatto, Matilde. *Rosalía de Castro y la condición femenina*. Madrid: Partenón,
   1981.
Alonso Montero, Xesús. *Rosalía de Castro*. Madrid: Júcar, 1972.
Barreiro Fernández, X. R. "Federalismo e rexionalismo galego no século XIX." *Grial*
   43 (1974): 49–53.
Blanco, Carmen. *Literatura galega da muller*. Vigo, Spain: Edicións Xerais, 1991.
Bouza Álvarez, José Luis. "*Los Cantares Gallegos* o Rosalía y los suyos entre 1860 y
   1863." *Cuadernos de Estudios Gallegos* 18 fasc. 56 (1963): 255–302.

————. "El tema rosaliano de 'negra sombra' en la poesía compostelana del sigo XIX." *Cuadernos de Estudios Gallegos* 8 fasc. 25 (1953): 227–78.

————. "En torno al simbolismo de *En las orillas del Sar*: Raíces pitagórico-platónicas y estoicas de los temas literarios de Rosalía de Castro." *Actas* 1: 143–54.

Briesemeister, Dieter. *Die Dichtung der Rosalía de Castro*. Munich: A. Bergmiller, 1959.

————. "Rosalía de Castro dentro da poesía feminina do seu tempo: Motivos e constantes." *Actas* 1: 239–49.

Bungard, Ana. "Análisis diegético de *Follas Novas*. Dinámica textual." *Actas* 2: 219–28.

Carballo Calero, Ricardo. "Bibliografía rosaliana." *Grial* 58 (1970): 389–400.

————. *Estudos rosalianos*. Vigo, Spain: Galaxia, 1979.

————. "Referencias a Rosalía en cartas de sus contemporáneos." *Cuadernos de Estudios Gallegos* 18.56 (1963): 303–13.

Carré Aldao, E. "Estudio bibliográfico crítico acerca de Rosalía de Castro." *Boletín de la Real Academia Gallega* 16.181 (Mar. 1926): 50–55; 17.189 (Dec. 1926): 237–40.

Costa Gómez, Antonio. "Rosalía de Castro e Emily Dickinson." *Grial* 18 (1980): 276–85.

Davies, Catherine. "A importancia de *Cantares Gallegos*: Libro de tradición e innovación." *Grial* 82 (1983): 443–52.

————. "Rosalía de Castro: Criticism 1850–1980. The Need for a New Approach." *Bulletin of Hispanic Studies* 61 (1983): 211–20.

————. *Rosalía de Castro e Follas Novas*. Vigo, Spain: Galaxia, 1990.

————. *Rosaliía de Castro no seu tempo*. Vigo, Spain: Galaxia, 1987.

Del Saz, Bernardo. "Bibliografía. *El caballero de las botas azules*." *El Museo Universal* (8, 9, 22, 29 Feb. 1868): n. pag.

De Paula Canalejas, F. "*Cantares Gallegos*." *El Contemporáneo* 6 (May 1864): n. pag.

Díaz, Nidia. *La protesta social en la obra de Rosalía de Castro*. Vigo, Spain: Galaxia, 1976.

Dupláa, Cristina. "Rosalía de Castro y el 'Rexurdimento' gallego: Posibles conexiones con la Renaixença catalana." *Actas* 3: 413–18.

Filgueira Valverde, Xosé. "Rosalía e a música." *Actas* 1: 33–56.

Fuente Bermúdez, José María de la. "A socioloxía de *Follas Novas*." *Galicia* 678 (14 Dec. 1924): n. pag.

Gamallo Fierros, Dionisio. "Una cima de la lírica del XIX: Rosalía de Castro." *Informaciones* (21, 27 July 1944): n. pag.

————. "¿Luz sobre la negra sombra?" *Nordés* 2-3 (1975): 55–84.

García Martí, Victoriano. Prologue. *Obras completas*. By Rosalía de Castro. Madrid: Aguilar, 1952.

García Negro, Pilar. "Rosalía á luz de Mara." *Actas* 1: 73–80.

González Millán, Xan. "Proceso textual y fantasía en *El primer loco*." *Actas* 1: 517–22.

Harvard, Robert G. "*Saudades* as Structure in Rosalía de Castro's *En las orillas del Sar*." *Hispanic Journal* 5 (Fall 1983): 29–41.

Kulp, Kathleen. *Manner and Mood in Rosalía de Castro. A Study of Themes and Style*. Madrid: José Porrúa Turanza, 1968.

Lapesa, Ramón. "Bécquer, Rosalía y Machado." *Ínsula* (Apr. 1954): 100–01.

Machado da Rosa, A. "Camões e Rosalia." *Atenea* 1–2 (Mar.–June 1973): 85–90.

———. "Heine in Spain. Relations with Rosalía de Castro." *Monatshefte* 49 (1957): 65–82.

———. "Rosalía de Castro, poeta incomprendido." *Hispánica Moderna* 20 (July 1954): 181–223.

March, Kathleen N. *De musa a literata: El feminismo en la narrativa de Rosalía de Castro*. Sada - A Coruña: Ediciós do Castro, 1993.

———. "Novela e feminismo." Spec. issue of *A Nosa Terra* (1990): 23–29.

———. "Rosalía de Castro como punto de referencia ideolóxico-literario nas escritoras galegas." *Actas* 1: 283–92.

Martín, Elvira. *Tres mujeres gallegas del siglo XIX*. 2nd ed. Barcelona: Aedos, 1977.

Mayoral, Marina. *La poesía de Rosalía de Castro*. Madrid: Gredos, 1974.

Murguía, Manuel. *Los precursores*. La Coruña, Spain: Biblioteca Gallega, 1885.

Naya Pérez, Juan. *Inéditos de Rosalía*. Santiago de Compostela: Patronato Rosalía de Castro, 1953.

Nogales de Muñiz, María Antonia. *Irradiación de Rosalía de Castro*. Barcelona: Tall. Gráf. Angel Estrada, 1966.

Odriozola, Antonio. "Las ediciones de Rosalía de Castro y su esposo en vida de ambos." *Actas* 1: 93–96.

Otero Pedrayo, Ramón. "El planteamiento decisivo de la novela romántica en Rosalía de Castro." *Cuadernos de Estudios Gallegos* 24.72–74 (1969): 290–314.

———. *Romantismo, saudade, sentimento da Raza e da Terra en Pastor Díaz, R. de Castro e Pondal*. Santiago de Compostela: Nós, 1931.

Pardo Bazán, Emilia. "La poesía regional gallega." *De mi tierra*. 1888. Rpt. Vigo, Spain: Xerais, 1984. 11–49.

Pérez Villaamil, A. *La personalidad enferma de Rosalía de Castro*. Vigo, Spain: n.p., 1947.

Piñeiro, Ramón. "A Saudade en Rosalía." *7 ensayos sobre Rosalía*. Vigo, Spain: Galaxia, 1952. 95–109.

Placer, Fr. Gumersindo. "Un subtema rosaliano: O suicidio." *Grial* (Apr.–June 1972): 138–57.

Poullain, Henri. *Rosalía de Castro e a sua obra literaria*. Vigo, Spain: Galaxia, 1989.

Rodríguez Sánchez, Francisco. *Análise Sociolóxica da Obra de Rosalía de Castro*. Vigo, Spain: AS-PG, 1988.

Rof Carballo, J. "Rosalía, ánima galaica." *7 ensayos sobre Rosalía*. Vigo, Spain: Galaxia, 1952. 111–49.

Rosalía de Castro: Unha obra non asumida. Santiago de Compostela: Xistral, 1985.

Ruiz Silva, A. "Reflexiones sobre *La hija del mar*." *Actas* 1: 367–80.

Sánchez Mora, Elena. "Rosalía de Castro ante la crítica feminista." Spec. issue of *A Nosa Terra* (1990): 30–36.

Stevens, Shelley. *Rosalía de Castro and the Galician Revival*. London: Tamesis Books, 1986.

Tirrel, Sister Mary Pierre. *La mística de la saudade. Estudio de la poesía de Rosalía de Castro*. Madrid: Ediciones Jura, 1951.

Varela Jácome, Benito. "Emilia Pardo Bazán, Rosalía de Castro y Murguía." *Cuadernos de Estudios Gallegos* 6 (1951): 405–29.

CAROLINA CORONADO
(1823–1911)

Susan Kirkpatrick

BIOGRAPHY

Carolina Coronado was the first daughter of Nicolás Coronado and María Antonia Romero, both from landowning families of Extremadura that had been persecuted under Fernando VII for their liberal views. Coronado's early childhood was spent in her birthplace, the village of Almendralejo, and in the provincial capital, Badajoz. Her education was no better than that of other young ladies of the upper classes—needlework, painting, piano, a smattering of Italian and French. She excelled in painting and piano, but literature was her true vocation; influenced by the classic Spanish poets she read in her father's library, she began to compose poems at an early age.

Coronado insisted throughout her life that the obstacles her social milieu put in the way of women with literary aspirations were nearly insurmountable. The preface of her first book of poetry claimed that she was forced to compose her poems in her head and retain them by memory, because no time for writing was allowed her. In a letter she pointedly remarked that even the most progressive fathers frowned at seeing their daughters pick up a newspaper instead of a darning needle ("Cartas" 228). Unquestionably, in the Spanish society of the period, women who wished to engage in intellectual or artistic endeavors faced hostility and ridicule. Yet the external evidence shows that Coronado was highly successful in winning support and approval for her literary career.

In 1839 one of her early compositions, "A la palma" ("To the Palm"), was published in the Madrid periodical *El Piloto* under the sponsorship of Donoso Cortés, an Extremenian intellectual and politician. A poem signed by a woman was a rarity in the Spanish press of the 1830s, and its publication brought Coronado immediate attention from the young Romantic poet José de Espronceda, who wrote a poem to her. After placing a number of poems in the periodical press, Coronado soon determined to publish her collected poetry in a volume. To this end, she initiated a correspondence with the respected and influential dramatist Juan Eugenio Hartzenbusch, whose help she solicited in editing her poems and finding a publisher for them. Hartzenbusch, who offered a helping hand to a number of women writers in the succeeding decade, became Coronado's mentor and promoter.

Coronado's first book of poetry, published in 1843, consisted mostly of short lyrical poems showing the influence of Coronado's models, Fray Luis de León and Juan Meléndez Valdés. In one cycle of poems, the lyrical subject addresses and characterizes a variety of garden and wild flowers; in another, the poet assumes the persona of Sappho. The poetry of this collection in no way transgresses the limits of the ladylike, as it was defined in the period; but "El marido verdugo" ("The Executioner Husband"), an indignant outburst against wife beaters, suggests a vein of feminist anger and criticism running through the childlike innocence of Coronado's poetic persona. Indeed, the collection of Coronado's letters to Hartzenbusch in the Biblioteca Nacional de Madrid reveals that she intended to include in this volume a poem that indicts society for denying women the right to self-expression. Hartzenbusch, reflecting the paternalistic bias of his support, advised her to omit the poem, which she did. Later, however, when she was not so dependent on her mentor's approval, she published many poems on this theme.

With the publication of the 1843 *Poesías*, Coronado achieved a considerable measure of fame and influence. Periodicals around the peninsula solicited her contributions, articles about her appeared, and she was made an honorary member of a number of provincial *liceos* (literary societies). A dramatic incident heightened her notoriety: In 1844 a published notice of Carolina Coronado's death prompted a number of premature poetic laments on her passing. The rumor of her death had been precipitated by an attack of catalepsy, a symptom of the nervous illness that she suffered in her early twenties.

During these years Coronado published a great deal, no longer limiting her topics to birds, flowers, and wooded nooks, but reflecting on history, politics, and, above all, the condition of women. Evidently this subject struck a chord in her female readers, for many of them wrote to her, sent her samples of their own writing, and asked for her assistance in publishing their work. Coronado responded generously. In journals where she had influence, she sponsored poems by unknown women writers, responded in verse to poems dedicated to her by women poets, and carried on warm epistolary friendships with such poets as Robustiana Armiño, Ángela Grassi, and Vicenta García Miranda.

Around 1845 a cycle of poetry addressed to "Alberto" suggests an amorous episode in Coronado's life, but the identity of Alberto—or whether he really existed—has never been established. A number of the poems indicate that Alberto perished at sea. Shortly afterward, Coronado made a vow of celibacy that was later to cause her some inconvenience. Continuing health problems—perhaps generated by the sense of suffocation, the need of the airs of a wider world that she expressed in her poetry—induced her parents to take her to Madrid in the spring of 1848. The capital city fêted her arrival: She was received in aristocratic salons, crowned with laurel in the Madrid *liceo*, and offered new avenues of publication by editors. Two years later the family moved to Madrid, and Coronado began to write articles on literary topics for Madrid journals. In an essay for *El Semanario Pintoresco Español*, she scandalized some readers by asserting a profound likeness between Saint Teresa and Sappho: Whereas Teresa's love materialized Jesus, she argued, Sappho's passion spiritualized her human lover; ideal love inspired both to reach the heights of feminine heroism. In her determination to honor the achievements of women, Coronado also began a series of articles on contemporary women poets, "Galería de poetisas españolas" ("Gallery of Spanish Women Poets"), for *La Ilustración*. Seeking to extend the scope of her talent, she started writing fiction, too. But still she longed for a wider sphere of existence. In 1851 she began a tour of Europe, accompanied by her father. (Whatever the intimate struggles in the heart of the Coronado family may have been, the bare facts of the biography suggest that Carolina's desires ultimately shaped family decisions.) Her description of this journey, in the form of letters to her brother Emilio, were published in *La Ilustración* throughout 1851. The highlight of the trip was Paris, where she was introduced to the leading literary figures of the day.

In 1852 Coronado published her second book of poetry, including in it the poems of her first collection as well as the poetry that she had written since. The widening arena of the poet's concerns is reflected by the topics of the volume's various sections: amorous poetry to Alberto, philosophical and religious reflections, commentary on contemporary history and politics (the turbulence of 1848 looms large here), poems to sister poets about the condition of women, and satirical and comic verse. This volume contains almost the entire corpus of Coronado's poetic production, for soon after its publication her life took a turn that seemed to mute her lyrical muse.

In July 1852, Carolina Coronado was married in Gibraltar in a Protestant ceremony to Horace Perry, a well-to-do American diplomat stationed in Madrid. The couple had to travel immediately to Paris to persuade Catholic authorities there to release Coronado from her vow of celibacy so that she could be married in the Catholic Church. The newlyweds settled in Madrid, where Coronado established herself as the hostess of an important salon. Children soon followed. The first, Horacio, died scarcely out of infancy in 1854; his devastated mother interred his body in a niche in the cathedral's most popular chapel. Two daughters, Carolina and Matilde, were born later. During these early years of her marriage, Coronado did not give up writing entirely. She published some short fiction and the novel *La Sigea* (1854), and composed the novel *Jarilla*, which was not published until 1873. In 1857 Coronado resurrected her series on women poets, publishing two more articles in *La discusión*. In the political turbulence of the 1860s, the Perrys used their influence to protect political figures on both the Right and the Left from reprisals. In 1872, Coronado published an anthology of her best poems (*Poesías*), including some written after the 1852 collection. The following year, she published two pieces of fiction, *Jarilla* and *La Rueda de la Desgracia* ("The Wheel of Misfortune").

In 1873, Coronado's daughter Carolina died of a sudden illness. The poet's reaction to this loss was violent. She would not permit the burial of her daughter's body; instead, she had it embalmed and placed in a closet in a Madrid convent sacristy. Nor could she bear to continue living in the house where Carolina had died, or even in Madrid; the Perry family moved to Portugal and settled in a secluded mansion on the outskirts of Lisbon. Although Horace Perry lost a good deal of his fortune through promoting and defending the interests of the first transatlantic telegraph cable company, the family lived comfortably in Lisbon until Coronado's death. Her eccentricities and imperious nature grew more marked in her old age. When her husband died, she kept his embalmed body surrounded by candles in her garden chapel. She refused to be separated from her surviving daughter, Matilde. Her jealous possessiveness reached such an extreme that she allowed her daughter (then near forty) to marry only on the condition that Matilde sleep in her mother's bedroom. From time to time during her last years she wrote occasional verse, but when she died in 1911, her creative career had long been over.

MAJOR THEMES

Carolina Coronado's first volume of poetry (1843), though published at the height of Spanish Romanticism, found its models in the lyrical tradition that ran from Horace through Fray Luis de León and Juan Meléndez Valdés. In centering on a poetic persona that retreats from society to find pleasure and consolation in the natural world, this tradition was regarded as more appropriate for a young woman than the tormented passions of the Romantic mode. Her preferred verse form was the *lira*, an Italianate stanza introduced during the Renaissance, but her diction shows the influence of Meléndez Valdés's late-eighteenth-century sentimentalism. Many of the poems deal with the lyricist's response to the natural world of the Extremaduran countryside—trees, brooks, birds, glades—though her poetic language tends to generalize rather than particularize nature.

The most original and satisfying of these nature poems are those addressed to various flowers—"Al lirio," "A la siempreviva," "Al jazmín" ("To the Wild Iris," "To the Immortelle," "To the Jasmine"). In these, the poetic voice invokes and revises the long poetic tradition associating flowers and women as objects of sensual delight. Instead of objectifying the flowers, these poems project a shared subjectivity with them: Reading the flowers' secret language, the poet discloses her own emotional life. In poems like "Al lirio" and "El girasol" ("The Sunflower"), the feminine subjectivity thus delicately sketched centers on a conflict between the modesty and fragility of the woodland flower and its desire for recognition, for glory. "Los cantos de Safo" ("The Songs of Sappho") develop a related theme—the woman poet's conflict between love and poetic achievement. Indeed, awareness of the problematic position of women in relation to writing is implicit in much of this poetry. "Rosa bianca" ("White Rose"), for example, suggestively presents the self-alienation and muteness of a woman who has been objectified as a flower by a male poet.

In the poetry written after 1843 and collected in the 1852 volume, the theme of women's suffering becomes explicit. In a period suffused with the emancipatory rhetoric of liberalism, Coronado comments tartly on her male compatriots' blindness to women's oppression: "¡Libertad: ¿qué nos importa? / ¿qué ganamos, qué tendremos? / ¿un encierro por tribuna / y una aguja por derecho?" ("La libertad" 72) (Freedom! What does it matter to us? / What will we gain, what will we have? / A sequesterment as our speaking platform / and a needle as our right?). Images of suffocation convey the situation of women, whose "lively intelligence" and "burning genius" are smothered in silent tedium ("Cantad, hermosas"; "Sing, Lovely Ones"). In "Último canto" ("Last Song") the poet compares herself to a captured insect expiring in a jar for want of air; she concludes by representing herself as a chained eagle: "roca inmóvil es mi planta, / águila rauda mi ser . . . / ¡Muera el águila a la roca / por ambas alas sujeta; / mi espíritu de poeta / a mis plantas de mujer!" (31; my feet are immobile rock, / my being a swift eagle . . . / Let the eagle die, / both its wings bound to the rock / as my poet's spirit / is to my woman's feet!). The imagery denoting the strain of winged poetic aspirations against the restrictions of the feminine role recurs in many poems. Reflecting on women's historical condition in "El castillo de Salvatierra" ("Salvatierra Castle"), Coronado indulges in the fantasy of liberation through soaring flight with the pigeons, only to find herself rebuked by the patriarchal thunder of an approaching storm. The pull of women's social destiny against their artistic aspiration is expressed in the dominant image of "La flor de agua" ("The Water Lily") as the tug of the water lily's floating petals against its roots; but the poem's conclusion suggests that the pain of that continuous struggle is alleviated by feminine solidarity when the water lilies "enlazan sus raíces / a la planta compañera, / y viven en la ribera / sosteniéndose entre sí" (195; link their roots / with those of their neighboring plant / and live along the bank / supporting each other).

The qualities that characterize Coronado's most successful amorous and religious poems can best be understood in the context of this imagery of feminine claustrophobia. For example, in "La luna en una ausencia" ("The Moon During an Absence"), the contrast between the dark, solitary olive grove and the luminous moon becomes increasingly charged with meaning through the association of the moon not only with another time—a previous occasion when the beloved was present—but also with another space—that which the beloved now occupies. The power of the moon image here is its association with an expanded world, a concrete time and place to which it—"swift messenger"—links the female lyrical subject in her restricted solitude.

In "El amor de los amores" ("The Love of Loves"), perhaps Coronado's

most frequently anthologized poem, an expansive movement likewise characterizes the lyrical speaker's quest for the beloved, whose existence she intuits
fleetingly in natural phenomena; from the mountain solitude where she first waits
for the beloved, she goes to the valley, then to the seashore, where she turns
her gaze to heaven: "Mi amor, el tierno amor por el que lloro / eres tan solo
tú, ¡señor Dios mío!" (67; My love, the tender love for which I weep / is you
alone, my lord God!). Yet the imposition of a conventional mystical meaning
on the poet's quest in the concluding stanzas lacks conviction; the power of this
poem is its evocation of the quest itself as the restless, unsatisfied movement of
the female subject.

   In her fiction, Coronado chose the genre of historical novel, which had been
popular in Spain since the 1830s; setting her narratives in the distant past allowed
her more freedom to criticize oppressive social structures. *Adoración* and *Paquita*
(1850), two stories that constitute Coronado's first published fiction, show little
skill with narrative form, but the latter offers indignant commentary on the role
of women in marriage. *Jarilla*, her first novel, paints with a free hand the
fratricidal wars of the nobility in the time of Juan II of Castile. Another novel
written during the same period, "La Exclaustrada" ("The Secularized Nun"),
is lost, but its title suggests that it may have explored themes similar to those
of her most successful novel, *La Sigea*, which centers on the suffering of two
intellectual women as a consequence of court intrigues and religious fanaticism.
The protagonists are Luisa Sigea of Toledo, a sixteenth-century scholar and poet,
and the Infanta María of Portugal, who brought Sigea to her court to teach her
ancient languages. Both protagonists must submit to a destiny different from the
one they would have chosen, and the narrator comments outspokenly on male
determination to subordinate women. Yet part II of the novel, published in 1854,
after Coronado had been married for three years, is much more conciliatory than
part I, which had been published four years earlier in *El Semanario Pintoresco
Español*.

   A shift in attitude is also apparent in the criticism Coronado published in the
same years. The incomplete series of articles to which she gave the title "Galería
de poetisas españolas" has the distinction of being the first attempt by a woman
writer to offer a critical portrait of a generation or group of women poets to
which she herself belonged. In 1850 she published two of these portraits, in
which she characterizes and praises the work of Ángela Grassi and Robustiana
Armiño; in 1857 she renewed the series with essays on Josefa Massanés and
Gertrudis Gómez de Avellaneda, and an introduction in which she explained
that her views on women and poetic vocation had changed since the 1840s. No
longer did she feel herself to be such a passionate champion of women's right
to poetic self-expression: "I must confess that today's society needs women
more than it does literary ladies. The absence that is starting to be felt is not
that of genius but of modesty; the light that we are beginning to need is not
academic enlightenment but the glow of the hearth" ("Galería. . . . Introducción" 3). Thus exalting women's domestic role, Coronado, who began writing

in protest against the restrictions of that role, closed the cycle of her poetic production. The key to this shift in attitude is not to be found solely in Coronado's personal life, though her experience of marriage and motherhood no doubt played a part. Above all, her views reflected the rapid consolidation in the 1850s of a new cultural ideal of womanhood that granted women authority—including the power to speak and write—exclusively in the sphere of domestic life. In the 1840s, a period of ideological flux and an expanding press and readership in Spain, Coronado was among the pioneering women who seized the opportunity to claim a place and a voice for their sex in literary culture. But by the same token, she helped to set the paradigm for her generation of women writers when, a decade later, the cultural consensus among the middle and upper classes made it clear that women's place in literature must conform to the role that modern bourgeois society assigned them.

SURVEY OF CRITICISM

Carolina Coronado's poetry was highly praised by critics in the 1840s. In his prologue to her first book of poetry, J. E. Hartzenbusch declared "novelty, concision and beauty" (ix) to be the principal traits of her work, which he regarded above all as "true poetry of feeling" (xi). Antonio Ferrer del Río, in his *Galería de la literatura española* (1846), places Coronado at the forefront of the "poetesses" and declines to examine her work (309). The qualities singled out for praise fit so well the paradigm of femininity that took hold in the nineteenth century that this view of Coronado as an essentially feminine poet persisted into the twentieth century; for example, Juan Valera wrote in 1902 that in comparison with other women poets, her writing represented "most distinctively and exclusively the eternal feminine" (370). Even Margarita Nelken, writing in 1930, echoes with a certain condescension the view that Coronado's poetry was feminine. This image may help to account for the absence of any serious critical study of her work until very recently.

Two biographies of Coronado were published in the 1940s: Ramón Gómez de la Serna's *Mi tía Carolina Coronado* and Adolfo de Sandoval's *Carolina Coronado y su época*. In the first, Gómez de la Serna writes engagingly of the family traditions and recounts anecdotes concerning his great-aunt, but the data are far from reliable. Sandoval's more scholarly study, based on a number of documents gathered from the nineteenth-century press, is by no means a definitive biography, since published statements by and about Coronado were frequently contradictory and often highly inaccurate. A biography by Isabel María Pérez González combines the materials provided by the two earlier biographies with new information published by Miguel Muñoz de San Pedro from the papers left by Coronado. In addition to offering sensible accounts of Coronado's principal works, this book provides a useful and accurate bibliography of the secondary literature. Unfortunately, Pérez's study does not use or mention an essential documentary source: the Biblioteca Nacional's collection of letters written by Coronado to J. E. Hartzenbusch between 1842 and 1852. Isabel Fonseca Ruiz has published important excerpts from these letters, which, besides bringing to light a previously unpublished poem—and the paternalistic censorship exercised by Hartzenbusch over his protégée—reveal the intellectual and domestic struggles that gave rise to the protofeminist sensibility of much of Coronado's poetry. Alberto Castilla's biography uses the Hartzenbusch-Coronado correspondence and other new sources to provide the most up-to-date account of Coronado's life.

Most of the secondary literature on Coronado has been journalistic or biographical. Serious literary study of her writing faces a difficult obstacle: the absence of an edition of her complete works, which have never been collected. Aside from a new edition of *Jarilla* in 1943 and two very incomplete anthologies (by Julio Cienfuegos Linares and Antonio Porpetta), her work has not been reprinted in the twentieth century. The new edition of Coronado's poetry by Noël Valis, published in 1991, therefore contributes significantly to the reevaluation of this poet. In the 1980s serious critical studies of individual aspects of Coronado's work began to appear. Lee Fontanella discussed her use of mystical diction in a 1981 article; in 1983 Monroe Hafter published a study of her narrative writing. Tomás Ruiz-Fábrega called attention to the feminist theme in her work in 1981. Following this line, in the most extended analysis of Coronado's poetry to date, Susan Kirkpatrick both explores the strategies with which Coronado constructs a gendered lyrical persona and documents her leadership in encouraging the women of her generation to write. It is to be hoped that these recent studies signal the renewal of interest in one of nineteenth-century Spain's most influential women writers.

BIBLIOGRAPHY

Works by Carolina Coronado

"Cartas a Juan Eugenio Hartzenbusch." MS. 20.806, cartas 195–230. Biblioteca Nacional, Madrid.
Poesías de la señorita doña Carolina Coronado. Madrid: Alegría y Charlain, 1843.
"Galería de las poetisas: Introducción a las poesías de la señorita Armiño." *La Ilustración, Periódico Universal* 12 June 1850: 187.
Paquita, Adoración. Madrid: Imprenta Española, San Fernando, 1850.
"Safo." *El Semanario Pintoresco Español* Nueva Epoca 5 1850: 187.
Poesías de la señorita doña Carolina Coronado. [Madrid]: n.p., 1852.
La Sigea. Madrid: Anselmo Santa Coloma, 1854.
"Galería de poetisas españolas contemporáneas. Introducción." *La Discusión* 21 June 1857: 3.
Jarilla. 1873. Barcelona: Montaner y Simón, 1943.
"Las poetisas españolas: Doña Josefa Massanés." *La Discusión* 21 June 1857: 3.
Poesías. Madrid: M. Tello, 1872.

La Rueda de la Desgracia. Manuscrito de un conde. Madrid: M. Tello, 1873.

Poesías. Badajoz, Spain: Arqueros, 1953. [Preface by Julio Cienfuegos Linares] *Carolina Coronado (apunte biográfico y antología).* Ed. Antonio Porpetta. Madrid: Torremozas, 1983.

Poesías. Ed. and intro. Noël Valis. Madrid: Castalia, 1991.

Works about Carolina Coronado

Castilla, Alberto. *Carolina Coronado de Perry.* Madrid: Editorial Beramar, 1987.

Ferrer del Río, Antonio. *Galería de la literatura española.* Madrid: Mellado, 1846.

Fonseca Ruiz, Isabel. "Cartas de Carolina Coronado a Juan Eugenio Hartzenbusch." *Homenaje a Guillermo Gustavino.* Madrid: Asociación Nacional de Bibliotecarios, 1974. 171–99.

Fontanella, Lee. "Mystical Diction and Imagery in Gómez de Avellaneda and Carolina Coronado." *Latin American Literary Review* 9 (1981): 47–55.

Gómez de la Serna, Ramón. *Mi tía Carolina Coronado.* Buenos Aires: EMECE, 1942.

Hafter, Monroe Z. "Carolina Coronado as Novelist." *Kentucky Review Quarterly* 30 (1983): 403–18.

Kirkpatrick, Susan. *Las Románticas: Women Writers and Subjectivity in Spain, 1835–1850.* Berkeley: U of California P, 1989.

Muñoz de San Pedro, Miguel. "Carolina Coronado: Notas y papeles inéditos." *Indice de las Artes y las Letras* 64 (1953): 1, 21–22.

Nelken, Margarita. *Las escritoras españolas.* Madrid: Editorial Labor, 1930. 199–207.

Pérez González, Isabel María. *Carolina Coronado: Epopeya de una mujer.* Badajoz, Spain: Diputación Provincial de Badajoz, 1986.

Ruiz-Fábrega, Tomás. "Temática feminista en la obra poética de Carolina Coronado." *Kániña* 5 (1981): 83–87.

Sandoval, Adolfo de. *Carolina Coronado y su época.* Zaragoza: Librería General, 1944.

Valera, Juan, ed. *Florilegio de poesías castellanas del siglo XIX.* Vol. 3. Madrid: Fernando Fé, 1902.

Valis, Noël. "La autobiografía como insulto." *Dispositio* 15.40 (1990): 1–25.

———. "The Language of Treasure: Carolina Coronado, Casta Esteban, and Marina Romero." *In the Feminine Mode: Essays on Hispanic Women Writers.* Ed. Noël Valis and Carol Maier. Lewisburg, PA: Bucknell UP, 1990. 246–72.

LEONOR DE LA CUEVA Y SILVA
(First Half of Seventeenth Century)

Teresa S. Soufas

BIOGRAPHY

The composition of both her varied corpus of poetry and her play *La firmeza en la ausencia* (N.d.; ''Steadfastness in Absence'') provides evidence of the education that Leonor de la Cueva y Silva surely received during her early years as the daughter of Agustín de la Rua and Leonor de Silva, minor nobles in the once-famed Renaissance market town of Medina del Campo in northwestern Spain. Born early in the seventeenth century, Cueva is scarcely known today in spite of her contribution to Golden Age letters. In the few brief modern references to her life and literary achievements, the accounts of her brothers' activities are used to identify the family's status because their social, political, and religious undertakings and careers are more public in nature and thus more easily accessible in historical documents.

One brother, Antonio de la Cueva y Silva, was named arms bearer to Prince Fernando, as well as captain and commissary of the cavalry in Flanders, distinctions listed in the military records and celebrated in a sonnet by his sister. A second brother, Jerónimo de la Rua, served as canon in Medina del Campo; and another, Juan de la Rua, was a military officer in Seville. Cueva's sister, María Jacinta de la Cueva, is mentioned in the documents prepared upon Antonio's commission in 1645.[1] In the twentieth-century references to Cueva, she is also described as the niece of the poet Francisco de la Cueva y Silva, whose interest in astrology eventually led to his trial for such practices. He, too, is honored in verse by Cueva, whose sonnet composed upon his death praises him as ''another Cato of miraculous sciences'' (Serrano y Sanz, *Apuntes* 338).[2] Manuel Serrano y Sanz asserts, without further explanation or reference, that uncle and niece enjoyed a close relationship (*Apuntes* 301).

There is no evidence that Cueva married. Thus she joins a list of noted women authors from the sixteenth and seventeenth centuries whose productivity and energies, it would seem, were channeled into writing, studying, and scholarly pursuits instead of the traditional roles of wife and mother. Feminist scholars such as Merry Wiesner, Ann R. Jones, and Margaret King suggest the importance of external normative pressures exerted upon literary women of these earlier periods.[3] At a time when the patriarchal culture associated women's public speech and writing with sexual promiscuity, a woman might opt for celibacy in order to participate in the male-dominated discourse of learning and authorship, leaving behind the culturally expected silence associated with the ideal woman, and so sidestepping the link between sexual activity and verbal communication. Suggestive, then, of this polemical tension between the stereotypical distaff and the pen—a tension that the authors, their contemporary commentators, and modern scholars acknowledge—is the unmarried status of Cueva and other female colleagues in Spain and Portugal, among them Luisa Sigea (1530–60), Luisa Carvajal y Mendoza (1566–1614), María de Zayas y Sotomayor (1590–1661?/1669), Violante do Ceo (1601–93), and Ana Caro Mallén de Soto (seventeenth century).

MAJOR THEMES

Cueva's complete works have not been anthologized, nor has all of her poetry been published. Her entire corpus of poems is housed in the Biblioteca Nacional de Madrid in a handwritten manuscript that is part of a collection from the late sixteenth (begun in 1596) and early seventeenth centuries. This manuscript includes poetry by Miguel de Cervantes, Francisco de la Cueva, Juan Fernández de Ledesma, Luis de Góngora, Pedro Liñan de Riaza, Juan de Salinas, and Lope de Vega, as well as the poems of Leonor de la Cueva. Her contributions consist of two *romances* (ballads) about Alvaro de Luna and other poems in varied verse forms such as the sonnet, the *lira* (a five-line stanza of three heptasyllables and two hendecasyllables), the *décima* (a ten-line stanza), and other *romances*. Cueva, like the majority of Golden Age poets, utilizes the traditional lyric forms of Spain, such as the *romance*, as well as the Italianate sonnet. Some of her poetry has been published in the two collections by Serrano y Sanz and the more recent anthology by Clara Janés.

Cueva's writings also attest to her familiarity with topoi and literary conventions popular in her day. Poetic themes well represented in the lyric poetry of the more famous Golden Age male poets are treated by Cueva. By means of her woman-centered expression and through the voice of complaint, however, she frequently questions the conventions and the constraints that she simultaneously resists and adheres to in her writing.

What is particularly significant in Cueva's works is the persistent reaffirmation of the tension between absence and presence and the memory's part in preserving this tension. The states of constancy and absence foregrounded in the title of her play, *La firmeza en la ausencia*, exemplify these dialectical components of her poetic discourse that suggest the unsettled and unstable quality of life. This perspective not only encompasses the general baroque sensibility concerning human inability to know and perceive with certainty, but also suggests a more personal expression of an underlying ambiguity and ambivalence with regard to the agency of the woman writer.

The physical absence of a beloved is the situation described or lamented in several of Cueva's poems as well as in her play. At times the poetic voice is a masculine one, expressing the pain of separation from the loved one but simultaneously complaining about her suspected fickleness. In Cueva's "Soneto a Floris" ("Sonnet to Floris"), the poetic voice asks: "¿Cuándo se ha de acabar, Floris divina, / La rigurosa pena de no verte / Y el cobarde temor de tu mudanza?" (Serrano y Sanz, *Apuntes* 337; When, Divine Floris, must / the arduous pain of not seeing you / and the cowardly fear about your inconstancy come to an end?). These sorts of antithetical conventions and sentiments described in love poetry over the centuries are very much a part of many of Cueva's poems, but beyond the courtly and/or Petrarchan traditions her poems suggest a preoccupation with the problematical status of seventeenth-century woman as marginalized author and intellectual, as well as objectified beloved and topic of literary and artistic representation. Whereas in her poetry romantic love is often reported to be an unhappy or unrequited condition by both the male and the female voice, there is repeated insistence upon the woman's response to all aspects of the experiences.

Frequently this response suggests a dialectical awareness of the relative freedom enjoyed by an educated seventeenth-century woman like Cueva who understands the pressures, demands, and expectations of social and literary conventions. One of her female personae celebrates in verse not only her ability to recognize the dangers of attraction to a handsome, seductive lover, but also her freedom and independence from love's stereotypical consequences that the poetic voice complains of elsewhere in poems about failed love and abandonment. In these latter examples, a female narrator often laments her disappointment and anger and the public humiliation that she suffers due to the fickleness of a lover once trusted. Cueva does not necessarily articulate a sense of women's moral superiority; rather, she presents a female-centered recognition that becomes a means to gain a sort of equilibrium in the human interactions whose traditions give the advantage of social liberty to the male. The social and literary systems are thus examined and challenged to the extent that women writers like Cueva confront the prevailing normative values even as they write. As is the case with many of her contemporary sisters, Cueva does not altogether abandon societal expectations. She does not depict radical alternatives through her literature; rather, she identifies and selects from among the limitations placed upon woman's public and private interests, activity, identity, and communication.

One way in which Cueva challenges the traditions is to celebrate female subjects who do not meet the conventional standards of beauty or conduct. In one *romance*, she describes the best qualities of Andronio's beloved, who is said to be "desaliñada" (disheveled) and "sarnosa" (mangy) ("Poesías" fol. 230). In another poem, whose title announces its subject's beauty as well as her lack of discretion, Cueva's poetic narrative recounts how this woman becomes queen of Egypt. Romantic love and/or marriage rewards the literarily atypical female beloved in several of these lyrics, but more frequently love is a negative experience described poetically in terms of *desengaño* (revelation of truth). The female voice in these cases articulates firm resolution to get beyond the uncertainty of suspicions and unrequited love, and to accept the *desengaño* without resistance.

In her poems that more openly and bitterly confront the situation of the abandoned or deceived woman—portrayed so often in Golden Age literature— Cueva emphasizes the conventional double standard of the time: men are able to live with public attention focused on their erratic love life, while women are not. She also examines a woman's lack of success in seeking fulfillment of a desire for wholeness. She thereby articulates the discomfort of ambiguity that emerges from such descriptions; there is only an in-between state. The ambivalent nature of the experiences of her discreet female characters disappointed in love suggests a parallel to the nature of life experienced by educated literary women like Cueva, whose professional and personal choices remain constrained by the society in which they live.

Cueva continues her scrutiny of women's responses to social and literary traditions in her play *La firmeza en la ausencia*. Its protagonist finds herself in the disquieting situation of so many female characters of Golden Age drama: She is desired by two men, observed by both, wooed relentlessly by the one she does not love, and suspected of faithlessness by the one for whom she truly cares. Cueva, however, adjusts her presentation of this conventional situation by focusing upon the female character's response instead of the males'; the latter is found, for instance, in the Calderonian honor dramas. Her protagonist, Armesinda, is unmarried, orphaned, and determined not to acquiesce to the materially comfortable solutions to her social and emotional dilemma. Cueva allows her to ponder, at several points during the action, what her recourses are once she hears that her beloved has married another. She receives constant entreaties from the king to become his mistress, if not his wife. Believing marital happiness with the man of her choice to be impossible, Armesinda considers a list of alternatives. Among these are marrying a man whom she does not love, becoming a courtesan in the king's palace, running away from the court to live alone, entering a convent, and committing suicide. After much contemplation, all possibilities except the convent are ruled out because they can only bring about her emotional, social, physical, and/or spiritual destruction.

Throughout the three acts, Armesinda is the only character who denies the king what he desires, for her *firmeza* is never broken. In the end, Cueva rewards Armesinda when Juan returns from war and she learns that the account of his marriage was a tale invented by the king to trick her into shifting her affections to him. The male culture and discourse in which Armesinda lives and communicates are shown to be a medium of deceit and cowardice, but one over which the female is able to triumph. In spite of the privileged and classist perspective unquestionably evident in Cueva's articulation of gender issues, her insistence upon a female character's consideration of all the possibilities that the represented society offers is, nevertheless, a strategy suggestive of a sisterly message of hope beyond class distinction. Without depicting a radical divergence from social patterns, Cueva's works ultimately recount the variety of alternatives that may be contemplated for and by women.

SURVEY OF CRITICISM

Cueva is virtually unknown to twentieth-century readers, though the brief attention directed to her works in the Serrano y Sanz collections, for example, does provide some access to her poetry and drama. An unmistakable sexist bias, however, permeates the commentary in these editions, which promote male authors as models rather than approach literary production as a two-gender accomplishment. Manuel Serrano y Sanz's ungenerous statements in this regard include his articulated doubts about the authenticity of female authorship in some cases, and in others, about the ability of women authors to write without the editing or collaboration of male authors. He suggests, for instance, that the sixteenth-century writer Luisa Sigea may have relied greatly on the aid of her father when composing her prose and poetry (*Antología de poetisas líricas* xxvii). Though at one point he describes Cueva as one of the most important female poets of the seventeenth century, Serrano y Sanz nevertheless directs only faint praise toward her poetry in further commentary, saying that among her many poems "there are some that do not lack ease and wit" (*Apuntes* 300; *Antología* xxv). Only the critical study of her play by Teresa Soufas approaches Cueva's work from a feminist theoretical context.

Future editions and critical studies of Cueva's poetry and drama await publication. There is a need for scholarly attention to her work. Such investigation will emphasize the fact that our understanding of Golden Age Spanish literature is incomplete without the woman-centered perspective that female authors such as Cueva contribute. Her writings must be studied in the context of those of her seventeenth-century sisters, among them Ana Caro, María de Zayas, Silvia Monteser, Cristobalina Fernández de Alarcón, Catalina Clara Ramírez de Guzmán, and Ana Francisca Abarca de Bolea, all of whom are an integral part of Spain's Golden Age.

NOTES

1. The sources of the biographical information on Cueva include Cayetano Alberto de la Barrera y Leirado, *Catálogo bibliográfico y biográfico del teatro antiguo español* (Madrid: Rivadeneyra, 1969) 121; Clara Janés, *Las primeras poetisas en lengua cas-*

tellana (Madrid: Editorial Ayuso, 1986) 210; Manuel Serrano y Sanz, *Antología de poetisas líricas*, vol. 1 (Madrid: Real Academia, 1915) xxiv–xxv, 364–65; and *Apuntes para una biblioteca de escritoras españolas* (Madrid: Atlas, 1975) 300–01.

2. The translations into English are my own. In the quotations from the autograph manuscript of Cueva's poetry, I have modernized the spelling and punctuation.

3. Ann R. Jones notes that "in a woman, verbal fluency and bodily purity are understood to be contrary conditions" ("Surprising Fame: Renaissance Gender Ideologies and Women's Lyric," in *The Poetics of Gender*, ed. Nancy K. Miller [New York: Columbia UP, 1986] 78). Merry E. Wiesner likewise states that "[t]hose [women] who chose the life of learning were generally forced to give up a normal family life. Most lived chaste lives of scholarly solitude in 'book-lined cells.' They chose celibacy because their desire for learning required it; their male admirers . . . felt no woman could be both learned and sexually active" ("Women's Defense of Their Public Role," in *Women in the Middle Ages and the Renaissance: Literary and Historical Perspectives*, ed. Mary Beth Rose [Syracuse, NY: Syracuse UP, 1986] 13). Margaret King adds that chastity was "the learned woman's defiance of the established natural order and of the learned man's attempt to constrain her energies by making her mind the prison for her body" ("Book-Lined Cells: Women and Humanism in the Early Italian Renaissance," *Beyond Their Sex: Learned Women of the European Past*, ed. Patricia H. Labalme [New York: New York UP, 1980] 78).

BIBLIOGRAPHY

Works by Leonor de la Cueva y Silva

"Poesías Líricas." Original Ms. Madrid: Biblioteca Nacional de Madrid, n.d.
Selected Poetry. Serrano y Sanz, *Antología de poetisas líricas* 364–92.
La firmeza en la ausencia. Serrano y Sanz, *Apuntes para una biblioteca de escritoras españolas* 302-28.
Selected Poetry. Serrano y Sanz, *Apuntes para una biblioteca de escritoras españolas* 329–39.
Selected Poetry. Clara Janés, ed., *Las primeras poetisas en lengua castellana* 140–47.

Works about Leonor de la Cueva y Silva

Barrera y Leirado, Cayetano Alberto de la. *Catálogo bibliográfico y biográfico del teatro antiguo español, desde sus orígenes hasta mediados del siglo XVIII.* Madrid: Rivadeneyra, 1969. 121.
Janés, Clara, ed. *Las primeras poetisas en lengua castellana.* Madrid: Editorial Ayuso, 1986. 210.
Serrano y Sanz, Manuel. *Antología de poetisas líricas.* Vol. 1. Madrid: Real Academia, 1915. xxiv–xxv, 364–65.
———. *Apuntes para una biblioteca de escritoras españolas desde el año 1401 al 1833.* Madrid: Atlas, 1975. Biblioteca de Autores Españoles. Vol. 268. 300–01, 329, 368. Rpt. of 1903 ed. Madrid: Sucesores de Rivadeneyra.
Soufas, Teresa S., ed. *Obras completas.* [In progress]
———. "Regarding the Woman's Response: Leonor de la Cueva y Silva's 'La firmeza en la ausencia.' " *Romance Languages Annual* 1 (1990): 625–30.

ROSA CHACEL
(b. 1898)

Shirley Mangini

BIOGRAPHY

Rosa Chacel Arimón was born in Valladolid, Spain, on June 3, 1898, a significant year for Spain both politically and intellectually. Encouraged by parents and other relatives who had a solid cultural background, Chacel was a precocious child who learned to read at age three. In 1906 she began to study drawing at the local art academy. The impact of art on her writing can be observed in her constant allusions to the plastic arts and her tendency to describe sensations with visual metaphors.

In 1908, Chacel's family moved to the Maravillas district of Madrid. The name of this neighborhood became the title of her 1976 novel, which provides a fictionalized version of her childhood there. At that time, Chacel began to read many of the classics she found in an uncle's library, among them works of William Shakespeare, Feodor Dostoyevsky, Plato, Honoré de Balzac, and Gustave Flaubert. In 1910, she entered the Art and Trade School in Madrid, and in 1911 she studied at the Domestic and Professional School for Women. Four years later, the mature young woman entered the San Fernando School of Fine Arts, where she met her future husband, the artist Timoteo Pérez Rubio. Her encounter with one of the school's instructors, the illustrious writer Ramón del Valle-Inclán, represented a turning point in her career from art to literature. She left the school in 1918 and began to visit such literary enclaves of Madrid as the Ateneo, the most important cultural club at the time. She also frequented the coffeehouse literary and artistic cliques, presided over by the Vanguard writers of the time. During these years, Chacel became familiar not only with the work of Valle-Inclán but also with that of the other "greats" of the times: Miguel de Unamuno, Ramón Gómez de la Serna, Juan Ramón Jiménez, and, in particular, the influential "dictator" of cultural modes, José Ortega y Gasset.

In 1921, Pérez Rubio and Chacel were married. The following year, Chacel published her first brief prose piece, "El amigo de voz oportuna" ("The Friend with a Timely Voice"), in the Madrid journal *La Esfera*. That same year the couple left for Rome, where Pérez Rubio had received a scholarship at the Spanish Academy. Two important works accompanied Chacel: James Joyce's *Portrait of the Artist as a Young Man* and the first volume of Sigmund Freud's *Complete Works*; both were to have significant impact on her future direction. During the Rome period, the young couple traveled frequently in Italy and other parts of Europe, including Munich, Innsbruck, Paris, and Normandy. These were indeed exciting times. In 1924–25, Chacel witnessed the blossoming of the most important Vanguard writers of the time: the surrealists. In Rome, the futurists were producing their avant-garde works, especially at the Bragaglia Theater, which Chacel frequented. She avidly read Ortega y Gasset's literary and philosophical treatises and the works of Marcel Proust. During this period she wrote her first story, "Chinina Migone," published in the *Revista de Occidente* in 1928.

Chacel began writing her first novel, *Estación. Ida y vuelta* (1930; "Station. Round Trip") in the midst of this literary renaissance. Although Ortega y Gasset had committed to publishing the entire novel, the series in which it was to be published was discontinued. Thus, only the first chapter appeared in his *Revista de Occidente* in 1927. Chacel returned to Madrid that year and reacquainted herself with the activities of the Madrid literary scene by rejoining the café cliques and by contributing to the major literary journals, especially *La Gaceta Literaria*. Although until very recently, few literary historians have included Chacel among the members of the Generation of 1927, she played an integral part in the activities of the group. In interviews, Chacel has expressed the embarrassment and discomfort she experienced in the presence of her male contemporaries, once describing her presence at their literary gatherings as a form of "torture" (Porlán 24). Chacel has further emphasized in interviews and in her diaries that she was short and overweight, and did not possess the attire befitting a cultured, high-society woman. Yet she has consistently denied that she was a pariah within her generation of writers. In fact, Chacel has adamantly repudiated the existence of a distinct, feminine literature and has denied the importance of the exclusion of female writers from the canon, despite the fact that she was neglected by Spanish critics and the public until the 1970s. She has always felt that literature is a "man's job" and that women who do not blend into the literary "boys' club" deserve to be shunned and isolated (Mangini, "Entrevista" 10).

In 1930, two major events took place that would mark Chacel's life and work: the birth of her only child, Carlos, and the publication of *Estación. Ida y vuelta*. The book was met with confused and somewhat cantankerous reactions; its vague plot and stream-of-consciousness narrative disconcerted critics. It was, after all, a product of modernity, and women did not "fit in" the literary avant-garde scene.

That same year, Chacel began writing the biography of José de Espronceda's "scandalous" lover, Teresa de la Mancha, which José Ortega y Gasset had requested for his series "Vidas extraordinarias del Siglo XIX." The Civil War (1936), however, interrupted publication of the series. In 1933, Chacel traveled to Berlin, where she witnessed the beginning of Hitler's reign of terror, obliquely described years later in her second novel, *La sinrazón* (1960; "The Injustice"). At this time she also began to write her first book of poetry, *A la orilla de un pozo* (1936; "On the Banks of a Well").

Although Chacel has rarely taken a clear political stance, when the Civil War broke out she did collaborate in the leftist publications of the time. In 1938, she fled to Paris with her young son. When the war ended the following year, she was reunited with her husband in Geneva. The first chapter of her novel *Memorias de Leticia Valle* ("The Memoirs of Leticia Valle") appeared in Buenos Aires that same year. In 1940, after a brief stay in Nazi-dominated Paris and then Bordeaux—where Chacel began to write her diaries, entitled *Alcancía. Ida* and *Alcancía. Vuelta* ("Memory Box. Round Trip")—and published years later in 1982—she left for Rio de Janeiro with her family. From that time on, Chacel divided her time between Rio, where Pérez Rubio lived, and Buenos Aires, where she found intellectual exile more palatable. She began a career in translation to support herself. Her diaries document the frustration and alienation that she felt during these years. Instead of enjoying the recognition she had hoped for, she was living the life of the penurious exile, far from her native country, her husband, and her son. These frustrations remained intact until Chacel's return to Spain in the 1970s, and greatly influenced the evolution of her emotional and professional life.

Chacel transformed the biography of Teresa de la Mancha into the novel *Teresa* (1941; *Teresa* 1969) which was published in Buenos Aires, as was *Memorias de Leticia Valle* (1946). In the 1950s, she engaged in a flurry of activity while working laboriously on her second and favorite novel, *La sinrazón*. The silence about her life, as reflected in her scant diary entries during the 1940s, had ended. In 1959 Chacel was awarded a Guggenheim Fellowship for her proposal to write a book of philosophical essays on eroticism, later to be called *Saturnal* (1972; "Saturnalia"). She moved to New York, where she established a close friendship with one of the major female political exiles of the Spanish Civil War, Victoria Kent, and lectured at the Spanish Institute and at local universities. At this time, Chacel became greatly interested in the French novelist Michel Butor and the French *nouveau roman* (new novel) in general, whose characteristics have often been attributed to her novels. In a lecture delivered at Columbia University, she defended vanguard literature against the attacks of the novelist Francisco Ayala, once again underlining her commitment to Orteguian theory.

Chacel's second volume of stories, *Ofrenda a una virgen loca* ("Offering to a Crazy Virgin") was published in Mexico in 1961. Chacel returned to Madrid in 1962, and began to gain some notice in Spain during her sojourn there. Yet she returned to Rio the following year. During the 1960s, she began the account of the first ten years of her life, *Desde el amanecer* (1972; "From the Dawn"). She also reworked her book of essays on the writings of Cervantes, Galdós, Unamuno, and others, entitled *La confesión* (1971; "The Confession"). In 1971 Chacel returned to Spain because of the interest generated there by her work. Some of her writings were republished, and her complete short stories were issued under the title *Icada, Nevda, Diada* (1971). In 1972, when Chacel once again returned to her native land, *Desde el amanecer* and *Saturnal* were published. In 1974 she received a grant to complete her novel *Barrio de Maravillas* (1976; *The Maravillas District* 1992).

Upon the death of her husband in 1977, Chacel finally established permanent residence in Madrid. In 1978 her second book of verses, *Versos prohibidos* ("Forbidden Verses"), was published in Madrid. In 1980 and 1981, respectively, the artistic biography of her husband, *Timoteo Pérez Rubio y sus retratos del jardín* ("T.P.R. and His Garden Paintings"), and *Novelas antes del tiempo* ("Novels Before Their Time") saw print. During the 1980s, Chacel was invited to participate in numerous literary events around the country. In 1983, her collected diaries were published in two volumes by the prestigious publishing house Seix Barral. *Alcancía. Ida* is from the period 1940–1966, and *Alcancía. Vuelta* covers the period 1967–1981. Chacel published the second volume of her trilogy, *Acrópolis* ("The Acropolis") in 1984, an event that was widely publicized in Spain. At that time, her fame became more pronounced, prompting appearances around the country and in Mexico, and culminating in the coveted National Prize for Spanish Letters in 1987. In 1988 her novel *Ciencias naturales* ("Natural Sciences") appeared, thus completing the trilogy begun with *Barrio de Maravillas*. On her ninetieth birthday, Chacel was honored in her hometown of Valladolid by intellectuals from around the country. A bronze bust of the author was unveiled as Chacel was proclaimed "favorite daughter" of the city. She had finally attained the fame that had been denied her during a literary career that has spanned more than sixty years.

MAJOR THEMES

Many of Chacel's recurring themes can be found in her first novel, *Estación. Ida y vuelta*, which serves as a metaliterary manifesto for her future aesthetics. In this work, we find a fixation on memory, an element that dominates all of her subsequent work. Chacel, the self-proclaimed "priestess" of memory, has spoken of Mnemosyne—in Greek mythology, the personification of memory—as "her tutelary deity." Her obsession with memory is present in much of her writing. In *Estación. Ida y vuelta*, the ontologically autobiographical protagonist searches for the inscrutable truth through his doppelgänger relationship with his girlfriend, who later becomes his wife. "He" and "she"—neither has a name—are psychologically fused, since he is aware of her thoughts and emotions at all times. The "we" protagonist creates a constant nebulosity about male/female emotions and thought processes. When he becomes bored with the lack of excitement in their relationship, he finds himself fascinated by another woman. Love triangles and breakdowns in communication between lovers are themes that are often repeated in Chacel's novels. The protagonist then embarks on a journey to France to find himself. Upon receiving the news that "she" has borne him a son, he returns to Spain at which time Chacel takes over the story and expounds on her theories of the novel.

Estación. Ida y vuelta reveals a morose and almost morbid fixation on the underpinnings of the processes of the mind; it is highly solipsistic and philosophically oriented, as are most of Chacel's later works. Yet it is perhaps the most lyrical of her writings—other than her verse, which has received very little critical attention—and reveals the influence of vanguard poetry on her writing during the 1920s.

Estación. Ida y vuelta also gives testimony to Ortega y Gasset's theories expounded in *La deshumanización del arte* and *Ideas sobre la novela* and published the year that Chacel began writing her first novel (1925). It is also perhaps the finest Spanish example of European modernism. Chacel took Ortega y Gasset's theories and tailored her novel to them. She not only alludes to his ideas on perspectivism but also takes on his challenge that the novel has no obligation to provide a story. The plot and characters are of minimal importance, yet the characters possess an ontological presence that is the essence of the novel.

Estación. Ida y vuelta is an intellectual exercise, an exploration of the psyche, a pretext for Chacel's exposé of her aesthetic creed. Chacel reverses the role of literary criticism; Ortega's theories, which describe the vanguard literature of the times, are embraced by Chacel and turned into literature. The novel is, in fact—much in the tradition of such classical moderns as James Joyce, Marcel Proust, and Virginia Woolf—a voyage through the minds of characters that represents Chacel's journey through her own psychological, ontological, and aesthetic life. The "we" protagonist is, in reality, the psychological fusion of Chacel and her husband as she perceived it in the first years of their marriage (Mangini, "Entrevista" 111).

Chacel's novels often suggest a confession of guilt, which she describes in *La confesión* as a prime motivator for provoking memory, and which is found in her second and most ambitious novel, *La sinrazón*. This novel, which is based on a triangular love affair similar to the one in *Estación*, is in fact a rewriting of the first work. Once again Chacel expounds on the psychological and ontological considerations of the protagonist's psyche. Santiago purports to be writing his "confessions," which vaguely trace his unfaithfulness to the woman in his life. Yet his confession—as in most of Chacel's work—also alludes to unspeakable secrets that Chacel often refers to as *intríngulis* (hidden intentions). This procedure functions as both an aesthetic tool for shaping her oblique prose and a defensive autobiographical device for keeping the reader from "knowing too much."

Chacel's projection of life through a male protagonist may be a method for masking her feminine "weaknesses" vis-à-vis her male contemporaries. Yet underneath this "virile" mask is a feminine discourse that challenges Chacel's claim that she wrote as a male character spontaneously (Aguirre 5). Chacel's opinion that creating a "specifically feminine literature is the greatest stupidity that a human being can commit" (Aguirre 5) suggests a powerful fear of being excluded by her male colleagues, and could very well explain her apparent rejection of feminine discourse. Unwittingly, though, what makes Santiago ver-isimilar is his own perception of the emotional fusion between himself and his wife, a perception that reveals the female essence of his "confessions." This is also true of *Estación. Ida y vuelta*. The almost schizophrenic voice in many of Chacel's works substantially challenges her intention to omit any profound characterization of women. Paradoxically, the brillance of much of her prose derives from her desire to avoid what she actually accomplishes.

La sinrazón, like most of Chacel's work, is highly autobiographical. Chacel, moving back and forth between Rio and Buenos Aires at the time that she wrote the novel, creates a protagonist, Santiago, who is an Argentine. Visible in the book are many of the author's own experiences, including her journey through Nazi-occupied Europe. Characteristic of these first two interrelated works is the pessimistic philosophy about relationships: Love and communication are impossible because individualism and cruel egotism make each person a lonely island. Guilt—very often sexual guilt—widens the gulf even more, leaving one to contemplate in silence some form of destruction, the grim ignominy of isolation and mediocrity, or the alienation of exile.

Chacel's characters are similar to the sick and lonely souls one finds in Dostoyevski's work. Love, for Chacel, is always eroded by disillusionment and indifference; good faith, by jealousy and an almost diabolical sense of possession, often illustrated through the doppelgänger theme. Infidelity results, and the vicious circle is completed. Beauty, love, and eroticism are inextricably related for Chacel. Eros is part of the creative act and lives in its precarious form in all of her prose. In spite of this pessimistic stance on love and communion, Chacel is saved from destruction by her work. Hers is a phoenix-like task: She is destroyed by life but reborn through literature. Chacel has always considered herself a free spirit and feels her world akin to that of Joyce: "Each and every one of my novels belongs to Joyce's world, an intellectual and social bohemia, a risk-taking bohemia without money. Mental, sexual and religious freedom, irrepressible and total freedom" (Mangini, "Entrevista" 110).

The subject of guilt is also visible in Chacel's biographical novel, *Teresa*, in which the protagonist is both the perpetrator and the victim of her tragic destiny, and again in her Dostoyevskian *Memorias de Leticia Valle*. In this novel, the precocious child Leticia is entrapped in a subtle emotional web with her mentors, the married couple Doña Luisa and Don Daniel, who appear to have an enigmatic interest in the girl. Yet this perverse triangle seems to change when Leticia becomes the aggressor in the implicit tale of seduction. As with Santiago of *La sinrazón*, Leticia tells the story in the first person, carefully hiding the secret of the triangular intrigue within her confession of guilt, only hinting at the fact that the victim has become the victimizer.

This ambiguity characterizes Chacel's trilogy, initiated with *Barrio de Maravillas*, which evokes memories of her childhood. It deals with the formation of a friendship between two young girls and describes, through visual and affective ruminations, the delicate and fragile underpinnings of that friendship. Similar to the later works that complete the trilogy and divided chronologically by the wars and exile that marked Chacel's life, *Barrio de Maravillas* constantly refers to the plastic arts and presents a typically stylized, ambiguous version of the author's childhood until the outbreak of World War I. The second volume, *Acrópolis*, covering the period from 1914 to the advent of the Civil War, represents a dramatic moment in Chacel's novelized life. It is the coming to consciousness of a young adult; the anecdotes that substantiate the novel are merely vehicles for representing Chacel's sensations and undivulged secrets of the early 1920s.

Ciencias naturales, which deals with the end of the Civil War and the Republican exodus from Spain, and concludes with the death of the dictator Francisco Franco, completes the trilogy and renders the same review of history through an intelligent appraisal of senses and sensations. It is, again, an indirect, spiritual portrait of Chacel's life, this time introducing her intellectual contemporaries, with many literary allusions to the writers of the Generation of 1927. As is customary in Chacel's work, the impact of philosophers, ranging from Jean Jacques Rousseau to Henri Bergson to Ortega y Gasset, is perceptible. Chacel is, in fact, perhaps closer to her philosopher colleague María Zambrano— also a disciple of Ortega y Gasset—in her approach to literature than any other contemporary writer.

The trilogy is, like all of Chacel's work beginning with *Estación. Ida y vuelta*, a continuous interior monologue. In that sense, all of her novels are one novel, always inspired by the same sensations and memories, always obliquely describing a love affair, often suggesting homoeroticism as a key factor in the intrigue through the vague portrayal of gender roles. As Chacel tells us in the introductory note to *Ciencias naturales*: "In this story of exile, there is not one line that is a testimony of real facts. There is nothing more than an outline of souls lost in the labyrinth of freedom" (5). Perhaps this description crystallizes most succinctly the essence of Chacel's novels.

As has been observed, sexual guilt is one of the most powerful elements in the author's work. Yet Chacel suggests that sexual preferences are irrelevant; what really interests her is what happens to people psychologically in a love affair. Sexuality is always presented in such a vague fashion that we are left with a troubled and unresolved dilemma about the nature of many of the relationships in her novels. Chacel's reader is, invariably, intrigued, enticed, confused, and ultimately fascinated by her surreptitious prose, in which the only clear "facts" belong to the realm of the senses. She tells us time and again that memory and its relation to reality are unclear and questionable. The only reality that is important is the interior one, which dictates the irrational and arbitrary nature of life.

Chacel uses memory as a critical tool; she is an implacable and cryptic judge of her own life and of life in general. Her characters are never really likable, yet they are attractive because they are elusive. Chacel's text is constructed of untenable, formless materials that derive from the intellect as it is affected by memory and sensations. Rosa Chacel is, in fact, the only Spanish novelist who has never substantially changed her vanguard style and is one of the few living representatives of European modernism at its best.

SURVEY OF CRITICISM

Until recently, there has been little critical material available on the life and work of Rosa Chacel. Given her exile of many years and the fact that women writers of the Generation of 1927 were ignored, and their work—especially Chacel's—dismissed as "dehumanized" literature of little relevance to the post-war social realist movement, few critics noticed Chacel until her return to Spain in the 1970s.

Of particular interest is the book-length interview by Alberto Porlán, *La sinrazón de Rosa Chacel*. Ana Rodríguez's dissertation on Chacel—"La obra novelística de Rosa Chacel"—provides the most complete study of the author to date. Mangini's introduction to the 1989 edition of *Estación. Ida y vuelta* concentrates on the author's first work, though it also offers insights into Chacel's subsequent works. Other enlightening works dedicated to the author include issue 85 of *Anthropos*, the bibliographical notes in supplement 8 of *Anthropos*, and the catalog published by the Ministry of Culture after Chacel won the National Prize for Spanish Letters in 1987.

Since the awarding of this literary prize, numerous articles have been published in Spanish journals and newspapers. Chacel has also received significant attention from women writers in Spain, including Ana María Moix and Clara Janés. Hispanists in the United States now consider her among the most innovative of the Spanish vanguard writers. Rafael Conte writes in *El País* that Chacel is one of the "greatest representatives" of the literature of exile. He adds that she "has blessed us with some of the most complex, beautiful and subtle prose of our language" (30). The essayist Federico Jiménez Losantos describes her as not only the "greatest female prose writer in Castilian in this century . . . but simply among the most interesting writers of our times" (*ABC* n. pag.). The poet Pere Gimferrer states that her work represents "some of the best prose written in Castilian after the Generation of 98" (*ABC* n. pag.).

Since the publication of *Ciencias naturales* and the celebration of her ninetieth birthday, Chacel has become a subject of increased interest within the intellectual community. Clearly one of the most unusual female writers of the twentieth century, her career has experienced a revolutionary change from obscurity to major recognition.

BIBLIOGRAPHY

Works by Rosa Chacel

Novels

Estación. Ida y vuelta. Madrid: Editorial Ulises, 1930.
Teresa. Buenos Aires: Ediciones de Nuevo Romance, 1941.
Memorias de Leticia Valle. Buenos Aires: Emece, 1946.
La sinrazón. Buenos Aires: Losada, 1960.
Barrio de Maravillas. Barcelona: Seix Barral, 1976.
Novelas antes de tiempo. Barcelona: Bruguera, 1981.
Acrópolis. Barcelona: Seix Barral, 1984.
Ciencias naturales. Barcelona: Seix Barral, 1988.

Short Stories

"Chinina Migone." *Revista de Occidente* 19.55 (1928): 79–89.
Sobre el piélago. Buenos Aires: Ediciones Imán, 1952.
Ofrenda a una virgen loca. Xalapa, Mexico: Universidad Veracruzana, 1961.
Icada, Nevda, Diada. Barcelona: Seix Barral, 1971.

Poetry

A la orilla de un pozo. Madrid: Ediciones Héroe, 1936.
Versos prohibidos. Madrid: Caballo Griego para la Poesía, 1978.

Memoirs and Diaries

Desde el amanecer. Madrid: Revista de Occidente, 1972.
Alcancía. Ida. Barcelona: Seix Barral, 1982.
Alcancía. Vuelta. Barcelona: Seix Barral, 1982.

Essays

"El amigo de voz oportuna." 1922. Rpt. in *Quimera* 84 (Dec. 88): 35.
Poesía de la circunstancia. Cómo y porqué de la novela. Bahía Blanca, Argentina: Universidad Nacional del Sur, 1958.
La confesión. Barcelona: Edhasa, 1971.
Saturnal. Barcelona: Seix Barral, 1972.
Los títulos. Barcelona: Edhasa, 1981. [Prologue by Clara Janés]
Rebañaduras. Valladolid, Spain: Junta de Castilla y León, 1986.
La lectura es secreto. Madrid: Ediciones Júcar, 1989.

Biography

Timoteo Pérez Rubio y sus retratos del jardín. Madrid: Cátedra, 1980.

Translations

"Alarm!" Trans. Rolfe Humphries. . . . *And Spain Sings*. Ed. M.J. Bernadette and Rolfe
    Humphries. New York: Vanguard, 1937. 114–16.
"Twilight in Extremadura." Trans. Beatrice Patt. *Great Spanish Stories*. Ed. Ángel
    Flores. New York: Modern Library, 1956.
Teresa. Trans. Ángel Flores. *Spanish Writers in Exile*. Ed. Ángel Flores. Sausalito, CA:
    Bern Porter, 1969. 54–64. [Selections]
The Maravillas District. Trans. d. a. démers. Lincoln: U of Nebraska P, 1992. [Intro-
    duction by Susan Kirkpatrick]

Works about Rosa Chacel

Aguirre, Mariano. "Rosa Chacel: La literatura femenina es una estupidez." *El País* 30
    Jan. 1983: 5. [Interview]
Conte, Rafael. "Contra la memoria." *El País* 18 Nov. 1987: 30.
Egido, Aurora. "Los espacios del tiempo en *Memorias de Leticia Valle*." *Revista de
    Literatura* 43.86 (1981): 103–31.
Gimferrer, Pere. "Una conciencia puesta en pie hasta el fin." *ABC* 3 June 1988: n. pag.
Janés, Clara. Prologue. *Los títulos*. By Rosa Chacel. Barcelona: Edhasa, 1981. i–x.
Jiménez Losantos, Federico. "Rosa Chacel." *ABC* 3 June 1988: n. pag.
Johnson, Roberta. "*Estación. Ida y vuelta*, de Rosa Chacel: un nuevo tiempo para la
    novela." *Prosa hispánica de vanguardia*. Ed. Fernando Burgos. Madrid: Editorial
    Orígenes, 1986: 201–08.
Mangini, Shirley. "Entrevista con Rosa Chacel." *Insula* 492 (Nov. 1987): 110–11.
———, ed. *Estación. Ida y vuelta*. Madrid: Cátedra, 1989. 11–69. [Critical introduction]
———. "Women and Spanish Modernism: The Case of Rosa Chacel." *Anales de la
    Literatura Española Contemporánea* 12 (1987): 17–28.
Marra López, José Ramón. "Rosa Chacel: la búsqueda intelectual del mundo." *Narrativa
    española fuera de España (1939–1969)*. Madrid: Guadarrama, 1963. 133–47.
Moix, Ana María. "Rosa Chacel." *24 × 24*. Barcelona: Ediciones Península, 1972.
    141–46.
Myers, Eunice. "*Estación. Ida y vuelta*: Rosa Chacel's Apprenticeship Novel." *Hispanic
    Journal* 4.2 (1983): 77–83.
Porlán, Alberto. *La sinrazón de Rosa Chacel*. Madrid: Anjana Ediciones, 1984.
Revenga, Luis, ed. *Rosa Chacel: Premio Nacional de las letras españolas 1987*. Madrid:
    Ministerio de Cultura, 1988.
Rodríguez, Ana. "La obra novelística de Rosa Chacel." Diss. U of Barcelona, 1986.
———, ed. "Rosa Chacel: Memoria, narrativa y poética de las presencias: poesías,
    relatos, novelas y ensayos." *Anthropos* Suplementos 8 (May 1988): 164–71.
———. "Un sistema que el amor presidía." *Quimera* 84 (Dec. 1988): 30–35.
Rodríguez, Ana, and Antonio Piedra, eds. *Rosa Chacel: La obra literaria, expresión
    genealógica del Eros*." *Anthropos* 85 (June 1988).

ERNESTINA DE CHAMPOURCIN
(b. 1905)

Joy B. Landeira

BIOGRAPHY

Of the original members of the Generation of 1927 included in Gerardo Diego's 1934 anthology *Poesía española (Contemporáneos)*, only one woman, Ernestina de Champourcin y Morán de Loredo, is still living. Often referred to simply as the wife of poet Juan José Domenchina, Champourcin is a poet and critic in her own right, having published a novel, a book commemorating Juan Ramón Jiménez, a verse anthology, and fifteen other volumes of poetry, the latest of which appeared in 1991.

Champourcin was born on July 10, 1905, in Vitoria, in the Basque province of Alava. She has never accented her surname, since it is of Provençal origin, from the Latin *campus ursinos*. Not long after her birth, her family moved to Madrid, where she received a traditional Catholic education. Quite assiduous in her studies, chiefly literary ones, Ernestina soon became proficient in Spanish, French (which was spoken at home), and English. Although some laudatory book jackets claim that she began writing poetry in French at the age of eight, she wrote only one such poem. During her teen years, Champourcin had little interest in cooking or performing the domestic chores required of her gender. Instead, she preferred to read and write, and she became enthralled with the poetry of Juan Ramón Jiménez. At twenty-one, her first book of poetry, *En silencio* (1926; ''In Silence''), was published by Espasa-Calpe. As is often the case with first books, Ernestina later recognized its poor quality; nonetheless, she viewed it as a small literary ''happening'' in a feminist sense, since two other books by women—Cristina de Arteaga's *Sembrad* and María Teresa Roca de Togores's *Poesías*—were published that same year. An attention-getting controversy ensued as male writers took notice of these books, and critics—also male—refused to believe that the volumes had been written by women.

Before writing her second book of poetry, *Ahora* (1928; "Now"), Champourcin met her literary idol, Juan Ramón Jiménez, whose presence reverberates throughout this collection, even to the type of paper on which it was printed. Upon showing him the paper she thought to be perfect, Juan Ramón chose another, pronouncing her selection appropriate for advertising a beauty parlor. His influence in this volume, along with that of other contemporary writers—Federico García Lorca, Rubén Darío, and Antonio Machado—combines with her own early preferences for nature imagery, modernist exoticism, and surrealist metaphors; *Ahora* marks her presence in the Generation of 1927.

Champourcin's next book, *La voz en el viento* (1931; "Voice in the Wind"), covers the period 1929–31 and prolongs Jiménez's influence to the point of including an introduction reproduced in his own undecipherable handwriting. During the early 1930s, Champourcin was welcomed into Madrid's active and influential literary scene. At the *tertulias* (informal literary gatherings), she met Valentín de Zubiaurre, Pilar and Juan de la Encina, Gerardo Diego, Rafael Alberti, Concha Méndez, and Manolo Altolaguirre, along with Juan José Domenchina, whom she later married.

In 1934 Champourcin's inclusion in Gerardo Diego's monumental anthology solidified her fame. She was anthologized as one of only two women in the Generation of '27, the other being Josefina de la Torre. In later years, other women have been identified with the '27 poets, but these two were the only ones originally named to the group. For Champourcin, acknowledgment as a Generation of '27 poet meant official recognition and respect for her work, as well as literary "security" in the form of exclusive contracts with the Aguilar publishing house. To have been accepted among a group of such preeminent scholars was in itself a major victory.

The year 1936 saw many abrupt changes in Ernestina's life. Her first book for Aguilar, one of her finest, appeared in time for the last annual Feria del libro (book fair) in Madrid before the Spanish Civil War. Prefaced by "cinco glosas excéntricas" (five eccentric poems in gloss form) by Domenchina, *Cántico inútil* (1936; "Useless Chant") stands out among her works. The book, her last before exile from Spain, is her longest, most intricate, and most structurally varied volume, and best characterizes her work of the time. In addition to this landmark book of poetry, Champourcin's only published novel, *La casa de enfrente* ("The House Across the Street"), also appeared in 1936. A fictionalized autobiography, its pseudo-psychological prose, narrowly limited to the narrator's self-perception, makes for an immature, almost adolescent novel. Champourcin abandoned the novel genre altogether after a few other unsuccessful attempts, including a war novel, "Aristocracia y democracia" ("Aristocracy and Democracy"), which she claimed suffered from a lack of perspective.

These two literary efforts of 1936 were not the only mileposts that year for Ernestina de Champourcin. Her marriage to Domenchina meant total and lasting change in her life. Domenchina, thirty-eight years old at the time, and seven years her senior, had been a confirmed bachelor, a sedentary writer, and a fervent

Republican. In the literary *tertulia* at the Café Regina, he had met the head of the Republican government, Manuel Azaña, and eventually became his personal secretary. As a result of this affiliation, on November 7, 1936, when it was feared that Franco would enter Madrid, Champourcin and Domenchina married and fled with Azaña to the Casa de Cultura in Valencia. They remained with the Republican faction, moving to Barcelona and finally being forced into exile in France. In 1939, they spent three months in Toulouse, then moved to Mexico with Domenchina's mother, a widowed sister, and her two children.

Invited to Mexico by the country's cultural attaché, Alfonso Reyes, and the Casa de España, the Domenchinas settled in Mexico City. When the Casa de España was dissolved, its professors stayed on at the newly formed Colegio de México; Champourcin and her husband became translators. Ernestina, relying upon her language skills in Spanish, French, and English, formed the Asociación de Personal Técnico para Conferencias Internacionales. Her own literary production suffered, and she did not publish another book until 1952. Life was difficult in Mexico; she translated more than a dozen books, but most of her translating was done at international symposiums. On two occasions, in 1948 and 1950, she was brought to Washington, D.C., as chief translator. During these sessions she was able to renew her friendship with Juan Ramón Jiménez and his wife, Zenobia, who were living in Maryland.

When Champourcin resumed publishing in 1952, her poetry had changed. Her earlier surrealist metaphors and technical ability with poetic forms were replaced by a new thematic credo: "God is in all poetry." *Presencia a oscuras* (1952; "Darkened Presence") initiates a definitively religious theme that characterizes all her works published in Mexico. Champourcin and Domenchina shared the view that the poet's only life was "el diálogo con Dios" (the dialogue with God), as Domenchina stated in 1958 in *El estrañado* ("The Estranged One"). Her husband's strong literary presence, combined with the absence of influences of her former fellow poets, may account for some of the obvious change in orientation of her poetry. Eight years lapsed before the appearance of Champourcin's next book.

In 1959 Juan José Domenchina died in Mexico, never having realized his obsession to return to his beloved Spain. Champourcin then began publishing poetry at a very rapid rate, all of it religious. The books of this period include *El nombre que me diste* (1960; "The Name You Gave Me"); *Cárcel de los sentidos* (1964; "Prison of the Senses"), which collects poems from 1953 to 1963; *Hai-kais espirituales* (1967; "Spiritual Haikus"); and *Cartas cerradas* (1968; "Closed Letters"). From 1968 to 1974 Champourcin edited an anthology, *Dios en la poesía actual* ("God in Current Poetry"), which had three editions, enabling her to remain in contact with her preferred religious themes and with other religious poets. Champourcin did not wait for Franco to die to return to Spain; she moved back to Madrid in 1973. Her last book of religious poetry, *Poemas del Ser y del Estar* (1974; "Poems of Being"), was published in the Spanish capital one year later.

Primer exilio (1978; "First Exile"), Champourcin's first book written entirely in Spain after exile, shows some abrupt, almost astounding changes in her poetry. Introducing a retrospective period, it incorporates qualities of her earlier works into a more worldly and philosophic vision. Subsequently she has recounted memories of her mentor Juan Ramón Jiménez in *La ardilla y la rosa: Juan Ramón en mi memoria* (1981; "The Squirrel and the Rose: Juan Ramón in My Memory"). She also has published more poetry: *La pared transparente* (1984; "The Transparent Wall"); an anthology of selected poems, *Antología poética* (1988; "Poetic Anthology"); what she claimed would be her last volume, *Huyeron todas las islas* (1988; "All the Islands Fled"); and *Poesía a través del tiempo* (1991; "Poetry Across Time").

In 1993, at the age of eighty-eight, Ernestina de Champourcin lives by herself in a second-floor apartment in a pleasant Madrid neighborhood on the Paseo de la Habana. There she strolls daily and lunches with some of her female writer friends, Concha Zardoya, Clara Janés, and Rosa Chacel. Nearly deaf and obliged to wear thick eyeglasses, she holds the paper close to her eyes when she writes, making slow, deliberate strokes. She remains devoted to literature and still enjoys reading and rereading the many signed first editions of poetry that her friends have given her over the years.

MAJOR THEMES

Because Ernestina de Champourcin was a poet of exile, one tends to assume that she wrote political poetry. In fact, she took no interest in politics and, if anything, made a concerted effort not to involve herself in affairs of that nature. Nor is her poetry "social," except in its desire to break the boundaries imposed by the human condition, in an attempt to unite with more universal absolutes. Transcendence, then, is the constant in Champourcin's poetry. The prewar years 1926–36 coincide with the first cycle, "amor humano" (human love), which represents her most creative and intellectual period. During this time, she experimented with a variety of poetic structures—from sonnets to free verse. Both platonic and sexual love, along with a fascination for the temporal and the cosmic, appear in the four books of this period: *En silencio, Ahora, La voz en el viento,* and, one of her finest, *Cántico inútil.* In *Cántico inútil,* many of the modernist and Generation of '98 tendencies are abandoned, with emphasis instead on exalted and exuberant surrealistic and mystical flights and fantasies in search of various types of unions: platonic/sexual, cosmic/temporal, individual/collective, and, above all, human and deital ones, which announce an orientation to God that overshadows all other themes in the second period.

Sixteen years passed between Champourcin's first literary period and the second cycle, "amor divino" (divine love). No longer surrealistic or worldly in any sense, the focus of the poetry published between 1952 and 1976 is definitively religious, though lacking the mystical quality of *Cántico inútil.* All six books of the "amor divino" period were written in Mexico. Much less varied in structure than the poems of the first period, the "amor divino" poems are predominantly *romancillos* (verses with fewer than eight syllables and assonantal rhyme), free verse, and religious forms such as litanies and short prayers. Inspiration from biblical passages and standard biblical imagery of light, water, fire, and silence appear throughout this cycle of standard religious poems.

Champourcin's third period, "amor anhelado" (longed-for love), coincides with her return to Spain. To date, it includes three works, *Primer exilio*, *La pared transparente*, and *Huyeron todas las islas*. In a sense retrospective, the poems of this cycle combine structures and themes from her first, most successful writings. No longer is religion an easy answer for spiritual longings, nor do earthly relationships reciprocate or satisfy. Poetry and cosmic unity become the only escape from a world filled with human anxiety, desperation, lack of communication, and loneliness. In *Huyeron todas las islas*, questions of exile abound—a spiritual rather than a political exile. Transcendence is accomplished through poetry, in which human exiles, like the islands of the Apocalypse, seek freedom from earthly constraints: "¡Van huyendo las islas a un mundo sin fronteras!" (The islands are fleeing to a world without boundaries!; 20).

It is impossible to close this section on major themes in Champourcin's work without mentioning the influence of two men—"the two Juans" in her life—Juan Ramón Jiménez and Juan José Domenchina. Whereas at first they aided her literary career by teaching her how to write and by introducing her into the proper literary circles, her later production seemed to suffer under their domineering influence. Champourcin's lifelong regard for her literary mentor, Juan Ramón, may have lowered her prestige among other poets of the Generation of '27, who were seeking innovations and going beyond the literary traditions set by the modernists. When Gerardo Diego asked Champourcin to submit comments on her own literary methods and attitudes for inclusion in his anthology, she instead praised the work of Juan Ramón, calling him the "maestro," and lamented the fact that he was not included in the anthology.

Domenchina's influence is more pervasive in her life, since his political ties led the couple to marry and immediately flee into exile. From 1939 to 1952, Champourcin did not publish any poetry; she was contributing to their survival by translating books and working at international conventions. Domenchina also worked as a translator, but at the same time was able to publish eight books of poetry and three editions of his *Antología de la poesía española contemporánea* (1941, 1946, 1947).

Thematically, Domenchina probably contributed to Champourcin's fervently religious poetry by promulgating the concept that poetry's only function should be to dialogue with God. After the death of her husband, Champourcin began to write religious poetry at a feverish pace. Although there can be no doubt about her own fervent religious commitment, the allegiance to religious themes simultaneously reflects the strong poetic presence of her dead husband and vestiges of self-censorship that render religious themes "safe." Despite the impressive quantity of the books written in Mexico, their quality is not on a par with her best and most serious (and currently most studied) poetry, which she wrote before she was married. The poetry written after Champourcin returned to Spain (1973) is technically not as intricate as her early work, but by abandoning the strictly religious orientation, she focuses more on humanity's alienation and experiments with new poetic forms.

SURVEY OF CRITICISM

Despite her mention in Gerardo Diego's landmark anthology, Champourcin's forced exile kept her from gleaning much early critical recognition as a member of the Generation of '27 or from forming any working relationships with other writers named to the group, such as Josefina de la Torre or the "poet-professors." Critics, among them Guillermo de la Torre, José Francisco Cirre, and Angel Valbuena Prat, included her work in anthologies and made brief references to her as a poet, or more often as the wife of Juan José Domenchina. Seldom, however, was there any real study of her poetry. Particularly during her years in Mexico, little notice was taken of Champourcin's writings. The first "contemporary" evaluation of her as a poet appeared in 1975, when she was interviewed in Spain by the editor and publisher Arturo del Villar. He has taken a great deal of interest in her work and has published *La pared transparente* and her memoirs of Juan Ramón Jiménez, *La ardilla y la rosa*.

Recently, more critical interest has been shown in Champourcin's work, principally by scholars in the United States, including Rafael Espejo-Saavedra, Joy B. Landeira, and Andrew P. Debicki. Debicki's essay, "Una dimensión olvidada de la poesía española de los '20 y '30: La lírica visionaria de Ernestina de Champourcin," is particularly recommended because it explores the originality of Champourcin's early lyric techniques. Debicki observes that "her work calls attention to its own creative process on the one hand, while yielding an imaginative and visionary world which dovetails with what is perhaps the most original vein of Spanish poetry emerging at the end of the 1927 period" (49).

BIBLIOGRAPHY

Works by Ernestina de Champourcin

Poetry

En silencio. Madrid: Espasa-Calpe, 1926.
Ahora. Madrid: Librería León Sánchez Cuesta, 1928.
La voz en el viento. Madrid: Compañía Ibero-Americana de Publicaciones, 1931.
Cántico inútil. Madrid: Aguilar, 1936.
Presencia a oscuras. Madrid: Rialp, 1952.
El nombre que me diste. Mexico City: Ecuador O O' O''-Finesterre, 1960, 1966.
Cárcel de los sentidos. Mexico City: Ecuador O O' O''-Finisterre, 1964.
Hai-Kais espirituales. Mexico City: Ecuador O O' O''-Finisterre, 1967.

Cartas cerradas. Mexico City: Ecuador O O' O''-Finisterre, 1968.
Dios en la poesía actual: Selección de poemas españoles e hispanoamericanos. Madrid: Biblioteca de Autores Cristianos, 1970, 1972, 1976. [An anthology edited by Champourcin]
Poemas del Ser y del Estar. Madrid: Alfaguara, 1974.
Primer exilio. Madrid: Rialp, 1978.
La pared transparente. Madrid: Los Libros de Fausto, 1984.
Antología poética. Madrid: Torremozas, 1988. [Anthology of selected poems]
Huyeron todas las islas. Madrid: Caballo Griego para la Poesía, 1988.
Poesía a través del tiempo. Barcelona: Anthropos, 1991.

Prose

"Aristocracia y democracia." 1936. [Unpublished novel]
La casa de enfrente. Madrid: Signo, 1936. [Novel]
La ardilla y la rosa: Juan Ramón en mi memoria. Madrid: Los Libros de Fausto, 1981.

Works about Ernestina de Champourcin

Asunce, José Angel. Prologue. *Poesía a través del tiempo*. By Ernestina de Champourcin. Barcelona: Anthropos, 1991. ix–lxxv.
Cano Ballesta, Juan. *La poesía española entre pureza y revolución (1930–1936)*. Madrid: Gredos, 1972. 69–71, passim.
———. Review. *El Sol* 13 (June 1936): n. pag.
Cirre, José Francisco. *Forma y espíritu de una lírica española*. Mexico City: Gráfica Panamericana, 1950. 164.
Debicki, Andrew P. "Una dimensión olvidada de la poesía española de los '20 y '30: La lírica visionaria de Ernestina de Champourcin." *Ojáncano* 1.1 (1988): 48–60.
Diego, Gerardo. *Poesía española (Contemporáneos)*. Madrid: Taurus, 1934.
Espejo-Saavedra, Rafael. "Sentimiento amoroso y creación poética en Ernestina de Champourcin." *Revista/Review Interamericana* 12.1 (Spring 1982): 133–39.
Jiménez Faro, Luzmaría. "Ernestina de Champourcin: Un peregrinaje hacia la luz." *Antología poética*. By Ernestina de Champourcin. Madrid: Torremozas, 1988. 9–17.
Jiménez, José Olivio. "Medio siglo de poesía española." *Hispania* 50 (1967): 945, n. 6.
Jiménez, Juan Ramón. *Españoles de tres mundos*. Buenos Aires: Losada, 1942. 107.
Landeira, Joy B. "Ernestina de Champourcin y Morán de Loredo." *Women Writers of Spain: An Annotated Bio-Bibliographical Guide*. Ed. Carolyn Galerstein. Westport: Greenwood Press, 1986. 88–91.
Marco, Joaquín. *Poesía española siglo XX*. Barcelona: EDHASA, 1986. 107.
Valbuena Prat, Ángel. *Historia de la literatura española*. Vol. 3. Barcelona: Gustavo Gili, 1953. 668–69. 3 vols.
Villar, Arturo del. "Entrevista de Ernestina de Champourcin." *La Estafeta Literaria* 556 (15 Jan. 1975): 10–15.
———. "Entrevista de Ernestina de Champourcin." *Alaluz* 18.2 (Fall 1986): 15.

CARMEN DE BURGOS ("COLOMBINE") (1867–1932)

Elizabeth Starčević

BIOGRAPHY

Born in Almería in southern Spain in 1867, Carmen de Burgos displayed early in life the signs of independence and rebellion that were to become her trademark. Although she became a very public figure, many details of her biography elude us and call for further study. Important sources of information about the author can be found, however, in Ramón Gómez de la Serna's prologue to her *Confidencias de artistas* (1916; "Artists' Confidences") and in Rafael Cansinos-Asséns' *La novela de un literato* (1982). From these sources, as well as from de Burgos's own account, the reader is able to construct a fascinating portrait of the future journalist and short-story writer.

Married at sixteen, against her family's wishes, to Arturo Alvarez, a local bon vivant, de Burgos soon took over his job at the small newspaper he ran. The marriage was an unhappy one, leading her to defy the Almerian social code by abandoning her husband and leaving for Madrid with a baby in her arms. Her early experiences at her husband's newspaper and her efforts to live independently while working as a teacher were later described in the unpublished reports de Burgos was asked to write for her school evaluations. Over a period of several years, she prepared herself to teach both at the elementary (1895) and secondary level (1898). Eventually, she became a teacher of future teachers in the Escuela Normal de Maestras (1899?). Information about this early period can be gleaned from the numerous articles de Burgos began publishing in the important newspapers and magazines of her time in 1901, among them *El Sol* and *El Heraldo* of Madrid. She also wrote a daily column in *El Diario Universal* (1904), "Lecturas para la mujer" ("Readings for Women").

Carmen de Burgos worked as a teacher and as a journalist, at times simultaneously and at times taking leaves from her pedagogical duties to engage in travels necessary for her reporting, a situation that provoked hostility among her teacher colleagues. Teaching, her major source of income, provided a forum in which she could elaborate her views on education and the role of women in society. As a journalist, de Burgos was acutely conscious of her status as the first female "roving reporter" in Spain, as her 1931 interview with José Montero Alonso clearly reveals: "There were women who wrote, of course . . . but they weren't really journalists . . . who did the same work of editing and being on the street. I was the first female editor of a daily newspaper" (n. pag.). Throughout World War I she reported from France and Germany and traveled in Spain, Portugal, and northern Africa. Her articles document the impact of the war on the poor and disenfranchised as well as on the economy of her beloved Almería.

De Burgos, an internationalist in every sense, published journalistic accounts that discuss social issues in a wide-ranging fashion, enriched by her experiences of travel and observation in other countries. An activist as well, she created the Sociedad de la Alianza Hispano-Israelita with the intention of corresponding with the Jewish settlements scattered throughout the world. This was the continuation of an effort begun in 1908, when she used her magazine *Revista Crítica* and its section on the Sephardic Jews as a vehicle to link the Jewish community in the diaspora. Once this short-lived magazine foundered, we find few references to the Sociedad de Alianza, and de Burgos's concern for the Jewish people does not appear as a topic discussed by other writers.

In 1904 de Burgos published the first public survey on divorce in *El Diario Universal*. Her views on this subject were in part influenced by the writings of Alfredo Naquet and Max Nordau, social commentators who were contributors to her *Revista Crítica*. Responses to the survey poured in from Spaniards of all classes. The varied reactions included commentary from important figures such as Emilia Pardo Bazán, who curiously reported that she had no opinion on the matter. As a result of this inquiry, de Burgos became the target of a slur campaign in one of the Catholic journals. She sought and achieved a rectification by first hitting and then threatening the editor until a retraction was printed. In 1906, when she again used the survey format to promote the cause of the vote for women, it was viewed as a joke. Nevertheless, she continued to fight for women's suffrage throughout her life: as a journalist, as a member of women's groups, in public forums, and as a provincial delegate of the Radical Socialist Party. The hostility that she encountered as a teacher, the ridicule she endured in her first attempts at journalism, and the lack of recognition for her work clearly illustrate the obstacles facing women early in the twentieth century. De Burgos's strength of character and her analysis of the need for united action propelled her to work with progressive groups to struggle for a better world for all people.

A multifaceted figure, Carmen de Burgos played a significant role in Madrid's cultural world. She became a consistent contributor of short stories to the flood of "little magazines" that began to appear in 1907 when Eduardo Zamacois founded *El Cuento Semanal*. Along with many of her female contemporaries, such as Emilia Pardo Bazán, Sofía Casanova, and Concha Espina, to mention only a few, de Burgos provided the reading public with weekly pleasures that painted a variegated world of romance, exotic scenarios, nightlife, and local color.

De Burgos's home became the locus of a literary salon where Spanish intellectuals such as Gabriel Miró, Enrique Díez-Canedo, Andrés and Edmundo González Blanco, and others came to share their thoughts and writings. It was here that the works of John Ruskin, Oscar Wilde, Colette, and Giacomo Leopardi were made accessible to the Spanish reading public through de Burgos's translations and through her employment of other young writers as translators. Her unceasing participation in the sociocultural events of her time brought her in contact with Ramón Gómez de la Serna. She was his inspiration, his support, and his lover for many years. He would eventually betray their friendship by entering into a brief affair with de Burgos's daughter but would renew their contact near the end of her life. The significance of her role in his development, and the impact the two had on Madrid's cultural life at that time, merit further study.

Another relationship that remains obscured is that of de Burgos and Vicente Blasco Ibáñez. She collaborated with him, knew him personally, and wrote about his work with deep feeling, yet Ibáñez's writings seem to ignore this. Criticism by Concepción Núñez Rey indicates that de Burgos's writings denied their intimacy. Similarly, little is known about her contacts with such women contemporaries as Pardo Bazán.

De Burgos's life was productive and complex. She relished this complexity, describing herself as a person of many yo's (I's). Writing under many pseudonyms, the best-known of which is Colombine, her discussions often demonstrate a similarity in both themes and approaches to the work of Concepción Arenal and of course to de Burgos's contemporary, Emilia Pardo Bazán. An extraordinarily prolific writer, de Burgos produced more than ten novels, about seventy short stories, several biographies, and many essays, poems, travelogues, and books on cooking, hygiene, and advice of a practical nature. She translated from the German, French, Italian, English, Russian, and Portuguese. Add to this the hundreds of articles she published, and we must wonder why she is not better known. This was the fate, however, of many women of her period, such as Sofía Casanova, Margarita Nelken, and Blanca de los Ríos. Some speculate that their work was buried literally and figuratively by the ravages of the Spanish Civil War and the many years of dictatorship that followed under Franco. It seems logical to assume that in de Burgos's case, her unorthodox personal behavior, her socialist politics, and her persistent focus on issues of concern to women—such as work, divorce, sexuality and the vote—would suffice to stifle all information about her during a period of political repression.

Carmen de Burgos died of a heart attack on October 9, 1932, while speaking at a public meeting of the Círculo Radical Socialista. Her final words were "I die happy because I die a Republican. Long live the Republic!" Although she was recognized in her time as a precursor of feminism and an indefatigable fighter for social rights, her activities and her writings remain a fertile field for the study of the accomplishments of this fascinating figure who defied her society's constraints to live a life of productivity and struggle during an exciting moment in Spain's history.

MAJOR THEMES

The scope of Carmen de Burgos's production includes all genres. Her early works of poetry, short story, and novel deal with life in her birthplace, Almería. Stylistically romantic, with heavy folkloric and *costumbrista* (emphasizing local color) tones, the fiction of this period, which includes the novels *El último contrabandista* (n.d.; "The Last Smuggler") and *Los inadaptados* (1909; "The Misfits")—the latter also the name of a short story published in 1918—treats issues of absentee landlords from the north of Spain and the difficult economic conditions that give rise to a romanticizing of the "outlaw." These works also lament the progressive disappearance of the strong and individualistic culture of the region.

Fiction writing obviously did not provide enough money to supplement her teacher's income. Journalism proved more lucrative, and de Burgos was a contributor to the important magazines and newspapers of her time. The following are but a few among the hundreds of articles that appeared in *El Diario Universal* and *El Heraldo* from 1904 to 1907: "El pleito del divorcio" ("The Divorce Suit"), "Libros y mujeres" ("Books and Women"), "El alcohol en los niños" ("Alcohol in Children"), "Jorge Sand y Emile Zola" ("George Sand and Emile Zola").

Another means of making money that was very popular at the time was to write practical instruction books. Directed mainly to women, de Burgos's more than thirty titles include *La protección y la higiene de los niños* (1904; "The Protection and Hygiene of Children"); *La mujer en el hogar* (1909?; "Women in the Home"); *¿Quiere usted comer bien?* (1917, 1931, 1936, 1949; "Do You Want to Eat Well?"). The author joked about how her cookbooks brought her recognition but not always money; once she was even paid in sacks of rice. It should be noted that this is the one area where de Burgos's name seems to have endured; both Spaniards and Latin Americans report seeing her cookbooks in their parents' homes.

Equally interesting works of a nonliterary nature include de Burgos's several books on travel, such as *Cartas sin destinatario* (1910, 1918; "Letters with No Addressee"), and her two volumes of interviews and essays on important Spanish and European women artists of her time, *Confidencias de artistas* (1916). Among her biographies, the best-known is her work on the social critic and author Mariano José de Larra, *Fígaro (Revelaciones "Ella" descubierta, epistolario inédito)* (1919; "Figaro [Revelations 'She' Discovered, Unpublished Correspondence]"). Revealing new information on Larra and lovingly describing his varied contributions, it was well received by the Real Academia Española, by

Larra's family, and by such writers as Azorín and Armando Palacio Valdés. It also circulated outside of Spain.

In her constant quest to improve conditions for women and to make a better world for all people, Carmen de Burgos turned her pen to articles, speeches, short stories, and novels that treat the questions of marriage, women's rights, education, and divorce. One of the strongest critiques of the infamous law on adultery—which punished the wife but not the husband—can be found in her short story "El artículo 438" (1921; "Article 438"). The title refers to the part of the Civil Code that deals with adultery. It points out the glaring inequality in the courts' treatment of women and highlights women's lack of economic control over their life. In a flowery and passionate style, de Burgos describes the tragedy of a young and innocent wife who is pushed by her husband into the arms of his best friend in order to rob her of her dowry. The husband murders his wife but is acquitted by the court for defending his honor. The story also treats the infantilization and exploitation of wives, and offers negative views on prevailing codes of parenting that prevent mothers from bonding with their children.

One among dozens of stories, "El artículo 438" is a forceful condemnation of the disadvantageous legal status of women in Spanish society; among de Burgos's works, it was often cited as a tragic representation of the need to change women's situation. Although stories such as this one and "La rampa" (1912; "The Ramp"), "El abogado" (1915; "The Lawyer"), and even "Villa María" (1916) treat social issues both seriously and at times humorously, others, like "Ellas y ellos o ellos y ellas" (1916; "Hes and Shes or Shes and Hes") and "La princesa rusa" (1922; "The Russian Princess"), provide a panoramic view of an artistic and exotic life of cafés, drugs, and sexual abandon.

Carmen de Burgos's novels, like those of Benito Pérez Galdós, offer a portrait of Madrid and its developing classes, and in particular reveal her knowledge of the latest information on sexuality, surely obtained through her familiarity with foreign literatures as well as through her friendship with Dr. Gregorio Marañón. Her novels highlight women's need for sexual fulfillment at the same time that their biting portraits of women's social and economic dependence reveal an acute analysis of class—a job as a matron in a public toilet becomes an anxiously sought salvation from starvation for one of her characters. One sees here, as in her other novels that look at women's problems in society, the influence of August Bebel's *Woman Under Socialism*.

Of great interest in this sociopolitical vein is the novel *La rampa* (1917), which de Burgos dedicated to all the poor and disoriented women who came to her, asking which road to take. It follows the descending trajectory of a lower-middle-class young woman who is unable to maintain herself economically. In a straightforward, realistic, and heavily descriptive style, Madrid is seen through the eyes of both the protagonist and other women as they come in contact with the institutions of their degradation: the maternity ward, the foundling home, the church, the department stores in which they work as part of the developing class of single working girls, and the families for whom they must slave. Victims of men and of men's rules, they are stripped of all human quality and end up scrubbing floors for the nuns. The novel, which contains fascinating details about such aspects of women's lives as budgets, clothing, work, and friendship, ends tragically and points to the need for societal solutions to female inequality.

Similarly, *Quiero vivir mi vida* (1931; "I Want to Live My Life") examines the institution of marriage and the unnatural demands it places on women. De Burgos provides a complex study of the main character, who is forced into roles that do not suit her personality. Though not profound, this view of a middle-class wife's lot is fascinating and tragic. The seeming independence of the protagonist is undermined by the descriptions of her inability to break the bonds of tradition. This work, which evoked both anger and sadness in the readers of her time, challenged the conventional view of woman's place; its violent and tragic ending was an extremely provocative conclusion for the period.

In her many trips to Portugal, where she shared a house with Gómez de la Serna, Carmen de Burgos became interested in the work of the Russian theosophist Helen Blavatsky (1831–1891), who, with others, advocated a worldwide eclectic religion based largely on Brahmanic and Buddhist teachings. Two of de Burgos's novels criticize excesses in religiosity: *El retorno* (192?; "The Return"), which depicts spiritualist phenomena in Estoril, Portugal, and *Los espirituados* (1923; "The Spiritists"), which also shows the negative side of religious zeal.

Also noteworthy is de Burgos's *La mujer moderna y sus derechos* (1927; "The Modern Woman and Her Rights") which surveys the situation of women throughout the world and their progress toward achieving the vote and legal equality. A work that clearly can be considered a precursor to Simone de Beauvoir's *The Second Sex*, it deserves translation into English and extensive study. Carmen de Burgos's work stands as a rich tapestry that allows us to observe a range of women's issues in the context of an international struggle for social change. Both in word and in deed, de Burgos displayed her passion for a better world.

SURVEY OF CRITICISM

Although she was well known during her life as a participant in the major cultural, social, and political activities of her period, the work of Carmen de Burgos has not been widely discussed in either Spain or the United States. Some interest in her writing has been shown by two newspapers in Spain, *El País* and *La Voz de Almería*, and by several graduate students. The only full-length study to date on the author is Starčević's *Carmen de Burgos, defensora de la mujer* (1976). It situates the fascinating life and activities of this important feminist precursor within the developments occurring in Spanish life and letters. The book examines the role of women in her fiction and provides revealing interviews with de Burgos's surviving contemporaries. It also contains the first extensive bibliography on the author. Further bibliography may be found in Starčević's doctoral dissertation, which formed the basis for the book.

In 1990, an article on de Burgos by the Spanish historian Paloma Castañeda was published in the feminist magazine *Poder y Libertad*. It is a brief biographical survey that places the author among Spain's many "forgotten women" whose works need to be rediscovered. In 1989 a collection of seven of her short stories was published in Spain and edited by Concepción Núñez Rey. This volume contains a very useful biographical introduction to the author, to her work, and in particular to the stories included in the volume. Utilizing Gómez de la Serna's work to clarify his relationship with de Burgos, Núñez Rey's study also offers the latest bibliographical sources available and facilitates further research on the author.

Finally, Carmen de Burgos's short story "Puñal de claveles" (1931; "A Fistful of Carnations"), has been republished (1991) in a volume that also includes a commentary by Starčević, who relates the story to Federico García Lorca's *Bodas de sangre* (1932). Her study highlights the fact that both works were inspired by the same event and use the mysterious countryside of Almería as their backdrop. The edition also contains an introduction and analysis by Miguel Naveros, a distant relative of de Burgos. It is hoped that these recent volumes signal a growing interest in the rich and varied work of this important internationalist feminist author.

BIBLIOGRAPHY

Major Works by Carmen de Burgos ("Colombine")

The most complete source of Carmen de Burgos's works is *Obras completas*. Madrid: Compañía Ibero-Americana de Publicaciones, 1929.

Novels and Short Story Collections

Cuentos de Colombine. Valencia: Sempere, 1908.
Los inadaptados. Valencia: Sempere, 1909.
Confidencias de artistas. Madrid: Sociedad Española de Librería, 1916.
Ellas y ellos, o ellos y ellas. Madrid: Alrededor del Mundo, 1917.
La rampa. Madrid: Renacimiento, 1917.
El retorno: Novela espiritista. Lisbon: Lusitania Editora, 192?.
La malcasada. Valencia: Sempere, 1923.
Mis mejores cuentos. Madrid: Prensa Popular, 1923. [This collection includes "El artículo 438," "El abogado," "El novenario," "Los huesos del abuelo," and "La mujer fría"]
Quiero vivir mi vida. Madrid: Biblioteca Nueva, 1931.
El último contrabandista. Barcelona: Ramón Sopena Editor, n.d.

Short Stories in Magazines

"En la guerra: (Episodios de Melilla)." *El Cuento Semanal.* 29 Oct. 1909: n. pag.
"La rampa." *Los Contemporáneos.* 11 Aug. 1912: n. pag.

"La indecisa." *El Libro Popular*. 12 Sept. 1912: n. pag.
"El abogado." *Los Contemporáneos* 340 (1915): n. pag.
"El hombre negro." *La Novela Corta*. 8 July 1916: n. pag.
"Villa María." *La Novela Corta*. 8 July 1916: n. pag.
"Los inadaptados." *Los Contemporáneos*. 5 Dec. 1918: n. pag.
"El artículo 438." *La Novela Semanal*. 1 Oct. 1921: n. pag.
"La princesa rusa." *La Novela Corta*. 30 Sept. 1922: n. pag.
"Los huesos del abuelo." *Los Contemporáneos*. 7 Dec. 1922: n. pag.
"La melena de la discordia." *La Novela Semanal*. 21 Mar. 1925: n. pag.
"Las ensaladillas." *La Novela Corta*. 26 Apr. 1925: n. pag.
"Viudas de novios." *La Esfera*. 29 May 1929: n. pag.

Biography

Fígaro (Revelaciones "Ella" descubierta, epistolario inédito). Madrid: Alrededor del
mundo, 1919.

Essays

El divorcio en España. Madrid: Viuda de Rodríguez Serra, 1904.
La mujer moderna y sus derechos. Valencia: Sempere, 1927.

Poetry

Notas del alma. Madrid: Fernando Fé, 1901.

Travel

Cartas sin destinatario. Valencia: Sempere, 1910, 1918.
Mis viajes por Europa. Madrid: V. H. Sanz Calleja, 1917.

Practical Books

La cocina moderna. Valencia: Sempere, n. d.
La protección y la higiene de los niños. Valencia: Administración de El Campeón del
Magisterio, 1904.
La mujer en el hogar. Valencia: Sempere, 1909(?), 1918.
¿Quiere usted comer bien? Barcelona: Ramón Sopena, 1917.
El arte de ser mujer. Madrid: Sociedad Española de Librería, 1920.

Translations

Keller, Helen. *Historia de mi vida*. Madrid: Viuda de Rodríguez Serra, 1904.
Leopardi, Giacomo. *Su vida y sus obras*. 2 vols. Valencia: Sempere, 1911.
Ruskin, John. *Las Piedras de Venecia*. Valencia: Sempere, n.d.
Tolstoy, Leon. *La guerra ruso-japonesa*. Valencia: Sempere, n.d.

Articles

"La mujer en el código penal." *La Correspondencia de España* 21 Sept. 1902: n. pag.
"Lecturas para la mujer." *El Diario Universal* 22 Jan. 1904: 3.
"El pleito del divorcio." *El Diario Universal* 22 Jan. 1904: 1.
"El alcohol en los niños." *El Heraldo* 24 July 1906: 3.

"La educación en Suiza." *El Heraldo* 24 July 1906: 1.

"Periodista italiana." *El Heraldo* 15 Aug. 1906: 1.

"El voto de las mujeres." *El Heraldo* 19 Oct. 1906: 1.

"Madame Curie." *El Heraldo* 4 Nov. 1906: 1.

"Las mujeres policías." *El Heraldo* 27 Feb. 1907: 1.

"El libro del mes. *Cuentos de Colombine* por Carmen de Burgos. Autocrítica." *Revista Crítica* 1. 1 (Sept. 1908): 45–53.

"Las mujeres de Blasco Ibáñez." *Prometeo* 2. 4 (Feb. 1909): 69–71.

"Sección sefárdica. Reanudando." *Prometeo* 3. 13 (1910): 81–82.

"Viajando por Dinamarca—El Castillo de Hamlet." *La Esfera* 22 May 1915: n. pag.

"El incendio de Bergen." *La Esfera* 29 Jan. 1916: n. pag.

"Mis recuerdos de Max Nordau." *La Esfera* 17 Feb. 1923: n. pag.

Works about Carmen de Burgos

Cansinos-Asséns, Rafael. *La novela de un literato. I (1882–1914)*. Ed. Rafael M. Cansinos. Madrid: Alianza Editorial, 1982.

"Carmen de Burgos. Falleció en Madrid." *La Nación* 9 Oct. 1932: n. pag.

"Carmen de Burgos—La Velada—Homenaje del partido republicano radical socialista." *El Heraldo* 19 Oct. 1932: n. pag.

Castañeda, Paloma. "Escritoras olvidadas: Carmen de Burgos." *Poder y Libertad* 13 (1990): 48–51.

Castrovido, Libertad. "In memoriam. Una gran periodista." *El Liberal* 11 Oct. 1932: 1.

"Colombine y Nocedal: Insultos Castigados." *El País* 29 May, 1904: n. pag.

"Los escritores ante la figura y obra de Carmen de Burgos." *La Libertad* 23 Oct. 1932: 9.

Gómez de la Serna, Ramón. "Cuento de Calleja." *Prometeo* 2.11 (1909): n. pag.

González Blanco, Andrés. "Letras españolas. Cuentos de Colombine." *Revista Crítica* 1 Feb. 1909: 24–32.

"Hemeroteca: Distintas tendencias del feminismo, Carmen de Burgos." *Desde el feminismo*. 1985: n. pag.

"Un libro muy interesante de Carmen de Burgos: *La mujer moderna y sus derechos*." *La Esfera*. 28 July 1928: 8–9.

"El Lyceum Club Femenino entra en el cuarto año de la vida." *Nuevo Mundo* 24 Oct. 1931: n. pag.

Montero Alonso, José. "Carmen de Burgos (Colombine) fue la autora de la primera encuesta periodística en torno al divorcio." *Nuevo Mundo* 24 Oct. 1931: n. pag. [Interview]

Naveros, Miguel, ed. *"Puñal de claveles"* por Carmen de Burgos "Colombine." Almería: Editorial Cajal, 1991. [Introduction]

Núñez Rey, Concepción, ed. and comp. *"La flor de la playa" y otras novelas cortas por Carmen de Burgos, Colombine*. Madrid: Castalia, 1989.

"El pleito del divorcio." *El Siglo Futuro* 6 Apr. 1904: 1.

Rueda, Salvador. "Fémina—Para Carmen de Burgos." *Revista Crítica* Apr. 1909: 206–07.

Starčević, Elizabeth. *Carmen de Burgos, defensora de la mujer*. Almería: Librería-
    Editorial Cajal, 1976.
———. ''La mujer en la obra de Carmen de Burgos.'' Diss. City U of New York, 1977.
———. ''La pasión afirmada.'' Naveros 17–21.

ANA DIOSDADO
(b. 1938)

Phyllis Zatlin

BIOGRAPHY

Unquestionably the most successful woman playwright of the postwar Spanish stage—indeed, the only visible woman playwright in the 1970s—Ana Isabel Alvarez-Diosdado was born in Buenos Aires on May 21, 1938, during the Spanish Civil War. Her father, noted Spanish actor and director Enrique Diosdado, was associated in South America with the acting company of the exiled Margarita Xirgu. The internationally acclaimed Spanish actress was Diosdado's godmother.

Diosdado's parents divorced in Montevideo when she was still a toddler. Her mother died not long after, and she was raised by her father and his second wife, the actress Amelia de la Torre. She made her stage debut at the age of six, appearing in Xirgu's production of Federico García Lorca's *Mariana Pineda*. With the strong role models provided by her stepmother and Xirgu, there was never any question about Diosdado's pursuing a professional career. Nevertheless, when the family returned to Spain in 1950, the young girl devoted herself exclusively to her studies. Upon graduation from an elite French academy, she enrolled in the Universidad Complutense of Madrid. Disillusioned by the poor quality of the teaching, she dropped out, turning to acting and, with the active encouragement of her father, to writing. Throughout her career she has maintained this dual focus.

Diosdado's first significant creative work, the novel *En cualquier lugar, no importa cuando* ("Anyplace, Anytime"), appeared in 1965. A second novel, "Campanas que aturden" ("The Bewildering Bells"), was runner-up for the Planeta Prize in 1969 but has never been published. That same year Diosdado began preparing adaptations of foreign plays. It was in 1970, however, with her first original stage play, that she established herself as a writer of importance.

Olvida los tambores (1972; "Forget the Drums") was a major box office hit in Madrid, enjoying an initial run of more than 450 performances, and has been staged repeatedly in Spain and abroad and shown on television. Receiving critical as well as public acclaim, it won the prestigious Mayte Prize.

The next several years were ones of intense theatrical activity for Diosdado, including four additional premieres in the Spanish capital: *El Okapi* (1972; "The Okapi"); *Usted también podrá disfrutar de ella* (1973; "You, Too, Can Enjoy Her"); *Los comuneros* (1974; "The Commoners"); and *Y de Cachemira, chales* (1976; "And Shawls from Kashmir"). *El Okapi* was staged by the Amelia de la Torre-Enrique Diosdado company, the only one of her works to star her father and stepmother. Diosdado directed *Y de Cachemira, chales*. While the response to these productions was not uniformly favorable, *Usted también podrá disfrutar de ella* rivaled Diosdado's first play in its critical and box office success. Recipient of the Fastenrath Prize of the Real Academia Española, it ran for more than five hundred performances. Diosdado simultaneously continued her work as a translator, and in 1974 *Juan y Manuela*, the first of her original television series, was aired with Diosdado portraying Manuela.

With Franco's death in 1975, the Spanish stage entered a difficult period of transition from dictatorship to democracy. Disconcerted, Diosdado, like several other successful authors, temporarily withdrew from writing original stage plays. In 1979 she married Carlos Larrañaga, a well-known leading man of stage and film, and thus became part of a second theatrical family.

By the early 1980s, Diosdado had a new play in mind that would have a cast of young actors. The absence of established names made the idea seem risky to theatrical producers; the text, initially titled "Al amanecer" ("At Dawn") and later renamed *Los ochenta son nuestros* (1988; "The Eighties Are Ours"), had to be set aside. In February 1983 Diosdado's controversial version of Ibsen's *A Doll's House* premiered in Madrid. Diosdado's original ending, created to underscore Torvald's inability to change, was retained in performance only because of her insistence on her rights as translator/adapter. That fall Diosdado played the role of a divorce lawyer in her new television series, *Anillos de oro* ("Wedding Rings"). Her thirteen hour-long scripts featured a variety of matrimonial cases within the individual segments as well as a frame story relating to the lawyer and her own family situation. The series proved enormously popular, reaching an estimated fifteen million viewers and making Diosdado a celebrity. In 1986 she wrote and starred in another series, *Segunda enseñanza* ("Secondary Education"), in which she played a teacher and single mother. Both series have been rerun in Spain and have aired in several other Spanish-speaking countries.

In October 1986, with the production of *Cuplé* (1988; "Ballad"), Diosdado returned to the stage with her first original play in ten years. The play, staged by her own company, ran for four months in Madrid and toured the provinces. In 1986 she also published her third novel, *Los ochenta son nuestros*, a narrative version of the play of the same title. The long-delayed *Los ochenta* finally reached the Madrid stage in January 1988 with a cast headed by Carlos Larrañaga's daughter Amparo. The play proved to be the biggest commercial success of the 1987–88 season and was revived in Madrid the following year, this time under Amparo's direction. In the meantime Diosdado premiered her eighth stage play, *Camino de plata* (''Silver Path''), which ran for seven months in 1988–89 before going on tour. The three-person cast featured Diosdado, her husband, and their daughter-in-law.

In the 1990–91 season, Carlos Larrañaga directed Diosdado's ''Trescientos veintiuno, trescientos veintidós'' (''Three Twenty-one, Three Twenty-two''), a comedy juxtaposing the problems of two couples, one newlywed and the other middle-aged. For 1992–93, Diosdado had two new projects pending: a version of Oscar Wilde's *Lady Windermere's Fan*, in which the author-character Wilde appeared, and a television series *Yo, la juez* (''I, the Judge''), in which Diosdado portrayed the pivotal figure of a professional woman.

Over the years, besides her work as actress, novelist, translator, and author of stage and television plays, Diosdado has been actively involved in two writers' guilds and has written for radio, film, and newspapers.

MAJOR THEMES

Diosdado's fame as a writer rests primarily on her original stage plays. Although these vary in theatrical technique and theme, they reflect certain continuing concerns on ideological and personal levels. Her works frequently speak out against materialism and plead for greater individual freedom and political harmony. Diosdado posits love and understanding as a solution to political divisiveness. On the personal level, she tends to deal with love relationships, sex roles, and the anguish of unfulfilled ambitions. Her focus on sex roles, in particular, overtly invites feminist analysis. Moreover, her general approach to social and historical issues coincides with contemporary feminist definitions of women's writing, for she typically deconstructs the binary oppositions of patriarchy (right/wrong, good/bad, conservative/liberal) and presents, instead, a multifaceted and open viewpoint. In spite of her general reliance on the strategies of the well-made play, her more innovative works have explored a kind of open-ended textuality in their construction.

In several ways, *Olvida los tambores* introduces themes that characterize Diosdado's theater. The action revolves around two young couples who represent diametrically opposed life-styles: a nonconformist youth culture and a traditional middle-class materialism. The first act, with its rapid comic pace and surface humor, prepares the audience to take the side of the idealistic Alicia and her composer husband, Tony, against Alicia's conservative sister, Pili, and her husband, Lorenzo, a businessman. But the second act reveals that the militant Tony is just as hypocritical and sexist as those against whom he rebels: he has started a love affair with his sister-in-law Pili in order to get even with Lorenzo for denying him a loan. When Lorenzo becomes aware of the betrayal, he kills himself in an automobile accident. The true idealist is not Tony but the cheerful and thoughtful Pepe, Tony's lyricist; Pepe, it should be noted, is a quasi-androgynous figure who reappears in later works.

In the context of the contemporary world, Diosdado has presented the eternal conflict of the two Spains, liberal and conservative. In doing so, she not only avoids the liberal male tradition of identifying the progressive or "good side" with a male figure, and the conservative or "bad side" with a female figure, but she also ultimately deconstructs the liberal/conservative dichotomy. Neither Alicia nor Pili is truly satisfied with her marriage or life-style; indeed, by the play's end, Pili, who realizes that both her husband and her brother-in-law have treated her as an object, is potentially far more radical than her sister. Tony speaks out against the consumer society and traditional sex roles, but his actions indicate that he has not freed himself from the old codes. Lorenzo is caricatured as a stuffed shirt, but his emotions run far deeper than Tony's. His death could have been avoided had the others shared Pepe's tolerance and sensitivity.

The staging of Diosdado's next play, *Los comuneros*, was delayed by the censors. In this work she directly confronts Spanish political history by focusing on the popular uprising against King Carlos I in the sixteenth century. Expressionistic in mode, it simultaneously portrays the king as a boy and as an old man. The two oneiric figures witness the episodes leading up to the defeat and execution of the rebellion's leaders. The dying king echoes Pepe's message of tolerance; he has come to understand that there is no single truth, and wishes he had averted civil war. Although the text includes two challenging female roles, it invites a feminist analysis not so much because of the treatment of these female characters as because of the deconstruction of binary oppositions. The boy king, like Tony in *Olvida los tambores*, is prone to view the world in terms of good/bad, us/them. His viewpoint underpins patriarchal history and, specifically, the political divisiveness of the Franco years. Diosdado's idealized old king incarnates a nonauthoritarian stance that accepts a multiplicity of opinions. Moreover, the introduction of two contradictory narrative voices provides a kind of open-ended textuality. It is this expressionistic feature, in combination with the play's episodic structure, that explains the difficulties posed for the director and audience in performance.

In *Usted también podrá disfrutar de ella*, Diosdado continues her attack on the consumer society: the capitalist manipulation of the masses and the exploitation of women. The "Her" of the title refers to a perfume whose advertising promotion features a discreetly nude model. When the perfume becomes connected in the media with the deaths of several children, the model, Fanny, becomes the object of widespread animosity. Javier, a reporter who goes to interview her, briefly becomes her lover. Disillusioned with life, he erroneously believes that she will commit suicide. He writes the story of her destroyed life, then kills himself. But Javier's suicide may also be viewed as the response to a midlife crisis, the irrational act of a man who sees himself as a failure. His negativism contrasts with the cheerful and constructive outlook of the photographer Manolo—a character reminiscent of Pepe in *Olvida los tambores*—or with the greater endurance and understanding of Javier's wife, Celia, and the model, Fanny. Once again Diosdado has depicted her female characters as stronger and more resilient than their male counterparts, and has created an ideal male figure, Manolo, who incarnates the kind of sensitivity that has often been identified as feminine.

Usted también podrá disfrutar de ella is a structurally innovative work whose action encompasses six locations at five moments in time. The scenes from the past are evoked in expressionistic fashion by a narrator who is investigating the death. The narrator's psychological analysis offers an exploration of an individual's state of mind that would lead to suicide. The result is a theatrical equivalent of the kind of multistrand subjective novel frequently associated in postwar Spain with women writers.

Diosdado's final play of the 1970s appeared within a year of Franco's death and may be seen as a science fiction allegory of Spain's future. The setting of *Y de Cachemira, chales* is a department store that has become a comfortable refuge for three survivors of an atomic war. The elderly Juan assures his two young companions that there is no life outside the store, but the unexpected arrival of another character, Dani, has a radicalizing effect and places Juan's assertion in doubt. Ultimately the patriarchal figure Juan dies, and the others flee to freedom and the unknown. Diosdado deconstructs Juan's binary opposition (known/unknown, safety/danger) and suggests, as she had in *El Okapi*, that the complacent materialism of Francoist Spain had stifled the nation's development in the postwar period.

In some ways *Cuplé* picks up the metaphor of Spain after Franco where *Y de Cachemira, chales* left off. The patriarchal figure has already died when the action begins, but there are no easy solutions for the survivors. Carmen, the role created by Diosdado, is a middle-aged woman who has inherited her longtime lover's wealth but has never had the freedom to live her own life. The fast-moving first act, like that of *Olvida los tambores*, is built on classic comic devices: mistaken identities and role reversals, including sex roles. For example, Carmen's new "maid," Grau, turns out to be a disillusioned former history teacher who, finding himself unemployed, has resorted to domestic service. Carmen has given up her career as a nightclub singer to fulfill the traditional, stay-at-home role; her lover's second wife, Leni, is a young radical involved in the Green movement. The inversion of traditional sex roles notwithstanding, the text's criticism primarily pinpoints economic and political themes: unemployment, exploitation of workers, terrorist acts (sometimes by the capitalists themselves) and the diversion of Spanish capital to Swiss banks.

While Diosdado focused on the elderly in *El Okapi*, her concern for young people and their particular problems appears in several of her works, including *Olvida los tambores* and episodes from her television series. *Los ochenta son nuestros* differs from these in having a cast that consists solely of teenagers. In its theatrical structure the play is somewhat related to *Usted también podrá disfrutar de ella* and *Los comuneros*: Two characters in the present evoke scenes from the past that will clarify what led up to a death.

From a feminist perspective, *Los ochenta son nuestros* is of interest because of its focus on the young people's questioning of their own identities, including their sexuality and their relationships with each other and with their parents. The play openly deals with rape and how an act of sexual assault can affect the victim and her friends. Below this surface thematic level, and perhaps more significant, is Diosdado's continued deconstruction of binary oppositions. The liberal/conservative dichotomy, exposed in earlier works, here finds expression in terms of social and economic conflict: prejudice based on class differences and the fear that privileged members of society may have of marginal groups.

The upper-middle-class characters in *Los ochenta son nuestros* vary widely in their concern for humanity. At one extreme, Miguel has befriended El Barbas, a homeless drug addict. At the other, José is so hostile to those outside his social class and, indeed, to anyone who is different, that he has contributed to the death of Miguel's friend and ultimately kills his own friend Rafa accidentally. The violence-prone José incarnates the rigid us/them, good/bad mentality that has become associated with patriarchy and machismo. His attitude, like that of the boy king in *Los comuneros*, can lead only to death. The play overtly contradicts José's simplistic view of El Barbas as "the other." More subtly, however, the play portrays not only the young women but also the liberal, sympathetic male characters as rejecting machismo in some way. The heterosexual Miguel has a nurturing attitude toward El Barbas. Juan Gabriel, Rafa's older brother, has been strongly attracted to Miguel and, at the least, is bisexual. Rafa, reminiscent of related characters in *Olvida los tambores* and *Usted también podrá disfrutar de ella*, is a quasi-androgynous peacemaker.

In *Camino de plata*, like the *Anillos de oro* television series, the emphasis is on personal relationships. The role played by Diosdado in this stage play is that of Paula, a housewife in her early forties who is given "early retirement" by a husband who has decided to divorce her. His response to her depression is to send her to a psychiatrist, Fernando. The gradual evolution of Paula follows a typical pattern of feminist consciousness raising for a displaced homemaker. Once she establishes her need for self-realization, she is able to gain her independence, emotionally and financially.

Like the frame story of *Anillos de oro*, *Camino de plata* deals with a professional relationship that turns into love. In the television series, the protagonist is widowed unexpectedly and ultimately marries her law partner, a younger man characterized by cheerfulness and sensitivity. In *Camino de plata*, after she ceases to be his patient, Paula becomes Fernando's lover. When her ex-husband eventually wants her back, Paula cannot return to her former life. She rejects the security of a conventional family to be with Fernando.

Paula's will to rebuild her life is reminiscent of Fanny's strength in *Usted también podrá disfrutar de ella* and Lola's resolve in *Anillos de oro*. Diosdado's female characters may go through periods of depression, but they invariably find the means to reconstruct their lives. Fernando, like Paula, is capable of making mistakes and succumbing to self-doubt. There is a ring of authenticity in both these characters and the contemporary situations in which they find themselves.

The divorce cases of *Anillos de oro* and *Camino de plata* highlight male/female relationships and sex roles, a theme that in fact permeates much of Diosdado's theater, starting with the two married couples in *Olvida los tambores* and continuing through the play performed in 1990–91, "Trescientos veintiuno, trescientos veintidos." In particular, she has repeatedly focused on men who face a midlife crisis when they find that they have not achieved their professional ambitions.

In this latest work, Diosdado once again introduces an androgynous male character, Jorge, who, in a classic reversal of sex roles, reveals on his wedding night that he is a virgin—and that he has strong bisexual tendencies. Variations on this sensitive male character appear in *Usted también podrá disfrutar de ella*, *Anillos de oro*, *Los ochenta son nuestros*, and *Camino de plata* and attest to Diosdado's ability to create male characters who challenge patriarchal norms.

SURVEY OF CRITICISM

Diosdado's prize-winning first play, *Olvida los tambores*, enjoyed immediate box office success. In choosing it for his annual anthology of the best Spanish plays of the season, F. C. Sainz de Robles announced that critics had unanimously hailed the work for its literary values and its treatment of contemporary social themes. Although in fact there was unanimous agreement on Diosdado's impeccable craftsmanship, there were dissenting voices with respect to the play's content. Writing for *Razón y Fe*, Florencio Segura questioned whether this could be called "young theater" and hastened to identify the work as a "comedy of manners," comparing it with the theater of Jacinto Benavente (1866–1954).

The division in critical opinion became more pronounced with subsequent plays, including Diosdado's second major hit, *Usted también podrá disfrutar de ella*. While on the one hand Sainz de Robles praised the treatment of human discontent and anguish, and declared Diosdado to be one of the best playwrights in the contemporary Spanish theater, some critics shrugged the work off as a "well-made play." Fernando Lázaro Carreter, theater critic for *Gaceta Ilustrada*, astutely observed that the formal perfection of Diosdado's texts tended to evoke the erroneous impression that her message, too, was conformist.

There is a paucity of scholarly theater criticism in Spain, and what does appear tends to ignore Diosdado. In his 490-page *El teatro desde 1936* (1989), César Oliva devotes only six lines to Diosdado, labeling her work "bourgeois comedy" (458). Eduardo Haro Tecglen, theater critic for *El País*, Spain's most important newspaper, focuses primarily on her commercial success. He links *Cuplé* with comedies by playwrights in vogue in the 1950s and 1960s, and includes *Camino de plata* among "works to make the bourgeoisie laugh" (22). Writing for the

American journal *Estreno*, Eduardo Galán calls this last text melodramatic and filled with concessions to a lower-middle-class audience.

Diosdado's recent works have fared better in the pages of *El Público*, a monthly publication subsidized by the Ministry of Culture. To find serious studies of contemporary Spain's major woman dramatist, however, one must turn to Hispanists in the United States. This is perhaps true in part because of the American scholars' greater objectivity, but even more so because of a strong American focus on feminist studies and contemporary theater. In his early assessment, Farris Anderson found that Diosdado's theater effectively captured the emptiness of contemporary society. In the plays of the 1970s, Ana María Fagundo has found an existential preoccupation with transcendental problems posed in today's world. Concentrating on *Usted también podrá disfrutar de ella*, Joan Cain has emphasized the playwright's mastery of theatrical techniques.

Approaching the works from a feminist perspective, Iride Lamartina-Lens has analyzed sex roles in several plays, concluding that Diosdado's women figures incarnate strength of character. In a series of studies beginning in 1977, Phyllis Zatlin has highlighted Diosdado's innovative approaches to theatrical structure as well as her deconstruction of traditional sex roles. Collectively, the American studies, in contrast to the passing judgment of Spanish critics, point to a theater of substance that illuminates a changing Spanish social reality.

BIBLIOGRAPHY

Works by Ana Diosdado

Plays

Olvida los tambores. Madrid: Escelicer, 1972. *Teatro español, 1970–71*. Ed. F. C. Sainz de Robles. Madrid: Aguilar, 1972. 1–75.

El Okapi. Madrid: Escelicer, 1972. *Teatro español, 1972–73*. Ed. F. C. Sainz de Robles. Madrid: Aguilar, 1974. 1–72.

Los comuneros. Madrid: Ediciones MK, 1974. Madrid: Preyson, 1983.

Usted también podrá disfrutar de ella. *Teatro español 1973–74*. Ed. F. C. Sainz de Robles. Madrid: Ediciones MK, 1975. Madrid: Aguilar, 1975. 1–78.

Y de Cachemira, chales. Madrid: Preyson, 1983. [Staged in 1976]

Anillos de oro. 2 vols. Madrid: Espasa-Calpe, 1985.

Cuplé. Madrid: Ediciones Antonio Machado, 1988.

Los ochenta son nuestros. Madrid: Ediciones MK, 1988.

Camino de plata. Madrid: Ediciones Antonio Machado, 1990.

"Trescientos veintiuno, trescientos veintidós." Madrid: Sociedad General de Autores de España. [Forthcoming]

Novels

En cualquier lugar, no importa cuando. Barcelona: Planeta, 1965.

"Campanas que aturden." 1969. [Unpublished]

Los ochenta son nuestros. Barcelona: Plaza y Janés, 1986.

Television Programs

Juan y Manuela.
Anillos de oro.
Segunda enseñanza.
Yo, la juez.

Essays

El teatro por dentro: Ceremonia, representación, fenómeno colectivo. Barcelona: Aula
    Abierta Salvat, 1981.

Adaptations and Translations

Casa de muñecas. Madrid: Ediciones MK, 1983. [Adaptation of *A Doll's House* by
    Henrik Ibsen]
La gata sobre el tejado de zinc caliente. Madrid: Ediciones MK, 1984. [Trans. of *Cat
    on a Hot Tin Roof* by Tennessee Williams]

Translation

"The Okapi." Trans. Marion Peter Holt. [Sponsored by the National Endowment for
    the Arts; unpublished]

Works about Ana Diosdado

Anderson, Farris. "From Protest to Resignation." *Estreno* 2.2 (1976): 29–32.
Bremón, Anunchi. Interview with Diosdado. *El País Semanal* 1 (July 1984): 10–14.
Cain, Joan. "Ana Diosdado: Winner of the Fastenrath Prize." *Letras Femeninas* 5.1
    (1979): 54–63.
Fagundo, Ana María. "El teatro de Ana Diosdado." *Alaluz* 18.2 (1986): 51–59.
Galán, Eduardo. "Cartelera." *Estreno* 15.2 (1989): 44.
Haro Tecglen, Eduardo. "Obras para que la burguesía se ría." *El País* 3 Oct. 1988,
    Weekly international edition: 22.
Lamartina-Lens, Iride. "Sex Roles in the Theater of Ana Diosdado." Fifth Annual
    Wichita State University Conference on Foreign Languages. Wichita, April 1988.
Lázaro Carreter, Fernando. Rev. of *Usted también podrá disfrutar de ella. Teatro español,
    1973–1974*. Ed. F. C. Sainz de Robles. Madrid: Aguilar, 1975. 7–8.
Oliva, César. *El teatro desde 1936*. Madrid: Alhambra, 1989. 458.
Santa-Cruz, Lola. Interview with Diosdado. *El Público* 39 (1986): 28–30.
Segura, Florencio. " 'Olivida los tambores,' ¿un teatro joven?" *Razón y Fe* 879 (1970):
    347–50.
Zatlin-Boring, Phyllis. "Ana Diosdado and the Contemporary Spanish Theater." *Estreno*
    10.2 (1984): 37–40.
———. "The Theater of Ana Diosdado." *Estreno* 3.1 (1977): 13–17.
———. "Traditional Sex Roles in the Theatre of Ana Diosdado." *Mid-Hudson Language
    Studies* 10 (1987): 71–77.

LIDIA FALCÓN O'NEILL
(b. 1935)

Gloria Feiman Waldman

BIOGRAPHY

Lidia Falcón was born in Madrid on December 13, 1935, as bombs fell on the city only months before the Spanish Civil War officially began. Her politics were shaped by her militant family of outspoken writers, feminists, and revolutionaries. Her grandmother, Regina de Lamo, whose pen name was Nora Avante, was an anarchist, trade-unionist, avowed feminist, and political companion of Companys, the president of the Generalitat of Catalonia during the Spanish Republic. Her mother, Enriqueta O'Neill, was the writer Regina Flavio who published thousands of articles on politics, fashion, and women's issues, and wrote detective novels, romances, radio scripts, and even action comics to earn a living, just as Falcón would later do. Her aunt, Carlota O'Neill, was the well-known dramatist and editor of *Nosotras*, the Communist Party publication during the war. Falcón was indeed born a feminist.

Her father, César Falcón, was a Peruvian journalist and writer who had worked in Spain since 1926, covered the war, and founded an agitprop theater group. He fled Spain with the defeat of the Republicans; his daughter never heard from him again. Because of their high political profile, three-year-old Lidia and her family of women—her mother, aunt, grandmother, and two cousins—moved to Barcelona to escape recognition and to find a way to survive in postwar Spain. By that time, Falcón's grandfather had been killed in a bombing, her aunt Carlota had been sentenced to four years in prison, and her uncle Virgilio Leret, who had been in charge of the Republican naval base in Melilla, had been executed.

Falcón recounts the tragic circumstances that defined her early years from 1939 to 1949 in *Los hijos de los vencidos* (1978; "Children of the Defeated"), a poignant and disquieting narrative that describes an era of repression, poverty, and the need to live a double life. In an interview Falcón portrayed herself as a "mischievous child, very alive, pathologically optimistic" (Vallina 31), who wrote her first articles defending equal rights for women when she was just twelve years old, and published her first short story when she was eighteen. In 1953 she married Alfred Borrás, who abandoned her three years later, leaving her with a five-month-old son, Carlos Enrique, and a two-year-old daughter, Regina. Not only did Borrás abrogate all sense of responsibility to his family, but he also refused to grant Falcón an annulment or a separation. Since she was neither a widow nor separated, she had no legal status in Spanish society at that time, and was not even considered the legal guardian of her children.

Falcón wanted to study medicine or pharmacy but did not have the economic means to do so, a recurrent situation in her life. Instead she studied dramatic arts at the Instituto del Teatro in Barcelona and in 1957 began to study law and journalism, eventually receiving degrees in both fields. During those years of virtually no sleep, surviving on anchovy sandwiches and amphetamines (Bayo 66), she worked as a proofreader of manuscripts, translator, model, bookseller, waitress, and telephone operator while simultaneously writing pulp novels, westerns, and war comics under a pseudonym. Falcón met Eliseo Bayo, her companion for twenty-four years, in journalism school in 1959, the same year she joined the clandestine Unified Socialist Party of Catalonia (PSUC). She completed her legal studies with a specialization in family law, and won the Durán y Bas Prize of the Bar Association of Barcelona. She opened her own practice and taught at the university until she was dismissed by her male mentor, who decided that women should not teach law.

During the 1960s Falcón began to forge her reputation as Spain's most outspoken feminist. The combined example of her political activism and published works speaks of a commitment to women's issues that earned her both public recognition and persecution by the Franco regime. Her first two pioneering works were *Los derechos civiles de la mujer* (1963; "The Civil Rights of Women") and *Los derechos laborales de la mujer* (1964; "The Labor Rights of Women"). During those same years, in her law practice she defended political prisoners, workers, and labor leaders as well as women in matrimonial cases. In 1969 *Mujer y sociedad. Análisis de un fenómeno reaccionario* ("Women and Society. Analysis of a Reactionary Phenomenon") finally appeared, after more than a year under government censorship. It was an extraordinary text for its time, making available in a single volume a wide range of material on women and history, women and politics, women and literature, women and sociology, and women and revolution.

In 1972 Falcón was arrested with her daughter Regina, seventeen years old at the time, for publishing and distributing antifascist literature. She was sent to La Trinidad prison in Barcelona, from which she was released after six months because her mother had committed suicide, ultimately frustrated and discouraged by a life of political and economic struggle. This prison experience, together with her subsequent nine-month stay in the infamous Yeseriás prison in Madrid in 1974, where she was beaten and kicked in the liver, formed the basis of Falcon's dramatic exposé, *En el infierno. Ser mujer en las cárceles de España* (1974; "In Hell. To Be a Woman in the Jails of Spain").

The reasons for Falcon's 1974 incarceration are more politically complex than the events that precipitated her first imprisonment. Together with twenty-one other Spanish intellectuals, including Eliseo Bayo, Eva Forest, and Alfonso Sastre, she was accused of pro-ETA (Basque terrorist organization) activity and implicated in both the ETA assassination of Prime Minister Luis Carrero Blanco and the bombing of the Cafeteria Rolando in Madrid, a spot frequented by police. It was there on September 13, 1974 that nine people were killed and some sixty wounded in what was deemed by some an attempted right-wing frame-up of the Left, and by others, an ETA-inspired action against the police. *Viernes y 13 en la calle del Correo* (1981; "Friday the Thirteenth on Correo Street") recounts Falcón's version of the nightmare that she and Bayo lived through from 1974 to 1975 and her release after nine months, with the crime still unsolved. Newspapers worldwide covered the events, and Falcón and the others were catapulted to international fame.

Falcón returned from prison to a Spain where, although Franco languished for five more months, the feminist movement had been born and had taken full advantage of the United Nations' declaration of 1975 as the International Year of the Woman. For the first time since the formation of the Spanish Republic, women were marching in the streets and demanding the rights that had been theirs under the Constitution of 1931: divorce, contraception, abortion, and child care. With the emergence from clandestinity of political parties that had long awaited Franco's death, the prolific and tireless Falcón launched a frontal attack on the machismo, favoritism, and reformism of the Spanish Communist Party. In her novel *Es largo esperar callado* (1975; "The Long Silent Wait"), Athenea, the outspoken heroine, is a doppelgänger for Falcón: honest, direct, stubborn, and willing to face isolation from the Left in order to maintain her revolutionary integrity.

Combining her background in journalism with her feminist commitment, Falcón had as her immediate goal the creation of a publication that would encourage open debate, offer a feminist point of view on national and international issues, and stimulate the creation of a feminist culture. In 1976 she founded *Vindicación Feminista*, thereby incurring three government injunctions against herself as publisher and Carmen Alcalde as editor, for defending abortion and attacking the church. These injunctions, common during the Franco era, continued during the transition to democracy. The police could fine the publication, close it, and/or arrest the personnel. None of these obstacles permanently discouraged Falcón or ever caused her to alter the content or tone of her publications, as is evident, for example, in the title of a 1978 *Vindicación Feminista* article, "The Spanish Constitution—Neither Here, nor There—The Penis Continues to Be King," which reveals not only her outrageous style but also her highly critical view of post–Franco Spain, where the dictator may have died but the patriarchal structure continued.

Vindicación Feminista closed in 1979 for economic reasons, and in the same year Falcón began publishing the theoretical journal *Poder y Libertad* and also founded the Vindicación Feminista clubs in Barcelona and later in Madrid, as places where women could attend lectures, seek psychological and legal counseling, and simply gather. The publishing house Vindicación Feminista Publicaciones was also created in 1979, and continues to publish both national and international titles.[1] In addition, in 1979 Falcón made what is perhaps her most dramatic contribution to Spanish feminism, the founding of the first feminist party in Spain, the Partido Feminista, which was finally legalized in 1981, after two years of petitioning the government for recognition.

Falcón, who had studied to be an actress, always had a special predilection for the theater. Her mother was an actress, her aunt Carlota was a playwright, and her father founded the political theater company Teatro Proletario (contemporaneous with Federico García Lorca's La Barraca), for which he wrote the political pieces that Lidia's mother presented on stage. Falcón's overtly feminist theater, unique in Spain, dramatizes the plight of Spanish women, often taking its plot line from her own legal cases or from prominent cases reported in the press. Although only two of her eleven plays have been published—*No moleste, calle y pague, señora* (1984; "Don't Bother Us, Shut up and Pay, Lady") and *Tu único amor* (1991; "Your Only Love")—many have been performed. In 1982 an abbreviated version of her play "Las mujeres caminaron con el fuego del siglo" ("The Women Walked with the Fire of the Century") was performed at the International Theater Festival in Athens. The full-length version has been performed in Puerto Rico, New York, Montclair State College in New Jersey (where she was writer in residence in 1985), and SUNY Buffalo. "Tres idiotas españolas" ("Three Idiotic Spanish Women"), an adaptation of *Cartas a una idiota española*, (1974; "Letters to an Idiotic Spanish Woman"), was part of the 1987 International Feminist Theater Festival organized by Falcón in Madrid. Her theatrical production has consistently been a powerful vehicle for the expression of her major concerns.

Falcón became well known to North American feminists after her 1982 American college tour, during which she lectured at over thirty universities. She has subsequently returned to speak on various occasions, including events at the PEN American Center, the United Nations, the City University of New York Academy for the Humanities and Sciences, the International Women Playwrights Conference at SUNY Buffalo, and St. Johns University in New York, where she was on a panel with Gloria Steinem and Matilda Cuomo, wife of the governor. She has traveled to the former Soviet Union, Japan, Venezuela, Israel, and Canada to lecture; to Brussels for the Tribunal on Crimes Against Women in 1976; and to Nairobi, Kenya, to participate in the United Nations–sponsored

Decade for Women Conference in 1985. She was officially honored by the Senate of Puerto Rico in 1984 for her contribution to feminism and her efforts to protect women against crimes of violence.

There have been many changes in Lidia Falcón's life. In 1986 she moved from Barcelona to Madrid and began to study painting and drawing. We see the flourishing of this artistic expression in the illustrations for articles in *Poder y Libertad*, the book cover for Kate Millett's *En pleno vuelo* (1991; *Flying*), and the poster for the 1987 International Feminist Theater Festival.

In 1990 Falcón closed the Vindicación Feminista Club in Madrid due to economic pressures and moved to the medieval mountain village of Bustarviejo, an hour from Madrid. Her production, however, has never wavered. Tireless, she fights with the zeal of a true revolutionary, building daily on the acts of the past, without personal reward as her incentive but with the satisfaction of seeing realized some of the vindications she has fought for throughout her adult life. Despite lingering physical ailments from the terrible times in jail and the toll on her body of those difficult early years, Falcón shows no signs of slowing down.

MAJOR THEMES

Falcón's production is truly prodigious and still growing, a new book appearing almost every year. In a society that rejects serious theoretical exploration, Lidia Falcón writes scholarly, elaborately researched, and thoughtful books that discuss the hard questions of contemporary feminist theory and political thought. Her books indeed fall under the category of critical and more critical. Is her description of women in Spanish prisons in the 1970s less dramatic than Concepción Arenal's? Is her sardonic look at Spain and its foibles any less biting than Mariano José de Larra's? Are her real-life accounts of personal betrayals and political deception (*Es largo*, *Hijos*) any less complex than Francisco de Quevedo's or Joaquín Costa's? Are her many books and thousands of articles documenting her pain and rage over her country any less anguished than those of Miguel de Unamuno or Antonio Machado? Are they any less anguished than those of her female forebears, including her own mother and grandmother, who patiently yet furiously filled the pages of Spanish dailies with their words of admonishment and exhortation to the small-minded men in power who eternally controlled and limited female horizons?

For Falcón, feminism is the revolution of the 1990s, the only coherent political philosophy that will lead us into the twenty-first century. Her books and her life center on this premise. The central question that is first posed in *Mujer y sociedad* is why have women, independent of their religious beliefs, geographic situation, or the period in which they have lived, found themselves and still find themselves without civil, political, and social rights? Falcón addresses this question in both *La razón feminista* volumes. *La razón feminista, 1. La mujer como clase social y económica. El modo de producción doméstico* (1981; "Feminist Reason, 1.

Women as a Social and Economic Class. Means of Domestic Production'') posits that women are a separate and exploited class, and as such should organize their own fight for liberation. She has astutely said that it is one thing to belong to a class, and quite another to have class consciousness.

La razón feminista, 2. La reproducción humana (1982; "Feminist Reason, 2. Human Reproduction") deals with the exploitation of women with regard to reproduction. Falcón analyzes how reproduction has been viewed cross-culturally and over the centuries, and she challenges the general acceptance of "maternal love" with numerous statistics about the history of infanticide, aggression, and child abuse from the Middle Ages to the International Year of the Child in 1979. She arrives at the conclusion that the myth of mother love is operant in direct relation to demographic exigencies (pt. 5, "Amor de madre"). Starting with the premise that women expend their health and time in reproduction, Falcón offers the radical proposal that women's labor in this area should be financially compensated and that not to compensate for work done is a question of politics, not of biology. In this same chapter, she elaborately describes contemporary theories and practices of genetic engineering and reiterates the position she has staunchly maintained over the years: that in vitro reproduction represents women's ultimate liberation.

It often seems that Falcón has been singlehandedly prodding and pushing Spain into the future vis-à-vis women's issues. Her 1991 book, *Violencia contra la mujer* ("Violence Against Women"), is the first of its kind in a country that, according to the author, "has never undertaken a systematic study of the extent and cause of the violence it perpetuates against women" (25). Falcón uses firsthand cases as well as extensive documentation to reveal how women are abused throughout the world to keep them in a state of subordination.

Falcón's investigation of women's relation to political power and the apoliticization of the feminist movement, the first of its kind in Spain, was presented in *Mujer y poder político. Fundamentos de la crisis de objetivos e ideología del Movimiento Feminista* (1992; "Women and Political Power. Reasons for the Crisis in the Objectives and Ideology of the Women's Movement"), her doctoral dissertation written for the Universidad Autónoma de Madrid. It is an exhaustive analysis of the evolution of the feminist struggle from the French Revolution to the present, documenting the opposition to feminism by the workers' movement and the socialist movement, and the long fight that women have had to wage in order to be recognized as workers, citizens, and political subjects. Confronted with the dilemma of reform or revolution, Falcón insists the answer must be reform *and* revolution (504). As Falcón sees it, the major problem with feminism today is that it has no political vision: "The feminist movement is making the same errors as the workers' movement. It is concentrating on social services, cultural enrichment, classes, conferences, books and publications, period'' (qtd. in Prego 54–55).

Falcón moves easily between fiction and nonfiction, and between a strong critique of inherent structures of male dominance found in Spanish society and a sense of optimism toward possibilities for future change. She situates her novel *El juego de la piel* (1983; "Skin Games") in what is for her an unusual venue—

Europe during the 1970s. In it she describes the communes, drug addiction, and juvenile delinquency that the heroine experiences until she returns to Barcelona, where she finds herself through the incipient feminist movement. The novel *Rupturas* (1985; "Breakups") is the Spanish equivalent of Marilyn French's *The Women's Room*. Situated in a university setting, it explores Spain's era of transition to socialism, feminism, and a new sense of possibility, through the lens of the forty-five-year-old apolitical female protagonist.

Falcón's fiction may be read as thinly veiled social history. Each work is a pretext to examine another facet of Spanish society: the drug-addicted and disaffected youth of the 1970s (*El juego*); the sexist and power-hungry Communist Party, and its betrayal of the real struggle to end fascism in Spain (*Es largo*); the beginnings of the feminist movement in the 1970s and its effect on a middle-class, apolitical married woman (*Rupturas*); and, finally, the clandestine world of anti-Franco activities in her last book, *Camino sin retorno* (1992; "No Way Back"). This novel incorporates many of Falcón's previous themes and centers on a five-hour conversation between Elisa and her ex-husband, Arnau, in which they explore leftist politics, male deception, women who love too much, self-discovery, and the recognition that women need each other to move to the next stage of personal and national consciousness.

Camino sin retorno, Falcón's best fictional work to date, and the most novelistic, multidimensional, and stylistically sophisticated, establishes an internal rhythm and maintains a complex narrative structure. Elisa engages in a collage of conversations with the major secondary characters that moves smoothly from the present to the past and back to the present, but not before exposing Elisa's conservative childhood and adolescence, imbued with traditional religious training, her ten-year militancy in an offshoot of the Communist Party, and her incarceration in a Spanish prison. Falcón cleverly weaves together characters and events alluded to in her previous books. The middle-aged revolutionary and staunch feminist named Octubre, falsely imprisoned for her involvement in the Calle Correo bombing, recalls Falcón herself, and Elisenda is reminiscent of the drug-addicted hippy protagonist of *El juego* who eventually embraces feminism. The reader is also reacquainted with some of the women whose dramatic stories were told in *En el infierno* as well as the unacknowledged female militants from *Es largo esperar*. This novel, which only an insider like Falcón could have written, is her homage to the militant women who were tortured in Franco's jails and psychiatric wards, never offered leadership positions in their own party, never acknowledged in the new democratic Spain, and never vindicated.

It has been revealed through personal correspondence that two new books are scheduled for publication in 1993: the second volume of her memoirs, "El amor acosado (1949–1956)" ("Troubled Love"), which uses her adolescence, young married life, and separation as a backdrop for an account of female repression during the Franco years, and a novel, *Postmodernos*, a profound and biting description of the defeat of the Left in Spain after Franco's death.

One of Falcón's major contributions to Spanish feminism is the internationalization of the parameters of its struggle. Falcón is an advocate for the world's women, and her writing encompasses this broad perspective. Her speaking engagements at academic centers throughout the United States and in other parts of the globe have served to present not only her controversial theses but also the Spanish female circumstance to new audiences. Personifying the adage that no one is a prophet in her own land, Falcón has garnered more generous recognition abroad for her stewardship of Spain's feminist movement since the 1970s than in her own land. Perhaps this is because she tells the stories no one wants to hear. Certainly not the Spanish male, chastised in her series of critical reflections, *El alboroto español* (1984; ''Spanish Uproar''), and her controversial indictment of macho Spanish reality, *El varón español a la búsqueda de su identidad* (1986; ''The Spanish Male in Search of His Identity''). Her writings have marginalized her from the socialist as well as the official feminist culture. Falcón, who has been called ''*the* opposition'' (B.B. 25), has persistently maintained women's issues in the public eye and continues to espouse vanguard positions that have yet to be embraced by the mainstream.

SURVEY OF CRITICISM

It is unforgivable that a writer of the stature of Lidia Falcón has received so little serious critical attention. Her Marxist-Leninist dialectical approach to radical feminism, not in favor these days, proposes a total overthrow of patriarchal structures in order to usher in a new era where women will not do two-thirds of the world's work, yet receive only 7 percent of the world's wages and only 1 percent of the world's wealth.

The bulk of the criticism about her work can be found in leading Spanish newspapers and magazines, where the line between commentary on the book and commentary on the author's personality is often indistinguishable. Since her writing is so extreme and confrontational, the critical response has been equally extreme. A sampling of the newspaper criticism that Falcón and her work have been subjected to since she first started publishing in the 1960s reveals the biases inherent in the general discourse about women in the Spanish press. The criticism of the 1960s included appreciations of her physical appearance and attractiveness—by both male and female journalists—as a significant detail to complement her serious interest in women's rights. Once the critics, generally male, were faced with her growing body of work, they reluctantly had to deal with its feminist content, at least summarily. And once they recognized Falcón's virulent attacks on patriarchy and its manifestations in Spanish society, they became increasingly hostile in their reviews.

Some of that early newspaper criticism was anonymous, as in the following examples from a 1968 article referring to a talk Falcón gave in Madrid on the sexual behavior of the Spanish male: ''This young lawyer who practices in Barcelona, where she collected the data for her survey, treaded on old 'taboos' with the same sweetness and simplicity that a housewife would use to break an egg . . . realizing important work on behalf of women . . . while on the other hand, showing no feminist leanings'' (''El comportamiento sexual del hombre español'' n.pag.). In a 1969 interview about *Mujer y sociedad* in the Barcelona daily *Tele/eXpres*, María Cruz Hernández first establishes Falcón's place in Spanish feminism and then continues, ''The fact that Lidia Falcón, besides being smart is *guapa* (good-looking), is stupendous propaganda for all the women who fight for women's rights'' (''Tres formas de rebelión de la mujer'' n.p.).

In 1970 author Miguel Delibes wrote what he certainly must have thought was a polite review of *Mujer y sociedad* but what a feminist reader would call patronizing. Unfortunately, it is representative of the tone of much of the pseudoserious criticism of Falcón's work: ''From my point of view Lidia Falcón tends to dramatize everything a bit . . . her book is indisputably intelligent, but perhaps too fervent, excessively passionate'' (''La emancipación de la mujer'' n.p.).

One can compare María José Obiol's generally dismissive review of *Rupturas* in 1986, where he admonishingly says that the ''flawed novel could, however, be read, and maybe even agreed with, if the language were not, as always, so acidic'' (n.pag.), with feminist critic Elizabeth Starčević's 1987 analysis of the same book. Starčević alludes to the novel's complexity, and sees it as a ''significant link in Falcón's continual endeavor to use her writings as a means of engaging the reader in a process of discovering aspects of women's lives hitherto absent from literature'' (177). Starčević recognizes how Falcón uses fiction to elaborate her theoretical ideas about feminism and observes that although the author offers no specific solutions, she does posit feminism as the arena for change and an ideology with which to work (187).

In Spain the more serious critics of Falcón's work have been Ana María Moix; Carmen Alcalde, who has written stirring prologues to *Cartas* and *En el infierno*; María José Ragué-Arias, who introduced Falcón's feminist theater to a North American audience in the highly informative 1984 *Estreno* issue dedicated to Spanish female dramatists; Carlos París, who wrote the prologue to *Mujer y poder político* and incisive newspaper articles; Marisa Híjar, who described Falcón in the pages of the widely read *Diario 16* as ''a tenacious and impenitent pen that has appeared in the country's press in a continuous way''; and Rosa Montero, who said that ''in Falcón's journalistic writing there is a fullness and brilliance'' (qtd. in Híjar n.p.).

North American Hispanists have studied Falcón's fiction (Starčević, Waldman) and her theater (O'Connor, Waldman), have translated her (Gazarian, Waldman), and have interviewed her (Gabriele, Gazarian, Levine and Waldman, García Castro and Nichols). North American journalists have captured her singularity and selfless dedication to redress wrongs against women (Berliner, Connell, Stephen, Morrissey, and Douglas). In Puerto Rico, journalists Jane Ransom and Eneid Routté-Gómez, academician Margarita Benítez, and feminist author Margarita Ostolaza have publicly recognized the undeniable influence Falcón has exercised in revitalizing the feminist movement there.

As the leading feminist in Spain, Falcón refuses to compromise her vision of a world where women are equal. She has been criticized by both men and women for being too radical, too strident, too passionate, a diva (Marqués 47), a witch, a man hater, "mujer tentacular" (B.B. 25 "a tentacled woman"), the "Lilith of Spain," the "Shiva of Spain," and the "falcon of Spanish feminism."

Falcón's place is ensured in the "Hall of Fame of International Feminism." For her, "Feminism is the eternally betrayed revolution, a revolution that has always been postponed" ("Spain: Women Are the Conscience of Our Country" 626). It is Falcón's lifework to make that revolution real, through her written and spoken words and through her example of tireless dedication. Her prophetic words, "The future will be feminist or it will not be at all," in her article, "Hispanic Women Playwrights," embody Lidia Falcón's philosophy.

NOTE

1. Vindicación Feminista Publicaciones has published the latest editions of fifteen of Falcón's books and the following works by non-Spanish feminists: *Paternidad voluntaria*, Hildegart (1985); *El poder de las mujeres y el estado del bienestar*, Helga María Hernes (1990); *SCUM Manifiesto*, Valerie Solanas (1990); *El derecho de la mujer*, Tove Stang Dahl (1991); *En pleno vuelo*, Kate Millett (1991); and *Mujeres del mundo*, ed. Robin Morgan (1992). It also distributes other works by feminist authors.

BIBLIOGRAPHY

Major Works by Lidia Falcón

Novels

Cartas a una idiota española. Barcelona: Dirosa, 1974. Madrid: Vindicación Feminista Publicaciones, 1989.
Es largo esperar callado. Barcelona: Pomaire, 1975. Barcelona: Hacer-Vindicación, 1984.
El juego de la piel. Barcelona: Argos Vergara, 1983.
Rupturas. Barcelona: Fontanella, 1985.
Camino sin retorno. Barcelona: Anthropos, 1992.
Postmodernos. Madrid: Ediciones Libertarias, 1993.

Plays

"En el futuro." 1957. [Unpublished]
"Un poco de nieve blanca." 1958. [Unpublished]
"Los que siempre ganan." 1970. [Unpublished]
"Con el siglo." 1982. [Unpublished]
"Dones i Catalunya." 1982. [Unpublished]
"Las mujeres caminaron con el fuego del siglo." 1982. [Unpublished]
"Parid, parid malditas." 1983. [Unpublished]
"Siempre deseé el amor." 1983. [Unpublished]

No moleste, calle y pague, señora. Estreno 10.2 (1984): 28–31. *Dramaturgas españolas de hoy.* Ed. Patricia W. O'Connor. Madrid: Fundamentos, 1988. 59–69.
"La hora más oscura." 1987. [Unpublished]
"Tres idiotas españolas." 1987. [Unpublished]
Tu único amor. Art Teatral 3.3 (1991): 19–24.

Autobiography

Los hijos de los vencidos (1939–1949). Barcelona: Pomaire, 1978. Madrid: Vindicación Feminista Publicaciones, 1989.
Viernes y 13 en la calle del Correo. Barcelona: Planeta, 1981.
"El amor acosado (1949–1956)." [Forthcoming]

Nonfiction Books

Los derechos civiles de la mujer. Barcelona: Nereo, 1963.
Los derechos laborales de la mujer. Madrid: Montecorvo, 1964.
Mujer y sociedad. Análisis de un fenómeno reaccionario. Barcelona: Fontanella, 1969.
En el infierno. Ser mujer en las cárceles de España. Barcelona: Ediciones de Feminismo, 1977.
La razón feminista, 1. La mujer como clase social y económica. El modo de producción doméstico. Barcelona: Fontanella, 1981.
La razón feminista, 2. La reproducción humana. Barcelona: Fontanella, 1982.
El alboroto español. Barcelona, Fontanella, 1984.
El varón español a la búsqueda de su identidad. Barcelona: Plaza y Janés, 1986.
Violencia contra la mujer. Barcelona: Círculo de Lectores, 1991. Madrid: Vindicación Feminista Publicaciones, 1991.
Mujer y poder político. Fundamentos de la crisis de objectivos e ideología del Movimiento Feminista. Madrid: Vindicación Feminista Publicaciones, 1992.

Selected Articles

Falcón has published over one thousand articles since the 1960s in books, all major Spanish newspapers, and magazines on diverse topics of current interest, particularly women and their relationship to national and international issues.
"La opresión de la mujer: una incógnita." *La liberación de la mujer año O.* Barcelona: Gránica, 1977. 45–57.
"Por qué no estrenan las mujeres en España?" *Estreno* 10 (1984): 16–17.
"Spain: Women Are the Conscience of Our Country." Trans. Gloria F. Waldman. *Sisterhood Is Global.* Ed. Robin Morgan. New York: Anchor-Doubleday, 1984. 626–31.
"Carmen Sarmiento o la mirada que perdurará." Prologue. *Los marginados.* By Carmen Sarmiento. Madrid: Servicio de Publicaciones del Ente Público RTVE, 1985. 9–16.
"El castigo de Flora Tristán." *Flora Tristán. Peregrinaciones de una paria.* Ed. José M. Gómez Tabanera. Madrid: Istmo, Colegio Universitario, 1986. lxxxii–lxxxviii.
"El asalto al poder, desde el feminismo." *Poder y Libertad* 8 (1987): 4–6.
"Vindicación Feminista o el ideal compartido." *Revista de Estudios Hispánicos* 22 (1988): 53–65.
"Cincuenta años de lucha." *Poder y Libertad* 11 (1989): 4–9.

"Kate Millet o el escándalo." *Poder y Libertad* 13 (1990): 42–47.

"Pornografía: ni libertad ni sexualidad." *Poder y Libertad* 14 (1990): 38–46.

Prologue. *Viajes a la marginación.* By Carmen Sarmiento. Madrid: Mondadori, 1990. 9–15.

"Hispanic Women Playwrights." Trans. Gloria F. Waldman. *International Women Playwrights: Voices of Identity and Transformation.* Ed. Anna Kay France and P. J. Corso. Metuchen, NJ: Scarecrow Press, 1993.

"Women Playwrights: Identity and Transformation." Trans. Gloria F. Waldman. *International Women Playwrights.* France and Corso.

Translations

Lettres a une idiote espagnole. Trans. Françoise Campo. Paris: Edition des femmes, 1975.

Breve til en Spansk täbe. Trans. Benedicte Wern. Copenhagen: Gyldendal, 1977. [Trans. of *Cartas a una idiota española*]

Enfers. Trans. Françoise Campo. Paris: Edition des femmes, 1979. [Trans. of *En el infierno. Ser mujer en las cárceles de España*]

Works about Lidia Falcón

Alcalde, Carmen. "De condición ¿reaccionaria?" *Destino* 2 Mar. 1968: n.pag.

Balsebre, Armand. "Lidia Falcón. El hombre como enemigo." *Mujer* 10 July 1976: 30–33.

Bayo, Eliseo. "Lidia Falcón. La mujer al poder." *La Gaceta Ilustrada* 1976: 66–71.

B.B. "Lidia Falcón arremete contra todos en *El alboroto español.*" *El Noticiero Universal* 21 Feb. 1985: 25.

Benítez, Margarita. "Lidia Falcón y el feminismo." *El Mundo* (Puerto Rico) 1 May 1983: 12A.

Berliner, Eve. "A Spanish Revolutionary, in New York, Speaks for the World: The Revolutionary Will of Lidia Falcón of Spain." *New York Arts Weekly* 12 Jan. 1983: n.p.

Connell, Noreen. "Feminist Movement in Spain." *NOW—NYS Action Report* (Spring/ Summer 1985): 9.

"El comportamiento sexual del hombre español." *Pueblo* 22 Nov. 1968: n.p.

Cruz Hernández, María. "Los derechos laborales, civiles y políticos de la mujer." *Tele/ eXpres* 2 Aug. 1965: n.p.

———. "Tres formas de rebelión de la mujer." *Tele/eXpres* 11 July 1969: n.p.

Delibes, Miguel. "La emancipación de la mujer." *El Noticiero Universal* 24 Feb. 1970: n.p.

Falcón, Pilar. "Lidia Falcón, feminista de toda la vida." *Diario de Barcelona* 10 Mar. 1984: 18.

Gabriele, John P. "Lidia Falcón y el feminismo español: una entrevista." *Hispania* 74 (1991): 947–50.

García Castro, Mary, and Geraldine Cleary Nichols. "Lidia Falcón y el partido feminista de España: Personalidad, ideas y práctica." *Cuéntame tu Vida. Revista de Mujeres* 10 (1987): 5–13.

Gazarian, Marie-Lise Gautier. "Lidia Falcón." *Interviews with Spanish Writers.* Elmwood Park, IL: Dalkey Archive Press, 1991. 126–36.

Híjar, Marisa. "La catalana cuando escribe . . . ." *Diario 16* 30 Apr. 1981: n.p.

Levine, Linda Gould, and Gloria F. Waldman. "Lidia Falcón." *Feminismo ante el franquismo: entrevistas con feministas de España.* Miami: Ediciones Universal, 1980. 67–85.

Marqués, Josep-Vicent. "Histriónico empaque de una diva." *El País* Oct. 1989: 47–48.

Mieza, Carmen. "Lidia Falcón." *La mujer del español.* Barcelona: Marte, 1977. 164–80.

Moix, Ana. "En el infierno, el cadáver de las flores." *Vindicación Feminista* Sept. 1977: 12.

———. "Lidia Falcón, el feminismo, una alternativa política." *El Viejo Topo* July 1977: 15–18.

———. "Lidia Falcón: la impertinencia de la reflexión." *Vindicación Feminista* Feb. 1977: 10.

Montero, Mayra. "Lidia Falcón o la vindicación de la mujer." *El Mundo* (Puerto Rico) 6 Jan. 1984: 113.

———. "Mujeres." *El Mundo* (Puerto Rico) 3 Mar. 1985: 57.

Morrissey, Caroline, and Carol Anne Douglas. "Feminism in Spain." *Off Our Backs* (Oct. 1982): n.p.

Obiol, María José. "Crónica de sucesos de una mujer." *El País* 27 Feb. 1986: n.p.

O'Connor, Patricia W. "¿Quiénes son las dramaturgas contemporáneas españolas y qué han escrito?" *Estreno* 10 (1984): 9–12.

———. "Women Playwrights in Spain and the Male-Dominated Canon." *Signs* 15.2 (1990): 376–90.

Ostolaza, Margarita. "Así son los hombres." *El Nuevo Día* (Puerto Rico) 7 Feb. 1984: 35.

París, Carlos. "Intrahistoria." *Diario 16* 14 June 1990: n.p.

Porta, Miguel. "Feminismo in vitro." *Leviatán* 11 (1983): 120–30.

Portugal, Ana María. "Lidia Falcón, yo nací feminista." *Viva* Nov. 1987: n.p.

Porcel, Baltasar. "Lidia Falcón en guerra." *Destino* 24 Jan. 1970: 24–25.

Prego, Victoria. "A las feministas nos han desprestigiado." *Elle* Feb. 1990: 53–56.

Ragué-Arias, María José. "Introducción a la obra de Lidia Falcón." *Estreno* 10 (1984): 26–27.

———. "Spain: Feminism in Our Time." *Women's Studies International Quarterly* 4.4 (1981): 471–76.

Ransom, Jane. "Lidia Falcón: Freedom Fighter." *San Juan Star* 12 Feb. 1984: 2–3.

Routté-Gómez, Eneid. "Notes on Women." *San Juan Star* 5 Feb. 1984: 32.

Simó, Isabel-Clara. "Lidia Falcón, 'Dones i Catalunya,' un camino abierto para el teatro feminista." *Estreno* 10 (1984): 3–5.

Starčević, Elizabeth. "*Rupturas*: A Feminist Novel." *Anales de la Literatura Española Contemporánea* 12. 1–2 (1987): 175–89.

Stephen, Beverly. "Fem Issues Are Global in Nature." *N.Y. Post* (1983): 55.

Vallina, Isabel. "Lidia Falcón, ternura radical." *Dunia* (June 1987): 31. [Interview]

Waldman, Gloria F. "En respuesta al 'Así somos' de Angela Luisa." *El Nuevo Día* (Puerto Rico) 1 Feb. 1984: 58.

———. "Lidia Falcón: 'Las mujeres caminaron con el fuego del siglo,' visto desde dentro." *Estreno* 10 (1984): 2–3.

———. "Lidia Falcón: Passion from a Feminist Base." *Pandora's Box* (York College, CUNY) 24 Nov. 1982: 3–4.

————. "Lidia Falcón." *Women Writers of Spain: An Annotated Bio-Bibliographical Guide*. Ed. Carolyn Galerstein. Westport: Greenwood Press, 1986. 107–10.

————. Personal correspondence. 3 and 18 August 1992.

————. "Vindicación feminista: Lidia Falcón, Esther Tusquets y Mercé Rodoreda." *La Torre, Revista General de la Universidad de Puerto Rico* 115 (1982): 10–25. Rpt. as "Tres novelistas españolas." *Linden Lane* 2.2 (1983): 36–37.

ÁNGELA FIGUERA AYMERICH (1902–1984)

John C. Wilcox

BIOGRAPHY

Ángela Figuera Aymerich was born in Bilbao, a seaport on the north coast of Spain, on October 30, 1902. Despite her comment, "My biography is of no importance whatsoever. Except to me, of course" ("Poética [1954]"), the critic in search of details about her life finds a rich amount of material in such sources as Germán Bleiberg and Julián Marías (1953, 573; 1964, 298), José Luis Cano (521–22), Carmen Conde (17–18), Julio Figuera Andú ("Nota" 7–10, "Datos"), J. P. González Martín (88–92, 220), Alfredo Gracia Vicente (1–2), Charles Ley (110), Jacinto López Gorgé (25), Leopoldo de Luis (*Poesía social* 57–58), Joaquín Marco (11–14), Antonio Núñez (4), Federico Sainz de Robles (420), and Eleanor Wright (*Poetry* 154–57; Galerstein 111–13).

Some of Ángela Figuera's strongest memories were of the life of Bilbao—its gulls, river, and sea—and the delicate beauty of that region of Spain—its trees, grass, and fine rain. She was the eldest of nine children, to whom she devoted a great deal of care and attention owing to her mother's poor health. In Bilbao she was educated at a primary school run by French nuns. She then went to a "grammar" school where she was one of five "señoritas" among one-hundred boys and one of the first women in Spain to receive a secondary education. Her best grades were in mathematics, but she preferred literary studies. Her father was opposed to her studying a subject as impractical as literature at the university—he wanted her to be a dentist—so Ángela studied on her own at home in Bilbao and went to the University in Valladolid to take the first set of examinations toward her degree.

In 1927 Figuera's father died suddenly, leaving the family penniless. Although she and her grandmother had to assume responsibility for the family, Figuera was fortunate in that the father of her future husband made sure that she was able to obtain her university degree; he had her move to Madrid to live with him and his family. She subsequently graduated from the Central University of Madrid and in 1930 began her teaching career, at which time her family moved from Bilbao to Madrid to be with her. In 1933 Ángela did extremely well in competitive professional examinations and won a teaching post in Huelva, in the south of Spain. On January 15, 1934, she married her cousin, an engineer named Julio Figuera Andú, and moved to Huelva, where she published her first poems in the magazine *Blanco y Negro*. In 1935 their son died in childbirth.

With the outbreak of the Spanish Civil War in July 1936, Julio Figuera Andú enlisted in a militia on the Republican side and for the next few years moved about Spain. On December 30, 1936, their second son, Juan Ramón, was born in war-torn Madrid, where Ángela was studying for further professional examinations. She and her family were evacuated to Valencia, and shortly afterward, Ángela was assigned a teaching post at the Alcoy Institute. In 1938, her husband having been sent further south, she secured a teaching position at the Murcia Institute where the reunited family spent the last seven months of the war.

In 1939, with Franco's victory in April, Figuera found herself stripped of her teaching post, penniless, and on the street. She returned to Madrid, where she devoted herself to her family and her spare time to writing. Although her early attempt for the Adonais Prize failed, José Luis Cano encouraged her with his approval of her work, as did her husband, who, involved at that time in publishing a book on physics, urged her to submit her first collection of poems to the same publisher. As a result, *Mujer de barro* (1948; "Woman of Clay") finally saw the light of day.

From 1943 to 1948 the family summered at Burgo de Osma (just south of Soria and northeast of Madrid). Their bicycle trips throughout that area inspired her second book, *Soria pura* (1949; "Pure Soria"). The reprisals and injustices meted out by the Franco regime contributed to the changed theme, intention and tone of her third book, *Vencida por el ángel* (1950; "Vanquished by the Angel"), in which, as Cano implies, she rejects the more self-centered aesthetic views of most of her precursors of the 1920s and 1930s (522). Gabriel Celaya's *Las cosas como son* (1949) intensified Figuera's vision of socially committed poetry and greatly influenced her next publications: *El grito inútil* (1952; "The Useless Cry"), *Víspera de la vida* (1953; "The Evening Before Life"), and *Los días duros* (1953; "Harsh Days").

It is reported that in 1953, at a public reading of her poetry, Figuera declared herself a disciple of Pablo Neruda as well as a friend of Gabriel Celaya and Blas de Otero, which in the climate of that time was tantamount to aligning herself with the communists (Ley 110). With her insistence on "solidarity, justice, and peace," Wright notes (*Poetry* 154), Figuera began to cut a striking "persona . . . a feminine voice in a literary world with few published poetesses." Attempting to actualize her poetic stance of solidarity, peace and justice, Figuera took a librarian's course and worked in the evenings "really for nothing" (Núñez 4) for the "bibliobús" (bookmobile) that went into Madrid's poorer neighborhoods to lend books, until that service was discontinued.

In 1957 Figuera was awarded a grant to conduct a bibliographical study in Paris, where she spent the months of August and September studying the French poets. Most importantly, she was introduced at that time to Neruda. Figuera took the opportunity to enlighten him on the state of poetry in Spain, in particular the work of Blas de Otero, Gabriel Celaya, and Victoriano Crémer, and to show him the manuscript of her unpublished book, *Belleza cruel* ("Cruel Beauty"), a compendium of what she later called her "furious poems" (*poemas rabiosos*). Neruda confessed that she changed his opinion about poetry in Franco's Spain— a view he expounded in a letter to Spanish poets, drafted in Paris on September 27, 1957 (finally published in 1986 in Figuera's *Obras completas* 294–96; Quance, "Introducción" 16, 22 n.12). Figuera had clearly impressed Neruda, and that the feeling was mutual is corroborated in the elegy she wrote on his death (*Obras completas* 340–43).

In 1958 Figuera's most famous book, *Belleza cruel*, was published in Mexico City with an important prologue by the poet León Felipe. After reading Figuera and the poets of the Generation of '36, Felipe "retracted his statement that the [exiles] had taken Spain's poetry" away with them (Wright, *Poetry* 154). The Union of Spanish Intellectuals in Mexico City awarded *Belleza cruel* the Nueva España Poetry Prize for 1958, one of a long list of prizes Ángela Figuera amassed during her poetic career.

In 1959 her husband's work took him to Avilés, Asturias, where Figuera joined him in 1961 and published *Toco la tierra. Letanías* (1962; "I Touch the Earth. Litanies"). Though her work was translated into numerous languages— French, Portuguese, Russian, Swedish, Italian, Dutch, Basque, Romanian, Turkish, Arabic, Czechoslavak, German (Marcos 136-38, 139)—after 1962 she considered her poetry dated (Núñez 4) and stopped publishing, with the exception of children's books. From Avilés, she made frequent visits to Madrid to see her grandchildren, who inspired *Cuentos tontos para niños listos* (1979; "Silly Tales for Clever Children") and the posthumously published *Canciones para todo el año* (1984; "Songs for the Whole Year"). In 1971 she and her husband moved back to Madrid where she remained until her death on April 2, 1984.

MAJOR THEMES

Ángela Figuera's poetry evolves through three cycles. The first, from 1948 to 1949, evinces a predominantly optimistic worldview: The major theme is love of womankind and nature. The second, from 1950 to 1953, is predominantly pessimistic: The major themes are social and political depredation, the inauthenticity of established religion, the frustrations and powerlessness of woman as writer and mother. The third phase, from 1958 to 1962, balances a critique of

Spain with positive concepts, and suggests to future Spanish generations how they might rebuild their country.

Figuera was forty-six when she published the eighty poems that constitute her first book, *Mujer de barro*—an important volume whose originality has been ignored. Of interest to today's readers are the ways Figuera—in albeit few poems—subtly undermines traditional perceptions; demystifying the male lover, the male child, and male poetic precursors. *Mujer de barro* is divided into three sections: "Mujer de barro," which treats the experience of a young woman in love; "Poemas de mi hijo y yo" ("Poems About My Son and Me"), which sings of a young mother's love for her child; and "El fruto redondo" ("The Round Fruit"), which reflects on poetry and poetics. The first poem of the first section is significantly titled "Mujer" ("Woman"). It is a deliberate but subtle challenge to traditional poetic figures used by men to designate females ("flower," "tree," "bird"). Against such passive, stereotypical symbols, the female speaker of Figuera's first text insists, "I'm not just a flower, I do the flowering," and "The seed may be given to me, but I bring forth the fruit" ("Flor, no: florezco . . . / Me entregan la simiente: doy el fruto" [26]). As Figuera implies elsewhere, woman is not a configuration of hallowed poetic clichés (e.g., "mother-of-pearl," "Madonna lilies"); she is "barro" ("clay," "earth," "mud"), which is fertile and provides food ("Barro" 27; "Morena" [27; "Dark Haired Girl"]; "Tierra" [34; "Earth"]). Although many of the poems in this section do sing of the delight a young female speaker experiences with her male lover, others detail the conflicts that arise as that love develops. For instance, for the man, love develops into a desire to control, whereas for the woman, it remains a gift; without a word the man's hands set upon the woman's warmth and are transformed into tenacious "claws of fire" (32) as they grasp at her flesh. In "Deseo" (37; "Desire"), the sexually frustrated woman perceives her lover as a cold, mute stone and herself as alive with fire. The speaker feels within her the grounds for ecstasy, and she pities her man for being unaware of it.

"Poemas de mi hijo y yo" sing of the delight and despair a young mother experiences as she nurtures her baby and rears her child. The joyous speaker, in presenting aspects of her baby's infancy and childhood, perceives her creation as a blond beauty *and* a little savage who grows and masters surrounding reality until he is too proud to hold her hand. The poems hint at traditional Spanish verse, echoing Federico García Lorca's *Libro de poemas* and *Canciones* and Juan Ramón Jiménez's "Historias," published in the *Segunda antolojía poética*. However, as J. P. González Martín suggests, Figuera distances herself—here and elsewhere—from such male precursors by the immediacy of her realism (90).

In "El fruto redondo," the book's third section, Figuera initiates a conscious reflection on her poetics. Outwardly she perceives her humdrum existence as wife, mother, housewife as "marvelous," even though others see her as doing very little. Inwardly, however, though no one listens, she struggles to explain her poetics. The dialogue she initiates with nature leads to an exploration not only of her own real anguish, in great part associated with her stillborn baby, but also of the words she uses to express this anguish. She claims that hers is not a poetry of the "naked word" or ethereal essences but, rather, one that springs from her hot flesh: "Pero mis versos nacen redondos como frutos, / envueltos en la pulpa caliente de mi carne" (54; But my lines are born round like fruit / wrapped in the warm pulp of my flesh).

Figuera's second book, *Soria pura*, is meditative poetry inspired by the natural beauty of the Duero River and the landscape around Burgo de Osma. Spiritual peace and sensual satisfaction are the major themes. Figuera expresses her experience of ecstasy in pantheistic terms; the peaceful nature of the earth, river, trees, and clouds blissfully penetrates the speaker of the poems and spiritually regenerates her as she meditates on the beauty with which she has had the good fortune to surround herself. Although Antonio Machado is the confessed inspiration for this frame of mind, strains of Jiménez and García Lorca are again to be heard.

Despite these confessed precursors, Figuera's vision is too female-centered to be theirs, and the entire collection is traversed by poems evoking her sexual fulfillment:

> Entre las cañas tendida;
> sola y perdida en las cañas . . .
>   ¿Quién me cerraba los ojos,
> que, solos, se me cerraban?
>   ¿Quién me sorbía en los labios
> zumo de miel sin palabras?
>   ¿Quién me derribó y me tuvo
> sola y perdida en las cañas?
>   ¿Quién me apuñaló con besos
> el ave de la garganta?
>   ¿Quién me estremeció los senos
> con tacto de tierra y ascua?
>   ¿Qué toro embistió en el ruedo
> de mi cintura cerrada?
>   ¿Quién me esponjó las caderas
> con levadura de ansias?
>   ¿Qué piedra de eternidad
> me hincaron en las entrañas?
>   ¿Quién me desató la sangre
> que así me derramaba?
>   . . . Aquella tarde de Julio,
> sola y perdida en las cañas. ("Cañaveral" 94)
>
> Lying in the reeds;
> alone and lost in the reeds . . .
>   Who closed my eyes,

which, by themselves, were closing?
  Who, without a word, sipped
juice of honey from my lips?
  Who pushed me down and held me
alone and lost in the reeds?
  Who knifed with kisses
the bird in my throat?
  Who shook my breasts
with a touch of earth and ember?
  Which bull charged in the ring
of my closed waist?
  Who swelled my hips
with leaven of yearning?
  What stone of eternity
thrust into my entrails?
  Who unleashed my blood
for it to shed itself on me?
   . . . That evening with Julio,
alone and lost in the reeds.

Although Figuera's choice of verbs evokes images of male dominance, she simultaneously creates a sense of sufficiency where the presence of another seems less important than her own sensuality. What male poet could relate the shock of immersing himself in icy-cold water to the delights of orgasm, as Figuera does in "Río" (77)? She inveighs against the prissiness of Spain's female poets. In an until recently unpublished poem, she criticizes her "hermanas poetisas" for living life as if they "were paying it a courtesy call" (*Obras completas* 302).

Between the publication of *Soria pura* in 1949 and of her next book, *Vencida por el ángel* in 1950, Ángela Figuera's work underwent a vast change. She suggests the reasons for her evolution in the "Poetics" she wrote in the 1950s and 1960s, and the interviews she gave in the 1970s and 1980s. With the Spanish Civil War and World War II, her verse left home and took to the streets and battlefields in solidarity with the oppressed. The hatred, injustice, suffering, and hunger she witnessed horrified her and led her to use her poetry—a painful scream—to protest that evil state of affairs. Such are the major preoccupations of the second phase of Figuera's work—*Vencida por el ángel*, *El grito inútil*, *Los días duros*, and *Víspera de la vida*—in which her lines are longer and her verse, now free, avails itself of such repetitive techniques as anaphora and apostrophe (Quance, "Introducción" 14). These poems should be read today as indications of the ways in which the poet uses her writing, consciously or not, to subvert and undermine the patriarchal order. In many poems—such as "Esta paz" ("This Peace") and "Madres" ("Mothers")—women are urged to rebel; "Rebelión" ("Rebellion") begins with the line "Serán las madres las que digan: Basta" (179; The mothers will be the ones who declare: Enough). Figuera presents, in a series of allegorical poems, a singularly negative perspective on fascist Spain: Spain is a prison ("La cárcel"), and all its land lies fallow and infertile ("Regreso" ["Return"]). This period of Figuera's work could be read today as a conscious manifestation of female rage and anger turned inward, resulting in a sense of guilt, egotism, and uselessness: She implores God to make her suffer ("Habla" ["Speak"]); she believes that as a woman she is a useless object, impregnated now only with her own death ("El grito inútil" ["Useless Cry"]); and she sees her state as that of an animal that has escaped slaughter ("Posguerra" ["After the War"]).

In *Vencida por el ángel*, one of Figuera's most powerful books, the speaker presents herself as hitherto having lived inured to her country's depredation and society's profound ills. Those self-protective walls have finally caved in, and the speaker has been "conquered" by the "angel" of death, anguish, and grief that dwells in her. In "Bombardeo" ("The Bombing"), the speaker, analogous to Mary, the Mother of Jesus, wraps her arms around her belly to protect her unborn child from the bombs and subtly implies the loveless inhumanity of the victors in the Civil War. In this book Figuera begins to present the untenable hypocrisy of the official, established religion of her country and to suggest a religion that she perceives as truly Christian. The poet has become aware of the fact that metaphorically she lives amid the stink of unburied dead, and that she is surrounded by starving children who have never tasted a crust of fresh bread.

The vision of the nineteen poems that constitute Figuera's next book, *El grito inútil*, is colored by the guilt of the survivor. In the hollowness they have become, survivors experience "the quiet vengeance of millions of dead people" ("Posguerra" 174–75) and perceive both themselves and their country as sterile. Numerous poems view society from an ironic perspective and its institutions as socially and politically debased, and present human beings as floundering in an existential quagmire. Although Figuera declares that to effect change, mothers of the world will have to rebel against the oppressive nature of the established order ("Rebelión" 179–80), she reiterates the uselessness of her poetry. Her only function can be to scream and weep over the present state of affairs. As a disenfranchised woman and a poet, Figuera empathizes with the powerless and disenfranchised of her country—farmers, day laborers, manual workers—as well as with downtrodden women, who are vividly presented as trapped in excruciating poverty. Despite her predominantly negative vision, she urges her readers onward toward the ideal of solidarity and holds quixotically to the belief that somewhere there must exist beauty and hope (in nature, with children and youths, with mothers, farmers, and workers).

Los días duros, Figuera's next book, reveals how the poet's age, her sex, the political upheavals through which she lived, and the numerous social injustices of which she was made aware contribute to her bolder vision of reality. The title poem of the collection alludes to *Mujer de barro* by referring to "mi dócil barro femenino" (125; my docile feminine clay), and indicates that age and experience have made the speaker more aware of the strengths of women. In this first poem, Figuera articulates a feminist perspective in very muted tones:

times are hard and bitter, but she "cannot faint like a softie" (127). The last poem of this section, "Madres," presents an even clearer feminist voice that by the final poem of the book, "Destino," has become strident. Coitus is no simple pleasure for a woman because her "destino" is to live with the consequences of its pain and suffering. Figuera compares the separate realities of men and women and critiques the male, whose "belly knows no affliction" and "frees himself for himself and enchains me / to the rhythm and servitude of the species" (141). Added to this is the fact that coitus is an even greater pain for women because they learn that the fruit of their wombs will become fodder for wars and for the slavery of the factory.

The vision projected in Figuera's next book, *Víspera de la vida*, is predominantly one of the meaninglessness of life in which the only certainty is death. The sense of uselessness that besets Figuera stems in part from her condition of being a woman at that particular time and in that particular place, defenseless and monotonously giving birth to men. Despite the bleakness of this vision, however, she fondly recalls her own beginnings—her childhood, when all was clear and purposive—and intermittently affirms life's basic goodness and mystery, in furtherance of which the visionary woman poet in her decrees that when she dies, her veins are to be cut open so that her blood may reirrigate the earth.

If in the second phase of her poetic evolution Figuera's vision is predominantly pessimistic, in the third phase—which includes *Belleza cruel* and *Toco la tierra. Letanías*—her pessimism is counterbalanced by determined optimism and desperate hope. When *Belleza cruel*, the collection of nineteen "furious poems," is contrasted with the previous four books, the poet is seen "to be searching for a point of equilibrium between exaltation and lugubriousness" (Bosch 6). It was published in Mexico in 1958 but did not appear in Spain until 1978, three years after Franco's death, probably because the theme of Spain—its cruelty and beauty—is overtly textualized. Today's reader no doubt could reread these works as a woman writer's desire to subvert the Francoist, patriarchal order, especially in those poems in which Figuera foregrounds the condition of downtrodden women, thereby implicitly condemning the society that thwarts and fails them.

In one poem of magic realism, "La justicia de los ángeles" (231–32), Figuera contrasts the very different deaths and burials of a rich, important man and an impoverished woman, Petra. The latter died caring for her nine illegitimate children, and to reward her for her unsung devotion, during the night a host of angels remove the flowers from the rich man's grave and deposit them on Petra's. A woman's ironical criticism of Francoist culture is found elsewhere. Like Carmen Conde, whom she cites in her poem "Guerra," Figuera has learned that Spain's women gave birth to internecine warfare; the poem ends, "Parí la GUERRA" (222; I gave birth to WAR). The "I" who speaks here identifies with the masculine power structure precisely to undermine it. In reaction to the lifeless state Franco created, Figuera urges in "Puentes" the building of "bridges" to the outside world—symbolic bridges of union of self with other, of Spaniard with foreigner—that Francoism, in its male isolation, had burned after the Civil War.

Figuera's poetic voice is stronger than ever in *Toco la tierra. Letanías*, her last volume of verse. When she reflects on Spain and on her own poetry, she weighs the good with the bad. The good is represented by the land and its crops, as well as by children, youth, and workers. The bad is Spain's ruined past and the hunger and poverty that prevail. Her poetry has grappled with such issues as religion and the oppressive powers at work in Spain and in the world. Her criticism of the self-interest of the powerful is trenchant and uncompromising.

Numerous poems in this final collection, as in *Belleza cruel*, are preoccupied with Spain. It is a country in ruin and decay but Figuera, the poet, has gone on loving it and urges its youth to find a way to cultivate it, literally and meta-phorically. In this volume Figuera also reflects on her poetics. She sees her work as down-to-earth; her poetry, rooted in the land, avoids idealistic flights of fancy and empathizes with those who have to sweat to survive each day. These ideas are also alluded to in the powerful sonnet ''Aunque la mies más alta dure un día'' (''Although the Tallest Stalk of Wheat Lasts Just a Day''), where Figuera declares:

> Mujer de carne y verso me declaro,
> pozo de amor y boca dolorida,
> pero he de hacer un trueno de mi herida
> que suene aquí y ahora, fuerte y claro. (284)

> Woman of flesh and verse I declare myself to be,
> well of love and grieving mouth,
> but I must make a thunder of my wound
> that it ring out loud and clear in the here and now.

In addition, the until now uncollected poem ''Poeta puro'' develops a comparable idea of Figuera's commitment.

Figuera's lines never cease to urge her readers to help, in whatever humani-tarian way possible, the defenseless, the oppressed, and those who perform society's menial and unglorified tasks. She also beseeches them not to cry over her when she dies. In her ''Poéticas,'' Figuera explains that she did not write for posterity, for pleasure, or for pure beauty; she wrote out of necessity, when she was inspired, or when she was moved by an event. She believed in trying to make the world perfect, despite people's meanness of spirit, and she claimed not to care if her poetry was ephemeral, provided that one single human being had been touched or consoled by it. The unassuming, self-denying aspect of her personality, which was manifested in the fact that she did not publish her first poems until she was forty-six, remained a constant until the very end of her ''robust'' and impressive life.

SURVEY OF CRITICISM

In the 1950s reaction to Ángela Figuera was mixed. Brief notes (Sainz de Robles, Aub) see her as indistinct from Latin American women poets (Storni, Ibarbourou, Mistral). Only Rafael Millán gave her the recognition she deserves (12). Carmen Conde approved of the first period of her work but equivocates on the second. Both José Luis Cano and Gonzalo Torrente Ballester insisted that she is a "Christian" poet, even though she accuses and condemns.

In the 1960s attention was paid to Figuera's style (Valbuena Prat 3: 851; Luis, "*Toco*"; López Anglada 250–51). Ciplijauskaité analyzed her aesthetic as evolving from a search for a beauty that is vague and imprecise toward one that is fully "rooted" in reality. The 1960s also introduced into Figuera criticism the notion of her maternal instinct (Luis, "Notes" 40; Bosch; Mantero).

In the 1970s more attention was paid to the content of Figuera's writing. Núñez published an indispensable interview with Figuera that contains commentary on her evolution. There were some helpful appraisals of her development (González Martín) as well as some limited ones (García de la Concha 340; Villa-Fernández). Emilio Miró ("Dos antologías") and Julian Marcos emphasized the social and humanistic impetus of her work, while José Manrique de Lara and Johannes Lechner stressed the intellectual range of her thought. At the end of the decade, Carlos Álvarez jumped through mental hoops to prove to his audience that Figuera must be thought of as a "poeta" (poet) not a "poetisa" (poetess) because her vision demonstrates "strength," which does not mean, he is quick to assure his audience, that her poems are "sexless" (5–6).

The 1980s began with an important interview conducted by Alicia Ramos. Santiago Daydí-Tolson was negative toward her work, but Joaquín Marco, Eleanor Wright (*Poetry* 154–57), and Emilio Miró ("Algunas poetas") offered an antidote to this, as did the special number *Zurgai* devoted to her in 1987. A feminist rereading of her work began with Nancy Mandlove, who analyzed Figuera's patterns of negation/affirmation, and Roberta Quance ("Introducción"), who argued that Figuera reinscribes the feminine in archetypal masculine discourses.

BIBLIOGRAPHY

Works by Ángela Figuera

Poetry

Mujer de barro. Madrid: Saeta, 1948.
Soria pura. Madrid: Ediciones Jura, 1949.
Vencida por el ángel. Alicante, Spain: Ediciones Verbo, 1950.
El grito inútil. Alicante, Spain: Such y Serra, 1952.
Los días duros. Madrid: Afrodisio Aguado, 1953.
Víspera de la vida. Madrid: Colección Neblí, 1953.

Belleza cruel. Mexico City: Compañía General de Ediciones, 1958. [Prologue by León Felipe]

Toco la tierra. Letanías. Madrid: Ediciones Rialp, 1962.

Cuentos tontos para niños listos. Monterrey, Mexico: Ediciones Sierra Madre, 1979.

Canciones para todo el año. Monterrey, Mexico: Editorial Trillas, 1984.

Obras completas. Madrid: Hiperión, 1986.

Prose

"Poética [1954]." *Poesía femenina española viviente*. Ed. Carmen Conde. Madrid: Ediciones Arquero, 1954. 151.

"Poética [1965]." *Poesía social española contemporánea. Antología (1939–1968)*. Ed. Leopoldo de Luis. 3rd ed. Madrid: Ediciones Júcar, 1982. 57–58.

"Poética [1967]." *Poesía española contemporánea: Antología (1939–1964). Poesía amorosa*. Ed. Jacinto López Gorgé. Madrid: Alfaguara, 1967. 27–28.

"Mis queridos amigos en la poesía [1968]." "De la correspondencia de Ángela Figuera." *Antología de Ángela Figuera*. Ed. Alfredo Gracia Vicente. Monterrey, Mexico: Ediciones Sierra Madre, 1969. 3–4, 5–6.

Translations

Antología bilingüe (español-inglés) de la poesía española moderna. Trans. and sel. Helen Wohl Patterson. Madrid: Ediciones Cultura Hispánica, 1965. Included in this volume are the following poems: "Giving." 131; "Only Before the Man." 135–36; "Without a Key." 131–32.

Recent Poetry of Spain. A Bilingual Anthology. Trans. Louis Hammer and Sara Schyfter. Old Chatham, NY: Sachem Press, 1983. Included in this volume are the following poems: "If You Haven't Died For an Instant." 147, 149; "Insomnia." 141; "The Jail." 143, 145; "My Lover's Flesh." 141; "Symbol." 149; "When My Father Painted." 145–47; "Women of the Market." 141, 143.

The Defiant Muse. Hispanic Feminist Poems From the Middle Ages to the Present: A Bilingual Anthology. Trans. Kate Flores. Ed. and intro. Ángel Flores and Kate Flores. New York: The Feminist Press at the City U of NY, 1986. Included in this volume are the following poems: "Destiny." 75, 77; "Market Women." 71; "Mothers." 73, 75.

"Accusative Case." Trans. Diana L. Vélez. *Alaluz* 19.1–2 and 20.1–2 (1987–88): 29–30.

"Unity." Trans. Noël Valis. *Alaluz* 19.1–2 and 20.1–2 (1987–88): 28.

Works about Ángela Figuera

Álvarez, Carlos. Prologue. *Belleza cruel*. By Ángela Figuera. Barcelona: Editorial Lumen, 1978. 5–6.

Aub, Max. *Poesía española comtemporánea*. Mexico City: Ediciones Era, 1969. 213.

Bleiberg, Germán and Julián Marías. *Diccionario de literatura española*. 2nd ed. Madrid: Revista de Occidente, 1953. 573. 3rd ed. 1964. 298.

Bosch, Rafael. "La poesía de Ángela Figuera y el tema de la maternidad." *Insula* 186 (1962): 5–6.

Cano, José Luis. *Poesía española del siglo XX: De Unamuno a Blas de Otero*. Madrid: Guadarrama, 1960. 521–22.

Ciplijauskaité, Biruté. *El poeta y la poesía: Del romanticismo a la poesía social*. Madrid: Insula, 1966. 410–12.

Conde, Carmen. Introduction. *Poesía femenina española viviente*. Ed. Carmen Conde. Madrid: Ediciones Arquero, 1954. 17–18.

Daydí-Tolson, Santiago. *The Post-Civil War Spanish Poets*. Boston: Twayne, 1983. 93–99.

Fagundo, Ana María. "Twentieth Century Spanish Poetry by Women." *Alaluz* 19.1–2 and 20.1–2 (1987–88): 14–22.

Figuera Andú, Julio. "Datos biográficos y recuerdos de Ángela Figuera." [Unpublished]
———. Preliminary note. *Obras completas*. By Ángela Figuera. 7–10.

García de la Concha, Víctor. *La poesía española de posguerra: Teoría e historia de sus movimientos*. 2nd ed. Madrid: Editorial Poesía Española, 1973. 339–40.

González Martín, J. P. *Poesía hispánica: 1939–1969 (Estudio y antología)*. Barcelona: El Bardo, 1970. 88–92.

Gracia Vicente, Alfredo. Foreword. *Antología de Ángela Figuera*. By Ángela Figuera. Monterrey, Mexico: Asociación de Estudiantes de Arquitectura, 1969. 1–6.

Lechner, Johannes. *El compromiso en la poesía española del siglo XX*. Vol. 2. Leiden: Universitaire Pers, 1975. 71, 125.

Ley, Charles David. *Spanish Poetry Since 1939*. Washington D.C.: Catholic U of America P, 1962. 109–10.

López Anglada, Luis. "La mujer en la poesía española contemporánea." *Panorama poético español (Historia y antología: 1939–64)*. Madrid: Editora Nacional, 1965. 250–51.

López Gorgé, Jacinto. Rationale. *Poesía española contemporánea: Antología (1939–1964). Poesía amorosa*. Ed. Jacinto López Gorgé. Madrid: Ediciones Alfaguara, 1967. 25–28.

Luis, Leopoldo de. Notes to the first edition. *Poesía social española contemporánea: Antología (1939–1968)*. 3rd ed. Madrid: Ediciones Júcar, 1982. 9–42.
———. "*Toco la tierra* de Ángela Figuera." *Papeles de Son Armadans* 26.78 (1962): 327–29.

Mandlove, Nancy. "Historia and Intra-Historia: Two Spanish Women Poets in Dialogue with History." *Third Women* 2.2 (1984): 84–93.

Manrique de Lara, José Gerardo. "Prosaísmo árido y ardiente humanidad en la poesía de Ángela Figuera." *Poetas sociales españoles*. Madrid: Ediciones y Publicaciones Españolas, 1974. 53–56.

Mantero, Manuel. "Ángela Figuera y la maternidad a la redonda." *Poesía española contemporánea: Estudio y antología (1939–1965)*. Barcelona: Plaza y Janés, 1966. 83–86.

Marco, Joaquín. *Poesía española: Siglo XX*. Barcelona: Edhasa, 1986. 128.

Marcos, Julián. Prologue. *Ángela Figuera Aymerich: Antología total (1948–1969)*. Ed. Julián Marcos. Madrid: C.V.S. Ediciones, 1975. 11–14.

Millán, Rafael. *Veinte poetas españoles*. Madrid: Agora, 1955.

Miró, Emilio. "Algunas poetas españolas entre 1926 y 1960." *Literatura y vida cotidiana*. Actas de las Cuartas Jornadas de Investigación Interdisciplinaria: Seminario de Estudios de la Mujer de la Universidad Autónoma de Madrid. Zaragoza: 1987. 314–17.
———. "Dos antologías: Juan Alcaide y Ángela Figuera." *Insula* 327 (1974): 5.

———. "La poesía desde 1936." *Historia de la literatura española*. Ed. José María Díez Borque. Vol. 4. Madrid: Taurus, 1980. 355–56.

Núñez, Antonio. "Encuentro con Ángela Figuera." *Insula* 327 (1974): 4.

Quance, Roberta. "Bibliografía selecta sobre la vida y la obra de Angela Figuera." *Obras completas*. By Angela Figuera. 449–52.

———. Introduction. *Obras completas*. By Ángela Figuera. 11–19.

Ramos, Alicia. *Literatura y confesión*. Madrid: Editorial Arame, 1982. 11–21.

Sainz de Robles, Federico Carlos. "Escritores españoles e hispanoamericanos." *Ensayos de un diccionario de la literatura*. Vol. 2. Madrid: Aguilar, 1973. 420.

Torrente Ballester, Gonzalo. *Panorama de la literatura española contemporánea*. 2nd ed. Vol. 1. Madrid: Ediciones Guadarrama, 1961. 397.

Valbuena Prat, Ángel. *Historia de la literatura española*. Vol. 3. Barcelona: Gustavo Gili, 1960. 851.

Villa-Fernández, Pedro. "La denuncia social en *Belleza cruel* de Ángela Figuera Aymerich." *Revista de Estudios Hispánicos* 7.1 (1973): 127–38.

Wright, Eleanor. "Ángela Figuera Aymerich." *Women Writers of Spain: An Annotated Bio-Bibliographical Guide*. Ed. Carolyn L. Galerstein. Westport, CT: Greenwood Press, 1986. 11–13.

———. *The Poetry of Protest under Franco*. London: Támesis, 1986.

Zurgai (Revista de poesía). (Bilbao). Dec. 1987.

GLORIA FUERTES
(b. 1918)

Ellen Engelson Marson

BIOGRAPHY

Gloria Fuertes's life and literature are inseparable. Details of her youth and adolescence are brazenly and often humorously testimonialized in the body of a poetry that probes the identity of its author. She was born in 1918 in a garret on La Espada Street in a working-class district of Madrid. It was perhaps amid the trees of the Plaza del Progreso and along the prostitute-lined streets where she played that the future poet absorbed the refrains, syntax, and flavor of a popular language that was later crucial to her unique voice (Cano, *Vida y poesía* 11).[1]

Fuertes's mother was a seamstress and a maid; her father was a concierge of a government building and a janitor first at the Institución Gota de Leche and later at a mansion on Zurbano Street (Cano 11). In spite of her "torn shoes" (*Historia de Gloria* 276 [1981; "Gloria's Story"]), Fuertes writes that she was happy and extroverted and wanted to become a clown (Núñez 3), but behind the clown there are many glimpses into painful times. She was the youngest of nine siblings, only three of whom survived; the others were victims of "infant mortality or civil war" (*Historia* 87). Her early years were hard. She felt unwanted by her parents, who "made her" when they were no longer in love (*Historia* 148); jealous of her brother, Angelín, whom they loved a little (*Historia* 321); and continually in need of affection—"Fifteen years passed between my first baby bottle / and my first kiss of love" (*Historia* 148). In a revealing moment, she discloses that her mother, who was gracious and clever, also had a terrible temper that marked Fuertes deeply because of the suffering it caused all members of the family. Although Fuertes the poet will be haunted by images of elusive love—"Ah, there are kisses in my room / and there are no lips on my flesh" (*Antología poética 1950–1969* 62 [1970; "Poetic Anthology"])—she will channel this emotional starvation into an authentic commitment to abandoned sectors of humanity.

The young Gloria, whose first toy was a rented typewriter, whose first doll was herself, and whose first friend was that doll she never had, addressed envelopes and counted eggs to earn a few pesetas. She tells us in her verses that she spoke at an early age, but instead of saying "papa," she said "rare things in a strange language" and invented an exotic bird for whom she spun her imaginative tales (*Obras incompletas* 58–59 [1980; "Incomplete Works"]). Reveling in her precocious creativity, she proudly recounts that "cuando se me ocurrió el primer poema, / me caí de la cuna de risa" (*Historia* 354; when my first poem came to me / I fell from my cradle laughing). The rebellious spirit was already brewing in this young child who "stopped being illiterate by age three" (*Historia* 64).

Fuertes confessed in an interview with Ana María Moix that since there were no books in her house, she had to write, illustrate, and even sew together the first one she ever read (40–41). Her mother, like so many other mothers of daughters, enrolled her in the Instituto de Educación Profesional de la Mujer (Institute of Women's Professional Education) where she studied cooking, hand and machine embroidery, hygiene, physiology, child-care, and confection. Suspicious of activities such as athletics and (most definitely) poetry as not befitting a daughter of a laborer, her mother also recommended grammar and literature (*Obras* 27). Given the rebellious and critical tone of her poetry, one marvels that Fuertes complied with this typical agenda for female education.

Fuertes casually informs us that at age nine she was hit by a car; at fourteen, by the Civil War; and at fifteen, by the death of her mother, at the time when she needed her most (*Obras* 41). She then lived with her father on Abascal Street. Fuertes refers often to her hunger, so severe that she went to work as a bookkeeper in a factory that produced shells for the Popular Front, but she managed to continue writing. Her adolescence, particularly grim, saw the blossoming of first love as the Civil War raged. It was precisely this amorous passion, mingled with the horror of the shells, deaths, and gnawing hunger, that gave birth to Fuertes's verses and bound her forever to her *pueblo* (people) in a communal protest against those who interrupted their struggle for freedom. It was the "uncivil" war (*Historia* 13) with its bomb "birthed by a heartless man" (*Obras* 268) that made Gloria Fuertes know she was a pacifist.

In 1939 Fuertes, still suffering from hunger, wrote her first story for children and submitted it to *Maravilla*, one of two magazines that published children's stories. The magazine not only printed the story but also offered her a job as an editor for ten pesetas a day, a position she kept for more than a decade. In 1942 a young, then unknown poet named Carlos Edmundo de Ory sent Fuertes a sonnet that she published. In a letter to José Luis Cano, she wrote of the friendship that developed between them and of the poems they occasionally composed together (Cano 15). Ory, along with Eduardo Chicharro and Silvano Sernesi, went on to form the *postista* (post-isms) poetic group, an offshoot of the surrealist movement, and Fuertes became its only female member.

In the 1950s Fuertes returned to her working-class neigborhood and became a regular at the bar run by an ex-bullfighter, Antonio Sánchez; there, armed with a bottle of wine and a plate of stuffed olives, she wrote her poems and stories (Cano 15). She founded a *tertulia* (literary group) of female poets--among them María Dolores de Pueblos and Acacia Uceta—that expanded into the Versos con Faldas (Verses with Skirts), a group that for two years gave weekly poetry readings in Madrid, and collaborated on various poetry magazines of the moment: *Rumbos, Poesía Española, El Pájaro de Paja,* and *Poesía de España.* In 1950 Fuertes published her first volume of poetry, *Isla ignorada* ("Unknown Island"), which although not wildly acclaimed, gained her recognition as a promising young poet. In 1952, she founded the poetry magazine, *Arquero,* with Antonio Gala, Rafael Mir, and Julio Mariscal. In 1954 two new books appeared: *Antología y poemas del suburbio* ("Anthology and Poems of the Slums"), published by Lírica Hispana in Caracas, and *Aconsejo beber hilo* ("I Advise Drinking Thread"), included in the Arquero collection. Still not able to live from her poetry and plagued by office bosses who were less than pleased with her creative endeavors during working hours, Fuertes decided to return to school. She earned a librarian's degree from the International Institute of Madrid in 1955, and claims that her years as a librarian advising avid readers were the happiest of her life: "My boss was the book. I was free!" (*Obras* 28). This newfound freedom led to the 1958 publication of *Todo asusta* ("Everything Is Scary"), which won honorable mention in the International Competition of Hispanic Lyric Poetry in Venezuela.

In 1961, armed with, in her words, an "anemic curriculum vitae" (*Obras* 28) of only a few out-of-print volumes of poetry, Fuertes was awarded a one-year Fulbright Fellowship that brought her to Bucknell University in Pennsylvania, where she taught twentieth-century Spanish poetry, novel, and theater. By her own account, in spite of the fact that her knees were trembling on her first day of class, Fuertes was able to win over her students with unaffected humility—much as she relates to her humble "colleagues" in her poetry—by revealing to them that it was the first time she had entered a university (*Obras* 28). She remained at Bucknell for three years until, despite her comfortable salary and her incipient love of North America, she longed to return to Spain to witness an end to fascism (Waldman, personal interview).

In Madrid, Fuertes continued to give Spanish classes to American students at the International Institute while her literary activity proliferated. The volume of poetry *Que estás en la tierra* ("You Are on the Earth"), made up of verses written over a ten-year period and arranged by the poet Jaime Gil de Biedma for José María Castellet's Collioure collection, appeared in 1962 and established her as a serious poet (Ynduráin 28). Three years later, *Ni tiro, ni veneno, ni navaja* (1965; "Neither Shot, nor Poison, nor Blade"), written during Fuertes's stay abroad, won the Guipúzcoa Prize. *Poeta de guardia* ("Poet on Duty"), considered by many critics her most significant volume of verse (Ynduráin 31; Cano, *Vida* 20), appeared in 1968 along with *Cangura para todo* ("Cangura for Everyone"), her first collection of children's stories and winner of an honorable mention for the prestigious International Hans Christian Andersen Prize. In 1969 she was awarded an Accessit Vizcaya Prize for *Cómo atar los bigotes al tigre* ("How to Tie the Tiger's Whiskers"). *Antología poética*, which included selections from her previous books of poetry and an indispensable prologue by Francisco Ynduráin, appeared one year later and further solidified her literary position among the male poets of the period. The year 1973 saw the publication of two more volumes: *Sola en la sala* ("Alone in the Parlor"), a collection of anguished poems not originally intended for publication and written during a difficult period of the poet's life, and *Cuando amas aprendes Geografía* ("When You Love, You Learn Geography"), awarded the Petrach Prize for Provenzal Poetry for Feminine Poetry. In 1980 Fuertes wrote an introduction to her *Obras incompletas,* and in 1981, produced *Historia de Gloria*, her most autobiographical volume to date.

Fuertes was granted the March Foundation Scholarship for Children's Literature (1972), and with it came the financial freedom for which she longed: "I gave myself a scholarship and for the first time I worked only for me" (*Obras* 28). Free to travel across the diverse regions of Spain, she brings her poetry to the ordinary people, especially the illiterate and the poor. Relentlessly seeking to broaden her readership, she reveals the social nature of her art when she writes that although "we need a poetic state in our hearts and in our nations . . . while there are more people who write poetry than who read poetry, we will get nowhere" (Batlló 338). Believing that it is not enough to make a poetry for the people—rather one must make a people for poetry (*Historia* 107)—Fuertes calls for an international campaign to teach the illiterate to read and the literate to read poetry (Batlló 338). José Luis Cano claims that Fuertes is probably the only poet who has dared to read her poems in a pub frequented by couples—managing to make them interrupt their caresses to listen to hers (17). In addition to her recitations, she has recorded her poetry and is intrigued by the medieval tradition of setting verses to music. Mocking the power of commercial advertisements, she proposes that if society were to "propagandize poetry as it does detergents, or to launch the slogan—'Live poetically'—maybe it would change people's attitude toward a book of poetry" (Núñez 3).

Gloria Fuertes, writer of poetry, children's stories, and unpublished theatrical works, lives alone on Alberto Alcocer Street in Madrid. An avid educator who relies on today's youth as the hope for future generations, she now dedicates herself, perhaps for this reason, primarily to the writing of children's stories. Many of her collections have been adopted as official school texts, and through her stories she delights in introducing impressionable minds to poetry and all its possibilities. As a collaborater on a television show, "Un globo, dos globos, tres globos," she is most proud of having been voted best children's writer by twenty-thousand young viewers. Fuertes's popularity is enormous; there are

schools named for her in Andalusia, there is a square bearing her name in a
pueblo of Málaga, and even King Juan Carlos paid tribute to her when he gave
her a tie made exclusively for him and said to her in appreciation, "Tú me haces
mucho bien" (Levine and Waldman; You do me a lot of good). Gloria Fuertes,
the public persona, has finally found the love and adulation that eluded her as
a motherless adolescent.

MAJOR THEMES

The social poets of the first generation of post–Civil War Spain, among them
Gabriel Celaya, Victoriano Crémer, Eugenio de Nora, and Blas de Otero, were
inspired by the concept that poetry is communication, converted into slogan by
Vicente Aleixandre and reelaborated theoretically by Carlos Bousoño.[2] Although
historically justified, these younger poets interpreted the idea of poetry as communication so literally that in many cases they ceased to write poetry. David
Bary observed that the social poet, putting clarity before authenticity, was forever
condemned to obscurity.[3] Fuertes, chronologically akin to Celaya, is nevertheless
often associated with the poets of the second generation of post–Civil War Spain,
among them José Ángel Valente, Ángel González, Claudio Rodríguez, and
Francisco Brines. For these complex writers for whom poetry is an act of knowledge, social commitment is reinterpreted to include the role of the poet as
discoverer, in collaboration with the reader, of a segment of everyday reality
unknown before the poetic experience. Anxious to communicate their revelations,
they experience the limitations and inadequacies of a clichéd and ineffective
language.

But Gloria Fuertes, perhaps as an isolated female writer, prefers not to be
aligned with any group. She is at once the "novice bullfighter of letters / on the
roads of Spain" (*Obras* 168) and the lone goat who "belongs to no flock"
(*Obras* 212). A poet by vocation, formed and deformed by the Civil War, who
feels compelled to find love and peace for herself and her *pueblo*, Fuertes
acknowledges that being a woman writer in a *machista,* or male-dominated,
country overpopulated by famous mediocre men has been an obstacle (Moix 41).
Her works recount her frustrations at being rooted in a restrictive partriarchal
society that encouraged her mother to wish she had given birth to a boy, impeded
her from fighting in the Civil War, and blocked women from writing (*Obras*
72). As a woman poet and political outcast, Fuertes was doubly marginalized
in Franco's Spain. She has been "on the edge" (al borde) of life's experiences—
jail, friendship, art, fame, suicide, love—and even "on the edge of waking up"
(*Obras* 42). It is on this edge that she finds herself naturally bonded to all those
at the margin of daily life—prostitutes, criminals, beggars, the destitute, and
the diseased—whom she longs to comfort and for whom she hopes to create a
better world.

Although many of the younger Spanish women poets minimalize their marginalization by avoiding references to gender (Ugalde 131), Gloria Fuertes is

clearly aware of herself as a woman poet. She not only writes from her hands, her eyes, and her heart but also, as none of her male counterparts can claim, from her ovaries (*Historia* 272). Once filled with dreams of becoming a captain (unarmed, of course), capable of transporting her poems to the moon, Fuertes realizes that it is quite enough to be a woman (*Obras* 256). Even more, she warns that it is up to her gender to undo the damage wrought by men (Moix 41). With the same intensity that she seeks affection, she longs to be recognized in her role as a female poet. Birds nest in her arms, thinking her a tree; ants gather, thinking her the earth; swans flock, thinking her a fountain: her poetic possibilities, wildly unleashed when fused with nature, are unnoticed only by men (*Obras* 49). Hungry for a glance, the needy child becomes the beggar/poet.

Fuertes sees strength in women poets as a group. In "Canción de las locas" (*Obras* 105; "Song of the Madwomen"), as the world is about to explode with evil, the mad women writers are asleep in the branches of a tree, symbolic of a fecund creativity, awaiting the Final Judgment. In "Enfermera de pulpos" (*Obras* 286; "Nurse to Octopuses"), the octopus and the poet, both dependent on their ink, are divided by gender. The male poets/octopuses are portrayed as removed from reality, greedy, untrustworthy in matters of love, and pompously stuffy, while their female counterparts simply play their harps in the afternoon, suggesting that it is their authentic voices that will eventually be heard. Our poet integrates herself into this sisterly community with her unique voice intact. It is in the silence and solitude of her "empty cradle"—one of the many female spaces that abound in Fuertes's verses—that she sees herself as "equal to all women / but similar to none" (*Historia* 198). The very solitude that intermittently leads her to thoughts of suicide and despair ultimately provides the arena for self-discovery. It is solitude personified as a sassy Andalusian prostitute who assures the poet that she deserves something better (*Obras* 186). Fuertes, along with the reader, drowns and resurfaces again and again in a silence, alternately painful and serene, in search of the words that delineate her being and free her from her patriarchal bonds. She begins her solitary dive toward what José Ángel Valente has called "point zero," the only place where a voice filled with stagnating echoes of a fallacious past becomes purifed: "Al calor del silencio / se maduran mis versos" (*Obras* 308; "In the heat of silence / my verses ripen"). At times the "point zero" leads her to another metaphorical level, the negative silence implicit in a language that is simply not adequate, and it is the tension and passion of this polarity that gives birth to her poetry.

The difficulties inherent in the poetic process become a constant theme. Surrendering with a veiled sexual submission to her poetry, her only constant lover— "Poetry takes over / and I submit" (*Historia* 347)—and often seduced by thoughts of suicide—"with a gentle chord in my throat / that gives me music and drains my blood" (*Obras* 169)—Gloria Fuertes knows that although hers is a difficult task, it is her ultimate salvation: "It seems that I'm going to die and I write" (*Obras* 294). Liberated in bouts of madness—she feeds herself food she does not eat, mails unwritten letters, and has at her disposal future centuries—

Fuertes's poetic voice grows in strength until in *Historia de Gloria* it reaches Amazonian proportions. She proclaims herself a mountain and boldly resorts to terrorist tactics that include holding up her readers to rob them of their indifference (57). Voices call out to her and converge upon her, and amid the fluid contradictions of her being, preconceived notions disappear and dissolve into awareness. At these most divine moments, the poet melts into a state of androgyny. It is precisely in this harmonious coming together of male and female— her referral to God in masculine and feminine terms, her penchant for transvestites, her hen that laid golden eggs and became a rooster—that Fuertes's identity emerges (Sherno, "Room of Her Own" 96).

Together with this androgynous perspective that informs Gloria Fuertes's poetry, there are other dimensions of self-discovery, already noted, that are more exclusively female centered. Deprived of her mother, childless herself, and constantly searching for her own matrilineal roots, Fuertes becomes obsessed with themes of maternity and birth. In an early autobiographical poem, "Isla ignorada" (*Antología* 49), the speaker, at first similar to the island, actually becomes the island during the poetic process. Surrounded by the existential nothingness of the sea, she finds the lost "green world" of her childhood and intuits her vocation as poet (Sherno, "Room of Her Own" 87). As poet/mother, ensconced in those serene nooks of solitude and love, she later gives birth both to herself ("I am my daughter" [*Historia* 326]) and to her poems, finally rejoicing in the "prologuillo" of *Historia de Gloria* that "this is not a book, it is a woman" (57). The painless process that Fuertes conceptualizes in her prose as "heart-mind-fingers, and between the fingers-creative thighs, the amazing birth of a new poem" (*Obras* 32), finds life in her verses:

> Soy una y estoy sola.
> La lluvia me serena.
> (ya está la poesía junto a mí),
> ya somos dos, poema. (*Historia* 363)

> I am one and I am alone.
> The rain calms me.
> (already the poetry is near me),
> now we are two, poem.

Identifying with Ángela Figuera's horror at the possibility of producing a son to go off to war, Fuertes prefers to keep her unborn child safe in her womb (*Obras* 122) and instead give birth to poems that can perhaps put an end to war.

Gloria Fuertes, echoing Hélène Cixous's belief that "woman must put herself into the text as into the world and into history—by her own movement,"[4] transcends her worst moments of existential anguish and transforms despair into hope as she unfolds "herstory." Her name, in all its glorious forms, and intimate details of her biography, are defined more boldly with each new volume: "Each act that I commit is poetry; the poet is not a poet if she doesn't live what she writes, if what she writes hasn't happened to her (qtd. in González Rodas 33). Fuertes's own sufferings are recalled and reflected with biting humor in her portraits of noncommunication and alienation, endemic in the decaying bourgeois society that oppresses her. Her own loves are retold in some of her most poignant poems, not as the erotic unfoldings of her younger literary sisters but, rather, as lonely yearnings in the form of anticipated phone calls, unwritten letters, and nocturnal visits, and as symbolic unions, the drinking of a lover's name inscribed in the melting snow (*Obras* 189–90). Fuertes continually demythifies the traditional notion of idyllic love, assuring us that the "matter of the nightingale" cannot be true (*Obras* 80) in a hostile world with a different agenda for its living dead. In the jolting poem "Me crucé con un entierro" (*Obras* 90–91; "I Came upon a Burial"), the speaker, encountering a burial procession, is casually drawn into a conversation with the dead man, who makes her wonder if perhaps her unrequited love makes her more dead than he. The poet, confirming and reconfirming her own existence in a gritty reality quite removed from the "very holy purity" of Juan Ramón Jiménez (*Obras* 332), feels obliged to tell her story as a reflection of what has happened or will happen to her people (*Obras* 22).

In her urgency to show solidarity with humanity, Fuertes has a preference for short poems that often take the form of a telegram, a letter, a file card, a confession, a recipe, or a brief news item. She chooses an unrhymed verse, uncounted syllables, and an exaggeratedly colloquial language laced with popular sayings, slang, curse words, and prosaic expressions rarely associated with poetry, to establish an immediate and open rapport with her reader and ease the frustrations of communication. Writing to her beloved poor in the *vosotros* form (plural familiar), Fuertes laments her inability to help her offspring. With maternal assurances she promises not only to sing their song but also that "others will come" (*Obras* 114). It is the poet/mother, in deep alliance with her children—the poor, the hungry, and the forgotten—who anxiously narrows the distance between reader and author and between child and mother, by demythifying the traditional image of an ivory tower poet. Andrew Debicki, in his analysis of "El vendedor de papeles" (*Obras* 52; "The Paperboy"), writes that the reader in this reversal of expectations is jolted into rethinking her preconceived notion of poetry. She is convinced by Fuertes that poetry, to be found everywhere, can indeed be peddled in the streets (83).

Seeing, feeling, smelling, sensing poetry everywhere, in mundane objects, forlorn beings, and even bodily functions, Fuertes, the "poeta de guardia," not only becomes the eyes of her progeny but also enables her reader to share her discoveries, the two now further bonded in an act of collusion. The poet delights in endless lists and namings as a means of substantiating her very existence and establishing a rapport with her own reality. Alicia Ostriker's evaluation of the poet May Swenson may be applied to Fuertes, in that the two exhibit a desire to create an intimacy with their world, with "no trace of the archetypal 'masculine' will to . . . control it."[5] If for Gabriel Celaya poetry was an "arm to transform the world," for Gloria Fuertes it is a warm "embrace" to cure the universe. From poet/mother to poet/doctor in a world inhabited by egotists, loveless bureaucrats, cheapskates, exploiters, hunters, and sexists, Fuertes wants to be a bandager of broken hearts and an "immense aspirin" to soothe her friends and enemies alike (*Obras* 270). She works furiously to discover the contagious poem that will spread its love (*Obras* 45) and cure the world of the virus of sadness that threatens rich and poor (*Obras* 234–35).

Fuertes is relentless as well in her criticism of other maladies of an ailing twentieth century: a world filled with greedy, arrogant "monsters" who have never said "I love you" (*Historia* 90). Marriage, in this milieu, becomes a frightening proposition for women who must hear a monotonous "ponte, venga, vamos, quiero" (*Historia* 69; put it, come, let's go, I want) from their husbands, who, clearly exonerated by glandular disorders, are more excited by their sisters-in-law than by their wives. Fuertes continues her attack against loveless men in her powerful critique of war. Outraged by a government that protects the rights of animals but condones the slaughter of humanity (*Obras* 56–57), the poet tries to disinvent war and humorously suggests that if there were a war, all soldiers should declare themselves on strike. Using stereotypical female images to conjure up the final solution of women to the rescue, Fuertes writes: "We've exchanged the gun for a broom / let's sweep the trench" (*Obras* 337).

In a world that is already topsy-turvy, where the sick are healthier than the well, where the heroes are the humble, where animals are smarter than humans, Gloria Fuertes resorts to further subversive tactics to unravel the patriarchal structures that gave birth to such a nightmare. At times, she writes "deliberately poorly" (*Historia* 65), to shake the reader into taking notice of the content of her verses. Elevating the importance of women's work, she lists the ingredients of her poetry in the form of a recipe: "mucha pena / mucha rabia / algo de sal" (*Obras* 141; a lot of anguish / a lot of wrath / a dash of salt). This bit of humor, serving to engage the reader's attention as well as to mollify the poet's fury, exists on two levels: on one it attracts the reader through puns, double entendres, hyperboles, paronomasias, and incongruent intertextualities; on the other, it surpasses the text and allows, through intellectual distancing, a reinterpretion of reality (Persin, "Humor" 119–20). Fuertes introduces surrealist images and expressionist deformations to shock the reader and to destroy the "normal" perspective of the world. In "Zoo de Verbena" (*Obras* 163), for example, someone in the street calling attention to this festive zoo invites passersby to enter and see the incredible array of animals: a hornless bull, an udderless cow, a marine monster and the father who birthed him. In another "reversal of expectations," the reader is forced to rethink this chaotic state of affairs more compassionately upon finding out, at the end of the poem, that the main attraction is an extinct animal, a happy man. Always underlying this destruction is the re-creation by both the poet and the reader of a better place turned right-side up.

Even God, presented as an earthly resident, is seen from an unexpected perspective (*Obras* 47). Implicit in this reversal is a powerful critique of the traditional dehumanized vision of the Almighty. Fuertes's God, although incorporating androgynous characteristics, is a regular person who has to be loved to exist, who can be reached by telephone, who feels comfortable in bars, and who calls the omnipotent Plumber to fix the leaking faucets when she/he cannot stop crying for humanity. Fuertes, in constant touch with God—speaking, soothing, and occasionally even berating this humanized presence—re-creates herself in her/his image. She, too, although accessible to all, identifies primarily with the poor, whose problems she seeks to solve through her love. In the tongue-and-cheek poem that closes her last published volume of poetry, *Historia de Gloria*, Fuertes, skillfully juxtaposing images of transcendental union and maternal magnitude, invites the reader to savor her through her textual body and emerge refreshed from this poetic odyssey:

> Al terminar de leer este libro
> —o lo que sea—,
> esta poesía
> —o lo que sea—,
> en ti se habrá posado un milagro
> —o lo que sea—,
> te has distraído unos minutos
> y has "entrado en la Gloria"
> sin necesidad de morirte. (336)

> As you finish this book
> —or whatever it is—,
> this poetry
> —or whatever it is—,
> a miracle will have happened to you
> —or whatever it is—,
> you will have distracted yourself for a few minutes
> and you will have "entered into *la Gloria*"
> without having had to die.

SURVEY OF CRITICISM

"A poetess," explains Alicia Ostriker, "is a poet who is sensitive and knows how to feel, perhaps very intensely, but does not know how to think or judge. She has no authority to change our minds . . . I suspect that many of the poetesses writing today are men."[6] Gloria Fuertes, addressing the precarious status of women poets before it was a fashionable issue, published a poem directed toward the male sector of the literary world (*Todo asusta* [1958]), in which she made clear her resentment at being called a poetess: "Hago versos, señores, hago versos / pero no me gusta que me llamen poetisa" (*Obras* 137; I write verses, gentlemen, I write verses / but I don't like to be called a poetess). Perhaps out of ignorance, many critics, both male (Aub, García Page, Miró, González-Muela) and female (Conde, Valdivieso) and as recently as 1991 (Cano), have persisted in their use of this deprecating label.

The definition of Gloria Fuertes in these terms has not, however, prevented her inclusion in many of the vintage anthologies of her time, among them José Luis Cano's *Antología de la nueva poesía española* (1958), Luis Jiménez Martos's *Nuevos poetas españoles* (1961), Leopoldo de Luis's *Poesía social* (1965, 1969), José María Castellet's *Un cuarto de siglo de poesía española (1939–1964)* (1966), Antonio Molina's *Poesía cotidiana* (1966), José Batlló's *Antología de la nueva poesía española* (1968), and Jerónimo-Pablo González-Martín's *Poesía hispánica. 1939–1969* (1979). Nor did it inhibit many leading Hispanic critics from writing general analyses of her poetry (Ciplijauskaité, González-Muela, Cano, González-Martín). Francisco Ynduráin and Pablo González Rodas wrote important introductions to her *Antología poética* and *Historia de Gloria* respectively. And José Luis Cano completed a thoughtful book about Fuertes's life and work published by Torremozas in 1991.

Although these general works invariably include a discussion of the social content of Gloria Fuertes's writings, Ynduráin's introduction being particularly noteworthy in this regard, other studies examine her work exclusively from this perspective (Bellver and Caballero Bonald). Catherine Bellver stresses three aspects of Fuertes's particular brand of "social consciousness": protest directed against injustices in general, an identification with the downtrodden based not on pity but on personal experiences, and an overriding "uplifting note of hope." While the critics often emphasize the importance of humor in Fuertes's verses, North American critics in particular explore this central role in a more systematic way. Timothy Rogers concentrates on Fuertes's comic sense of life. Reflecting on her use of humor to evoke the despair and absurdities of existence as a means of helping herself and her reader cope, he writes: "The jocular tone which vibrates like a resonant leit-motiv is what draws us to her voice and in the absurdities of the experiences which it offers to us, we can either find the humor and smile or we can despair. Gloria Fuertes, I believe, would prefer that we smile" (96). Margaret Persin, going further, examines how Fuertes uses humor both on a linguistic level to encourage "her reader to take a close look at how language can be self-referential in a comic way" ("Humor" 124) and on a semiotic level to manipulate "the reader's response in a specific way, to lead the reader in a certain direction" ("Humor" 125).

Gloria Fuertes's particular use of language never goes unnoticed. Although Santiago Daydí-Tolson dismisses her poetry for her "defiant and boorish language that reveals a radically rebellious attitude" and a "lack of poetic inventiveness and acumen" (*The Post-Civil War Spanish Social Poets* 99, 100), most critics have chosen to emphasize in different terms her deliberate inclusion of a colloquial and at times vulgar language. Luz María Umpierre understands that Fuertes, through the use of a hackneyed voice and what Michael Riffatere calls an "inversion of values," negates traditional male language and attitudes and seeks a transformation of society, linking her to the American poet Adrienne Rich. Andrew Debicki writes that Fuertes's inappropriate language does not reflect expressive inadequacies but, rather, introduces a new and different text—ads, verses from other poets, prayers—that conflicts in the reader's mind with the expected one (89). Substantiating his thesis with enlightening analyses of several of Fuertes's verses, Debicki shows that it is precisely in the confrontation of the two texts that a new level of meaning emerges (82). Margaret Persin, Candelas Newton, and Nancy Mandlove, with differing terminology, also present important intertextual analyses of Fuertes's use of clichéd language.

North American literary critics have generated great interest in a feminist reading of Fuertes's poetry, with particular regard to her reinvention of language. Harriet Turner, in a comparative study of Gabriela Mistral, Gloria Riestra, Rosario Castellanos, and Fuertes, insightfully analyzes the new poetic persona that emerges in each case in the cross between word and world. Nancy Mandlove, basing her study on the models of Mary Daly's *Gyn/Ecology* and Susan Griffin's *Woman and Nature*, writes that Fuertes's authentic female voice is rooted in the subversive opposition of text and context (official patriarchal history and unofficial herstory). And Sylvia Sherno, to be singled out for her feminist studies of Fuertes, reveals and perceptively analyzes the poet's multiple rebellious stratagems against an established patriarchal order. For Sherno, Fuertes's poetry "becomes a 'blank page' that not only defies the language of accepted male texts, but is ripe with the potential of female creativity" ("Textuality" 20). Her use of images of miniature and immensity serves "to explore issues of being and non-being" ("Room of Her Own" 86). Her poetry viewed as a journey inward can be interpreted either as an "archetypal rebirth story [Annis Pratt] or as a spiritual quest [Carol Christ]" ("Room of Her Own" 86). Finally, the subversive nature of Fuertes's writings may be underscored in light of her language of negation, which empowers her "both to reject conventions and to establish her own womanly discourse" ("Textuality" 21).

Gloria Fuertes was able, in spite of many obstacles, to establish herself as a serious female literary figure among her male colleagues. Pablo González Rodas, in his insightful and sensitive introduction to *Historia de Gloria*, credits her with having divided Spanish "feminine poets" of the twentieth century into two groups: those who came before her and those who followed (28). Margaret Persin, also emphasizing Fuertes's role as a pioneer, writes that as the bard of the community, she proves that the "female voice is capable of expressing the poetic song of the twentieth century" ("Humor" 134). Sylvia Sherno claims that the "issues she explores in her work have distinguished her as one of post–Franco Spain's leading feminist poets" ("Textuality" 19).

If women authors have traditionally been modest and shied away from writing in the first person, that is not the case with Gloria Fuertes. The rebellious voice of this lone fighter gains strength in its crusade against social injustices, inequalities, and hatred as it sings the cause of peace. The poet's only arm, her pen, serves to bridge the gap between her space of solitude and her expanding embrace of solidarity as her voice moves beyond the confines of her urgent texts, missives, and telegrams to reach its destination: humanity.

NOTES

1. All quotes in this section from José Luis Cano are in *Vida y poesía de Gloria Fuertes*. The poems cited throughout the article from *Antología poética* are from the second edition (1972), referred to as *Antología*; from the ninth edition (1984) of *Obras incompletas* referred to as *Obras*, and from the fifth edition (1990) of *Historia de Gloria*, referred to as *Historia*.

2. Carlos Bousoño, "Poesía como comunicación," *Teoría de la expresión poética*, 4th ed. (Madrid: Gredos, 1966) 17–57.

3. David Bary, "Sobre el nombrar poético en la poesía española contemporánea," *Papeles de Son Armadans* 44 (1967): 161–89.

4. Hélène Cixous, "The Laugh of the Medusa," trans. Keith Cohen and Paula Cohen, *New French Feminisms*, ed. Elaine Marks and Isabelle de Courtivron, (New York: Schocken, 1981) 245–46.

5. Alicia Ostriker, "May Swenson and the Shapes of Speculation," *Shakespeare's Sisters. Feminist Essays on Women Poets*, ed. Sandra M. Gilbert and Susan Gubar (Bloomington: Indiana UP, 1979) 223.

6. Alicia Ostriker, *Writing Like a Woman* (Ann Arbor: The U of Michigan P, 1983) 146.

BIBLIOGRAPHY

Major Works by Gloria Fuertes

Poetry

Isla ignorada. Madrid: Musa Nueva, 1950.
Aconsejo beber hilo. Madrid: Arquero, 1954.
Antología y poemas del suburbio. Caracas: Lírica Hispana, 1954.
Todo asusta. Caracas: Lírica Hispana, 1958.
Que estás en la tierra. Barcelona: Seix Barral, 1962.
Ni tiro, ni veneno, ni navaja. Barcelona: El Bardo, 1965.
Poeta de guardia. Barcelona: El Bardo, 1968.
Cómo atar los bigotes al tigre. Barcelona: El Bardo, 1969.
Antología poética (1950–1969). Barcelona: Plaza y Janés, 1970. [Contains selections
    from *Isla ignorada*, *Antología y poemas de suburbio*, *Aconsejo beber hilo*, *Canciones para niño*, *Pirulí*, *Ni tiro, ni veneno, ni navaja*, *Poeta de guardia*, and *Cómo atar los bigotes al tigre*]
Cuando amas aprendes Geografía. Málaga: Curso Superior de Filología, 1973.
Sola en la sala. Zaragoza: Javalambre, 1973.
Obras incompletas. Madrid: Cátedra, 1980. [Includes edited versions of all volumes from
    Antología y poemas del suburbio through *Sola en la sala*]
Historia de Gloria (Amor, humor y desamor). Madrid: Cátedra, 1981.

Poetics

"Respuestas, cuestionario." *Antología de la nueva poesía española*. By José Batlló.
    Madrid: El Bardo, 1968. 337–38.

"Poética." *Poesía social. Antología (1939–1968)*. By Leopoldo de Luis. 2nd ed. Madrid: Alfaguara, 1969. 151–52.

Prologue. *Obras incompletas*. By Gloria Fuertes. Madrid: Cátedra, 1980. 21–38.

Books for Children

The following is a selection of Gloria Fuertes's children's books.

Canciones para niños. Madrid: Escuela Española, 1952.

Villancicos. Madrid: Magisterio Español, 1954.

Pirulí (versos para párvulos). Madrid: Escuela Española, 1955.

Cangura para todo (cuentos para niños). Barcelona: Lumen, 1968.

Aurora, Brígida y Carlos (versos para párvulos). Barcelona: Lumen, 1970.

Don Pato y Don Pito (versos para niños). Madrid: Escuela Española, 1970.

La pájara pinta (cuentos en verso). Madrid: Alcalá, 1972.

El camello-auto de los Reyes Magos (poemas para niños). Madrid: Igreca de Ediciones, 1973.

El hada acaramelada (poemas para niños). Madrid: Igreca de Ediciones, 1973.

La oca loca. Madrid: Escuela Española, 1977.

La momia tiene catarro (cuentos). Madrid: Escuela Española, 1978.

El dragón tragón (cuentos). Madrid: Escuela Española, 1979.

Tres tigres con trigo. Madrid: Yubarta, 1979.

Theater

"Prometeo." [Premiered in the Teatro de Cultura Hispánica, 1952]

"El chinito Chin-cha-the." [Children's theater]

"Guiones, cuentos y poesías." [Spanish television]

Translations

"Prayer." Trans. unknown. *Arena* 23 (1965): 67.

Recent Poetry of Spain. A Bilingual Anthology. Trans. Louis Hammer and Sara Schyfter. Old Chatham, NY: Sachem Press, 1983. Included in this volume are the following poems: "Biographical Note," 151; "Don't Run Away from Pain," 163; "Homage to Rubén Darío," 161; "Hospital-old-age Asylum for the Poor," 159; "I Fell," 157, 159; "The Lady-Termite," 159, 161; "Let's Not Waste Time," 153; "Look at Me Here," 157; "The Man's Departure," 155; "Nighttime Tears," 155; "The Truth Inside the Lie," 161.

Off the Map. Selected Poems by Gloria Fuertes. Ed. and trans. Philip Levine and Ada Long. Middletown, CT: Wesleyan UP, 1984.

The Defiant Muse. Hispanic Feminist Poems from the Middle Ages to the Present: A Bilingual Anthology. Ed. and intro. Ángel Flores and Kate Flores. New York: The Feminist Press at the City U of NY, 1986. Included in this volume are the following poems: "The Bird's Nest in my Arms," Trans. Kate Flores, 85; "I Don't Know," Trans. Kate Flores, 81; "I Make Poems, Gentlemen!" Trans. Kate Flores, 83; "Not Allowed to Write," Trans. L. Smith and Judith Candullo, 83; "To Have a Child these Days," Trans. Kate Flores, 85.

Works about Gloria Fuertes

Aub, Max. "Gloria Fuertes." *Una nueva poesía española (1950–1955)*. Mexico City: Imprenta Universitaria, 1957.

Bellver, Catherine G. "Gloria Fuertes, Poet of Social Consciousness." *Letras Femeninas* 4.1 (1978): 29–38.

Benítez, Rubén. "El maravilloso retablo popular de Gloria Fuertes." *Mester* 9 (Jan. 1980): 29–30.

Caballero Bonald, José Manuel. "Gloria Fuertes: *Qué estás en la tierra.*" *Insula* 203 (Oct. 1963): 5.

Cano, José Luis. "Humor y ternura en la poesía de Gloria Fuertes." *Poesía española contemporánea. Las generaciones de posguerra.* Madrid: Guadarrama, 1974. 174–80.

———. "La poesía de Gloria Fuertes." *Insula* 269 (Apr. 1969): 8–9.

———. *Vida y poesía de Gloria Fuertes.* Madrid: Torremozas, 1991.

Castellet, José María. Prologue. *Un cuarto de siglo de poesía española (1939–1964).* Barcelona: Seix Barral, 1966. 111–13.

Ciplijauskaité, Biruté. "Direcciones de posguerra: comunión y conocimiento." *El poeta y la poesía (Del Romanticismo a la poesía social).* Madrid: Insula, 1966. 383–484, passim.

Concha, Víctor G. de la. *La poesía española de posguerra. Teoría e historia de sus movimientos.* Madrid: Prensa Española, 1973.

Conde, Carmen. *Poesía femenina española viviente.* Madrid: Arquero, 1954.

Daydí-Tolson, Santiago. "Hacia un panorama crítico de las voces femeninas en la poesía española contemporánea." *Monograph Review/Revista Monográfica* 6 (1990): 46–60.

———. *The Post-Civil War Spanish Social Poets.* Boston: Twayne, 1983. 99–102, passim.

Debicki, Andrew P. "Gloria Fuertes: Intertextuality and Reversal of Expectations." *Poetry of Discovery. The Spanish Generation of 1956–1971.* Lexington: The UP of Kentucky, 1982. 81–101.

Fernández Molina, Antonio. "Gloria Fuertes. *Ni tiro, ni veneno ni navaja.*" *Asomante* 2 (Apr.–June 1968): 60–61.

García Page, Mario. "Un artificio fónico recurrente en la lengua poética de Gloria Fuertes: la paronomasia." *RLit* 48 (1986): 407–31.

González-Martín, J. P. *Poesía hispánica. 1939–1969. Estudio y antología.* Barcelona: El Bardo, 1979.

González-Muela, Joaquín. "Antologías de poesía nueva." *La nueva poesía española.* Madrid: Ediciones Alcalá, 1973. 129–54.

———. "Gloria Fuertes. 'Poeta de Guardia'." *La nueva poesía española* 13–29.

González Rodas, Pablo. Introduction. *Historia de Gloria (Amor, humor y desamor).* By Gloria Fuertes. Madrid: Cátedra, 1981. 27–50.

Grande, Félix. *Apuntes sobre poesía española de posguerra.* Madrid: Taurus, 1970.

Jiménez, José Olivio. *Diez años de poesía española (1960–1970).* Madrid: Insula, 1972. Passim.

Levine, Linda Gould, and Gloria Waldman. Personal interview. 1991.

Long, Ada. Introduction. *Off the Map. Selected Poems by Gloria Fuertes.* Ed. and trans. Philip Levine and Ada Long. Middletown, CT: Wesleyan UP, 1991. 3–8.

Luis, Leopoldo de. Introduction. *Poesía social. Antología (1939–1968).* 2nd ed. Madrid: Alfaguera, 1969. 9–42.

Mandlove, Nancy. "*Historia* and *Intra-historia*: Two Spanish Women Poets in Dialogue with History." *Third Woman-Hispanic Women: International Perspectives* 2.2 (1984): 84–93.

———. "Oral Texts: The Play of Orality and Literacy in the Poetry of Gloria Fuertes." *Siglo XX/Twentieth Century* 5.1–2 (1987–88): 11–16.

———. "Used Poetry: The Trans-parent Language of Gloria Fuertes and Angel González." *Revista Canadiense de Estudios Hispánicos* 7.2 (Winter 1983): 301–06.

Miró, Emilio. "Gloria Fuertes [*Sola en la sala*]—Concha Lagos." *Insula* 324 (Nov. 1973): 6.

———. "Poesía. Una antología y dos nuevas colecciones." *Insula* 288 (Nov. 1970): 7.

Moix, Ana María. "Gloria Fuertes: Poeta para niños, o el difícil encanto de peinarse las canas a los 12 años." *Vindicación Feminista* 5 (Nov. 1976): 40–41.

Newton, Candelas. "La palabra 'convertida' de Gloria Fuertes." *Letras Femeninas* 13.1–2 (1987): 6–11.

Núñez, Antonio. "Encuentro con Gloria Fuertes." *Insula* 270 (May 1969): 3.

Persin, Margaret H. "Gloria Fuertes and (Her) Feminist Reader." *Revista/Review Interamericana* 12.1 (Spring 1982): 125–32.

———. "Humor as Semiosis in the Poetry of Gloria Fuertes." *Recent Poetry and the Role of the Reader*. Lewisburg, PA: Bucknell UP, 1987. 119–36.

Quiñones, Fernando. *Ultimos rumbos de la poesía española*. Buenos Aires: Columba, 1966.

Rogers, Timothy J. "The Comic Spirit in the Poetry of Gloria Fuertes." *Perspectives on Contemporary Literature* 8 (1982): 88–97.

Rubio, Fanny. "La poesía española en el marco cultural de los primeros años de posguerra." *Cuadernos Hispanoamericanos* 276 (June 1973): 441–67.

Sherno, Sylvia. "Carnival: Death and Renewal in the Poetry of Gloria Fuertes." *Modern Language Notes* 104 (Mar. 1989): 370–92.

———. "Gloria Fuertes and the Poetics of Solitude." *Anales de la Literatura Española Contemporánea* 12.3 (1987): 311–26.

———. "Gloria Fuertes' Room of Her Own." *Letras Femeninas* 16.1–2 (1990): 85–99.

———. "The Poetry of Gloria Fuertes: Textuality and Sexuality." *Siglo XX/Twentieth Century* 7.1–2 (1989–90): 19–23.

———. "Weaving the World: The Poetry of Gloria Fuertes." *Hispania* 72 (May 1989): 247–55.

Turner, Harriet S. "Moving Selves: The Alchemy of *Esmero* (Gabriela Mistral, Gloria Riestra, Rosario Castellanos, and Gloria Fuertes)." *In the Feminine Mode. Essays on Hispanic Women Writers*. Ed. Noël Valis and Carol Maier. Lewisburg, PA: Bucknell UP, 1990. 227–45.

Ugalde, Sharon Keefe. "Spanish Women Poets on Women's Poetry." *Monografic Review/Revista Monográfica* 6 (1990): 128–37.

Umpierre, Luz María. "Inversión de valores y efectos en el lector en 'Oración' de Gloria Fuertes." *Plaza* 5–6 (1981–82): 132–44.

Valdivieso, L. Teresa. "Significación del discurso poético: Un poema de Gloria Fuertes." *Letras Femeninas* 2.2 (Fall 1976): 15–22.

Waldman, Gloria. "Gloria Fuertes." *Women Writers of Spain: An Annotated Bio-Bib-*

liographical Guide. Ed. Carolyn L. Galerstein. Westport, CT: Greenwood Press, 1986. 119–21.

———. Personal interview. 1986.

Ynduráin, Francisco. Prologue. *Antología poética (1950–1969)*. By Gloria Fuertes. Barcelona: Plaza y Janés, 1970. 9–45.

ADELAIDA GARCÍA MORALES
(b. 194?)

Yvonne Jehenson

BIOGRAPHY

Adelaida García Morales was born in Badajoz and raised in Seville, in the province where her parents were born. She received her degree in philosophy in 1970 from the University of Madrid, studied script writing at the Official School of Cinematography in Madrid, and has been a secondary school teacher of Spanish language and literature as well as of philosophy. In Algiers, she served as translator for OPEC and has worked as a model and as an actress. For five years she lived in the village of La Alpujarra in Granada, the setting of one of her novels. One of two unpublished works, the novel "Archipiélago," was a finalist for the Sésamo Prize in 1981.

Although she is a recent literary discovery, García Morales's four published novels to date have been very successful. *El Sur* (1985; "The South") was begun in 1981 and made into a movie by Víctor Erice in 1983. The movie is very different from the novel; the characters have been changed, and the poignant monologue to the dead father—essential to the novel—is replaced with dramatic action. The movie ends where the novel becomes most interesting, with the narrator's trip south in search of her father's past. It avoids such social taboos as the suggestion of incest, which are central to the novel. The movie, nevertheless, gave García Morales wide exposure. *Bene,* her second novel, is even more controversial in its treatment of social taboos. It is a companion piece to *El Sur*, with which it was published in 1985 as *El Sur seguido de Bene* ("The South Followed by Bene"). *El silencio de las sirenas* (1985; "The Silence of the Sirens"), begun in 1979, was published in the same year. *El silencio de las sirenas,* dedicated to Víctor Erice, won both the Herralde Novel Prize and the Icaro Prize given by the periodical *Diario 16.* In 1990 García Morales published her fourth novel, *La lógica del vampiro* ("The Vampire's Logic").

García Morales is an intensely private person. The fragments of her biography that she chooses to reveal are fundamental to an understanding of her works. Her novels are childhood memories, fictional permutations of her personal experiences. Until she was ten, she lived far from the city, restricted and isolated from the companionship of other children. She grew up with adults viewed as rigid and conventionally oppressive, and as distant as those she portrays in her novels. She admits that she is an introvert for whom the imaginative is more important than the real. Her epigraphs reiterate this penchant. *El Sur* begins with a quote from Johann C.F. Hölderlin: "What can we love that is not a shadow?" and the epigraph to *El silencio de las sirenas* is from Fernando Pessoa: "For God permits that which does not exist to be intensely illuminated."

MAJOR THEMES

Adelaida García Morales's works incorporate a wide variety of signs from other texts in order to create new networks of meaning. Her use of intertextuality is primarily polemical and subversive. Intertextuality becomes a feminist strategy in her works, a counterreply that highlights or negates the previous text and leads to a new statement and new meaning.

In *El Sur seguido de Bene,* García Morales deliberately subverts traditional genre conventions. She focuses on marginal characters and uses the fantastic mode, which, because it is marginal to the canonical genres, images the possibility of radical cultural transformation. She attempts to dissolve, to shatter the boundary lines between the imaginary and the symbolic.[1] García Morales thereby creates a space for a discourse that seems forever suspended on the point of meaning, a meaning that never takes place. Although García Morales's fantastic world is deliberately removed from contemporary sociorealism, a dialogic relationship exists between the narrators' society and their intense and ultimately aborted desire to transgress their limits.

In *El Sur seguido de Bene,* García Morales uses two literary modes, that of the fantastic and that of the bildungsroman. The term "fantastic" is used here in its Latin sense of *phantasticus*—that which is made visible, that which is uncovered. The focus in *El Sur* is on the brooding figure of Adriana's dominant father, who overwhelms the household by imposing silence and isolation on the women who are confined within. The child Adriana grows up alienated from her uncaring mother and adoring her dominant, brooding father, who harbors a dark secret: he has abandoned the woman he once loved and their son. This repressed past eventually destroys him. The child narrator seeks to learn about her father after his violent suicide. She goes to the south of Spain, thereby attempting to prolong his presence in her life and to become a part of his past, of that romantic dream he has shared with "the other woman." Her adoration of her father prompts her to dream that they will marry one day and to make a sacrificial pact with God that entails her dying before she is ten so that her father's soul can be saved. This incipient note of incest, merely implied vis-à-vis her father, becomes explicit at the end of the story. Adriana encourages her half brother's incestuous love for her by admitting to him that she loves him.

García Morales also uses the generic codes of the bildungsroman in order to inscribe the development of young Adriana. She takes Adriana through the different stages of female development and exposes her to the dissonances and conflicts of life that are conventionally necessary for the hero to achieve maturity and harmony. But this developmental process does not work for the heroine. The story of her development is inscribed in the master's plot. Instead of Adriana's reinscribing the genre and her place in it, she becomes circumscribed by it. Her father emplots the various stages of her development, only to abandon her through his suicide. Even the intensely private García Morales admits in an interview that "when suffering is no longer conceptual, but visceral, as in this case, it is irrelevant to speak of 'accepting' a suicide and a half-destroyed childhood'' (Sánchez Arnosi 4).

The master's plot also partakes of a double standard. Her father imposes "rigid norms" on Adriana, yet she feels that they are norms that he himself had ridiculed (32). Her ultimate growing-up experience—seeking her dead father in the south—results in the most devastating moment of recognition. She realizes that just as he had abandoned the woman he had loved and their son, so he could also have abandoned her. The realization that the father for whom she is ready to die is actually a coward does not free Adriana, nor does it bring her the maturity or understanding with which the conventional bildungsroman ends: "Understanding was not enough to reconcile me with your existence, nor mama's, nor mine, nor those two beings who also suffered from your abandonment'' (52). The novel ends with a frustrating and painful sense that this is an ironic version of the traditional bildungsroman. The dissonances and conflicts of life that mark each stage of the hero's development are certainly here, but they do not work for the female. They do not serve Adriana as the basis for progressing to a higher stage marked by continuing independence. The female protagonist in García Morales's bildungsroman never becomes independent. She ends as she begins—with the father. By Adelaida García Morales's own account, the brother with whom Adriana incestuously bonds at the end is but the shadow of the paternal figure.

García Morales explores similar themes in *Bene*. A dominant, mysterious figure with a terrible secret pervades the pages of *Bene*. This time, however, the dominant figure is not a man but a woman, the half-gypsy maid Bene, a dreadful supernatural figure who invades the space of Angela, the narrator. The love that Angela's brother, Santiago, feels for Bene becomes "a supernatural possession" that eventually causes his death (99). Aunt Elisa is convinced that Bene has bewitched Angela's father with whom she claims Bene is sexually involved. Bene, then, despite the positive connotation of her name, seems to embody the traditional evil figure of the gothic-fantastic mode. But García Morales reverses the topos to bring a feminist consciousness to the gothic-fantastic convention. Is Bene a persecutor or a victim? Aunt Elisa hates Bene. But how reliable is Aunt Elisa?

The hesitation inscribed structurally in García Morales's fictional worlds forces the reader to reflect. Aunt Elisa has forbidden Angela to speak to gypsies because they are members of the lower class. Bene and her sister Juana are part gypsy, and Bene is also the family's maid. Aunt Elisa accuses Angela's father of going on pleasure trips during his many absences. Angela believes that the suffering occasioned by her mother's death and his own inability to cope with two young children are more likely the reasons for her father's frequent absences. Even the suspicious Doña Rosaura sees Bene as the victim of her father/lover, who forced her into a shameful life when she was only fourteen. Obviously possessed by a force that subjects her to his will, Bene is afraid to sleep for fear of her own dreams. She is the object of Angela's father's and brother's desire and is the sexual possession of her ghost father/lover. She has no authentic self, and has been rendered deathlike and alien in the ghost's presence and otherworldly in Santiago's dreams, where she has no feet. No one, however, has actually found Bene guilty of any wrongdoing. Even Aunt Elisa gets bored spying on her. It becomes clear that the negative perception of Bene can be societally determined, that "evil" is at one with the category of Otherness. Bene is a gypsy, a maid, and "different."

Adelaida García Morales's reversal of the fantastic subtext serves to emphasize that the "Other" is not feared because she is evil, but that she is "evil" because she is the Other, alien, different, and unfamiliar.[2] Bene eventually hangs herself. Even then, how much autonomy does she exercise? Her sister, Juana, sees her, once more, as the object of her father/lover, who has "taken her" with him. The novel ends when the young narrator merges with the ghost of Bene's father. It is a willing surrender for which the reader has been prepared by Angela's admitted satisfaction that the ghost now seems to seek her rather than Bene. The erotic nuances of the necrophilic embrace and Angela's inability or unwillingness to fend for herself are similar to Adriana's in *El Sur*. Angela, too, ultimately turns to the male, in this case to a union with her dead brother, Santiago. As fantastically eerie as the atmosphere appears, *Bene's* defenseless, overwhelmed women characters are inscribed in the metonymical world of *El Sur*, which is once again presented as a portion of the real world. This literary device serves to uncover aspects we either do not encounter or repress in prosaic reality.

In *El silencio de las sirenas,* García Morales exposes the courtly-love tradition as the romantic search for that which can never be made present. Although she pinpoints the novel's relationship with the romantic tradition, the irony implicit in these clichés is explicit. She presents the romantic heroine Elsa as a type— "a paradigm of the woman in love" (Ciplijauskaité 171). She underlines Elsa's estrangement from the other characters, portraying her as a "totally inactive" figure (53) who inhabits "another space" in her "inhuman immobility" (26–27).

García Morales presents Elsa's love story as a pastiche, a compendium of romantic intertextualities. In Elsa's diary, we have the epistolary romantic tradition. In her hypnotic trances we see the courtly-love tradition in which Agustín, Elsa's idealized lover, merges with Edward, and Elsa with Ottilie, of Goethe's *Elective Affinities*. In Elsa's waking "trances" Franz Kafka becomes as much of a model as Goethe, and Kafka's *Silence of the Sirens* becomes the subtextual impetus for García Morales's *El silencio de las sirenas*. Even the idealized Agustín understands Elsa's reinscription in the courtly-love tradition. He explains to the narrator, María, that he has never felt that Elsa's letters are actually addressed to him but rather to an ideal lover, and Elsa herself admits that she seeks the nonexistent: "I do not want a man! I only want to feel love as I now experience it" (147). García Morales has Elsa hold a conscious dialogue with the traditional romantic topos of the pale and wan lover who dies a victim of the disdainful mistress of the courtly-love tradition, only to reverse it. In *El silencio,* it is not Tristan, Grisóstomo, or Romeo who loses Isolde, Marcela, or Juliet. Unlike Goethe's literary ending, where the hero, Edward, goes insane over Ottilie's death, or Elsa's oneiric wish that Edward-Agustín suffer intensely because of her death, García Morales gives the lie to the entire romantic convention. In real life, the narrator María knows that things happen differently: "I feared that Elsa's death would not impress him [Agustín] as it had in the dreams in which she had loved him so much" (168).

In her latest novel, *La lógica del vampiro*, García Morales depicts the patriarchal and fantastic world of her first three novels. It is a rarefied world where the characters are alienated, trapped in a game whose rules are unknown to them and where mysterious figures continue to exert obsessive control. *La lógica del vampiro* depicts the odyssey of Elvira, a young woman in search of the true circumstances of her brother Diego's death. Diego's friend Pablo sugests that their mutual friend Alfonso, the "vampire," had something to do with Diego's apparent suicide. Through demonic powers of suggestion, Alfonso creates "unresolvable conflicts" in others that lead to their anguish and/or destruction. As a result of Alfonso's influence, an irrevocable rupture occurs between Diego and his lover, Mara. Diego, encouraged by Alfonso to dwell on his estrangement and limitations, kills himself. Sonia, Alfonso's musically untalented protégée, is obsessed with the futility of perfecting her piano performance. Alfonso controls them all by unveiling their deepest needs and then encouraging them to dwell upon their inadequacies. As a result, they become his pawns. There is Alfonso's wife, Teresa, who alludes to the horror of her life with Alfonso and who is described as silent, marginal, and "a vegetable" (137); Sonia, the mediocre musician, who is sickly and marked by lassitude and loss of willpower; and the vacant-eyed, twenty-eight-year-old Mara, who is described as a mere reflection rather than an entity in her own right. She poignantly longs to be able to feel any kind of personal desire once again.

Elvira, the narrator of *La lógica*, is different. More defiant than the other characters in *La lógica*, more defiant than her adolescent female predecessors in *El Sur* and *Bene* or the romantic heroine Elsa of *El silencio*, she chooses not to turn to the male. The hiatus of five years between García Morales's novels is marked in the character of Elvira. She is a woman who refuses, despite her loneliness and her incipient love for Alfonso, to be inscribed in his plot. Elvira is a forty-year-old geography teacher who lives alone. She has returned to the Seville of her youth because of her younger brother's death. Immediately attracted to Alfonso, as are all the characters except Pablo, she nevertheless sees the "disagreeable influence" he has over everyone.

Elvira is skeptical of both Alfonso's version of her brother's death and his desire to undermine the reliability of Pablo's version. But she, too, is vulnerable. Alfonso has unveiled her "lack." He reminds her of how lonely her life has been and makes her concentrate on its emptiness. He provokes her jealousy by spending time in the room next door with Mara. Their soft murmurs are designed to remind Elvira of her own loveless life. Alfonso stops by to visit her, caresses her leg, and then leaves. Excited, euphoric, and "intolerably empty" (93), she begins to experience the "unresolvable conflicts" Alfonso creates, and finally understands why Diego killed himself. He, too, must have experienced such intolerable inner conflicts. Elvira, however, is the only character who confronts Alfonso directly; she orders him to cease controlling her. She publicly announces to the victimized circle surrounding Alfonso that much worse than her brother's death is "that monstrous something of which we are all aware" (170). Elvira leaves Seville and Alfonso, knowing that she might have succumbed, like the others, if he had loved her.

Elvira, aware of her vulnerability, is nevertheless determined not to be used. Adriana and Angela transgress conventional taboos. Elsa lives out her literary ideal to the end. She plans her own death, thereby choosing a literary fulfillment traditionally reserved for males. As painful as García Morales's endings are, they emphasize both the reality of the patriarchal worlds that circumscribe her women and the women's deliberate defiance within these worlds.

SURVEY OF CRITICISM

Although only recently discovered within Spain, Adelaida García Morales is becoming known outside Spain. Her reputation has been strengthened by Víctor Erice's film version of *El Sur* and by the award given to *El silencio de las sirenas*. In interviews and articles, critics agree on this young writer's talent for creating probing imaginative worlds that deal with subjects not traditional in Spanish letters.

Because her works are so recent, reviews are still sparse. They focus on the analysis of García Morales's individual works. Of the five studies listed in the bibliography, Milagros Sánchez Arnosi's interview is perhaps the most interesting, for it uncovers areas of García Morales's personal life that are fundamental to an understanding of her literary work. She reveals elements of her childhood that are fictionally transferred to the worlds of *El Sur* and of *Bene* and that explain salient features of those works.

Luis Suñén's review of *El silencio de las sirenas* points to the major themes of García Morales' works, especially the quest for the inexplicable not as a means of contrast with, but as complement to, the real. Biruté Ciplijauskaité studies *El silencio de las sirenas* as a subversion of the traditional love story and the protagonist Elsa as a paradigm of the heroine within that tradition. Currie Thompson gives a psychoanalytic reading of *Bene*. Her approach is twofold: she sees *Bene* as the tale of the separation of two siblings, Adriana and Santiago, and the narrator's resistance to that separation; and as an account of the twelve-year-old Adriana's awareness that her secure sanctuary (her inner and outer space) is being invaded by a sinister masculine force. Elizabeth Ordóñez studies three of García Morales's novels (*El Sur*, *Bene*, *El silencio*) as positioned between the imaginary and the symbolic, occupying a duration of uncertainty. She attempts to show how García Morales explores the varied manifestations of desire in her work.

García Morales's knowledge of literary traditions is extensive. Her works are fertile ground for the continuing investigation of her use of genre theory in order to explore, by her own account, the feminine world that is of such vital interest to her.

NOTES

1. Rosemary Jackson, *Fantasy: The Literature of Subversion* (New York: Methuen, 1981) 178.
2. Frederic Jameson, *The Political Unconscious: Narrative as a Socially Symbolic Act* (Ithaca, NY: Cornell UP, 1981) 140.

BIBLIOGRAPHY

Works by Adelaida García Morales

El silencio de las sirenas. Barcelona: Editorial Anagrama, 1985.
El Sur seguido de Bene. Barcelona: Editorial Anagrama, 1985.
La lógica del vampiro. Barcelona: Editorial Anagrama, 1990.

Translation

The Silence of the Sirens. Trans. Concilia Hayter. London: Collins, 1988.

Works about Adelaida García Morales

Ciplijauskaité, Biruté. "Intertextualidad y subversión en *El silencio de las sirenas* de Adelaida García Morales." *Revista Hispánica Moderna* 41.2 (Dec. 1988): 167–74.

Ordóñez, Elizabeth J. "Writing Ambiguity and Desire: The Works of Adelaida García Morales." *Women Writers of Contemporary Spain: Exiles in the Homeland*. Ed. Joan L. Brown (Newark, DE: U of Delaware P, 1991). 258–77.

Sánchez Arnosi, Milagros. "Adelaida García Morales: La soledad gozosa." *Insula* 472 (Mar. 1986): 4.

Suñén, Luis. "En pos de la quimera: una nueva de Adelaida García Morales." *El País* 6 Feb. 1986: 8.

Thompson, Currie K. "Adelaida García Morales' *Bene* and that Not-so-obscure Object of Desire." *Revista de Estudios Hispánicos* 22.1 (Jan. 1988): 99–106.

CONCEPCIÓN GIMENO DE FLAQUER (1852?–1919)

Maryellen Bieder

BIOGRAPHY

One of the few women of her generation to sustain a career as a writer, Concepción Gimeno was born in Alcañiz (Teruel) in December 1850 or 1852 (Bieder, "Feminine Discourse" 460–62; Simón Palmer 363), although she later gave 1860 as her date of birth (Bolaños 18; Valle 6). The modernized spelling "Jimeno" frequently replaced the author's own usage in her day, as it does today. Her life and writings span the same period as the most famous woman author of her generation, Emilia Pardo Bazán, but the two women moved in different literary circles and addressed different readerships. Journalist, novelist, and *literata*, Gimeno reached both female and male readers in Spain and Latin America with her essays, her fiction, and her weekly illustrated magazines.

Educated at schools in Zaragoza, Gimeno initiated her writing career in a local magazine in 1869. Surprisingly, and in contrast with other literary women, she did not pen verses. Her first article, "A los impugnadores del bello sexo" ("To the Detractors of the Fair Sex"), anticipates the revisionist defense of women and the figurative language that characterize her future writing. Tracing a familiar pattern for young women from provincial families, Gimeno completed her education in Madrid, where she was introduced into literary circles through the *tertulias* (literary gatherings) held by senior men of letters. Recognizing that societal expectations equated women with beauty, she foregrounded her good looks as the visible confirmation of her femininity. Her youth and her careful espousal of the values and virtues of traditional womanhood assured her admiration and support among literary men, even as she directly challenged commonplace disparagements of women and their capabilities. Although she rewrote gender representation and wove new roles for women into the carefully modulated fabric of her texts, she continued to find male sponsors for her career.

In Madrid, Gimeno moved in social circles, attending the duchess de la Torre's literary salon, where she gave recitations and met such major literary figures as Juan Valera and Carolina Coronado (Gimeno, "La duquesa" 162). Coronado, known at this time for her encouragement of young women writers, became something of a mentor to Gimeno. The young writer also participated in the literary and cultural activities initiated by Patrocinio de Biedma, Faustina Sáez de Melgar, Josefa Pujol de Collado, and Sofía Tartilán, who together formed an informal community of literary women. Gimeno maintained these associations with other writing women for the rest of her life. In 1871 her name appeared as one of the editors of a new magazine for women, *La Mujer*, founded by Faustina Sáez de Melgar. Her early articles appeared in such leading women's magazines as *Cádiz* and *El Correo de la Moda*, as well as in Madrid newspapers.

In 1873 Concepción Gimeno launched her own periodical, *La Ilustración de la Mujer* ("The Illustrated Magazine for Women"), the editorship of which soon passed to Sofía Tartilán. That same year a Madrid newspaper, *La Época*, serialized her first novel, *Victorina; o Heroismo del corazón* (1873; "Victorina, or Heroism of the Heart"), before its publication in two volumes. This was her only novel to be published as a newspaper *folletín* (serial), and the only one in the multivolume format in fashion at midcentury. By the time Gimeno completed her first book of essays, *La mujer española: Estudios acerca de su educación y sus facultades intelectuales* (1877; "The Spanish Woman, Essays on Her Education and Her Intellectual Capacity"), she had attracted sufficient attention to present her book to King Alfonso XII and read him a chapter from it. Royal patronage of Gimeno's writing signaled social sanction of her ideas; her dedication of two later books on women to royal princesses, sisters of the late king, confirmed the value she attached to that approval.

After marrying the journalist Francisco de Paula Flaquer in 1879, Gimeno appended Flaquer's surname to her own, signing all her publications "Concepción Gimeno de Flaquer." In this way, she foregrounded her status and respectability as a married woman, a practice adopted by many, but not all, women authors of her time. After her marriage, she continued to write, publishing both a second novel, *El doctor alemán* (1880; "The German Doctor"), and a volume of essays on women, *La mujer juzgada por una mujer* (1882; "A Woman's View of Women"). With her husband, Gimeno traveled to various European capitals, including Paris, where she met Victor Hugo and absorbed the new social and literary currents.

In 1883, the couple moved to Mexico City, where they spent the next six years and where Gimeno started an illustrated magazine, *El Album de la Mujer, Ilustración Hispano-Americana* ("The Woman's Album, a Hispano-American Illustrated Magazine"). As owner and editor of her magazine, she joined the small band of Spanish women, including Patrocinio de Biedma, Josefa Pujol de Collado, and Emilia Pardo Bazán, who controlled their own periodicals. The longevity of *El Album de la Mujer* is striking; it published an issue a week in folio format from September 1883 through 1889, at which time the couple returned to Spain. Despite having a woman editor, the contributors were preponderantly male. It was a magazine about women and to a large degree for women, but not written primarily by women.

Before launching *El Album*, Gimeno solicited contributions from Spain's principal writers, receiving permission to include works by both literary men and literary women. The magazine serialized novels by Carolina Coronado, Emilia Pardo Bazán, and Julia de Asensi, as well as Gimeno's own *Victorina*, all works previously published in Spain. In addition, in 1888 it offered, in installments, her new short novel, *Maura*, inspired by a trip to Havana the previous year. Juan Valera contributed an occasional article, and commented in a letter to Marcelino Menéndez y Pelayo that he considered the magazine useful in building a readership for himself in Mexico and Latin America (272). Gimeno maintained her ties to the female literary community in Spain during these years, sending some of her articles to their magazines for republication. While in Mexico, she published a volume of essays, *Madres de hombres célebres* (1884; "Mothers of Famous Men"), and her third novel, *Suplicio de una coqueta* (1885; "A Coquette's Suffering"), retitled in the fourth edition *¿Culpa o expiación?* (1890; "Sin or Atonement?").

Shortly after returning to Madrid in early 1890, Gimeno enhanced her scholarly and social reputation by becoming the second woman—Emilia Pardo Bazán having preceded her—to lecture at the Ateneo de Madrid, the capital's most prestigious (male) literary society. Juan Valera introduced her lecture, "La civilización mexicana antes de la llegada de los españoles" ("Mexican Civilization Before the Arrival of the Spaniards"). A year later, Gimeno returned to the Ateneo to speak on "Las mujeres de la Revolución francesa" (1891; "Women of the French Revolution"), and in 1895 she discussed women's intellectual faculties and the need for education in "Ventajas de instruir a la mujer" ("The Advantages of Educating Women"). These lectures attracted a large female audience and received widespread notice in newspapers. Press reviews commented on Gimeno's pleasing appearance, demeanor, and attire; they also acknowledged the control of language she demonstrated in both her written text and her oral delivery. And they recognized her ability to engage and critique male language, seeing her speech as proof that a woman could use language with the same polemical and persuasive effect as men (Matheu 134; "Opiniones" 146).

In Spain, Gimeno resumed publication of her magazine, rebaptized *El Album Ibero Americano* ("The Ibero-American Album") and featuring a lead column on the Americas written by Flaquer. Covering art, science, literature, fashion, and society, as its subtitle indicated, *El Album* continued weekly publication until at least 1910, an impressive record of twenty-eight years in an era when short-lived periodicals predominated. It attracted occasional pieces from Spain's principal writers but drew its contributions mostly from the broader communities of literary men and, to a lesser degree, literary women. The periodical also served to showcase Gimeno's publications and public appearances.

In addition to publishing her lectures, Gimeno compiled some of her essays into a volume entitled, on the model of Plutarch, *Mujeres. Vidas paralelas* (1890; "Women. Parallel Lives"). She drew her examples from many cultures and epochs, ranging from the women of ancient Greece to early-nineteenth-century women writers of Spain. Appealing to a more conservative readership by underscoring her own adherence to established gender categories, she contributed to a women's genre with her social conduct manual, *En el salón y en el tocador* (1899; "In the Drawing Room and the Boudoir"). During these years, notices of the literary gatherings hosted by Gimeno in her home occasionally found their way into the society columns of Madrid newspapers.

In the first decade of the twentieth century, Gimeno published five collections of essays and one novel, *Una Eva moderna* (1909; "A Modern Eve"), her only contribution to the popular short novel format that sold in weekly series on newsstands. Her books of essays embraced studies of the changing social roles and self-definitions of women (*La mujer intelectual* [1901; "The Intellectual Woman"]), cultural differences among women (*Mujeres de raza latina* [1904; "Latin Women"]), and lives of historical women (*Mujeres de regia estirpe* [1907; "Women of Royal Blood"]). She continued to give lectures to organizations in Madrid, as well as to the press club in Rome. At the Ateneo she spoke on "El problema feminista" ("The Feminist Problem") and "Influencia y acción social de la mujer" ("Women's Influence and Social Action") in 1903 and 1908, respectively. As the titles of her lectures demonstrate, her emphasis shifted from historical models for women to the need for contemporary women to participate in social issues. In 1906 Gimeno became the first president of the Women's Section of the Ibero-American Union.

When Spanish Senator Emilio Alcalá Galiano argued in a 1907 parliamentary speech that women should be granted the franchise on the same terms as men, Gimeno's name capped his list of prominent Spanish women from Queen Isabel to the present (Bieder, "Feminine Discourse" 472). A few years before, in her lecture "El problema feminista," Gimeno herself had rejected the vote for women as a corrupting influence on their lives (*El problema feminista* 13–14). By 1908, however, she dedicated the lecture "Iniciativas de la mujer en higiene moral social" ("Women's Initiatives in Moral and Social Hygiene") to the senators and deputies who supported granting women "el voto administrativo" (limited voting rights). In 1909 her last novel, *Una Eva moderna*, fictionalized the Senate debate over the vote for women and, although endorsing the franchise, argued against women entering the political arena. The social content of this novel is offset by the religious nature of her last nonfictional work, a volume on the veneration of the Virgin Mary (*La Virgen Madre y sus advocaciones* [1907; "Invocations of the Virgin Mother"]).

The *Unión Ibero-Americana* announced in 1911 that Gimeno was in Buenos Aires on a lecture tour. Six years later, she reached Asunción, Paraguay, on her five-year trip around Latin America (Díaz-Pérez 59). Since her years in Mexico, she had commanded respect and appreciation in the Americas as a model for the modern woman (Díaz-Pérez 42). In Spain by this time, however, the social concerns and fictional modes of younger women writers had shifted away from those of Gimeno's generation, and brash young male writers found her an anachronism (Cansinos Asséns 272; Almagro 45). She apparently died in 1919.

Although numerous short sketches of Gimeno appeared throughout her lifetime, no biography of her exists. The fullest treatment of the early decades of her life comes from the pen of a Mexican writer, Eduardo del Valle, who reproduces Gimeno's account of her life. Her trace surfaces in her essays and survives in tributes to her by male and female colleagues, in brief sketches in the memoirs of literary men, and in turn-of-the-century dictionaries of Spanish women writers.

MAJOR THEMES

For almost fifty years, in her fiction and her essays, Concepción Gimeno contributed to the debate over women's attributes, rights, and sphere of action. A major figure in the women's literary community in Spain, she voiced the conflictive identities of the female in the society of her day. Virtue and beauty, abnegation and sacrifice, economic and legal equality, education and career opportunities, intellectual compatibility in marriage, earned income and life insurance—Gimeno espoused them all. Presenting herself as both a conventionally feminine woman and a modern feminist, she invoked and reshaped the definitions of each. She attributed her commitment to the equality of women to her Aragonese heritage, since that region retained Roman laws granting women economic and legal rights denied them in other areas of Spain. Her audience was the educated middle class, both female and male, who applauded her intertwining of moral precepts and social progress. Gimeno successfully negotiated the extremes of the contemporary feminist debate, avoiding identification with the emancipation movement—a foreign import that threatened to defeminize women—while rejecting the strictures that limited women to the home, without access to education or a compatible marriage partner. Her invariable touchstone throughout was motherhood, extolled as the essential and most exalted function of women. (Although Gimeno had no children, she nevertheless grounded her definition of the female in motherhood as consistently as did other women of her century.) Quintessentially woman, Gimeno was at the same time an active journalist and indefatigable publicist for her ideas, her magazines, and her books. In short, she embodied the synthesis of competing agendas that she termed ''moderate feminism.''

Indeed, despite her reform agenda, Gimeno did not break with the categorization of women but, rather, echoed the taxonomic preoccupation of her era. She reworked familiar representations of women—the pretty woman, the ideal woman, the Old Eve, and the New Eve—drawing careful distinctions between excess and appropriate feminine behavior. But she also explored new categories—the woman scholar, the woman scientist, the woman doctor—that met the challenge of changing opportunities. She defended women against derogatory stereotypes, seeking to erase negative expectations and to free women to redefine themselves. Rejecting the traditional woman as passive, self-centered, and superficial, she countered with her new agenda: the active, self-determined, other-oriented woman. In the modern woman who "struggles, resists and overcomes," Gimeno conveyed her conviction that women must implement change by taking responsibility for their own lives (*La mujer intelectual* 16).

In the book that established Gimeno as a champion of women's issues, *La mujer española*, she rebuts the restrictive definitions of women that place limitations on their activities. She denounces with particular ardor the negative stereotype of the *literata*, the category to which she as a writer was assigned. To support her claims for women's literary and cultural productivity, she appends a catalog of contemporary women writers and artists (*La mujer española* 239–46). Her later essays on women authors—María de Zayas, Cecilia Böhl de Faber, Carolina Coronado, and Gertrudis Gómez de Avellaneda—attempt to identify a tradition of women's letters in Spain. From her earliest essays, such as one on Catalan heroines ("Las heroínas catalanas"), she highlighted the contributions the women of Spain have made to their country's history by depicting the endeavors of individual women across the centuries. In these lives of exemplary women, Gimeno redefined inherited boundaries of female behavior. In her lecture on Mexico, she reversed the dictum that woman is the root cause of all cultural upheavals and argues instead that all great historical events depend on the actions of the virtuous and honorable woman. In this way, her essays counter commonplace denigrations of women and opposition to female self-definition with positive representations of historical women.

Gimeno also questioned why the contemporary debate over the regeneration of Spanish society overlooked the role women could play in shaping the future of the country. Building on women's most conventional roles—wife and mother—she projected women's potential to influence the direction of the nation and empower themselves by marrying only honorable and patriotic men and by exercising moral motherhood in molding the lives of their children (*Evangelios de la mujer* 259). She confronted the conflict between women's traditional acquiescence to male-defined patterns of behavior and their current awareness of the marginal status this behavior had produced: "The Spanish woman exaggerated her obedience, behaving frivolously to please you, and today she is beginning to curse this docility because, although you call her the joy of your life, you don't involve her in resolving Spain's fundamental problems" (*El problema feminista* 38).

As the range of Gimeno's titles indicates, she attempted to contribute to all the existing modes of women's writing, from the feminist polemic to devotional literature. She defined her approach as a moderate feminism that seeks change without disruption to the social fabric or patriarchal institutions. Nor did she dislodge the privileges and obligations of the traditional Spanish woman. Instead, she anchored her views in the model of the Christian woman and employed carefully selected quotations from contemporary Catholic writers to underscore her tie to the church. Within this framework, she developed her constant themes: education (the cornerstone of change), the right to enter liberal professions, employment opportunities, equal compensation, a woman's control of her own money, financial security, and a defense of writing women. At the same time, she suggested the historical inevitability of change. As the eighteenth century proclaimed the rights of men and the nineteenth century gave rights to women in some countries, the twentieth century, she asserted, would grant all women the rights she propounded (*Mujeres de raza latina* 31). Indeed, she repeatedly designated the new century as "the century of the woman." Her vision of the future projected the equality of men and women through education and common values, with both sexes engaged in the scientific and moral perfection of society (252).

Gimeno's style is frequently aphoristic and sententious as she pens social and moral precepts for the Spanish woman in an era of change. In flowing sentences and flowery, sentimental language, she reiterates the inherited values of Spanish womanhood alongside her calls for redefinition and reform. Following the fashion of her day, she formulates and collects *pensamientos* (sayings) about women from ancient and contemporary writers that displace negative commonplaces and confirm her affirmative portrayal of women. Historical and mythic models multiply in her metaphorical characterizations—for example, when she evokes the woman from Madrid as "a Sphinx, a Proteus, an indecipherable hieroglyphic" (*Mujeres de raza latina* 7). At the surface level, Gimeno's language is rarely disruptive, allowing a wide range of readers to endorse her work. She tempers strong pronouncements on equality or injustice by embedding them in familiar discourse on motherhood and moral virtues. She also borrows the language of religion to legitimize proposed social change—for example, when she invokes the advent and glorification of women (*Mujeres de raza latina* 252). This tension between the familiar and the new, between tradition and change, between surface and subversion, characterizes all her writings.

The moral conflicts that Gimeno addresses in her essays define the parameters of her novels. Writing within the cautionary mode dominant in nineteenth-century women's fiction, she structures her novels on the moral opposites that set the boundaries of her female protagonists' world. Circumscribed by their essential definitions as daughters, wives, and mothers, her heroines are caught in a struggle between duty and desire. The motif of marriage as sacrifice, in which the daughter marries to rescue her father from financial ruin, recurs in most of her novels. With marriage defined as duty, desire occurs only outside wedlock, and traps the protagonist in a moral dilemma between her duty to society and her own emotions. Thus the site of this conflict is adulterous desire. The responsibility for maintaining social order centers on the woman, and in Gimeno's novels "the noblest figure, the most sympathetic character is always a woman" (*La mujer juzgada* 5). From her first novel, *Victorina*, the trope "heroism of the heart" defines the protagonist's triumph of will over the temptations of desire. In this novel the protagonist gains control over her passion, and thus her own life, by entering a convent, an example of self-sacrifice that brings about the regeneration of her lover as well. Other protagonists heroically renounce love while remaining within the social sphere as married women.

With *Suplicio de una coqueta*, Gimeno moves increasingly away from the excesses of romantic plotting and character construction toward more realistic patterns of conflict, action, and speech, without abandoning the sentimental mode (Bieder, " 'El escalpelo' "). She incorporates contemporary settings and social customs, as well as more flexible dialogue. Despite locating the source of the moral dilemmas that bind her heroines in arranged marriages, Gimeno avoids addressing the patriarchal authority that allows financially irresponsible fathers to sell their remaining asset, their daughters, to escape economic bondage. Nevertheless, fathers, supplementing the convention of the absent mother, tend to be positive figures who provide their daughters with the modern education and broad cultural horizons that enable them to develop a strong moral character. (In a familiar topos, an orphaned protagonist is morally weak and unable to resist committing adultery in her heart.) Within the restricted territory her novels explore, Gimeno's protagonists exercise a moral choice that signifies their control over their lives. Her exploration of rebellion against a passionless life closes either with the protagonist's voluntary reinscription into patriarchal institutions or with the punishment of her insubordination by death, both modes of closure characteristic of the nineteenth-century sentimental novel.

SURVEY OF CRITICISM

At the time of their publication, Concepción Gimeno's books received brief notices in newspapers and magazines but few full reviews. One candid critical judgment of Gimeno the novelist came from her contemporary Juan Valera, who, after reading *Suplicio de una coqueta*, observed that the author had "extraordinary ability, talent and even humor and feeling" (272).

Although Gimeno maintained close ties to both male and female literary circles, the two groups assessed her work differently. Josefa Pujol de Collado praised Gimeno's first book to her female readers as a work "filled with the purest precepts of valiant morality in form" and "daring in content," and that serves to "summon the weaker sex to the field of learning" (107). Pujol identifies here the inherent tension between Gimeno's adherence to a conventional moral framework and her bold call for women to redefine themselves. While apparently invoking the didactic nature of her writing, Pujol simultaneously suggests its more active agenda.

Male critics find Gimeno a more problematic figure and frequently invoke nonliterary categories in their evaluations of her. A review of *La mujer juzgada por una mujer* in an important cultural magazine lauds her "erudition, wit, mature judgment and great spirit of impartiality" (Cárdenas 126). Other critics draw a distinction between Gimeno "the serious woman writer" and silly, superficial *literatas* (Roca qtd. in Díaz-Pérez 58). Idealizing the woman at the expense of the writer, one sketch presents her as "a distinguished and beautiful woman with refined talent and a feminine heart" whose books bring glory to woman as wife and mother (Salvador 278, 280). (Not surprisingly, Luciano Salvador considers the issue of female equality a matter for men to resolve.) Nevertheless, the vigor and forthrightness that at times characterize Gimeno's writing provoke some critics to label her prose "manly," an adjective similarly applied to the writings of Emilia Pardo Bazán and Gertrudis Gómez de Avellaneda. Her friend and fellow writer Teodoro Guerrero voiced the anxiety resulting from such violations of the gendered boundaries of language when he declared that "her lyre is at times so virile it masks the woman." But Guerrero also acknowledged that Gimeno had moved away from the language and imagery of late romanticism that dominated women's writing without going to the opposite extreme of naturalist excess. Díaz-Pérez, one of the last men to write about Gimeno, attempted to synthesize her "virile intellect" and her defense of traditional womanhood by defining her as "an elegant and virtuous lady who writes out of a love of letters and a love for the sex whose pride she is" (53).

One of the most significant writers in the female literary community in Spain in the late nineteenth and the early twentieth centuries, Concepción Gimeno is perhaps its most visible public representative. In 1900 Marie de la Rute, editor of *Nouvelle Revue Internationale*, identified "Mme. de Flaquer" as Spain's feminist writer par excellence. An author who enlarges our idea of women's letters in Spain, Gimeno represents the trajectory and contradictions of the feminist debate and embodies the inherent tension between the woman and the writer.

BIBLIOGRAPHY

Works by Concepción Gimeno de Flaquer

Novels

Victorina, o Heroísmo del corazón. 2 vols. Madrid, 1873.
El doctor alemán. Zaragoza, 1880.
Suplicio de una coqueta. Mexico City, 1885.
Maura. Serialized in *El Album de la Mujer* 6.10. (Jan.–June 1888).
¿Culpa o expiación? Mexico, 1890. [4th ed. of *Suplicio*]
Una Eva moderna. El Cuento Semanal 3.152 (1909).

Essays

"Las heroínas catalanas." In *Las mujeres españolas, lusitanas y americanas pintadas por sí mismas.* By Faustina Sáez de Melgar. Barcelona: n.d. 232–44.
La mujer española: Estudios acerca de su educación y sus facultades intelectuales. Madrid, 1877.
La mujer juzgada por una mujer. Barcelona, 1882.
Madres de hombres célebres. Mexico City, 1884.

"La duquesa de la Torre y su salón literario." *El Album de la Mujer* 6.10 (Jan.–June 1888): 162–63.

Civilización de los antiguos pueblos mexicanos. Madrid, 1890.

Mujeres. Vidas paralelas. Madrid, 1890.

Mujeres de la Revolución francesa. Madrid, 1891.

Ventajas de instruir a la mujer. Madrid, 1896.

En el salón y en el tocador. Madrid, 1899.

Evangelios de la mujer. Madrid, 1900.

La mujer intelectual. Madrid, 1901.

El problema feminista. Madrid, 1903.

Mujeres de raza latina. Madrid, 1904.

Mujeres de regia estirpe. Madrid, 1907.

La Virgen Madre y sus advocaciones. Madrid, 1907.

Iniciativas de la mujer en higiene moral social. Madrid, 1908.

Works about Concepción Gimeno de Flaquer

Almagro San Martín, Melchor de. "Domingo, 7. La Rattazzi." *Biografía del 1900.* Madrid: Revista de Occidente, 1943. 40–46.

Barbier, José, Filomeno Mata, et al. *Concepción Gimeno de Flaquer.* Mexico City, 1884.

Bieder, Maryellen. " 'El escalpelo anatómico en mano femenina': The Realist Novel and the Woman Writer." *Letras Peninsulares* 5.2 (Fall 1992): 1–19.

———. "Feminine Discourse/Feminist Discourse: Concepción Gimeno de Flaquer." *Romance Quarterly* 37 (1990): 459–77.

Bolaños Cacho, Miguel. "Siluetas españolas: Concepción Gimeno de Flaquer." *El Album de la Mujer* 10 (Jan.–June 1888): 18.

Cansinos Asséns, Rafael. *La nueva literatura.* Vol. 2. *Las escuelas (1898–1900–1918).* 2nd ed. Madrid, 1925.

Cárdenas, José de. "Boletín bibliográfico." *Revista Contemporánea* 9.43 (Jan.–Feb. 1883): 126–27. [Rev. of *La mujer juzgada por una mujer*]

Diego, Estrella de. *La mujer y la pintura del XIX español.* Madrid: Cátedra, 1987. 158–61, passim.

Díaz–Pérez, Viriato. "Concepción Gimeno de Flaquer." *Ensayos II–Notas.* Palma de Mallorca: Luis Ripoll, 1988. 50–60.

Guerrero, Teodoro. "Concepción Gimeno de Flaquer." *La Ilustración Española y Americana* 34.36 (1890): n. pag.

Matheu, José M. "Concepción Gimeno de Flaquer en el Ateneo." *El Album Ibero Americana* 9 (1891): 134.

"Opiniones de la prensa sobre la conferencia de Concepción Gimeno de Flaquer." *El Album Ibero Americano* 9 (1891): 146–47.

Pérez, Martín. "Concepción Jimeno de Flaquer." *La Ilustración Nacional* 35 (16 Dec. 1890): 547.

Pujol de Collado, Josefa. "Concepción Gimeno de Flaquer." *La Ilustración de la Mujer* (Barcelona) 3 (1885): 107.

Rute, Marie de la (Madame Rattazzi), ed. *L'Espagne.* Spec. issue of *Nouvelle Revue Internationale* 5–7 (Apr. 1900): 229.

Salvador, Luciano. "Bocetos literarios: Concepción Jimeno de Flaquer." *Revista Contemporánea* 91 (July–Sept. 1893): 227–80.

Simón Palmer, María del Carmen. *Escritoras españolas del siglo XIX*. Madrid: Castalia, 1991. 363–74.

Valera, Juan, and Marcelino Menéndez y Pelayo. *Epistolario de Valera y Menéndez Pelayo*. Madrid: Espasa-Calpe, 1946. 347, 271–73.

Valle, Eduardo del. ''Biografía de Concepción Gimeno de Flaquer.'' *¿Culpa o expiación?* By Concepción Gimeno de Flaquer. 4th ed. of *Suplicio*. Mexico City, 1890. 2–23. [Preface]

CLARA JANÉS
(b. 1940)

Anne M. Pasero

BIOGRAPHY

Daughter of the well-known poet and editor Josep Janés, Clara Janés was born
on November 6, 1940, in Barcelona. She studied at the universities of Barcelona
and Pamplona, graduating from the latter with a degree in philosophy and letters.
She also took courses abroad in Perugia, at Oxford, and at the Sorbonne, where
she studied comparative literature and the Czech language. Since the age of
nineteen, she has devoted herself to a literary career. She has been awarded two
Ciudad de Barcelona literary prizes, the first in 1972 for her biography *La vida
callada de Federico Mompou* (1975; "The Silent Life of Federico Mompou"),
and the second in 1983 for her book of poetry *Vivir* (1986; "To Live").

Janés is primarily considered a poet. Her early works of poetry include *Las
estrellas vencidas* (1964; "The Conquered Stars") and *Límite humano* (1973;
"Human Limit"), which reflect her metaphysical anguish over the spatial and
temporal limits of human existence. After a temporary hiatus and period of
reflection, Janés's fascination with the life and work of Czechoslovak poet Vladimir Holan inspired her return to poetry and the publication of *En busca de
Cordelia y poemas rumanos* (1975; "In Search of Cordelia and Romanian
Poems"), *Antología personal* (1979; "Personal Anthology"), and *Libro de
alienaciones* (1980; "Book of Alienation"). In addition to selections from her
previous works, *Antología personal* includes poems from *Kampa*, published in
its entirety in 1986. A transition occurs with the publication of *Eros* (1983) and
Vivir (1986), in which the poet articulates a more concrete, specifically female
and life-affirming view. *Fósiles* (1987; "Fossils") and *Lapidario* (1988; "Lapidary") have in common their focus on the permanence of natural objects as a
symbolic extension of the self. In her latest work, *Creciente fértil* (1989; "Fertile

Crescent''), Janés continues to develop themes of female identity and expression elaborated in *Eros* and *Vivir*.

Janés's works in prose consist of two novels published early in her career, *La noche de Abel Micheli* (1965; ''The Night of Abel Micheli'') and *Desintegración* (1969; ''Disintegration''); the extensive biography of the composer and musician Federico Mompou (1975); a work of pedagogy and psychology in epistolary form dedicated to her daughter, *Cartas a Adriana* (1976; ''Letters to Adriana''); a travelogue, *Sendas de Rumania* (1981; ''Romanian Roads''); and two short stories, ''Tentativa de olvido'' (1982; ''Attempted Oblivion'') and ''Deja que todo se llene de hierba'' (1986; ''Let All Be Covered with Grass''). A more recent novel, *Los caballos del sueño* (1989; ''The Dream Horses''), relates to *Desintegración* in that both works treat woman's increasing need for self-expression, especially in the realm of male-female relationships.

The literary activity of Clara Janés extends beyond creative writing. Stimulated by her acquaintance with the Czech land and people and her travels abroad, she has published translations of works by the major Czech poets Holan and Jaroslav Seifert, and also by such minor figures as Bohumil Hrabal, Jiří Orten, and Karel Čapek. She has also translated from the French (Marguerite Duras, Nathalie Sarraute, and others), and from the Turkish and Romanian. In addition to her career as a writer and translator, Janés is a literary critic; she has published editions of the works of the Spanish writers Pureza Canelo, Juan-Eduardo Cirlot, and Rosa Chacel. She also has compiled an anthology of early Spanish women poets, *Las primeras poetisas en lengua castellana* (1986; ''The First Women Poets in Castilian'').

Janés belongs to a generation of women writers succeeding the few included among the post–Civil War social poets (Gloria Fuertes, Ángela Figuera). Along with poets such as María Victoria Atencia, Blanca Andreu, Ana Rossetti, Julia Castillo, and others writing today, Janés is primarily concerned with what the French feminists Hélène Cixous, Monique Wittig, and Luce Irigaray have described as *l'écriture féminine* (feminine writing)—the process by which women's writing reflects and responds to the problem and essence of being female. This generation of Spanish women poets differs from the preceding one in that it focuses on the question of female gender and its representation through language. Janés, one of the more important Spanish women poets writing today, utilizes theme, language, and imagery to explore and express her dual identity of woman and writer.

MAJOR THEMES

The poetry of Clara Janés is a quest for discovery and definition of the female essence. To that end, her writing has undergone significant phases of development as she has evolved toward a more complete expression of female identity. From an initial phase of questioning and denial (*Las estrellas vencidas*, *Límite humano*), Janés began to define the extensions of the female self as first related to a specific geographical place and subsequently to a metaphorical one, boundless and unlimited (*En busca de Cordelia, Libro de alienaciones, Kampa*). Within this context, from a traditional association of woman with nature, Janés moved toward the more creative identification of the female with an imaginary, symbolic realm open to endless and erotic possibilities. Then, from the association of woman with place/space, both real and imaginary, Janés turned to writing of her own specifically female nature—her body (*Eros, Vivir, Creciente fertil*). In "writing the body," as French feminist theorists describe it, Janés explores the very concrete and physical difference that is female, and from there projects a sexuality/textuality that is fluid and liberating. The focus on the body, through the writing of her own female discourse, enables Janés to transcend those limits, both external and internal, that initially entrapped her. The "other" she acknowledges is her personal unconscious within, that unexplored territory to which she now has access.

Pervading Janés's initial works of poetry is a desperate sense of searching for affirmation, both psychical and physical, in a world the poet sees crumbling before her. Her questions are of a metaphysical nature and probe the essence of a seemingly vacuous and sterile reality. This phase characterizes her first book of poetry, *Las estrellas vencidas*. Although the poet finds herself thrust into life, she is unable to affirm her corporeal and spiritual identity. There prevails a sense of questioning vis-á-vis one's place in the natural order of things. Her presence, which the poet has yet to assert fully, attempts to negate nothingness. The tension, still to be resolved, persists between *ser* and *no-ser*, "being" and "nonbeing." The setting is the surrounding city, a concrete and specific plane from which the poet projects her philosophical speculations. From the outset, a tenuous relationship is implied between the finite limits of one's physical existence and an ever-changing and less clearly delimited universe. Janés hints at—but does not yet elaborate—the affinity between the female body and the surrounding cosmos, suggesting that one mirrors the other.

In her next work, *Límite humano*, written between 1963 and 1965, Janés begins to rebel against the limits imposed on human, terrestrial existence and to aspire toward a more transcendent and metaphysical plane. Accompanying her frustration when faced with the inevitable passage of time is a desire for permanence. The fugacity of terrestrial matters provokes a note of desperation. Love provides only a fleeting possibility of hope that precludes any real escape from the solitude of the human, and female, condition. The limits that circumscribe temporality also determine the finite nature of human (male-female) relationships. Janés has not yet achieved a state of integration of self and other that will allow transcendence of sexual boundaries and liberation of the female unconscious about which the French critic Cixous has written.

An important evolution in Janés's poetry occurred with the publication of *En busca de Cordelia y poemas rumanos*. This work more directly confronts the question of self (Cordelia). Janés is seeking not only that symbolic female self that resides within her but also the metaphorical means by which to express it.

In *En busca de Cordelia*, a reconciliation is achieved between the two apparently unconnected spheres, physical (Romania) and metaphorical (Cordelia). Janés thus begins to associate her personal female identity with the landscape of distant, exotic places.

As indicated by the title, Cordelia represents the being Janés so urgently seeks and ultimately encounters, a being that transcends spatial and temporal limits to achieve a mythical-universal dimension. In this book, the purpose of travel (*viajar*) becomes evident, for it carries one beyond the boundaries imposed by daily human existence. Romania, like other mysterious, faraway lands, represents not only an escape from enclosure but also an affirmation of one's imaginative, creative faculties. The introductory poem to *Poemas rumanos*, "Sosiego" (35; "Peace"), indicates an extension of the physical domain onto the symbolic one. The walls of the city now merge with the walls of the poet's physical existence; her body becomes a literal landscape for the metaphorical one she has imagined:

Ábreme las riberas del sosiego, Bucarest,
deja que en tus aceras se remanse
ese silencio
que violento se agolpa
dentro de la muralla
de mi cuerpo.

Open for me the shores of peace, Bucarest,
May your sidewalks be stilled
by that silence
that violently pounds
within the wall
of my body.

The question of landscape becomes an essential one in the poetry of Janés, for it symbolizes a projection of her physical being onto a more abstract, infinite, and all-encompassing plane. The relationship of the female corpus to external place reflects the female need for liberation and the desire for self-expression, erotic and otherwise.

In *Libro de alienaciones*, published in 1980 but written in about 1973, the poet is inclined on the one hand toward a complete denial of being, as in her earlier work, but at the same time is drawn toward an expression of self through landscape—literal, metaphorical, and female. What appear as antithetical perspectives are, in fact, complementary. The first half, "Isla del suicidio" ("Island of Suicide"), is in every respect a projection of the poet's inner turmoil onto an external landscape. The identification of self with surrounding nature, the fusion of internal and external landscapes, is explicit in "En el oscuro pozo de la mente" ("In the Dark Well of the Mind"); the poet continues to lament the condition of nonbeing, viewing it as a sea raging to be released from physical confines. The desire to bring about a reconciliation, to trap that fleeting image of resolution with self, is incessant and unrelenting. In another poem, the sea is associated with an unfulfilled and unexpressed eroticism, still to be harnessed:

> Que el mar se duerma
> y se duerma la angustia
> que me acosa . . . (42)

> May the sea sleep
> and the anguish that haunts me
> also sleep . . .

Likewise, Janés identifies herself specifically with the island of Pitiusa, a metaphorical reference to the female body and to its psychic landscape, which is "mental, lapidary and deserted" (26). The island represents a place of confinement for the female, who is denied the freedom to merge with surrounding elements:

> Isla aislada,
> de alma cerrada,
> de palabra quebrada,
> de piel resquebrajada . . . (12)

> Isolated island,
> of soul enclosed,
> of broken word,
> of splintered skin . . .

The title poem, "Libro de alienaciones," describes an entity yet to be born, yet to be engendered from within the security of the uterus. The poet still despairs at the apparent futility and randomness of the quest. As an independent, autonomous being, she has yet to affirm herself/her place within the cosmos, separate from and still a part of the mother who conceived her. She fears finding herself adrift, abandoned to the immensity of the ocean, and perceives herself as physically fragmented. Paralyzed by the horror of nonbeing, she considers confinement within the abyss of her limited existence less frightening than the unknown beyond. A change in orientation begins to occur in *Libro de alienaciones*. From an initial perception of woman as the passive depository of all human suffering, Janés moves to assume a more active, affirming stance, wishing to penetrate and reengender herself as the most viable source of sustenance. In her quest for fulfillment, she initiates a return to the female essence: she moves in the direction of "writing the body" as a means of female self-expression.

Kampa marks a dramatic transition in the work of Janés. Written during the same period as *Libro de alienaciones* but not published until 1986, it takes a decidedly different tack and is clearly indicative of the poet's evolution toward a free and open assertion of female self. In the introduction to her *Antología personal*, Janés confirms that in *Kampa* she has achieved a kind of resolution, "a knowledge that engenders fulfillment" (9). Consisting of four cycles, the second composed entirely of poetic-musical sounds, *Kampa* was inspired by the poet's friendship with Holan, much of whose work she has translated into Spanish. Kampa, the island where Holan lived, becomes for Janés the symbol of her liberation, both physical and spiritual. The island now functions as a metaphor for both the female body and uninhibited creative expression; it suggests a boundless space that fuses naturally with the surrounding oceanic cosmos. If, as Cixous perceives it, water represents the comfort of the mother's womb, then the island is that child about to be born, just as Janés gives birth to her text.

In *Kampa*, for the first time, Janés speaks of her fulfillment in erotic terms. For Janés, expressing the erotic means breaking down established limits—within the self and between self and other—so that the woman can freely convey her formerly repressed sexual desire. Her *jouissance* or sensation of pleasure comes from the awareness of having dissolved boundaries in order to reconcile internal conflicts. Having achieved an integration of the self, she is able to merge freely with another *equivalent* being. She now actively asserts her erotic desire, stressing female power over suffering, female initiative over victimization. The nonverbal and verbal spheres are united as the body becomes a concrete source of a more abstract symbolic experience.

"Writing the body" enables Janés to extend her vision outward metaphorically, as she contemplates the domain opened up to her by projected love for the other. For Janés, the island of Kampa represents all of the symbolic geographic terrain now accessible to her. She re-creates such female figures as Eurydice and Sappho, giving them a new and autonomous dimension as self-sustaining entities. By doing so, Janés engages in a kind of "revisionist myth-making" undertaken by women writers to topple male stereotypes. Eurydice is not just a passive, tragic object of Orpheus's love:

> Y tú, avanza,
> acosada cabeza aún de los abismos
> con el rostro encendido
> y el cabello derramado entre los vientos.
>
> . . .
> teje un lamento
> al malhadado y fiel Orfeo. (83–84)

> And you go forward,
> with your head still haunted by the abyss,
> with your face alight
> and your hair spilling in the wind.
>
> . . .
> weave a lament
> for the faithful and unfortunate Orpheus.

Nor is Sappho deprived of a male counterpart or inhibited in her sexual expression as she exclaims:

Sediento amor,
ansioso como la arena, insaciable de olas.
Asediante, acosante, asolador . . . (85)

Thirsty love,
anxious like the sand, insatiable for waves.
Besieging, pursuing, destroying . . .

Janés, through techniques such as this, connects her personal view of the cosmos to a universal one that encompasses all women.

In *Eros* and *Vivir*, Janés becomes even more candid, direct, and explicit about her own eroticism. She now revels in the freedom to express her sexual/sensual instincts openly. Such a liberation has been achieved gradually, through a transcendence of barriers and a poetic creation of an open and erotic landscape. Having been described by Rosa Chacel as one of the great love poets (7), Janés displays in *Eros* the entire spectrum of her eroticism, from the most sublime of experiences to the unabashedly sexual. The introductory poem, "Eros," provides the key to the work's orientation: Janés, affirming rather overtly that "loving the other is first loving oneself" (9), exults in erotic gratification. Throughout the work, the poet's focus is on sexual pleasure and erotic discovery, elaborated in specific, sexual terms:

Estuve con un joven
y supe al fin lo que era

. . .

la densidad precisa de jugos derramados . . . (43)

I was with a young man,
and discovered at last what it was

. . .

the exact density of flowing juices . . .

She elaborates further:

el filo más suave, erecto y encendido
planea y arremete las costas de amor. (46)

the gentlest cutting edge, erect and inflamed
glides into and assails the shores of love.

The references to female body parts (vulva, breast, hips) are explicit and joyous: "Mi pecho es redondo y casi virginal" (34; My breasts are round and almost virginal). Her sexuality has become an entity unto itself, to be explored and savored:

Sus yemas insaciables se centran en la vulva,
inician nueva forma de oración . . . (50)

His insatiable fingertips center on my vulva,
and initiate a new kind of prayer . . .

The boundary of the self is no longer fixed and self-contained; it is presented in a constant state of flux and transformation:

Yo te engendro de una sombra mortal
y por mi carne vagas,
humor que ya en los labios hormiguea. (38)

I engender you from a mortal shadow
and you wander through my flesh,
sensation that already burns on my lips.

Woman's essence is open and permeable, actively responsive to the sexual forces being generated within and without.

Vivir follows the trajectory initiated in *Eros*. It is a vehement affirmation of all that is life-giving, beginning with the purely erotic and gradually encompassing multiple facets of human existence. The basis for the book is established in the introductory poem, ''Teoría'' (9), in which the poet pays homage to the power of love as a force that inspires life and transcends the passage of time.

Two of the work's most impressive poems, ''Convite'' (29–32; ''Feast'') and ''Albores de San Juan'' (59–60; ''Dawning of San Juan''), have an explicitly erotic orientation. In ''Convite,'' Janés offers herself as a human sacrifice to the fiery passion of love, to be consumed (literally) and thus regenerated:

pido que se me coma
    . . .
comunión canibal suplico,
génesis en el otro. (32)

I beg to be eaten
    . . .
I beg for a cannibal communion,
genesis in the other.

''Albores de San Juan'' reflects the joyful pleasure and anticipation that accompany an uninhibited expression of love during the feast of San Juan:

la yerba más suave se nos hace caricia
y pacen los caballos en núbiles dehesas
el agua subterránea por mi carne murmura
mientras el sol desliza sus alas a lo lejos. (59)

the gentlest grass caresses us
and the horses graze in nubile pastures

the subterranean water ripples through my flesh
while the sun spreads its wings in the distance.

The entire book represents, in fact, a celebration of living inspired by Janés's
newly discovered delight in self.

Following *Fósiles* and *Lapidario*, Janés published *Creciente fértil* in 1989. In
its entirety, this book affirms the pleasure of erotic fulfillment to which Janés
aspires throughout her poetic pursuit. The gods it exalts are female, re-created
from another time and place—queens of the ancient Sumerian, Hittite, and
Babylonian civilizations—and transported to the present moment. They are mythical women reenacting the most primordial erotic experiences. For example, on
one occasion Janés portrays herself as Ishtar, the Babylonian and Assyrian goddess of love and fertility. "Creciente fértil" is a metaphorical reference to the
ancient Fertile Crescent as well as to the whole of the female body and more
specifically to the womb. It also suggests the country of Turkey, whose flag
bears the crescent moon, and thereby reconnects geographical place with female
desire. Throughout the work, as in her previous books of poetry, references to
exotic lands correspond to the expression of uninhibited sexual joy:

Cuando llevado por mi mano
suave entraste en mí
            . . .
aun no sospechabas
que se encuentra en mi cuerpo,
entre praderas y mantojos,
la sagrada puerta de lasily-Kaya. (37)

When led by my hand
you gently entered me
            . . .
you still did not suspect
that you would find in my body
amid meadows and brush
the sacred gate of lasily-Kaya.

In this most recent work, Janés speaks for and about women, creating a mythical
dimension, universal in time and space. The most assertively sexual of her works
thus far, *Creciente fértil* represents what Janés describes as a progression in her
continual search for a specifically female form. This form reflects the woman
poet's obligation to sing praise to the female being, now firm in its essence.

SURVEY OF CRITICISM

Criticism of Janés's work remains limited, but interest both in Spain and
abroad has increased dramatically during the past few years, as indicated by the
number of conference presentations and articles devoted to her writing and to

her place among contemporary Spanish women poets. Many of the articles deal with individual books and give a limited view of their thematic and stylistic orientation. The more general studies of Sharon Ugalde and John Wilcox are significant in that they not only present an overall picture of the poet's work but also treat the question of the female text and feminism from a specific, theoretical focus. Ugalde discusses issues central to the work of Janés, such as the search for identity, the female voice, and the revisionist approach to language and imagery. Wilcox stresses the female voice and perspective in his discussion of *En busca de Cordelia* and especially *Eros*, where he underlines the poet's quest for self, her candid eroticism, and her vindication of the sorceress figure.

In terms of feminist theory, criticism of Janés's work is in need of the kind of approach that Ugalde and Wilcox suggest above. Their analyses, together with this chapter, help to situate the author's writings in both the larger context of contemporary Spanish poetry and that of women's writings today.

BIBLIOGRAPHY

Works by Clara Janés

Poetry

Las estrellas vencidas. Madrid: Agora, 1964.
Límite humano. Madrid: Oriens, 1973.
En busca de Cordelia y poemas rumanos. Salamanca: Alamo, 1975.
Antología personal. Madrid: Rialp, 1979.
Libro de alienaciones. Madrid: Ayuso, 1980.
Eros. Madrid: Hiperión, 1983.
Kampa. Madrid: Hiperión, 1986.
Vivir. Madrid: Hiperión, 1986.
Fósiles. Barcelona: Z.I.P., 1987.
Lapidario. Madrid: Hiperión, 1988.
Creciente fértil. Madrid: Hiperión, 1989.
Emblemas. Madrid: Caballo Griego para la Poesía, 1991.

Prose

La noche de Abel Micheli. Madrid: Alfaguara, 1965.
Desintegración. Madrid: Eucar, 1969.
La vida callada de Federico Mompou. Barcelona: Ariel, 1975.
Cartas a Adriana. Madrid: S.A.R.P.E., 1976.
Sendas de Rumania. Barcelona: Plaza y Janés, 1981.
"Tentativa de olvido." *Doce relatos de mujeres*. Ed. Ymelda Navajo. Madrid: Alianza, 1982. 23–36.
"Deja que todo se llene de hierba." *Insula* 473 (1986): 3.
Federico Mompou: Vida, textos, documentos. Madrid: Banco Exterior, 1986.
Los caballos del sueño. Barcelona: Anagrama, 1989.
Jardín y laberinto. Madrid: Debate, 1990.
El Hombre de Adén. Barcelona: Anagrama, 1991.

Anthologies/Editions

Obra poética de Juan-Eduardo Cirlot. Madrid: Cátedra, 1981.
Pureza Canelo. Madrid: Ministerio de Cultura, 1981.
Los títulos. Barcelona: Edhasa, 1981. [Critical edition of Rosa Chacel's volume]
Las primeras poetisas en lengua castellana. Madrid: Ayuso, 1986.
Las primeras poetisas españolas. Antología. Madrid: Ayuso, 1986.

Selected Articles

"Fe de una vocación poética o el libro-cosmos." *Nueva Estafeta* 12 (1979): 104–06.
    [Rev. of *Habitable* by Pureza Canelo]
"Cirlot y el surrealismo: el tema del amor." *Cuadernos Hispanoamericanos* 363 (1980):
    494–514.
"Un poema checo del siglo XIV." *Nueva Estafeta* 16 (1980): 57–62.
"Cirlot y el surrealismo: El material poético." *Nueva Estafeta* 53 (April 1983): 55–61.
"Holán, del otro lado del abismo." *Quimera: Revista de Literatura* 28 (1983): 22–25.
"La palabra poética de María Zambrano." *Cuadernos Hispanoamericanos* 413 (1984):
    183–87.
"Holán, el árbol más alto." *Cuadernos Hispanoamericanos* 432 (1986): 5–7.
"Jaroslav Seifert: Modernidad y clasicismo de un poeta indomable." *Insula* 41 (1986):
    3.
"Ilhan Berk." *Pasajes* 7 (1987): 63–64.
"Aproximación a un poeta turco contemporáneo: Ilhan Berk." *Cuadernos Hispanoam-
    ericanos* 468 (1989): 57–60.
"Vladimir Holán: Conocimiento y selva." *Revista de Occidente* 104 (1990): 83–92.

Works about Clara Janés

Allegra, Giovanni. "Amore e 'umanismo' di Clara Janés." *Uomini e Libri: Periodico
    Bimestrale di Critica ed Informazione Letteraria* 79 (1980): 38.
Chacel, Rosa. "Palabras de Rosa Chacel." *Poesía en el Campus* 3 (May 1988): 7–8.
    [Tribute to Clara Janés]
Ciplijauskaité, Biruté. "Hacia una nueva esencialidad," *El Ciervo* (May 1989): n. pag.
Gándara, Alejandro. "Círculos de tiza: Biografía de los sentimientos en relación de tres
    personajes." *El País* 9 Apr. 1989: n. pag. [Rev. of *Los caballos del sueño*]
García Nieto, José. "*Los caballos del sueño*". *ABC Literario* 1 Apr. 1989: n. pag.
    [Review]
García Ortega, Adolfo. "Clara Janés: Una pasión literaria." *Insula* 483 (Feb. 1987): 8.
    [Rev. of *Kampa*]
Garro, Elena. "Anuncio del martirio." *Nueva Estafeta* 17 (Apr. 1980): n. pag. [Rev. of
    Antología personal]
Golanó, Helena. "Entrevista con Clara Janés." *Insula* 461 (1985): 8–9.
Irigoyen, Ramón. "Clara Janés, escritora y catalana." *Interviú* 708.12 (27 Nov.–3 Dec.
    1989): 99–100, 102.
Martínez Ruiz, Florencio. "*Lapidario*." *ABC Literario* 28 May 1988: n. pag. [Review]
Miró, Emilio. "Clara Janés: La perfección de la materia." *Insula* 503 (Nov. 1988): 11.
    [Rev. of *Lapidario*]

Rodríguez Fischer, Ana. "Cabalgada hacia el ser." *El Norte de Castilla* 15 Apr. 1989: n. pag. [Rev. of *Los caballos del sueño*]

Ugalde, Sharon. "Huellas de mujer en la poesía de Clara Janés." Modern Language Association Convention. Washington, D.C., 1989.

———. "La sujetividad desde 'lo otro' en la poesía de María Sanz, María Victoria Atencia y Clara Janés." *Revista Canadiense de Estudios Hispánicos* 14.3 (1990): 511–23.

Wilcox, John. "Clara Janés: Hacia su poemario de los años ochenta." Unpublished ms.

Zambrano, María. "La voz abismática." *Diario 16* 7 Dec. 1986: III. [Rev. of *Kampa*]

CARMEN LAFORET
(b. 1921)

Roberta Johnson

BIOGRAPHY

Carmen Laforet, Spain's first winner of the prestigious Nadal Prize for the novel (1944), had an exceptional childhood compared with other Spanish women her age. Born on September 6, 1921, she lived until age eighteen in Las Palmas on the island of Gran Canaria. The more carefree atmosphere of the Canary Islands, far from the turmoil that characterized Spanish political and social life from Primo de Rivera's dictatorship to the end of the Second Republic and the Civil War (1923–1939), as well as her own family's orientation, created an ambience in which the spirited Carmen was encouraged to develop her talents and interests. Her mother, trained as a schoolteacher, shepherded her children through readings in the Spanish classics, and the family library was entirely at her disposal. She steeped herself especially in the works of the great nineteenth-century Canary Island realist novelist, Benito Pérez Galdós. Her father, an avid sportsman, made no distinction in any activity between Carmen and her two younger brothers; her brothers were her first literary audience, listening to her fanciful childhood tales.

A key event in Laforet's formative years was her mother's untimely death when Carmen was thirteen. She considered her father's behavior on the occasion reprehensible; he soon married his longtime mistress, whose intellect and character Laforet found much inferior to her mother's, and she began disassociating herself as much as possible from family life. She attended school, and although she frequently played hookey she did well, especially in literature. She enjoyed going to the beach and wandering about the city on her own. At the end of the Civil War, she blackmailed her father into allowing her to go to the mainland to live with relatives and attend the University of Barcelona by threatening to make public some rather scabrous letters he had written to his mistress.

Laforet arrived in war-torn and hungry Barcelona from the Canary Islands, which had seen no direct action in the Civil War, and beheld with fresh eyes the devastation that the three-year struggle had wrought on the Spanish mainland. This is the Barcelona she depicts in her first novel, *Nada* (1945; *Nada* 1958, *Andrea* 1964). World War II was now under way, and neutral Spain received a number of illegal refugees from nations where the war was raging. Laforet became friends with a Polish girl and her family, who were engaged in finding safe hideouts for Polish refugees; adventuresome and free-spirited Carmen joined in their clandestine efforts to save Polish nationals. Neither the Civil War nor World War II is depicted directly in her novels, nor are her clandestine activities represented, but they remind us that Laforet's formative years were filled with a politically charged ambience that is manifest in her writing in more subtle ways.

Laforet also took up with a set of bohemian artists in Barcelona, long known as a center for the visual arts and architecture. Art has always been central to Laforet's life; her father was an architect, several ancestors engaged in various artistic endeavors, and three of her five children are painters. While Laforet herself has never painted, her novels and stories are heavily interlarded with visual and other sensual imagery. During her two years in Barcelona she wrote and published several short stories, a prelude to the first long novel she wrote shortly after moving to Madrid, in which she recalls the two years she had just spent in Barcelona and converts them into the timeless stuff of literature.

In Madrid, Laforet lived with another set of relatives and continued her university career (in law), but once again she found activities that suited her artistic and freedom-loving nature better than formal university studies. She met with other literary minded young people to read and discuss such hallowed writers as Pablo Neruda and also worked on her first full-length novel, *Nada*. When she finished it at age twenty-two, she sent the manuscript to the Barcelona-based publisher Destino, which had just announced a new literary competition—the Nadal Prize for the novel. To her great surprise and that of many others (for she was very young and a woman!), she won the prize. Her novel was published the following year, catapulting her instantly into the national spotlight.

Shortly thereafter Laforet married Manuel Cerezales, a journalist. Within a year the first of her five children was born, and the responsibilities of marriage and motherhood, coupled with the burden of being a nationally known personality, slowed her writing production. She did, however, publish a second novel, *La isla y los demonios* (1952; "The Island and the Devils"), based on her girlhood in the Canaries. In the interim she wrote short stories and journal articles on personal, human interest, and travel topics. A collection of her short stories was published in 1952 under the title *La muerta* ("The Dead Woman"). In 1951 Laforet wrote a column entitled "Puntos de vista de una mujer" ("From a Woman's Point of View") for *Destino*, a weekly magazine published in Barcelona.

In 1954 Laforet underwent a mystical religious experience, and for seven years she sought religious instruction, trying to find her place within the Catholic Church. Like most Spaniards, she had been baptized, but her family was not particularly religious. Because of the strong emphasis on the church as an institution under the Franco regime and the rigidity with which dogma was presented, Laforet found it difficult to practice her newfound faith, and after seven years her intense religious activity waned. Her third novel, *La mujer nueva* (1955; "The New Woman"), grew out of her religious exploration. After a period of rest from writing (she was exhausted by the public interest in her Christian experience) and several trips abroad, she began work on a trilogy, "Tres pasos fuera del tiempo" ("Three Steps out of Time"), that was to explore life in Spain during the first two decades of the Franco regime. She began to haunt the periodical libraries in search of the recent past she and her compatriots had experienced but had not yet put into literary perspective. The first volume of the trilogy, *La insolación* ("Sunstroke") was published in 1963, but by the time Laforet received the galley proofs for the second volume, "Jaque mate" ("Checkmate") several years later, her concept of the trilogy had changed dramatically. She planned extensive revisions for the second volume, which she has never made; the galleys still lie in an old trunk.

Laforet made two extensive and personally important trips in 1965 and 1967, the first to the United States at the invitation of the State Department, after which she published her travel notes as *Paralelo 35* (1967; "Parallel 35"), reissued as *Mi primer viaje a U.S.A.* (1985; "My First Trip to the U.S.A."). The trip in 1967 was to Poland, sponsored by the journal *Actualidad*, for which she did a series of articles on that country. Laforet returned to the United States for lecture engagements on five different occasions during the 1980s and found that being in this country rekindled her interest in writing; she has published several journal articles about the visits.

Marital difficulties reached the crisis stage in the early 1970s, and Laforet finally separated from Manuel Cerezales in 1972, when her youngest son, Agustín, was old enough to fend for himself. She sought self-imposed exile in Rome for several years, hoping that distance from Spain and its oppressive atmosphere for women would allow her to return to her writing. But this did not occur, and she now lives in Madrid with a married daughter. The reasons a writer, especially one with so much talent and promise, suddenly ceases to write are complex, even impossible to pinpoint. Laforet's situation as a famous woman writer, married to a journalist of lesser note in Francoist Spain, where it was official policy that women should have no lives beyond their husbands and family, surely contributed to her anguish. It must also be considered, however, that about the time she became stymied on the trilogy, a new style of novel-writing had dawned in Spain. Belatedly Spanish novelists had discovered the European and American modernists—Marcel Proust, Virginia Woolf, James Joyce, William Faulkner—and with the publication of Luis Martín-Santos's *Tiempo de silencio* in 1962, Laforet's rather straightforward realistic approach to the novel began to look dated. That she was aware of this radical shift in narrative technique when she received the galley to the second volume of "Tres pasos fuera del tiempo" is entirely possible.

MAJOR THEMES

Laforet's four long novels and many of the novelettes and short stories share a basic theme or paradigm that closely parallels the limitations placed on her life when she arrived in Barcelona after the Spanish Civil War. The protagonist of many of her works is enmeshed in a particular set of social and psychological circumstances from which he or she attempts to escape. After contact with a different milieu, the protagonist arrives at a decision about his or her appropriate role in life. The pattern is essentially that of a rite of passage. In three of the four novels the protagonist is a young person who is orphaned of one or both parents, a loss that thrusts him or her into a situation of semi-independence and an opportunity for exploration and growth. That the protagonist who is seeking to adjust her life situation is usually a girl or woman can certainly be interpreted as a feminist approach, although Laforet denies such an orientation.

For many readers, Laforet's name is synonymous with her first novel, *Nada*; her three other long novels and her shorter works have received much less attention from the public and critics, although most of her works continue to be in print. Whether *Nada* is Laforet's best novel is debatable (the other novels contain certain technical improvements and a less labored style), but in this work Laforet hit upon a particularly fortuitous narrative device that she did not repeat in later narratives. Andrea, the protagonist, tells her own story—her year in Barcelona immediately after the Civil War, spent with a set of strange relatives while she attended the university—from a more mature perspective several years after the events she recounts. The dichotomy between the more mature stance of the narrator and the innocence and naïveté of the girl who lived the experiences creates a tension and existential ambiguity lacking in other works. The title *Nada* suggests this existential ambiguity, and the novel's appearance at the height of the existential movement in France encourages its interpretation as representative of the modern malaise.

Laforet's stated purpose for the novel was rather less philosophical and universal; she set out to recapture the ambience of post–Civil War Barcelona in the early 1940s. She accomplished this goal in a manner that is prototypical of her style with a strong emphasis on the senses—sights, smells, sounds. Andrea's relatives live in an apartment that represents a closed microcosm of bizarre decadence; the place has been divided into two sections, one of which has been sold, occasioning piles of extra furniture in every corner. It is filthy and in total disrepair. The grandmother, aunts, uncles, and maid who inhabit the apartment likewise show the wear and tear of time and misfortune. The elder aunt, Angustias, who typifies the attitude toward women during the Franco era, is by her own assessment "over the hill." She has worked and supported the others in the family since her wealthy father's death, but having never married (a woman's chief destiny), she decides to enter a convent. Laforet's approach to such a "traditional" woman is, however, far from simple, for Angustias is in love with her married boss, a situation that may be influential in her decision to take vows. The two uncles (Juan, married and with a child; Román, single) are Cain and Abel figures whose experiences during the Civil War seem to have caused unexplainable tensions between them. Juan eventually goes completely mad, and Román commits suicide. Her Aunt Gloria, married to Juan, is the one strong character of the household, a fact that Andrea realizes slowly. Gloria protects Juan's ego (he thinks himself a fine painter) while secretly supporting the family by gambling at her sister's tavern.

Andrea's family contrasts with that of her university friend Ena, who represents modern, forward-looking Spain. Ena's father is a successful businessman, and her mother, while maintaining her appropriate role within the family, has a bit of a life of her own as an excellent musician. Ena is very much a free spirit, as is Andrea, who delights in wandering about the city alone, an activity that horrifies Angustias. At the end of the novel, Ena invites Andrea to move with her family to Madrid, continue her studies, and work in her father's office. The last scene depicts Andrea leaving her relatives' house in Barcelona to enter Ena's father's car for the trip to Madrid. She believes at the time that very little has happened to her during her year in Barcelona, but it is clear from the narrative that she has left innocence behind and now has a more jaded and adult view of the world. Andrea has emerged from a long, dark night of hunger, loneliness, and oppression, but Spain and her female citizens had to survive more than thirty years of Franco's regime and very limited options.

La isla y los demonios takes place during the Spanish Civil War on the island of Gran Canaria, and like *Nada* it is the story of the maturation of a young girl, this time a kind of Joycean *Portrait of the Artist as a Young Man* in reverse. Marta, the sixteen-year-old protagonist, is a budding writer crafting a series of Legends of Alcorah, a reference to a god of the native Canary Island people. Canary Island folklore combines with the themes of art, fantasy, and maturation that envelop Marta's young life. She resides with a half brother and his wife (her mother is an invalid and eventually dies), who are not interested in her artistic pursuits. In fact, the half brother is interested only in Marta's feminine purity and the fact that she stands to inherit the mother's estate. Marta eagerly awaits the arrival of an uncle and two aunts from the mainland, who will live on the island until the hostilities cease. The uncle, a musician, and his wife, a poet, are accompanied by a painter friend; but these adults also fail to live up to Marta's expectations. Their lives are less lofty than she had imagined. The musician is hypochondriacal, his wife embittered and unsympathetic, and the other aunt is clearly having an affair with the painter, who turns out to be a weak, cowardly man whose wife has stayed behind to contribute to the war effort. When the war ends, Marta escapes from her island prison by accompanying her aunts and uncle back to the mainland to attend the university. Disillusioned with her early literary efforts, Marta burns her notebook of girlish literary efforts as a sign of her dawning maturity. As in the case of Andrea's "escape," the reader is left to wonder how positive a change the move to Madrid will be for Marta, especially considering that she will be living with the dour, conservative aunt.

La insolación likewise deals with a young person—this time Martín, a boy growing up amid the harsh realities of Civil War and Francoist Spain. The title of the projected trilogy "Tres pasos fuera del tiempo" refers to Spain during the Franco years. The country was in many ways "out of time"; still preoccupied with the aftermath of its own recent war, it remained isolated from World War II and other events in Europe. Martín's life is suffused with the prevailing sociopolitical ambience at the most personal level; these are the lean years of privation and hunger, and his health and growth are threatened by insufficient protein in his diet. His personal story, set in the context of a politically charged Spain, centers, like Marta's and Andrea's, on his sexual and artistic maturation; but unlike Marta, who rejects her art, Martín reaffirms his artistic vocation. His family, above all his father, a military man, reflects many of the values of traditional Spain, and his horizons are broadened by contact with a more liberal, freethinking family, the Corsis. The Corsis, however, lack the positive aspects with which Ena's family is endowed. The Corsi children are motherless like Martín, and the two fathers represent opposite poles of the political spectrum: Martín's father is a conservative Francoist, while the Corsis' father is a black marketeer, loyal to no regime or ideology. The Corsis enjoy a large measure of personal freedom, a reflection of their father's ambiguous sociopolitical situation, while Martín's father is a rigid disciplinarian.

Laforet boldly introduced two taboo subjects into *La insolación*—the situation of Republican sympathizers in Franco's Spain and homosexuality. Martín and the Corsi children unwittingly discover an ex-Republican soldier hiding in the Corsis' summer home, and Martín suffers an irreparable break with his father when the father believes (incorrectly) that his son has homosexual tendencies. In the wake of these two cataclysmic events, Martín determines to pursue the artistic career he had allowed to languish during the summer holidays with his father at a seaside town. It is interesting to note that Marta, the female adolescent artist, gives up her literary pretensions, while the male creator continues his artistic endeavors, perhaps a subconscious or conscious recognition on Laforet's part that the path to a public career as a writer or artist in Franco's Spain is much smoother for a man than for a woman.

La mujer nueva is Laforet's only novel to deal with a mature protagonist, a married woman who, like herself, undergoes a religious conversion. As in her novels with younger protagonists, *La mujer nueva* centers on the woman's search for a fulfilling life path. After her mystical experience, Paulina—the echoes of Saint Paul are apparent—separates from her husband and child to take up an independent life of religious study and good works. Ironically, the mystical experience occurs while Paulina is on a train to Madrid, attempting to escape further involvement with her lover. Her life becomes a triangle centered on three choices: (1) return to her husband and child; (2) break with her husband, whom she married during the Civil War in a ceremony considered illegal in Franco's Spain, in order to marry her lover; (3) enter a convent. In consonance with the opportunities for women during the 1950s in Spain, it does not occur to Paulina to live an independent life outside the institutions of the church or marriage.

Laforet heightens the limitations on Paulina's choices as an adult woman in Francoist Spain by depicting her as a single working parent during the early postwar years when her Republican husband went into exile, and she lived alone and taught school. As a reflection of the values of the times, when marriage and family were the paramount occupations for women, Paulina returns to her husband and son. Although this may be Laforet's least successful novel in an artistic-narrative sense, it is quite adept in depicting the general social ambience in Spain in the 1950s, especially the superficial religiosity that became the socially acceptable norm and that clashes at every turn with Paulina's deeply felt religious experience. Furthermore, the novel was a good medium for portraying the limited choices for women during this period.

Laforet's shorter fiction can be grouped into several thematic categories that diverge in rather startling ways. Those with a decidedly feminist message and those that center on the theme of Christian charity, with emphasis on traditional roles for women, seem particularly at odds. The short story "Rosamunda," one of Laforet's most accomplished pieces of short fiction, included in *La muerta*, centers on a woman who had pretentions to a stage career but was forced by social convention to marry and have a family. The woman, now in her frumpy middle years, attempts to realize her frustrated ambitions in the theater. She leaves her family and runs off to the city, but soon returns, defeated and ridiculous, to her husband and children. Although the protagonist's fate is negative, the message and underlying quest can be interpreted in a feminist manner. Of similar intent is one of Laforet's masterpieces, the novelette "El noviazgo" ("The Engagement"), included in *La llamada* (1954; "The Vocation"), which depicts a working woman whose life is limited by the dictates of a male society. Alicia, of good family but beyond the first bloom of youth, must work as a secretary to support herself and her mother after her father's death. She has long loved her boss; when he, after being widowed, asks Alicia to marry him (obviously expecting her to be a kind of nurse in his old age), she suddenly sabotages the engagement and the marriage is called off. The feminist turn of these pieces, which reveal the tragedy of a woman trapped by the exigencies of society, contrasts sharply with the message for women (and men) in stories like "El aguinaldo" ("The Christmas Gift," in Laforet's *Novelas I* 1957), and the novelette "El piano" (in *La llamada*), composed during Laforet's "Christian" period. These stories depict women finding happiness within the traditional confines of home, family, and Christian charity work.

SURVEY OF CRITICISM

Aside from two books of the "life and works" variety, criticism of Laforet's oeuvre has concentrated almost exclusively on *Nada*, which has elicited a large number of significant and worthwhile articles. Immediately upon its publication in 1945, *Nada* attracted the attention of older, established writers. Juan Ramón Jiménez, the poet who won the Nobel Prize in 1955, and Francisco Ayala, who was a well-established writer of fiction and essays, wrote public letters about the event, and Ramón Sender, one of Spain's most prolific novelists since the 1940s, wrote Laforet a letter from his exile in the United States. Azorín, a living remnant of the Generation of '98, wrote an article for *Destino* in which he recognized Laforet's refreshing new kind of novel. More recent academic interpretations have found endless dimensions in *Nada*; with each new critical turn from psychoanalytic to semiotics, the novel invariably undergoes yet another reading.

Nada has been interpreted variously as a "venture in mechanistic dynamics" (Eoff), a romance (Foster), and a Cinderella story (Higginbothom). A major division in criticism of the novel centers on whether the outcome is positive or negative. Robert Spires, for example, employing strategies of recent narratology, finds Andrea's experience essentially affirming, while Ruth El Saffar, also analyzing narrative voice, finds an undercurrent of disillusion. A number of articles center on the bildungsroman or initiation ritual aspect of *Nada*. Marsha Collins links the form of the novel with the search for identity, and Juan Villegas interprets *Nada* as an example of the archetypal mythic structure in which the hero's (or heroine's) life is a quest following a very specific trajectory: a leave-taking (separation from home and family), a search for freedom and personal identity through a series of adventures in a hostile environment, and the initiation's conclusion, which affirms the self. Carlos Feal Deibe explores the initiation ritual in the novel from a psychoanalytic perspective.

Elizabeth Ordóñez enriches this reading of *Nada* by adding a feminist and sociological perspective. Emphasizing the importance of the family paradigm, she sees the novel as a reflection of Spain's post–Civil War political and social values. For Ordóñez, Andrea's "new life" with Ena's family at the end of *Nada* is, rather than a liberation, a reaffirmation of patriarchal and bourgeois values. Sara Schyfter adds another dimension to the feminist approaches by interpreting Andrea's uncle Román as the dangerous side of the male's attraction for the female, and Geraldine Nichols points out the sexual obstacles portrayed in the novel. Michael Thomas, on the other hand, believes that *Nada* projects a positive view of Andrea's year in Barcelona as one of learning and development. Several feminist interpretations (Jones, Lamar Morris) also find a positive message in Andrea's narration.

Drawing on deconstructive notions of narratology, Rosa Perelmuter Pérez shifts discussion of Andrea's development to conflicting narrative moments, revealing that, rather than the protagonist's change over time, the real theme of the novel is the problematic coincidence of two narrative functions in one character. John Kronik, focusing on language and structures, analyzes the novel as a suffocated text. More traditional approaches to stylistics have been applied to Laforet's elaborate language in *Nada*, including analyses of animal imagery (Glenn), water imagery (Thompson), and painterly devices (Johnson, *Carmen Laforet*).

Even though Carmen Laforet was unable to sustain either the quality or the quantity of her novelistic production, she will remain an important contributor to post–Civil War literature. She was the first woman novelist of note during that period and a pioneer in developing narrative means to circumvent the establishment and portray the painful realities of the Civil War and its aftermath. Two of her techniques—elliptical narration and paradigmatic structures such as the family microcosm—were widely appropriated by the many fine novelists who were her contemporaries and successors. Finally, Laforet's presence as a woman novelist of national prominence opened the doors of Spanish publishing to the numerous women novelists who have followed in her wake since the 1940s.

BIBLIOGRAPHY

Works by Carmen Laforet

Nada. Barcelona: Editorial Destino, 1945. [Novel]
La isla y los demonios. Barcelona: Editorial Destino, 1952. [Novel]
La muerta. Barcelona: Editorial Destino, 1952. [Collection of short stories]
La llamada. Barcelona: Editorial Destino, 1954. [Collection of short stories]
La mujer nueva. Barcelona: Editorial Destino, 1955. [Novel]
Novelas I. Barcelona: Editorial Planeta, 1957. [Collection of novels and short stories]
La insolación. Barcelona: Editorial Planeta, 1963. [Novel]
Paralelo 35. Barcelona: Editorial Planeta, 1967. [Travel notes]
La niña y otros relatos. Madrid: Editorial Magisterio Español, 1970. [Collection of short stories]
Artículos literarios. Ed. Heather Leigh. Eastbourne, UK: Stuart-Spencer Publications, 1977[?].
Mi primer viaje a U.S.A. Madrid: P.P.P. Ediciones, 1985. [Reissue of *Paralelo 35*]

Translations

Nada. Trans. Inez Muñoz. London: Weidenfeld and Nicolson, 1958.
Andrea. Trans. Charles F. Payne. New York: Vantage Press, 1964. [Translation of *Nada*]

Works about Carmen Laforet

Ayala, Francisco. "Testimonio de la nada." *Realidad. Revista de Ideas* 1 (1947): 129–32.

Carrasco M., Hugo. "Las narraciones concurrentes en *La isla y los demonios*." *Estudios Filológicos* 17 (1982): 23–38.

Cerezales, Agustín. *Carmen Laforet*. Madrid: Ministerio de Cultura, 1982.

Collins, Marsha S. "Carmen Laforet's *Nada*: Fictional Form and the Search for Identity." *Symposium* 38 (1984–85): 298–310.

Decoster, Cyrus C. "Carmen Laforet: A Tentative Evaluation." *Hispania* 40 (1957): 187–91.

El Saffar, Ruth. "Structural and Thematic Tactics of Suppression in Carmen Laforet's *Nada*." *Symposium* 28 (1974): 119–29.

Eoff, Sherman. "*Nada* by Carmen Laforet: A Venture in Mechanistic Dynamics." *Hispania* 35 (1952): 207–11.

Feal Deibe, Carlos. "*Nada* de Carmen Laforet: La iniciación de una adolescente." *The Analysis of Hispanic Texts: Current Trends in Methodology*. First York College Colloquium. Ed. Mary Ann Beck et al. Jamaica, NY: Bilingual Press, 1976. 221–41.

Foster, David William. " 'Nada' de Carmen Laforet." *Revista Hispánica Moderna* 32 (1966): 43–55.

Galerstein, Carolyn L. "Carmen Laforet and the Spanish Spinster." *Revista de Estudios Hispánicos* 11 (1977): 303–15.

Glenn, Kathleen M. "Animal Imagery in *Nada*." *Revista de Estudios Hispánicos* 11 (1977): 381–94.

Higginbothom, Virginia. "*Nada* and the Cinderella Syndrome." *Rendezvous* 22 (1986): 17–25.

Horrent, J. "L'Oeuvre Romanesque de Carmen Laforet." *Revue des Langues Vivants* 35 (1959): 179–87.

Illanes Adaro, Graciela. *La novelística de Carmen Laforet*. Madrid: Gredos, 1971.

Johnson, Roberta. *Carmen Laforet*. Boston: Twayne, 1981.

———. "Light and Morality in Carmen Laforet's *La insolación*." *Letras Femeninas* 12 (1986): 94–102.

———. "Personal and Public History in Laforet's Long Novels." *Feminine Concerns in Contemporary Spanish Fiction by Women*. Ed. Roberto C. Manteiga, Carolyn L. Galerstein, and Kathleen McNerney. Potomac, MD: Scripta Humanistica, 1988. 43–53.

Jones, Margaret E. W. "Dialectical Movement as Feminist Technique in the Works of Carmen Laforet." *Studies in Honor of Gerald E. Wade*. Ed. Sylvia Bowman et al. Madrid: José Porrúa Turanzas, 1979. 109–20.

Kronik, John. "*Nada* y el texto asfixiado: proyección de una estética." *Revista Ibero-americana* 47 (1981): 195–202.

Lamar Morris, Celita. "Carmen Laforet's *Nada* as an Expression of Woman's Self-Determination." *Letras Femeninas* 1 (1975): 40–47.

Newberry, Wilma. "The Solstitial Holidays in Carmen Laforet's *Nada*: Christmas and Midsummer." *Romance Notes* 17 (1976): 76–81.

Nichols, Geraldine. *Des/cifrar la diferencia: Narrativa femenina de la España contemporánea*. Madrid: Siglo XXI, 1992. 133–151.

———. *Escribir, espacio propio: Laforet, Matute, Moix, Tusquets, Riera y Roig por sí mismas*, Minneapolis: Institute for the Study of Ideologies and Literature, 1989. 127–45.

———. "Sex, the Single Girl, and Other Mesalliances in Rodoreda and Laforet." *Anales de la Literatura Española Contemporánea* 12 (1987): 123–40.

Ordóñez, Elizabeth. "*Nada*: Initiation into Bourgeois Patriarchy." *The Analysis of Hispanic Texts: Current Trends in Methodology*. Second York College Colloquium. Ed. Lisa E. Davis and Isabel C. Tarán. Jamaica, N.Y.: Bilingual Press, 1976. 61–78.

Perelmuter Pérez, Rosa. "Acontecimiento y escritura en *Nada* de Carmen Laforet." *Taller Literario* 1 (1980): 11–15.

Pilar Palomo, María del. "Carmen Laforet y su mundo novelesco." *Monteagudo* 22 (1958): 7–13.

Rice, Mary. "La novela femenina del siglo XX: Bombal, Laforet y Martín Gaite." *Mester* 15 (1986): 7–12.

Ruiz-Fornells, Enrique. "Una novelista española ante los Estados Unidos: Carmen Laforet." *La Chispa 1983*. Ed. Gilbert Paolini. New Orleans: Tulane UP, 1983. 241–53.

Schyfter, Sara E. "The Male Mystique in Carmen Laforet's *Nada*." *Novelistas femeninas de la postguerra española*. Ed. Janet W. Diaz. Madrid: José Porrúa Turanzas, 1984. 88–93.

Servodidio, Mirella d'Ambrosio. "Spatiality in *Nada*." *Anales de la Narrativa Española Contemporánea* 5 (1980): 57–72.

Spires, Robert C. "La experiencia afirmadora de *Nada*." *La novela española de posguerra*. Madrid: Cupsa Editorial, 1978. 51–73.

———. "*Nada* y la paradoja de los signos negativos." *Siglo* 3 (1985–86): 31–33.

Thomas, Michael D. "Symbolic Portals in Laforet's *Nada*." *Anales de la Novela de Posguerra* 3 (1978): 57–74.

Thompson, Currie K. "Perception and Art: Water Imagery in *Nada*." *Kentucky Romance Quarterly* 32 (1985): 291–300.

Ullman, Pierre L. "The Moral Structure of Carmen Laforet's Novels." *The Vision Obscured: Perceptions of Some Twentieth-Century Catholic Novelists*. New York: Fordham UP, 1970. 201–19.

Villegas, Juan. " 'Nada' de Carmen Laforet o la infantilización de la legendaria." *La estructura mítica del héroe*. Barcelona: Planeta, 1973. 177–201.

MARÍA TERESA LEÓN
(1904–1988)

Beth Wietelmann Bauer

BIOGRAPHY

One of thousands whose lives were torn asunder by the Spanish Civil War (1936–39), María Teresa León stands out for the depth and prominence of her involvement in the political and cultural life of her country and for the artistry with which she has recounted her experiences of war and exile. Over the course of a writing career that began in early adolescence, León experimented successfully with many genres, including short stories, novels, poetry, plays, fictionalized biography, and scripts for radio and television. She is best known, however, for her autobiography, *Memoria de la melancolía* (1970; "Memory of Melancholy"). To read these powerful memoirs is to encounter a woman given to deeply felt reflection and yet moved to valiant and tireless action by political circumstance and by her steady commitment to human solidarity, justice, and art, each in the service of the other.

Upon alighting in Oran, Algeria, from the plane that carried her into a thirty-eight-year exile at the end of the Civil War, León was called upon to introduce herself, her husband (the poet Rafael Alberti), and their companions, high-ranking officials of the defeated Republican government: "This gentleman is General Antonio Cordero, War Minister, and this other one is Mr. Núñez Mazas, Minister of the Air Force. That man over there is a poet and I am . . . a soldier" (*Memoria* 226; Rodrigo, "La miliciana" 187–88; Rodrigo, "Una mujer" 38). Perhaps it should come as no surprise that the daughter of an army officer would define herself in these terms. But León's militarism, which was shaped by her affiliation with organizations like the Communist Party and the Alliance of Antifascist Intellectuals, was of a far different political stripe than that of her father, whom she remembers surrounded by generals and the dying embers of Spain's former colonial glory.

As a young girl, León found herself increasingly at odds with the bourgeois values of her financially comfortable and socially well-connected family. Yet her parents seem at least to have recognized their daughter's literary inclinations, for she recalls in *Memoria* being taken, on the day of her First Communion, to meet the renowned writer Emilia Pardo Bazán. The doyenne of Spanish letters dedicated a copy of her novel *El tesoro de Gastón* (1897) to the young María Teresa, with an added wish that she would continue along a literary path (*Memoria* 25; Bravo Villasante 13). Later expelled from a Catholic girls' school for reading prohibited books, León found appealing role models in the home of her aunt and uncle, the eminent philologists María Goyri and Ramón Menéndez Pidal, and in their daughter Jimena. She proudly remembered studying with her cousin and listening to gramophone recordings of the popular ballads collected by Menéndez Pidal and Goyri, the first woman to obtain a doctorate from a Spanish university.

León began to write stories and articles at the age of fourteen or fifteen, and published many of them between 1921 and 1928 in *El Diario de Burgos*, the local newspaper, under the name of a D'Annunzio heroine, Isabel Inghirami. In this same paper she published her first highly polemical piece, a defense of a young unwed mother who in shame had drowned her baby (Rodrigo, "La miliciana" 174). Both the awareness of social ills that lead to such tragic crimes and the consciousness of women's concerns typified León throughout her career. She herself came face to face with restrictive laws and social conventions when she struggled to free herself from a miserable marriage into which she had entered at the age of sixteen. Few lines in her autobiography express more bitterness than those in which she recalls how her confessors urged her to endure matrimony at all costs and how her estranged husband, Gonzalo de Sebastián, allowed her only a few closely monitored hours at the side of their gravely ill son (*Memoria* 79–81). When her son Gonzalo recovered, León reconciled with her husband and they had a second son, Enrique, in 1925. By 1929, however, further marital difficulties led to a final separation that, along with the Civil War, was to keep her apart from her two sons for many years (Sebastián 78).

From the alienation of her early years, a time reminiscent of the fictional life of Clarín's heroine Ana Ozores (*La Regenta*, 1884–85), León went on to lead a life of action and commitment alongside Rafael Alberti, whom she met in 1929 and married after divorce laws were liberalized under the Second Spanish Republic (1931–36). The account of their activities in the decade between 1930 and 1940 includes a dizzying series of names, trips, organizations, and historical and cultural events. In 1932, León and Alberti traveled, under the auspices of the newly formed Spanish Republic, to Berlin, the Soviet Union, Denmark, Norway, Belgium, and Holland to study the European theater movement. Back in Spain in 1933, and inspired by their trip to Russia, they founded the journal *Octubre*, whose first issue—which the editors sold on street corners—included pieces by Antonio Machado, Alejo Carpentier, Emilio Prados, Maxim Gorki, and Luis Cernuda. Their house on Marqués de Urquijo Street was a center for leftist ideology, for art, and for the promotion of fraternity in both a political sense and on a more intimate level (Rodrigo, "La miliciana" 176). The friends mentioned in *Memoria de la melancolía* in connection with that house and those years are legion, and include Federico García Lorca, Manuel Altolaguirre, Ignacio Sánchez Mejías, Miguel de Unamuno, José Bergamín, Luis Buñuel, and Pablo Neruda.

In 1934 León and Alberti again traveled to the Soviet Union, this time to attend the First Congress of Soviet Writers. Their return home was delayed by the outbreak of the October Revolution, which in turn precipitated another journey to the United States in order to raise funds for the Asturian mine workers who had suffered in this bloody prelude to the war. By the end of 1935 Alberti and León were back in Spain, working on behalf of the Popular Front. When the Spanish Civil War broke out in July 1936, they were in Ibiza. Certain that the Nationalist troops who had assassinated Federico García Lorca were after them as well, they hid in the mountains until Republican troops took control of the island in August (*Memoria* 156–66). León and Alberti then returned to Madrid, where they played a centrol role in the Alliance of Antifascist Intellectuals, headquartered throughout the war in the elegant Heredia-Spínola Palace. In her memoirs, León speaks fondly of the camaraderie that warmed the old mansion, noting with irony how even in the leanest of times, when dinner was but a few wormy lentils, the friends and members of the Antifascist Alliance ate from fine porcelain emblazoned with the Heredia-Spínola coat of arms.

With the exception of a brief trip to the Soviet Union in 1937, to attend the Second International Writers Congress, a sojourn highlighted by a long meeting with Stalin, León and Alberti lived out the Civil War with their comrades in Madrid near the line of combat. When the constant bombing of Madrid forced the closing of the Zarzuela Theater, where León served as director of the Theater of Art and State Propaganda, she founded an itinerant company that took theater to the trenches. The Guerrillas del Teatro performed both classical drama and newer works of social protest, traveling by truck to the battle lines, warding off hunger and fear with song and laughter (Rodrigo, "La miliciana" 181–82). Particularly vivid among León's memories are the war vignettes: the jingling reins of horses pulling the cart of a mortally wounded driver, the anonymous bravery of common soldiers, their wives, and families.

León's own valor and her intense belief in the social value of art are evident not only in her work with the Guerrillas del Teatro but also in her collaboration with the Junta for the Protection and Defense of the National Artistic Treasure, a group formed at the outset of the war to conserve invaluable artifacts and collections. As Franco's troops neared Toledo, María Teresa and a friend were called upon to supervise the evacuation of paintings by El Greco; similarly, after the Prado was hit by German incendiary bombs in November 1936, she was authorized to see that the masterpieces of Spain's foremost museum were safely transported to Valencia. Wood for crates and trucks was scarce, but León scraped together what was needed and then spent what she described in her memoirs as the longest night of her life waiting for radio messages as the transport vehicles passed each of the checkpoints on their way south (*Memoria* 217–20; Rodrigo, "La miliciana" 184–85; "Una mujer" 36–37).

After Franco's triumph in 1939 and their initial stop in Oran, León and Alberti went to Paris, where they worked as translators for Radio Paris-Mondial until collaboration between the Vichy government and the new Spanish dictatorship made it impossible for them to stay. At the close of 1940 they embarked on the long voyage to Argentina, birthplace of their daughter Aitana and their home for twenty-three years. León filled the emptiness of her exile with the written word, composing page upon page of the many novels, stories, biographies, screenplays, radio programs, and memoirs she published or produced during the Argentina years. Faithful to the utopian visions of social solidarity and equality that she had embraced as a young woman, she traveled with her family in 1957 to the People's Republic of China, an experience she describes with admiration and with deep feeling for the Chinese people and their history in *Sonríe China* (1958; "China Smiles").

This awareness of her connection with all people and the search for a country in which her sense of social justice might be realized stand in stark contrast to León's lonely estrangement from the country of her birth. Her nostalgia for Spain and for the close friendships of her youth seemed to intensify as time took her farther and farther from the life she had known, and it was in her final years of exile in Rome that she penned the most eloquent record of her longing, *Memoria de la melancolía*. León and Alberti finally returned to Spain in 1977, following the death of Francisco Franco (1975) and the legalization of the Communist Party. By the time she set foot upon Spanish soil, however, León was lost in her memories, unable to recognize what was once hers. Fortunately, her spirit is still present in the rich written legacy that she has left for readers everywhere.

MAJOR THEMES

It is impossible to do justice to the vast corpus of León's work in a brief summary. Nonetheless, her writings are traversed by a series of common themes and attitudes that resurface at the end of her career in *Memoria de la melancolía*. Central among these are the realities of war and exile, alienation and violence, and, in contrast, intense feelings of friendship and solidarity. A stylistically rich and lyrical composition, León's autobiography is quite different from that of her husband, with which it is sometimes compared. Whereas Alberti's *La arboleda perdida* (1959) is a straightforward, chronological account that ends with the period when the poet met León, *Memoria de la melancolía* embraces a much longer period and its time line is much more jagged. Though they begin with the author's youth, León's memoirs are propelled back and forth by the consciousness of the aging exile who writes in Rome in the 1960s. Events from the mature writer's present intrude upon the past, and Proustian objets trouvés— frequently photographs—also determine the sinuous course of her narrative (Albornoz 46). Though she frequently uses the autobiographical first person, León also refers to herself in the third person, and she sometimes reaches out to address her readers. The common ground on which she meets the reading public is that of shared emotion. Just as she offers up her feelings and recollections in highly expressive prose, she also demonstrates an enormous capacity to identify with the complex inner worlds and external realities of others. With its shifting time frame and focalization, *Memoria de la melancolía* is technically reminiscent of the modern novel (Albornoz 46); like the latter, it demands active participation by the reader, and it highlights the expressive power of language as both vehicle of consciousness and record of experience.

There is no denying the prominence in *Memoria de la melancolía* of scenes from the Second Republic and the Civil War, and it is also evident that León witnessed these events from a key vantage point. Her travels and her affiliation with the Alliance of Antifascist Intellectuals and the famed International Brigade put her in contact with prominent artists and thinkers from both Spain and the rest of Europe. Prior to writing this autobiography, León had incorporated her war experiences into other works of both fiction and nonfiction. *La historia tiene la palabra* (1944; "History Has the Floor"), for example, is a detailed account of her efforts to preserve works of art threatened by gunfire and bombs. Her first novel, *Contra viento y marea* (1941; "Against Wind and Tide"), juxtaposes the struggling Cuba of 1898 with vignettes from the Spanish Civil War, and her second, *Juego limpio* (1959; "Clean Game"), is set in the Heredia-Spínola Palace and narrated primarily by a fictional actor from the Guerrillas del Teatro. Also, many of the stories in *Cuentos de la España actual* (1936; "Stories of Contemporary Spain") and *Morirás lejos* (1942; "You Will Die Far Away") deal with war-related themes, including hunger, political allegiance, class differences, bravery, and need. Several of these works, along with the history that engendered them, resurface in the immense tapestry of memory, love, and violence that León weaves in her autobiography, where well-known names and battles are interspersed with equally vivid impressions of the lost moments of war: the ballads, the imaginary feasts invented by famished soldiers, the oddly safe sound of bullet showers, the trampled doll lost by a little girl of unknown origin and sad destiny.

The sense of belonging and commitment that was León's throughout the bitterly divisive and brutal Civil War is juxtaposed throughout her work with her years of errantry and her feelings of loss. The themes of exile and estrangement permeate much of her writing, even the densely surrealistic and legendary stories of her last collection. Thus, in the story "Las estatuas" ("The Statues") from *Fábulas del tiempo amargo* (1962; "Fables of the Bitter Time"), the narrator cries: "I can't stand it anymore! Undo me. Untie the cord that connects me to the womb of my land!" (*Una estrella roja* 180). Similarly painful feelings of uprootedness are foregrounded in León's third and last novel, *Menesteos, marinero de abril* (1965; "Menesteus, April Mariner"), a reelaboration of the mythical tale of the lovestruck Athenian captain who died searching for Hades near the site where the Spanish city of Cádiz was founded. And, Spain's most famous exile of the medieval period is the subject of one of León's fictionalized biographies, *Don Rodrigo Díaz de Vivar, el Cid Campeador* (1954). A companion work, *Doña Jimena Díaz de Vivar, gran señora de todos los deberes* (1960; "Doña Jimena Díaz de Vivar, Great Lady in All Duties"), focuses on the wife of the epic hero and attempts to portray the dignity of women who worked alongside the warriors of old.

Many of León's writings evince a special sensitivity to the lives of women and to the children entrusted to their care. The protagonists of the stories in *Cuentos de la España actual,* León's most sustained experiment with Soviet-style social realism, often are women who adopt a revolutionary stance in the face of exploitation by the bourgeoisie and the powers that be ("Liberación de Octubre" ["October Liberation"]; "El derecho de la Nación" ["The Right of the Nation"]). Also notable among her fictional works devoted to female experience and psychology is the collection of stories entitled *Las peregrinaciones de Teresa* (1950; "Teresa's Peregrinations"). The nine stories in the collection are united by a protagonist named Teresa who becomes a kind of "everywoman" as she assumes different identities and circumstances in each story. Through Teresa, León explores many women's issues: how the desire for freedom gets trapped between the home and the convent ("El noviciado de Teresa" ["Teresa's Novitiate"]); a woman's dissimulation and sexual dissatisfaction in her marriage to a good man ("Tres pies al galgo" ["Splitting Hairs"]); public responses to female madness ("Madame Pimenton"); the despair of a forty-year-old woman abandoned by her wayward husband ("Los otros cuarenta años" ["The Other Forty Years"]). Some of the stories in *Las peregrinaciones de Teresa* are marked by obvious anticlerical and anti-Franco bias, yet all resonate with the ambiguities, the descriptive details, and the touches of legend and folklore that define León's evocative style. A good example of a work of nonfiction marked by León's concern for members of her sex is *Sonríe China*, much of which is devoted to her impressions of Chinese women and the abuses that they suffered under traditional patriarchy.

It is in *Memoria de la melancolía*, however, that León most directly describes her consciousness of being both a woman and a writer. She recalls that from an early age she took pleasure in the term *femme de lettres*, and she gratefully acknowledges her link both with other Spanish women writers from María de Maetzu to Concha Espina, and with the feminists and female intellectuals who frequented the Lyceum Club Femenino in the Madrid of the 1920s and 1930s. Occasionally, the aging narrator of *Memoria de la melancolía* reaches out to specific women, including her own mother in a description of the changing nature of daughterly love (118–21). On another occasion, the same María Teresa is moved by current events to address the women of Vietnam: "I feel that I would like to be seated in any jungle shelter, next to any Vietnamese woman, her hand in mine. I urgently need to tell her that I am an old woman from Spain.

I am not worth anything to you. Take consolation in knowing that I, too, paid the price of freedom in tears'' (100).

León's more intimate memories—the girls' schools, the limits placed by middle-class society on female conduct, the first encounters with male desire and with an amorous uncle, the disastrous early marriage, relationships with mother and grandmother, role models, the experience of aging—speak of and to issues confronted by women everywhere. Interestingly, these are often the recollections that León tends to address indirectly, speaking of herself in the third person, alluding to feelings evoked by events while omitting facts and details (Albornoz 46). The use of innuendo and the vacillation between self-revelation and concealment, while perhaps indicative of shame or pain associated with León's girlhood and adolescence, might also be read as a reflection of social restrictions placed upon female self-expression. León eventually found her voice, one that declaimed verses from public stages and enlivened radio programs, but it was a voice ever modulated by memories of the past and of her own struggle for personal and political freedom.

SURVEY OF CRITICISM

Given her active role in the Spanish Civil War and in the intellectual life of her country, both in situ and in exile, it is not surprising that her life has been the focus of many studies devoted to María Teresa León. Both the summary biography and personal reminiscences provided by contributors to the volume published in honor of León by the Junta de Castilla y León are informative in this regard, as are the articles of Antonina Rodrigo. The latter, in particular, help clarify events that appear disjointedly in *Memoria de la melancolía*, which the Spanish writer Rosa Chacel has called ''a flock of memories that escape from the nest and go fluttering all around'' (49). Specifying that she does not pretend to offer a serious literary evaluation, Chacel refers to *Memoria de la melancolía* as León's ''best'' book, and stresses the invaluable wealth of memories that are subtly intertwined in León's poetic antidote to our collective amnesia. Chacel also speculates that the book's fragmented design is a product not of inexperience (as León herself suggests when she apologizes for flitting from one subject to the next) but of a need for distance and perspective. In a similar vein, Aurora de Albornoz detailed the careful artistry that unifies León's seemingly spontaneous and disorganized account, and in so doing has underscored the following aspects of her narrative technique: use of free indirect style and stream of consciousness; similarity to the ''new'' Latin American novel; connections with Proust; music-like repetition of motifs and meditations; and above all the forceful presence of the narrative voice as it moves from first to second to third person and from the narrative to the contemplative to the lyrical mode (43–46). Gregorio Torres Nebrera observes that *Memoria de la melancolía* is not just a personal record, but also a testimony to the efforts of an entire group of middle-class Spanish intellectuals who opted for a revolutionary and feminist stance during the 1920s and 1930s (29).

Particularly interesting with regard to León's place among her female peers is Shirley Mangini's comparison of *Memoria de la melancolía* with the autobiographies of two other female Civil War exiles, Victoria Kent—a radical socialist and director of prisons during the Second Spanish Republic—and Federica Montseny—the first high-ranking female member of the government in Spain during the Republic and an anarchist leader during the war. While observing that all three women shared the conscious moral aim of decrying fascism and expressing their solidarity with those who had endured the hardships of exile, Mangini also underscores differences in the form and focus of their memoirs (209). Whereas León's very literary and lyrical work highlights her lifelong role as an intellectual and artist, Kent and Montseny focus on their claustrophobic post–Civil War years of hiding in France. Kent wrote a philosophical and novelized account of her struggle against madness and despair, and Montseny employed a direct, autobiographical style tinged with bitterness toward Vichy France. But in their passionate portrayal of the horrors of war and exile all three women are united and bound in "the urgent solitary voice of a collective testimony" (209).

León's short stories have been studied by Carmen Bravo-Villasante and Joaquín Marco, who trace a similar trajectory in the style and content of her stories. These critics note that the early stories (*Cuentos para soñar* [1929; "Stories for Dreaming"]) and *La bella del mal de amor* [1930; "The Beauty Unhappy in Love"]) are very lyrical, modernist pieces based on fairy tales, folklore, and ballads. In keeping with major artistic trends of the times, *Rosa-Fría, patinadora de la luna* (1934; "Rosa-Fría, Moon Skater") incorporates surrealistic imagery reminiscent of the paintings of Marc Chagall, Joan Miró, and Salvador Dalí. With *Cuentos de la España actual* (1936) and some of the stories of *Morirás lejos* (1942), León deviates from her earlier work in an attempt to practice a didactic social realism heavily influenced by Soviet writers. But the densely allusive and mythical legends of the 1962 *Fábulas del tiempo amargo* return to and develop León's earlier experiments with poetic and surrealistic prose. Joaquín Marco stresses the aesthetic value of these later stories, which he finds richly imaginative and laden with a poetry heightened by León's fascination with the exotic, the primitive, and new sensations. He also underscores the contrast between these final tales and the ideologically charged stories of *Cuentos de la España actual*. For Marco, the latter are "an indispensable example of revolutionary literature" (11) written by a woman who not only lived through a Spanish "revolution" but also was very familiar with posttsarist writers such as Ilya Ehrenburg, Vsevolod Ivanov, and Maxim Gorki. These are stories in which León portrays the world of the powerless and exploited, particularly women and children. In these often tragic tales of class hatred and the struggle for survival, Marco also finds reminiscences of Zola, of the Pérez Galdós of *Misericordia* (1897), and of the César Vallejo of *Tungsteno* (1931). Marco stresses León's attention to her art—psychological depth, lyrical moments, and descriptive power—even in her most politically slanted pieces. Much of what is fresh about *Cuentos de la España actual*, Marco affirms, is its portrayal of a woman's point of view and specifically of the thoughts and actions of militant women (17–18).

León's three novels have been studied by Gregorio Torres Nebrera, who traces their movement from the documentary to the mythical. He emphasizes the relatively vague characterization and simple construction of *Contra viento y marea*, a two-part work in which sketches from the Spanish American War of 1898 are loosely tied to scenes from the Spanish Civil War through a common character, the idealist who fights for freedom, and through repeated themes like the dignity and suffering of the masses. The Civil War is also the backdrop for León's second novel, *Juego limpio,* which for Torres is closer to an autobiographical account than to fiction. He notes the novel's technical and thematic artistry, including the use of multiple narrators and points of view, the confessional quality of the memoirs of the chief narrator, and the novelistic development of the contrast between war games and "clean games," between deadly "play" and the plays performed by the intensely life-affirming Guerrillas del Teatro (37–38). For Torres Nebrera, León's final novel, *Menesteos, marinero de abril* (1965), is her finest, one in which the adaptation of an ancient Greek legend and the plot structure of the Byzantine novel impose an artistic distance from which the writer explores some of her favorite themes: memory, loss, exile, adventures in foreign lands, paradises lost and found. Thus, Torres Nebrera sees *Menesteos* as an extension of León's great obsession: Spain, as it is both diminished and monumentalized in human memory (40).

María Teresa León's place in Spanish letters has yet to be established. Many of her writings are not readily available, and many have not received the critical attention they deserve. *Memoria de la melancolía* is certainly, as many have observed, a vital reference for those who wish to know the exiles of the Spanish Civil War. It is also a moving portrait of the artist as both a young and an old woman. María Teresa León was well attuned to the ways in which memory and consciousness both fix and transform the past, and those who meet her in her memoirs will wish for further literary encounters with this exceptional woman.

BIBLIOGRAPHY

Works by María Teresa León

Novels

Contra viento y marea. Buenos Aires: Ediciones Aiape, 1941.
Juego limpio. Buenos Aires: Goyanarte, 1959. Barcelona: Seix Barral, 1986.
Menesteos, marinero de abril. Mexico City: Alacena/Era, 1965.

Short Stories

Cuentos para soñar. Burgos, Spain: Hijos de Santiago Rodríguez, 1929.
La bella del mal de amor (cuentos castellanos). Burgos, Spain: Hijos de Santiago Rodríguez, 1930.
Rosa-Fría, patinadora de la luna. Madrid: Espasa-Calpe, 1934. Barcelona: La Gaya Ciencia, 1973.
Cuentos de la España actual. Mexico City: Editorial Dialéctica, 1936.
Morirás lejos. Buenos Aires: Americalee, 1942.
Las peregrinaciones de Teresa. Buenos Aires: Botella del Mar, 1950.
Fábulas del tiempo amargo. *Revista Poesía Universal Ecuador O O' O''* (1962): n.p. [Collection of short stories]
Una estrella roja. Madrid: Espasa-Calpe, 1979. [Includes *Cuentos de la España actual*, *Morirás lejos*, and *Fábulas del tiempo amargo*]

Autobiography and Fictionalized Biography

El gran amor de Gustavo Adolfo Bécquer. Buenos Aires: Losada, 1946.
Don Rodrigo Díaz de Vivar, el Cid Campeador. Buenos Aires: Peuser, 1954.
Doña Jimena Díaz de Vivar. Buenos Aires: Losada, 1960. Madrid: Biblioteca Nueva, 1968.
El Cid Campeador. Buenos Aires: Fabril, 1962.
Memoria de la melancolía. Buenos Aires: Losada, 1970. Barcelona: Editorial Laia/ Ediciones Picasso, 1977. Barcelona: Editorial Bruguera, 1982.
El soldado que nos enseñó a hablar. Cervantes. Madrid: Altalena, 1978.

Miscellaneous (History, Travel, Theater)

"Huelga en el puerto." *Octubre* [Madrid] 1933. *Teatro de agitación política. 1933–39*. Madrid: Cuadernos para el Diálogo, 1976.
Crónica General de la Guerra Civil. Vol. 1. Madrid: Alianza de Intelectuales Antifascistas, 1937.
La historia tiene la palabra. Buenos Aires: Patronato Hispano-Argentino, 1944. Madrid: Hispamérica, 1977.
Nuestro hogar de cada día. Buenos Aires: Fabril, 1958.
Sonríe China. Buenos Aires: Jacobo Muchnik, 1958. [With Rafael Alberti]

Works about María Teresa León

Abellán, José Luis, ed. *El exilio español de 1939*. 4 vols. Madrid: Taurus, 1976.
Albornoz, Aurora de. "El lugar de María Teresa León." *María Teresa León* 41–48.
Bravo-Villasante, Carmen. "María Teresa León, mujer de letras: Los cuentos de María Teresa León." *María Teresa León*. 13–22.
Chacel, Rosa. "María Teresa." *María Teresa León* 49–54.
García de Nora, Eugenio. *La novela española contemporánea (1939–1967)*. Vol 3. Madrid: Gredos, 1970. 242.
Lloréns, Vicente. "La emigración republicana de 1939." Abellán. Vol. 1. 165.
Mangini, Shirley. "Three Voices of Exile." *Monographic Review* 2 (1986): 208–15.
Marco, Joaquín. Prologue. *Una estrella roja*. By María Teresa León. Madrid: Espasa-Calpe, 1979. 7–22.

María Teresa León. Valladolid: Junta de Castilla y León, 1987. [Essays, remembrances, biography, and bibliography]

Marra López, José Ramón. *Narrativa española fuera de España 1936–1961*. Madrid: Guadarrama, 1963. 495–96.

Rodrigo, Antonina. "María Teresa León, la miliciana de mejor aire." *Mujeres de España*. Barcelona: Plaza y Janés, 1977. 172–92.

——. "María Teresa León: Una mujer en la Guerra Civil." *Vindicación Feminista* 23 (1978): 36–38.

Sáenz, Pilar. "María Teresa León." *Women Writers of Spain. An Annotated Bio-Bibliographical Guide*. Ed. Carolyn Galerstein. Westport: Greenwood Press, 1986. 174–77.

Sáenz de la Calzada, Carlos. "Educación y pedagogía." Abellán. Vol 3. 274.

Sanz Villanueva, Santos. "La narrativa del exilio." Abellán. Vol 4. 181.

Sebastián, Gonzalo de. "¡Cómo me gustaría! Carta de Gonzalo Sebastián de León a María Teresa León." *María Teresa León* 77–78.

Torres Nebrera, Gregorio. "María Teresa León, esbozo a tres tintas (memorias, biografías, novelas)." *María Teresa León* 27–40.

——. *La obra literaria de María Teresa León. Memorias. Biografías. Novelas*. Trabajos del Departamento de Literatura 5. Badajoz, Spain: Universidad de Extremadura, 1986.

LEONOR LÓPEZ DE CÓRDOVA
(Late Fourteenth–Early Fifteenth Century)

Theresa Ann Sears

BIOGRAPHY

Leonor López de Córdova, a fourteenth-century Spanish noblewoman, lived and suffered through the turbulent years of the battle between Pedro I, the "Cruel" (1350–69), and his illegitimate half brother, Enrique de Trastámara (1369–79), for domination of Spain. In Leonor's veins ran the blood of legends both royal and literary. Her father, Martín López de Córdova, Master of Calatrava and Alcántara by King Pedro's grace, was the nephew of Don Juan Manuel (1282–1348), a powerful figure in both politics and literature. Martín himself figures prominently in the major contemporary source for the history of the period, *Crónicas de los Reyes de Castilla.*[1]

Sancha Carrillo, Leonor's mother, was niece to Alfonso XI (1312–50), Pedro's father. Sancha died young, a fact Leonor uses to explain her marriage to Ruy Gutiérrez de Finestrosa, son of an influential member of Pedro's court. There has been some controversy as to Leonor's age when she married: seven years old, according to Reinaldo Ayerbe-Chaux and Amy Kaminsky; or seventeen, in the *Colección de documentos inéditos*, which contains her "Testamento o Relación que deja escrita para sus descendientes." The young couple's strong ties to Pedro on both sides and through several generations served to guarantee that they would spend many of the troubled years of their marriage apart and that Ruy Gutiérrez's considerable inheritance would disappear because of Enrique de Trastámara's triumph and the revenge he took upon the losing side.

Leonor's life, as she relates it in her "Testamento," was an eventful and often desperate one. Her text provides a more personal parallel to the tale of royal intrigue and violence than we find in the *Crónicas*. Born in King Pedro's house in Catalayud, a city in northeastern Spain that lies at the crossroads connecting

Soria, Zaragoza, Guadalajara, and Teruel, Leonor remained a member of his household until he was overthrown. Little is known about that time, for Leonor is our only source of information, and she does not elaborate. After her marriage, she joined her in-laws, who were caring for King Pedro's children at Carmona, near Seville. When Enrique treacherously murdered his half brother, Pedro, Leonor was still in Carmona, which, as a stronghold for Pedro's supporters as well as residence of the now-orphaned princes and princesses, was placed under siege by Enrique's forces.

Carmona was eventually taken, and those who had defied Enrique were imprisoned in the Seville Arsenal, in spite of King Enrique's promise to free them if they surrendered. The imprisonment lasted nine years, and it continued the vicious game of exchanged lies, intrigue, and vengeful murder that characterized the fraternal conflict that the *Crónicas* portray so vividly. The men of Leonor's family, including a brother of thirteen, were shackled with seventy pounds of iron on their feet, and not even death served to free them from such an indignity. Despite their entreaties, the jailers waited until after their victims had died to cart them off to the blacksmith, a treatment usually reserved for Moors. Even those who managed to survive these and other punishments were not safe: What Leonor calls "pestilences" swept the prison periodically, further reducing their numbers. Only Enrique's death in 1379 freed the hardy survivors, and Leonor's gratitude for the death-bed reprieve is clear when she calls Enrique, with no apparent trace of irony, "the high and illustrious king" of "high and illustrious memory" (37).

If Enrique's death served to strike the leg irons from his one-time prisoners, it nonetheless left them with shackles no less heavy for being invisible. Tainted by their past, Leonor and her family had to find their way in a world from which all support, both economic and political, had evaporated. Ruy Gutiérrez left his wife and family behind as he spent seven years searching for a means to recoup their losses. Leonor at one point lost hope of ever being reunited with him, and began to make arrangements to enter the Order of Guadalajara, a religious community founded by her great-grandparents, where her mother had lived before the king chose her as a bride for Leonor's father.

During Ruy Gutiérrez's absence, Leonor remained with the household of a maternal aunt, a member of a branch of the Carrillo family that had supported Enrique out of resentment for past injustices by Pedro, including, according to the *Crónicas*, the seduction of a wife. Here her affairs evidently prospered sufficiently to encourage her husband's return, and they took up life as the tolerated, if not always warmly welcomed, impoverished members of a major family. This situation apparently lasted for some twenty years, although Leonor's account telescopes the time involved. The victories they enjoyed from that point on were small, though fiercely fought: gaining housing, arranging for a private entrance from their home to the aunt's, so that they would appear of proper status and not beggars, tradesmen, or strangers who must knock at the front door.

But even this guarded peace was not undisturbed. The periodic attacks of plague continued, and eventually provided the mechanism for the third exemplary death in Leonor's story, following those of her father and brother. Tragedy struck this time when one of Leonor's servants—a Moor—contracted the plague; despite the household's danger, she refused to cast him out, prevailing instead upon a longtime family retainer to shelter him. When each of those who had cared for the sufferer died, Leonor finally asked her twelve-year-old son to watch over the servant. With almost literary irony the servant survived while all of his caretakers, including Leonor's young son, did not. Her sorrow and humiliation not yet completed, Leonor had to endure her son's burial outside the city because of the fear of contagion, and the blame and censure from family and neighbors, not only for bringing the plague into the city but also for her son's death.

Leonor's text ends at this point, with her exile once more from family and settled surroundings, but her life did not. She figures in the *Crónicas de los Reyes de Castilla* in her own right, as a powerful adviser to and influence upon the queen regent of Spain, Catalina of Lancaster, Pedro's granddaughter. From this height fate tumbled her to the extent that in 1412 only the intervention of the coregent Prince Fernando saved her from Catalina's proposed punishment for undue influence and apparent bad advice: burning at the stake. It was evidently this last fall from grace that inspired her to record her life in written form.

In her "Testamento," Leonor reveals what happens to the women and children who all too often figure in the *Crónicas* only as victims and pawns. With the same headlong style, typical of the chronicles, that so strongly communicates the rush of events—sentences strung together with "and"'s and semicolons— Leonor tells us how women coped. Whereas the official histories involve sweeping travel over vast stretches of territory that are all the more impressive in light of the available methods of transportation, a woman's story is concentrated on home and hearth, be it prison or palace. She does not move unless forced to do so.

For women, escape from treachery and abuse was never as easy as it was for men, who needed only to change sides to gain some advantage, whether political or personal. While the men were fighting and traveling, women were left behind; and if they were important enough, they were also left vulnerable to attack by enemies. The *Crónicas* relate all too many instances of royal women kidnapped, raped, seduced, and even murdered because of the political stands of the male members of their families. Leonor López de Córdova's story provides a remarkable record of the need and ability of women to cope under extreme duress, to make a home wherever necessary, with intelligence, political acuity, piety, and sheer determination.

MAJOR THEMES

In her one extant text, "Testamento," Leonor stresses those themes that are central to nearly all aristocratic texts of the Middle Ages and early Renaissance.

Her guiding spirit throughout all of her adversity is the Virgin Mary, as well as God the Father, but it is to the Virgin that Leonor specifically appeals in times of peril or sorrow and to whom she gives thanks when she survives or overcomes the dangers that come her way. All that occurs, good and bad, does so by God's will, but the intercession of the more approachable Mother of God enables one to meet the challenges that result.

One of God's indisputable gifts, in Leonor's eyes, is that of noble birth, and she makes it clear throughout her ''Testamento'' that diminished fortunes do not in any way imply a fundamental change in the social order. She carefully presents her lineage and that of those around her, and while she clearly mourns and resents the loss of wealth and privilege due to political circumstances, she yearns after them as manifest symbols of implicit worth. She thus bitterly recounts her jailers' failure to honor the family's status by unshackling them before their deaths, and is carefully triumphant after her success in arranging housing in Toledo that reflects her place in society and within her noble family.

Because of the importance given to nobility of birth, the family as such becomes another major concern of Leonor's autobiography, but its involvement in the political upheaval of the period makes it a more complex and ambiguous motif. Pride in and loyalty to family shine through the story, but there are suggestions of rents in the whole cloth of Leonor's narrative. Her maternal relatives, the Carrillos, who eventually served as the instruments of Leonor's rescue from penury, were allied with Enrique, Leonor's captor. The same relatives intrigued against Leonor in Toledo, and eventually engineered her removal from the household following her son's death from the plague. As with the larger political alliances, the support of a powerful family can be useful and wonderful, but in times of stress or turmoil it often cannot be relied upon, since it rarely reflects any real sentiment.

In such situations, when neither blood, nor history, nor money produces lasting bonds, one must depend on the more ephemeral ties of loyalty, both personal and political. Consequently, loyalty and treachery form the centerpiece of Leonor's complex of themes. Her emphasis on loyalty as a supreme value causes her to simplify the events of her time, so that men's actions become, if not precisely admirable in all cases, then certainly a good deal less universally sordid. Pedro, of course, is seen as the good and rightful king, and Enrique as the unlawful and treacherous usurper—someone who, by himself and with his supporters, is deceitful and disloyal in matters both large and small. Leonor quotes her father's reply to one of Enrique's converts: ''It is better to die loyal, as I have done, than to live as you live, having been a traitor'' (36). She gives us no inkling of the equally treacherous behavior of Pedro and his supporters, portrayed in the *Crónicas*, where Pedro, along with Leonor's father and eventual father-in-law, lures Prince Juan of Aragón to his death at López de Córdova and the Finestrosas' hands, while literally clasped in their fraternal embrace. Leonor also fails to mention—and perhaps knew nothing about—an episode in which Pedro arranged for her father's murder as punishment for failure to kill several

Córdova relatives. Her father's titles to Calatrava and Alcántara were to be the assassin's reward. Although the plot was never realized, it proves a point made only implicitly in Leonor's telling: Loyalty is of but dubious use in a morally clouded universe, and it is no wonder that her contemporaries did not consider it a justification for having allied oneself with the losing side.

All of the above serves to create a strong sense of the precarious nature of life and the extent to which, under certain types of pressure, all positive values— loyalty, truth, love, family—fall away, and one is left with only faith in God and in one's own efforts for whatever protection they might afford. In spite of Leonor's fervent belief in the efficacy of prayer, the small triumphs she manages to extract from political collapse and chaos around her come not as gifts of divine benevolence but as the results of her untiring efforts to bring them about. Bereft of husband, father, brother, and king—all of whom ought to provide for her in the patriarchal system—Leonor humbles herself sufficiently to find refuge, and eventually renewal of status, through association with maternal relatives who are both family allies and political enemies, perfect symbols for the ultimate tenuousness of life in her time.

Leonor's political astuteness makes her success possible, as she paints herself navigating family intrigue with skill and a calculated humility that does not entirely conceal a fierce and relentless pride. When forces beyond her control drive her from even this haven, she will employ the same abilities to find or build herself another. So well does she succeed, before the inevitable fall, that she manages to write herself into the insistently androcentric *Crónicas* as a political player as influential (for a time) as any man, a rarity for a text in which women are consistently relegated to the role of political and sexual pawns in the chess game of men's affairs.

SURVEY OF CRITICISM

Critics have done little with Leonor López de Córdova's "Testamento" other than edit it and situate it as a historical source text parallel to the *Crónicas de los Reyes de Castilla*. The original manuscript is in Córdoba, in the the archives of the Royal Convent of San Pablo. It was apparently first published in a collection of manuscripts during the period 1842–95, but there is no record of a "public" for the text until the twentieth century's renewed interest in "nonliterary" texts. Leonor clearly expected the "Testamento" to be read only by family members.

Reinaldo Ayerbe-Chaux, editor of a scholarly edition of the "Testamento" (1977), was "one of the first to recognize Doña Leonor's narrative as a literary text intended to vindicate the writer and her family" (Kaminsky and Johnson 70). Amy Katz Kaminsky and Elaine Dorough Johnson, basing their work on Ayerbe-Chaux's edition and analysis, translated the "Testamento" into English and published it, along with a brief discussion of the work as an example of feminine autobiography, in "To Restore Honor and Fortune: 'The Autobiography of Leonor López de Córdova.' " They correctly situate the text "within the patriarchal institutions of state, church, and family'' (72) and emphasize the extent to which Leonor must depend on herself and a ''matrifocal family'' for vindication and reestablishment of her household. Kaminsky and Johnson also point out that the enemies who bring about Leonor's downfall, first in her aunt's house and later in the royal court, are also female. This demonstrates that the female world existed separate from but analogous to the masculine world that surrounded it and from which it took its rules and structures. Such a separate female world may historically be a remnant of Arabic influence on Spanish social attitudes. In practical terms, however, the ongoing political disturbances meant that men would be absent much of the time.

Leonor López de Córdova's ''Testamento'' is both a literary and a historical text, a rare and early document openly composed by a woman willing to identify herself by name, birth, and gender. The Spanish edition by Ayerbe-Chaux and the English translation by Kaminsky and Johnson should encourage further study of this manuscript and the fascinating life of its resolute author.

NOTE

1. Cayetano Rosell, ed., *Crónicas de los Reyes de Castilla, Biblioteca de Autores Españoles*. Vol. 68 (Madrid: Real Academia Española, 1953).

BIBLIOGRAPHY

Work by Leonor López de Córdova

''Testamento o Relación que deja escrita para sus descendientes.'' *Colección de documentos inéditos para la historia de España*. Vol. 81 Madrid: Imprenta de la Viuda de Calero. 33–44. 1883.

Translation

''To Restore Honor and Fortune: 'The Autobiography of Leonor López de Córdoba.' '' Trans. Amy Katz Kaminsky and Elaine Dorough Johnson. *The Female Autograph*. Ed. Domna C. Stanton. Chicago: U of Chicago P, 1984. 70–80.

Works about Leonor López de Córdova

Ayerbe-Chaux, Reinaldo. ''Las memorias de doña López de Córdova.'' *Journal of Hispanic Philology* 2 (1977): 11–33.
Firpo, Arturo Roberto. ''Un ejemplo de autobiografía medieval: las 'Memorias' de Leonor López de Córdoba (1400).'' *Zagadnienia Rodzajów Literackich: Woprosy Literaturnych Zanrov/Les Problèmes des Genres Littéraires* 23.1 (1980): 19–31.
Kaminsky, Amy Katz, and Elaine Dorough Johnson, trans. ''To Restore Honor and Fortune'' 70-73.

MARCELA DE SAN FÉLIX (SOR MARCELA) (1605–1687)

Electa Arenal

BIOGRAPHY

During Spain's Golden Age the convent often became a subversive space, a women's subculture that intensified the world at large. José María Díez Borque claims that convents reflected the "complex and contradictory ways of being and appearing" of the period and were part of daily life (Arenal and Sabat-Rivers vii). The writings of many nuns illustrate the interweavings of lives fashioned both within and without monastic walls. For women, enclosure could be stricter on the outside. Few learned and lived that paradox more dramatically than Sor Marcela de San Félix, whose case holds a particular fascination because of her kinship to one of the period's cultural icons.

At the age of sixteen, Marcela del Carpio (her baptismal name), abandoned *el siglo*—the "century," as secular life was called—and joined a reformed Trinitarian community a few blocks from her turbulent home. The monastery was refuge for several other daughters of theatrical and literary families; it was attached to the church where Cervantes had been buried a few years earlier, and where her father, Lope de Vega, often said Mass. It was he who made sure that the ceremony marking her bethrothal to Christ was most worldly, the music superb, the preacher eloquent, the entire event worthy of being re-created in his poem "Epístola a Don Francisco de Herrera Maldonado." She, on the other hand, could now see her father at a safe distance, because Lope visited his daughter almost daily while he was still alive—some fourteen years. For Marcela, consecration to God allowed, along with periods of inspirational and mystical solitude, the opportunity to teach, to participate in the governance of the convent, to converse with outstanding theologians, to write, to act, and to produce plays.

The only known writing by Marcela before she became a nun was a forced assignment when she was thirteen years old: the copying, for her father's curious and insistent patron, the duke of Sessa, of Lope's love letters to Marta de Nevares. The last of the dramatist's passionate liaisons, de Nevares became her stepmother and moved into the household a few years before Marcela moved out. In the *Vida* ("Life"), recorded in convent annals after her death, Sor Marcela is said to have remarked that her parents "held her in low esteem and that to flee their troubles she had to come to this refuge like a criminal fleeing from the law" (Arenal and Schlau 231). The same document witnesses her recognition of the paradoxical nature of her active role and fame in monastic life—a result of having attempted to escape from the world: "Poor me! I have come to play a greater role [here] than out in the world, where I was destitute, and unworthy even of being noticed" (Arenal and Schlau 232). Feliciana and Antonia Clara, Marcela's two half sisters and members of the same household, suffered precisely that fate. Of the three, only Marcela achieved a modicum of autonomy and authority. Satisfaction, a victorious survivor's pride, smiles under the semblance of self-pitying humility.

Marcela del Carpio was listed as a child of unknown parents in the Toledo church where she was baptized on May 8, 1605. The godfather, dramatist José de Valdivielso, was a close friend of her father, Lope de Vega. The mother, Micaela de Luján, a former actress with whom Lope had seven children (though she herself was legally married to an actor), disappeared or died when Marcela was very little. At the age of eight, Marcela and her six-year-old brother Lope Félix were taken with their nanny to live at Lope's residence in Madrid. Soon after that Lope became a priest, although he never took his vow of celibacy seriously. Marcela, not surprisingly, aspired, perhaps more than many young Catholic women, to a life, if not of moral perfection, at least of less hypocrisy. One of the few references to Marcela in Lope's letters regards the provision of money by the duke of Sessa for fabric for a gown. The need to extirpate temptations and desires would later become one of Marcela's literary themes. That she was determined to win the battle for religious integrity that her father so conspicuously and constantly lost is evidenced by her announcement at fifteen of her decision to take the veil.

There were other factors, of course, most prominently Marcela's recognition of the limited options open to women of strong personality and talent. Whether the recognition was conscious or unconscious is a matter for speculation, but clearly intelligent, articulate, expressive, and beautiful women in Lope's circles (and in his plays) were admired but objectified; their proper devotion in the end was considered to be to an earthly man. It is not unlikely that the young and observant Marcela came to her own conclusions about these matters. Her father's flirtatiousness, mentioned in the epistle cited above, and which, according to the convent biography, led Sor Marcela to prohibit his visits for a short time after he had inappropriately admired her hands, may have provided a further motive. Nevertheless, when he died, Madre Marcela requested that the hearse be routed along the street on which the convent stood so that she could pay her last respects. A nineteenth-century painting by Suárez Llanos presents a romanticized version of the event (Arenal and Schlau 284).

The seventeenth-century portrait of Sor Marcela that hangs in Lope's house, now a museum, reveals an older woman of forceful character and mature beauty. Her dramatic self-depictions emphasize a volatile and at times ferocious temperament. In part, the verbal self-portraits drawn in her comical dialogues and plays were catalytic strategies; as mistress of novices, doorkeeper, provisions officer, and mother superior, Sor Marcela consistently held positions of authority and power, and understood that the sisters would benefit from a humorous chance to vent resentment and anger.

Before she died in 1687, at the age of eighty-two, Sor Marcela had completed four or five manuscripts and, at the behest of her confessor, burned all but one of them. Remaining were a 505-page collection of plays and poems and a brief biography of a sister nun. The convent had allowed, and at times required, Sor Marcela to put to use and to develop her considerable literary vocabulary and skills. Her range was impressive: On one hand, she allegorized the ideals and conflicts of religious life, criticizing with daring humor the foibles of convent domesticity; on the other, she described with lyric eloquence the unity with herself and with God achieved through solitude.

MAJOR THEMES

The long, undated extant manuscript by Sor Marcela de San Félix, all in verse, includes six *coloquios espirituales* (spiritual colloquies—allegorical religious plays), eight *loas* (poem-dialogues that preceded the plays), twenty-two *romances* (ballads), five *romances esdrújulos* (a ballad form in which the final word of each line is accented on the antepenultimate syllable, providing an exaggerated rhythmic pattern, often used comically), and examples of various popular verse forms. Circumstantial evidence allows us to date three of the poems with certainty: the "Romance a la soledad de las celdas" (1646; "Ballad to the Solitude of Cells"), a *loa*, and a *romance* written for the final vows of Isabel del Santísimo Sacramento (1655). Only one selection of her prose survived. In a compendium of nuns' lives, Electa Arenal found the brief, previously unlisted "Noticias de la vida de la madre soror Catalina de Sant. Joseph, Religiosa Trinitaria Descalza" (1641?; "An Account of the Life of the Mother Soror Catalina de Sant. Joseph, a Nun of the Order of Discalced Trinitarians"), the biography of a Trinitarian sister whose virtues Sor Marcela had been asked to praise.[1] That completes her extant works. She is said to have composed the music for her Christmas plays, but not a trace of that music has been found. Although she did not write her own *Vida*, unless it was among the works destroyed as an act of obedience, autobiographical elements, distilled in her poems and prose and caricaturized in her plays, fill her works.

The contemplative path led not only to spiritual salvation but also to artistic freedom. The in-house nature of Marcela's literary production gave room for poetic license and expressive liberty she would not otherwise have enjoyed. The greater part of her writing was addressed exclusively to her convent companions, which explains the spontaneity and farcical humor of the plays. This sense of privacy permitted her to mock and to praise her literary heritage—Lope's legacy—an important secondary theme in some works. It stimulated the elaboration of religious lessons in a series of plays that also became vehicles for theological disquisitions and for entertainment that diffused the tensions and frustrations of the cloistered community. Asceticism, etched severely in the biography of Sor Catalina, turned into *erótica a lo divino* (spititual eroticism) in the *romances*:

> Sufre, que noche, y día
> Te ronde aquesas puertas:
> Exhale mil suspiros,
> Te diga mil ternezas.
>   . . .
> Ay, si me viese yo,
> Como el alma desea;
> O morir de abrasada,
> O herida con tus flechas.
>
> Permit me, night and day,
> to keep watch at your doors:
> to breathe a thousand sighs,
> and murmur soft endearments.
>   . . .
> Oh, that I might find myself,
> as my soul desires,
> either dying in love's fierce flames,
> or wounded by your shafts.
>   (Arenal and Schlau, 242; ''Romance a un afecto amoroso''
>   [''Ballad of a Loving Passion''])

The cultural and autobiographical contexts of Sor Marcela's writings reveal a daughter's pride and disdain for her father—a transference of the seduction. Both in the poem Lope wrote when she took the veil and in an anecdotal episode—part of the convent's anonymous and unpublished biographical pages dedicated to her—mention is made of Lope's flirtatious behavior toward his daughter. She writes proudly and with humor about her father, turning him into a synechdochal trope for literary accomplishment. A symbol of modern poetic greatness, his name is placed beside those of the poets of antiquity: ''Aquí de Terencio y Plauto / aquí de Lope de Vega / que de lo antiguo y moderno / fueron luz de los poetas'' (Arenal and Sabat-Rivers 10; Here Terence and Plautus / Here Lope de Vega / poetic lights / ancient and modern''). Lope is the paradigm of poetry. Marcela constructs and deconstructs the image of the poet through the use of diminutives, hyperboles, contradiction, affirmations, and negatives of ridicule.

She insists on her incapacity and ignorance, yet praises her logical mind and intense literary labors. Strategic variations on (false) modesty and illusions of grandeur found in the works of many nuns have a particularly personalized stamp in Sor Marcela's verses. Playing a male role in one of her *loas*, she calls herself "discípulo / de aquella fecunda Vega / de cuyo ingenio los partos / dieron a España nobleza" (Arenal and Sabat-Rivers 393; Disciple / of that fecund Vega [. . .] / the offspring of whose wit / gave Spain nobility).

Very little was known about convent theater until recently. The ambivalent church attitudes regarding theatrical performances, religious or otherwise, led to silence but not absence. In other words, performances in churches and monasteries went generally unacknowledged and unrecorded. Among sources that indicate lively theatrical activities in both are legal documents fining actors and directors, and proclamations prohibiting ladies from lending their clothing to nuns as costumes. Recent research (Weaver,[2] Arenal and Schlau) indicates that nuns created a significant dramatic literature and regularly engaged in creating theatrical as well as musical events. An excuse was provided by the need to follow tradition—to observe holy days and celebrate professions. Allegorical plays instructed, inspired, and entertained. They also relieved the monotony of enclosure. Nativity plays, among the most popular, reenacted and interpreted the origins of the Holy Family from a female viewpoint. The nuns empathized, and even more identified, with Mary. Often the crèche provided the centerpiece for music, dance, procession, and dramatization. Sor Marcela included in her plays words and images specific to her religious order. The theme of capture and ransom, for instance, referred to the semidiplomatic function both Trinitarians and Mercedarians undertook for Spanish hostages (Cervantes among them) in North Africa. Under the allegorical dress, vignettes of monastic life come to life:

> Sácame de aquel pernil,
> pues te lo envió mi madre
> la Gula.

> Slice me a bit of that ham,
> for it was dispatched to you
> by my mother, Greed. (Arenal and Schlau 253)

In a theater by and for women, Sor Marcela's two male stock characters, the *licenciado* (scholar) and the *estudiante* (student), with a twist heighten comicity, open the cloistered space, parody customs and types, and underscore the circumspection of nunly life. Her aim was partly to strengthen the faith of her Trinitarian sisters. Sor Marcela revitalized religious ideas and elements of mystical literature through the theatrical techniques and popular language she brought to the convent. If she used the *coloquio* form to extend daily lessons in spirituality (perhaps especially to the unlettered), she also wished to provide an escape valve for jealousies, resentments, and tensions among the sisters and their leaders and to inspire religious collectivity. The interpersonal dynamic of spectators-author-actors seems almost modern—an anticipation of twentieth-century participatory or psychological drama.

Where her comic bent, the other side of Sor Marcela's contemplative, ascetic temperament, shines forth most clearly is in the *coloquios* and especially in the *loas*. The only other dramatist to use the more informal and perhaps humanistic title *coloquio*, rather than *auto*, as a rubric to describe religiocomical plays of few characters and simple structure like hers, was Fernán González de Eslava. He, too, was addressing a marginalized group, the Indians of New Spain, whom he wished to convert to Catholicism. A jocular, dynamic, outrageous voice makes fun of illnesses and disease; of food—its consumption, preparation, and scarcity; of pretense and bombast with regard to lineage, honor, fame; of nuns, prelates, poets; of mythology and muses; of the custom of writing *loas*; of herself. Sor Marcela employed the popular form of short theater with slapstick humor, constructing ingenious critiques of literary and theatrical conventions, of misogyny, of convent tribulations, and even of power battles in men's monasteries. The *gracioso* (comic character), appearing in the guise of either the *licenciado* or the *estudiante*, amplifies Sor Marcela's own voice(s), allowing her to speak of the mundane dimensions of being a writer, and of the interactions between the cloister and the world *extramuros* (outside the cloister): "¡Ay, quién se fuera en un coche / a pasear por el Prado!" (How I'd love to ride in a coach / for a ramble through the Prado! [Arenal and Schlau 253]).

The longest of six *coloquios*, the 1,542-line *Coloquio espiritual intitulado Muerte del Apetito* ("A Spiritual Drama, Entitled The Death of Desire"), took about two and a half hours to perform. Its allegorical characters are Mortificación (Mortification) and Desnudez (Simplicity), who wage a battle against Apetito (Desire) to win Alma (Soul). This work and three others—the *Coloquio espiritual de la estimación de la Religión* ("Colloquy in Praise of Religion"), *Coloquio espiritual "De Virtudes"* ("Colloquy on Virtues"), and *Coloquio espiritual del Celo Indiscreto* ("Colloquy on Overzealousness")—together form a dramatized treatise on contemplative life, a sort of theatrical manual on the formation of nuns. In them Sor Marcela discusses such major themes of religious calling as prayer, the symbolism of the sacraments, and the meaning of humility, obedience, and detachment.

The *Coloquio espiritual del Santísimo Sacramento* ("Colloquy for the Holiest of Sacraments" [Corpus Christi]) is Sor Marcela's only play that belongs to the most typical genre of religious theater of Counter-Reformation Spain—the *auto sacramental* or Corpus Christi play. Marcela played the role of Fervor, thus embodying her own practical ascetic theology, her antagonism to laxity and indulgence, and her belief in emotional preparation for the mystical experience of Union, and the renewal of holy matrimony.

A Nativity piece, in romance form, *Ofrecimiento que hacen las religiosas al Niño Jesús* ("Offering by the Sisters to the Newborn Jesus"), is the text for a short dramatic ritual in which all the nuns participated. Each was represented by several verses that mentioned her by name and highlighted some particular trait, usually a virtue—her offering to Jesus. Three saints (Ildefonso, Paula, and Teresa) were part of the procession, probably represented by sculptured wooden images carried by the sisters.

Sor Marcela's *romances* can be divided into two groups: occasional (liturgical festivities, professions) and devotional (divine and maternal love, meditation and religious discipline). Stylistically they are traditional in their octosyllabic lines and assonant rhyme; some are *romancillos* of seven-syllable lines. Drawing from both sacred and profane sources, Madre Marcela fashioned poems of sanctified sensuality—on the theme of religious love and marriage expressed in metaphors of erotic ardor. "Romance a una soledad" ("Ballad to a Solitude"), one of the most beautiful among them, is a poem of ecstatic experience in a serene, contemplative mode. In this poem Sor Marcela inscribes personal thoughts on religious orthodoxy and re-creates herself, a self earned through solitary retreat from the bustle of everyday life in the religious community.

SURVEY OF CRITICISM

Not until the nuns prepared to make a copy of Sor Marcela de San Félix's manuscript for the marqués de Molins and for the Academia Española de la Lengua—where Menéndez Pelayo consulted it in 1881 to write a speech for his acceptance into that august body—was official approval obtained. This statement of unobjectionability was required of every text circulated or printed. Previous to that, little attention had been paid over the course of two hundred years to Sor Marcela's plays and poems, and none to the short biography.

The first scholar to mention Sor Marcela and to present a selection of her poetry was the *marqués* de Molins, who in 1870 cited fragments of her most pious lines and included three *romances* in the appendix of his book on the sepulcher of Cervantes, "to make known . . . the talent and taste of Lope's saintly daughter" (Arenal and Sabat-Rivers 6). Menéndez y Pelayo chose to praise her poetry, emphasizing its piety and purity and its sixteenth-century, rather than seventeenth-century, aesthetic. He also compared some of her verses favorably with those of her father.

The only substantial presentation of Sor Marcela's work to appear was that of Manuel Serrano y Sanz. In his monumental bibliographic anthology, *Apuntes para una biblioteca de escritoras españolas*, he published four *romances*, the *liras*, *endechas*, and *villancico*; four of the six *coloquios*; and three of the eight *loas*. A long passage of one of these, full of ribald and irreverent humor, was omitted, presumably by the nineteenth-century nun who made the copy he consulted and who, shocked and embarrassed, must have viewed it as the height of bad taste (Arenal and Schlau 238–39).

Julio de Ramón Laca, in a 1967 book of Lope memorabilia, referred to Sor Marcela as "a delicate female figure" (103) and transcribed some of her poems (367–85). María Isabel Barbeito (1982) was responsible for the first serious modern treatment of Sor Marcela. The beatific, adoring daughter is finally replaced by a woman of integrity, a writer of maturity, wit, and psychological perspicacity worthy of earning the attention of twentieth-century readers.

Although an unauthorized version based on the incomplete nineteenth-century copy appeared in 1987, it was not until the following year that Sor Marcela de San Félix's complete works were published. The first selection of her work in English forms part of *Untold Sisters: Hispanic Nuns in Their Own Works*, published in 1989. The essay that accompanies the Spanish texts and Amanda Powell's translations summarize the overall significance of Sor Marcela's life, which spanned most of an extraordinary century of Spanish cultural history. For Arenal and Schlau, it "illuminates four important issues: illegitimacy and self-legitimation; the problems and benefits of being the daughter of a famous father; censorship and self-censorship; and asceticism as a structure for autonomy and sublimated sensuality" (229).

NOTES

1. See Electa Arenal and Stacey Schlau, *Untold Sisters* (Albuquerque: U of New Mexico P, 1989) 268–77.
2. Elissa Weaver, "Spiritual Fun: A Study of Sixteenth Century Tuscan Theater," *Women in the Middle Ages and Renaissance: Literary and Historical Perspectives*, ed. Mary Beth Rose (Syracuse, NY: Syracuse UP, 1976) 173–205.

BIBLIOGRAPHY

Works by Marcela de San Félix

Complete Works

Literatura conventual femenina: Sor Marcela de San Félix, hija de Lope de Vega. Obra completa. Ed. Electa Arenal and Georgina Sabat-Rivers. Barcelona: Promociones y Publicaciones Universitarias, 1988. Includes *Coloquio espiritual intitulado Muerte del Apetito*, 121–67; *Coloquio espiritual de la estimación de la religión*, 168–213; *Coloquio espiritual del nacimiento*, 214–45; *Coloquio espiritual "De Virtudes,"* 247–71; *Coloquio espiritual del Santísimo Sacramento*, 273–315; *Coloquio espiritual del Celo Indiscreto*, 317–52; "Loas para diferentes coloquios," 353–424; "Romances en esdrújulos," 425–50; "Romances," 451–581; "Seguidillas, Liras, Endechas y Villancicos," 583–603. [No original dates]

Selected Works

La sepultura de Miguel de Cervantes. Marqués de Molins. Madrid: Rivadeneyra, 1870. Includes "Romance a una soledad," 213–17; "Romance de un pecador arrepentido," 217–21; "Romance a un afecto amoroso," 221–25.
Lope de Vega, parientes, amigos y "trastos viejos." Julio de Ramón Laca. Madrid: Deral, 1967. Appendix 2 includes "Romance a una soledad," "Romance a [sic]

un pecador arrepentido," "Romance a la soledad de las celdas," "Romance al
jardín del convento," and fragments of other *romances*. 367–85.
Apuntes para una biblioteca de escritoras españolas desde el año 1401 al 1833. Manuel
Serrano y Sanz. Madrid: Atlas, 1975. Biblioteca de Autores Españoles. Vol. 270.
235–98. Rpt. of 1903 ed. Madrid: Sucesores de Rivadeneyra.
Marcela Lope de Vega. Obra poética completa. Ed. José A. Ramírez Nuño and Clara
Isabel Delgado Ramírez. Córdoba: Monte de Piedad y Caja de Ahorros de Córdoba,
1987.
Antología poética de escritoras de los siglos XVI y XVII. Ed. Ana Navarro. Madrid:
Castalia, 1989. Includes "Sor Marcela de San Félix," 221; "Romance a una
soledad," 222–26; "Romance de un Alma que temía distraerse al salir de un
retiro," 227–31; "Romance al jardín del convento," 232–37.
Tras el espejo la musa escribe: Lírica femenina del Siglo de Oro. Ed. Julián Olivares
and Elizabeth Boyce Olivares. Madrid: XXI, 1992.

Translations

Untold Sisters. Trans. Amanda Powell. By Electa Arenal and Stacey Schlau. This bilingual
volume includes the following titles: "An Account of the Life of Mother Soror
Catalina de Sant. Joseph, a Nun of the Order of Discalced Trinitarians," 273–
77; "A Spiritual Drama, Entitled *The Death of Desire*," 250–68; "To a Solitude,"
278–81.
Flores del agua/Water Lilies: Spanish Women Writers. Trans. Amanda Powell. By Amy
Kaminsky. Minneapolis: U of Minnesota P. [Forthcoming]

Works about Marcela de San Félix

Arenal, Electa, and Georgina Sabat-Rivers, eds. and intro. *Literatura conventual femen-
ina: Sor Marcela de San Félix, hija de Lope de Vega. Obra completa.* Barcelona:
Promociones y Publicaciones Universitarias, 1988. [Prologue by José María Díez
Borque]
Arenal, Electa, and Stacey Schlau. *Untold Sisters: Hispanic Nuns in Their Own Works.*
Trans. Amanda Powell. Albuquerque: U of New Mexico P, 1989. 229–50, 282–
85.
Barbeito Carneiro, María Isabel. "La ingeniosa provisora Sor Marcela de Vega." *Cua-
dernos Bibliográficos* 44 (1982): 59–70.
———. "Marcela de San Félix (Sor)." *Escritoras madrileñas del siglo XVI (Estudio
bibliográfico-crítico).* Vol. 1. Madrid: Universidad Complutense, 1986. 438–61.
Kaminsky, Amy. *Flores del agua/Water Lilies: Spanish Women Writers.* Minneapolis:
U of Minnesota P. [Forthcoming]
Menéndez y Pelayo, Marcelino. *La mística española.* Madrid: Afrodisio Aguado, 1956.
Molins, Marqués de (Mariano de Roca de Tagores). *La sepultura de Cervantes.* Madrid:
Rivadeneyra, 1870.
Ramón Laca, Julio de. "La célebre monja Marcela." *Lope de Vega, parientes, amigos
y "trastos viejos."* Madrid: Deral, 1967. 103–57.
———. *Lope de Vega, sus amores y sus odios.* Segovia, Spain: Renacimiento, n.d.

MARÍA DE SAN JOSÉ (MARÍA DE SALAZAR) (1548–1603)

Stacey Schlau

BIOGRAPHY

Although it is certain that María de San José was born in Toledo in 1548, so little is known about her early years that even the names of her parents, probably converted Jews, have been confused. They are given by some as Sebastián de Salazar and María de Torres, and by others as Pedro de Velasco and María de Salazar. The only other information available about the first part of her life is that she appears to have acquired learning during the years she spent as lady-in-waiting to the highly educated Luisa de la Cerda, whom she served from early childhood. She gained connections and access to dominant literary culture in this aristocratic milieu.

According to her *Libro de recreaciones* (1585; "Book of Recreations" 1989), in 1562, when she was fourteen and a lady-in-waiting, María met Teresa of Ávila, then a Carmelite nun who had not yet begun founding convents. Mother Teresa and her companions spent six months at the palace consoling Doña Luisa after the death of her husband. María, fascinated with the austere but affectionate nuns, spied on Teresa when she prayed and entered the mystic state. She wanted to be a part of the movement and the world to which the Carmelite nuns belonged. Her religious vocation did not crystallize until 1568, however, when the future Saint of Ávila briefly stopped at the Toledo palace en route to complete the founding of a convent in Malagón, an activity made possible by Doña Luisa's donation of land.

It was in Malagón, in May 1570, that María de Salazar took the veil and the name María de San José. A year later she made her final vows. Barely four years after that, in 1575, Mother Teresa—who in later years called María de San José "my bookworm" (*Epistolario* 1025)—chose her as a mother superior.

Although Teresa wanted her to be abbess in a new convent at Caravaca, these plans were changed due to the intervention of Fray Jerónimo Gracián. In that year, Gracián, who was Teresa of Ávila's protégé and confessor, and who later became an important leader in the Discalced Carmelite order, began to play a significant role in María de San José's life. He persuaded Teresa to open a convent in Seville, so that the order might establish a foothold in Andalusia, and she chose María de San José as its head.

María de San José's *Libro de recreaciones* provides a major source of information concerning Teresa of Jesus' difficult journey from Beas (Castille) to Seville (Andalusia), accompanied by María de San José, other nuns, priests, and lay persons. Moreover, the most realistic portrait of Saint Teresa, painted by the Carmelite lay brother Juan de la Miseria, owes its existence to María de San José, who persuaded her spiritual mother to sit for it. Other facts about the relationship between Teresa and her protégée may be found in St. Teresa's letters (*Epistolario*). Written between 1576, when the Saint of Avila left Seville after the inauguration of the convent, and 1582, the year of her death, the letters document a loving, albeit stormy, relationship between two strong-willed women: the younger sometimes forgetting humility, and the elder at times overly harsh and demanding.

María de San José's difficult years as prioress in the fledgling cloister of Seville tested her mettle and prepared her for future persecution. In 1578, two failed nuns and two clerics brought before the Inquisition accusations of scandalous and heretical behavior by the nuns of the Carmelite community and particularly their prioress. María de San José was removed from office and imprisoned for more than six months. Only when the new Discalced Carmelite superior general took office was she cleared of the charges and reinstated. Subsequently, she was unanimously reelected convent leader, and remained in that office until her transfer to Lisbon at the end of 1584.

As in Seville, María not only founded but also was elected first prioress of the Lisbon convent. She served several terms as convent leader between 1585 and 1600, with a seven-year hiatus from 1590 to 1597. There she was a friend of such esteemed and influential personages as Fray Luis de Granada, Fray Jerónimo Gracián, San Juan de la Cruz (St. John of the Cross), and Cardinal-Prince Albert, viceroy of Portugal.

María de San José also assumed an active role in the conflicts that emerged among Discalced Carmelites during the years when the new order became institutionalized, immediately after Teresa of Ávila's death. She clearly and consistently spoke in favor of the spirit of the new Discalced Carmelite Rule, which meant following Teresa's Constitution without modification. For instance, during the controversy of 1590–91 regarding nuns' freedom to choose their confessors, she, along with Jerónimo de Gracián, San Juan de la Cruz, and Ana de Jesús, participated in writing a brief to the pope requesting affirmation of that right. The Discalced Carmelite vicar general, Nicolao Doria, had the brief annulled and punished its authors. Jerónimo de Gracián was expelled from the order, San

Juan died, and the two nuns were imprisoned. María de San José, deprived of voice and vote for two years, spent one year in solitary confinement in the Lisbon convent.

After Doria's death in 1594, María de San José enjoyed six years of peace under the new general. When he died, however, the persecution began again, and reached its climax in 1603. In September of that year, María was smuggled out of her convent and exiled to a remote convent in Cuerva, Castille, whose prioress had orders not to treat her as a member of the community. She died a few weeks after her arrival.

María de San José left behind several works, written primarily during her eighteen years of cloistered life in Lisbon. Major writings from this period include *Libro de recreaciones*, "Carta que escribe una pobre y presa Descalza" (1593; "Letter from a Poor, Imprisoned Discalced Nun," 1989), "Ramillete de mirra" (1594; "Bough of Myrrh") and *Instrucción de novicias* (1602; "On the Instruction of Novices"). Together with several poems and short testimonial and documentary works, these texts not only reveal María de San José's intellectual and literary talent but also affirm in content and style a Spanish genealogy of women's writing, largely hidden until recently.

MAJOR THEMES

María de San José might well be an intellectual foremother of Sor Juana Inés de la Cruz. Like the seventeenth-century poet of New Spain, she draws on literature and theology rather than mystical experience. Her defense of women, critique of persecution and stupidity, and use of irony continually remind the reader of Sor Juana's incisive analysis of patriarchal society. Unlike the Mexican Hieronymite, however, this Spanish Carmelite had a community of responsive women to whom she was devoted and who became her audience. She writes as a woman, for women, representing women.

Madre María outlines in writing the form and content of the first generation Discalced Carmelite women's movement. She uses prose dialogues among semifictitious sisters and, occasionally, poetry. At once a self-appointed historian of the order and a fierce defender of the potential for autonomy within the Reform, a spiritual daughter of the founder and much-loved mother of novices and colleagues, María de San José adds an intellectual element to Teresa de Jesús's vision of a pure inner spirituality within the Catholic Church. Her integrated intellectuality, clearly visible in the *Libro de recreaciones*, challenged and threatened the attempts made by male ecclesiastic officials to increase restrictions on nuns' minds and bodies.

María de San José's best-known work, *Libro de recreaciones*, summarizes and elaborates many key ideas and techniques of her narrative prose. It juxtaposes women's unswerving fidelity to the spirit of Teresa's reform of religious life with the arrogance and ambition of some of the men, particularly those officials of the order who sought to limit nuns' freedom as set forth in Teresa's Constitution. Decrying the betrayal of basic elements of the Reform, such as inner spirituality, and lamenting the clerical stupidity that hindered women's fuller, reasoned participation in religion, María pleads for the recording of women's history, thus providing the rationale for writing the *Libro*.

The work is a tour de force, a vehicle for the order's "theologian" and "bookworm" to display her thorough knowledge of the Bible, the texts of the holy fathers of the church, the history of monastic orders, and contemporary theological polemics. For its time, it was daring to the point of heresy, which partly explains why its author was harshly persecuted until her death and why it was not published until the twentieth century. Indeed, a critique of accusations of heresy, especially those regarding the rules that governed nuns' conduct, is one of its major motifs. The *Libro* was also a vehicle for María to express her feminist intellectuality, her knowledge of a female lineage and heritage, and her sense of community with women of her order.

María declares that her purpose in composing the work is "to depict the conversations and life of the nuns" (47). Consciousness of style and the impact of theatrical techniques explain her choice of the dialogue form. At the beginning of the *Libro de recreaciones*, she makes explicit the dilemmas of self-presentation. In discussion with her real/imaginary religious sisters, cast as shepherdesses, the narrator decides that the safest, most discreet, and artistically richest way to draw a self-portrait will be through dialogue. She, Madre María, becomes Gracia, while other characters, some drawn directly from individual nuns, some a composite of personalities, are Justa, Atanasia, Dorotea, and Josefa. The author uses discussion among these nun-shepherdesses to project the literary-pastoral framework of the book.

The book is fashioned on the pattern of the daily religious "entertainment" hour established in Reformed Carmelite rules; each "recreation" represents the lecture-discussion of a different day. Twenty years before she wrote the *Libro de recreaciones*, the young courtier María had been attracted to religious life by the intelligent and serious discussions among Teresa and her companions. In this sense, we can see her writing as an effort to develop and pass on the tradition of women's engagement in matters of consequence. Authority for this enterprise comes from proximity to Teresa. Justa instructs Gracia to "say what you saw and heard her do . . . since you were with her in the founding of some of the convents" (57–58).

In one of her most feminist passages, María recognizes the impact of custom in preventing women from exercising God-given talents. She uses ironic reversal, exposing ridiculous viewpoints by seeming to espouse them while offering explanations for the opposing point of view: Women by right should be prohibited from writing and relegated to the needle, as custom would have it, *because*— and here is the catch—they have not been educated.

María de San José, in the tradition of Christine de Pizan and the early feminists of the *querelle des femmes* (debate over women), recognizes a lineage of courageous, virtuous, and intellectual women to whom she and her religious sisters are connected. She defends the right of women to learn and use Latin, to teach, to consult, and to write. She traces religious history, comparing and contrasting Gentile and Hebrew beliefs and practices that were adopted or continued in Christianity. That Justa is scandalized by Gracia's incursions into such thorny subject matter lends humor and emphasis, as well as canny protection against male censorship. The author anticipates and mocks such objections as uncultured, ignorant, and "womanish." Atanasia overrides Justa's resistance and supplements Gracia's discussion by challenging the less sophisticated woman's fear and partial knowledge. She interjects that while it is true that the greatest influence on the "new [Christian] law" was the "ancient [Hebrew] law": "I will give you an example of one practice which the Church uses that it did not learn from the synagogue, and that is the consecration of virgins" (106). The author thus implies that nuns, like those who appear in the *Libro de recreaciones*, are the most important advance of Christianity over Judaism.

Through the character of Gracia, María repeatedly declares her literary ambition, for which other nun-characters criticize her. They also urge her not to be anxious about influence nor to feel the need to use Father Gracián as a model. Atanasia juxtaposes Gracián's style ("delicate and fine tidbits") to María's (92; "garlic and onions"). The passage seems to echo Saint Teresa's view that women's writing is a reflection of daily life, as opposed to the "delicious" concoctions of such male writers as Jerónimo Gracián.

In all her writing, María de San José is more ambivalent than most nun-authors in her expression of the introductory formulas of humility required of women who were to live their lives "dead to the world." She is also more literary. María's education prepared her to employ the discourse of the elite. Her metaphors and similes refer to architecture, painting, and music, to civil and ecclesiastic law, and to the natural order of animals, minerals, and plants. Using highly elaborated structures and controlled modes of expression, she affirms the primacy of female intellectuality, community, and lineage in an unusually direct manner, through religious history and symbol, and against all opposition.

SURVEY OF CRITICISM

Little has been written about María de San José's work, although some of her historical narratives and poems have been anthologized in compendia of Carmelite writings, and several texts have been published in their entirety. Selections of her work, as well as studies of her life and writings, have been published almost exclusively by male members of the order. In chronicles and historical surveys, since the sixteenth century and especially during the twentieth, Discalced Carmelite scholars have tried to reconstruct Saint Teresa's life and the early years of the Reform. Their dedication to preserving documents about this period has motivated them to garner extant information about María de San José's life. They have saved some of her writing from being lost forever. In short, her connection with Saint Teresa has been the main impetus for religious research on the most intellectual nun of the first generation of the order.

Internecine politics of the order, particularly the controversy regarding nuns' right to choose their own confessors, have to a large extent determined how various chroniclers of the Carmelite order have presented María de San José. Fray Francisco de Santa María, for instance, the seventeenth-century chronicler who wrote volume II of *Reforma de los Descalzos* in 1644, accuses her of being "extravagant" and causing scandals because her ties to Jerónimo Gracián were too close. On the other hand, in the 1930s Silverio de Santa Teresa, in his *Historia del Carmen Descalzo* suggests that María de San José incarnated better than any of her generation the virtues, talents, and good qualities of the Teresian Reform (471).

A broadly drawn summary of María de San José's life and major works appears in the introduction to her *Escritos espirituales* ("Spiritual Writings"), edited by Simeón de la Sagrada Familia in 1979. The essay includes a selection of bibliographic sources; a chronological survey of major events in her life; a list of and explanatory paragraph about each of the works included; and a collection of quotes from religious authorities about María's religious, historical, and intellectual significance. Despite its brevity and sketchiness, the editor's presentation, which summarizes previous studies, is the most comprehensive available to the Spanish-language reader.

Manuel Serrano y Sanz's monumental compendium *Apuntes para una biblioteca de escritoras españolas*, originally published in 1903, has been a significant source of information about early modern women writers for contemporary feminist scholars, despite grave problems with accuracy. The entry on María de San José, as with so many in his two volumes, is filled with factual errors. For example, he confuses her with another María de San José from Avila, and therefore gives the wrong date and place of birth, family, and date and place of profession. Nevertheless, Serrano y Sanz includes excerpts from several works, among them the *Libro de recreaciones*. He and Vicente de la Fuente (whose work on Saint Teresa predates the reprint of Serrano y Sanz's *Apuntes*) are among the few male secular scholars who have recognized María de San José.

An introductory feminist analysis of María de San José's life and work, upon which this essay draws, and selected texts in modern Spanish and English, appear in *Untold Sisters: Hispanic Nuns in Their Own Works*, by Electa Arenal and Stacey Schlau. Discussion of María de San José is included in a chapter that examines her life and work and that of another of Saint Teresa's favored spiritual daughters, Ana de San Bartolomé (1549–1626), as representative of the first generation of Discalced Carmelite nuns. Arenal and Schlau conclude that María de San José and Ana de San Bartolomé "helped create the aura surrounding Teresa of Ávila's life, thus sanctifying the terrain on which they could legitimately speak of themselves" (45). María de San José was "dangerously independent in thought, word, and deed, woman-centered in her perspective." Her works are significant today, for they ''highlight the potential for female autonomy and self-direction which were implicit in Teresa of Ávila's movement'' (30).

BIBLIOGRAPHY

Works by María de San José

Escritos espirituales. Edition and notes. Simeón de la Sagrada Familia. Rome: Postulación General, 1979. This volume includes the following titles: *Libro de recreaciones*. 1585. 45–227 [The quotations in this article from the *Libro* are from this edition]; ''Elegía.'' ca. 1591/92. 527–42; ''Carta que escribe una pobre y presa Descalza.'' 1593. 271–80; ''Ramillete de mirra.'' 1594. 283–340.
Avisos para el gobierno de las religiosas. N.d. Ed. Juan Luis Astigarraga. Rome: Instituto Histórico Teresiano, 1977.
Instrucción de novicias. 1602. Ed. Juan Luis Astigarraga. Rome: Instituto Histórico Teresiano, 1978.

Translations

Untold Sisters: Hispanic Nuns in Their Own Works. By Electa Arenal and Stacey Schlau. Trans. Amanda Powell. Albuquerque: U of New Mexico P, 1989. This bilingual volume includes the following titles: ''Book of Recreations,'' 92–108; ''Elegy,'' 112–17; ''Letter from a Poor, Imprisoned Discalced Nun,'' 110–12.

Works about María de San José

Arenal, Electa, and Stacey Schlau. *Untold Sisters: Hispanic Nuns in Their Own Works*. Trans. Amanda Powell. Albuquerque: U of New Mexico P, 1989.
de la Fuente, Vicente. *Escritos de Santa Teresa*. Biblioteca de Autores Españoles. Vols. 53, 55. Madrid: Ediciones Atlas, 1952. 53: 261–64, 555–61; 55: 442–49.
Serrano y Sanz, Manuel. *Apuntes para una biblioteca de escritoras españolas desde el año 1401 al 1833*. Madrid: Atlas, 1975. Biblioteca de Autores Españoles. Vol. 270. 333–50. Rpt. of 1903 ed. Madrid: Sucesores de Rivadeneyra.
Silverio de Santa Teresa. *Historia del Carmen Descalzo en España, Portugal y América*. Vol. 6. Burgos, Spain: El Monte Carmelo, 1935–52. 10 vols.
Simeón de la Sagrada Familia, ed. Introduction. *María de San José (Salazar) (1548– 1603): Escritos espirituales*. 2nd ed. Rome: Postulación General, 1979.
Teresa de Jesús, Santa. *Epistolario. Obras completas*. Ed. Luis Santullano. Madrid: Aguilar, 1970. 731–1315.

CARMEN MARTÍN GAITE
(b. 1925)

Joan Lipman Brown

BIOGRAPHY

On December 8, 1925, Carmen Martín Gaite was born in Salamanca, a stoutly traditional provincial capital in Spain. The second daughter of a successful attorney and his wife, she enjoyed the advantages of a cultured and liberal home. Because her parents sought to avoid the parochialism of religious schooling, she and her sister began their education at home with private tutors. The family spent their summers in Galicia, the province of Spain near Portugal, where her mother had grown up. There the young girl took immense pleasure in being a tomboy; this summer home appears in her novel *Retahílas* (1974; "Yarns"). Martín Gaite has explained that her parents' plans for their children to further their education at a well respected liberal secondary school in Madrid were dashed by the Spanish Civil War of 1936–39. In an "Autobiographical Sketch" she notes simply that "the war, which broke out in the summer of '36 . . . destroyed those plans and so many others" (Brown, *Secrets* 24).

The Feminine Institute of Salamanca that Martín Gaite attended instead was a "huge, cold, dilapidated old house" (Brown, *Secrets* 25) identical to the school described in her novel *Entre visillos* (1958; *Behind the Curtains* 1990). In 1943, after completing her studies there, she enrolled at the University of Salamanca, where she contributed to the student magazine and enjoyed success as a dramatic actress in student productions. She traveled to Portugal and to France as an exchange student, experiences that she credits with broadening her horizons. In 1948, with a degree in Romance Philology, Martín Gaite moved to Madrid, where she has lived ever since.

In the Spanish capital, Martín Gaite fell in with a group of companions who would become the major writers of the Spanish postwar era. Her friends included

Ignacio Aldecoa, Medardo Fraile, Alfonso Sastre, Jesús Fernández Santos, and Rafael Sánchez Ferlosio, whom she married. "None of them was a very good student, or dreamed of being a professor," she recalls. "All of them carried in their blood the virus of literature" (qtd. in Brown, *Secrets* 27). Influenced by their pursuit of literary rather than scholarly goals, Martín Gaite also concentrated on writing fiction. She did, however, complete her doctorate twenty years later and has subsequently achieved recognition as a social historian of eighteenth- and twentieth-century Spain.

Martín Gaite and Sánchez Ferlosio were at the center of this group of friends, now called the Generation of Midcentury, who began to define Spanish literature of the postwar era. After an extended honeymoon in Italy, where Martín Gaite became engrossed in the literature of that country, the couple moved into the spacious Madrid apartment that her father had given them as a wedding present. Friends gathered there at all hours for wide-ranging discussions, exchanges of foreign books, and readings of each other's works. The commitment to literature that was cemented by this group of friends has been central to Martín Gaite's life as well as her art.

Martín Gaite's literary achievements have been rewarded both by the reading public and by professional literary critics. Her novels have been awarded Spain's most respected prizes over the years. In recognition of her lifelong achievement as a writer, she was honored with the prestigious Prince of Asturias Prize in 1988; in the same year, the Modern Language Association of America designated her a first-tier living author by electing her an honorary fellow. Her fiction is renowned for its accessible narrative style, which seems almost spoken rather than written. Martín Gaite is also recognized for the new techniques she intro- duced into the Spanish novel, beginning with those of fantastic literature in her 1954 "El balneario" ("The Spa"; Gijón Prize 1955) and culminating in the metanarrative innovations of her 1978 *El cuarto de atrás* (*The Back Room* 1983; National Prize for Literature 1979).

Like her generational colleagues in the 1950s, Martín Gaite contributed to documentary realism, the aesthetic that produced chronicles of everyday life in Franco's Spain. Her novel *Entre visillos* (1958; winner of the Nadal Prize of 1957), the novella *Las ataduras* (1960; "Binding Ties"), and most of her short stories belong to this genre. The technique of a synchronic narrative collage was explored in her 1962 *Ritmo lento* ("A Slower Rhythm"), and Martín Gaite tried her hand at the *novela negra* (a popular action-suspense genre) with her 1976 *Fragmentos de interior* ("Inner Fragments"). Of all her technical experiments, however, the one with which she is most closely identified is the conversational or dialogue structure, used in the 1974 novel *Retahílas* and again in 1978 in *El cuarto de atrás*.

MAJOR THEMES

In contrast with her technical experimentation over four decades, Martín Gaite's major themes are enduring and constant. She is a profoundly social novelist, concerned with the relationship between the individual and society and with the connection between individuals. All other themes are variations on these two overarching concerns. She is one of the very few writers whose work reflects the changing political and social landscape of contemporary Spain.

Martín Gaite's criticism of the immediate postwar era, when Franco's dictatorship was at its strongest, is evident in her earliest fiction. Her first major work, the novella "El balneario," considers the dilemma of the person whose life is severely circumscribed but who secretly lusts for adventure and risk. In this prizewinning short novel that launched Martín Gaite's career, a spinster arrives at a spa for her safe, dull summer holiday; soon, however, she becomes embroiled in a terrifying, surrealistic adventure. This exciting episode is later revealed to have been a dream. Martín Gaite has offered an explanation of the central theme of "El balneario": "Lives of intrigue and complicated psychological impulses hold a mixture of fascination and terror for those who live ordinary lives. . . . What no one will ever be able to explain is who is the actual agent (or true narrator)" of the stories in which "repressed fantasy materializes" (Brown, " 'El balneario' " 165; *Secrets* 37–38).

Martín Gaite's first full-length novel, *Entre visillos*, moves from the inner regions of the mind to an external overview of a provincial town recognizable as Salamanca. As with all of her novels written under censorship, its social themes are studiously apolitical. The major concerns of this work are the tyranny of gender-specific role definitions, especially for women, and the oppressive conformity of small town society.

Entre visillos chronicles a year in the life of a young provincial girl in the late 1940s or early 1950s, through her own eyes and through those of an iconoclastic young male teacher who has recently arrived. Although the town is perceived as stultifying by both main characters, it is the young girl, Natalia, who most poignantly reveals how its social order restricts personal choice. By resisting the tacit social imperative to snare a husband above all other pursuits, the intellectual girl casts herself in the role of nonconformist. She demonstrates Martín Gaite's keen awareness of the restrictions placed on women in a traditional society, and of the tendency of women in such a society to rely on the values and judgments of others. The novel's accomplished technique is cinematic in the ways of the Italian neorealist cinema: It offers multiple "takes" on everyday life, from which the reader assembles a complete view. Martín Gaite's adeptness at presenting female society, and especially the nuanced interactions of adolescent girls, was unparalleled in the Spanish novel at the time *Entre visillos* was published.

The issues that predominate in "El balneario" and *Entre visillos* are the same themes that are explored in Martín Gaite's short stories. Originally published in two volumes in 1954 and 1960, her short stories, including several later new ones, were collected in a single anthology in 1978. A chronological analysis of all of Martín Gaite's short stories indicates that they have served as a workshop for her longer narratives (Brown, "Martín Gaite's Short Stories"). The themes of social inequity, gender-specific role restrictions, and escape into fantasy are all explored in these brief narratives.

Psychological probing of the superior nonconformist character, who cannot adapt to a society that he (accurately) sees as corrupt, is the central theme in Martín Gaite's second full-length novel, *Ritmo lento*. The narrative is composed of a pastiche of recollections offered to a psychiatrist by a disturbed yet brilliantly lucid young man. Points of conflict between this character and the society that surrounds him indicate society's deficiencies rather than his own: Society, unable to tolerate complete rationality and honesty, must silence his criticism in order to reinforce its values. One example of David's brutal honesty is his observation that women contribute to their own oppression by upholding the cultural norms that trap them. In its complex presentation of social criticism through a first-person perspective, *Ritmo lento* was a pioneer of the new subjective novel that appeared in Spain in the late 1960s and early 1970s.

The theme for which Carmen Martín Gaite is best known—that of the problem of communication between individuals in the modern world—is concretized in the structure of two of her novels. The first, *Retahílas*, consists of a night-long conversation between a forty-five-year-old woman and her young nephew, a man in his twenties. The novel chronicles one of the evanescent opportunities for meaningful communication that the author has described in several essays. The two protagonists are brought together unexpectedly, in the ancestral home in which the woman's grandmother (the young man's great-aunt) is about to die. Neither knows much about the other's true personality. Both speakers are intensely interested in one another; the nephew, Germán, is especially fascinated by his aunt Eulalia. Under these propitious circumstances, the two characters exchange a series of interlocking monologues that are best categorized as verbal missives.

The topics covered by these spoken letters include the oppressiveness of gender-specific role definitions, the deleterious effects of aging on physical beauty, the difficulty of sustaining a relationship over time, and the decay of language among contemporary speakers. The position that gender roles should be based on personal preference rather than on sex is articulated by the nephew, who seeks to transcend "sex role polarities" (Ordóñez 238). The aunt, facing the first signs of aging as she confronts the end of a valued relationship with her husband, voices pessimism regarding the passage of time, which she associates with decay. Nowhere is this negative assessment more troubling than in the realm of language, on which communication hinges. Published in the last year of the Franco dictatorship, *Retahílas* reflects the cultural malaise of the Franco era without overtly criticizing the regime.

Fragmentos de interior, the first of Martín Gaite's novels written after Franco's demise ended censorship in 1975, presents more explicitly the themes that were introduced in *Retahílas*. This fast-paced novel chronicles the adventures of a family and its servants over the course of three days in 1975. Along with illicit activities, dangerous escapades, and a dramatic range of emotions, this novel of suspense includes social commentary. The inability of men and women to form lifelong relationships, the devaluation of the older woman in contemporary society, and the changing relationship of the upper and lower classes in modern Spain are vividly sketched. Despite the presence of these themes, however, *Fragmentos de interior* is a less reflective novel than others by Martín Gaite; it highlights political, sexual, and class intrigue. The novel is an early manifestation of the suspense genre that captivated Spain in the early 1980s, when the advent of a free press meant that fiction writers could throw off their yokes of responsibility as social critics and historians.

Balancing writers' desire for the new luxury of escapism, the freedom of democratic Spain brought with it a renewed obsession with the past. Like her compatriots, Martín Gaite felt pulled to reexamine the events of the Civil War and the protracted postwar era in Spain. Unlike most of her counterparts, however, she was keenly aware of the pitfalls—primarily the huge potential for tedium—inherent in a self-centered retrospective. She circumvented the hazards of the testimonial by creating a hybrid novel: a fantastic memoir.

Her most famous novel consists of an interview, conducted during a raging late-night storm by a mysterious man dressed in black, with a woman writer who exactly resembles Carmen Martín Gaite. Fantastic elements abound: The man's arrival and departure are marked by the appearance of a huge cockroach, the visitor offers the narrator a series of substances that loosen her memory, and as they speak a pile of pages grows next to the writer's typewriter. These pages bear the title *El cuarto de atrás*. The title has a dual meaning: It refers both to a real playroom and to the back room of the mind.

The two facets of the title reveal the novel's two central themes. One might be called "growing up female in Franco's Spain." In the novel, Martín Gaite recalls what it was like to come of age as a bright young woman during the Spanish Civil War and postwar years. Details of feminine socialization, previously excised from accounts of the period, are recalled by the narrator during her discursive conversation with Alejandro, the man in black. She describes the mandatory social service commitment required of young women who attended classes in which they learned how to be helpmates to their future husbands; the rituals of having clothing made to order, both by prestigious dressmakers and by common seamstresses; the specter of spinsterhood held out to young women as a "bad end." Perhaps surprisingly, considering her status as a bourgeois provincial girl, the narrator was largely immune to the social directives of the Franco regime; her mother and father supported her literary ambitions and helped her attain the education she so eagerly sought. However, the deprivation of the Franco era affected even a financially secure family such as her own. The "back room" of her childhood home, in which she and her sister played freely and happily, was commandeered by her mother as a storage room during the war, used for hoarding food and other necessities that were only intermittently available.

As Martín Gaite later explained in a key interview, in *El cuarto de atrás* she establishes "a parallel between the back room in my house in Salamanca . . . and the garret of the mind, a sort of secret region full of jumbled contents, separated from the cleaner and more orderly outer chambers of the mind by a curtain that is drawn only infrequently" ("Carmen Martín Gaite," *La Gaceta del Norte* 4). The novel's second main theme has to do with this other back room, and especially with the secrets it holds. "The memories that can surprise us are hidden in the back room," the author affirmed in the 1979 interview. "They always emerge from there, and only when they wish to do so; it is useless to harass them." The unreal nature of childhood recollections, composed of what the adult thinks he or she remembers, is compounded in the case of Martín Gaite and her generation by the unreal-seeming violence and destruction they witnessed as children during the war. These perturbing memories, buried under years of external repression and internalized restraint, are difficult to retrieve.

In *El cuarto de atrás*, the fantastic man in black, with his arsenal of pharmacological and verbal inducements to speech, serves as a facilitator of "lost" childhood memories. He also functions to introduce the novel's most important subtheme: the question of what literature should be. The metaliterary aspects of the novel include overt criticism of Martín Gaite's "El balneario," as well as lively discussion of the functions of literature. The novel has been shown to reveal as well as illustrate Martín Gaite's personal theory of literature, involving the elements of escape, memory, communication, and catharsis (Brown and Smith).

The question of what makes good literature, along with the social issues that are recurring themes in Martín Gaite's fiction, are also the subjects of many of her nonfiction publications. A personal approach to literary analysis and theory is found in *El cuento de nunca acabar* (1983; "The Never-Ending Story"). Issues of communication and the socialization of women are analyzed in *La búsqueda de interlocutor y otras búsquedas* (1973; "The Search for a Conversational Partner and Other Searches"), and the role of women writers in Spanish literature is detailed in *Desde la ventana: Enfoque femenino de la literatura española* (1987; "From the Window: A Feminine Focus on Spanish Literature"). Socialization and courtship customs in eighteenth-century Spain are studied in *Usos amorosos del siglo XVIII en España* (1972; "Love and Courtship Customs in Eighteenth-Century Spain"); these topics are addressed with regard to Spanish women of Martín Gaite's own generation in *Usos amorosos de la postguerra española* (1987; "Love and Courtship Customs of Postwar Spain," Anagrama Essay Prize 1987).

While her nonfiction and her fiction for adults reflect social realities, Martín Gaite's loftiest aspirations for women are concretized in her three children's novels: *El castillo de las tres murallas* (1981; "The Three-Walled Castle"), *El pastel del diablo* (1985; "The Devil's Pie"), and *Caperucita en Manhattan* (1990; "Little Red Riding Hood in Manhattan"). The protagonist of each of these works is a young girl who triumphs heroically over adversity. In these simple stories, the nature of good and evil reflects the worldview of their creator:

cowardice, conformity, and materialism are vanquished by bravery, imagination, and the veneration of people over possessions.

SURVEY OF CRITICISM

Joan Lipman Brown's review of the Modern Language Association *Bibliographies* of the 1980s indicates that there are more scholarly entries for Carmen Martín Gaite than for any other contemporary Spanish woman writer ("Women Writers of Spain: An Historical Perspective," in *Women Writers of Contemporary Spain: Exiles in the Homeland).* The bulk of scholarship on Martín Gaite is composed of specialized essays. Critics have responded primarily to *El cuarto de atrás,* whose metaliterary orientation has strong appeal to literary scholars. Central among critics' observations has been the importance of ambiguity in the novel (Castillo), the significance of the work's two literary modes (Brown, "A Fantastic Memoir" and chapter 10 of *Secrets),* the innovation of the novel's depiction of the artist as woman (Levine), the importance of popular culture in the work (Sieburth), and the complexity of the novel's intertextual and metaliterary codes (Servodidio and Spires).

Criticism of other individual works, such as John W. Kronik's valuable "A Splice of Life: Carmen Martín Gaite's *Entre visillos,"* is less frequent than comparative studies of one or more novels. Two seminal comparative studies are Catherine G. Bellver's "Carmen Martín Gaite as a Social Critic" and Phyllis Zatlin Boring's "Carmen Martín Gaite, Feminist Author." Noteworthy entries in histories of contemporary Spanish literature include Gonzalo Sobejano's pioneering study of her first three novels and Ignacio Soldevila Durante's review of her works through 1980.

To date, only one comprehensive analysis of the author and her literature has appeared: Joan Lipman Brown's *Secrets From the Back Room: The Fiction of Carmen Martín Gaite* (1987), which offers a comprehensive analysis of Martín Gaite's fiction through 1984. Intended for a broad audience, including English-speaking readers as well as Hispanists, it begins with an overview of Martín Gaite's historical and literary era. Chapter 2 is an "Autobiographical Sketch" written by Carmen Martín Gaite expressly for this volume. Subsequent chapters are devoted to each of Martín Gaite's works, including her volume of poetry, *A rachas* (1976; "In a Gust of Wind"), and her first children's novel. The book includes an extensive, annotated bibliography of primary and secondary sources.

The critical anthology *From Fiction to Metafiction: Essays in Honor of Carmen Martín Gaite,* edited by Mirella Servodidio and Marcia L. Welles (1983), is an indispensable resource. This volume, composed of articles written in Spanish and English, includes an introduction by the editors, a short essay by Carmen Martín Gaite about her experiences in New York, an interview (reprinted from the Spanish journal *Ínsula),* and fifteen essays. The contributors (Brown, Durán, El Saffar, Feal, Glenn, R. Gullón, Kronik, Levine, Ordóñez, Palley, Servodidio, Sobejano, Spires, Thomas, and Welles) each address a different aspect of Martín

Gaite's opus. From an analysis of the intertextual codes of *El cuarto de atrás* (the most studied work in this collection) to a lyrical musing on the unity among all of Martín Gaite's narratives, this volume includes thoughtful and important critical insights.

Two more recent review essays are useful in understanding both Carmen Martín Gaite and her literature. The first, published by Isabel Roger in 1988, is entitled "Carmen Martín Gaite: Una trayectoria novelística y su bibliografía." The article summarizes Martín Gaite's literary output and the major critical works it has elicited; it is accompanied by a bibliography that, although not annotated, is extensive. The most recent overview of Carmen Martín Gaite is Joan Lipman Brown's "Carmen Martín Gaite: Reaffirming the Pact Between Reader and Writer," in the volume *Women Writers of Contemporary Spain: Exiles in the Homeland* (1991). This essay takes the position that Martín Gaite's nonfiction works, which have been largely overlooked by literary critics, shed great light on her fiction. This point is demonstrated in the context of all of the author's major works to date, and is accompanied by a primary and an annotated secondary bibliography.

Since the mid-1950s, the literature of Carmen Martín Gaite has won her a loyal and enthusiastic readership. Since she began writing fiction in the early 1950s, she has published five novels, two novellas, fifteen short stories, a collection of casual verses, and three children's books. Her works have spanned not only decades but also literary movements and techniques. Throughout her career, Martín Gaite has demonstrated constancy in her enduring network of social themes. Critical recognition has accompanied her popular success. Carmen Martín Gaite—the girl from the provinces—is now the most studied contemporary woman author of Spain.

BIBLIOGRAPHY

Major Works by Carmen Martín Gaite

Fiction

El balneario. Madrid: Afrodisio Aguado, 1955. [Includes the novella "El balneario"]
Entre visillos. Barcelona: Destino, 1958.
Las ataduras. Barcelona: Destino, 1960.
Ritmo lento. Barcelona: Destino, 1962.
Retahílas. Barcelona: Seix Barral, 1974.
A rachas. Madrid: Peralta, 1976.
Fragmentos de interior. Barcelona: Destino, 1976.
El cuarto de atrás. Barcelona: Destino, 1978.
Cuentos completos. Madrid: Alianza, 1978.
El castillo de las tres murallas. Barcelona: Lumen, 1981.
El pastel del diablo. Barcelona: Lumen, 1985.
Dos relatos fantásticos. Barcelona: Lumen, 1986. [*El castillo* and *Pastel*]

Caperucita en Manhattan. Madrid: Siruela, 1990.
Nubosidad variable. Barcelona: Anagrama, 1992.

Nonfiction

El proceso de Macanaz: Historia de un empapelamiento. Madrid: Moneda y Crédito,
    1970. Rpt. as *Macanaz como otro paciente de la Inquisición*. Madrid: Taurus,
    1975.
Usos amorosos del siglo XVIII en España. Madrid: Siglo Veintiuno, 1972.
La búsqueda de interlocutor y otras búsquedas. Madrid: Nostromo, 1973.
El cuento de nunca acabar. Madrid: Trieste, 1983.
Desde la ventana: Enfoque femenino de la literatura española. Madrid: Espasa-Calpe,
    1987.
Usos amorosos de la postguerra española. Barcelona: Anagrama, 1987.

Translations

The Back Room. Trans. Helen R. Lane. New York: Columbia UP, 1983.
Behind the Curtains. Trans. Frances M. López-Morillas. New York: Columbia UP, 1990.

Works about Carmen Martín Gaite

Bellver, Catherine G. "Carmen Martín Gaite as a Social Critic." *Letras Femeninas* 8
    (Fall 1980): 3–16.
Brown, Joan Lipman. " 'El balneario' by Carmen Martín Gaite: Conceptual Aesthetics
    and *'L'étrange pur'*." *Journal of Spanish Studies: Twentieth-Century* 9.3 (Winter
    1978): 163–74.
———. "Carmen Martín Gaite: Reaffirming the Pact Between Reader and Writer."
    Women Writers of Contemporary Spain: Exiles in the Homeland. Ed. Joan L.
    Brown. Newark: U of Delaware P, 1991. 72–92.
———, and Elaine M. Smith. "*El cuarto de atrás*: Metafiction and the Actualization of
    Literary Theory." *Hispanófila* 90 (1987): 63–70.
———. "A Fantastic Memoir: Technique and History in *El cuarto de atrás*." *Anales
    de la Literatura Española Contemporánea* 6 (1981): 13–20.
———. "Martín Gaite's Short Stories, 1953–1974: The Writer's Workshop." Servodidio
    and Welles 37–48.
———. *Secrets From the Back Room: The Fiction of Carmen Martín Gaite*. University,
    MS: Romance Monographs, 1987.
———. "*Tiempo de silencio* and *Ritmo lento*: Pioneers of the New Social Novel in
    Spain." *Hispanic Review* 50.1 (Winter 1982): 61–73.
———. "Women Writers of Spain: An Historical Perspective." *Women Writers of
    Contemporary Spain* 13–25.
"Carmen Martín Gaite: Su 'Yo' fuerte." *La Gaceta del Norte* 18 Mar. 1979: 4. [Interview]
Castillo, Debra. "Never-Ending Story: Carmen Martín Gaite's *The Back Room*." *PMLA*
    102:5 (1987): 814–28.
Calvi, María Vittoria. *Dialogo e conversazione nella narrativa de Carmen Martín Gaite*.
    Milan: Arcipelago Edizioni, 1990.

Kronik, John W. "A Splice of Life: Carmen Martín Gaite's *Entre visillos*." Servodidio and Welles 49–60.

Levine, Linda Gould. "Carmen Martín Gaite's *El cuarto de atrás*: A Portrait of the Artist as Woman." Servodidio and Welles 161–72.

Matamoro, Blas. "Carmen Martín Gaite: El viaje al cuarto de atrás." *Cuadernos Hispanoamericanos* 351 (Oct. 1978): 581–605.

Ordóñez, Elizabeth J. "The Decoding and Encoding of Sex Roles in Carmen Martín Gaite's *Retahílas*." *Kentucky Romance Quarterly* 27 (1979): 237–44.

Palley, Julian. "El interlocutor soñado de 'El cuarto de atrás' de Carmen Martín Gaite." *Ínsula* 404–05 (1980): 22.

Pope, Randolph D., Amy Kaminsky, Andrew Bush, and Ruth El Saffar. "*El cuento de nunca acabar*: A Critical Dialogue." *Revista de Estudios Hispánicos* 22 (Jan. 1988): 107–34.

Roger, Isabel. "Carmen Martín Gaite: Una trayectoria novelística y su bibliografía." *Anales de la Literatura Española Contemporánea* 13 (1988): 293–317.

Seiburth, Stephanie. "Memory, Metafiction and Mass Culture: The Popular Text in *El cuarto de atrás*." *Revista Hispánica Moderna* 43.1 (June 1990): 78–92.

Servodidio, Mirella. "Oneiric Intertextualities." Servodidio and Welles 117–27.

———, and Marcia L. Welles, eds. *From Fiction to Metafiction: Essays in Honor of Carmen Martín Gaite*. Lincoln, NE: Society of Spanish and Spanish-American Studies, 1983.

Sobejano, Gonzalo. *Novela española de nuestro tiempo (en busca del pueblo perdido)*. 2nd ed. Madrid: Editorial Prensa Española, 1975. 493–502.

Soldevila Durante, Ignacio. *La novela desde 1886*. Madrid: Alhambra, 1980. 239–43.

Spires, Robert C. "Intertextuality in *El cuarto de atrás*." Servodidio and Welles 139–48.

Zatlin-Boring, Phyllis. "Carmen Martín Gaite, Feminist Author." *Revista de Estudios Hispánicos* 11 (Oct. 1977): 322–28.

MARÍA MARTÍNEZ SIERRA ("GREGORIO MARTÍNEZ SIERRA") (1874–1974)

Alda Blanco

BIOGRAPHY

Born María de la O. Lejárraga on December 28, 1874, in San Millán de la Cogolla, this prolific playwright, novelist, and essayist chose to sign her literary production with her husband's name, Gregorio Martínez Sierra, until his death in 1947. After Gregorio's death and until her own on June 28, 1974, in Buenos Aires, she used the name María Martínez Sierra.

The signature "Gregorio Martínez Sierra" was a pseudonym that assured the author literary anonymity and invisibility. It afforded her a much-needed shield against a firmly entrenched male literary establishment that did not look kindly upon women writers. Anonymity, Carolyn Heilbrun has suggested, "eases women's pain, alleviates the anxiety about the appropriateness of gender."[1] María Martínez Sierra's use of the pseudonym is, on the one hand, a symbolic act that signals a central problematic for the Spanish female author at the turn of the century, and on the other, "a name of power, the mark of private christening into a second self, a rebirth into linguistic primacy."[2] For María Martínez Sierra, the use of the pseudonym was a strategy that she felt empowered her as a woman writer and as a feminist.

María Lejárraga spent her childhood years in San Millán de la Cogolla. In 1880 her family moved from La Rioja to Madrid, where she graduated from high school and studied to be a language teacher, at the Teacher's Training College, the career she pursued until 1909. During the summer of 1897 she met Gregorio Martínez Sierra, seven years her junior, and they immediately began their literary "collaboration." By November 30, 1900, the date of their wedding, this literary couple had already published four titles with the signature "Gregorio Martínez Sierra." In 1905 she received a scholarship from the Teacher's Training

College to travel abroad to study European pedagogy. During this trip she visited Belgium, a country that, according to María herself, had a profound impact on her personal and political development. For it was in Belgium that she learned the pleasure of solitude, a way of life she always cherished, and became acquainted with the Casa del Pueblo, the Socialist Meeting Hall, a cultural space that came to symbolize for her the viability of and need for socialism.

In 1911, after many years of hard work and literary disappointments, "Gregorio Martínez Sierra" finally triumphed on the Madrid stage with the play *Canción de cuna* (1910; *The Cradle Song* 1916, 1922), which was not only publicly acclaimed but also received a prize from Spain's Royal Academy. Although prior to the resounding success of this dramatic work "Gregorio Martínez Sierra" had written a handful of plays, her literary production had mainly included novels, short stories, and poetry. As early as 1906 "Gregorio Martínez Sierra" had received some degree of recognition with the publication of the novel *Tú eres la paz* ("You Are Peace"), but it was the combination of her playwriting and Gregorio's staging that firmly placed "Gregorio Martínez Sierra" in the literary limelight until 1932, when this voice unexpectedly fell silent. When it resurfaced again in 1952, with the publication of her beautiful autobiography, *Una mujer por caminos de España* ("A Woman on the Roads of Spain"), this voice was accompanied by the signature María Martínez Sierra.

Although her marriage disintegrated, she did not relinquish her use of the pseudonym "Gregorio Martínez Sierra" until her husband's death in 1947. In 1906 Gregorio had met Catalina Bárcena, the actress who became not only his lifetime companion but also the leading lady in the majority of the hit plays performed in Spain and Latin America. The lack of biographical or autobiographical information about Gregorio and María's marriage precludes any hypothesizing on the nature or the form of their marital arrangement. All that is known is that Gregorio did not separate from María until 1922, when his only child by Catalina was born.

Whereas María Martínez Sierra seems to have chosen invisibility as regards her literary production, the same is not the case with her feminist and socialist political activity. In 1914 she began to participate in the feminist movement at the national and international levels, becoming Spain's secretary to the International Woman Suffrage Alliance (IWSA). Coinciding with her feminist activism was the publication of "Gregorio Martínez Sierra's" feminist essays, beginning in 1916 and appearing intermittently until 1932. In 1930 she was elected president of Spain's Feminine Association for Civic Education (AFEC), an organization of middle-class women devoted to the promotion of economic and legal rights for women. She also was active in the Lyceum Club, headed by María de Maeztu, whose main objectives were to reform women's legal position, to create day care centers for children of working women, and to provide a meeting place for women and their cultural activities.

Although in the early 1930s she seems to have moved away from feminism as a political movement, becoming active instead in the Socialist Workers Party of Spain (PSOE), she continued to approach, interpret, and write about Spanish reality from a feminist perspective. In the 1933 elections, the first in which women could vote, she was elected to the Spanish Parliament on the PSOE ticket for the region of Granada. Her autobiography, *Una mujer por caminos de España,* narrates her participation in this electoral campaign as a Socialist propagandist. In this important historical document, María Martínez Sierra re-creates key scenes from her many public appearances and moments of great expectations and of equally great disappointments for the Second Republic and for the women of Spain. Masterfully weaving a wealth of detail—associated with women's writing—and a reflective analysis of each scene, this narrative draws its reader into a world of struggle, hope, and disillusion that exists today only in the tales of our grandparents or that, for the most part, has been forgotten.

In protest over the brutal governmental repression of the Asturian working class in 1934, María Martínez Sierra resigned her seat in the Spanish Parliament and devoted herself to organizing on behalf of the National Committee of Women Against Fascism headed by Dolores Ibarruri. With the outbreak of the Spanish Civil War on July 18, 1936, the Loyalist government sent her to Switzerland as commercial attaché, but shortly thereafter she left her post, for reasons that we are unable to ascertain, and went to live in the south of France until her departure for her American exile in 1952. She traveled about Latin America, finally settling in Buenos Aires in 1953, where she made her living as a writer and translator until her death in 1974, at the age of one hundred. Little is known of her life in Argentina. She continued writing stories and articles that were published in Buenos Aires, principally in the newspaper *La Prensa.* It is worth noting that letters to other friends in exile, dated in the late 1950s and available at the Fundación Pablo Iglesias in Madrid, were signed María Lejárraga, the maiden name she had never used during her writing career.

MAJOR THEMES

In general, the work of "Gregorio Martínez Sierra" has fallen out of favor with readers, theater audiences, and critics. Yet nowadays an argument can be made for the historical importance and place of her literary production from a feminist perspective. "Gregorio Martínez Sierra's" plays, novels, and essays elaborate a language and thematics that significantly contribute to a specific—albeit marginal—type of literature that was written in Spain in the first third of the century by a handful of women: feminist literature. Moreover, the themes and female perspective of her literary production coincide with the general tenets of the turn-of-the-century international women's movement, and in particular with those of the English feminist novelists so eloquently discussed by Elaine Showalter in *A Literature of Their Own.* In this way, her work can be inscribed both within a Spanish literary tradition and within an international feminist tradition.

Furthermore, "Gregorio Martínez Sierra" was by far the most prolific and successful author among the Spanish feminist writers of the period—a group that included Carmen de Burgos, Margarita Nelken, and María Teresa León, to name but a few. Although her short stories, poetry, and novels did not elicit critical or public praise—with the exception perhaps of *Tú eres la paz*—numerous plays were staged and critically acclaimed each year, and her essays often set the terms of the debate on the "woman question" and feminism. It was not infrequent for those interested in the "woman question" to quote "Gregorio Martínez Sierra's" opinions or solicit her views.

What characterized the literary and theatrical production of "Gregorio Martínez Sierra," as contemporaries often noted, was the presence of feminist themes and perspectives. Closely linked to the questions and problems posed by women's issues of the period, her literary production explores the ways in which gender constructs the social and psychic life of its characters. At the center of numerous plays and novels stands the young, independent woman character, the Spanish equivalent of the "New Woman" for whom a career, marriage, and motherhood are the three desirable and necessary aspects of a woman's life that not only can but also should be combined without major problems or contradictions. "Gregorio Martínez Sierra" creates female characters whose struggle for self-determination does not preclude their being the embodiment of feminine virtue, a combination at odds with contemporary notions of womanhood, in which independence was associated with the masculine, and passivity with the feminine. Narrative tension and conflicts arise in the plays when the female protagonist confronts the deeply embedded sexist tradition, usually represented by a traditional and severe mother who attempts to impede the character's desire for independence. The resolution of the plays is always one of victory: the heroine triumphs over tradition. Yet because "Gregorio Martínez Sierra" constructs the female characters as both strong-willed and sweetly feminine, hers is not a literature of great feminist confrontations nor of tragically insoluble problems for the woman in search of her freedom. Nevertheless, "Gregorio Martínez Sierra" always emphasizes that women can obtain their much-desired liberty through work, education, and equality, the basic tenets for the development of the "modern woman."

From a contemporary perspective it could be argued that "Gregorio Martínez Sierra's" feminism is rather meek and uninteresting, given its easy, happy solutions. But in fact the exemplary model that she proposes for her female characters is that of a woman capable of controlling and determining her life and way of living. The feminist impulse of the independent female characters can be summarized in the emblematic words spoken by a woman character in a one-act play entitled *No le sirven las virtudes de su madre* (1945; "Her Mother's Virtues Are Not Useful to Her") when she applauds her granddaughter's desire to "live in and for herself" (8). Because in Spanish culture during the first third of the century, womanhood was articulated strictly in terms of women's role as daughter, wife, and mother, the suggestion that her life could and should be self-determined is more radical and utopian than timid or accommodating.

The need for gender equality in the public and private spheres is one of the main themes that runs through the work of "Gregorio Martínez Sierra." Her plays and novels explore the many areas of social and domestic life in which equity for women does not exist. This primary conflict is resolved by proposing the necessary equality between the sexes. Moreover, equality is linked to justice, happiness, and well-being not only for the female character but also for all those around her. Equality is the necessary precondition for the existence of balance, happiness, harmony, and serenity. For example, in the plays organized around the conflicts of the career woman (1919; *Cada uno y su vida*, "To Each His Own") or the working woman (1915; *Amanecer*, "Dawn"), the resolution of the primary conflict—happiness in love and work—is achieved through the professional partnership of the couple or the close collaboration between husband and wife.

In the plays where the woman does not work outside the home, nor even aspires to do so, the domestic equality "Gregorio Martínez Sierra" proposes is one of moral equality between men and women within marriage, a notion put forth by feminist writers of the period in contrast to what they saw as the double standard of male morality. Rather than suggest that women's equality is attainable through sexual license, a play such as *Mujer* (1925; "Woman") demands men's self-control and marital fidelity.

Canción de cuna, the writer's most renowned play, nationally and internationally, is a rather curious and enigmatic piece for today's feminist reader, given its lack of conflict and critique of patriarchy. Yet this gently sweet two-act play elaborates several feminist themes of the period: that mother love is not predicated upon biology, that it can take the place of romantic and sexual love, and that woman, as the vehicle through which man can attain self-knowledge, has the power of regeneration.

"Gregorio Martínez Sierra" sets the play in a convent, an emblematic space for the feminist writer within two literary traditions. In the Spanish literary tradition, the convent is associated with two important protofeminist writers: Teresa of Avila and Sor Juana Inés de la Cruz. It is no coincidence, therefore, that two of the characters' names are Teresa and Sor Juana de la Cruz. For "Gregorio Martínez Sierra" the convent is the place where women are free to fulfill their maternal love urges without having to be biological mothers. The convent can also be seen as the Spanish elaboration of the utopian tradition within feminist literature at the turn of the century, best exemplified by Charlotte Perkins Gilman's *Herland*, which casts an all-female society as a utopian space. The veneration of motherhood, the disjunction between mother love and its biological origin, and the convent as utopia situate this play firmly within a Western feminist tradition. These themes are the cornerstones of "Gregorio Martínez Sierra's" novels and plays, and also of her important essays on the "woman question."

"Gregorio Martínez Sierra" wrote four volumes of feminist essays between 1916 and 1932: *Cartas a mujeres de España* (1916; "Letters to the Women of Spain"), *Feminismo, feminidad, españolismo* (1917; "Feminism, Femininity,

Spanishness''); *La mujer moderna* (1920; ''The Modern Woman''), and *Nuevas cartas a las mujeres* (1932; ''New Letters to Women''). The essays, mostly written in the epistolary form, show an intellectual affinity for and commitment to bourgeois feminism of the period. They skillfully weave different aspects of feminist discourse: theory, concrete analyses of women's plight, social and political tactics for the feminist struggle, and psychic strategies for the emotional survival of women in society and within the couple. In these essays, the middle-class female reader could frequently find translations and summaries of important Western contemporary feminist theory, as well as news from the international feminist movement.

In the essays published before 1932, ''Gregorio Martínez Sierra'' constructs her theoretical arguments regarding gender and the need for feminist practice on the essentialist premise that sexual difference is innate. This theoretical position coincides with that of Western feminism in the early century, which articulated ''woman'' and ''man'' as natural categories, in which ''woman'' was positively associated with nature and peace, and ''man,'' her opposite, was negatively linked to culture and war. By 1932, the publication date of her last feminist essays, *Nuevas cartas a las mujeres*, she questions this theoretical position by proposing instead that sexual difference is socially and culturally constructed by men. This important theoretical shift responds to the collapse of bourgeois feminist theory after World War I. Because a sector of the international feminist movement had actively supported this war, it was no longer possible for feminists to theorize ''woman'' as ''naturally'' or ''inherently'' peaceful and, therefore, as the regenerator of ''naturally'' violent ''man.'' Confronted with this devastating wartime collusion, she seeks to understand the reasons why women— including feminist women—could so easily give up their theoretical principles. For the first time in her long career as a feminist thinker, she turns to literature as a way of comprehending the production and reproduction of sexual ideology. ''Gregorio Martínez Sierra's'' conclusion is resounding. Male writers, she argues, have played a fundamental role in the creation of sex roles, given their historic power over the representation of women. Women, having internalized this oppressive masculine construction, merely imitate it. This important theoretical move had far-reaching implications not only for ''Gregorio Martínez Sierra's'' feminist theorizing but also for her future literary production.

The following extraordinary fragment from the *Nuevas cartas* is possibly one of the period's most lucid analyses of the way in which woman's image in a patriarchal society has been culturally produced and reproduced. More than a mere description of this phenomenon, the narrator blames male writers for having falsified woman's real image:

Men have been able to create, one after another, the impossibly pure and chaste figures of women who decorate, adorn, illuminate, perfume, and idealize their novels, stories, and plays, because men have dreamed them, and dreams are, in a way, a reality for the mind that forges them. But a woman who ''sees herself

on the inside,'' who ''knows herself by heart'' intimately, personally, and inex-
orably, cannot dream herself absurdly outside of reality. And, to that effect, today's
women writers are beginning to put on paper a female reality which is at odds
with the ideal of the ''innocently pure angel'' or ''the little bird fallen out of the
tree'' (everything has wings) consecrated by centuries of male fantasy. (176)

This fragment can also be seen as María Martínez Sierra's first effort to
overcome her deeply felt anxiety of authorship. Her new cultural analysis forced
her to unravel the paradoxical strategy of her feminist essays, which had served
her so well but now could be seen as limiting and even as falsifying: the fact
that a masculine signature articulated and adopted a feminist position. In one of
her essays, a male narrator proposes for the first time the need for a literature
written by women, because only women are capable of imagining and writing
themselves as they really exist. Moreover, only women writers, she argues, with
their own images, can counteract the false representation of woman constructed
by the male imagination. The paradox of the feminist essays has now become
a contradiction. By suggesting that women's oppression is largely due to the
fact that culture and literature are in male hands, a text with a male signature,
however feminist, will by definition distort the real image of the woman. Trapped
by her own narrative strategy and at a theoretical impasse, María Martínez Sierra
had either to authorize her own voice and become a woman writer, or to continue
writing behind a male signature, hoping that other women—and women writers—
would not confuse her voice with Gregorio's signature. The theoretical dilemma
apparent in this book, coupled with the fact that María Martínez Sierra devoted
herself to her beloved Republic between 1930 and 1936, helps explain the abrupt
halt in ''Gregorio Martínez Sierra's'' literary production after 1932. Her voice
was heard again in 1952, the publication date of her autobiography, *Una mujer
por caminos de España*.

SURVEY OF CRITICISM

To date, there is no complete biography of María Martínez Sierra. This is due
perhaps to the lack of biographical tradition in Spanish letters, coupled with the
marginalization of the majority of women writers from the literary canon, a
situation that has led to the ''disappearance'' of writing women from the critical
and biographic imagination. The most important biographic information can be
found in Patricia W. O'Connor's *Gregorio and María Martínez Sierra* (1977)
and in Ricardo Gullón's *Relaciones amistosas y literarias entre Juan Ramón
Jiménez y los Martínez Sierra* (1961). Gullón reprints a series of fascinating
letters written by María Martínez Sierra to Juan Ramón Jiménez that span the
length of their friendship.

Joaquín Entrambasaguas justifiably complains in his 1958 introduction to
''Gregorio Martínez Sierra's'' *Tú eres la paz* that this author has generally been
studied too little by literary critics. With a handful of notable exceptions, this

is still the case. Criticism by contemporaries of "Gregorio Martínez Sierra" tends to be rather impressionistic and normative. For today's literary critic, particularly the feminist critic, these essays prove to be more useful at the metacritical level than as scholarly critiques. Through them we witness the ways in which critics were constructing "Gregorio Martínez Sierra's" literary production to fit their particular notion of Spanish literary history. There is the tendency to downplay the feminist themes and to avoid a discussion of María Martínez Sierra's authorial hand.

The most complete overview of "Gregorio Martínez Sierra's" literary production in general, and her theater in particular, can be found in the two books written by Patricia W. O'Connor, the most prolific critic of "Gregorio Martínez Sierra": *Gregorio and María Martínez Sierra* and *Women in the Theater of Gregorio Martínez Sierra* (1967). A rather thorough and extensive review of "Gregorio Martínez Sierra's" novelistic production is available in Entrambasaguas's introduction to *Tú eres la paz*.

Perhaps it is the question of authorship that has most intrigued modern critics to date. Although during Gregorio and María's lifetime it was well known in literary and theater circles that it was she who was the author of the plays, novels, and essays, the undeniable recognition of her authorship has been made possible only recently by Patricia W. O'Connor's thoroughly documented book, *Gregorio and María Martínez Sierra*, which finally accords to María Martínez Sierra her rightful place as author of "Gregorio Martínez Sierra's" work. Although in 1961 Gullón had categorically stated that María was the author of "Gregorio Martínez Sierra's" literary texts, his short introductory essay to the letters between the Martínez Sierras and Juan Ramón Jiménez is not documented, as is O'Connor's work. O'Connor concludes her important investigation, in no uncertain terms, by writing that "material discovered after her death in 1974 firmly establishes her as author—far more than merely inspirer or editorial assistant—of much of what was published under the name of her husband" (133).

O'Connor finally puts to rest the critical polemic that had so often haunted the literary production of "Gregorio Martínez Sierra." It had originated in an inherent discrepancy between what the critics perceived as the "feminine sensibility" of the writing itself—and in later years its feminist perspective—and the fact that the work was signed by a man. Some disconcerted critics therefore sought to reconcile the male signature with its "feminine" voice. Thus Julio Cejador, a contemporary of "Gregorio Martínez Sierra," elaborated the notion of María and Gregorio's literary collaboration in his *Historia de la lengua y literatura castellana* (1919), a view that would be taken up by a handful of other critics. Entrambasaguas, for example, is willing to accept Cejador's notion of spousal "collaboration" only after having completed, in his words, an "unfruitful" stylistic comparison of Gregorio and María's individual production in which he is unable to differentiate between their writing styles.

Yet there were other critics for whom even the idea of Gregorio and María's collaboration was offensive. Federico Sainz de Robles, for example, staunchly denied María's authorial participation by privileging his position as witness to that literary era: "Thank goodness that there are still some of us alive who know for certain that Martínez Sierra is the sole author of innumerable and admirable plays and admirable novels and essays" (*Raros y olvidados* 107). Echoing Sainz de Robles's stance, other critics simply omitted any mention of María in their discussions of Gregorio Martínez Sierra's literary corpus. Their gesture of exclusion served to affirm the dominant male literary establishment's sentiment that writing, in spite of its perceived "femininity," was a man's job.

It was not until the publication of one of María Martínez Sierra's two autobiographies, *Gregorio y yo* (1953; "Gregorio and I"), that she confirmed for the first time what many already knew: She had penned the majority of the works that had been widely read and so greatly applauded by theatergoing audiences under the signature "Gregorio Martínez Sierra." Finally emerging from her literary invisibility, she frames this autobiographical text by subtitling it *A Half-Century of Collaboration* and reveals the nature of her "collaborative" role in the affectionately biting dedication to her deceased husband: "For the Shadow who maybe will have leaned over my shoulder—as he did so many other times when he had a body and eyes with which to look—to read what I was writing." In *Gregorio y yo* she does not seek to appropriate the work or to amend the conscious self-effacing decisions taken at an early age. Rather, she includes in this literary autobiography a contextual analysis of the sociocultural and personal reasons that kept her from signing her literary production, and of adopting Gregorio's name as her pseudonym.

In the last few years critical attention has turned, for the first time, to the two autobiographies written by María Martínez Sierra: *Una mujer por caminos de España* and *Gregorio y yo*. The former has been reissued (1989) by the Spanish publishing house Castalia and includes a lengthy introduction by Alda Blanco. Basing herself on the important documentation provided by O'Connor, Blanco's reading situates Martínez Sierra in the context of feminist literary criticism and suggests that "Gregorio Martínez Sierra's" use of the pseudonym can be read as symbolic and symptomatic of the anxiety felt by women writers in turn-of-the-century Spain. María A. Salgado has written the first critical essay on *Gregorio y yo*, "*Gregorio y yo*: La verídica historia de dos personas distintas y un solo autor verdadero" (1989).

A continued feminist rereading of María Martínez Sierra's writings will show the way in which the author articulated and worked through the pressing international feminist polemics of the time. Although her plays, novels, and essays may seem out-of-date to today's readers, they nevertheless significantly contributed to the debates that took place in Spain about the "woman question" in the early part of the century. It was perhaps María Martínez Sierra who arrived at the most important theoretical formulation with regard to the cultural construction and reproduction of gender by proposing the pivotal role played by male-authored literature and the need for women to become writers in order to counteract the Spanish misogynist tradition.

NOTES

1. Carolyn Heilbrun, *Writing a Woman's Life* (New York: Norton, 1988) 40.
2. Susan Gilbert and Sandra Gubar, *No Man's Land: The Place of the Woman Writer in the Twentieth Century* (New Haven: Yale UP, 1988) 241.

BIBLIOGRAPHY

Works Signed by "Gregorio Martínez Sierra"

El poema del trabajo. Madrid: Eusebio Sánchez, 1898.
Diálogos fantásticos. Madrid: A. Pérez y P. García, 1899.
Almas ausentes. Madrid: Biblioteca Mignón, 1900.
Flores de escarcha. Madrid: G. Sastre, 1900.
Horas de sol. Madrid: Ambrosio Pérez, 1901.
Pascua florida. Barcelona: Salvat, 1903.
Sol de tarde. Madrid: Tipografía de la Revista de Archivos, 1904.
La humilde verdad. Madrid: Henrich, 1905.
Motivos. Paris: Garnier, 1905.
Teatro de ensueño. Madrid: Imprenta de Samarám, 1905.
La tristeza del Quixote. Madrid: Biblioteca Nacional, 1905.
Tú eres la paz. Madrid: Montaner y Simón, 1906.
Aldea ilusoria. Paris: Garnier, 1907.
Aventura. Madrid: Blas, 1907.
La casa de la primavera. Madrid: Renacimiento, 1907.
La feria de Neuilly. Paris: Garnier, 1907.
Aventura. Madrid: Renacimiento, 1908.
Beata primavera. Madrid: Renacimiento, 1908.
Hechizo de amor. Madrid: V. Prieto, 1908.
Juventud, divino tesoro. Madrid: Renacimiento, 1908.
El peregrino ilusionado. Paris: Garnier, 1908.
Torre de marfil. Madrid: El Cuento Semanal, 1908.
El agua dormida. Madrid: Sucesores de Hernando, 1909.
La selva muda. Madrid: Blas, 1909.
La sombra del padre. Madrid: Tipografía de la Revista de Archivos, 1909.
El ama de casa. Madrid: Sucesores de Hernando, 1910.
El amor catedrático. Barcelona: E. Domenech, 1910.
Canción de cuna. Madrid: R. Velasco, 1910.
Todo es uno y lo mismo. Madrid: Revista de Archivos, 1910.
Lirio entre espinas. Madrid: Velasco, 1911.
El palacio triste. Madrid: Renacimiento, 1911.
Primavera en otoño. Madrid: Prieto, 1911.
La suerte de Isabelita. Madrid: Velasco, 1911.
Madam Pepita. Madrid: Renacimiento, 1912.
El pobrecito Juan. Madrid: Prieto, 1912.
El enamorado. Madrid: Renacimiento, 1913.
Madrigal. Madrid: Renacimiento, 1913.

Mamá. Madrid: Renacimiento, 1913.
Margot. Madrid: Renacimiento, 1913.
Los pastores. Madrid: R. Velasco, 1913.
Sólo para mujeres. Madrid: R. Velasco, 1913.
La tirana. Madrid: Renacimiento, 1913.
La vida inquieta. Madrid: Renacimiento, 1913.
Las golondrinas. Madrid: Juan Pueyo, 1914.
La mujer del héroe. Madrid: R. Velasco, 1914.
La pasión. Madrid: Renacimiento, 1914.
Amanecer. Madrid: R. Velasco, 1915.
El amor brujo. Madrid: R. Velasco, 1915.
Abril melancólico. Madrid: Renacimiento, 1916.
Cartas a mujeres de España. Madrid: Clásica Española, 1916.
El diablo se ríe. Madrid: Renacimiento, 1916.
Navidad. Madrid: Renacimiento, 1916.
El reino de Dios. Madrid: Pueyo, 1916.
La adúltera penitente. Madrid: Renacimiento, 1917.
Esperanza nuestra. Madrid: Renacimiento, 1917.
Feminismo, feminidad, españolismo. Madrid: Renacimiento, 1917.
Calendario espiritual. Madrid: Estrella, 1918.
Cartas a las mujeres de América. Buenos Aires: Juventud, 1918.
Cristo niño. Madrid: Estrella, 1918.
Rosina es frágil. Madrid: Estrella, 1918.
Sueño de una noche de agosto. Madrid: Renacimiento, 1918.
Cada uno y su vida. Madrid: Estrella, 1919.
El corazón ciego. Madrid: Estrella, 1919.
Fuente serena. Madrid: Estrella, 1919.
Granada. Madrid: Estrella, 1920.
La mujer moderna. Madrid: Estrella, 1920.
Vida y dulzura. Madrid: Renacimiento, 1920.
Don Juan de España. Madrid: Estrella, 1921.
El ideal. Madrid: Estrella, 1921.
Kodak romántico. Madrid: Estrella 1921.
Cada uno y su vida. Madrid: Prensa Gráfica, 1924.
Torre de marfil. Madrid: Estrella, 1924.
Mujer. Madrid: Estrella, 1925.
Rosas mustias. Madrid: Prensa Gráfica, 1926.
Seamos felices. Madrid: Estrella, 1929.
Eva curiosa. Madrid: Pence, 1930.
La hora del diablo. Madrid: Estrella, 1930.
No le sirven las virtudes de su madre. Revista literaria 748 (1945): 6–8. [Extract from
     Eva curiosa, 1930]
Triángulo. Madrid: Estrella, 1930.
Nuevas cartas a las mujeres. Madrid: Ibero Americana de Publicaciones, 1932.

Works Signed by María Martínez Sierra

Cuentos breves. Madrid: Imprenta de Enrique Rojas, 1899.
La mujer ante la república. Madrid: Ediciones de Esfinge, 1931.

Una mujer por caminos de España. Buenos Aires: Losada, 1952. Madrid: Castalia, 1989.
Gregorio y yo. Mexico City: Biografías Gandesa, 1953.
Viajes de una gota de agua. Buenos Aires: Librería Hachette, 1954.
Fiesta en el Olimpo. Buenos Aires: Aguilar, 1960.

Translations

The Cradle Song. Trans. John Garrett Underhill. *Poet Lore* 28 (1916): 625–79.
Love Magic. Trans. John Garrett Underhill. *Drama* 25 (1917): 40–61. [Trans. of *Hechizo de amor*]
The Lover. Trans. John Garrett Underhill. *Stratford Journal* 5 (1919): 33–44. [Trans. of *El enamorado*]
Poor John. Trans. John Garrett Underhill. *Drama* 10 (1920): 172–80. [Trans. of *El pobrecito Juan*]
Ana María. Trans. Mrs. Emmon Crocker. Boston: n.p., 1921. [Trans. of *Tú eres la paz*]
The Cradle Song and Other Plays. Trans. John Garrett Underhill. New York: Dutton, 1922.
Plays of Gregorio Martínez Sierra. Trans. John Garrett Underhill. 2 vols. New York: Dutton, 1923.
The Romantic Young Lady. Trans. Helen Granville-Barker and Harley Granville-Barker. New York: French, 1923. [Trans. of *Sueño de una noche de agosto*]
Take Two from One. Trans. Helen Granville-Barker and Harley Granville-Barker. New York: French, 1925. [Trans. of *Todo es uno y lo mismo*]
Idyll. Trans. Charlotte Marie Lorenz. *Poet Lore* 37 (1926): 63–72. [Trans. of *El ideal*]
The Kingdom of God: A Play in Three Acts. Trans. Helen Granville-Barker and Harley Granville-Barker. London: Sidgwick, 1927. [Trans. of *El reino de Dios*]
Holy Night: A Miracle Play in Three Scenes. Trans. Philip Hereford. London: Sheed, 1928. [Trans. of *Navidad*]
A Lily Among Thorns. Trans. Helen Granville-Barker and Harley Granville-Barker. Ed. T.H. Dickinson. Boston: n.p., 1930. 457–71. [Trans. of *Lirio entre espinas*]
The Two Shepherds. Trans. Helen Granville-Barker and Harley Granville-Barker. *Plays for the College Theatre*. Ed. G. H. Leverton. New York: n.p., 1932. 341–62; London: Sidgwick, 1935. [Trans. of *Los pastores*]
Let Us Be Happy. Trans. T. S. Richter. N.p.: n.p., n.d. [Trans. of *Seamos felices*]
Reborn. Trans. Nena Belmonte. New York: n.p., n.d.

Works about "Gregorio Martínez Sierra" and María Martínez Sierra

Blanco, Alda. "In Their Chosen Place: On the Autobiographies of Two Spanish Women of the Left." *Genre* 19 (1986): 431–45.
———. Introduction. *Una mujer por caminos de España*. By María Martínez Sierra. Madrid: Castalia, 1989. 7–46.
Cansinos Assens, Rafael. *La nueva literatura*. Madrid: Editorial Paez, 1925.
Cejador y Frauca, Julio. *Historia de la lengua y literatura castellanas*. Vol. 11. Madrid: Tipografía de la Revista de Archivos, 1919.
Douglas, Frances. "Gregorio Martínez Sierra." *Hispania* 5.5 (1922): 257–69; 6.1 (1923): 1–13.

Entrambasaguas, Joaquín. Introduction to *Tú eres la paz. Las mejores novelas contemporáneas.* Vol. 3. Barcelona: Planeta, 1958. 543–98.

Goldsborough Serrat, Andrés. *Imagen humana y literaria de Gregorio Martínez Sierra.* Madrid: Gráficos Cóndor, 1965.

Gullón, Ricardo. *Relaciones amistosas y literarias entre Juan Ramón Jiménez y los Martínez Sierra.* Río Piedras, Puerto Rico: Ediciones de la Torre, 1961.

Massa, Pedro. "Los cien felices años de María Martínez Sierra." *Los domingos del ABC* 3 Mar. 1974: 22–25.

O'Connor, Patricia W. "Death of Gregorio Martínez Sierra's Co-author." *Hispania* 58 (1975): 210–11.

———. *Gregorio and María Martínez Sierra.* Boston: Twayne, 1977

———. "Gregorio Martínez Sierra's Maternal Nuns in Dramas of Renunciation and Revolution." *The American Hispanist* 2 (1976): 8–12.

———. "La madre española en el teatro de Gregorio Martínez Sierra." *Duquesne Hispanic Review* 4.1 (1967): 17–24.

———. "A Spanish Precursor to Women's Lib: The Heroine in Gregorio Martínez Sierra's Theatre." *Hispania* 55 (1962): 865–72.

———. *Women in the Theatre of Gregorio Martínez Sierra.* New York: American Press, 1967. 8–12.

Owen, Arthur L. Introduction. *El ama de casa.* By Gregorio Martínez Sierra. Chicago: Sonborn, 1927. xi–xiv.

Sainz de Robles, Federico Carlos. *Raros y olvidados.* Madrid: Editorial Prensa Española, 1971.

Salgado, María A. "*Gregorio y yo:* La verídica historia de dos personas distintas y un solo autor verdadero." *Hispanófila* 96 (1989): 35–43.

———. Teatro de ensueño: Colaboración modernista de Juan Ramón Jiménez y Gregorio Martínez Sierra." *Hispanófila* 38 (1970): 49–58.

Scari, Robert M. "Los Martínez Sierra y el feminismo de Emilia Pardo Bazán." *Romance Notes* 20 (1980): 310–16.

ANA MARÍA MATUTE
(b. 1926)

María Carmen Riddel

BIOGRAPHY

Ana María Matute, one of the most important and prolific writers of the postwar years in Spain, is representative of a group of women whose literary production contributed to the intellectual regeneration of Spain after the Civil War (1936–39). Born in Barcelona on July 26, 1926, she was the second child of a family of five. Her father was a Catalan industrialist whose work often took the family to Madrid. The children spent many summers with their maternal grandparents in Mansilla de la Sierra, a village of the Rioja region. Thus, Matute became well acquainted with both rural and urban life in Spain.

Stricken by a serious illness at the age of nine, Ana María spent a long period convalescing at her grandparents' home. Shortly thereafter, the Civil War began. The family lived in Barcelona throughout the conflict. Unable to go to school and prevented by her disorder from leaving the house, Ana María once again experienced a lengthy confinement. Forced to remain at home, she began to read widely and to write. During this period she prepared a journal for the other children in the family and wrote plays for their marionette theater.

The family's frequent moves from Barcelona to Madrid, which made Ana María feel she was an outsider in both cities, the primitive living conditions in Mansilla de la Sierra, and long periods of confinement left their mark on her. Most of her works reflect alienation and loneliness, and manifest her opposition to social injustice. Above all, the Civil War and the disruption it brought to the social fabric of the country profoundly affected her. She witnessed the physical destruction of cities and individuals, and perceived the psychological damage inflicted by war. The darkness and pessimism of some of her characters, their selfish, violent, and dramatic reactions, reflect experiences that she viewed as scarring and degrading.

When circumstances permitted, Ana María attended Catholic schools and was taught exclusively by nuns. She has often indicated that she was dissatisfied with the rigid discipline and poor instruction she experienced as a student. Having concluded her secondary education at the age of sixteen, she studied music and painting and continued to read avidly. Shortly after leaving school, Ana María began to write professionally and to participate in the cultural life of Barcelona. She befriended the young, idealistic, and rebellious writers who, like herself, opposed the Franco dictatorship and experienced its stifling limitations. Carlos Barral and Juan Goytisolo were among the members of this group who would later become well known. She met them regularly at informal gatherings where they discussed literature in general and their own projects in particular.

In November 1952, Ana María married Ramón Eugenio de Goicoechea, also a writer. Until their separation in 1963, the family lived mostly in Madrid. Ana María did not particularly enjoy life in the capital, but the move enabled her to become acquainted with the young writers of another important urban center in Spain. Thus, she was painfully aware of Spain's dismal intellectual and cultural ambience during those years. Her active participation in the endeavors of the fledgling writers in Madrid and Barcelona connected her with the group that was breathing new life into Spanish literature in the postwar period. Their insightful works during the 1940s and 1950s contributed to the gradual regeneration of the devasted intellectual world. The significance of Matute's early work derives in large part from that fact.

In 1954 her son, Juan Pablo, was born. Motherhood was significant in her professional life and development. The experience of childhood, which had always concerned her, became much more poignant with the birth of her child. She immersed herself in the world of children and began to write for and about them. Matute published the bulk of her work in the 1950s and 1960s. Her novel *Los Abel* (1948; "The Abel Family") launched her professional career. She has published a total of eight novels, one novelette, nine short story collections, two short stories, two collections of short stories for children, and numerous essays and articles. Her last novel, *La torre vigía* ("The Watchtower"), appeared in 1971. Although she has published little in recent years, she continues to write in Barcelona, where she resides.

Matute has received many prestigious literary awards, including the Planeta Prize in 1954 for *Pequeño teatro* ("Little Theater"); the National Literary Prize Miguel de Cervantes in 1959 for *Los hijos muertos* (1958; *The Lost Children*); the Nadal Prize in 1960 for *Primera memoria* (*School of the Sun* 1963, 1989; *Awakening* 1963), and the National Prize for Children's Literature in 1965 for *El polizón del Ulises* ("The Ulysses Stowaway"), and again in 1983 for *Sólo un pie descalzo* ("Only One Bare Foot").[1]

MAJOR THEMES

Ana María Matute's early writing is rooted in the emerging novel of social realism in Spain. The political oppression and widespread economic deprivation that characterized the country during the late 1940s and early 1950s led many young writers to oppose the status quo in their works. However, the strong censorship imposed by the church and the state severely limited criticism of the Franco regime and its policies. As a result, novelists often attempted to describe faithfully the living conditions of the Spanish people without making direct commentary. Criticism of the authoritarian and anti-intellectual social order was implicit in the novels, and authors expected the intelligent and active participation of the reader in the condemnation of a situation that was unsatisfactory to almost everyone.

Matute's literary production reflects the thematic interests that concerned many of her contemporaries. She opposes social injustice and condemns the living conditions of peasants and workers. Her preoccupation with the effects of the Civil War on individuals and on the population at large is best exemplified in her novels by the frequent appearance, under one guise or another, of the Cain/Abel fratricide theme. She treats childhood, adolescence, and adulthood as closed worlds in conflict, each affecting the others deleteriously. Her young and adolescent characters find adjustment to the social group traumatic, and they often resist and regret the inexorable passage of time. It is this use of recurring themes that places her work within the mainstream of the Spanish novel during the postwar years.

Matute's literary production can be divided into two categories, the basis for which is determined by the implied reader. In one instance her writing is aimed at the adult; in another, it is aimed at the child or the young adolescent. Her attitude is not as pessimistic when she writes for children as when she writes for adults. However, even in her literature for children she explores the above-mentioned themes. As Noël Valis succinctly puts it: "Matute's literature for children is, above all, a personal expression of reality, a subjective vision which continues and connects with her books written for adults" (408). In her literature for children she pits fantasy against the reality of the adult world. In her adult fiction she uses poetic subjectivity against the reality of an unsatisfactory social situation. In general terms her work can be said to move from a concern with the living conditions of the group to concern with the existential problems of the individual.

Most critics who have dealt with Matute's work point out the poetic subjectivity of her discourse, which contrasts with the more objective writing of her contemporaries. Miguel Delibes, Rafael Sánchez Ferlosio, Jesús Fernández Santos, and others were exploring the possibilities of the novel of social realism and were attempting an objectivity that Matute did not pursue in her writing. Ronald Schwartz has aptly referred to her style as "subjective realism" (116). It could be said that her poetic style places her work askew of her contemporaries' more conventional production. Moreover, it is in the shaping of the content of her novels, rather than in the major themes of her work, that she reveals contradictions and conflicts that are characteristic of female writing. Therefore, while her production is bound thematically to that of the midcentury generation of Spanish writers, the individual's problems are best detected in the deep structures of her novels.

Two concepts developed by American feminist critics appear particularly relevant to an analysis and interpretation of Matute's work. Elaine Showalter has argued that women writers have to contend with the literary guidelines established by males as well as with the feminine life experiences that are the basis of their work. In other words, they must use literary forms that reflect the male perception of reality to convey a message that is the product of their experience as women. This results in literary works characterized by narration on two levels, or what Showalter has termed a "double-voiced discourse."[2] The dominant or overt narrative adheres to the traditional male-established literary conventions, while the submerged or muted narrative is used to communicate a feminine viewpoint. Moreover, because women in the Western world have traditionally been assigned the private sphere of life, one of the first obstacles the female writer must overcome is her inhibition concerning public expression, or what Sandra Gilbert and Susan Gubar identify as "the anxiety of authorship."[3]

To overcome this anxiety of authorship, women writers develop stratagems that distinctly mark their works at the structural level. These stratagems are more or less obvious, depending on the intensity of the conflict the woman writer experiences within herself. Women writers must contend in their expression with a difference that emerges in them when they combine the dependency of traditional femininity with the autonomy of a writer. Being a woman and a writer is contradictory and conflictive. Ana María Matute's subjective poetic style is her individual way of opposing the social order, but that style simultaneously expresses a feminine point of view and camouflages female assertiveness, which was unacceptable in the very repressive ambience of postwar Spain.

The double-voiced discourse manifests itself throughout Matute's work. Generally the second voice of the discourse, the subversive one, is associated with some aspect of the novels' lyricism. The prevalence of this feature indicates that it is central to the deep structures of her literary creations. In fact, an analysis of the variations and changes in this type of discourse reveals a pace of development in her production more closely linked to her difference than to the development of the contemporary Spanish novel.

Matute's works were not always published in the order in which they were written. *Los Abel* was her first published work, but the first novel she wrote was *Pequeño teatro*. In order to trace the development and changes in her literary production, attention must be paid to the order in which her works were written rather than to the order in which they were published. Matute writes initially in search of a voice. This marks a double textual level in her novels: an exterior, more conventional text and an interior, individual text that often contradicts and subverts the first one. The second textual level, the second voice of the double-voiced discourse, carries the repressed content providing the motivation of the main female character. The protagonists of these early works escape their world and the first textual level by slipping into the second one, thus protecting their endangered or threatened interior.

The duality in *Pequeño teatro's* discourse was noticed immediately by critics. About this novel Juan Luis Alborg, for example, wrote: "*Pequeño teatro* possesses a disequilibrium . . . because the author navigates between two waters: one of a reality amassed by a peculiar pulse and that of another 'objective reality' which she does not succeed in portraying satisfactorily" (194). In this work Matute fuses two generic modalities, dramatic (Díaz, "La 'Comedia dell'Arte' ") and lyric, within a narrative model, the bildungsroman or novel of formation. The conflict central to the bildungsroman is between the individual approaching adulthood and the social order into which he or she must be incorporated. In *Pequeño teatro* the narrative model leads the main character to a socially acceptable marriage. On the other hand, the dramatic modality leads her to a resolution based on love. Throughout the novel, Matute presents a counterpoint between the social roles demanded of the characters in a small Basque community, the "objective reality" to which Alborg refers, and those roles they must carry out as dramatic characters, that "other reality amassed by that peculiar pulse."

The opposition of the main character, Zazu, to the performance of either role is carried in *Pequeño teatro* by its lyricism. Zazu resists the social roles demanded of her, and refuses as well to accept the conventional amorous ending of a play. That is to say, she rejects marriage and love, the respective dictates of the narrative and dramatic models that are used in the novel. Finding herself without space, she drowns herself in the sea. She chooses limitless death in the ocean rather than life's constraints and limitations. The suicide is the culmination of Zazu's subjectivity, but it is also the incident that concludes the conflict and the tale. Since the suicide can be read on all levels, it fuses or confuses the poetic and the narrative-dramatic voices of the discourse in this work.

Pequeño teatro, like most of Matute's novels, is subjective. Its lyricism demands narration in the first person, but the suicide of the main character makes it impossible to transmit the story in that manner. To reconcile the subjectivity with the third-person omniscient narration, Matute uses a variable and multiple vision. That is, she divides or separates voice from vision.[4] While the novel is told in the third person by an omniscient narrator, the story is presented from the interior of a different character in each section of the novel. The poetic element in *Pequeño teatro* is contained in those interior visions. The visual poetic discourse is static, and it contradicts and postpones the dynamic narrative discourse.

The second stage in Matute's development is exploratory. She attempts to determine the process whereby an adolescent becomes a woman. The work that best exemplifies this second stage is *Primera memoria*, the first novel of a trilogy entitled *Los mercaderes* ("The Merchants"). The novel is a bildungsroman narrated retrospectively by a mature woman. The double voice emerges from the contrast between the point of view of the adolescent who is living the events and that of the adult woman who is writing about them. In *Pequeño teatro* the opposition to a conventional ending was carried by lyrical interior visions. In *Primera memoria* it is the lyrical and disenchanted tone of the novel that subverts the traditional narrative discourse.

Another difference between these two works is in the resolution of the conflict between interior idealism and the various exterior demands to conform. If the main character in *Pequeño teatro* chooses self-destruction to protect her endangered interior, the character in *Primera memoria* chooses to sacrifice her interior in order to survive externally. Matia, the main character in *Primera memoria*, approaches her entrance into the adult world by accepting its demands, but she enters that world alienated and jaded. Matia accepts and rejects the adult world simultaneously.[5] The writing of the novel could be interpreted as an attempt on the part of the adult narrator to bridge and heal the gap created within the female character at the point of passage from late childhood to early adolescence. This conflict between exterior and interior, between one voice and the other, parallels the conflict in Matute the woman writer.

Once Matute reaches maturity, both personally and professionally, the double-voiced discourse that characterized her early works becomes more explicit and pronounced. The conflict provoked by combining femininity and authorship, which she had to overcome in order to produce, becomes an asset at this point. She openly maintains the duality in her writing and creates a literary space in which there is a dialogue and a counterpoint between the contradictions within her double-voiced discourse. This is evident in *La trampa* (1969; ''The Trap''), a fragmented and structurally complicated novel that demands the reader's active participation.

The narration in *La trampa* is controlled by four consciences that simultaneously present an interior and an exterior tale. However, the subjective voice, which previously remained covered by a conventional text, emerges in this work as the main voice. The conventional narrative becomes functional in that it serves to maintain a connecting thread between the interiors presented. It also provides a contrast that permits the reader to perceive the effect of the past on the present lives of the characters.

Matute's subjectivity is maintained in *La trampa*, the structure of which leans on retrospection and introspection. Here, Matute presents a dialogue between present and past, process and product, disorder and order, maturity and youth, voice and silence, poetic and narrative discourse. Since the fragmentation of the novel invites reader participation, the dialogue is between reader and text as well. In this wide-ranging dialogue, it is the process that is emphasized and that acquires importance, rather than the conclusion to which either the parallel interior or exterior tale may lead. Of the four stories presented simultaneously, none is as significant as their articulation or as the relationship established among them.

La trampa concludes the trilogy *Los mercaderes*. The adult Matia is again the protagonist and one of the four narrating consciences of the novel. Throughout the development of the exterior tale, she writes a diary in which she provides the reader with the past events of her life and with her present concerns. In a feminist analysis of *La trampa*, Linda Gould Levine explains that in her sections of the novel, Matia explores the experience of motherhood in a manner that resembles Matute's relationship with her son: "with one essential difference. Matute has been quoted as saying: 'My son is my reason for living; literature my reason for being.' In Matia's case, neither seems to define her as clearly" (302). Nevertheless, Matia intensely ponders her maternity and engages in the process of writing throughout the novel.

La trampa deals with, and attempts to relate and reconcile, feminine essence and existence. Matute's foregoing statement is, therefore, important to an understanding of this novel. Maternity is a feminine life experience. It is, therefore, an existential experience. Literature in Matute's case, the action of writing in Matia's case, belongs to individual essence. The character and the author define themselves through the process of writing, which affords them the opportunity personally to reinterpret the past.[6] Matute combines in her character Matia maternity and narrative agency, femininity and voice; the creation of the novel emerges from this fusion.

Matute incorporates in her fiction a variety of literary modes and models. For example, elements of the commedia dell'arte[7] appear in *Pequeño teatro*, and Matute revises fairy tales and traditional legends in *Primera memoria* (Anderson). *Los hijos muertos* is a generational novel, and *La torre vigía* is a fantastic medieval tale. Throughout her writing Matute maintains a poetic style. Nevertheless, the literary model that seems to serve her purposes best is the bildungsroman. Even those of her novels that cannot be classified under this category often have embedded subplots that conform to the bildungsroman model. This enables her to deal simultaneously with the social group, with the individual, and, above all, with the conflicts between these two entities.

The devastation of Spain's intellectual world, as a result of the Civil War and its aftermath, left the young midcentury writers without significant and immediate precursors. Matute, being both a woman and a writer, doubtless felt that discontinuity and illegitimacy. The social space she presents in her fiction is not significantly different from that of her contemporaries. Her characters, however, are alienated and disconnected from the group by physical or mental problems, social class, or orphanhood. In other words, her characters are, like her, "different." They lack important links to the social order and acceptable options or places within it. For these reasons, her characters find adjustment costly and difficult, and they experience the passage of time and its demands for change in a negative and traumatic manner.

Matute's thematic concerns, reflected primarily in the social ambiences she creates in her fiction, indicate that her aims were similar to those of her contemporaries, and place her work unquestionably within the same frame. On the other hand, the structures of her novels, the peculiar and subversive combination of literary modes and models, and the prevalence of her poetic vision reveal conflicts, often played out in the experiences of her characters, that can be interpreted as parallel to those of the individual woman writer.

Matute has openly rejected the feminist label (Riddel, Interview). Nevertheless, she has constantly grappled with the contradictions created by her personal and professional life and her maternal and intellectual activities. The reconciliation of oppositions, manifested in her later works by the new dialogical relationship between the narrative voice and the poetic elements of her discourse, indicates that she has succeeded in accommodating femininity and autonomy.

SURVEY OF CRITICISM

Matute is one of several midcentury writers who has received considerable attention from Spanish and non-Spanish critics alike. Many of her works have been translated into various languages and published abroad. There is a large body of criticism dealing with every aspect of her literary production as well as several doctoral dissertations devoted to her work. The two most comprehensive works in English are *Ana María Matute*, by Janet W. Díaz, and *The Literary World of Ana María Matute*, by Margaret E. W. Jones. Both books provide a wealth of factual information and concern themselves with Matute's recurrent themes and narrative style. They differ in their organization and emphasize different details or aspects of her fiction. Nevertheless, the analytical and interpretative approaches of the two works are quite similar.

Matute is one of the few female writers whose work is treated in virtually all books dealing with contemporary Spanish literary history. Literary critics of the stature of Gonzalo Sobejano, Juan Luis Alborg, Eugenio de Nora, José María Martínez Cachero, and others have acknowledged her contribution to the contemporary Spanish novel and to the intellectual regeneration of postwar Spain. Until recently, however, her work has generally been considered as part of the Spanish postwar novel at large, and has been analyzed and interpreted from a traditional perspective. Critics have pointed out Matute's preoccupation with certain themes, and have established the similarities and differences between her works and those of other writers. The relationship between her literature for children and her adult fiction has been noted. The autobiographical elements in her novels also have been researched, and there have been several analyses of her style.

Matute's literary production has been, on the whole, judged favorably by critics, but largely in terms of its conformity to established literary standards and models. Almost all critics agree that Matute's novels have many points in common with those of her contemporaries, but most of them would also agree with Díaz's statement that "Matute's style has always been extremely personal and subjective, dominated by primarily a lyric vision of reality, or a deceptive childlike conception" (*A.M.M.* 146). Sometimes that extremely personal and subjective style is considered an asset. Alborg maintains that none of her novels can be judged completely successful, but that lack of success should be over-looked in view of the excellent quality of her personal tone and narrative style (192). At other times, the elements of her subjective style have been considered a defect. Some of her works—*Pequeño teatro*, for example—have been perceived as arbitrary, lacking verisimilitude, and being overly fantastic (Nora 293–94). Others, such as *Los soldados lloran de noche* (1964; ''The Soldiers Cry by Night''), have been criticized for not giving formal plot much importance (Díaz *A.M.M.* 135, 146).

Matute's work is now being reconsidered in the light of new literary theory. Feminist literary criticism in particular is furnishing scholars with new perspectives from which to approach her work. Critics such as Linda Gould Levine, Michael S. Doyle, Geraldine Cleary Nichols, and others have published articles that analyze the structures of her novels and interpret their meaning according to recent literary, social, and feminist concerns.

From this later perspective, Matute transformed her initial disadvantage, her ''difference,'' into a literary and artistic asset. The repression of content in her work necessitated the subversion of forms and, therefore, in many instances more elaborate writing than that of her male contemporaries. While critics have explored many aspects of her works, few have paid much attention to the broad range of problems and conflicts inherent in writings by women that manifest themselves in her novels. A thorough study of the structures of these novels and a persuasive and feminist interpretation of her literary production are yet to be done. New critical perspectives open up the possibility of a rereading of Matute's production. This rereading may shed some light on the relationship between the woman writer and the contemporary Spanish novel, and it may also lead to a fairer and more accurate assessment of Matute's contribution to the development of the postwar novel in Spain.

NOTES

1. Janet W. Díaz, *Ana María Matute* (New York: Twayne, 1971); and Margaret E. W. Jones, *The Literary World of Ana María Matute* (Lexington: UP of Kentucky, 1970). All the biographical information on Matute and most of the bibliographical information on her work were obtained from these two sources.

2. Elaine Showalter, ''Feminist Criticism in the Wilderness,'' *The New Feminist Criticism: Essays on Women Literature and Theory*, ed. Elaine Showalter (New York: Pantheon Books, 1985), 263. The term ''double-voiced discourse'' was borrowed from Susan Lanser and Marilyn Beck. However, Showalter has further elaborated the concept.

3. Sandra Gilbert and Susan Gubar, *The Mad Woman in the Attic: The Woman Writer and the Nineteenth Century Imagination* (New Haven: Yale UP, 1979) 49–51.

4. Gerard Genette, *Narrative Discourse: An Essay in Method*, trans. Jane E. Lewin (Ithaca, NY: Cornell UP, 1980) 186, 192.

5. Elizabeth Abel, Marianne Hirsch, and Elizabeth Langland, eds., *The Voyage In: Fictions in Female Development* (Hanover, NH: UP of New England, 1983) 12. In the introduction to this book, the editors state: ''The tensions that shape female development

may lead to a disjunction between surface plot, which affirms social conventions, and a submerged plot, which encodes rebellion.''

6. Joanne S. Frye, *Living Stories, Telling Lives: Women and the Novel in Contemporary Experience* (Ann Arbor: U of Michigan P, 1986) 110. Frye states: "the protagonist's act of self-narration provides a crucial aspect to . . . subversive representation: as she recognizes that her past life has been lived in relation to the cultural grid, her claim to narrative agency gives her the capacity to reinterpret her previous experience as a basis for a new self-definition.''

7. The commedia dell'arte was a type of theater that did not rely on a written script. Prior to a performance, professional actors agreed on stock situations involving common characters then improvised their lines on stage. It developed in Italy during the sixteenth century and became very popular. Eventually it spread and influenced theater throughout Europe.

BIBLIOGRAPHY

Major Works by Ana María Matute

Novels

Los Abel. Barcelona: Ediciones Destino, 1948.
Pequeño teatro. Barcelona: Editorial Planeta, 1954.
En esta tierra. Barcelona: Editorial Exito, 1955.
Los hijos muertos. Barcelona: Editorial Planeta, 1958.
Primera memoria. Barcelona: Ediciones Destino, 1960.
Los soldados lloran de noche. Barcelona: Ediciones Destino, 1964.
La trampa. Barcelona: Ediciones Destino, 1969.
La torre vigía. Barcelona: Editorial Lumen, 1971.

Short Novels and Short Stories

Los niños tontos. Madrid: Ediciones Arión, 1956.
El tiempo. Barcelona: Editorial Mateu, 1957.
Fiesta al noroeste. Barcelona: Pareja y Borrás, 1959. [Short novel]
El arrepentido. Barcelona: Editorial Rocas, 1961.
Historias de la Artámila. Barcelona: Destino, 1961.
Libro de juegos para los niños de otros. Barcelona: Editorial Lumen, 1961.
Tres y un sueño. Barcelona: Editorial Destino, 1961. [Short novel]
Algunos muchachos. Barcelona: Ediciones Destino, 1969.
La virgen de Antioquía y otros relatos. Madrid: Narrativa Mondadori, 1990.

Children's Fiction

Paulina, el mundo y las estrellas. Barcelona: Editorial Garbo, 1960.
El país de la pizarra. Barcelona: Editorial Molino, 1961.
Caballito loco. Barcelona: Editorial Lumen, 1962.
El polizón del Ulises. Barcelona: Editorial Lumen, 1965.
Sólo un pie descalzo. Barcelona: Editorial Lumen, 1983.

Miscellaneous

A la mitad del camino. Barcelona: Editorial Rocas, 1961.
El río. Barcelona: Editorial Argos, 1963.

Translations

Awakening. Trans. James H. Mason. New York: Hutchison, 1963. [Trans. of *Primera memoria*]
The Lost Children. Trans. Joan MacLean. New York: Macmillan, 1963.
School of the Sun. Trans. Elaine Kerrigan. New York: Pantheon, 1963. Rpt. New York: Columbia UP, 1989. [Trans. of *Primera memoria*]
The Heliotrope Wall and Other Stories. Trans. Michael S. Doyle. New York: Columbia UP, 1989. [Trans. of *Algunos muchachos*]

Works about Ana María Matute

Alborg, Juan Luis. *Hora actual de la novela española*. Vol. 1. Madrid: Taurus, 1958.
Anderson, Christopher L. "*Primera memoria*: A Fairy Tale Gone Awry." Conference on Romance Languages and Literatures. U of Cincinnati, 14 May 1987.
Atlee, A. F. Michael. "El enigma de Ana María Matute." *Explicación de Textos Literarios* 3.1 (1984–85): 35–42.
Brown, Joan Lipman. "Unidad y diversidad en *Los mercaderes* de Ana María Matute." *Novelistas femeninas de la postguerra española*. Ed. Janet Pérez. Madrid: José Porrúa Turanzas, 1983. 19–32.
Burns, Adelaide. "The Anguish of Ana María Matute in *Los mercaderes*." *Hispanic Studies in Honour of Joseph Manson*. Ed. Dorothy M. Atkinson and Anthony H. Clarke. Oxford: The Dolphin Book Co., 1972. 21–42.
Díaz, Janet W. *Ana María Matute*. New York: Twayne Publishers, Inc., 1971.
———. "The Autobiographical Element in the Works of Ana María Matute." *Kentucky Romance Quarterly* 15 (1968): 139–48.
———. "La 'Commedia dell'Arte' en una novela de Ana María Matute." *Hispanófila* 40 (Sept. 1970): 15–28.
———. "Variantes del arquetipo femenino en la narrativa de Ana María Matute." *Letras Femeninas* 10.2 (Fall 1984): 28–39.
Domingo, José. "Análisis de una sociedad conformista." *Insula*. 274 (Sept. 1969): 7.
Doyle, Michael Scott. "Trace-Reading the Story of Matia/Matute in *Los mercaderes*." *Revista de Estudios Hispánicos* 19.2 (May 1985): 57–70.
El Saffar, Ruth. "En busca del Edén: Consideraciones sobre la obra de Ana María Matute." *Revista Iberoamericana* 47. 116–117 (July–Dec. 1981): 223–31.
Flores-Jenkins, Raquel. "El mundo de los niños en la obra de Ana María Matute." *Explicación de Textos Literarios* 3.2 (1975): 185–190.
Gómez-Gil, Alfredo. "Ana María Matute (N. en Barcelona, 1926)." *Cuadernos Americanos* 178.5 (Sept.–Oct. 1971): 250–54.
Jones, Margaret W. "Antipathetic Phallacy: The Hostile World of Ana María Matute." *Kentucky Foreign Language Quarterly* Supp. 13 (1967): 15–16.

———. *The Literary World of Ana María Matute*. Lexington: The University Press of Kentucky, 1970.

———. "Religious Motifs and Biblical Allusions in the Works of Ana María Matute." *Hispania* 155.3 (Sept. 1968): 416–423.

———. "Temporal Patterns in the Works of Ana María Matute." *Romance Notes* 12.2 (Spring 1971): 282–88.

Kubayanda, José. "*La torre vigía* de Ana María Matute: Aproximación a una narrativa alegórica." *Estudios Hispánicos* 16.3 (Oct. 1982): 333–45.

Levine, Linda Gould. "The Censored Sex: Woman as Author and Character in Franco's Spain." *Women in Hispanic Literature: Icons and Fallen Idols*. Ed. Beth Miller. Berkeley: U of California P, 1983. 289–315.

Marra-López, José Ramón. "Novelas y cuentos." *Insula* 186 (1962): 4.

Martínez Cachero, José María. *Historia de la novela española entre 1936 y 1975*. Madrid: Editorial Castalia, 1979.

Martínez Palacio, Javier. "Una trilogía novelística de Ana María Matute." *Insula* 219 (Feb. 1965): 1, 6, 7.

Nichols, Geraldine Cleary. "Modes of Exclusion, Modes of Equivocation: Matute's *Primera memoria*." *Ideologies and Literature* 1.1–2 (1985): 156–87.

———. "Privation in Matute's Fiction for Children." *Symposium* 39.2 (Summer 1985): 125–38.

Nora, Eugenio de. *La novela española contemporánea*. Vol 2. Madrid: Gredos, 1962.

Núñez, Antonio. "Encuentro con Ana María Matute." *Insula* 219 (Feb. 1965): 7.

Ordóñez, Elizabeth. "Forms of Alienation in Matute's *La trampa*." *Journal of Spanish Studies* 4 (Winter 1976): 179–89.

Ortega, José. "La frustración femenina en *Los mercaderes* de Ana María Matute." *Hispanófila* (U of North Carolina) 54 (May 1975): 31–38.

Riddel, María Carmen. Personal interview with Ana María Matute. Barcelona, 12 July 1985.

Rovira, Rosalina R. "La función de la mujer en la literatura contemporánea española." *Explicación de Textos Literarios* 3.1 (1974): 21–24.

Schwartz, Ronald. "Ana María Matute and *Primera memoria*." *Spain's New Wave Novelists*. Metuchen, NJ: Scarecrow Press, 1976. 113–31.

Shelby, J. Townsend. "Retrospection as a Technique in Matute's *Los hijos muertos* and *En esta tierra*." *Revista de Estudios Hispánicos* 14.2 (1980): 81–95.

Sobejano, Gonzalo. *Novela española de nuestro tiempo*. Madrid: Editorial Prensa Española, 1975.

Spires, Robert C. "Lenguaje-técnica-tema y la experiencia del lector en *Fiesta al noroeste*." *Papeles de Son Armadans* 70. 289 (1973): 17–36.

Stevens, James R. "Myth and Memory: Ana María Matute's *Primera memoria*." *Symposium* 25. 2 (Summer 1971): 198–203.

Valis, Noël. "La literatura infantil de Ana María Matute." *Cuadernos Hispanoamericanos* 389 (November 1982): 407–15.

Winecoff, Janet. "Style and Solitude in the Works of Ana María Matute." *Hispania* 39.1 (March 1966): 61–69.

Wythe, George. "The World of Ana María Matute." *Books Abroad* 40 (1966): 17–28.

Zatlin-Boring, Phyllis. "The World of Childhood in the Contemporary Spanish Novel." *Kentucky Romance Quarterly* 23 (1976): 467–79.

JULIA MAURA
(1906–1971)

Patricia W. O'Connor

BIOGRAPHY

Julia Maura y Herrera was born on April 5, 1906, in the family's Madrid home on the Calle de la Lealtad (subsequently renamed Antonio Maura). She was the third of five children of Julia Herrera y Herrera, countess of Mortera, and Gabriel Maura y Gamazo, duke of Maura. Her paternal grandfather, Antonio Maura, who was particularly influential in his granddaughter's life, was head of the Conservative Party, prime minister to Alfonso XIII, and president of the government. He was named to the Royal Academies of Language, History, and Jurisprudence.

Because of her mother's fragile health, the family spent more time in their mountain retreat in the Sierra de Guadarrama than in Madrid. There, Julia enjoyed a privileged education with private tutors, engaged in numerous imaginative games with her siblings, and began to write stories based on her observations. As a teenager, she traveled abroad extensively with her family, and after her debut at about age sixteen, made Madrid her home. In 1931 Julia Maura married Andrés Covarrubias Castillo, marquis of Villatoya, with whom she had five children. In a 1990 conversation with Maura's eldest son, the current marquis of Villatoya recalled that although his mother was first and foremost a loving, caring parent, she was also a witty, fun-loving, and brilliant conversationalist.

Scant personal information appears in standard biographical references, but in the opening essay of *Estos son mis artículos* (1953; "These Are My Articles"), Julia Maura conducts a mock interview with herself. Her statements, as well as her writings, suggest that she both respected and resented the "angel-in-the-house" model of feminine virtue. Nevertheless, in her mock interview, Maura foregrounds the wife and mother rather than the author. Claiming that her writing

is a pastime and affirming that she is merely a "good mother"—comments
solidly in the tradition of the genteel "lady author"—Maura states that she is
neither envious nor proud, precisely because she does not take her professional
life seriously. Her principal aspiration is, she says, a continued peaceful home
life. Demonstrating ambivalence, however, she adds that she would also love
to create a play powerful enough to bring an audience to its feet, whether in
admiration or in protest. The confrontational nature of the interview underlines
the division between Maura's private and public personae. This wealthy, titled
woman, member of an important, conservative family, might well have misgiv-
ings about the propriety of her public expression, of working and receiving
money, and of taking time from family and social obligations to write.

Although Maura wrote numerous newspaper articles, essays, short stories,
and novels, she is best known for her plays. The most-performed female dramatist
of the post–Civil War period, Maura saw approximately twenty of her works
produced between 1944 and 1967. Despite—or perhaps because of—her considerable professional success, she suffered disappointments and reverses. Although treated as an exotic newcomer early in her career, she later felt that critics
had turned on her and were determined to silence her. She was able to prove,
for example, that negative reviews of her work had been written before critics
had even seen the performances. Furthermore, in 1953, a widely publicized
accusation that Maura had plagiarized Oscar Wilde in three *ABC* articles sparked
rumors that she had never written anything, that she had in her employ a male
ghost writer. Maura explained that her use of Wilde's words to criticize the
critics was a trap set for her enemies in the press to see if they would attack
her; the plan was then to reveal the true author when she was attacked. In one
of her short pieces, "Era un jardín sonriente ("Once upon a Time, in a Smiling
Garden"), included in *Artículos de fe* (1959; "Articles of Faith"), Maura uses
a touching allegory to describe her painful experience.

MAJOR THEMES

Many of Julia Maura's works have provincial rather than urban settings;
involve aristocratic, powerful, or wealthy characters; focus on gender and/or
generational issues; utilize humor; and are written in conventional forms. Although superficial or random readings of Maura's works might suggest acquiescence to patriarchal values, through a series of "dark doubles" as well as
through authoritative male voices, Maura demonstrates rebellion at the same
time that she illustrates the classic "anxiety of authorship" that marks so much
of women's writings.[1] By means of traditional and well-crafted plots, she often
questions her own identity as well as the established male order. Expressing
ambivalence and seeming to confront herself in the role of "angel" or "monster," Maura gives lip service to some conventions of her time and class while
clearly opposing others. She consistently writes of strong, mature, intelligent,
virtuous, and proud women tested by envy, gossip, and male prejudice. Innocent

of the accusations against them, these women, like Iphigenia, Antigone, and Ophelia before them, are punished. Although not offered up on altars, buried alive, or ordered to a nunnery, Maura's female characters implicitly suffer unjust punishments.

Unable to free herself of guilt for her presumption and pride, Maura seems to play out inner conflicts in various scenarios. In curious foreshadowings of—and subsequent reflections on—her own fate after the plagiarism scandal, Maura's heroines often end their lives isolated and silenced. Having internalized many of the values of her time and social class, Maura often emphasizes the ennobling and stabilizing aspects of motherhood as well as the willingness of women to sacrifice for their children. Although few works deal with courtship per se, the social necessity of marriage for women is conceded. Marriage relationships, however, are rarely satisfactory, and the double standard is accepted as inevitable. Maura's women philosophically resign themselves to men's transgressions as a cross they must bear, and consistently place family above self. Many of her works focus on unchanging values in contrast to relatively minor cosmetic adjustments observable between generations.

The writer (frequently female) and the "old maid" are recurring images through which Maura shows her ambivalence, alternately humanizing and reinforcing negative stereotypes. Male characters, less developed than the female ones, are generally womanizing, selfish, brutal, proud, opportunistic, childish, and weak. Several minor male figures, however, depart from tradition to express progressive positions in defense of women. Maura may have chosen to speak through male characters to utilize the masculine "voice of authority" as well as to avoid association with a potentially feminist position. Speaking through a male alter ego may also have been a liberating fantasy for this talented, driven woman, limited by her social, geographical, and historical circumstances. Not surprisingly, Maura's defenses of women expressed in her articles and essays are cleverly diplomatic.

Maura's first play, *La mentira del silencio* (1944; "The Lie of Silence"), establishes certain paradigms—including the silencing of women—that subtly subvert the patriarchal order. Irene, a beautiful, proud woman approaching forty, is the heroic figure. Although she is of humble origins, her beauty and intelligence attract the attention of the wealthy Eduardo, who, against the wishes of his aristocratic family, marries her. As the play opens, Eduardo has shot and killed his business associate, Jorge, because the latter had learned that Eduardo was stealing from the company. After discovering the circumstances of the crime, the defense lawyer concludes that the only way to save Eduardo's life and the family's reputation is to prove that the murder was a crime of passion.

To establish his case, lawyer Albareda fabricates an affair between Irene and Jorge. Irene, faithful despite an imperfect relationship with an immature husband, is proud of her virtue and hesitates to be a party to a lie that will not only destroy her reputation but also damage the relationship with her son, a student in London. Albareda argues that acknowledging the father's crime will have permanent and disastrous repercussions on the son's life; he claims that not only will the "sin" of the woman be accepted as "normal," but that an immoral mother is preferable to a criminal father. The lawyer insists that his fictitious defense scenario has negative consequences only if a daughter is involved, thereby suggesting that a "philandering gene" presents no problem for male children.

Only when the attorney convinces Irene that her son will suffer if the truth is told does Irene relent. She agrees to maintain silence. When called to testify as planned, Eduardo tells the truth about the murder but is believed by no one; indeed, many see him as the heroic gentleman willing to sacrifice himself in order to protect his wife's reputation. The truly admirable and strong character is, of course, Irene—in sharp contrast to the men.

La eterna doña Juana (1954; "The Eternal Femme Fatale") is a play inspired by Vicki Baum's novel *Grand Opera* (1942). The title character and protagonist is Sandra Vali, one of Maura's "dark doubles." An aging diva, Sandra is in Barcelona briefly to sing the title role in *Carmen*. Like her stereotypical male counterpart, Don Juan, she strongly attracts those of the opposite sex, whom she manipulates to her advantage. Although Maura does not portray Sandra as evil, she does show her as a misguided, pathetic, and ultimately unfeminine career woman. Having repressed her maternal instinct, Sandra has chosen not to acknowledge the existence of her only child in order to maintain as long as possible the youthful, sophisticated image favorable to her career. The daughter Sandra hardly knows, now an adult, is married, pregnant, and abandoned by her husband. Because the daughter knows of Sandra's power over men, she pleads with her to convince the husband to return. Having agreed to help, Sandra invites the son-in-law to her dressing room without revealing their relationship. In a curious and slightly daring (for the times) twist, the husband, long attracted to Sandra as an international celebrity, attempts to seduce his mother-in-law. In the course of Sandra's eventually successful maneuver to get the husband to return to her daughter, she recovers some maternal instinct and is thus partially redeemed in the eyes of conservative theatergoers.

Maura's first play after the plagiarism scandal, *La riada* (1956; "The Torrent"), alludes to this searing episode in her life. Although she continued to write and publish sporadically after this scandal, it is interesting to note that in *La riada* she reflects the shame and embarrassment she experienced at the hands of critics and journalists, but transfers these feelings to a village woman victimized by envy and gossip. The play's protagonist, Inés, long married to Antonio, the village's leading cattleman, causes tongues to wag when she leaves a red carnation on the casket at the austere burial of Víctor, the local Don Juan. In reality, and contrary to the public belief that she and Víctor had been lovers, Inés had placed the flower there as an expression of gratitude for a compliment he had paid her on her beauty. As a village woman no longer young, she had appreciated the reassurance provided by the gesture.

Antonio, the stereotypical, overbearing, and brutal husband who demands obedience and absolute decorum from his wife, considers himself dishonored by murmured suggestions that Inés and Víctor were lovers. Unconvinced by Inés's passionate declaration of innocence, Antonio becomes suspicious of an employee long respectfully devoted to Inés and kills him. This violence coincides with the resolution of the mystery surrounding Víctor's death: it is revealed that a young girl killed Víctor in self-defense when he attempted to rape her. As the play ends and the police lead Antonio away, Inés declares, Bernarda Alba style, that her house will henceforth be sealed and the sound of evil tongues will never again penetrate her fortress-prison home. The villagers, envious of Inés's beauty and position, have their revenge, and social ills continue unchanged.

Although this rural melodrama implies that patriarchy is a root cause of women's suffering and isolation, foregrounded are such specific symptoms and results as gossip, envy, and pride. Violence, including rape, is portrayed as a fact of life for women, and the admirably strong protagonist, an earthy, beautiful woman, becomes a victim partially because she has internalized the system that attributes value to women on the basis of youth and beauty.

Jaque a la juventud (1965; "Warning to Youth") is a departure in several ways from Maura's earlier works. Urban in setting and contemporary in mood, this play does not have a female protagonist but features composite characters representative of two generations. The ambivalent note characteristic of much of Maura's work is accentuated here. The central conflict revolves around the pregnancy of María, the unmarried daughter of a well-to-do family. To complicate the traditional solution, the father of the expected baby is already married. The various reactions to María's problem reveal shifting values and the clash of two generations: one currently in power, and the other anxious to assume control.

The play suggests that the young people, victims of rapidly changing social patterns, need more parental supervision. It also positively presents the charitable solution to María's problem suggested by the young people: to acknowledge the pregnancy openly, accept the blameless new member of the family, and hope that María will one day find love and happiness. The final decision, however, involves the purchase of a husband: María's opportunistic, flippant, womanizing cousin Tano. Once again the woman, victimized by the paternalistic system, is doomed to live a lonely existence because of the perceived sin. No blame is attached to the father of the baby, nor is there any hint that he has any responsibility to María or his child. Furthermore, the materialistic new husband prospers. Freed of all financial worries, he may now devote himself to pleasure within the limits of discretion.

Maura's three novels of the 1940s, written in a style reminiscent of earlier decades, contain the most conservative portraits of—and patriarchal asides on—women. The most conventional is *Como la tierra y el mar* (1945; "Like Land and Sea"). Here newlywed María gazes happily at the wedding ring that symbolizes the realization of her lifelong dream: to be a married woman. Thinking back to her progressive education in a French boarding school, she recalls that even there young girls were taught the importance of pleasing a man. The narrator frequently interrupts the narrative flow to digress about the natural inclinations and social constructs that account for the behavior of men and women. This ungendered narrator accepts without question the spiritual superiority of men, and women's inability to be generous when dealing with their assumed natural enemies, other women. The narrator does find, however, that women mature, never to return to their childish ways, while men are forever immature and in need of the guidance of the wife/mother. This judgmental voice advises women to overlook men's transgressions with maternal indulgence while it defends husbands' rights to enjoy the company of members of the opposite sex, a right never extended to wives.

In *¡Quién supiera escribir!* (1945; "If Only I Could Write!"), more a series of short stories than a novel, Maura employs a descriptive style reminiscent of the turn of the century in which a third-person omniscient narrator offers moralizing vignettes of provincial life. The first two chapters introduce an authorial "dark double," Rosario, the frustrated writer of the framing device that gives structural unity to a series of intercalated stories. Ill-humored Rosario, married and living in rural Extremadura, attributes her "writer's block" to lackluster surroundings. One day she sees the announcement of a series of lectures in Madrid for novice writers. Since her husband—pleased to be free of his shrewish wife for a few days—offers no objections, Rosario departs for Madrid.

Anticipating the revelation of creative secrets that will launch her on a successful course as a novelist, Rosario arrives early for the first lecture. Disappointed with its content, however, she requests an appointment with the speaker. In the course of their conversation, the male authority figure (and the masculine mask of the author) details Maura's writing philosophy as he advises her to observe her surroundings carefully, use material from her life, and emphasize human inclinations—love, hate, envy, greed—as a source of inspiration. When Rosario returns to Extremadura, she attempts to use her neighbors as points of departure for her novel. Lacking both empathy and imagination, however, she fails. The framing device now complete, Maura's male alter ego/narrator takes up the pen to demonstrate in six stories how Rosario has failed to recognize the excellent material of her surroundings.

Maura wrote numerous short stories and essays in the course of her career. *Eva y la vida* (1950; "Eve and Life") contains ten short stories that illustrate traditionally assumed feminine virtues and vices, while *Estos son mis artículos* is a collection of forty brief articles, most of which had already appeared in newspapers and magazines. In a succinct prologue, Maura dedicates this volume to detractors as well as to fans and addresses the accusation of plagiarism. Among the many themes treated, those most repeated involve women and the art of writing. *Artículos de fe* offers over one hundred short essays on a variety of subjects. Several of these pieces indirectly ridicule male supremacist attitudes. *Historias crueles* (1963; "Cruel Stories") is a volume of six short stories. Probably a projection of Maura's own psychological state, the women in most of the stories are bitterly disappointed.

Although Julia Maura produced a few lighthearted, witty comedies, novels, and prose pieces, much of her work is serious. Insightful in creating compelling characters, adept at producing tightly structured plays, and equally brilliant at producing taut, realistic dialogue, she consistently illustrates ambivalence characteristic of women writers' "anxiety of authority." In the latter regard, Maura both verbally defends—principally in novels and short stories—and negatively portrays male supremacist attitudes. Woman-centered, her works primarily depict domestic problems of Spanish women of the period, caught between the dictates of social customs—forged to serve the interests of men—and their own need for personal autonomy. Strong and intelligent, these characters are consistently frustrated, limited, and silenced. Principal antagonists are rigid expectations that women must marry; must suffer the infidelities of philandering husbands; must be obedient, self-effacing wives; and must be the models as well as the guardians of morality. Lies, slander, and envy appear again and again as crosses that talented, assertive women unjustly bear.

Wealthy, titled, and a member of one of Spain's most prestigious families, Maura had no practical need to prove herself professionally or economically. She was driven, however, to write in a time and place in which both her social position and her gender worked against her; feminine expression in Spanish theater was difficult and rare, while envy and male chauvinism were commonplace. After the plagiarism accusation of 1953, Maura increasingly withdrew from writing, and her final works reflect understandable disillusionment and bitterness.

SURVEY OF CRITICISM

There are no books or major studies devoted to Julia Maura. Some theater historians mention her briefly, and she is included in the more complete literary biobibliographical encyclopedias and dictionaries of Spanish literature. Critics treat her as a commercially successful dramatist of the Franco era who was a follower more than a leader. Important biographical and historical information is contained in interviews by Marino Gómez-Santos published in the Madrid newspaper *Pueblo* in 1960.

Gonzalo Torrente Ballester fails to mention Maura in his review of Spanish theater of the first half of the twentieth century, *Teatro español contemporáneo* (1957). In his detailed *Historia del teatro español* (1975), Francisco Ruiz Ramón summarizes Julia Maura's theater in one sentence: "The sentimental comedy of manners or minor thesis play is represented in the theater of Julia Maura" (318). In a prologue to Maura's *Artículos de fe*, José María Pemán, a respected writer of conservative views, patronizes Maura as he praises her articles for, among other things, their "frivolity," a quality often negatively associated with women writers but one he finds "convenient for making intelligence tolerable" (7).

In *Cuentistas de hoy* (1952), Mario B. Rodríguez describes Maura's style as "simple and concise" (34), and he attributes to her a keen understanding of feminine psychology as well as skill in portraying scenes of daily life. Curiously,

Janet Pérez makes no reference to Maura in her *Contemporary Women Writers of Spain* (1988), probably because she limited her study—the title notwithstanding—to novelists. Patricia W. O'Connor provides a brief overview of her work in both *Dramaturgas españolas de hoy* (1988) and "Women Playwrights in Contemporary Spain and the Male-Dominated Canon" (1990); in "Lark in a Hostile Garden" (1992), she discusses the plagiarism scandal.

Because of the superior quality of her works, her position as a pioneer woman dramatist, the vision of female experiences her works document, and the unjust treatment she has received at the hands of envious, biased critics, Julia Maura deserves an enlightened reevaluation and greater acknowledgment.

NOTE

1. "Dark doubles" are negative authorial projections that dramatize self-fragmentation by seeming both to accept and to reject patriarchal strictures. See Sandra Gilbert and Susan Gubar, *The Madwoman in the Attic* (New Haven: Yale UP, 1979) 78. In the same work Gilbert and Gubar define the "anxiety of authorship" as a pervasive but barely conscious feeling of inadequacy felt by women who sense that their creative activity is inappropriate (51).

BIBLIOGRAPHY

Works by Julia Maura

La mentira del silencio. Madrid: Biblioteca Teatral, 1944.
Ventolera. Madrid: Aguilar, 1944.
Como la tierra y el mar. Madrid: Aguilar, 1945.
¡Quién supiera escribir! Madrid: Aguilar, 1945. [A series of short stories]
Eva y la vida. Madrid: Aguilar, Ediciones Cristol, 1950. [Short stories]
Siempre. Madrid: Alfil, 1952.
Chocolate a la española. Madrid: Alfil, 1953.
Estos son mis artículos. Madrid: Aguilar, 1953. [Short essays]
La eterna doña Juana. Madrid: Alfil, 1954.
La riada. Madrid: Alfil, 1956.
Artículos de fe. Madrid: A. Vassallo, 1959. [Short essays]
Historias crueles. Madrid: Aguilar, 1963. [Short essays]
Jaque a la juventud. Madrid: Alfil, 1965.

Unpublished Plays

"Lo que piensan los hombres." 1945.
"¿Dónde estará la verdad?" 1946.
"La sin pecado." 1947.
"El placer de los dioses." 1948.
"El mal amor." 1950.
"El mañana no está escrito." 1952.

"Poker de damas." 1953. [With Manuel Martínez Remis]
"La calumnia." 1965.
"Un crimen de abril y mayo." 1966.

Works about Julia Maura

Gómez-Santos, Marino. "Julia Maura cuenta su vida." *Pueblo* 21 (July 1960): n.p.
———. *La tijera literaria: Enciclopedia histórico-antológica de las más famosas obras en lengua castellana*. Madrid: Siglo Ilustrado, 1972.
O'Connor, Patricia W. *Dramaturgas españolas de hoy*. Madrid: Fundamentos, 1988.
———. "Lark in a Hostile Garden." *Estudios sobre escritoras hispánicas en honor de Georgina Sabat-Rivers*. Ed. Lou Charnon-Deutsch. Madrid: Castalia, 1992. 233–45.
———. "Women Dramatists in Contemporary Spain and the Male-Dominated Canon." *Signs* 15.2 (Winter 1990): 376–90.
Pemán, José María. Prologue. *Artículos de fe*. By Julia Maura. Madrid: A. Vassallo, 1959.
Rodríguez, Mario B. *Cuentistas de hoy*. Boston: Houghton Mifflin, 1952.
Ruiz Ramón, Francisco. *Historia del teatro español: Siglo XX*. Madrid: Alianza Editorial, 1975.

MARINA MAYORAL
(b. 1942)

Concha Alborg

BIOGRAPHY

Marina Mayoral was born in Mondoñedo, Lugo, in the province of Galicia in 1942. She studied in Santiago de Compostela before going to Madrid, where she received a doctorate in Romance Philology at the Universidad Complutense. She also holds a degree in psychology from the Escuela de Madrid. Since 1978 she has taught Spanish literature at the Universidad Complutense. She also spent a year as a visiting professor at the University of Pennsylvania. She was married to the well-known literary critic Andrés Amorós, with whom she had two sons. She is now married to Jordi Teixidor, an accomplished painter from Valencia, with whom she lives in Madrid.

Mayoral's research activities have been many. She has focused her attention on the Galician writers Rosalía de Castro and Emilia Pardo Bazán, with whom she feels a sense of kinship based on common love for their native land. Her studies on the post-Romantic poet include *La poesía de Rosalía de Castro* (1974; "The Poetry of Rosalía de Castro"), which was her doctoral dissertation; *Rosalía de Castro y sus sombras* (1976; "Rosalía de Castro and Her Shadows"); and a critical edition of *En las orillas del Sar* (1978). In addition, she has prepared the critical editions of several works of Pardo Bazán: *Cuentos y novelas de la tierra* (1984), *Los pazos de Ulloa* (1986), *Insolación* (1987), and *Dulce dueño* (1989). Mayoral's approach to these two writers is not feminist and could even be called phallic, considering her frequent utilization of Freud and other masculine points of view.

In 1979, her reputation as a literary critic established, Mayoral began publishing novels that were well received by the press. She was soon considered one of the most promising of the new women novelists by such critics as Carmen

Martín Gaite, Manuel Cerezales, and Concha Castroviejo. Prior to this date, she had written a few short stories that she subsequently published in *Morir en sus brazos y otros cuentos* (1989; ''To Die in His Arms and Other Stories''). Her first novel, *Cándida otra vez* (1979; ''Cándida Once Again''), won the second prize of Ámbito Literario, an innovative publishing house; the novella *Plantar un árbol* (1981; ''To Plant a Tree'') earned her the Gabriel Sijé de Novela Corta Prize and *Al otro lado* (1981; ''On the Other Side'') was awarded the Novelas y Cuentos Prize. The two novels that immediately followed are lengthier: *La única libertad* (1982; ''The Only Liberty'') and *Contra muerte y amor* (1985; ''Against Love and Death''), a finalist for the Planeta Prize. Mayoral considers writing fiction her primary goal; she is mainly interested in historic themes and science fiction (Alborg, Interview). She has recently started to publish in Galician: *Unha árbore, un adeus* (1988; ''A Tree, a Goodbye''), a longer version of *Plantar un árbol*; *O reloxio da torre* (1988; ''The Tower's Clock''); and *Chamábase Lluís* (1989; ''His Name Was Luis'').

MAJOR THEMES

A first reading of Mayoral's novels reveals common threads: some of the same characters reappear, story lines continue, and all have the presence of Galicia as an unmistakable characteristic. The first two novels, *Cándida otra vez* and *Plantar un árbol*, take place in Mayoral's native land. The author has created, in the fashion of Juan Benet or Gabriel García Márquez, a fictitious town, Brétema, which embodies all that is meaningfully Galician for her: a semifeudal society where social classes are still very much in place. Although she admittedly is not concerned with social commentary, it is evident in Mayoral's novels that inequities exist between the working class and the privileged class, exemplified in *Contra muerte y amor* by the poor section of Brétema, La Tolda, and the well-to-do neighborhood, La Rosaleda. Even when the novels take place in Madrid, as in the case of *Al otro lado* and *Contra muerte y amor*, the characters are always Galician and their childhood and adolescence weigh heavily on them, determining their lives as adults in the big city.

The themes in Mayoral's novels are the traditional ones of liberty, death, and love as suggested in her titles. Death seems to be the most prevalent, since violent, untimely, or mysterious endings are the fate of many of her characters. For her, death is omnipresent. Love and marriage are less enduring than friendship. Other relationships come into play as well, involving homosexuality and incest, a marked change in theme from the censored writings of the Franco era. Some critics have interpreted Mayoral's emphasis on the affective as melodramatic, but she claims that this is how she perceives life (Alborg, Interview).

Given her knowledge of literary criticism, it would be easy for Mayoral to cultivate contemporary narrative techniques, but instead she chooses a more traditional approach in her fiction, dispensing with complex devices. Nevertheless, her novels tend to have involved, intricate action with an element of mystery and intrigue reminiscent of the so-called *novela negra* (detective story). In some instances, following the newest tendencies of the contemporary Spanish novel, the reader has to wait for a future novel to uncover the resolution of the plot. The detective story seems to flourish only in capitalistic, democratic societies and was, therefore, absent from the Spanish writing scene during the Franco years (Zatlin).

Also worth noting is Mayoral's use of the technique of perspectivism, which incorporates different narrative points of view, forcing the reader to take an active part by deciding which one constitutes the "real" version. Mayoral has said in her unpublished essay "Algunas notas sobre la novela" ("Notes on the Novel") that truth is relative: "objective Reality, that which a possible good would see, does not exist. That is why in my novels, the reader has to create his or her own reality, one that emerges from the often contradictory views of the characters."

Humor is a fundamental aspect of Mayoral's writing. Whether by a witty play on words, a funny episode, or the irony of a situation, the reader is often amused. Mayoral herself, in the tradition of Alfred Hitchcock, makes cameo appearances as an acquaintance of the characters. Her technique of poking fun at herself is, in her own words, like "a wink to the reader" (Alborg, Interview). Her use of humor has made her a popular novelist of her generation.

The strength of Mayoral's novels, however, lies in the richness and originality of her characterizations. A wide range of characters from different social classes, ages, and occupations relate to each other in a weblike pattern. The professional— doctor, lawyer, or journalist—contrasts with the more unusual boxer, artist, or detective. Strong female protagonists are of special interest in all her novels, but she also portrays substantial male characters.

Although Mayoral does not proclaim herself a militant feminist, in her novels she does defend a better position for women in society. With the possible exception of Cándida—the first of the many members of the aristocratic Monterroso del Cela family to appear in her narrative—who is somewhat type-cast in her "strong woman" role, all of her female characters are unique personalities who serve as models to the female reader.

Silvia, the protagonist of *Al otro lado*, stands out as a sensitive woman who has suffered despite her privileged social status. Her portrayal is achieved in part through the first-person narration of her sister Olga, an equally well-developed character. From early childhood Silvia demonstrates special powers in dealing with death. Olga readily accepts Silvia's gift, as does the reader. Thus the psychic element is eventually taken for granted, and Silvia's ability to foresee the death of those around her transforms her into an "angel of death" figure.

A contrast to the ethereal Silvia is the realistic and pragmatic Olga, who narrates four chapters of the novel, including the important opening and closing ones. A doctor, she lives alone despite the fact that Alfonso, her lover of some fifteen years, wants to marry her. This situation is implicitly contrasted with Silvia's three marriages and the wedding that opens the novel.

Olga's interest in feminist issues and her solidarity toward other women explains her questioning of the institution of marriage: "Is it so difficult to understand that one can love a man, even be faithful to him all of one's life, without wishing to share all of life's moments with him?" (85–86). Mayoral has indicated in interviews that most of her female characters are feminists, while very few of her male ones would fall into that category. She believes that the inspiration for her portrayal of strong women characters who reject stereotypical patterns and manifest individualistic traits is rooted in role models from her own family.

The portrayal of women in *La única libertad* demonstrates this point amply. Notable among these female characters are Etelvina, the inquisitive, suspicious narrator; Matilde, the maid turned muse; the daring Inmaculada de Silva; and the repressed Cecilia. However, the most memorable characters are the three cantankerous great-aunts: Benilde, Ana Luz, and Georgina, who reveal Mayoral's sensitivity in portraying elderly figures.

Mayoral's ability to characterize women continues to reveal greater depth. Esmeralda, in *Contra muerte y amor*, for example, is a progressive lawyer working in Madrid. Despite her successful career, she cannot free herself from her family background and childhood in Galicia. Although the sign on her door says "María García Novoa," she still feels like the vulnerable Esmeralda (or worse yet, "Tunda's daughter"), a name that painfully conjures up memories of the past. From the beginning of the novel, the discourse of the omniscient narrator is interwoven with the voices of Esmeralda's past. Distance cannot erase the echo of her father's words, her mother's advice, and her teacher's comments when she left Brétema to study in Madrid. The depth of her character is revealed through the fusing of past and present that constitutes her personality.

The female characters in the short stories of *Morir en sus brazos y otros cuentos* are also remarkable. They include the novice who escapes from the convent in "Sor Clara" ("Sister Clara"), the elderly woman who lives happily with two men in "Febrero, cuando florecen las forsitias" ("In February, When the Forsythias Bloom"), and the wife—some twenty years older than her husband—of the title story of this volume. Motherhood, the outstanding theme in this collection of stories, is of particular interest, especially since this topic has been virtually absent from Mayoral's work.

Throughout her fiction, Mayoral's female and male characters grapple with the fundamental issues of love and death. As suggested by Luis Cernuda's epigraph to *La única libertad*, love is the only liberty for which one lives; but love, in Marina Mayoral's novels, is in fact far from idyllic. Germán Gullón has pointed out that the relationships between men and women are all poorly timed (59–70). Often the female characters are frustrated in their search for love; in several instances they find happiness in incestuous relationships.

This particular theme is explored early in Mayoral's narrative. In her first novel, Cándida takes her much younger brother as her lover. In *La única libertad* there are two cases of incest that are developed further. In one of the "disposable" chapters of the book, which in fact parallels the narrator's own story, several characters elaborate upon the relationship between Doña Petronila Alonso and her son Eduardo, suggesting that it is incestuous. In the course of her inquiries into the history of La Braña, Etelvina finds out that her father is really her mother's twin brother, and therefore her uncle. This incestuous love is described in detail by her uncle Alberto in a long exposition that constitutes the climax of the novel. His comment, "To love someone is never a crime, even if society condemns it" (367), underscores the futility of love, since in these few instances where love exists, society has denounced it.

The reader of Mayoral's fiction can observe a definite development in her work; not only have her novels grown in length—from the mere one hundred pages of *Cándida otra vez* to the four hundred of *La única libertad*—but they have also grown in complexity. *Contra muerte y amor* is a tour de force of perspectivism. Aside from her characteristic themes of love and death, Galicia versus Madrid, and social class differences, the novel highlights the use of humor and suspense while incorporating more of the Galician language.

It is not surprising then, that most recently Mayoral has published three works in Galician. In *Unha árbore, un adeus*, Laura, the fifty-year-old protagonist, reflects upon her past while she plants a magnolia tree in her hometown in Galicia. Her thoughts center on her relationships with the men in her life: her father, her husband, and Paco, her first love. Aside from the theme of relationships between women and men, this novel is of great interest for its exploration of the sexuality—added in the Galician version—of a mature woman in crisis. *O reloxio da torre* deals with a middle-aged woman and her twin brother, and their incestuous desire for each other. The differences between the female and male psyche manifest themselves in the two versions of the same events recorded in each twin's diary.

Chamábase Lluís introduces a new facet to Mayoral's work, testimonial writing in which the family and friends of the drug addict Lluís comment on his life. The testimony of his mother, a cleaning woman, is reminiscent of the testimony of Rigoberta Menchú in the contemporary Guatemalan classic, *Me llamo Rigoberta Menchú*, because of its insight into lower-class life. With *Chamábase Lluís*, Marina Mayoral has joined the group of Galician writers, such as Xosé Luis Méndez Ferrín and Ramón Lorenzo, who are cognizant of the sociopolitical issues that affect their homeland.

SURVEY OF CRITICISM

Besides the article by Germán Gullón, which places Mayoral in a generational context, and another by Phyllis Zatlin, which examines the relationship of Mayoral's fiction to the detective story, Mayoral criticism consists of a few short studies of specific novels. Carmen Díaz Castañón discusses *La única libertad*, while José Manuel García Rey focuses on *Plantar un árbol* and *Al otro lado*. An interview with Milagros Sánchez Arnosi contains informative remarks about

La única libertad; similarly, an interview with Ángel Vivas contains some insightful comments on the author's concept of the novel as a genre.

Papers about Mayoral's work include Alborg's presentation on metafiction and the visual arts in Mayoral's novels. Alborg has also published ''Marina Mayoral's Narrative: Old Families and New Faces from Galicia'' in *Women Writers of Contemporary Spain: Exiles in the Homeland*, which explores many of the aspects mentioned here, as well as Mayoral's short stories, intertextuality, and the conflict among the social classes.

With the publication of nine books of narrative, it can no longer be said that Mayoral is just a promising writer. Her contribution to both Galician and Spanish letters is notable.

BIBLIOGRAPHY

Works by Marina Mayoral

Fiction

Cándida otra vez. Barcelona: Ámbito Literario, 1979.
Al otro lado. Madrid: Magisterio Español, 1981.
Plantar un árbol. Orhieuela, Spain: Ministerio de Cultura, 1981.
La única libertad. Madrid: Cátedra, 1982.
Contra muerte y amor. Madrid: Cátedra, 1982.
Unha árbore, un adeus. Vigo, Spain: Galaxia, 1988.
O reloxio da torre. Vigo, Spain: Galaxia, 1988.
Chamábase Lluís. Vigo, Spain: Xerais, 1989.
Morir en sus brazos y otros cuentos. Alicante, Spain: Aguaclara, 1989.
''En los parques, al anochecer.'' *Relatos eróticos*. Ed. Carmen Estévez. Madrid: Castalia, 1990. 85–107.

Literary Criticism

La poesía de Rosalía de Castro. Madrid: Gredos, 1974.
Rosalía de Castro y sus sombras. Madrid: Fundación Universitaria Española, 1976.
Análisis de cinco comedias. Madrid: Castalia, 1977. [With Andrés Amorós and Francisco Nieva]
Análisis de textos (Poesía y prosa españolas). Madrid: Gredos, 1977.
Rosalía de Castro. Madrid: Cátedra, 1986.
El oficio de narrar. Ed. Marina Mayoral. Madrid: Cátedra, 1989.

Critical Editions

En las orillas del Sar. By Rosalía de Castro. Madrid: Castalia, 1978.
Cuentos y novelas de la tierra. By Emilio Pardo Bazán. Santiago de Compostela, Spain: Sálvora, 1984.
Los pazos de Ulloa. By Emilia Pardo Bazán. Madrid: Castalia, 1986.
Insolación. By Emilia Pardo Bazán. Madrid: Espasa-Calpe, 1987.
Dulce dueño. By Emilia Pardo Bazán. Madrid: Castalia, 1989.

Works about Marina Mayoral

Alborg, Concha. "Las artes plásticas en la narrativa de Marina Mayoral: de metaficción a metaarte." MLA Convention. Washington D.C., 27–30 Dec. 1989.

——. Interview with Marina Mayoral. 28 Dec. 1987.

——. "Marina Mayoral's Narrative: Old Families and New Faces from Galicia." *Women Writers of Contemporary Spain: Exiles in the Homeland.* Ed. Joan L. Brown. Newark: U of Delaware P, 1991. 179–97.

Cadenas, C. B. "Cuando los personajes lo son." *Nueva estafeta* 50 (Jan. 1983): 94.

Díaz Castañón, Carmen. "Historia de una familia." *Cuadernos del Norte* 12 (1982): 89–90.

García Rey, José Manuel. "Marina Mayoral: La sociedad que se cuestiona en medio de una dudosa realidad." *Cuadernos Hispanoamericanos* 394 (1983): 214–21.

Gullón, Germán. "El novelista como fabulador de la realidad: Mayoral, Merino, Guelbenzu . . . ." *Nuevos y novísimos.* Ed. Ricardo Landeira and Luis T. González del Valle. Boulder, CO: Society of Spanish-American Studies, 1987. 59–70.

Sánchez Arnosi, Milagros. "Entrevista a Marina Mayoral." *Ínsula* 431 (1982): 4–5.

Tarrío Varela, Anxo. "Marina Mayoral, una voz para Galicia." *Ínsula* 514 (1989): 20.

Valencia, Antonio. Prologue. *Al otro lado.* By Marina Mayoral. Madrid: Magisterio Español, 1981.

Vivas, Ángel. "Un paseo con el amor y la muerte." *Leer* June 1985: 37–39.

Zatlin, Phyllis. "Detective Fiction and the Novels of Mayoral." *Monographic Review/ Revista Monográfica* 3. 1–2 (1987): 279–87.

ANA MARÍA MOIX
(b. 1947)

Linda Gould Levine

BIOGRAPHY

In 1970 José María Castellet published an anthology of poetry that he suggestively titled *Nueve novísimos*. Among the daring young poets who appeared in the collection was one woman—to whom he dedicated the volume—Ana María Moix. At the time, Moix was twenty-three years old; a scion of the Catalan bourgeoisie; the sister of the future writer Terenci Moix; a familiar presence in the chic leftist Barcelona bar Boccaccio; the initiator, while in her teens, of an avid correspondence with Ana María Matute and Rosa Chacel, who was still an unknown figure in the Spanish literary world;[1] and already the author of two books of poetry. It was not surprising that Moix was accorded the rare honor of being anthologized with eight male poets. Her literary vocation was clearly defined from the time she was twelve years old and wrote her first book, sarcastically entitled "Todos eran unos marranos" ("They Were All Pigs"). The evolution of this early passion for letters is comically retold in the "Poética" ("Poetics"), the tongue-in-cheek autobiography she wrote for Castellet's anthology, in which she also describes her upbringing in a conservative Barcelona household.

Foremost in Moix's humorous account is the continual but silent ideological war between her "monarchic and sentimental" father, who was convinced that Jean-Paul Sartre was the "reincarnation of the devil" (221), and her brother, Ramón (Terenci Moix), who categorically informed her that she could never be a writer if she was not socially committed. To facilitate her indoctrination into the world of the engagé, he surreptitiously loaned her copies of Sartre's works, which were carefully hidden in comic books lest their father discover his "proselytism'' on ''Satan's'' behalf (222). Unfortunately, Moix read the comics instead of Sartre, much to the despair of her brother, and of her mother as well, who was convinced that ''no good would come from a girl who read books'' (222).

Despite this rather inauspicious inauguration into the world of letters, Moix clearly managed to disprove her family's prophecy of doom. In fact, she converted the raw material of her problematic adolescence into the satirical vignettes of her monthly column ''Nena no t'enfilis: diario de una hija de familia'' (''Don't You Dare, Girl: A Daughter's Diary''), published in the magazine *Vindicación Feminista* in the late 1970s, in which she poked fun at the whole ideological gamut of her upbringing: sexism, male chauvinism, tradition, and progressive leftist politics. A more poignant rendition of this reality, together with her tenderness for her deceased brother Miguel, appeared in her first novel, *Julia* (1970), published shortly after two volumes of poetry, *Baladas del Dulce Jim* (1969; ''Ballads of Sweet Jim''), dedicated to Miguel, and *Call Me Stone* (1969).

If the titles of these two works of poetry revealed Moix's penchant for popular culture and song lyrics characteristic of the *novísimos* (the ''very new'' poets), they were also a prelude to an explosion of literary activity that soon followed. In the space of the next three years, Moix published an additional book of poetry, *No Time for Flowers y otras historias* (1971; ''No Time for Flowers and Other Stories''); a book of interviews, *24 × 24* (1972); a collection of short stories, *Ese chico pelirrojo a quien veo cada día* (1971; ''That Red-Headed Boy I See Every Day''); and two novels, *Julia* and *Walter, ¿por qué te fuiste?* (1973; ''Walter, Why Did You Leave?''). The back cover of *No Time for Flowers* announced a new book of narrative in preparation, ''Las virtudes peligrosas'' (''Dangerous Virtues'').

The critics generously applauded Moix's writings: *No Time for Flowers* was awarded the Vizcaya del Ateneo de Bilbao Prize in 1970, and *Walter* was a finalist in the 1972 competition for the Barral Novel Award. Moix was hailed as one of the brightest new talents to appear in Barcelona and compared in precociousness with Carmen Laforet thirty years before (Ordóñez 38). While her poetry and fiction demanded careful reading because of their hermetic images, her journalistic pieces and interviews immediately delighted the literary community with their comical and irreverent jabs at such sacred figures as Salvador Dalí, Carlos Barral—affectionately called ''Carlos Barral I''—(*24 × 24* 101)— her brother Terenci, and others.

Then suddenly Moix's creative muse grew silent. The 1970s passed without further word of ''Las virtudes peligrosas'' or the emergence of any additional collections of verse or narrative bearing her name. Moix's abrupt retreat from the world of fiction baffled her followers, and rightly so. Yet, Moix did not abandon literature; her muse merely transferred itself from poetry and narrative to different spheres as her passion for literature found new direction in the 1970s. She translated into Castilian the works of Marguerite Duras, Mercè Rodoreda, Samuel Beckett, Louis Aragon, and other favorite authors. She wrote book reviews and satirical pieces, among them the column for Lidia Falcón's feminist magazine *Vindicación Feminista*, where for two years she also directed the section on culture and society and reviewed the works of such diverse authors as Rosa Chacel, Gloria Fuertes, Jean Rhys, Virginia Woolf, and Felicidad Blanc. She also co-authored with Castellet a book in Catalan on the painter Maria Girona, and wrote stories for children. However, precisely because her engagement with literature in general, and women artists in particular, is so apparent in these endeavors, one cannot help asking why the translator, the critic, and the storyteller for children was unable to find the words that would have created a personal tapestry as compelling as that of her early writings.

Shortly before *Las virtudes peligrosas* was finally published in 1985, Moix revealed in an interview with Geraldine Nichols that alcoholism and depression had blocked her creative process for many years (*Escribir* 108, 122). This candid portrayal of a private struggle provides a telling link between text and life and amplifies Moix's previous references to the psychological stress she suffered in her adolescent years when her brother Miguel died (Jones, "Literary Structures" 105). It also adds an autobiographical note to the specter of death, decay, and alcoholism that constantly hovers over many of her characters, leading the protagonist of her novel *Julia* to attempt suicide and eventually die in a sanatorium.

Although Moix's transference of autobiography into fiction in the early 1970s was often marked by witty satire and feminist fervor, in her inner war between parody and despair the latter eventually won. This kind of literary suicide not only mirrors Julia's self-destructive act but also fulfills the author's call for silence foreshadowed in the pages of *Walter*. If in this novel Moix's protagonist, Ismael, continually struggles against the futility of language, his creator, too, eventually surrenders to the "enemy lines" (Levine, "Behind the 'Enemy Lines' " 97) and seeks her distance from "the foul words" (*Walter* 10) that sully the whiteness of her text. The words of other writers, in particular those of women—Duras, Sylvia Plath, Woolf, Katherine Mansfield, Chacel, Mary Shelley, Rodoreda—are there to be discovered, publicized, and acknowledged. But Moix's creation of a new poetic and female space, suggested in many pages of her early verse and fiction, is drowned out in the late 1970s and early 1980s by her overriding belief that words are meaningless and that truth eludes. It is not surprising that one of her favorite authors in the 1970s was Beckett (Jones, "Literary Structures" 115), who also had grappled with silence as a response to life's imperfections. Thus, in some paradoxical sense and despite Moix's connection with other women writers, the world she has chosen to inhabit is a solitary one. Yet if she is the lone trumpeter she always wanted to be ("Poética" 222), she is also the seer and the artificer whose wit and satire demythify norms and conventions, and propose liberating paths of salvation for women in society.

MAJOR THEMES

Despite the interruptions and silences that mark Moix's literary evolution from 1973 to 1985, her fiction—from *Ese chico pelirrojo* to *Las virtudes peligrosas*—

reveals a tremendous sense of unity as the author returns in 1985 to the phantoms and obsessions that filled her world in the early 1970s. The themes of the double, the pull between the fantastic and the real, the obsession with the past and memory, the propensity toward abstract and intellectual concepts combined with strong doses of humor and subversive hit-and-run attacks on patriarchy, appear as constants in all her texts, including her volumes of poetry.

Moix's first book of short stories, *Ese chico pelirrojo*, casts the reader into a hallucinatory world in which males and females merge in androgynous patterns, children become birds, vampires become humanized, and men become so obsessed with the sexual configurations of phone books that they are institutionalized. That is, conventional reality is slowly undermined by the forces of the imaginary that convert the familiar into the strange, reproducing echoes of a Kafkaesque world. Yet carefully blended with this leap into absurdity is the clash between the traditional Spanish society that forms the backdrop of many of these stories and Moix's implicit desire to subvert that world and reveal its oppressive structures. She assumes for herself the role of Lilith, the woman to whom the narrator of "Dedicatoria" ("Dedication") addresses his tale. Gone from the pages of this story is the image of Lilith, the cursed first wife of Adam, the demonic spirit of evil; rather, she is cast as a kind of Nietzschean superwoman, "beyond good and evil" (47), whose ultimate task is to give voice to that which has not been named. Appropriating, yet also reinventing for herself, Adam's role, she first reveals "the name of each one of the parts of her body and their desires" (56), then does the same for the male narrator, joyfully introducing each limb and organ to its female counterpart.

Moix's desire to name the forbidden, to introduce into the body of her writing the body of woman, not only mirrors a current in contemporary feminist literature but also provides a counterpoint to the other voices heard in her text—the voices of patriarchal morality. The young girl in the title story of the volume, "Ese chico pelirrojo," is instructed by her mother not to tell anyone that she has just begun to menstruate. When she awkwardly reveals to the nuns at school that she has become a woman, they angrily tell her to be quiet. The body cannot be named, the process has no explanation. Is it any wonder the girl gets pregnant nine months later, Moix seems to ask. Where is Lilith when we most need her?

While authors like the Mexican Rosario Castellanos incorporate the satire of biblical myth and patriarchal naming into a vast rewriting of national history (*El eterno femenino*), Moix situates her critique of machismo within the conflicting sexual codes that permeated the Catalan society of the 1960s. In "Yo soy tu extraña historia" ("I Am Your Strange Story"), she humorously relates the dilemma of a vampire who is seduced and humanized by a freethinking socialist woman, only to confront the worst fear of his life: "la impotencia dental" (133; dental impotence). Moix resuscitates the spirit of Lilith in "Ella comía cardos" ("She Used to Eat Thistles"), a tale of a young woman who seduces her studious young cousin and dares to create her own sense of morality, only to be extinguished by alcoholism and self-destructiveness at the end. These scenarios—

suggestive, humorous, and often macabre—resurface in a more coherent structure—though without the element of the absurd—in Moix's first novel, *Julia*,
reprinted by Lumen in 1991. The story Moix tells is a compelling one, based
in part on her own experiences. A brief comparison of the self-portrait of her
"Poética" and the cast of characters she depicts in her novel reveals, in particular,
a close affinity between her brothers Miguel and Ramón, and Julia's siblings
Rafael and Ernesto.

Julia's profound alienation from self, family, and society is circumscribed in
a third-person narrative in which she relives, during one sleepless night, fourteen
years of personal history. Humor and pathology are juxtaposed as the reader
becomes privy to the memories and obsessions that lurk in her psyche: the
haunting image of a sexual assault she suffered at age six that she shared with
no one; her intense longing to find maternal love and her transference of this
desire to her university professor, Eva; her sense of loss when her brother dies;
her close relationship to her paternal grandfather, whose ethic of freedom and
choice is sharply contrasted to her maternal grandmother's conviction that "a
woman who doesn't go to mass and pray isn't proper" (161); and her disgust
with the Catalan university students who are convinced that their social poetry
and strikes will restructure society. This disquieting narrative, set against the
backdrop of Spanish history of the 1950s and 1960s, with its concomitant shadow
of Civil War divisions and the beginning of the new Spanish *apertura* (openness
in social attitudes), culminates in Julia's failed attempt to free herself from the
images of her past through an overdose of pills.

Lilith's power has seemingly been muted, and thus effectively wiped out of
Julia's life. Her inability to name and publicly express a wide range of emotions—
the terror she faced at being attacked, the desire she feels for Eva, the repulsion
she experiences when she is kissed by her friend Carlos, the discomfort she notes
when someone mentions the "anti-baby pill"—not only reveals the profound
suppression of the topics of lesbianism and rape in Spanish society but also the
fact that Julia has no voice at all. Disregarded by a patriarchal society that values
male over female, comfortable only with the borrowed words of her grandfather
or the signs in Latin that she decodes with ease (Bush 147), Julia is left in a
voiceless psychic space filled with threatening phallic images that negate and
obfuscate her own bodily experiences. Moix pointedly suggests here a theme
that becomes even more apparent in later works—that there is indeed no escape.
Julia's cry for silence—the crystallization of her passage through society and a
theme evocative of Sylvia Plath's *The Bell Jar*—thus becomes the only response
possible. When Julia fails to extinguish her own voice, she has nothing left but
the nightly re-creation of her past horror.

It is not surprising that Moix reintroduces this character into the more complex
narrative world of her next novel, *Walter, ¿por qué te fuiste?*, reprinted by
Lumen in 1992. There, Julia is joined by her two brothers and a cast of cousins—
Lea, Ricardo, and María Antonia—whose monologues in first, second, and third
person coexist with both her own and those of Ismael, the protagonist of the

work. If Ismael fulfills his timeworn literary role of outcast, witness, and participant in this new search for the metaphorical whale of the past, Julia, too, fulfills the destiny Moix carved out for her in her first novel and dies at the age of twenty-three, a victim of depression, alcoholism, and despair. Her last act before her death is to ask that Ismael deliver a packet of letters to Lea. It is a fitting request, given their mutual adoration and physical attraction toward their older cousin, who had made love to each, thus blurring gender distinctions and providing a compelling example of male/female doubling (Bellver 36) and bisexuality. Ismael's seven-year search for Lea not only justifies his return to his childhood haunts of some twenty years past and the nonlinear narrative perspective of the novel but also captures in a profound sense the meaning of writing for Moix. It is the process of being burdened down with words, memories, and images that need to be simultaneously articulated and destroyed, lest they destroy the bearer herself.

Although Julia's words never reach their destination, Ismael's struggle to come to terms with his past leads to a richly textured narrative that can be read on different levels. The bizarre and imaginary scenarios that characterized many of the stories of *Ese chico pelirrojo* resurface in this novel as Moix artfully combines the real and the surreal, eroding our notion of "psychological realism" (Bush 152) and presenting us with such unusual characters as the circus star Albina, half woman and half horse. Albina's presence in the novel seems to respond, in part, to Moix's desire to satirize all forms of conventional sexuality, including heterosexual relationships, since Albina's greatest fantasy is to make love "missionary style" with a fellow circus performer, The Great Yeibo/Ismael. On another, more compelling level, Albina functions as a metaphor for all of Moix's characters. Obsessed with a past they are unable to incorporate into the present, victims of a generation that grew up in a world of conflicting postwar values, trapped between the legacy of convention preached by family and their desire for sexual freedom and political expression, they are all only half human, incomplete, and disfigured.

Nowhere is Moix's sense of the futility of existence more apparent than in this novel. Despite the models of Rosa Luxemburg, Simone de Beauvoir, Pablo Neruda, Antonio Gramsci, and others who appear as mentors and guides for a searching generation, many of her male characters opt for comfort over commitment, while her female characters die or disappear or fail to convert their desire for freedom into a meaningful life's work. Experiences and the words that describe them are ultimately judged as "piles of manure" (37) by the witness, Ismael. Yet, despite this rejection of the human condition and literary creation, it is apparent that Moix uses her novel as a vehicle to revindicate and name, Lilith style, a wide range of experiences, primarily those lived by women.

It is difficult to think of a writer who more daringly or humorously entered the forbidden zone of the female body in the early 1970s than Ana María Moix. Much as Juan Goytisolo denuded and celebrated the male body in his *Don Julián* and *Juan sin tierra*, in *Walter* Moix carefully strips away myth after myth of the tabooed world of female sexuality. She pokes fun at a nonexistent sex education that makes María Antonia fear becoming pregnant because she masturbated; she criticizes the sexist notion that a woman who wants premarital sex is a "whore" (202); she sarcastically labels menstruation "monstruation" (196) because of society's treatment of it; she tenderly re-creates Lea's love affair with Julia; and she enables the reader to suspend all conventional belief and relish the arduous lovemaking between Ismael and Albina. Not until the publication of Esther Tusquets's novels in the late 1970s does one find a more complex portrayal of woman's sexuality. It is not surprising that the censors recommended forty-five cuts in *Walter*, among them passages related to Albina (Nichols, *Escribir* 110) and María Antonia's humorous speculation that if "her mother did it with her father," then Franco must have done "it" with his wife (Levine, "The Censored Sex" 309). Clearly, Moix's words can be viewed as threatening as well as instrumental in transforming societal taboos, even though Ismael would have us believe the contrary.

Yet despite this initial sense of defiance, Moix ultimately falls victim to Ismael's conviction that the writer is a "parrot-like chatterbox" (16) and that "silence and a blank mind" (38) are preferable to useless verbiage. If words indeed are "for sale," as she tells us in *No Time for Flowers* (54), the writer must either become a pimp or whore or abstain from writing altogether. It is no wonder that twelve years elapsed before the publication of Moix's next volume for adults, *Las virtudes peligrosas*, awarded the Ciudad de Barcelona Prize in 1985.[2] Much like Ismael, burdened for seven years with Julia's letters, and much like Julia herself, condemned to reenact nightly the traumas of her past, Moix is obliged to return in this volume to the obsessive themes of her past. Her adolescent characters have now grown up and no longer inhabit the Barcelona world of the 1950s and 1960s; rather, they reside in a more timeless and spaceless dimension that adds an abstract and intellectual quality to this brilliant volume. But their desire to free themselves from their own mind-sets as well as from tenuous webs of convention and reality unites them with their younger sisters and brothers of Moix's early fiction.

Despite the nihilistic tone that infuses the five stories of this collection and emphasizes Moix's unchanging belief that "texticide" (Levine, "Behind the Enemy Lines" 106) is the best remedy for the proliferation of words in the universe, her subtle demythification of patriarchy brings new power to her prose. The title story of the collection, "Las virtudes peligrosas," casts the reader into an ambiguous and enigmatic reality in which two women's obsession for each other can be read on many levels: as a rendition of a "lesbian love" (Levine, "Behind the Enemy Lines" 99) that has not yet converted female desire into female discourse, as French critic Luce Irigaray deems necessary;[3] the portrait of a "narcissistic" woman (Nichols, *Escribir* 114); or the transformation of an "unmediated and fantastic love" with Lacanian overtones into a silent "lover's discourse" (Bush 155). While Moix herself has suggested that "Las virtudes" is a story about "beauty" and "narcissism" (Nichols 114), her shifting narrative perspectives create an open-ended tale that probes the complexities of female passion and the male inability to deal with it. Her somber portrayal of the army general's retreat into madness when faced with the "nameless" power of his wife's attraction to another woman; his realization that he has no "arms" to use in this "unheard of" "battle"; and his fear that he is being asphyxiated by reptiles are only some of the ironic reversals of phallic power now directed against men that Moix presents in this story. In other tales of this collection, the author sympathetically portrays a woman who experiences the emptiness of being her husband's poetic muse ("Los muertos"; "The Dead"); she comically explores a "problem's" inner despair when he realizes that he is destined to be not a philosophical problem but the most mundane one of all—a sexual problem ("El problema"); and she imaginatively rewrites the fairy tale canon ("Érase una vez"; "Once upon a Time").

In the latter story Moix most clearly articulates anew her theory of writing and the role of the narrator ("uno para contarlo"; the one to tell it) as a reborn Ismael, an enslaved witness of repetitive realities expressed in timeworn linguistic signs and formulas. Yet, at the same time that she presents "uno para contarlo" as someone forced to tell and not experience, and "érase una vez" as an entity who can live only "once," she allows some of her female voices the privilege of rebelling against their fixed linguistic roles. Most notable are her portrayal of Sleeping Beauty as an anti-Freudian feminist who drinks tons of coffee to avoid the prescribed one hundred years of sleep and her creation of a dark-skinned Snow White who pays no notice to the desperate attempts of the racist and sexist dwarves to lighten her skin so she can win the prince.

Although the castle of literature appears to have crumbled here, a feminist reader cannot help but rejoice in its ruin. Much as an elusive bond of solidarity between two women defeats the controlled world of an army general, so Moix, following in the footsteps of Julia Kristeva and Hélène Cixous, strikes a mighty blow at the phallologocentric order. In this sense, she restores to words the power they have lost in a world that devalues truth, thus suggesting that silence may not be the best response at all.

SURVEY OF CRITICISM

Moix's fiction has generated substantial interest in North American literary circles. Two collections of essays from the 1980s—*Nuevos y novísimos*, edited by Ricardo Landeira and Luis González-del-Valle, and Janet Pérez's *Novelistas femeninas de la postguerra española*—include a significant number of articles written about Moix's novels, a tribute to their continually provocative effect on the reader. Her prose lends itself particularly well to feminist and psychoanalytical interpretations. Some of these approaches involve discussions of the concept of doubling (Bellver; Bush; Jones, "Literary Structures"; Levine, "The Censored Sex"; Schyfter, "Rites without Passage"; Thomas). Others (Lee-Bonanno; Schyfter, "Rites without Passage") concentrate on the connection between the mother–daughter relationship and the lesbian experience as developed by Charlotte Wolff in *Love Between Women*. Lee-Bonanno draws an interesting parallel between Moix's protagonist, Julia, and Annis Pratt's characterization of the female who grows "down" or grows "up grotesque" in patriarchal society (5).

Other felicitous interpretations draw upon theories of intertextuality (Bush; Valis), linguistic subversion (Masoliver Rodenas, one of the few critics in Spain to examine Moix's writing), the struggle between silence and discourse in the author's fiction (Bush; Levine; Valis), and the influence of film and the mass media on society (Costa). Still others (Lee-Bonanno; Schyfter; Nichols, "*Julia*") utilize sociopolitical perspective with literary overtones to capture the problematic relationship between Moix's narrative techniques and her portrait of an estranged and disjointed generation. C. Christopher Soufas suggests the relationship between the "central authority of the narrator" in *Julia*, which circumscribes the protagonist's autonomy, and the control exercised by Franco and the Spanish state on its citizens (219). Linda Gould Levine ("The Censored Sex") situates Moix's writing within the context of gender and sexual repression in Franco's Spain, while Elizabeth Ordóñez offers an interesting perspective on the "psychological strain" wrought upon the "daughters, wives and mothers of the Catalan borgeoisie" (44). In an attempt to restore a balance to the criticism that has focused on the flawed relationship between mother and daughter in *Julia*, Ordóñez suggests that the "betrayal of mothers" in this text needs to be viewed "in relation to the self-betrayal or failure of the fathers" who sacrificed ideology to comfort (45).

Margaret Jones must be credited with publishing one of the first comprehensive articles on Moix that successfully identifies the major themes and obsessions in her fiction and poetry.[4] Her thoughtful observation in 1976 of Moix's creative utilization "of the same characters, themes and even plot incidents from book to book" ("Literary Structures" 114) is reinforced by Andrew Bush and by Levine ("Behind the Enemy Lines"), who discuss the recurring conflicts and linguistic strategies of the author's early fiction and poetry (Bush) that reappear in *Las virtudes peligrosas*. Levine's analysis focuses on the textual strategies Moix uses in this collection as well as on her demythification of male power and the male canon in several of the stories. She also compares Moix's creative rewriting of the fairy tale canon to the "revisionary mythmaking" of Carmen Martín Gaite and Esther Tusquets.[5] Bush insightfully views the "silent calling" of the two female protagonists of "Las virtudes peligrosas" as Moix's attempt to bypass the alienation from language experienced by her earlier characters, Julia in particular (154). Further criticism on both *Las virtudes peligrosas* and *Walter, ¿por qué te fuiste?* would be a welcome addition to the substantive and often repetitive analyses currently in print on *Julia*, Moix's most accessible novel.

Together with these critical perspectives, special mention must be made of the wonderful portraits provided of Ana María Moix, the person, by other women writers. Cristina Peri Rossi, Uruguayan writer and close friend of Moix, captures with wit and grace the different worlds inhabited by Ana María and herself in the early 1970s. Her lengthy poem, "Correspondencia con Ana María Moix," provides a personal and tender reading of Moix's obsession with Esther Tusquets and the voices of the past, her relationship to the Catalan *gauche divine* (divine left), and her chronic drinking habits. The same sense of respect and admiration for Moix's writing expressed by Peri Rossi is echoed by Ana María Matute and Esther Tusquets in their interviews with Geraldine Nichols. Elizabeth Ordóñez further underlines the bond of friendship among Moix, Tusquets, and Concha Alós, and applauds this working model of a communal spirit among women unencumbered by competitiveness and egotism (38–39).

Thus, the lone musician is ultimately joined by a chorus of other players in the solitude of her creative endeavor. A phone conversation with Moix in the summer of 1991 brought news of her translations of Sylvia Plath's *Letters* and Mary Shelley's *Frankenstein*, an endeavor that, together with her book reviews on female authors in the Spanish press, confirms her continuing fascination and connection with the hermetic and subversive world of women writers. There is also the suggestion that her current silence may be broken with the publication of a new novel. Certainly the reprinting of *Julia* and *Walter* by Lumen attests to the renewed interest her work has generated. Given the complex textual strategies and innovations of her rich body of fiction, we eagerly await the sound of her trumpet, which threatens to bring down the walls of Jericho and offer woman-made materials for its reconstruction.

NOTES

1. In Moix's interview with Geraldine Nichols (*Escribir* 104), she mentions that she discovered Chacel's novel *Teresa* in the back room of a bookstore where there were prohibited items. Shortly after, she began her fifteen-year correspondence with Chacel, who was then living in Brazil. Moix presents a compelling portrait of Spanish society's forty-year neglect of this great writer in the introduction to her interview with Chacel in *24 × 24* 141–46.

2. Although Moix did not publish *Las virtudes peligrosas* until 1985, at least two of the stories were published before then. See the bibliography for complete information.

3. Luce Irigaray, *This Sex Which Is Not One*, trans. Catherine Porter with Carolyn Burke (Ithaca, NY: Cornell UP, 1985) 214.

4. Although this chapter has been devoted to Moix's fiction—the most compelling genre of her literary works—her role as poet of the "novísimos" discussed by Andrew Bush and Ellen Engelson Marson has been reevaluated by Santiago Daydí-Tolson, who views her as a forerunner of "a growing and vigorous lyrical production of women determined to establish their own new voices" (53).

5. The term "revisionist mythmaking" appears in Alicia Ostriker's article "The Thieves of Language: Women Poets and Revisionist Mythmaking," in *The New Feminist Criticism*, ed. Elaine Showalter (New York: Pantheon Books, 1985) 314–38.

BIBLIOGRAPHY

Works by Ana María Moix

Poetry

Baladas del dulce Jim. Barcelona: Saturno, 1969.
Call Me Stone. N.p.: Esplugues del Llobregat, 1969.
No Time for Flowers y otras historias. Barcelona: Lumen, 1971. [Contains *No Time for Flowers*, *Call Me Stone*, and ''Homenaje a Bécquer'']
A imagen y semejanza. Barcelona: Lumen, 1983. [Contains *Baladas del dulce Jim*, *No Time for Flowers*, *Call Me Stone*, and ''Homenaje a Bécquer'']

Fiction

Julia. Barcelona: Seix Barral, 1970. Rpt. Barcelona: Lumen, 1991. [This article cites from the 1970 edition]
Ese chico pelirrojo a quien veo cada día. Barcelona: Lumen, 1971.
Walter ¿por qué te fuiste? Barcelona: Barral Editores, 1973. Rpt. Barcelona: Lumen, 1992. [This article cites from the 1973 edition]
''Vida, esplendor y caída de un problema sexual que no quiso serlo.'' *Vindicación Feminista* 28 (July 1979): 61–66. [An early version of the story ''El problema,'' which appears in *Las virtudes peligrosas*]
''Las virtudes peligrosas.'' *Doce relatos de mujeres*. Ed. Ymelda Navajo. Madrid: Alianza Editorial, 1982. 37–66.
Las virtudes peligrosas. Barcelona: Plaza y Janés, 1985.

Miscellaneous

''Poética.'' *Nueve novísimos*. Ed. José María Castellet. Barcelona: Barral Editores, 1970. 221–22.
24 × 24. Barcelona: Ediciones Península, 1972. [Interviews]
La maravillosa colina de las edades primitivas. Barcelona: Lumen, 1976. [A collection of children's stories]
Maria Girona: una pintura en llibertat. Barcelona: Edicions 62, 1977. [With José María Castellet]
La niebla y otros relatos. Madrid: Alfaguara, 1988. [A collection of children's stories]

Selected Articles

''Los Rolling Stones, a la recherche de una generación superada.'' *Vindicación Feminista* 1 (July 1976): 9.
''Virginia Woolf y el grupo de los Bloomsbury.'' *Vindicación Feminista* 2 (Aug. 1976): 7.
''Jean Rhys o la amarga aventura de vivir.'' *Vindicación Feminista* 3 (Sept. 1976): 7.
''Gloria Fuertes: Poeta para niños, o el difícil encanto de peinarse las canas a los 12 años.'' *Vindicación Feminista* 5 (Nov. 1976): 40–41.
''Carmen Alcalde: Una interpretación iconoclasta del feminismo.'' *Vindicación Feminista* 7 (Jan. 1977): 15.

"Lidia Falcón: La impertinencia de la reflexión." *Vindicación Feminista* 8 (Feb. 1977): 10.
"Rosa Chacel: Una larga y creativa aventura del conocimiento." *Vindicación Feminista* 12 (June 1977): 14–15.
"Isadora Duncan: Un arte, una blasfemia." *Vindicación Feminista* 14 (Aug. 1977): 11.
"Nacha Guevara: Genio y figura." *Vindicación Feminista* 17 (Nov. 1977): 9–10.
"Ariadna intenta vender el jardín de los cerezos." *Camp de l'arpa* 52 (1978): 47–49. [Review of Esther Tusquets's novel, *El mismo mar de todos los veranos*]
"Espejo de sombras, de Felicidad Blanc: Ejercicio de melancolía." *Vindicación Feminista* 19 (Jan. 1978): 6–7.
"La debilidad del sexo y la omnipotencia de los gobiernos." *Vindicación Feminista* 28 (July 1979): 45–48. [With Carmen Alcalde and Anna Estany]
"La fermentación de la primavera." *Camp de l'arpa* 71 (1980): 51–53. [Review of Esther Tusquets's novel, *El amor es un juego solitario*]

Translations by Ana María Moix

Cuanta, cuanta guerra. By Mercè Rodoreda. Barcelona: Edhasa, 1982 [Trans. of *Quanta, quanta, guerra*]
Veintidós cuentos. By Mercè Rodoreda. Madrid: Mondadori, 1988. [Trans. of *Vint-i-dos contes*]

Works about Ana María Moix

Bellver, Catherine. "Duplication and Doubling in the Novels of Ana María Moix." Landeira and González-del-Valle 29–41.
Bush, Andrew. "Ana María Moix's Silent Calling." *Women Writers of Contemporary Spain: Exiles in the Homeland*. Ed. Joan L. Brown. Newark, DE.: U of Delaware P, 1991. 136–58.
Castellet, José María. Prologue. *Nueve novísimos*. Barcelona: Barral Editores, 1970. 15–47.
Costa, Luis. "Hipocresía y cine en la obra de Ana María Moix." *Letras Femeninas* 4 (1978): 12–33.
Daydí-Tolson, Santiago. "Hacia un panorama crítico de las voces femeninas en la poesía española contemporánea." *Monographic Review/Revista Monográfica* 6 (1990): 46–60.
Jones, Margaret E.W. "Ana María Moix: Literary Structures and the Enigmatic Nature of Reality." *Journal of Spanish Studies: Twentieth Century* 4 (1976): 105–16.
———. "Del compromiso al egoísmo: la metamorfosis de la protagonista en la novelística española de postguerra." Pérez 125–34.
Landeira, Ricardo, and Luis González-del-Valle, eds. *Nuevos y novísimos: Algunas perspectivas críticas sobre la narrativa española desde la década de los sesenta*. Boulder, CO: Society of Spanish and Spanish-American Studies, 1987.
Lee-Bonanno, Lucy. "The Quest for Authentic Personhood: An Expression of the Female Tradition in Novels by Moix, Tusquets, Matute and Alós." *DAI* 46 (1985): 714A. U of Kentucky.
Levine, Linda Gould. "Ana María Moix." *Women Writers of Spain: An Annotated Bio-Bibliographical Guide*. Ed. Carolyn L. Galerstein. Westport: Greenwood Press, 1986. 219–20.

————. "Behind the 'Enemy Lines': Strategies for Interpreting *Las virtudes peligrosas* of Ana María Moix." Landeira and González-del-Valle 97–111.

————. "The Censored Sex: Women as Character and Author in Franco's Spain." *Women in Hispanic Literature: Icons and Fallen Idols*. Ed. Beth Miller. Berkeley: U of California P, 1983. 289–315.

————. Phone conversation with Ana María Moix. Summer 1991.

Marson, Ellen Engelson. "Mae West, Superman, and the Spanish Poets of the Seventies." *Literature and Popular Culture in the Hispanic World*. Ed. Rose S. Minc. Gaithersburg, MD: Ediciones Hispamérica, 1981. 191–98.

Masoliver Rodenas, Juan Antonio. "La base sexta contra Ana María Moix." *Camp de l'arpa* 9 (1974): 9–12.

Nichols, Geraldine C. *Escribir, espacio propio: Laforet, Matute, Moix, Tusquets, Riera y Roig por sí mismas*. Minneapolis: Institute for the Study of Ideologies and Literature, 1989. 103–25.

————. "*Julia*: 'This is the Way the World Ends. . . .' " Pérez 113–24.

Ordóñez, Elizabeth J. "The Barcelona Group: The Fiction of Alós, Moix, and Tusquets." *Letras Femeninas* 6 (1981): 38–50.

Pérez, Janet, ed. *Novelistas femeninas de la postguerra española*. Madrid: José Porrúa, 1983.

Peri Rossi, Cristina. "Correspondencia con Ana María Moix." *Palabra de escándalo*. Barcelona: Tusquets, 1974. 199–214. [Anthology of writings of various authors]

Schyfter, Sara. "The Fragmented Family in the Novels of Contemporary Spanish Women." *Perspectives on Contemporary Literature* 3.1 (May 1977): 23–29.

————. "Rites Without Passage: The Adolescent World of Ana Maria Moíx's *Julia*." *The Analysis of Literary Texts: Current Trends in Methodology*. Ed. Randolph D. Pope. Ypsilanti, MI: Bilingual Press/Editorial Bilingüe, 1980. 41–50.

Soufas, C. Christopher, Jr., "Ana Maria Moíx and the Generation of 1968: *Julia* as (Anti-)Generational (Anti-)Manifesto." Landeira and González-del-Valle 217–28.

Thomas, Michael D. "El desdoblamiento psíquico como factor dinámico en *Julia*." Pérez 103–11.

Vázquez Montalbán, Manuel. Prologue. *Baladas del Dulce Jim*. By Ana María Moix. Barcelona: Saturno, 1969. 7–10.

Valis, Noël M. "Reality and Language in Ana María Moix's *Walter ¿por qué te fuiste?*" *Ojáncano* 4 (Oct. 1990): 48–58.

ROSA MONTERO
(b. 1951)

Kathleen M. Glenn

BIOGRAPHY

Best-selling novelist, award-winning journalist, and self-declared feminist, Rosa Montero was born in Madrid on January 3, 1951. As a child she suffered from tuberculosis, and from the ages of five to nine did not attend school; instead, she remained at home, where she entertained herself by reading and writing. Every week her mother borrowed an armful of books from a relative's library and the child devoured them, even the pornographic works that she found quite boring. She also composed her own short stories and began a number of novels, writing four or five pages and then setting them aside in favor of a new subject. Thus, from an early age, literature was a source of immense pleasure for Montero, a marvelous game. When she was well enough to continue formal education, it was at a public school, an *instituto* attended by the children of working-class families. The building was falling apart, the classes huge, and individual attention unheard of. Montero recalls that when lessons were over, the girls raced down the stairs like wild animals let out of a cage.[1] The first day they knocked her down, but never again. She was an equally quick learner inside the classroom. Despite the limitations of the *instituto*, some of the teachers were excellent, and Montero believes that the years spent there were important in her development as a person. Moreover, she was spared the repressive, moralizing, asphyxiating atmosphere then prevalent in religious schools.

While still very young, Montero saw what it was like to grow up female in a man's world. When she was only ten, it was her responsibility to carry home heavy buckets of ice—the family did not have an electric refrigerator—even though her brother was five years older and far stronger than she. Family squabbles were frequent, with her extremely traditional, conservative father yelling at her mother, who was forced to keep her opinions to herself. Montero's reaction was to vow not to marry and suffer the same fate as her mother. When she was in her teens, a classmate lent her a copy of Simone de Beauvoir's *The Second Sex,* and the book helped clarify her perceptions of the feminine condition.

During her university years, Montero studied psychology and journalism and was active in several theater groups (Tábano, Canon) of the off-Broadway type. In 1969 she began writing for various publications, and some eight years later joined the staff of Spain's major newspaper, *El País.* In 1980 and 1981, when she was suffering from writer's block with respect to her journalistic work, she served as editor in chief of the paper's Sunday supplement; she now writes a weekly column as well as articles and the interviews that first brought her fame. Her skill at capturing the telling detail and puncturing inflated egos is apparent in the interviews collected in *España para ti para siempre* (1976; "Spain for You Forever") and *Cinco años de País* (1982; "Five Years of *El País*").

Montero's subjects—in some cases "victims" might be a more appropriate term—range from Manuel Fraga Iribarne, conservative politician and minister of information and tourism under Franco, to the Communist Santiago Carrillo, and from retired bullfighter Luis Miguel Dominguín to opera singer Montserrat Caballé. Montero's newspaper work has earned her a series of awards—the Mundo Prize in 1978, the National Prize for Periodismo (Journalism) in 1980, and the 1989 Derechos Humanos Prize, granted by the Human Rights Association of Spain—and has afforded her opportunities for travel outside Spain. In 1985 she spent a term at Wellesley College, where she taught courses on contemporary Spanish women writers and literary journalism.

Montero is the author of several short stories and the scripts for a situation comedy, *Media naranja* ("The Better Half"), televised in 1986, that featured a role reversal: the female lead decidedly modern, liberated, and determined, and the male lead timid and dominated by his mother. More recently, her version of a play by Scottish writer Sharman MacDonald, *When I Was a Girl I Used to Scream and Shout,* was staged in Madrid and several other Spanish cities. To date Montero has published five novels and a children's book: *Crónica del desamor* (1979; *Absent Love: A Chronicle* 1991), *La función Delta* (1981; *The Delta Function* 1991), *Te trataré como a una reina* (1983; "I'll Treat You Like a Queen"), *Amado amo* (1988; "Dear Master"), *Temblor* (1990; "Tremor"), and *El nido de los sueños* (1991; "The Nest of Dreams"). Writing, she insists, is like being passionately in love: Both are characterized by intoxication, fervor, and the feeling that one is eternal.

MAJOR THEMES

In a 1988 interview (Talbot 92), Montero stated that she sees the world from a feminist perspective, and this is particularly evident in *Crónica del desamor.* Thematically it is the most combative of her narratives, and it foregrounds issues of special interest to women: discrimination in the workplace, sexual stereotyping and the difficulty of escaping societal roles, female sexuality, methods of birth control, and the horrors of illegal and botched abortions. Most of the characters are young professional women in their thirties, the friends of free-lance journalist and single mother Ana Antón, who have rejected traditional modes of behavior but have not found complete satisfaction in new ones. They are now reexamining their values and wondering whether they have mistaken a lack of commitment for freedom. What does women's liberation really mean? Have women been sold a bill of goods along with the pill? All the female characters are dissatisfied with personal relationships that have gone sour, and most of them seem to feel unfulfilled without a man at their side. Neither their education nor their past experience nor society's expectations have fostered in them a sense of self-sufficiency. Rather than depict strong, fully liberated female characters who qualify as role models, Montero has chosen to portray women who continue to be victimized by patriarchal ideology (as in *Te trataré como a una reina*) or who are struggling to free themselves from it and forge their own identity (as in *Crónica*). The characters' disenchantment extends to the political arena, and they are critical of the failures of the government of the early post-Franco period.

The choice of *Crónica* for the title was deliberate, for Montero was well aware of the book's weaknesses. Characters are schematic and defined rather than individualized or developed. Episodes are loosely strung together or simply juxtaposed. One of the most impressive chapters from the standpoint of style is that devoted to el Zorro (The Fox) and a portrayal of the hippie drug scene, but this section is an almost independent unit. The book at times resembles a sociohistorical document and is, in fact, an account of Montero's own generation and world. She describes it as the typical first novel, *un vómito*, a pouring out of all the frustrations, bitterness, and anger that she felt. Giving vent to those emotions was a salutary experience that enabled Montero to pay greater attention to artistic concerns in her next book. The lack of distance from her first novel was not without its advantages, however, for the impassioned tone lends an unmistakable note of sincerity to the narrative and helps explain its popularity. Ten years after its initial publication, *Crónica* was in its seventeenth edition.

La función Delta is a further exploration of the conflicts experienced by women between the demands of a career and emotional needs, as well as a sustained reflection on love and death. The protagonist, Lucía, is torn between two different types of love: passion and tenderness. She associates the former with Hipólito, with whom she fancies she is madly in love, and the latter with Miguel, her companion of twenty years and her refuge. Lucía imagines herself to be strong and self-assured, but she depends upon others for a sense of worth and completeness. Ricardo, the third man in her life, suggests that her upbringing is in part responsible for her insecurity and lack of inner resources, and that she—like so many girls—was brought up to be a helpmate rather than an independent person. Love, for Lucía, is all important and a means of allaying the fear of death. When she learns that she is dying of cancer, she swings between blind terror and self-pity, denial and ultimate acceptance. A variation upon the theme of death is played out in the figure of Doña Maruja, an elderly neighbor who repeatedly attempts suicide.

The narrative present is the year 2010, when Lucía, confined to the hospital, writes down her recollections of the week preceding the premiere of the one and only film she directed. Ricardo, who plays the role of critic within the text, points out her many contradictions and presents a version of events that differs markedly from hers. His penchant for telling tall tales renders suspect much of what he says, but it is obvious that Lucía, too, is a far from reliable narrator. Frequent images of distorted vision emphasize her inability to see herself as she is or others as they are. The resultant ambiguity enriches the narrative and compels readers to decide for themselves who is more credible. Unlike the one-dimensional beings of *Crónica del desamor*, Lucía and Ricardo are nuanced, complex characters who change in the course of the novel. The alternation of chapters from her memoirs of the year 1980 and entries from her hospital diary in 2010 permits the juxtaposition and contrast of the views of a still young woman and those of an elderly one. *La función Delta* represents a significant advance in technique and maturity on Montero's part, and writing the book served as a partial catharsis of her fear of death.

With her third novel Montero set out to create a world far removed from her own. The action of *Te trataré como a una reina* revolves around a seedy nightclub and a group of characters who, in the main, are uneducated, physically unattractive to the point of repulsiveness, and desperately lonely. The need to love and be loved makes the women especially vulnerable to the romantic images projected by sentimental literature, popular songs, and films. Bella's points of reference are the boleros she sings; she longs for a heart that will beat in tune with hers, while Antonia fantasizes about kisses like those she has seen in the movies, and Vanessa dreams of stardom. No matter how hard they try to escape the narrow confines of their existence, they are losers, trapped in a world of leaking faucets, chipped paint, threadbare carpets, and faded illusions. The idea that there is no way out for them is dramatized in the final pages of the novel: Bella is in jail, Vanessa is in the hospital, and Antonia finds herself on the same train that over the years has borne her back to her mother's house. Misunderstanding and a lack of communication mark the lives of all the characters, who constantly misinterpret one another's words, actions, and motives. Sexual/textual authority is wielded by the men. They are the ones who initiate and terminate relationships, who compose boleros, report supposed crimes, and write up their affairs, casting themselves in important roles and relegating women to supporting parts. Montero, however, systematically undermines the writing of her male characters by using different perspectives on the same events and ironic juxtapositions. Like Francisco de Quevedo, a writer she admires, Montero has a keen sense of the ridiculous plus a gift for biting humor and scathing satire. She exposes the pretense, foolishness, and exaggerated self-importance of her characters, but also evokes compassion for the most defenseless of them, such as the pathetic Benigno or the simple Antonia. Montero has described her novel as a bolero, a grotesque melodrama (Monegal 11); the description is appropriate.

It is not surprising that women are merely bit players and a man is the main character of *Amado amo*, since it is a novel about power, and power has long been reserved for males. Montero here presents a devastating portrait of her weak, egotistical protagonist, ironically named César, who is the former art director of an advertising agency and is now suffering a professional and personal crisis. His is a world where status is measured in terms of private parking spaces and the number of windows in one's office, where competition is cutthroat, and where there are but two options: dominate or be dominated. César's attitude toward his boss/master alternates between hate and love (hence the title); he is exhilarated by a friendly slap on the back, plunged into despair by a curt word. His paranoia leads him to search for hidden meanings in the most casual of remarks and to detect enemies on every side. Ultimately, in order to save his own neck, he does not hesitate to betray a woman friend. After all, he reflects, women lack ambition and therefore their ruin is of no consequence; they are born underlings. César is a tragicomic figure, pitiable in his loneliness and insecurity, contemptible in his groveling before superiors. Montero is merciless in her dissection of him—recalling again the style of Quevedo. In *Amado amo* she has succeeded in distancing herself from her characters to a greater degree than in her previous works and has demonstrated increasing sophistication as a writer.

SURVEY OF CRITICISM

Montero's evaluation of her own work may be found in several interviews (Monegal; Talbot; Glenn). Most of the critical studies published to date focus on her first two novels. Emilio de Miguel Martínez's monograph *La primera narrativa de Rosa Montero* is a good starting point because of its fairly detailed plot summaries and perceptive observation on theme, structure, and style. In the case of *Crónica del desamor*, Miguel calls attention to Montero's desire to bear witness to the affective, sexual, and political frustration felt by her contemporaries, and to criticize certain situations and types of behavior that are manifestly unjust. He suggests that her background as an interviewer and reporter explains her tendency to give a quick sketch of characters when they are introduced, and then to confirm rather than modify that initial description, and to stress content over form. Ideological concerns clearly outweigh artistic ones—the reverse is true of *La función Delta*—yet we already find in *Crónica* considerable fluidity of expression, naturalness of dialogue, and skillful use of colloquialisms. Despite obvious differences, Miguel notes curious parallels in technique and tone between *Crónica* and the satiric prose of the fifteenth-century misogynist Alfonso Martínez de Toledo, author of *El Corbacho*. Although the male writer excoriated women and Montero defends them, the two share a critical-moralistic bent and use the stylistic device of *plurifurcación*. "Plurifurcation," as contrasted to "bifurcation," is the term Miguel employs to describe Montero's furnishing of multiple examples of the same phenomenon and her emphasis on shared experiences. With reference to *La función Delta*, Miguel points out the importance of Ricardo's comments as a counterpoint to Lucía's highly subjective version of events, the difference in tone between her diary and her reconstruction of the past, and the lyricism of the closing pages of the novel. In his final comparison of the two books, he concludes that in *La función Delta*, narrative elements prevail over essayistic ones, the individual over the collective, the imaginary over the testimonial, and the pleasure of constructing a literary universe over the pressing need to write about certain issues (106, 108).

In "The Feminist Message: Propaganda and/or Art?" Eunice D. Myers concurs with Miguel in her assessment of the strengths and weaknesses of the early novels, stating that the emphasis is upon the message in *Crónica*, where Montero examines male-female relationships, stereotypical roles, sexuality, motherhood, and career-related problems. Whereas Myers regards feminist ideology as central to the first two books, Roberto Manteiga observes that Montero is critical of some aspects of the women's rights movement and that her concerns are not exclusively feminist. In "The Dilemma of the Modern Woman: A Study of the Female Characters in Rosa Montero's Novels," he illustrates that those characters "vividly represent the complexities of what it means to be a woman in today's society" (123). He also draws an interesting comparison between Montero's views about marriage and those of Carmen Martín Gaite.

Kathleen M. Glenn, in "Reader Expectations and Rosa Montero's *La función Delta*," examines the novel as a fictive autobiography. She highlights the protagonist's self-deception, seen in her insistent criticism of other's defects but ability to ignore her own. Despite Lucía's protestations that she is fair-minded, self-sufficient, and mature, her words and deeds repeatedly betray her, and she fails to display the insight and maturity one expects from autobiographical narratives. Glenn's article on *Te trataré como a una reina* ("Victimized by Misreading") focuses on Montero's exposé of the ways in which men abuse their power to read the world and the ways in which female characters of the novel suffer from male stereotyping and male-generated myths. The supposedly objective "documents" provided by journalist Paco Mancebo are ridden with clichés, polarized images, and blatant sexism in their portrayal of Bella as a castrating bitch/monster madwoman, and the male object of her aggression as a model of respectability and innocence.

Studies by Biruté Ciplijauskaité, Concha Alborg, and Phyllis Zatlin include overviews of Montero's fiction through *Te trataré*. Ciplijauskaité acknowledges Montero's power of observation and remarkable linguistic sensitivity but plays down the literary merit of her novels, asserting that their popularity is partly due to their content and accessibility to the general public (191–92). In "Women Novelists in Democratic Spain," Zatlin situates Montero's work within the context of the open treatment of the female experience in narratives written during the late 1970s and the fascination with metafiction, a potentially subversive mode. Elaborating on her earlier remarks on *La función Delta* in ''The Contemporary Spanish Metanovel,'' Zatlin discusses the importance of Ricardo as reader of Lucía's manuscript and as critic whose observations affect what she writes in subsequent chapters. With respect to *Te trataré*, Zatlin views the boleros not only as an ironic commentary on the reality of Bella's existence but also as a metafictional device, ''another level of fiction within the narrative'' (38). Alborg, too, treats this aspect of Montero's writing, arguing that the novelist uses metafiction as an instrument to give emphasis to feminist theme (''Metaficción feminismo'' 73). Alborg's ''Cuatro narradoras de la transición'' also contains general comments on Montero's fiction. Last, in ''Rosa Montero ante la escritura femenina,'' Elena Gascón Vera applies the theories of French feminists Hélène Cixous, Monique Wittig, and Julia Kristeva to Montero's writing and seeks to determine the extent to which the Spanish novelist coincides with their ideas. She also attempts to create an alternative to the dominant male discourse by concentrating on the exploration and analysis of female sexuality.

Inasmuch as Montero is still quite young, it would be foolish to attempt to predict the future course of her fiction; it is reasonable, however, to expect that she will continue to mature as a writer and will make further contributions to the contemporary Spanish narrative.

NOTE

1. All biographical information is based on a July 10, 1989, interview of Montero. See ''Conversación con Rosa Montero.''

BIBLIOGRAPHY

Works by Rosa Montero

España para ti para siempre. Madrid: A.Q. Ediciones, 1976.
Crónica del desamor. Madrid: Debate, 1979.
La función Delta. Madrid: Debate, 1981.
Cinco años de País. Madrid: Debate, 1982.
Te trataré como a una reina. Barcelona: Seix Barral, 1983.
Amado amo. Madrid: Debate, 1988.
Temblor. Barcelona: Seix Barral, 1990.
El nido de los sueños. Madrid: Siruela, 1991.

Translations

Absent Love: A Chronicle. Trans. Cristina de la Torre and Diana Glad. Lincoln: U of Nebraska P, 1991.
The Delta Function. Trans. Kari Easton and Yolanda Molina Gavilán. Lincoln: U of Nebraska P, 1991.

Works about Rosa Montero

Alborg, Concha. "Cuatro narradoras de la transición." *Nuevos y novísimos: Algunas perspectivas críticas sobre la narrativa española desde la década de los 60*. Ed. Ricardo Landeira and Luis T. González-del-Valle. Boulder, CO: Society of Spanish and Spanish-American Studies, 1987. 11–27.

———. "Metaficción y feminismo en Rosa Montero." *Revista de Estudios Hispánicos* 22 (1988): 67–76.

Brown, Joan L. "Rosa Montero: From Journalist to Novelist." *Women Writers of Contemporary Spain: Exiles in the Homeland*. Ed. Joan L. Brown. Newark: U of Delaware P, 1991. 240–57.

Ciplijauskaité, Biruté. *La novela femenina contemporánea (1970–1985): Hacia una tipología de la narración en primera persona*. Barcelona: Anthropos, 1988.

Gascón Vera, Elena. "Rosa Montero ante la escritura femenina." *Anales de la Literatura Española Contemporánea* 12 (1987): 59–77.

Glenn, Kathleen M. "Conversación con Rosa Montero." *Anales de la Literatura Española Contemporánea* 15 (1990): 275–83.

———. "Fantasy, Myth, and Subversion in Rosa Montero's *Temblor*." [Forthcoming in *Romance Languages Annual*]

———. "Reader Expectations and Rosa Montero's *La función Delta*." *Letras Peninsulares* 1 (1988): 87–96.

———. "Victimized by Misreading: Rosa Montero's *Te trataré como a una reina*." *Anales de la Literatura Española Contemporánea* 12 (1987): 191–202.

Manteiga, Roberto. "The Dilemma of the Modern Woman: A Study of the Female Characters in Rosa Montero's Novels." *Feminine Concerns in Contemporary Spanish Fiction by Women*. Ed. Roberto C. Manteiga, Carolyn Galerstein, and Kathleen McNerney. Potomac, MD: Scripta Humanistica, 1988. 113–23.

Miguel Martínez, Emilio de. *La primera narrativa de Rosa Montero*. Salamanca, Spain: Universidad de Salamanca, 1983.

Monegal, Antonio. "Entrevista a Rosa Montero." *Plaza* 11 (Autumn 1986): 5–12.

Myers, Eunice D. "The Feminist Message: Propaganda and/or Art? A Study of Two Novels by Rosa Montero." *Feminine Concerns in Contemporary Spanish Fiction by Women*. Ed. Roberto C. Manteiga, Carolyn Galerstein, and Kathleen McNerney. Potomac, MD: Scripta Humanistica, 1988. 99–112.

Talbot, Lynn K. "Entrevista con Rosa Montero." *Letras Femeninas* 14 (1988): 90–96.

Zatlin, Phyllis. "The Contemporary Spanish Metanovel." *Denver Quarterly* 17.3 (1982): 62–73.

———. "Women Novelists in Democratic Spain: Freedom to Express the Female Perspective." *Anales de la Literatura Española Contemporánea* 12 (1987): 29–44.

MARGARITA NELKEN Y MAUSBERGER (1896–1968)

Eleanore Maxwell Dial

BIOGRAPHY

Born in Madrid on July 5, 1896, of German-Jewish parents, Margarita Nelken spent the first half of an unusually active life in that capital. She was trained as a pianist, an artist, an art critic, and a sociologist. Educated at home by private tutors, she therefore did not have to suffer through the process of rejecting her early education, as described by other notable Spanish women of her period in their memoirs: Isabel de Palencia, in *I Must Have Liberty*; Constancia de la Mora, in *In Place of Splendor*; and María Teresa León in *Memoria de la melancolía*. All three of these women came from distinguished Spanish families and were educated in leading convent schools of the day. An essential part of their education was language training, because speaking other languages was considered part of the "feminine polish." They were further instructed in the feminine arts of sewing and embroidering. Other subjects, for example art, were taught in a shabby manner; "questionable" parts of famous pictures, as mentioned by de la Mora, were deleted in art books to preserve the girls' modesty. Women were not taught to question what was happening in the world around them, and most assuredly not to earn a living for themselves.

This was precisely the kind of education that Nelken rails against in her most famous book, *La condición social de la mujer en España* (1919?; "The Social Condition of Women in Spain"). "The talents of Spanish women," she informs us angrily, "have been limited by their education and by the atmosphere that has stifled them for centuries. This does not mean that their aptitudes are inferior to those of women in other countries, where feminism is more advanced" (45). Her book, banned by a Spanish bishop, ironically sold more copies than it would have had it not been banned. It was controversial because Nelken used it as a forum to attack all the truisms that were inculcated in Spanish women in the course of their religious training and education: the unquestioning acceptance of masculine authority, the vision of marriage as both a sacrament and their best alternative, and the belief that working outside the home was not as meaningful for women as for men.

Nelken dedicated *La condición social* to her friends Matilde Ibuici and Paquita Bohigas, law students, as well as to all Spanish women tirelessly involved in dignifying the position of their sex. She herself expended great energy to bring about changes in the lives of women. She wrote and spoke ceaselessly and passionately to this end. To understand the indignation Nelken expressed through her books, newspaper columns, and speeches, from 1918 through 1939, one must consider Spain's position at the turn of the century in light of its defeat in the Spanish American War of 1898. Nelken grew up familiar with the anguish of the writers of the Generation of '98, a group of intellectuals who examined Spain's decline and pondered the country's future. She was deeply concerned about the general unrest in her country, the fate of strikers who were protesting working conditions, and the inequitable distribution of land and money. She was indignant about the plight of all oppressed Spaniards unable to change the conditions of their lives.

Most significantly, Nelken had a rare understanding of the repression of both men, whom she considered trapped in their circumstances because of women's dependence on them, and women, whose limited lives stood in marked contrast to the opportunities she herself was offered. An accomplished pianist, she also studied art from an early age. Eduardo Chicharro and María Blanchard, both well-known artists, were among her instructors. Nelken was proficient enough to exhibit her works in Madrid and Barcelona. At the age of fifteen she published articles of art criticism in the English review *The Studio* and in *Le Mercure de France*. In 1923 Nelken wrote somewhat regretfully that her poor eyesight was a determining factor in her choice of writing over painting as a career. Her interest in art, however, did not diminish during her lifetime. She was in charge of courses at the Prado Museum for fifteen years and served on the board of trustees of the Museum of Modern Art in Madrid until 1936. Her involvement with art is evident in *La aventura de Roma* (1923; "The Adventure in Rome"), a novel about a Spanish painter and an American woman who spend their time contemplating Roman art.

In *Las escritoras españolas* (1930; "Spanish Women Writers"), Nelken offers a panoramic view of women writers, beginning with such Latin authors as Pola Argentaria, wife of the poet Anneo Lucano, and Teofila, wife of the poet Canio Rufo, and ending with the nineteenth-century writer Emilia Pardo Bazán. She also wrote a column for women called "La vida y nosotras" ("Life and Us"), which she continued until she entered political life in 1931 as a deputy for the Socialist Workers Party, representing Badajoz. Nelken's *La mujer ante las Cortes Constituyentes* (1931; "Women and the Constituent Assembly") dates from this time. In it she reflects on the future of women in light of new legislation that would be passed, such as recognition of women as legal entities and the legalization of divorce. Nelken vehemently expresses her belief that only divorce offers women a guarantee of personal dignity. No matter how many legal rights they were given, married women were subordinated to their husbands by law, religion, and custom. Thus, only through divorce could unhappily married women achieve freedom. Before the Republic, marriage could only be annulled by the church in a slow, undignified, and infrequent process entirely in the hands of men. Women such as Constancia de la Mora, who suffered an unbearable marriage, were encouraged to seek annulments so that they could remain within the church. De la Mora describes in her memoir, *In Place of Splendor*, how she sat eagerly listening to the discussion of the divorce law in the Assembly, along with Ignacio de Cisneros, the future head of the Spanish Air Force. Their attention to the matter was certainly explicable, since they were the first people to be married after the law was enacted. During the Republic women received the right to vote, to get a divorce, and to be considered a legal entity.

Nelken was reelected as deputy in 1933, and in this capacity regularly participated in national and international meetings. In the same year, she traveled to Paris to lecture on Spanish politics and the work of the Constituent Assembly. In her *Por qué hicimos la Revolución* (1936; "Why We Made the Revolution"), she gives a stirring eyewitness account of early events of the Republic, ably capturing the tension of the period, particularly the miners' strike in Asturias in October 1934, a low point in the history of the Spanish Republic. At that time men, women, and children were treated as brutally by the Civil Guards as they had been under the dictatorship of Primo de Rivera in the 1920s. Nelken went to the region to verify some of these acts of cruelty. In 1936 she was again elected deputy, becoming the only woman to be elected to all three sessions during the Republic, as Esperanza García Méndez points out in *La actuación de la mujer en las Cortes de la II República* (39).

In 1937 Nelken joined the Spanish Communist Party and began collaborating in *Mundo Obrero*, the Communist newspaper. Many women avidly read her columns and, according to Carmen Alcalde's account in *La mujer en la guerra civil española*, they eagerly followed her suggestions on how to support the war effort. Passionate and outspoken in her speeches and columns, Nelken certainly must have offended as well as inspired the Spanish public. In a column, "Perdón y Olvido" ("Forgive and Forget"), for instance, she urges her readers not to forget the monstrous actions of their enemies in the Spanish Civil War and not to forgive them (138). Alistair Hennessy writes in *The Spanish Civil War, 1936–1939: American Hemispheric Perspectives* that the Cuban journalist Pablo de la Torriente Brau "joined the Loyalist forces in Spain after hearing an impassioned plea by La Pasionaria and Margarita Nelken for all able-bodied men to go to the front" (131). He died there within a few months.

Throughout the war Nelken continued to expend her great energy for the Loyalist cause and was awarded a medal by the government for her activities. After the defeat of the Republic, she lived briefly in France and Russia before going to Mexico in 1939. She had two children, Magda and Santiago. We know little of her marriage other than that her husband's name was Santiago de Paúl, a name passed on to their son. One of the great sorrows of her life was the death of this only son, a pilot who was killed in 1943, fighting on the side of the Allies on the Russian front in World War II.

In Mexico, Nelken worked for the Ministry of Education and wrote many books on painting and sculpture. She was the highly respected art critic of the newspaper *Excélsior*. She was also a poet and translator, and a frequent contributor to journals and periodicals published by Spanish exiles in Mexico, such as *Las Españas* and *Boletín de la Unión de Intelectuales Españoles*. Her articles appeared regularly in the Mexican journal *Cuadernos Americanos* and in *Cabalgata* (Buenos Aires). As active as Nelken was in the intellectual life of Mexico, it must have been difficult for her, for she had little opportunity to participate in the political life of her newly adopted country. The reins of power were tightly held by the inner circle of the PRI (Partido Revolucionario Institucional), the main political party. Although Mexican President Lázaro Cárdenas had generously welcomed thousands of Spanish exiles, they were not as free to enter politics as they had been in Spain.

Nelken hated fascism all her life. Juan A. Ortega y Medina relates in *El exilio en México. 1939–1982* that when the Austrian maestro Clemens Krauss conducted in Mexico City in the 1950s, Nelken denounced him in *Excélsior* for having collaborated with the Nazis in the death camps (268–69). Krauss died of a heart attack the following day. Some felt that his death might have been brought on by Nelken's actions. Margarita Nelken herself died on March 9, 1968, ever a staunch and intrepid feminist.

MAJOR THEMES

Nelken reiterates her major concerns throughout her career: politics, art, and the struggle of women for political and economic equality. Her four main sociopolitical works—*La condición social de la mujer en España*, *Las escritoras españolas*, *La mujer ante las Cortes Constituyentes*, and *Por qué hicimos la Revolución*—were all written before 1940, a period of unrest and upheaval. Although her treatment of women's issues in *La condición social* might not seem inflammatory to women today, Nelken's views were highly controversial to the conservative population of traditional Spain in the 1920s. Nelken insisted that Spanish women learn to fend for themselves. "And our feminist struggle," she proclaims, "is, above all, an economic question of terrible urgency" (15). She felt that women did not understand that regardless of their social class, they might one day be forced to support themselves. Nelken may have written successfully about working-class women but, as she herself points out, women's economic problems have a broader base; all women are ultimately affected. Writing of the difference in pay for men and women, she states: "I know of a large store where the saleswoman who has been employed the longest earns thirty-five pesetas a month. And in this same store any male employee begins with a much higher salary. . . . In Spain only women who do not need to depend entirely on their salary can earn a living" (59). Nelken points out that working girls led "lives of absolute submission and passivity, bowing to the men in their lives" (66).

Nelken's perception of charity in Spain sheds light on another vital issue. While she affirms that in other countries women who participate in charitable groups learn principles that can be applied in gainful employment, in Spain that kind of charitable spirit is entirely lacking. Nelken points out that in Belgium, also a very Catholic country, nuns had to be trained as teachers or nurses in order to earn certificates and be placed in charge of charitable organizations. "But not here," she states pointedly. "Here a habit gives omniscience to the wearer. Saintly as some of the women might be, some of them are little more than illiterates serving as nurses, as teachers, and even administering large sums of money" (31–32). Some charitable groups forced people to partake in religious services as a condition for being given food. The only program that Nelken found truly effective was Breakfast for Pupils in the municipal schools, founded by Doña Benita Ases de Monterola, which gave food to students who would otherwise have had nothing to eat before attending classes.

These ideas on charity, published in 1919 in *La condición social*, had previously been expressed by Nelken in a speech at the Ateneo of Madrid in 1918. She further maintained that women without money or means of earning a living "sell themselves legitimately and with hardly less cunning than a prostitute" when they marry (30). Once "the buyer" has been secured, women no longer bother about trying to please him. Such forthright statements contradicted the notion of marriage as a sacrament. Some women walked out, scandalized by what they heard.

Nelken delves into subjects that women in Spain were not supposed to think about, much less write about: prostitution, the subservience of women, the inequities of the legal system. The thesis she develops in her books is essentially that women, not educated to believe in their personal dignity, were socialized to accept that the most desirable goal in life was to be supported by someone else—husband, father, or brother. Nelken argues that this kind of treatment rendered them "perfectly useless to themselves and to others" (*La condición social* 31). One can picture the horrified expressions of traditionalists upon reading in her books that the School for Orphaned Daughters of Veterans turned out women whose only recourse was to become prostitutes, since they were not taught how to make a suitable living. Nelken points out that a greater number of women from distinguished families in Spain became prostitutes than in any other European country.

In her 1923 novel, *La trampa del arenal* ("The Quicksand Trap"), Nelken elaborates upon some of the ideas expressed in *La condición social*. Here the protagonist, Miguel Otura, finds himself trapped in a grotesquely unsuitable marriage. The author concentrates on the women in Miguel's life: his sisters, his mother, his wife, and his mother-in-law. Miguel also has a friend, symbolically called Libertad, who is in some ways Nelken's counterpart. She shows an independence of spirit that is not typical of the other women in the novel. Orphaned at an early age, Libertad works hard to educate herself. Her goal is to be able to support herself; at the novel's end she heads for Paris to continue her work as a translator. Miguel's sisters, on the other hand, are horrified at his suggestion that they all move to Madrid after their father's death so that they can attend school and support themselves. Their mother, the embodiment of traditional religious values, and the sisters themselves, would rather live in genteel poverty among people they know than try to change the circumstances of their lives. Miguel's wife, previously a shopgirl, sought to emulate the manners of the upper-class women who came into her store; after her marriage she drops any pretense of being refined. Miguel is unable to finish his education because of his marriage; he sees himself as doomed to struggle all his life to provide for his vulgar wife, his daughter, his sisters, and his mother. The central metaphor of the novel is that Miguel, like a man in a print in his father's office, is caught in quicksand and is inevitably pulled downward. Throughout *La trampa del arenal*, Nelken develops a perceptive view of the social conditions of women in Spain. In this novel, as in *La condición social*, she makes it clear that social forces at work in the country are deleterious to both men and women.

Nelken also discusses feminist issues in *La mujer ante las Cortes Constituyentes*. The cover of the original edition of this feminist study shows the head and shoulders of a pensive woman looking directly at the reader. Her head is divided into the main issues discussed: divorce, women's suffrage, the religious question, and labor laws and women. Here Nelken argues against immediately granting women the vote. This idea, voiced by such an ardent feminist, seems surprising at first glance. After encountering the women in *La trampa del arenal*, however, one can comprehend her reasoning. She believed that many women were under the control of a conservative church and that their voting would reflect this influence. She felt, as the Socialist Party did, that women's suffrage should be postponed.

Las escritoras españolas, written in a different vein, is also of great interest to feminists. It provides excellent source material for those interested in women writers in Spain, many of whom were overlooked in histories of Spanish literature. Some of the women she focuses on are Doña Luisa de Padilla, daughter of a hero of Lepanto, who wrote on a variety of themes; Isabel Rebeca Correa, a distinguished linguist, who combined a thirst for knowledge and poetic ability; Ana Caro Mallén, the seventeenth-century playwright called "The Tenth Muse from Seville"; and María Rosa de Gálvez, a notable playwright and friend of Manuel de Godoy.

SURVEY OF CRITICISM

Some of the women writers who took part in the turbulent political life of Spain in the 1930s were commenting on their country's plight in periodicals and books a decade or more before the establishment of the Republic. Writers such as Victoria Kent, Dolores Ibarruri (La Pasionaria), María Teresa León, Isabel de Palencia, and many others looked to the Republic with hope and optimism. They shared an indefatigable desire to better the position of women within it and worked tirelessly to achieve a better economic, social, and cultural atmosphere for all: Kent through her work as a prison director; La Pasionaria along with Nelken as an advocate of the rights of male and female workers; León as a preserver of the cultural and artistic heritage of Spain; and Palencia as an internationally known feminist and diplomat. The fratricidal conflict that was the Spanish Civil War and the subsequent defeat of the Republic meant imprisonment for many writer-activists; for others, including Nelken, it meant exile and a new career. Some of these writers, such as Victoria Kent, spent decades organizing public opinion against the Franco regime. Others, such as Nelken, flourished in the literary world of her adopted country. Nelken has been written about in books on both sides of the Atlantic. Criticism about her focuses on two areas of her life: her art and her feminism. Although both realms are significant, she is best known as a feminist.

The sociocultural book by Nelken that is most often cited by modern critics is *La condición social de la mujer en España*. When Maria Aurèlia Capmany researched her book *La dona a Catalunya* (1965), she discovered Nelken's text. She was astonished by the author's incisive tone and the relevance of her analysis for a Spain that was entering what would be the last decade of the Franco dictatorship (Introduction, *La condición social* 16–17). Shortly before Franco's death in 1975, a new edition of *La condición social* was published in Spain. In her introduction to this volume, Capmany notes that many of the deplorable conditions described by Nelken in the 1920s persisted in the Spain of the 1970s. Mary Nash bases several chapters of *Mujer, familia y trabajo en España (1875–1936)* on Nelken's *La condición social*. In 1963 Maria Laffitte (Condesa de Campo Alange) published *La mujer en España*, an extensive consideration of the cultural history of women in Spain from 1860 to 1960. Her comments about Nelken are directed toward her role as a feminist, as a member of the Constituent Assembly, and as a writer. Campo Alange admires her artistic accomplishments as well as her prose style, which she finds clear and correct.

In *Resistencia y movimiento de mujeres en España, 1936–1976*, Giuliana di Febo underscores Nelken's "very important role in the defense of Madrid, and the famous speeches she made to combatants via Radio Madrid" (75). She singles out Nelken's numerous writings on women during the war (referring to her column in *Mundo Obrero*) and her analysis of the Republic in *Por qué hicimos la Revolución*. Nelken also figures in several sections of Juan Ortega y Medina's *El exilio español en México. 1939–1982* dealing with members of both the literary community and the artistic world. In each area, the high quality of her work is acknowledged. She is mentioned several times in a book published in Spain with a similar title, *El exilio español*, edited by José Luis Abellán. Although her poetry is mentioned, many do not realize that some of her verses appeared in the book *Primer frente* (1944; "First Front"). Esperanza García Méndez makes a valuable contribution to our knowledge of Nelken as a deputy to the Constituent Assembly in her book *La actuación de la mujer en las Cortes de la II República*. She also specifically cites Nelken's commentary in newspaper columns during the 1930s, the period that marked the culmination of her work as a feminist, when legislation was being considered on divorce, prostitution, labor laws, and other feminist issues. Janet Pérez, in her insightful *Contemporary Women Writers of Spain*, alludes to Nelken as "an influential feminist, politician, sociologist, and critic during the epoch of the Second Republic" (42).

As new books document the Spanish Republic, the Spanish Civil War, and the exile of many Spanish intellectuals, Margarita Nelken will undoubtedly have a prominent place. To evoke her name is to recall a vibrant, assertive, energetic person and writer who will be remembered for her forthright style, the quality of her art criticism, and her insightful analysis of women's issues.

BIBLIOGRAPHY

Works by Margarita Nelken

Novels and Poetry

La aventura de Roma. Madrid: Sucesores de Rivadeneyra, 1923. [Novel]
La trampa del arenal. Madrid: Librería de los Sucesores de Hernando, 1923. [Novel]
Primer frente. Mexico City: Ángel Chapero, 1944. [Poetry]

Nonfiction

La condición social de la mujer en España. Barcelona: Minerva, 1919? Madrid: CVS Editions, 1975.
Las escritoras españolas. Barcelona: Labor, 1930.
La mujer ante las Cortes Constituyentes. Biblioteca para el Pueblo IV. No. 10. Madrid: Publicaciones Castro, 1931. Madrid: Secretaría de Educación, 1976.
Por qué hicimos la Revolución. 2nd ed. Barcelona: International Publishers, 1936.
La mujer: Conversaciones e ideario. By Santiago Ramón y Cajal. Buenos Aires: Editorial GLEM, 1941. 5–9. [Edition by Margarita Nelken]
Historia del hombre que tuvo el mundo en la mano: Johann Wolfgang von Goethe. Mexico City: Secretaría de Educación Pública, 1943.
Las torres del Kremlin. Mexico City: Imprenta Grafos, 1943.

Art

Tres tipos de Virgen: Fray Angélico, Rafael, Alonso Cano. Madrid: Imprenta de la Ciudad Lineal, 1929. Mexico City: Secretaría de Educación Pública, 1942.
Carlos Orozco Romero. Trans. Irene Nicholson. Mexico City: Ediciones Mexicanas, 1951. Mexico City. UNAM, Dirección General de Publicaciones, 1959. [Bilingual Spanish-English edition]
"Escultura mexicana contemporánea." *Enciclopedia mexicana de arte*. Vol. 11. N.p.: n.p., 1951. 1–39.
El expresionismo en la plástica mexicana de hoy. Mexico: INBA, 1964.

Translations by Margarita Nelken

Historia del arte. By Elie Fauré. 5 vols. Buenos Aires: Editorial Poseidon, 1943–44.

Works about Margarita Nelken

Abellán, José Luis, ed. *El exilio español.* Vol. 4. Madrid: Taurus, 1977.

Alcalde, Carmen. *La mujer en la guerra civil española.* Madrid: Editorial Cambio 16, 1976.

Capmany, Maria Aurèlia. "Un libro polémico sin polémica." *La condición social de la mujer en España.* By Margarita Nelken. Madrid: CVS Editions, 1975. 9–25. [Introduction]

di Febo, Giuliana. *Resistencia y movimiento de mujeres en España, 1936–1976.* Barcelona: Icaria, 1979.

García Méndez, Esperanza. *La actuación de la mujer en las Cortes de la II República.* 2nd ed. Madrid: Ministerio de Cultura, 1979.

Hennessey, Alistair. "Cuba." *The Spanish Civil War, 1936–1939: American Hemispheric Perspectives.* Ed. Mark Falcoff and Frederick B. Pike. Lincoln: U of Nebraska P, 1982. 101–58.

Laffitte, Maria [Condesa de Campo Alange]. *La mujer en España: Cien años de su historia.* Madrid: Aguilar, 1964. 206, 208, 241–43.

Nash, Mary. *Mujer, familia y trabajo en España (1875–1936).* Barcelona: Anthropos, Editorial del Hombre, 1983.

Ortega y Medina, Juan A. "Historia." *El exilio español en México. 1939–1982.* Mexico City: Fondo de Cultura Económica, 1982. 237–306.

Pérez, Janet. *Contemporary Women Writers of Spain.* Boston: Twayne, 1988.

TERESA PÀMIES
(b. 1919)

Janet Pérez

BIOGRAPHY

Teresa Pàmies i Bertran was born in 1919 in Balaguer, a small town in the Catalan mountain province of Lérida. Her father, Tomás Pàmies Pla, an extraordinarily durable influence in her life, was a colorful, romantic, eccentric, self-taught revolutionary born in the same town in 1889. A womanizer and a chauvinist, he was also a hardworking idealist, an admirer of the Soviet Union, and an organizer of workers' and peasants' cooperatives and syndicates. Teresa, the third child born of his second marriage and his first surviving offspring, followed in his footsteps, unlike her younger siblings. Their mother, Rosa Bertran, had inherited a house and a bit of land. She supported the family, thus allowing Tomás to spend his time in politics. She helped to raise money when he was jailed, and saved enough money so that the elder son could study in Barcelona.

This model of the primal family becomes almost a paradigm of Pàmies's fiction; a much-used archetype in her writings is the hardworking, self-abnegating woman who lives for an ungrateful activist. Teresa, accustomed as a child to her father's frequent incarcerations, often visited him in jail and brought him food and small necessities. She recalls in *Testament à Praga* (1971; *Testamento en Praga* 1971; "Testament in Prague") his imprisonment "for daring to claim the land for those who worked it, demanding the nationalization of properties of nuns and priests, the separation of Church and State, free lay schools, women's emancipation, rehabilitation of prostitutes, free love and so many other outrages" (52).[1]

Largely self-educated, Teresa became known in leftist and feminist organizations at a young age. Biographical information must be deduced, for the most part, from her heavily autobiographical "fiction," along with the scant additional data appearing on cover blurbs, one of which notes that she began working in a sweatshop at age eleven, while another indicates that she left school at age twelve to work as a dressmaker's apprentice. Both accounts may be true; her works (e.g., *Dona de pres* 1975; *Mujer de preso* 1975; "The Prisoner's Woman") certainly show familiarity with the seamstress's trade and textile manufacturing. A correspondent for the Socialist revolutionary press while still in her teens, she wrote war chronicles for the JSUC (Catalan Young Socialists Union). Pàmies became politically prominent during the Second Republic (1931–36), presiding at meetings, delivering speeches, and working in information and propaganda. She visited the Civil War battlefront, and traveled for the Republic in an attempt to obtain support from foreign governments. Her political experiences, wartime activism, family background, and exile are all rich sources of literary inspiration, supplying the narrative framework, settings, and models for characters in some two dozen books.

The Spanish Civil War separated the family. Pàmies's father worked in the leftist Central Committee of the region, from which he was later expelled for independent thinking and criticism of opportunism. Teresa and her father lost contact with the rest of the family, and she never saw her mother again. She and her father joined the Republican exodus on foot to France, where he spent time in a concentration camp, then worked on farms for room and board and helped supply food to the French Resistance during World War II. Teresa experienced the hardships of refugee camps, then spent time in Paris, where for three months she was jailed as an undocumented alien. Eventually she made her way to Latin America, living temporarily in the Dominican Republic and Cuba. She studied journalism in Mexico and remained there for nearly eight years. She moved to Prague in 1947, where she lived for some twelve years, working as an editor for Radio Prague's broadcasts in Catalan and Spanish.

Her father remained in France until 1953, when ill health contributed to his decision to join Teresa in Prague; there he worked as a municipal gardener, sometimes taking his youngest grandson with him so that Teresa could go to work. Accused of complicity in the execution of Falangists, he was denied a passport to return to Spain, and died in Prague in 1966.

Pàmies spent more than thirty years in exile. From 1959 until 1971, the year of her return to Catalonia, she lived mostly in France, visiting Spain only briefly. She married and bore at least five children: a daughter who died young of an incurable illness, and four sons. Many personal experiences, wartime hardships, and real-life characters appear almost unchanged in Pàmies's heavily "testimonial," autobiographical fiction, but her marriage and maternal trials remain cloaked in privacy.

Prior to publishing *Testament à Praga* and while still in exile, Pàmies completed *La filla del pres* (1967; "The Prisoner's Daughter") and won the President Companys Prize for Prose in the Catalan literary competition and celebration, Jocs Florals, held in Marseilles in 1967. She did not become known in Spain until 1971 with *Testament à Praga*, which had won the 1970 Josep Pla Prize. Three subsequent editions in Catalan and four in Castilian evince continuing public interest in this novel; deprived of the Republican perspective during most of the Franco regime, Spanish readers were increasingly avid for accounts of this silenced portion of their recent history. Pàmies's often polemic and intensely personal text alternates two viewpoints or narrative voices, that of Teresa and that of her late father. His voice is heard through his handwritten memoirs, composed in his final years (1958–66), which he instructed Teresa to type verbatim as his legacy to his four children. Teresa's narrative voice comments on, contradicts, modifies, clarifies, speculates, and reminisces in a mono-dialogue with her father in entries written during 1968–70. In one revealing passage, she reflects on his influence on her life: "Perhaps there was a time when I mythified you, but that helped me. In my adolescent political exaltation, mythifying my father neither slowed my career nor did me any damage. You were the man of integrity and valor whom I wished to resemble, and if any of your friends said that I did, it made me happy" (215–16).

Shaken and provoked by the Russian invasion of Czechoslovakia, Pàmies attempts to reconcile the crushing of one socialist people by another. Her recollection of what her father stood for politically is juxtaposed with thoughts of the final years when, already aged, sick, and becoming senile, he was somewhat of a burden. Attempting reconciliation with her father's spirit, she confesses her shortcomings but also denounces his philandering and lack of consideration for her mother, his absences when her brother and sister were born, and his ignorance of her mother's sacrifices, which included doing laundry in the public washhouse and picking olives to aid her husband in jail and feed the four children. At the same time, she attempts an ideological "rapprochement" with a party that continues to change, a party that no longer represents the ideal that she and her father first espoused.

Following her return to Catalonia in 1971, Pàmies devoted herself with characteristic energy to a career as a novelist. In the first decade, she published fourteen books in Catalan and four in Castilian, a rapidity suggesting that many must have been written wholly or partly in exile. When the Catalan daily *Avui* was established in 1976, she became a regular contributor, later writing also for the leftist Castilian weekly news magazine *Triunfo*. Her interest in women's problems and issues led to articles for women's magazines, including such nonfeminist publications as *Hogar y moda*.

MAJOR THEMES

Pàmies possesses an extraordinarily rich store of personal experience upon which to draw for her literary accounts; her themes and plots are almost without exception autobiographically grounded. Frequently repeated topics include labor conflicts, working-class problems, the organization of workers' parties, and political imprisonment. Political motifs appear insistently in *Crònica de la vetlla*

(1976; "Chronicle of Vespers"), set in Balaguer, where both Pàmies and her father participated with passionate enthusiasm in local politics. Prior to the Civil War, the most left-leaning Spanish political organization was the radical faction of the Socialist Party, to which she and her father belonged; the Communist Party became increasingly prominent with the war's outbreak, and was the only organized opposition to Franco. In exile both belonged to the Communist Party, (officially known in some countries as Socialist).

In Pàmies's writing, the Primo de Rivera dictatorship (1923–30) and early years of the Republic are evoked together with ideological rivalries among Socialist Party dissidents and the leftists' bitter, treacherous infighting, which Pàmies highlights more than the conflicts between Right and Left or the differences between the rich and the poor. Her intense involvement in these struggles and their role in her father's career are echoed in *Testament à Praga*. Ideological strife occupies less of the foreground in *Memòria dels morts* (1981; *Memoria de los muertos* 1981; "Memoir of the Dead"), a dreamlike reconstruction of the past provoked by a return to Balaguer and the discovery of her mother's grave, a surreal encounter with her mother's spirit that enabled Pàmies to experience peace. In this book, Teresa recalls learning that her mother was drowned in July 1942 under mysterious circumstances, variously interpreted as suicide, political intrigue, or vengeance. With her family in exile and her husband accused of war crimes, some wanted to bury her in a potter's field, but Tomás's brother intervened, paying excessive charges so that the devout Rosa could receive a Christian burial.

Ideology is likewise prominent in many of Pàmies's works focusing upon exile; modification of ideologies over time is a theme. The Spanish Civil War is another pervasive major theme that appears in *Crònica de la vetlla* and *Romanticismo militante* (1976; "Militant Romanticism"). War's shadow also looms in her novelized, romanticized biography of the fiery Communist orator La Pasionaria, *Una Española llamada Dolores Ibarruri* (1977; "A Spanish Woman Named Dolores Ibarruri") and in *Records de guerra i d'exili* (1976; "Recollections of War and Exile"). Occasionally present in *Testament à Praga* and *Memòria dels morts,* war occupies center stage in *Quan érem capitans* (1974; "When We Were Captains"), winner of the Joan Estelrich Prize. Subtitled "Memoirs of That War," this novelistic memoir depicts civil conflict from the committed Socialist perspective of a young woman familiar with many historical figures personally known to Pàmies. The pain and sorrow of losing the war and the anguish of exodus are passionately re-created.

The autobiographical basis of the theme of exile and exiles is too evident and significant to be termed a substratum; like war, it is a traumatic experience for Pàmies and much of her generation. Together with love of the Catalan homeland, exile—already prominent in *Testament à Praga*—becomes the primary, nearly exclusive focus of *Cròniques de nàufrags* (1977; "Chronicles of Shipwreck Survivors") and *Gent del meu exili* (1975; "Unforgettable Characters of My Exile"), in which it is portrayed from the perspective of others. Composed in epistolary form, *Cròniques de nàufrags* comprises experiences of some forty refugees of varying ages who struggle to survive with dignity in extremely trying circumstances. Still more personal is *Gent del meu exili*. The reader senses that Pàmies actually knew the people described, while the "letters" might have been stories heard from other exiles rather than trials witnessed at close quarters. Enormous pathos pervades these descriptions of war's innocent victims, predominantly women and children: the crazed woman whose three-year-old son was sacrificed in the Nazi holocaust; aging French sisters dying of cancer in Mexico; outcasts in a strange, reclusive world, imprisoned by loneliness and despair.

Works viewing exile from the perspective of Pàmies herself are *Quan érem refugiats* (1975; "When We Were Refugees") and *Va ploure tot el dia* (1974; "It's Going to Rain All Day"), a finalist for the Prudenci Bertrana Prize. In the latter work, a Catalan woman exile returning home after thirty years spends a rainy day lost in memories prompted by police questioning. *Quan érem refugiats* is an autobiographical text depicting the trials of women in French refugee camps and jails, the passage to South America, and life in the Dominican Republic and Cuba, all experienced firsthand by Pàmies. Interspersed are grim glimpses of Catalonia, treated harshly by Franco as a consequence of traditional Catalan separatism and the deeper rooting there of leftist and liberal parties. Homer's *Odyssey* has been seen as the prototype of exile literature, with the hero's twenty years of wandering. Wandering is still more prolonged for Pàmies and her characters, with the further difference that the woman's point of view, the plight of innocent victims, and the antiheroic nature of internment and incarceration provide striking contrast with the heroic prototype.

Newfound postwar Spain provides three major themes or facets of Pàmies's work: clandestine resistance to Franco; the difficulties faced by the defeated and the profiteering and abuses at the hands of the victors; and variants on travel books wherein Pàmies visits areas of Spain previously unknown to her. Four of the latter seem strangely atypical and out of context in Pàmies's overall production. The travel books explore the concept of the journey topos, life as a voyage; and unlike anything previously undertaken by Pàmies, their purpose is enjoyment. Earlier ideologial preoccupations and political intent are relegated to the background in *Busque-me à Granada* (1980; "Seek Me in Granada"), *Matins de l'Aran* (1982; "Mornings in the Aran Valley"), *Rosalia no hi era* (1982; "Rosalia Wasn't There"), and *Vacances aragoneses* (1979; "Vacation in Aragon").

The four travel works divide naturally into two groups, according to the author's relative familiarity with the areas: those closely resembling Catalonia— *Matins de l'Aran* and *Vacances aragoneses*, involving regions contiguous to Pàmies's native Pyrenees—and those with more "exotic" culture, history, and appearance, *Busque-me à Granada* and *Rosalia no hi era*. In her book on Galicia and Rosalía de Castro, feminism is again a prominent theme, as the author's visit to the beloved province of the nineteenth-century poet inspires a sense of identification with this literary foremother. Rosalía's status as a writer in a minority language of the peninsula (outlawed under Franco, as was Catalan), her loss of her mother and her experience of the loss of a child, and her devotion to the cause of the peasants are points of similarity with which Pàmies identifies strongly. Rosalía's criticism of male insensitivity and the suffering undergone by unwed mothers and illegitimate children also strikes a responsive chord in Pàmies (Rosalía herself was the offspring of an affair between a priest and an unmarried country girl). Pàmies attempts to re-create Rosalía as woman: her words, her thoughts, her life—and her early death from cancer.

Clandestine resistance to Franco is a major concern in *Amor clandestí* (1976; ''Clandestine Love'') and *Dona de pres*, both employing a woman's perspective on illegal political activism and depicting ways that political circumstances intrude upon private lives and change private feelings. *Dona de pres*, obviously insired by Pàmies's primal family, recounts the life of Neus, a convent-educated daughter of the small-town mercantile bourgeoisie in postwar Catalonia. She is swept off her feet by a member of the underground resistance, has an affair with him, and bears him a son. Her married lover is imprisoned, while pregnant Neus is ostracized and disowned. Facing life as a single parent and unmarried mother in a rigid, Victorian society, and stigmatized as ''the prisoner's woman,'' she steadfastly makes herself his emotional and financial mainstay. She serves as the ''secretary'' of the illiterate wives of other prisoners, leads campaigns to improve their lot, and raises her son to revere his father as a hero. ''Sisterhood,'' although never named by Pàmies, is a strong subtheme and among the virtues possessed by nearly all her heroines. Feminist themes—as important as the political ones in many of Pàmies's books—often echo her perception of her mother's sacrifices and her father's egotism. Emotional abuse (through infidelity, neglect, and verbal assault), financial exploitation, and abandonment of wives appear frequently, as do the neglect and abandonment of children. Unwanted pregnancies and the inaccessibility of contraceptives and abortion are repeated in a number of works, along with the double standards of morality and conduct, which are uniformly portrayed as causes of women's suffering.

A more contemporaneous view of post-Franco Spain appears in *Cartes al fill recluta* (1984; ''Letters to My Son the Recruit''). Centered on the narrative viewpoint of a mother writing to her son in military service, two temporal planes intersect: one corresponds to a series of letters written regularly by the mother over many months; the other, which she writes upon a single occasion of emotional stress, is stimulated by the abortive military coup attempted by conservatives wishing to reassert Falangist control by occupying the Cortes (Spanish Parliament) on February 23, 1984. Fragments of the single long missive alternate with the periodic notes, showing the traumatic effect on Pàmies (and other returned exiles) of the threat to Spain's democracy. Save for this work, political concerns become less important in Pàmies's writings after *Memòria dels morts* in 1981, being symbolically laid to rest along with her mother.

Another, earlier work whose major concern is political—although not inspired primarily by Spanish politics—is *Si vas a París, papá . . .* (1975; "If You Go to Paris, Daddy . . . "). The leftist student revolts of May 1968 in France inspire a meditation on French ideals (intuited or experienced during nearly twelve years of exile in that country) and their connections with contemporary Catalan political issues. Obviously, the year 1968 (which also saw the "Prague Springtime" and Russian suppression of that movement, as evoked with anguish in *Testament à Praga*) symbolizes for Pàmies the abyss that separates revolutionary dreams from the conservative and repressive actions of established governments of any political persuasion whatsoever. Another recent title by Pàmies, *Praga* (1987; "Prague"), although ostensibly one of a series of tourist guides to cities, recalls her disillusionment along with that of the Czech people. Covering the funeral of the Communist president, Klement Gottwald, for Radio Prague in 1953, she stressed for Spanish listeners the outpouring of grief, which was "authentic, because Czechs and Slovakians hadn't yet felt the tremendous jolt of revelation of the crimes committed in the name of the Socialist homeland" (70). She refers to the slow erosion of ideals in the Socialist bloc as a malignant tumor, growing until 1968, "when Czech Communists themselves tried to extirpate it and regenerate the Republic" (71). Pàmies's political maturation leaves her with sympathy for Socialist ideals but without radicalism; disillusioned, she is no longer unwilling to criticize Russia and other Communist nations.

Pàmies's ideology has evolved more in political matters than in feminist ones. She writes knowingly of divergences between Trotskyites and Leninists and of obscure differences between Marxist splinter groups in Catalonia, and communicates lucid perceptions of evolving Communist dogmas. Her feminism reflects time's passage less clearly: in comparison with younger feminists in Catalonia during the 1980s, Pàmies is unquestionably of another generation. More concerned with class than with gender (as is generally true of Third World feminism in its initial stages), she makes no mention of elimination of *machista* or sexist language, women's personal and sexual fulfillment, or equal pay for equal work. She does not advocate lesbianism or attack marriage as an institution, nor does she address such issues as educational opportunities for women in prison, provision of day-care centers, or equal access to professional and managerial careers and promotions. Her feminist concerns include male egotism, the oppression and exploitation of women and neglect of women and children, women's sacrifice to support their families in order to allow their husbands to pursue political or other goals, the nonexistence of divorce in Spain (prior to 1983), and lack of access to contraceptives and abortion. She treats adultery, but not subtler problems such as sex-role stereotyping, and tends to idealize mothers and motherhood—along with their exploitation. While she excoriates masculine vanity and insensitivity, Pàmies gives little thought to feminine self-realization beyond marital or quasi-marital relationships; even her female revolutionaries fall prey to masculine wiles.

Like her own mother, Pàmies's heroines are hardworking and uncomplaining, as is the heroine of *Dona de pres*, who complies with the expectation of "concrete, daily abnegation, [and] constant resignation'' (107). In the unexpectedly sentimental ending of the novel, Neus dies of tuberculosis, having deprived herself of medical care to devote herself to the prisoners' causes. Her lack of awareness, of protest, contrasts with the heightened consciousness of women portrayed by younger Catalan feminists (Esther Tusquets, Maria Antònia Oliver, Montserrat Roig, and Carme Riera) or more mature ones, such as Mercè Rodoreda and Nùria Pompeia. Pàmies does not disdain occasional recourse to the melodramatic, and appears unaware of the paradox implicit in a feminism that patriarchally idealizes a woman's sacrifice for men. On a personal level, she does not point out that her father's chauvinism and womanizing contradicted his leftist advocacy of women's emancipation, nor does she lament her mother's lack of liberation, although her sympathy for such women is apparent throughout her work.

Pàmies's texts repeatedly raise the theoretical problem of the relationships between autobiography and fiction, autobiography and truth. Although her father commanded her to copy his memoirs without changes or omissions, she was unable to resist "censoring" his amorous episodes (*Testament* 215), critiquing his inclusions and exclusions: "You devote folios and folios to your mistresses and girl friends and don't mention important events which we, your children, witnessed. For example, that All Saints' Day in 1926, a day we remember because that's when María was born and you weren't home'' (217). The self-centeredness of Tomás's memoirs runs counter to her expectations as a reader: "It's in this matter that your memoirs disappoint me, Father'' (219). Pàmies argues that her father's "biography" cannot give short shrift to her mother, because only thanks to her abnegation was he able to be what he was (220). Questioning the "truth" in autobiography, of real concern to contemporary critical theorists, is of necessity relevant to readers of Pàmies's other writings as well. Even her ostensible guide to Prague is filled with personal reminiscence and political judgments, along with her comments on Czech poets, music, theater, hotels, restaurants, monuments, night life, history, and bookstores, and repeated contrasts of the "tourists' Prague" with the working-class areas and neighborhoods known only to long-term residents that she experienced as an exile.

Implicitly, Pàmies raises questions of reception aesthetics and reader-response theory, as well as the correlation between author and narrator, author and character or persona, writer and audience. And when she discusses her own recollection of Tomás's "testament" with relatives in Barcelona a few years later, she is interrupted by shouts: "Your father couldn't possibly have thought that. Never!'' (220). In addition to questions raised by reader-response theory as to the integrity and reliability of the text, Pàmies herself is challenged as editor and narrator, in regard to her obvious subjectivity, her "censoring" of her father's memoirs, and her evolving ideological biases. Readers must exercise caution in extracting "facts" from her autobiographically based texts. Undoubtedly the safest way to read them is as fiction inspired by some of this century's most significant historical events.

Rural Catalonia, the growth of working-class political consciousness, the organization of political parties in the villages, and the relationship between Catalan interests and those of the central government are emotionally charged issues, as is the ideological strife preceding and imbuing the Spanish Civil War. The bitter infighting within leftist organizations in Spain and abroad, the trauma of war and exile, the anguish of exodus and the loss of family, the drama of clandestine resistance and persecution of the defeated—these are themes almost impossible to treat with objectivity, themes that are central to Pàmies's life and work. It is equally difficult to address feminist questions dispassionately. Pàmies, however, never pretends to be objective or dispassionate: Her recurrent themes are repeated within a variety of contexts, viewed from different moments in her life, and occasionally modified enough for the reader to become familiar with the external stimuli as well as the internal reactions from a variety of perspectives.

SURVEY OF CRITICISM

Due in part to her long exile (which made her an unknown in Spain), as well as to her writing primarily in a "minority" or vernacular language, Pàmies has received little critical attention. Unknown to the literary community and critical "establishment" alike until relatively late in life (her first novel was published when she was fifty-two), she was an obscure figure even in Catalonia until the mid-1970s. Most of the critical commentary has been written by Catalans, primarily in the post-Franco era, and reflects the political as well as the tendentious and journalistic aspects of her work.

Book reviews in such newspapers and periodicals as *Destino*, *La Vanguardia*, and *El Correo Catalán*, the vernacular *Avui*, and similar outlets, form nearly the totality of secondary works.

When Pàmies's first novel appeared in Spain, daily newspapers in Catalan were still not allowed by the Franco regime, and the Castilian press took little notice of writing in the vernacular languages (Catalan, Galician, Basque). The fact that Pàmies published her works in such rapid succession (two works in 1974, four in 1975, seven in 1976, and four more before the end of the decade) may also have interfered with early critical studies. The absorbing nature of events in Spain during this period of transition to democracy likewise distracted would-be critics.

Pàmies is not mentioned in literary histories, not even those in Catalan, with the exception of J. M. Serviá's *Catalunya. Tres generacions*, in which she is studied as part of three coexisting literary "generations" in Catalonia. There are few relevant scholarly treatments of any length, no analytical essays, and no study of her complete works beyond an introductory overview (Pérez, *Contemporary Women Writers*). Not only are there no structuralist or formalist exegeses of her novels, there are not even sociological or Marxist approaches (to which Pàmies's writing would be especially amenable). Nor are there dissertations or thematic or linguistic studies, despite the fact that her use of language and dialogue invites examination. There are no biographies, apart from her autobiographical writings. Only isolated aspects have been studied, as in the brief article by María Lourdes Möller-Soler, who in ten pages examines the impact of the Civil War on the life and works of Pàmies and two other Catalan women novelists. The only other article of any length, by Genaro Pérez, focuses upon the importance of mother and homeland as remembered in exile and "recovered" after the exile's return. The remainder of the scant bibliography on Pàmies comes almost exclusively from generally inaccessible reviews, usually brief and impressionistic, occasionally somewhat polemic. The criticism is far from proportional to Pàmies's importance as a chronicler of war, revolution, and exile; but neglect of women writers is too frequent and widespread for this to cause surprise. Pàmies stands almost alone in her generation as witness to women's participation in some of the major events of twentieth-century Spanish history.

NOTE

1. All quotations are from the Castilian editions.

BIBLIOGRAPHY

Works by Teresa Pàmies

Novels and Novelized Memoirs

La filla del pres. N.p.: n.p, 1967.
Testament à Praga. Barcelona: Destino, 1971.
Quan érem capitans. Barcelona: DOPESA, 1974.
Va ploure tot el dia. Barcelona: Edicions 62, 1974.
Dona de pres. Barcelona: Proa, 1975.
Gent del meu exili. Barcelona: Galba, 1975.
Quan érem refugiats. Barcelona: DOPESA, 1975.
Amor clandestí. Barcelona: Galba, 1976.
Aventura mexicana des noi. Pau, France: Arizpa, 1976.
Crònica de la vetlla. Barcelona: Editorial Selecta, 1976.
Los que se fueron. Barcelona: Roca, 1976.
Records de guerra i d'exili. Barcelona: Roca, 1976.
Romanticismo militante. Barcelona: Destino, 1976.
Cròniques de nàufrags. Barcelona: Destino, 1977.
Aquell vellet gentil i pulcre. Palma de Mallorca: Moll, 1978.
Memòria dels morts. Barcelona: Planeta, 1981.
Cartes al fill recluta. Barcelona: Portic, 1984.
Massa tard per a Cèlia. Barcelona: Destino, 1984.
La chivata. Barcelona: Planeta, 1986.
Segrets amb filipina. Barcelona: Destino, 1986.

Travel Books

Vacances aragoneses. Barcelona: Destino, 1979.
Busque-me à Granada. Barcelona: Destino, 1980.
Matins de l'Aran. Barcelona: Portic, 1982.
Rosalia no hi era. Barcelona: Destino, 1982.
Praga. Barcelona: Destino, 1987.

Essays and Biography

Si vas a París, papá . . . . Barcelona: Hogar del Libro, 1975.
Maig de les dones. Barcelona: Laia, 1976.
Una española llamada Dolores Ibarruri (La Pasionaria). Barcelona: Roca, 1977.
La mujer después de los cuarenta años. Barcelona: Publicaciones Europa-América, 1980.
Opinió de dona. Barcelona: Edicions 62, 1983.
Rebelión de viejas. Barcelona: La Sal, 1989.

Miscellaneous

Obras selectas inéditas. Barcelona: DOPESA, 1985.

Translations

There are no translations in English of works by Teresa Pàmies. Several of her works are available in Castilian, although it is difficult to know which are translations and which she originally wrote in that language, as she writes with equal facility in both Castilian and Catalan. In some cases, titles appeared simultaneously in both languages. Eight of the titles mentioned above appear to have been published only in Castilian; those listed below are cases where it is clear that the Castilian version appeared later (or that the original was in Catalan).
Testamento en Praga. Barcelona: Destino, 1971.
Mujer de preso. Barcelona: Ayma, 1975.
Memoria de los muertos. Barcelona: Planeta, 1981.

Works about Teresa Pàmies

Möller-Soler, María Lourdes. ''El impacto de la guerra civil en la vida y obra de tres autoras catalanas: Aurora Bertrana, Teresa Pàmies y Mercè Rodoreda. *Letras Femeninas* 12. 1–2 (Spring–Fall 1986): 34–44.

Pérez, Genaro J. ''Madre, patria y destierro en *Memoria de los muertos* de Teresa Pàmies.'' *Revista Canadiense de Estudios Hispánicos* 14.3 (Spring 1990): 579–88.

Pérez, Janet. *Contemporary Women Writers of Spain.* Boston: Twayne, 1988. 148–52.

Riera Llorca, Viçent. ''La crònica novel.lesca de Teresa Pàmies.'' *Serra d'Or* (May 1977): 325–27.

Serviá, Josep Maria. *Catalunya. Tres generacions.* Barcelona: Ediciones Martínez Roca, 1975. 133–51.

EMILIA PARDO BAZÁN (1851–1921)

Ruth El Saffar

BIOGRAPHY

One of Spain's most prolific and intellectually accomplished writers, Emilia Pardo Bazán has to her credit over twenty novels, nearly one thousand short stories, hundreds of essays, and several plays and volumes of poetry. Bursting onto the literary scene at a time when women were excluded from virtually every facet of intellectual life, her very presence challenged the barriers that kept women from developing talents other than the socially prescribed domestic ones. Not content merely to have achieved recognition of her own prowess, she also devoted a great deal of her time and energy to the cause of women. Her indefatigable struggle for the rights of women—for their sexual as well as their political and intellectual freedom—became the hallmark of her life and work.

Passionate though she was on the issue of women's rights, and innovative though she was in the area of literary style, Pardo Bazán's overall political profile is complicated by a deep conservative strain—a lifelong commitment to her noble origins and the Catholic faith with which those origins were inextricably associated. It is the mixed pull of the modern and the traditional that gives tension and energy to her work and that has so perplexed critics. Nonetheless, it is clear that Pardo Bazán parlayed her wealth and titles in the service of an intellectual and literary visibility that was to work ultimately for the benefit of all women. Viscerally aware of the penalties attendant on being a woman of intellect, she pointed out far in advance of the feminist movement in Europe and the United States how crippling it has been for women to be judged exclusively in terms of relationship, and not to be considered in and for themselves: ''The fundamental error that disturbs common opinion about creatures of the female gender . . . is that of attributing to them a destiny of mere relationship, not considering them in themselves, nor for themselves, but rather in and for others'' (''Una opinión sobre la mujer'' [''An Opinion About Women''], Schiavo, *Mujer* 158).

Pardo Bazán's parents were provincial nobles from the northwestern region of Spain known as Galicia. Born on September 15, 1851, as the only child of parents of education and means, every attention was lavished on her and every encouragement given for her intellectual growth. Her mother taught her to read; her father, that women can do anything men can do. She was sent to French schools and was tutored in math and science. Her passion for reading was indulged and even encouraged. She was allowed without remonstrance to forgo the usual training of the gentlewoman—allowed *not* to learn embroidery and the piano skills that constituted the usual education of a young lady of her social status.

Pardo Bazán was also allowed to marry the man of her choice and, after her marriage in 1868, to continue her travels and studies. In fact, her husband, Don José Quiroga, encouraged her to take classes surreptitiously at law school with him, which meant that though she could not actually attend the lectures, she read the texts he brought home and wrote papers for some of his courses. Her education did not stop there, however. Before she was twenty, she had become aware that in the active social life of Madrid that threatened to absorb her and her husband, there yawned a desperate void. Fear that she would not have time to carry out what had the imperative of a life mission drove her early into an encyclopedic quest for knowledge.

In 1871 Pardo Bazán wrote what became a prize-winning essay on the eighteenth-century Spanish philosopher Benito Jerónimo Feijóo, whose early espousal of feminism made him a lifelong figure of veneration for her. The year 1876 also saw the birth of her first child, Jaime, who became the inspiration for her first collection of poems. By then twenty-five years old, Pardo Bazán had fully embarked on a career as an autodidact, connoisseur of the arts, and writer. Her interest in contemporary intellectual life did not stop at the doors of literature and philosophy, but led also into politics and science. Many of her early essays in Galician journals represented efforts to inform her compatriots of recent scientific discoveries.

In the twelve-year period from 1878 to 1890, Pardo Bazán gave birth to two more children, extended the reach of her talent for controversy deeply into the realm of literature, published nine of her twenty-one novels, founded and published a monthly literary journal, traveled incessantly, and gave major lectures on Russian literature at the Ateneo, a gathering place for intellectuals in Madrid.

Perhaps the most notable event of those early years was the publication of a collection of essays entitled *La cuestión palpitante* (1883; ''The Burning Question''), in which Pardo Bazán sought to bring to the attention of Spanish readers the importance of naturalism as a literary movement. Although she never subscribed to the idea that human beings are ineluctably the mindless product of their environment, she was drawn by temperament to the naturalist technique of close description of the circumstances within which characters act. Her novels typically supply a full and often overly abundant accounting of her characters' surroundings, in keeping with the regionalist and *costumbrista* (slice-of-life vignette) trends practiced among contemporary writers.

Pardo Bazán's knowledge of and attraction to French ideas, her early interest in naturalism, and her temerity as a woman to broach matters of literary theory combined to produce considerable negative reaction to her work. She might as well have been espousing child prostitution, so hysterical were the recriminations her interest in naturalism provoked. The controversy aroused over *La cuestión palpitante* caused her husband such chagrin and embarrassment that he insisted, in a fit of anger, that Pardo Bazán give up her writing entirely. Instead, she gave up married life. In a short novel, *La dama joven* (1883; "The Young Woman"), written during the period of separation, she depicts her plight through the character of an actress who, unlike Pardo Bazán herself, succumbs to her husband's pressure to conform to the traditional role assigned women, giving up for his sake a brilliant theatrical career.

Although Pardo Bazán's flamboyant personality, love of polemic, and overpowering intellect made of her one of the leading literary figures of her day, and although she worked indefatigably to disseminate progressive ideas about science, literature, politics, and education, she was never truly able to overcome the "handicap" of being a woman in what was indisputably a man's world. From as early as her fledgling scientific essays on heat, she had drawn hostile published responses from men who expressed doubt that a woman could write knowledgeably on matters of science. Her many novels were ransacked for signs of a woman who was immoral, materialistic, or without faith. Even her closest male literary friends—Marcelino Menéndez y Pelayo, Clarín, and Juan Valera—could not always be counted on for support when the controversies around her became especially inflamed.

Despite the vicissitudes of her political and religious sentiments, Pardo Bazán remained constant in her devotion to feminist concerns. Her father had ingrained in her the conviction that women could do whatever men could, yet even her recognition as a major figure in the intellectual life of her times could not prevent her from being wounded by an environment implacably hostile to women as intellectuals. In 1895, at the age of forty-four and at the peak of her career, she wrote to a friend that the artist's vocation, which brings such plaudits to men, is to women a source of great pain: "What for a man are flowers are for us thorns. Each step toward art costs us some pain and some injury" (qtd. in Bravo-Villasante 192).

In 1891 Pardo Bazán founded the *Nuevo Teatro Crítico* ("New Critical Theater"), a journal that became a major vehicle for the propagation of feminist ideas. Her voice became more urgent and insistent over the years, especially in relation to the education of women. She felt so moved by John Stuart Mill's work that she was instrumental in having *On the Subjection of Women* translated into Spanish. She also espoused the cause of other contemporary women writers, particularly the poet Rosalía de Castro and the novelist and feminist Concepción

Gimeno de Flaquer. In later years she established the Biblioteca de la Mujer ("Women's Library"), in which she republished, among others, the works of the seventeenth-century *novela* writer, María de Zayas.

Although she eventually was elected president of the literary section of the Ateneo, Pardo Bazán was never accepted into the Spanish Academy. Five years before her death, by fiat and despite vigorous protest, the minister of public education appointed her to a professorship in Romance languages at the University of Madrid, thereby making her the first woman to occupy such a position. The times had passed her by, however, or perhaps they had not yet caught up with her. Few students attended the lectures: first six, then only two. An old man, hunchbacked and asthmatic, is reputed to have stayed when all the other students had left, saying that to close the position would be a "true national shame." She lectured to him alone until he, too, disappeared, and she was forced into retirement within a year of her appointment.

Pardo Bazán died of complications of diabetes at the age of sixty-nine. She fell into a seizure while she was writing an article on the Spanish novelist Juan Valera and never recovered. She left behind her fifty-four published books: literary criticism, biographical essays, novels, poems, short stories, theater, political essays, travelogues, and even a cookbook. She is considered among the best novelists of the nineteenth century in Spain, and one of the best short story writers in the history of Spanish letters.

MAJOR THEMES

Pardo Bazán belongs in every sense to the gestational period of Spanish letters, when political and scientific activity in western Europe was demanding that intellectuals awaken from the dream of literary Romanticism and the spiritual and monarchical ideologies in which Romanticism was incubated. While her earliest novel, *Pascual López* (1879), still carries the burden of a literary formation nurtured by the Romantics of the early nineteenth century as well as echoes of the Spanish classics, it also reveals an impulse to shake off those remnants of a tradition no longer viable.

Perhaps as important to Pardo Bazán's work as science and the challenge to the theocentric worldview that science represents, is the related literary theme of naturalism. Much of her enthusiasm for the Goncourt brothers was motivated by their espousal of a literature oriented toward a rendering of sensual reality. In her second novel, *Un viaje de novios* (1881; *A Wedding Trip* 1891, 1910), Pardo Bazán devotes herself to a minute representation of the travel experience of a newly married young woman who loses her husband on their honeymoon and winds up having an affair with a man she meets on the train. Much of the novel could well have emerged from the meticulous travelogues Pardo Bazán kept on her journey to southern France and Italy, but it also introduces the theme of the contradictory pulls of matrimony and adultery that will face so many of her female characters. It also foreshadows later works in which the novelist explores the tensions between desire and religious duty.

The two early novels show themes that persisted and developed as successful elements of her work as she learned to better integrate her scientific/naturalistic bent with her passion for the exploration of character. Later novels—*Insolación* (1889; *Midsummer Madness*, 1907), *Morriña* (1889; *Homesickness,* 1891), *Una cristiana* (1890; *A Christian Woman,* 1891) and its sequel, *La prueba* (1890; "The Test")—will deepen the question of a woman's interest in and search for control over her own sexuality.

In *Insolación*, Pardo Bazán explores, through the character of Asís, the effect of passion and sexual desire on the conscience of a widow who had considered herself "respectable." *Morriña* also examines the distance between the socially constructed view of propriety and the passions that find expression in human lives. Esclavitud, the illegitimate daughter of a priest and a "woman of ill repute," seeks to escape the shame of her birth by leaving her native Galicia to work in Madrid. She falls in love with the young man of the house in which she works and is seduced by him on the eve of his departure for Galicia. The novel ends with her plan to kill herself.

Adultery lurks in the background of *Una cristiana* as it did in *Un viaje de novios* and in the novel often considered Pardo Bazán's masterpiece, *Los pazos de Ulloa* (1886; *The Son of the Bondswoman*, 1908, 1976; *The House of Ulloa* 1991, 1992). The theme of forced and loveless marriage is one that crops up frequently in Pardo Bazán, and it provides a backdrop for her increasingly subtle psychological exploration of her female characters' suppressed feelings and desires. The sequel to *Los pazos de Ulloa*, *La madre naturaleza* (1887; "Mother Nature"), suggests what Pardo Bazán might imagine true love to be, but shrouds that love in tragedy. The two protagonists, Manuela and Perucho, discover on the day they consummate their passion that they are children of the same father and are therefore guilty of incest.

In all of these works, Pardo Bazán presents love and desire as experiences prohibited to women because of the conventions that dictate that they live out their lives in the confines of either marriage or the convent. Her works dramatize the poverty of the options by inviting the reader into the psychological complexity of women destined to such narrowing fates. In an 1891 essay in *Nuevo Teatro Crítico*, Pardo Bazán makes explicit what is rendered imagistically in her novels when she writes "women are drowning, caught in the tight webbing of a petty moral net" (qtd. in Bravo-Villasante 184).

Pardo Bazán's novelistic portrayal of women as aware of, and interested in matters of erotic concern, offered a view to which her male compatriots were unaccustomed. Her attention to the here and now, to the sights and sounds, the colors and fragrances of a powerfully eroticized natural world, combine with her own deepening feminist passions to produce works in which sexuality runs into—often with disastrous results—the walls of a social structure shown to be patrolled by brute male power. The victims, as has best been seen in *Los pazos de Ulloa* and *La madre naturaleza*, are men and women capable of love, and vulnerable to their feelings as well as the feelings of others. In *Los pazos*, the delicate and sensitive Nucha is married to a country manor owner who is blind to her sensibilities, openly preferring the maid Sabel for his sexual pleasures. With Sabel he has Perucho, the illegitimate son who grows up to become in the sequel, *La madre naturaleza*, the lover of his legitimate daughter Manuela.

In work after work, Pardo Bazán presents the tragedy of social customs that block the flowering of love and of talent, and the futile struggles of characters such as Nucha and Esclavitud to escape their fate. The novelistic challenge, limited by Pardo Bazán's commitment to realism and her close observation of existing conditions, was to create a credible image of the ''new woman'' whom she so regularly championed in her essays. The novel in which she best captures that elusive figure is *Memorias de un solterón* (1896; ''Diary of a Bachelor''). In this work the major character, Feíta, appears as a woman determined to be educated and capable of earning her own living. She refuses the offer of marriage made to her by the bachelor through whose memoirs the story is being told. Feíta brings to life the ideals of intellectual development, freedom of sexual choice, and personal efficacy that so eluded Pardo Bazán in earlier depictions of female characters.

The influence of realism and naturalism, along with her interest in the discoveries of science and in Spanish regionalism and *costumbrismo*, produced in Pardo Bazán a tendency to represent Spanish society as accurately as possible. Many of her novels and short stories take place in her native Galicia. Others come out of her direct study of life in the factories (*La Tribuna* 1882) or of her travels (*Un viaje de novios*). Interest in the shaping power of the environment leads in later novels to a concern with character itself. The novels of what is often called the second or transitional phase of her writing, those written between 1889 and 1897—*Morriña* (1889), *La sirena negra* (1908; ''The Dark Siren''), *Una cristiana*, *La prueba*, *Doña Milagros* (1894; ''Lady Miracles''), *Memorias de un solterón*, and *El tesoro de Gascón* (1897; ''Gascon's Treasure'')—have a much more clearly psychological focus. In these works, conflicts between a character's direct experiences of life and the expectations imposed on him or her are highlighted, with convention usually defeating the characters who strive to escape its power over them.

Despite Pardo Bazán's fascination with the relationship between environment and character, a persistent spiritualistic strain can be found even in her early work. That strain becomes, in the last major decade of her novelistic production, a dominant note. Starting with *La Quimera* (1905; ''The Chimera'') and continuing in *La sirena negra* and *Dulce dueño* (1911; ''Sweet Lord''), Pardo Bazán focuses clearly on the psychology of characters in confrontation with religious experience and death, for it is only through those realms, Pardo Bazán came to believe, that her characters could truly experience freedom from a social order she became increasingly pessimistic about being able to change. Many of her most interesting female characters overcome their socially imposed limitations by their deepening commitment to spiritual values. Her attention to minute detail also turns inward in these later works, focusing not on nature and the outer world but on interiors and on objects of art. The late work tends to veer toward the aesthetics of modernism and art for art's sake that were the hallmark of many Spanish and European writers of the turn of the century.

In every phase of her work, despite variations in emphasis from beginning to end, Emilia Pardo Bazán shows herself to be faithful to the norms and concerns of contemporary society and at the same time critical of those societal dominants. Very much a creature of her time because of her interest in science and its relationship to the realm of the spirit, she also reflects her age's preoccupation with a decaying nobility, with a nascent middle class burdened with all the pretenses and frivolities of the nobility it was displacing, and with the abjection of the urban underclass. Her finely attuned sensualism and her acute awareness of class and regional differences make her novels, like those of her realist contemporaries, images of an evolving urban culture. Her own sense of alienation from that culture and her feminist perspective give her work a highly iconoclastic and progressivist cast as she portrays women deviating from social norms, experiencing illicit sexual desires, and expressing an urge to shake free from a numbing and limiting sense of role.

SURVEY OF CRITICISM

Friend of all the major writers of her age, militant spokesperson for an emancipated womanhood, energetic propagator of literary, philosophical, and scientific innovation, critic and portraitist of late-nineteenth-century mores, and one of the most accomplished colorists among her fellow novelists, Pardo Bazán is a figure hard to ignore in any fair presentation of Spanish letters.

In her own time Pardo Bazán was in fact not ignored. Most of her novels suffered early and poorly wrought translations into French and English. Her love of polemic brought her into battle with many of the key figures in Spanish literary and intellectual life. Controversial though she often was, she also won admiration and lectured to large audiences throughout Spain in the 1880s and 1890s, at the height of her literary powers.

By the 1900s, though Pardo Bazán remained active, her literary fortunes were clearly on the wane. Her efforts in the theater were generally unsuccessful, and the production of her plays elicited largely unfavorable critical reaction in the journals and newspapers. The general rejection of the late-nineteenth-century novelists by critics and writers of the succeeding generation led to a decline of interest in Pardo Bazán in the early decades of the twentieth century.

The first major book on Pardo Bazán was written, not surprisingly, by a woman, Carmen Bravo-Villasante. An impressionistic, idealizing, and largely anecdotal tracing of Pardo Bazán's life and work, Bravo-Villasante's 1962 study nonetheless remains a major resource for the critics and scholars who have followed her.

Although Pardo Bazán is regularly mentioned in studies of the nineteenth-century novel in Spain, and is generally recognized for her naturalism and realism in works devoted to the Spanish novel, she has remained essentially unknown to non-Hispanists. Since the beginning of the twentieth century, only *Los pazos de Ulloa* has been republished in English translation. Book-length studies have also been relatively scarce. There is a 1957 book emphasizing Pardo Bazán's Catholicism by D. F. Brown. In 1971 Walter F. Pattison wrote a book on Pardo Bazán's life and work for the Twayne collection. Nelly Clemessy's two-volume French dissertation on Pardo Bazán's novelistic technique in 1973, and Juan Paredes Núñez's dissertation on Pardo Bazán's short stories in 1979 marked a decided upswing in interest among young scholars in her work. In the 1980s, studies tracing not so much the life or the works but identifying trends, began to emerge, two prime examples being Mauricio Hemingway's 1983 study of the novelistic phases in Pardo Bazán's work and Mariano López's 1985 analysis of the naturalist and spiritualist threads of Pardo Bazán's opus. However, in light of the massive impact Pardo Bazán had on her age, the power of her intellect, and the sheer volume of her literary output, the mere handful of books devoted to her seems at best an ungenerous tribute.

Articles have of course been more numerous, though in no year do they come near to matching in volume those written on Benito Pérez Galdós or even Juan Valera. Most frequently, they focus on the one or two novels that have come to be recognized as Pardo Bazán's best. Principal themes are her naturalism, the degree to which it is contested by her spiritualism, and the development of her writings. Some work has been done on separating out the romantic and realistic strands in the author's novels.

Only in recent years, as feminist criticism has become more sophisticated, have studies begun to analyze Pardo Bazán's irony and the complexity of her position as she writes, using male narrators to express values contrary to the dominant masculinist norms. Especially noteworthy as studies of Pardo Bazán's feminism are the articles by Carlos Feal Deibe, Ronald Hilton, Mary Lee Bretz, Ruth Schmidt, and Maryellen Bieder.

An example of the kind of feminist reading that could advance our under-standing of Pardo Bazán and other nineteenth-century women novelists can be found in Maryellen Bieder's study ("En-Gendering") of narrative voice in some of Pardo Bazán's novels. Bieder notes that although Pardo Bazán does not give the dominant discourse to the female voice, she writes into her work the ex-perience of being female in a patriarchal society. Her novels, according to Bieder, show how women exist and are judged in a context exclusively governed by a male perspective. Bieder illustrates how Pardo Bazán presents her central female characters as figures perceived and written by individual men and, by extension, by the norms of male society.

Obviously much remains to be done in Pardo Bazán studies. The critical tools honed by feminist scholarship in the 1980s, along with the general feminist impulse to recover and reread the works of women, should provide the impetus for carrying out in greater depth the analysis of Pardo Bazán's complex imaginative world. That world is one shaped to a large degree by the literary norms and sociopolitical concerns of her time and place. Critics who have chosen to ignore gender issues still have a great deal to consider when writing about Pardo Bazán. As our own sociopolitical lenses shift, we make possible new understandings, and bring to light unexpected aspects of the work. It is in the context of Pardo Bazán's complex response to a literary world that she both embraced and resisted that we can look forward to further insights into the motivation, intellectual passion, and literary achievement of one of Spain's most gifted and prolific writers.

BIBLIOGRAPHY

Works by Emilia Pardo Bazán

A complete list of Pardo Bazán's publications is beyond the scope of this article. The interested reader is invited to consult the sixty-page chronological listing offered by Nelly Clemessy at the end of her study. Included here, in chronological order, are the best known of her works, all of which can be found in the three-volume *Obras completas (novelas y cuentos)*. Ed. Federico Carlos Sainz de Robles. Madrid: Aguilar, 1964.

Novels

Pascual López. 1879.
Un viaje de novios. 1881.
La Tribuna. 1882.
El cisne de Vilamorta. 1885.
Los pazos de Ulloa. 1886.
La madre naturaleza. 1887.
Insolación. 1889.
Morriña. 1889.
Una cristiana—La prueba. 1890.
La piedra angular. 1891.
Doña Milagros. 1894.
Memorias de un solterón. 1896.
La salud de las brujas. 1897.
El tesoro de Gascón. 1897.
El niño de Guzmán. 1899.
Misterio. 1903.
La quimera. 1905.
La sirena negra. 1908.
Dulce dueño. 1911.

Short Stories and Short Novels

La dama joven. 1883.
Cuentos escogidos. 1891.
Cuentos de Marineda. 1892.

Cuentos de Navidad y Año Nuevo. 1894.

Cuentos nuevos. 1894.

Arco iris. 1895.

Novelas ejemplares. 1895.

Cuentos de amor. 1898.

Cuentos sacro–profanos. 1899.

Un destripador de antaño. 1900.

En tranvía, cuentos dramáticos. 1901.

Cuentos de Navidad y Reyes; cuentos de la patria; cuentos antiguos. 1902.

El Fondo del alma. 1907.

Sud-exprés, cuentos actuales. 1909.

Belcebú, cuentos breves. 1912.

Cuentos de la tierra. 1923.

Cuentos religiosos. 1925.

Essays

La cuestión palpitante. Madrid: 1883. [Collection of essays]

Translations

A Christian Woman. Trans. Mary Springer. New York: Cassell, 1891.

Homesickness. Trans. Mary J. Serrano. New York: Cassell, 1891.

The Swan of Vilamorta. Trans. Mary J. Serrano. New York: Cassell, 1891; New York: Mershon, 1900.

A Wedding Trip. Trans. Mary J. Serrano. New York: Cassell, 1891; Chicago: Henneberry, 1910.

The Angular Stone. Trans. Mary J. Serrano. New York: Cassell, 1892.

A Galician Girl's Romance. Trans. Mary J. Serrano. New York: Mershon, 1900.

The Mystery of the Lost Dauphin. Trans. Annabel Hord Seeger. New York: Funk and Wagnalls, 1906.

Midsummer Madness. Trans. Amparo Loring. Boston: C. M. Clark, 1907.

The Son of the Bondswoman. Trans. Ethel Harriet Hearn. New York: n.p., 1908; New York: Fertig, 1976.

The House of Ulloa. Trans. Paul O'Prey and Lucia Graves. New York: Penguin, 1991.

The House of Ulloa. Trans. Roser Caminals-Heath. Athens, GA: U of Georgia P, 1992.

Works about Emilia Pardo Bazán

Bieder, Maryellen. "En-Gendering Strategies of Authority: Emilia Pardo Bazán and the Novel." *Cultural and Historical Grounding for Hispanic and Luso–Brazilian Feminist Literary Criticism.* Ed. Hernán Vidal. Minneapolis: Institute for the Study of Ideologies and Literature, 1989. 473–95.

Bravo-Villasante, Carmen. *Vida y obra de Emilia Pardo Bazán.* Madrid: Revista de Occidente, 1962.

Bretz, Mary Lee. "Naturalismo y feminismo en Emilia Pardo Bazán." *Papeles de Son Armadans* 87 (1977): 195–219.

Brown, Donald F. *The Catholic Naturalism of Pardo Bazán.* Chapel Hill: U of North Carolina, 1957.

Ciplijauskaité, Biruté. "El narrador, la ironía, la mujer: Perspectivas del XIX y del XX."
    Homenaje a Juan López-Morillas. Ed. José Amor y Vázquez and A. David
    Kossoff. Madrid: Castalia, 1982. 129–49.
Clemessy, Nelly. *Emilia Pardo Bazán como novelista (de la teoría a la práctica)*. 2 vols.
    Madrid: Fundación Universitaria Española, 1981. [Trans. from the 1973 French
    dissertation by Irene Gambra]
Feal Deibe, Carlos. "Naturalismo y antinaturalismo en *Los pazos de Ulloa*." *Bulletin
    of Hispanic Studies* 48 (1971): 314–27.
———. "La voz femenina en *Los pazos de Ulloa*." *Hispania* 70 (1987): 214–21.
Giles, Mary. "Feminism and the Feminine in Emilia Pardo Bazán's Novels." *Hispania*
    63 (1980): 356–67.
Goldin, David. "Social and Psychological Determinants in *Morriña*." *Crítica Hispánica*
    3.2 (1981): 133–39.
González Martínez, Pilar. *Aporias de una mujer: Emilia Pardo Bazán*. Madrid: Siglo
    Veintiuno, 1988.
Hemingway, Mauricio. *Emilia Pardo Bazán: The Making of a Novelist*. New York:
    Cambridge UP, 1983.
Hilton, Ronald. "Pardo Bazán and Literary Polemics About Feminism." *Romanic Review*
    44 (1953): 40–46.
López, Mariano. "Esteticismo y evolución en la obra de Emilia Pardo Bazán." *Cuadernos
    Americanos* 234 (1981): 47–63.
———. *Naturalismo y espiritualismo en la novelística de Galdós y Pardo Bazán*. Madrid:
    Editorial Pliegos, 1985.
Oliver, Walter. "A Privileged View of Pardo Bazán's Feminist Ethos." *Romance Notes*
    28 (1987): 157–62.
Paredes Núñez, Juan. *Los cuentos de Emilia Pardo Bazán*. Granada: U of Granada P,
    1979.
Pattison, Walter F. *Emilia Pardo Bazán*. New York: Twayne, 1971.
Schiavo, Leda. "Emilia Pardo Bazán y Francisco Giner de los Ríos." *Insula* 30 (Sept.
    1975): 1, 14.
———. *La mujer española*. Madrid: Editorial Nacional, 1981. [A critical edition of
    Pardo Bazán's writings on feminism]
Schmidt, Ruth A. "Woman's Place in the Sun: Feminism in *Insolación*." *Revista de
    Estudios Hispánicos* 8 (1974): 69–81.
Valis, Noël M. "Pardo Bazán's 'El cisne de Vilamorta' and the Romantic Reader."
    Modern Language Notes 101 (1986): 298–324.

PALOMA PEDRERO
(b. 1957)

Iride Lamartina-Lens

BIOGRAPHY

Paloma Pedrero stands out as a promising young playwright of the 1980s who has gained national and international recognition for her multifaceted contribution to contemporary Spanish theater. Her creative and artistic versatility as playwright, stage and screen actress, theater teacher, director, and producer reflects an intimate knowledge of the diverse facets of the dramatic genre and a dynamic commitment to the Spanish stage.

Born in Madrid on July 3, 1957, Pedrero first showed an interest in theater at the age of fourteen, when she began to play the female roles in the yearly stage productions of an all-boys private school. While majoring in sociology at the University of Madrid, she also studied theater arts under the tutelage of such well-known instructors as Zulema Katz and Alberto Wainer. It is to Wainer that Pedrero is most indebted, for he not only served as her acting teacher and coach but also exposed her to dramatic writing and stage direction. From 1978 to 1981, Pedrero was both actress and coauthor of texts for an independent theater group, Cachivache, whose collective efforts produced several works in children's as well as experimental theater. Pedrero cites these years as crucially important to her development as actress and playwright. Although Cachivache has disbanded, she continues to maintain strong ties with the independent theater movement.

The dramatic political and social changes that emerged at the end of the forty-year Francoist regime in 1975 failed to generate the long-awaited plays of high quality that would deal candidly with the pressing issues in a rapidly changing society. Pedrero's dissatisfaction with the theater's state of affairs led her to request that her former husband, the well-known Spanish playwright Fermín Cabal, create a play of social and contemporary immediacy. Thanks in part to

Cabal's prompting, Pedrero decided to write the work herself. This effort resulted in her first play, "Imagen doble" ("Double Image"), which was never published but was revised a year later and became *Besos de lobo* (1985; "Wolf Kisses"). In spite of Pedrero's acknowledgment of Cabal's early mentorship of her work, little if any of his influence is visible in the realistic and uncompromising theater that she now produces.

In 1985 Pedrero's career as a dramatist was launched with the publication and staging of her second play, *La llamada de Lauren* ("Lauren's Call"). Introduced in 1984 as a one-act play, it was first runner-up for the Valladolid Teatro Breve Prize. In November 1985 an expanded version was staged in Valladolid and in Madrid. Directed by Wainer, the Madrid version starred Pedrero in the role of Rosa. Also in 1985 Pedrero wrote three plays that she directed: *Resguardo personal* ("The Voucher"); *Besos de lobo*; and *Invierno de luna alegre* ("Winter's Happy Moon"), winner of the prestigious Tirso de Molina Theater Award of 1987.

Since 1985 Pedrero has had extraordinary success in having her plays presented professionally, thus overcoming a major obstacle faced by young Spanish playwrights, especially women. By the early 1990s, not only have nine of her ten plays received some level of staging in Spain but four of her works have had international premieres: *La llamada de Lauren* in Toulouse, France; *El color de agosto* (1989; "The Color of August"), *Resguardo personal*, and *La noche dividida* (1989; "A Night Divided") in New York. In addition to her prolific work as a dramatist in the late 1980s, Pedrero's credits include cowriting several television and film scripts as well as performing on stage, screen, and television.

MAJOR THEMES

Pedrero is one of the most innovative and controversial female dramatists to enter the contemporary Spanish stage. Her plays not only reflect an ability to construct tightly knit scenes and to re-create realistic dialogue peppered with current street slang but also, and more importantly, they seem to echo many of the concerns and issues facing youth during these socially turbulent years. Pedrero's conscientious attempt to revitalize the interest of the younger generation in theater, as well as to uncover a way to connect with their angst and tenuous hopes, is clearly manifested in a straightforward and realistic style, coupled with a genuine concern for the psychological, spiritual, and ideological development of the individual. Throughout her work, Pedrero unabashedly challenges the established canons by addressing such provocative and complex issues as the search for sexual identity, men's and women's conflicting needs for both personal freedom and commitment to one another, the difficulty in establishing meaningful interpersonal relationships based on mutual equality and sensitivity, loneliness, alienation, frustration, and the quest for love. Thus her theater provides a model for understanding the immediate reality of her time while also encompassing a broader, more complex vision of the powerful underlying patriarchal influences on modern Spanish culture.

Although Pedrero insists that her theater does not adhere to any one ideological position, her work does contain unequivocal feminist overtones. She creates compelling, realistic characters who are motivated by a sense of personal freedom rather than limited to superficial political rhetoric. These individuals tend to be marginal to the dominant society, and their world is presented with the minute detail associated with hyperrealism. The author's objective—to dramatize the most ordinary experiences of daily existence—is primarily achieved through the impersonation of a lifelike dialogue. The constant repetitions, silences, and pauses inherent within this dialogue highlight the central characters' inability to focus on and articulate their alienation within the contours of a desolate and hopeless reality.

Pedrero's theater embraces intriguing linguistic recourses that incorporate the verbalization of the unspoken words and suggestive language of women, an inversion of the traditional vocabulary allocated to male and female characters and a rejection of the hierarchical dominance of established male discourse. This technique accentuates an uncelebrated feminine world that has remained unexplored until recently. In addition to this stark new dialogue and engaging personal vision, Pedrero employs metatheatrical devices juxtaposed with intertextual references to films and other literary works.

Pedrero's plays tend to fall into two categories: plays that have several characters who develop and mature over a span of time, and two-character plays whose action hinges upon an intense process of soul-searching and self-discovery within the confines of a few hours. *Besos de lobo* and *Invierno de luna alegre* belong to the first category, while all her other plays belong to the second. In each of the first two plays the female character serves as the catalyst for the action and is the pivotal point around which the four male characters focus and interact.

Besos de lobo, Pedrero's only rural play, is reminiscent of Federico García Lorca's *Doña Rosita la soltera* and a long tradition of Spanish literary works that target the plight of the unmarried woman and the social ostracism and/or ridicule to which she is subjected. In contrast with earlier plays, in which the women had little or no choice in their tragic destiny wrought by men's deceits, Pedrero's protagonist, Ana, sheds the age-old victim's cloak and consciously opts for the single life as a means to freedom. For several years, Ana's personal relationship with the four male figures in her life—father, suitor, friend, and lover—shifts from one of dependence to one of independence. Her ripening sense of self-sufficiency and control over her destiny culminates in the final scene when the long-awaited idealized lover arrives at the train station to "save" her from dreaded spinsterhood. Pedrero cleverly inverts the deeply engrained expectations of the fairy-tale happy ending by making Ana get on the same train from which Raúl had descended, thus suggesting an entirely new scope of possibilities.

The search for love and personal freedom is again foregrounded in *Invierno de luna alegre*. The action takes place in a rundown boardinghouse in Madrid; the characters are vagabonds and street performers. Olegario, a middle-aged ex-bullfighter, befriends Reyes, a homeless but musically talented and charming young woman who later becomes the source of his spiritual and economic well-being. Although Reyes establishes a unique and loving relationship with each of the four male characters, she is soon the element of discord among them, for they have misinterpreted her good intentions and are in love with her. The play assumes metatheatrical proportions as the author inserts several spectacles, replete with music and special lighting effects. These plays within a play serve to highlight the vicious male rivalry that will eventually cause Reyes to desert Olegario and pursue her own career goals. Although Reyes's presence is only temporary, her positive influence upon each of the male characters endures as she becomes the unquestionable motivating force behind their spiritual and emotional transformation.

Throughout the next group of plays, Pedrero examines the problem of the couple within the confines of marriage, friendship, and dating. *La llamada de Lauren*, the most metatheatrical and controversial of all her plays to date, concentrates on the married couple and probes repressed feelings of male sexual identity and ambiguity. The play takes place on a magical evening during Carnival, when traditionally one can assume another identity with a change of costume, lose all inhibitions, and revel in sensual pleasure. In the first scene, we find that the usually straitlaced Pedro has decided to surprise his wife, Rosa, with special costumes of Lauren Bacall and Humphrey Bogart. Pedrero sets the mood for the couple's voyage back in time by choosing the musical score, characters, and costumes of the 1944 American film *To Have and Have Not*, which launched Hollywood's quintessential couple of unmitigated sensuality. The male/female roles will be reversed, however, for he will dress as Bacall and she as Bogart.

What at first appears to be a harmless erotic game slowly takes on perturbing psychological innuendos. Pedro's transfiguration into the female role of Lauren and his identification with her become unmistakably real, culminating in his insistence on being sexually penetrated by Humphrey/Rosa. Through the donning of one mask, Pedro's other mask falls, and in a stirring moment of self-revelation he is forced to admit his sexual ambivalence to Rosa and himself. In spite of Rosa's confusion and disillusionment, she does not lose her sensitivity or love for Lauren/Pedro. The final scene vaguely suggests her ultimate support for her/his decision to go out alone, dressed as Bacall, and find her/himself. *Resguardo personal*, written four years later, may be considered the counterpoint of *La llamada de Lauren*, for it is the story of the total breakdown of communication between an estranged couple, their failed marriage, and the destructive force of a love gone sour.

Pedrero continues her examination of relationships in *El color de agosto*, in which the dynamic of the friendship between two women in their early thirties is unraveled from an insightful female perspective. In this work the focus is on an impassioned love/hate relationship, injected with lesbian overtones, that addresses past and present competitiveness over careers and men. Although both women once aspired to become artists, only María, the less talented of the two, has achieved professional and economic success. Laura has fared much worse during their eight-year separation and is now a model. Once reunited, they embark upon a painful journey of retrospection and introspection. Through a series of graphic and even violent scenes, the author renounces certain stereotypical images of women and openly embraces the previously taboo theme of female homosexuality.

In no other group of plays are Pedrero's hyperrealistic tendencies more fully expressed than in *Noches de amor efímero* (1991; "Nights of Ephemeral Love"), a trilogy of one-act plays that includes *Solos esta noche* ("Alone Tonight"), *La noche dividida* ("A Night Divided") and *Esta noche en el parque* ("Tonight in the Park"). These short works are closely linked by an underlying structural and thematic unity based on an ardent but fleeting moment of intimacy. Their individual narrations target familiar and readily identifiable situations of one-night stands between strangers, presented from a female perspective. In essence, the trilogy underscores the overall thrust of Pedrero's theater, which closely examines themes of estrangement in a depersonalized society, disillusionment with love and its beguiling expectations, and the incongruity between the human hunger for emotional stability and the fear of commitment. In spite of Pedrero's bleak Weltanschauung, it cannot be said that her plays are entirely pessimistic, for there is a deliberate attempt, especially on the part of the female characters, to gain control over their lives in an otherwise chaotic world of social and sexual disparity.

SURVEY OF CRITICISM

In general, it may be said that Paloma Pedrero's theater has been well received by younger audiences, especially women, and less so by older men and critics. The reason for this polarization of critical perception, often categorized by age and gender, becomes quite understandable when one considers the overall scope of her dramas. In Spain, critical reaction to her work has ranged from an expression of perplexity and even indignation by Francisco Álvaro, who labeled *La llamada de Lauren* "uninteresting, boring, extravagant, and obscene" (216), to a more favorable response by Fernando Lázaro Carreter, who praised her dramatic talent and potential ("Dos comedias" 10).

It is to North American scholars, however, that one must turn in order to gain a more insightful and profound analysis of Pedrero's work. Patricia O'Connor, in her anthology on current Spanish women playwrights, succinctly studies the dramatist's style, themes, and position among her contemporaries. Phyllis Zatlin explores Pedrero's major themes from a feminist perspective while delving into her stylistic dramatic devices. In Spain most of the criticism about Pedrero has been brief and published in magazines and newspapers. The lack of more substantial criticism on this pioneering dramatist may be attributed to insufficient exposure and her relatively recent arrival on the Spanish stage. However, increased interest in Pedrero is evidenced by a growing number of scholarly papers delivered at international literary conferences on the metatheatrical, ideological, and thematic facets of her work. Future scholars will no doubt continue the investigation of the suggestive possibilities of this fascinating new author.

BIBLIOGRAPHY

Works by Paloma Pedrero

"Imagen doble." 1984. [Unpublished MS]
La llamada de Lauren. Teatro breve 1984. Valladolid, Spain: Caja de Ahorros Provincial, 1985ᴉ. Madrid: Ediciones Antonio Machado, 1987.
Besos de lobo and *Invierno de luna alegre.* Madrid: Espiral/Fundamentos, 1987.
"Autoentrevista: escribir algo vivo y sin miedo." *Primer Acto* 222 (1988): 124–25. [Self-portrait]
"Las fresas mágicas." 1988. [Unpublished MS]
Resguardo personal. Dramaturgas españolas de hoy. Ed. Patricia O'Connor. Madrid: Espiral/Fundamentos, 1988. 97–105.
El color de agosto. Madrid: Ediciones Antonio Machado, 1989.
La noche dividida. Madrid: Ediciones Antonio Machado, 1989.
Esta noche en el parque. Estreno 16.1 (1990): 15–17.
"Una estrella." 1990. [Unpublished MS]
Noches de amor efímero. Murcia, Spain: Universidad, Secretariado de Publicaciones, 1991.

Translations

L'apelle de Lauren. Trans. André Camp. Paris: L'Avant Scène, 1989. N.pag.
"Lauren's Call." Trans. Nancy L. Rogers. 1990. [Unpublished]
"The Color of August." Trans. Phyllis Zatlin. 1991. [Unpublished]
"A Night Divided." Trans. Phyllis Zatlin. 1991. [Unpublished]
"The Voucher." Trans. Phyllis Zatlin. 1991. [Unpublished]

Works about Paloma Pedrero

Álvarez, M. " 'Invierno de luna alegre.' Sainete de la marginalidad." *El País* 22 July 1988: n.pag.
Álvaro, Francisco. "El teatro en España en 1985." *El espectador y la crítica.* Valladolid, Spain: Edición del Autor, 1986. 216.
Arco, Antonio. " 'Noches de amor efímero.' " *La Verdad* 20 Feb. 1991: 43.
Armiño, Mauro. "Paloma Pedrero: El largo viaje hacia el estreno." *Cambio 16* 841 (Jan. 1988): 104.
Áviles, Juan Carlos. " 'Invierno de luna alegre' de Paloma Pedrero: Teatro con corazón." *Guía Del Ocio* 20 Feb. 1989: 35.

————. "Mi marido es mi mujer." *Villa de Madrid* 18 Nov. 1985: n.pag.

Campos, Jesús. "Nuevos autores españoles." *Primer Acto* 212 (1986): 60–72.

Centeno, Enrique. "Dos mujeres en escena." *Cinco Días* 2 Aug. 1988: 31.

————. "Mujeres." *Diario 16* 17 Nov. 1990: n.pag.

de Carlos, C. "Paloma Pedrero: 'La obra se me ocurrió cuando paseaba por Vallecas.'" *ABC* 15 Dec. 1987: 100.

de la Hera, Alberto. " 'Invierno de luna alegre' de Paloma Pedrero: Un sainete urbano con sólo cinco intérpretes." *Ya* 19 Feb. 1989: n.pag.

Díaz Sande, J. R. " 'Invierno de luna alegre': Premio dudoso." *Reseña* 194 (1989): 9.

F. B. "*La llamada de Lauren* rompe máscaras." *El Público* 23 (1985): 23.

Fernández Torres, A. "Amor y desamor urbano." *Metrópoli* 16–22 Nov. 1990: n.pag.

Galán, Eduardo. "Paloma Pedrero: 'El escritor tiene que prestar su voz a los marginados.' " *Ya* 10 Feb. 1989: 39.

————. "Paloma Pedrero, una joven dramaturga que necesita expresar sus vivencias." *Estreno* 16 (1990): 11–13.

García, Alejandro. "Paloma Pedrero. La militancia femenina en el teatro." *El País* 18 Feb. 1989: n.pag.

García, William. "El cine como pre-texto y pretexto en *La llamada de Lauren* de Paloma Pedrero." NEMLA Conference. Toronto, Apr. 1990.

García Cazón, Juan. "Paloma Pedrero pinta el amor tierno y cruel." *ABC* 17 Nov. 1990: n.pag.

Gómez Porro, Francisco. "*El color de agosto*." *Dunia* (July–Aug. 1988): n.pag.

————. "Paloma Pedrero escribe y dirige 'Invierno de luna alegre'." *ABC* 10 Feb. 1989: n.pag.

Gómez Rufo, Antonio. "De todo en el verano." *El Globo* 8 Aug. 1988: 94.

J. M. M. "El color del éxito y del fracaso profesional." *El Público* 60 (1988): 31–32.

Lamartina-Lens, Iride. "Contemporary Spanish Women Dramatists of the Eighties and Nineties." MLA Conference. Chicago, Dec. 1990.

————. "An Insight to the Theater of Paloma Pedrero." *Romance Languages Annual* 2 (1991): 465–68.

————. "Introduction to *Esta noche en el parque*." *Estreno* 16 (1990): 14.

————. "María Manuela Reina and Paloma Pedrero: New Voices for a New Generation." NEMLA Conference. Hartford, Apr. 1991.

————. "La recuperación de una voz femenina en el teatro español contemporáneo." España frente al siglo XXI: literatura, arte y cultura. Ohio State U., Apr. 1990.

————. "Three One-Night Stands of Love: Paloma Pedrero's Variations on a Theme." *Discurso femenino actual*. Ed. Adelaida Martínez. [Forthcoming]

Lázaro Carreter, Fernando. "Dos comedias de Paloma Pedrero." *Blanco y Negro* 3 (Feb. 1989): 10.

————. "Intermedio con Paloma Pedrero." *Blanco y Negro* 16 (July 1989): 12.

————. " 'Invierno de luna alegre.' " *Blanco y Negro* 9 (Apr. 1989): 12.

————. " 'Noches de amor efímero'." *Blanco y Negro* 27 (Jan. 1991): 12.

López Negrín, Florentino. "Un paseo por la Moncloa." *El Independiente* 16 Nov. 1990: n.pag.

López Sancho, Lorenzo. "Tema antiguo, sainete nuevo, 'Invierno de luna alegre,' en el Maravillas." *ABC* 16 Feb. 1989: 98.

Makris, Mary. "Paloma Pedrero's *El color de agosto*." NEMLA Conference. Buffalo, Apr. 1992.

Monleón, José. " 'Invierno de luna alegre'." *Diario 16* 24 Feb. 1989: 28.

O'Connor, Patricia, ed. *Dramaturgas españolas de hoy*. Madrid: Espiral/Fundamentos, 1988.

———. Prologue. *La llamada de Lauren*. By Paloma Pedrero. Madrid: Ediciones Antonio Machado, 1987. 13–17.

———. "Six *Dramaturgas* in Search of a Stage." *Gestos* 5 (1988): 116–20.

———. "Women Playwrights in Contemporary Spain and the Male-Dominated Canon." *Signs* 15 (1990): 376–90.

Oliva, María Victoria. "Paloma Pedrero: El espaldarazo del Tirso." *El Público* 52 (1988): 41.

Ortiz, Lourdes. "Nuevas autoras españolas." *Primer Acto* 220 (1987): 10–21.

Parra, Javier. "Paloma Pedrero apuesta por un teatro que sea espejo de nuestra sociedad." *Ya* 18 Dec. 1987: n.pag.

Piña, Begonia. " 'Invierno de luna alegre.' La imposible historia de amor entre un viejo trompetista y una rockera." *Diario 16* 9 Feb. 1989: n.pag.

———. "El invierno de un torero desencantado." *Diario 16* 19 Feb. 1989: n.pag.

Podol, Peter. "Sexuality and Marital Relationships in Paloma Pedrero's *La llamada de Lauren* and María Manuela Reina's *La cinta dorada*." *Estreno* 17 (1991): 22–25.

Sangüesa, Agustina. "El realismo marginal de un sueño." *El Público* 66 (Mar. 1989): 23–24.

Serrano, Virtudes. Introduction. *Noches de amor efímero*. By Paloma Pedrero. Murcia, Spain: Universidad Secretariado de Publicaciones, 1991. 7–26.

S. F. "Los amores fáciles." *El Público* 82 (Jan.–Feb. 1991): 108.

Tecglen, Eduardo. "Orgasmos perdidos y hallados." *El País* 15 Nov. 1990: n.pag.

Torres, Rosana. "El salto de Paloma Pedrero." *El País* 10 Feb. 1989: n.pag.

———. "Se afianza una autora." *El País* 22 July 1988: n.pag.

Torres-Pou, Juan. "Bakhtin, teatro y feminismo: El elemento paródico en *La llamada de Lauren* de Paloma Pedrero." *Estreno* 19.1 (1993): 26–28.

Villán, Javier. "Ni abandonadas, ni seducidas." *El Mundo* 16 Nov. 1990: n.pag.

Zatlin, Phyllis. "Juegos metateatrales e intertextuales en el teatro de Paloma Pedrero." *Letras Femeninas*. [Forthcoming 1994]

———. "Paloma Pedrero and The Search For Identity." *Estreno* 16 (1990): 6–10.

SOLEDAD PUÉRTOLAS
(b. 1947)

Mary Jane Treacy

BIOGRAPHY

Soledad Puértolas is an intensely private person who veers away from self-revelation in her fiction just as she does in interviews with journalists and scholars. She insists on separating the personal from the public to such an extent that she claims to have abandoned a childhood predilection for poetry because it was too confessional, turning instead to narrative, which offered a much-desired distance in her writing. Puértolas keeps to the safe topics in her public statements—her literary interests, work habits, favorite themes—and provides very little information about the experiences and values that have formed her.

Puértolas was born in Zaragoza (Aragon) in 1947 and lived in that provincial city until she was fourteen years old. She was a sickly and solitary child, rather given to melancholy. The daughter of a chemist and the second of three sisters, she recalls having a "classic" middle-class girlhood, being groomed by her Sagrado Corazón Preparatory School to marry well and to take her place in the higher realms of society. Although at the time she accepted this traditional view of a woman's destiny, Puértolas now chuckles at her naive dream that she would marry a mayor. An abrupt change from this enclosed world came when her family moved to Madrid. Even in 1961, as she indicated to Concha Roldán in a 1989 interview, she found the capital city to be informal and dizzyingly out of control.

Madrid, providing Puértolas with her first sensation of real openness, of life's possibilities, indeed offered the young girl an existence full of adventures. During her formative years, her interests shifted from math and science during the *bachillerato* (high school) to political science and economics at the university, and finally to journalism, in which she received a degree. She married at twenty-one; spent three years in California, where she received a master's degree in

Hispanic literature from the University of California, Santa Barbara; then returned to Madrid, where she began writing fiction in earnest while also raising two sons (Roldán). She is now well known for her first novel, *El bandido doblemente armado* (1980; "The Double-Armed Bandit"), which won the Sésamo Prize in 1979, and the highly praised *Queda la noche* ("There's Still the Night"), which won the Planeta Prize in 1989.

Puértolas has placed writing at the center of her life. Although she recognizes that there has been intolerance in the past toward women in the arts and that, even today, women experience great difficulty in combining their roles as house-wife, mother, and professional, she claims to have no problem balancing work with family life. On the contrary, she believes that the family in general, and her sons' enthusiasm for her work in particular, contribute positively to her development as a writer (Roldán). Although Puértolas is keenly aware that she is a woman who writes in a literary world dominated by men—she is only the sixth woman to have won the prestigious Planeta Prize—she does not see herself as a woman writer. Indeed, she considers any critical emphasis on her sex as either prejudicial or unnecessary because she sees no real difference between the writing of men and women (Mora 188). Puértolas does not view gender as a category that determines an individual's experience; it is not an area that she explores in any depth. Moreover, she rejects the idea of feminist fiction because she insists that good literature does not attempt to teach or illustrate any type of doctrine, however worthy (Mora 188). Thus, Puértolas places herself in the tradition of ungendered, perhaps even disembodied, fiction writers and subjects her work only to the criteria of its aesthetic value.

MAJOR THEMES

Soledad Puértolas sets out to observe the human condition and, as she explained in an interview with Miguel Riera, what she discovers in the process is the passing of time, desolation, and solitude (48). It is no wonder that most of her characters do not engage with life or that they are alienated from others, for they prefer distance and escape to genuine interaction or development of any sense of community. The very young turn to frantic activity, flocking to discos and bars, finding yet another lover, and seeking the emotional thrills that will keep their loneliness at bay. Their elders take refuge in daily habits that are repeated like dull rites, while they look to social institutions—the family or order—to structure the fragments of lives they are too weak to live fully. Characters of all ages are apathetic, disillusioned, and without energy. The young Spanish narrator of *El bandido doblemente armado*, for instance, tells of his fascination with the members of the wealthy Lennox family, who are based on the characters of Raymond Chandler's *The Long Goodbye*. The son, Terry, gets involved in some dangerous business and is forced to leave the country, but he is able to play life for all its worth, while the Spanish narrator reflects that he has never taken any risks at all and has only been able to observe the vitality around him. Again, in *Todos mienten* (1988; "They All Lie"), a young male narrator reveals how Madrid's beautiful people become disenchanted with their courtship of wealth, style, and social standing. He discovers that, like himself, they hide their emptiness behind a social facade.

Chance wrenches Puértolas's characters out of their favorite escapes; it is a force that undermines the aimlessness of the Europeans who inhabit her works as well as the futile attempts of her American characters to create and control destiny. Chance may eventually prove to be benevolent, but it also provides the necessary jolt that obliges characters to confront and search for meaning in their lives. Often this is a plunge into mystery and possible crime—a con game, murder, or espionage. Although Puértolas borrows many of the plot devices of the thriller, she is not interested in the crime, its detection, or its outcome. To the contrary, she refuses to develop these mysteries, preferring instead to leave the plots unfinished, the clues dangling, and the characters confused about what has happened to them. What interests her is life's surprises, which lead characters into situations they have never expected and that push them toward a more accurate sense of reality: that life is a murky but not hopeless mess.

Puértolas appears to suggest that life has much to teach if one follows the twists and turns that chance may bring, and that the courageous can make an exciting adventure of their lives. This is the course taken by the young male characters who keep reappearing in her novels. They are either orphans who have no one to care for them or boys whose fathers are too emotionally distant or too conventional to provide any human warmth. They are thrown out into the world; yet instead of fearing the unknown or mistrusting adults' capricious behavior, they adapt to constant change and use their very instability as a source of self-knowledge. Puértolas promises no happy endings, but she does offer an alternative to despair.

Nowhere does Puértolas present her worldview so charmingly as in her stories for children. In *El recorrido de los animales* (1975; "The Animals' Journey"), young Arturo is transformed into different animals and actually takes on their characteristics as he learns about himself and the complexity of his human nature. *La sombra de una noche* (1986; "A Night's Shadow"), written a decade later, tells of a far unhappier boy who sets out one night to search for his father, who has not come home. Jacobo has to brave the night world of bars and brothels, even the danger of a smuggling ring, but he manages to prove his courage and his loyalty as he has his first life adventure.

Puértolas's notions about life and human nature are more problematic in the short stories and novels written for adults precisely because she universalizes the experience of a particular urban, upper-middle-class character. Most of her protagonists have access to wealth even if they have a (seldom mentioned) career, and all have sufficient leisure to travel and become involved in adventures. They are relatively young, unmarried, and have few responsibilities to family members. Almost all are male. It is not that these characters lead fulfilling lives— in fact, most suffer through ones that are quite dreary—but they have the comfort of belonging to the dominant social group and accept their privileges without reflection.

Puértolas does not include characters whose presence could disturb her focus on the search for self and meaning in life. There are no down-and-out characters in her writing—the unemployed, foreign exiles, disgruntled workers—nor are there any whose political views or political histories question the structure of contemporary society or examine how self-exploration could lead to social change. Even her one KGB agent (*in Queda la noche*) is apolitical, turning out to be a rather pathetic German woman whose unrequited lesbian love brings about her own destruction. Yet this turn of events is not a statement about homosexual identity or oppression in heterosexist society; in Puértolas's hands it becomes just another unexpected passion that mysteriously comes to light. The absence of characters who have different or powerless positions in society creates an illusion that the malaise of the bourgeoisie can stand for the experiences of all; and even this bourgeoisie seems primarily urban, heterosexual, and male.

Puértolas does not view human experience in political terms; consequently she does not examine how social structures can affect a character's perception of and responses to the world. Nevertheless, she does observe that middle-class women can be limited by their roles as wife and mother. A male character in *Burdeos* (1986; "Bordeaux") laments the fate of his dynamic, interesting daughter, who is being forced into a female world of marriage and household chores. The narrator's mother in *Todos mienten*, a widow, clings to her children in order to avoid a new marriage and new life, finally taking refuge in murder mysteries and her sister-in-law's flings at home decoration. The narrator's sister in *Queda la noche* realizes that she has gone from child to wife to mother and that, at forty-four, has never had control of her own life.

Minor female characters in these and other works confront wife beating, sexual objectification, and dependence on men, but, however many "women's issues" Puértolas may include in her work, she does not piece them together to form a pattern of female experience nor suggest that this pattern may be due to a social structure beyond the individual. On the contrary, Puértolas gives the impression that overt oppression is a thing of the past and that in the present women and men lead very similar lives. What differences remain between the sexes seem to be due either to the remnants of the past or to individual quirks. Raquel, the unhappily married sister in *Queda la noche*, attributes her woes to a traditional upbringing and claims that the narrator, some ten years her junior, has a freer, more open life. The novel supports this view, showing that the narrator has somehow left the confines of old-fashioned female experience and entered the apparently ungendered angst of modern life.

In her early works, Puértolas focuses on a male character's coming of age; women are shadowy figures in her children's tales, and when they appear as mothers, girlfriends, and wives in *El bandido doblemente armado* and *Todos mienten*, they still have little importance to the development of the protagonist or his plot. In a 1989 interview with Marimont Mora, Puértolas explains that male characters are easier to portray because she has less of a tendency to identify with them. She finds it difficult to create female characters who are not extensions of herself, and, since she does not want to write confessional literature, she has avoided female protagonists until quite recently. They are used in two of the three related stories that make up the 1986 novel *Burdeos*, but it is only in her latest work, *Queda la noche*, that Puértolas introduces a female narrator and protagonist, symbolically named Aurora (Dawn), whose thoughts and actions shape the novel.

One can almost sense Puértolas's struggle with her belief that a shared human condition makes men and women more similar than different. On the one hand, she creates female protagonists who are very similar to her male characters and has them face the same difficulties in order to fulfill what she considers to be human destiny: coming to know oneself. Nonetheless, she suggests that female protagonists have a particular illusion to overcome: they tend to use romance in order to escape from life's task. *Burdeos* is the first novel to explore this gender-specific theme through Lilly, who uses love affairs to avoid focusing on her first big career opportunity; the alcohol-soaked Lisa, who knowingly maintains her illusion that a man—any man—will rescue her; and Rose, who has recovered from the loss of love by turning inward to become a cultured woman "for her own pleasure" (25). The process of women's self-awareness and fulfillment is developed more in *Queda la noche*. Here Aurora's struggle—leaving the married politican who would have her at his beck and call to have brief affairs with several men before finally confronting solitude for the first time in her life—is contrasted with her sister's false independence, which takes her from an empty marriage to therapy and immediately back to marriage, this time to her psychiatrist.

Puértolas clearly sees many of the troubles and challenges that contemporary bourgeois women are facing, and her recent work gives female characters an increasingly important place. However, she is still less interested in gender than in experiences that she considers to be universal. This is consistent with her hope of using writing to express the harmony that can exist in life: "I am trying . . . to find those moments in life in which everything is resolved, which serve as a symbol or an emblem, and point out the harmony and mystery that are so infrequently seen" (Riera 48). As long as she searches for moments of peace in the human condition, Puértolas will continue to minimize differences of any sort (gender, class, sexual identification, national origin), for they threaten to bring about conflict and suggest a world that is fragmented, one divided into haves and have-nots, one that she herself sees but will not examine. However, if Puértolas continues to center her fiction on female characters and maintains her unflinching observations of women's lives, she may find that gender differences are significant in shaping an individual's experience of life. She may come to suspect that women's flight into romance may be more than a tradition or an escape from freedom; it may be a common practice that, if sufficiently probed, can open up new ways of thinking about a social construction of femininity, women's experiences of sexuality, and women's complex position in the social order.

SURVEY OF CRITICISM

In spite of her literary prizes and frequent interviews in the Spanish press, Soledad Puértolas has only recently begun to attract critical attention, and to date there is little published on her work. Thanks to a colloquium held at St. Anselm's College in 1990, North American Hispanists have become acquainted with her novels and her artistic concerns. Roberto Ignacio Díaz notes that Spanish critics have commented unhappily on Puértolas's preference for foreign settings, as in the novel *Burdeos*, and her lack of specificity even when using Spanish locales for her fiction. Francisca González-Arias explains that Puértolas seeks both a temporal and a spatial distance from the post–Civil War period of her youth. Refusing to dwell in the past or to be contained by purely national or political interests, the novelist prefers to stand back, take stock of contemporary life, and focus on the meaning(s) of universal human existence. According to Sonia Mattalia, this flight away from testimonial fiction is the hallmark of recent Spanish writing and is due to a general loss of faith in leftist traditions. Like others of her generation, Puértolas seems to reject the once widespread belief that fiction can capture or correctly interpret reality, or even that it can offer any totalizing vision of the world.

Beth W. Bauer states that Puértolas uses motifs from detective fiction to explore how her characters make sense of lives seemingly governed by chance. Unlike the classic detective story, which has the sleuth follow clues to ferret out the truth, Puértolas's works use subjective and limited narrators who try to piece together the puzzles of their lives and who never arrive at full knowledge. Thus the novels bring up the greater question of interpretation and suggest that there is no truth hidden behind events; rather, it is the individual in dialogue with a set of clues or mysteries who makes meaning in a creative and self-affirming act. The narrator, as Darcy Donahue points out, is thereby able to use his or her story to invent a self.

Critics appear to agree with Tomás Camarero Arribas that Puértolas's characters confront a reality that they cannot control, and that each event they face presents a step in learning about the self and about life. González-Arias elaborates that the process involves appreciating solitude, friendship, and, above all, celebrating life for its own sake. Symbolized by the rivers that reappear throughout Puértolas's fiction, life is continual motion and change. Like the wine that is savored in *Burdeos*, it is full of light and shadows, and it provides both security and danger.

BIBLIOGRAPHY

Works by Soledad Puértolas

Novels

El bandido doblemente armado. Madrid: Legasa, 1980.
Burdeos. Barcelona: Anagrama, 1986.

Todos mienten. Barcelona: Anagrama, 1988.
Queda la noche. Barcelona: Planeta, 1989.

Short Fiction and Nonfiction

El Madrid de "La lucha por la vida." Madrid: Helios, 1971. [A study of Pío Baroja's fiction]
El recorrido de los animales. Madrid: Júcar, 1975. [Children's story]
"A través de las ondas." *Doce relatos de mujeres*. Ed. Ymelda Navajo. Madrid: Alianza, 1982.
Una enfermedad moral. Madrid: Triestre, 1982. [Short stories]
La sombra de una noche. Madrid: Anaya, 1986. [Children's story]

Works about Soledad Puértolas

Bauer, Beth W. "*El bandido doblemente armado* and Beyond: Soledad Puértolas and the Mystery of Interpretation." Encuentro con Soledad Puértolas.
Camarero Arribas, Tomás. "Lógica de una narrativa en *Una enfermedad moral* de Soledad Puértolas." *Ventanal* 14 (1988): 133–57.
Díaz, Roberto Ignacio. "Borges y Soledad Puértolas: La geografía como recurso narrativo." Encuentro con Soledad Puértolas.
Donahue, Darcy. "La voz masculina en dos novelas de Soledad Puértolas." Encuentro con Soledad Puértolas.
Encuentro con Soledad Puértolas. Saint Anselm's College, Manchester, N.H., 10 Apr. 1990. [Colloquium]
Fajardo, José Manuel. "Escribo lo que puedo, no lo que quiero." *Cambio 16* 6 Nov. 1989: 138–39. [Interview with Puértolas]
González-Arias, Francisca. " 'De la solitude': The Poetics of Soledad Puértolas." Encuentro con Soledad Puértolas.
———. "Soledad Puértolas: La ciudad de las almas." *Historia y crítica de la literatura española*. Vol. 9. Ed. Francisco Rico. Barcelona: Grijalbo, 1992. 371–75.
Mattalia, Sonia. "Entre miradas: Las novelas de Soledad Puértolas." *Ventanal* 14 (1988): 171–92.
Mora, Marimont. "Soledad Puértolas/Premio Planeta a *Queda la noche*." *Tiempo* 23 Oct. 1989: 186–88. [Interview with Puértolas]
Riera, Miguel. "Los vacíos del tiempo: Entrevista con Soledad Puértolas." *Quimera* 72 (1987): 42–48.
Roldán, Concha. "Soledad Puértolas: Sugerencias." *Heraldo de Aragón* 14 Apr. 1989: n. pag. [Interview with Puértolas]
Talbot, Lynn K. "Entrevista con Soledad Puértolas." *Hispania* 71.4 (1988): 882–83.

CARME RIERA
(b. 1948)

Margery Resnick

BIOGRAPHY

Since 1977 Carme Riera has published an astonishing quantity of work. The sheer volume and range of her writing—seven books of fiction, four nonfictional works, and more than a dozen articles—bespeak prodigious energy and intellectual breadth. Her fictional protagonists, whose existences often teeter between chaos and control, seek autonomy in a world in which reason and rationality as defined by men lead women to vacillation, self-censure, fear, and too often an escape through fantasy. The reader's experience of Riera's often poetic prose is enhanced by the intellectual challenge of confronting the biological as well as the cultural construction of gender. While assuming a prominent place in the post-Franco revival of Spanish narrative, Riera has also established herself as a definitive critical voice in Spanish letters through her books on contemporary poetry in Barcelona.

Riera traces the roots of her passion for literature to events in her early life. She was born into a well-to-do family in Palma de Mallorca in 1948. Riera notes that the attraction of telling stories—of speaking without seeing or being seen by the listener—became apparent to her at the time of her first confession (Racionero, ''Entrevista'' 14). Her parents' comfortable home in Palma, with its extraordinary number of books, as well as her grandfather's house in Deià, filled with heavy furniture, shadows, and secrets harboring the unexpected and prohibited, provided the space and inspiration for her early poetry. Family events alluded to but unnamed, like the death of her grandfather, which she could only intuit from the noises in the house and expressions on others' faces, also motivated her to write (Racionero, ''Entrevista'' 14).

Riera's education at the primary school El Sagrado Corazón was characteristic of that of girls in post–Civil War Spain. The principal concern in this religious school was to teach girls the skills they needed to marry and to carry out their functions as wives in a bourgeois society. Thus, the curriculum emphasized the cultivation of rhetoric appropriate to the writing of letters, condolences, invitations, and excuses. Despite these limitations, Riera recalls that it was in this school that she learned to enjoy the control of style that set a course for her subsequent career.

When Riera moved to Barcelona to attend the university, she was immediately drawn to the city—its buildings, even its cemeteries. The active intellectual life of conferences, literary gatherings, and political meetings absorbed her energy. As she continued her studies toward a degree in Spanish philology, her involvement in activist politics decreased, and she embarked on a series of social service projects. During these years she studied, gave free classes at the Sacre Coeur primary school, and wrote poetry in the early hours of the morning. Perhaps it was the rigors of this schedule that set the pattern for the continued intensity of her creative life. Although she has characterized herself as "a teacher who writes from time to time" (Racionero, "Entrevista" 16), it is difficult to conceive of her writing as a collateral activity, given the numerous editions of her first two books of short stories, the Prudenci Bertrana Prize that she received for her novel *Una primavera per a Dominico Guarini* (1981; *Una primavera para Domenico Guarini* 1981; "A Spring for Domenico Guarini"), and the Anagrama de Ensayo Prize awarded to her for her critical book, drawn from her doctoral dissertation, *La escuela de Barcelona* (1988; "The Barcelona Group"). At present, Riera, a professor of Spanish literature at the Universidad Autónoma, resides in Barcelona with her husband, Francisco Llinás, a professor of physics.

MAJOR THEMES

Riera's narrative technique encompasses both conventionally constructed short stories and experimentation with avant-garde modes. Although she is bilingual, Riera writes her fiction in Catalan.[1] She herself has translated two of the Catalan works into Spanish. The complex interplay of levels of language and the intricate use of dialect has been preserved in the works in translation: *Palabra de mujer* (1980; "A Woman's Word"), the Spanish translation of Riera's first two books of short stories, *Te deix, amor, la mar com a penyora* (1975; "I Leave You, My Love, the Sea as a Token") and *Jo pos per testimoni les gavines* (1977; "The Seagulls Serve as My Witnesses"); *Una primavera para Domenico Guarini*; and *Cuestión de amor propio* (1988), originally published in 1987 as *Qüestió d'amor propio* ("A Matter of Self-Respect"). While each volume treats distinct subjects, characters, and situations, each also involves the examination of women's lives through a variety of fictional lenses. As they try to shape their lives, Riera's diverse characters confront the biological and cultural realities of being female players in a world in which the script is written by men.

"Te entrego, amor, la mar como una ofrenda," the first story of *Palabra de mujer*, whose title evokes the original version in Catalan, begins as a tale of traditional adolescent longing: that of a high school student for her teacher, with whom she has had an intense affair. The narrative bears all the characteristics of this kind of story—the young girl's passion, the neighbors' gossip, the father's exile of his daughter to the home of relatives to avoid scandal, and the daughter's desolation experienced in a life without the teacher's presence. When the young girl returns to school, the teacher insists on ending the relationship, so as to limit the damage it might cause. On the basis of conventional erotic expectations and Riera's artfully teasing style, the reader misreads the text, for not until the very end does one realize that the object of the girl's passion is female.

Riera presents us with a lesbian love affair in order to destabilize traditional social dichotomies. Despite the protagonist's subsequent heterosexual affairs that result in marriage and pregnancy, she never disengages from the *memoria impenitente* (obdurate memory) of her lesbian love—more enduring and important than any of the traditionally fulfilling experiences life offers her. The closing lines of the work allude to the wish for a death marked by burial in the sea. This ending connects the first story to the second. While never explicit, there is strong evidence that the second story in the collection, "Y pongo por testigo a las gaviotas," chronicles the same affair from the more mature perspective of the teacher. By making absolute identification impossible, Riera underscores the invisibility and silence that surround lesbian lives.

The world of the protagonist in "Y pongo por testigo . . . " is shaped by her memory of a lesbian affair. Like the protagonist in "Te entrego, amor . . . ," this narrator stubbornly clings to the memory of her passionate involvement with another woman as the organizing principle of her life. In this case, however, she refuses to accept subsequent heterosexual liaisons; she will not conform to social norms, for she recognizes that her emotional illness, which has caused her to live her life in a mental institution, began when she rejected a love that challenged established conventions. Although the protagonist yielded her autonomy to external forces fifteen years earlier, intense unhappiness has caused her to reexamine that decision, and she is no longer willing to remain silent or to exist invisibly within the confines of heterosexual life. Given her rebellion, the forces mustered to silence her are more sinister than those faced by the young girl in "Te entrego, amor . . . ," whose longings remained private. In the second story, the protagonist's doctors try to silence her by preventing the publication of her memoirs; indeed, she notes that prisoners have more freedom of expression than she. Yet, having once relinquished her ability to speak and live as she chose, she now refuses to be quiet: "I will not resign myself to shutting this manuscript in a drawer . . . "(33). Years of self-analysis (the illness has forced her resignation from her teaching post) have given this protagonist a fiercely defiant attitude regarding the social constraints that prevented her affair from coming to fruition and forced her to live in the past rather than the present. While she clearly possesses great insight into her own condition and the social milieu in which she exists, she is also only marginally anchored in reality.

Thus, the evocative connection with her lover with which "Y pongo por testigo . . . " ends is as ambiguous as the character herself. Though her doctors claim it is impossible, the protagonist continually reports visits from her drowned lover. The lover's perfume, a mixture of sea smells and roses, and a bit of algae wrapped around some strands of hair appear to provide irrefutable evidence of the lover's visit. Drawn in by the intensely personal prose style, the reader is more likely to accept the protagonist's view of events than the doctors'. These two stories have successfully erased the rigid demarcations between order and chaos to the extent that the conventional authorities of a rational world become stick figures, and the women's world of erotic desire is transformed into the reality the reader trusts. The themes of longing for unattainable love and condemnation to a life led exclusively in the past are central in almost all the stories in this collection.

Four stories in *Palabra de mujer*—"Como si el miedo . . . " ("As if Fear . . . "), "Arrugas como olas" ("Wrinkles Like Waves"), "Descasadas" ("Separated"), and "El detergente definitivo" ("The Final Cleanser")—reproduce the popular speech of Mallorcans trying to express themselves in a language not their own. The hybrid mix of Castilian and Mallorcan gives strength to the voices of the working-class women who narrate these tales. There is a kind of rueful self-knowledge evident in these works that sets the protagonists apart from other voices heard in the book. Although their lives contain an element of brutality absent in the stories of middle-class women, these characters earn independence from men by doing housework, ironing, and keeping other people's children clean. They understand their own situations, even if others do not. In "El detergente definitivo," for example, the protagonist is punished by incarceration in a mental institution for discarding her marriage photos and some postcards from her husband after his death. This gesture, which her nephew regarded as insane, is understood by the narrator to be sane, given that these objects underscore the misery of her marriage and her husband's sexual transgressions.[2] The protagonist of "Descasadas" uses commonplaces to excuse her autonomy: "I think that when a women has luck, she should respect her husband. . . . Of course, in our case we haven't had any luck with men" (170).

Despite their desperate condition, the women in these stories know that the madness of which they are often accused resides in the society that surrounds them, not within themseves. Although the protagonists continually confront the inadequacy of language to articulate full understanding of their lives, Riera presents the reader with such a rich mosaic of detail that we become capable of piecing together female experience from the threads that are expressed. The complex social and experiential forces that determine women's lives—sexual assaults by nuns, childhoods that render women incapable of making decisions, conflicting needs for dependence and autonomy that cannot be resolved within the social fabric—are chronicled in this book in such a fashion that the reader feels the weight of circumstance even if full comprehension remains unavailable.

Unlike the protagonists of the short stories in *Palabra de mujer*, Clara, the central character in Riera's first novel, *Una primavera para Domenico Guarini*, successfully sheds her dependence on identities bestowed upon her by others. The plot is fairly straightforward. Clara, a journalist for a Barcelona newspaper, is sent by her editor to Italy to cover the Guarini affair, which involves an act of vandalism against the Botticelli painting *Primavera*. She welcomes this opportunity as a chance to leave Spain at a time when physical and emotional distance from her daily life is essential. Having just discovered that she is pregnant, Clara must come to a decision as to whether to abort.

The novel begins with Clara's train journey out of Spain and ends a few weeks later with her return. The long trip, the encounter in Italy with her former lover, the experimentation with writing that the Guarini case affords, and her examination of her past allow her to come to a decision not only about her pregnancy but also about her ability to determine her own life. The complex narrative techniques employed by Riera in this work give a sense of authenticity to Clara's search. Her quest for identity takes place simultaneously within a social and a personal space. It is conveyed to the reader, therefore, in a way that reflects life as lived—nonlinear, creative, and brooding—at times rational and at times governed by myth and history. Just as Clara's achievement of autonomy requires her comprehension of all aspects of her life—her fantasies, her realities, and her strengths—so Riera demands that the reader assimilate and comprehend all the different strands that make Clara's understanding possible. Through Clara's conversations with herself, both she and the reader confront her most intimate doubts: Although she has been taught that maternity is the only way for a woman to make sense of her life, she is frightened of the idea of herself as a mother and doubts her ability to offer emotional sustenance to a child. The thought of childbearing throws her into a state in which she is overcome by primal images of "a repulsive magma, a black stain, a dirty, disgusting amalgam that grows bigger without restraint" (15).

Vignettes of the past are evoked and examined as Clara recalls her mother and unmarried aunts embroidering her dowry of sheets, tablecloths, towels, and aprons . . . all now moldering in a closet. She is moved by memories of her adolescent recognition of her own sexual desire and its condemnation by her religious upbringing. Her memories are often painful and filled with recollections of sexual abuse in a movie theater, threats of divine retribution for masturbation, images of the libertine tendencies of her father, and the consequent humiliation of her mother. Riera summons up the characters in books that formed Clara's ideas of love, as well as the repeated admonitions regarding a woman's passive, suffering role in the world. But Clara's conversations with herself are not merely fixed on memories of childhood. Her reflections concern present events as she confronts the evolution of her relationship with her former lover, Alberto. She contrasts the physical and emotional comfort she has drawn from him with his current inability to be sexually aroused by her. Most critically, she finally recognizes and comes to terms with the fact that Alberto's sexual energy is now directed toward a man, Piero, who has introduced him to the world of drugs.

The contemplation of the future in Clara's conversations with herself is pivotal in her growth. It is here that Clara examines her relationship to her current lover, Enrique, an indefatigable Marxist politician and polemicist whose child she carries. She elaborates and embraces a future that will depart from her past. She recognizes that her pleasure in the relationship derives from both Enrique's weakness and her ability to provide him with a quiet port where he can recover from the vicissitudes of the daily struggle while she in turn denies her own creativity. When Clara finally realizes the anachronistic quality of her position, she can no longer accept a future that posits a continuation of this past not far removed from that of her mother or from the traditional culture that provided models for women's roles. The clarity of vision that occurs requires the shedding of this persona, the Clara who is Enrique's helpmate and scriptwriter. As the future emerges in these conversations with self, it is clear that Clara's transformation will allow her to live her own life and write her own story. She is alone, and she accepts that isolation as the only means of attaining autonomy.

The intensely personal level of narrative is juxtaposed with several others that offer a counterpoint to Clara's introspection. Three derive from the Guarini case. The first comprises the texts of the journalistic pieces Clara sends back to Spain, recounting the Guarini trial in a distant, disinterested style. The second is Clara's experiment with fiction as she ignores the journalistic items sent to Spain and rewrites the history of the Guarini case, solving it within the context of Guarini's obsessive Neoplatonic love for his Laura. In Clara's fictitious version of the story, there is a complex juxtaposition of first- and third-person narration that reveals her talents as a novelist. Her resolution of the mystery is a compelling fictional text in which Guarini becomes a hero who risks everything for love. Ironically, as Clara hears herself defending Guarini as a Petrarchan model of love, she is able to confront her own wish to love and be loved totally and limitlessly. She thus discovers a part of herself that must be named before it can be mastered. She recognizes that her longings have been hidden in order to conform to contemporary views of love. Only by unmasking her conflicting desires for autonomy and dependence can she construct a sexual identity of her own.

Riera creates another narrative level by inserting an art historian's exegesis of Botticelli's *Primavera* into the text. While the professorial lecture purports to interpret the painting, it also helps the reader (and Clara) situate her current dilemma within the historical context of women's place in the world as evidenced in Renaissance art. Although this occurs only implicitly (Clara never comments directly on the lecture she overhears), it is impossible to ignore the impact that Neoplatonic myths continue to exert on contemporary life for both Clara and the reader.

Carme Riera's most recent novel translated from Catalan into Spanish is *Cuestión de amor propio*, a concise epistolary work composed of a single letter from Ángela, a Spanish writer, to her Scandanavian friend, Ingrid. The argument is a simple one. Ángela has been deceived by Miguel, a self-serving, egotistical author, who basks in the glow of fame afforded him by press and public. In addition to destroying Ángela's sexual confidence, Miguel tries to destroy her work. In a final twist, Ángela successfully develops a plan to avenge herself for his behavior. With the help of Ingrid, she plots to use his self-aggrandizing behavior against him, and thwarts his chance to win the Nobel Prize he covets.

Ángela utilizes the epistolary form to examine her relationship to men, the connections between life and literature, and the ephemeral world of publishing, in which gossip, innuendo, and the press play a decisive role. Unlike the Riera characters who change in the course of the fictions they inhabit, the protagonist of this novel has undergone prior transformation. A year of introspective reflection has given Ángela the distance and vision to identify the source of her problems. She cringes as she recounts the way in which Miguel unabashedly manipulated her, understanding her romantic desire for protection and tenderness from men that blinded her to his banal advances. She comes to view her positive response to flattery, her willingness to dismiss older women as uninteresting and bitter, her joy at receiving orchids and *cursi* (trite) love notes, her desire to be small, cared for, *cosificada* (objectified) as part of the world in which she was raised.

Ángela struggled during the year that precedes her letter to Ingrid to comprehend her failure to protect herself. As a woman who, following a traumatic marriage, had avoided serious relationships with men, she is perplexed by her vulnerability to Miguel. She recalls the genesis of their affair at a literary conference in Valencia, where his brilliant talk on *La regenta* fascinated her. Ironically, in order to capture his attention, Ángela had contradicted Miguel's thesis that Clarín's Ana Ozores was the first protagonist to explore sexuality openly in a Spanish novel. A discussion between them ensued in which Miguel argued that Ana Ozores's life was governed by sexual drives, while Ángela insisted that it was the desire for affection that shaped Ana's world. This chance meeting began an affair in which the two writers acted out a plot that Miguel had cunningly determined.

In retrospect, Ángela realizes that Miguel seduced her solely to elaborate a story. Soon after their brief liaison, Miguel publishes a novel in which the protagonist is transparently fashioned after Ángela—a betrayed, foolish, middle-aged woman who humiliates herself out of her hunger for affection and romance. Nonetheless, Ángela ultimately emerges as more than the victim of an obsolete bourgeois education that assigned passive, romantic roles to women. She has acquired a level of self-awareness that Miguel lacks. He is an insecure liar, incapable of Ángela's self-reflective irony. Riera's novel can be read on many levels: as a cautionary tale, as a revealing study of women's entrapment by romantic notions and traditional education, and as a fiction about the social realities in which the masculine script determines the female actors' lines. Without its conclusion, this novel would offer only a dismal perspective. The reader's final knowledge that Ángela's hard-won understanding of herself and, consequently, of Miguel will give her the ability to thwart his ambitions, confirms the protagonist's sense of power. No longer passive, Ángela will finally determine the story line of Miguel's life.

While the texture of Riera's fiction is often enhanced by her training as a literary scholar and humanist, her critical essays demonstrate traditional erudition. She has written a book about the Barcelona School of poets, *La escuela de Barcelona*, which became identifiable as a group in the 1950s and whose leading figures include Carlos Barral, Juan Agustín Goytisolo, and Jaime Gil de Biedma. She has also written an extensive study of the poetry of Carlos Barral, *La poesía de Carlos Barral* (1990; "The Poetry of Carlos Barral"). In addition, she has published the narrative for a photo essay on cemeteries in Barcelona, *Els cementiris de Barcelona* (1981; "Cemeteries of Barcelona"), and a children's biography of Ramon Llull, *Quasi bé un conte, la vida de Ramon Llull* (1980; "Almost a Story, the Life of Ramon Llull"). Although many of Riera's articles study specific aspects of the Barcelona poetic group, others broach distinct topics, including the question of whether there exists a specifically feminine language. Riera's interviews with Carmen Balcells (the well-known literary agent for Vargas Llosa, Augusto Roa Bastos, and Gabriel García Márquez) and with the Brazilian writer Nélida Piñón underscore the theoretical complexities surrounding the debate about feminine language as well as the contradictions revealed by women's writing and women's lives.

SURVEY OF CRITICISM

Carme Riera's work has not received the critical attention it deserves. No book-length studies of her writing exist, and very few of the critical articles provide serious analysis and contextualization of individual volumes. Riera herself notes that despite the immediate success of her first book, it was not mentioned in any journal for more than a year and several editions later (Nichols, *Escribir* 199). Only two studies situate Riera's works within a larger critical framework. One, an excellent article by Geraldine Nichols, "Stranger Than Fiction," examines fantastic elements in works by Matute, Rodoreda, and Riera. Here, stories from *Epitelis tendríssims* (1981; "Delicate Skin") are analyzed, using definitions of the fantastic elaborated by Tzvetan Todorov, Rosemary Jackson, and David Hume. Nichols utilizes this theoretical framework to underscore the ways in which fantasy's eradication of rigid social categories, transgression of commonly observed taboos, and blurring of the line between reality and fiction allow Riera to create an ingenious erotic landscape that challenges conventional expectations. While the article only hints at the connections between that body of Riera's work defined as "realistic" and the "fantasy" fiction examined here, the reader's ability to connect the subversive nature of Riera's fantasy with the subversive elements of her realistic prose is enhanced by the critic's insights. Nichols's article also heightens the reader's awareness of the ways in which Riera's narrative technique in all her works often blurs traditional distinctions between realistic and fantastic fiction.

The second critical study that perceptively contextualizes Riera's work is Elizabeth Ordóñez's "Beginning to Speak," which examines *Una primavera para Domenico Guarini* in the light of Riera's critical concerns about the creation of a feminine language. In this study, Ordóñez shows how Riera uses textual models both to measure and to reject available models for female behavior. She traces the parallels between the various "texts" of the Guarini affair and the protagonist's ability to define her own life free of the text that has been generated for her by patriarchal society.

Other criticism of Riera's works tends to be positive, short, and superficial. Interviews with Riera published in Spain and in the United States provide some insight into the genesis of her work as well as an understanding of the constraints and ambience that inform her writing; Nichols's dialogue with Riera in *Escribir, espacio propio* is the most instructive of these interviews. In addition to biographical information, she elicits Riera's opinions on the relationship of gender to the act of reading and writing; the importance of foreign literature to Spanish writers; Riera's sense of the interplay of Catalan, Mallorcan, and Spanish in her writing; and her own situation within the context of contemporary Spanish authors. Some crucial topics, such as Riera's insights regarding the social construction of gender and the connection between the writer and her audience, are also addressed.

One of the most glaring absences in the available work on Riera is the lack of any works in English translation. It is clear that her novels and short stories would enhance Anglo-American readers' understanding of the rich texture of Spanish fiction in the 1990s. Furthermore, were her works available in English, they could form an integral part of the study of gender and literature that is a dynamic element in university curricula today.

Riera's work since 1977 represents an extraordinary intellectual and imaginative accomplishment. The breadth of humanist scholarship in her critical work enriches the reading of her vital, engaging, and original fiction. The energy and range of her writing make her a crucial voice in the world of contemporary letters. She is a writer whose contributions have just begun to be examined, and whose work merits much more probing and careful discussion.

NOTES

1. This chapter deals primarily with the three fictional works that have been translated into Spanish. This decision was made for reasons of limitations of space. All titles in this chapter are given in Spanish. For a complete listing of the author's works, consult the bibliography.

2. It is important to note that many of the protagonists in these stories are characterized as madwomen if in their search for identity they reject the social construction of gender deemed appropriate. This subject as it appears in writing by contemporary Spanish women is fully examined by Lois-Kay Turner in her doctoral dissertation, "Estás loca: Feminine Constructs of Madness and Obsession in the Post–Civil War Spanish Novel" (Brown University, 1989). Though Turner does not specifically deal with Carme Riera's work,

her research on this topic is essential for anyone interested in this aspect of women's writing.

BIBLIOGRAPHY

Works by Carme Riera

Fiction

Te deix, amor, la mar com a penyora. Barcelona: Laia, 1975.
Je pos per testimoni les gavines. Barcelona: Laia, 1977.
Epitelis tendrissims. Barcelona: Edicions 62, 1981.
Una primavera per a Dominico Guarini. Barcelona: Edicions 62, 1981.
Qüestió d'amor propio. Barcelona: Laia, 1987.
Joc de miralls. Barcelona: Planeta, 1989.
Contra el amor en compañía y otros relatos. Barcelona: Destino, 1991.

Nonfiction

Quasi bé un conte, la vida de Ramon Llull. Barcelona: Ayuntamaiento de Barcelona, 1980.
Els cementiris de Barcelona. Barcelona: Edhasa, 1981.
La escuela de Barcelona. Barcelona: Anagrama, 1988.
La poesía de Carlos Barral. Barcelona: Península, 1990.

Articles

"Enseñar a dudar: Conversación con José Manuel Blecua, senior." *Quimera* 26 (1982): 20–25.
"Literatura femenina: ¿Un lenguaje prestado?" *Quimera* 18 (1982): 9–12.
"Carmen Balcells, alquimista del libro." *Quimera* 27 (1983): 23–29.
"El Río común de Juan Marsé y Jaime Gil de Biedma." *Quimera* 41 (1984): 56–61.
"Hace 40 años, en una noche come hoy." *El País* 16 Jan. 1985: 25.
"De *El retorno* a *Final de un adiós*: Algunas notas sobre la elegía en José Agustín Goytisolo." *Cuadernos Hispanoamericanos* 429 (1986): 155–67.
"Entrevista con Nélida Piñón: La vida es la literatura." *Quimera* 54–55 (1986): 44–49.
"El Otro Machado." *Quimera* 50 (1986): 46–50.
"Los personajes femeninos de doña María de Zayas, una aproximación." *Literatura y vida cotidiana*. Ed. María Angeles Durán and José Antonio Rey. Actas de las Cuartas Jornadas de Investigación Interdisciplinaria. Zaragoza, Spain: Seminario de Estudios de la Mujer, Universidad Autónoma de Madrid, 1987. [Written with Luisa Cotoner]
"Amistad a lo largo." *Quimera* 74 (1988): 48–55.
"La escuela de Barcelona, un habla expresiva fruto de la amistad." *Insula* 43 (Jan. 1988): 12–13.
"Punto de Vista en Azul: Entrevista con José María Merino." *Quimera* 82 (1988): 34–39.
"Algunas notas sobre la poesía de Carlos Barral, en torno a los recursos lingüísticos." *Homenaje al profesor Antonio Vilanova*. Barcelona: Universidad de Barcelona, 1989.

Translations

Palabra de mujer. Trans. Carme Riera. Barcelona: Laia, 1980.
Una primavera para Domenico Guarini. Trans. Luisa Cotoner. Barcelona: Montesinos, 1981.
Cuestión de amor propio. Trans. Carme Riera. Barcelona: Tusquets Editores, 1988.
On Our Own Behalf. Women's Tales from Catalonia. Ed. Kathleen McNerney. Lincoln: U of Nebraska P, 1988. Included in this volume are the following short stories: "A Cool Breeze for Wanda." Trans. Eulalia Benejam Cobb. 53–63; "I Leave You, My Love, the Sea as a Token." Trans. Alberto Moreiras. 31–46; "The Knot, the Void." Trans. Alberto Moreiras. 49–53; "Miss Angels Ruscadell Investigates the Horrible Death of Marianna Servera." Trans. Eulalia Benejam Cobb. 63–77; "Some Flowers." Trans. Alberto Moreiras. 46–49.

Works about Carme Riera

Camps, Susana. "Carme Riera: 'Cuestión de amor propio': Amor y dignidad." *Quimera* 82 (1988): 71.

Cotoner, Luisa. *"Una primavera per a Domenico Guarini* de Carme Riera." *Mirall de glac. Quaderns de Literatura Terrassa* (Spring-Summer 1982): 52–57.

Guillaume, Anne. "Entrevista a Carme Riera." *Ventanal* 14 (1988): 71–79.

Nichols, Geraldine Cleary. *Escribir, espacio propio: Laforet, Matute, Moix, Tusquets, Riera y Roig por sí mismas.* Minneapolis: Institute for the Study of Ideologies and Literature, 1989. 187–227.

———. "Stranger Than Fiction: Fantasy in Short Stories by Matute, Rodoreda, Riera." *Monographic Review/Revista monográfica* 4 (1988): 33–42.

Ordóñez, Elizabeth. "Beginning to Speak: Carme Riera's *Una primavera para Domenico Guarini.*" *La Chispa.* Ed. Gilbert Paolini. Proceedings of the Sixth Louisiana Conference on Hispanic Languages and Literatures. New Orleans: Tulane U, 1985. 385–93.

Orja, Juan. "Carme Riera, fiel a sus orígenes." *La Vanguardia* 14 Jan. 1988: 38.

Racionero, Luis. "Entrevista con Carme Riera: Cada vez tenemos menos imaginación." *Quimera* 9–10 (1981): 14–16.

———. "La maniera gentile de Carme Riera." *Quimera* 9–10 (1981): 12–13.

MERCÈ RODOREDA
(1908–1983)

Nancy Vosburg

BIOGRAPHY

Mercè Rodoreda y Gurguí was born in Barcelona on October 10, 1908.[1] An only child, she lived with her parents and grandfather in the Sant Gervasi district of that city. She attended school until age nine, when her parents withdrew her for financial reasons. In 1921 Rodoreda's uncle, Joan Gurguí, sixteen years her senior, returned from America, where he had spent twelve years rather unsuccessfully seeking his fortune. A letter that Rodoreda wrote to her daughter-in-law in 1957 indicates that she lived a happy life until then. Her uncle immediately took over the family's finances and moved them to a smaller house nearer the center of Barcelona. It was decided by the family that he would marry his niece on her twentieth birthday. In 1921, Rodoreda was enrolled briefly in a French monk's school, studying accounting and languages in order to help her uncle with his business. The marriage took place on her twentieth birthday; nine months later her only child, Jordi, was born.

Despite her lack of formal education, Rodoreda began writing during her teenage years, and by the early 1930s had published several short narratives in such journals and newspapers as the *Revista de Catalunya, Clarisme, Mirador,* and *Companya*. During the 1930s, she published four short novels, all of which she later renounced: *Sóc una dona honrada?* (1932; "Am I an Honest Woman?"), *Del que hom no pot fugir* (1934; "The Inevitable"), *Un dia en la vida d'un home* (1934; "One Day in a Man's Life"), and *Crim* (1938; "Crime"). These early novels reflect the influence of the avant-garde writers of Barcelona who comprised the Sabadell group, including Francesc Trabal, Joan Oliver, and "Armand Obiols" (the pseudonym of Joan Prat, with whom Rodoreda later shared exile in France and Switzerland).

Rodoreda's early novelistic attempts culminated in the 1938 publication of *Aloma*, which the previous year had won the most important Catalan literary prize of the 1930s, the Crexells Prize. Rodoreda was at that time working for the Ministry of Culture of the Catalan regional government, an institution that continued to survive despite the Fascist uprising of 1936. Nevertheless, with the fall of the regional government in 1939, Rodoreda, already separated from her husband, left her son with her mother and fled to Paris with Obiols, who left behind his daughter and wife (Francesc Trabal's sister).

Rodoreda's early years in exile were difficult. She was initially ostracized by many of her fellow exiles in Paris because of her relationship with Obiols. In June 1940, as the German Army advanced on Paris, Rodoreda and Obiols set off, first by train, then on foot, to Limoges. The arduous journey along the edge of the war zone is captured as motif and/or setting in later works such as "Orleans, 3 quilòmetres," published in the 1978 *Semblava de seda* (*Parecía de seda* 1981; "It Seemed Like Silk"), a collection of short stories, and her 1980 work *Quanta, quanta guerra* (*Cuánta, cuánta guerra* 1982; "So Much War"). Shortly after they arrived in Limoges, Obiols was sent to a work camp, where he spent a year and a half. For Rodoreda, the separation period was marked by poor health (and an ensuing partial hysterectomy), extreme poverty, and doubts about Obiols's true feelings toward her, as revealed in her letters to Anna Murià, then exiled in Mexico. In 1943, however, Rodoreda and Obiols were reunited in Bordeaux, where Rodoreda began writing poetry while eking out a living as a seamstress. The arrival of Obiols's wife in September 1946 provoked Rodoreda to flee to Paris; Obiols, having sent his wife and daughter back to Spain, joined her there within a few months. With sewing as her only source of income, Rodoreda's life continued to be unstable both economically and emotionally. She and Obiols were separated again in 1953, when he went to Geneva to take a translating/editing job with UNESCO. In 1954, however, Rodoreda was also offered a job with UNESCO and moved to Geneva, where she spent the next twenty years.

Although her novelistic pursuits were virtually truncated by the harsh conditions of exile, Rodoreda's letters to her friend Anna Murià reveal that throughout the 1940s and 1950s, she was writing poems and short stories, some of which appeared in Catalan journals in France and Mexico (such as the *Revista de Catalunya*, published for a brief period in Paris). Since she wrote in Catalan, her audience was naturally limited to Catalan exiles. Rodoreda stated in a 1946 letter to Murià that her stories were inspired by the writings of Katherine Mansfield, John Steinbeck, William Faulkner, Dorothy Parker, and Katherine Anne Porter. Carme Arnau has speculated that an unfinished novel, *Isabel i Maria* (1991; "Isabel and Maria"), discovered after Rodoreda's death, was begun during the late 1940s.

By the mid-1950s most restrictions in Spain on publications in the Catalan language had been lifted. Rodoreda reentered the Catalan literary scene with the 1958 publication of *Vinti-i-dos contes* (*Veintidós cuentos* 1988; "Twenty-two

Tales''), which had won the prestigious Víctor Català Literary Prize the previous year. In 1962 Rodoreda presented her novel *La plaça del Diamant* (*La plaza del Diamante* 1965; *The Pigeon Girl*, 1967; *The Time of the Doves*, 1981) for the Sant Jordi Literary Prize. Although it failed to win the award, the novel, hailed by Gabriel García Márquez as "the most beautiful novel published in Spain since the Civil War" (6), became a best-seller after its publication in 1963. It has been translated into Castilian and twelve other languages, and was adapted for the screen in 1982.

Rodoreda's next novel, *El carrer de les Camèlies* (1966; *La calle de las Camelias* 1970; ''Camellia Street''), won not only the Sant Jordi Prize of that year but also the 1967 Catalan Critics' Prize and the 1969 Ramon Llull Literary Prize. The year 1966 also saw the publication of *Jardí vora el mar* (*Jardín junto al mar* 1975; ''Garden by the Sea''), which Rodoreda later admitted she had written in 1959, and thus must be viewed as her first completed postwar novel. It was followed in 1967 by *La meva Cristina i altres contes* (*Mi Cristina y otros cuentos* 1982; *My Christina and Other Stories* 1984), a collection that included narratives published in Catalan newspapers in exile and two previously unpublished short stories. A completely rewritten version of Rodoreda's 1938 award-winning novel, *Aloma*, was published in 1969; it differs from the original primarily in that the point of view is reduced to that of the eponymous heroine, thus giving the work greater unity. *Mirall trencat* (*Espejo roto* 1978; ''Broken Mirror''), the saga of the destruction of an aristocratic Catalan family narrated from multiple perspectives, followed in 1974.

It appears that Rodoreda returned from exile in 1974, although there is some confusion surrounding the actual date of her return. In several newspaper interviews, she spoke of her ''twenty years'' in Geneva, and an article in a 1975 issue of *Tele/eXpres* suggests that she was living and writing in Catalonia. According to her American translator, the late David Rosenthal, however, Rodoreda did not officially reestablish residence in Spain until 1979. We know from her correspondence with Murià that Rodoreda was making occasional clandestine trips back to Catalonia to visit her mother as early as 1948. After her mother's death in 1962, she received a small inheritance, which she used to buy an apartment in Barcelona. According to Montserrat Casals (''El 'Rosebud' '' 46), Rodoreda saw her son Jordi for the last time in 1968; the circumstances of this visit, and their subsequent parting of the ways, have never been revealed, and it is not clear whether she was then living in Catalonia.

The year 1978 saw the publication of *Semblava de seda*, a collection of short stories whose title story had been published in a Catalan magazine in 1974. The other stories in the collection were written between 1938 and 1978, thus offering a diversity of styles and thematic concerns. In 1980, Rodoreda published two works, the novel *Quanta, quanta guerra* and the award-winning *Viatges i flors* (*Viajes y flores* 1981; ''Journeys and Flowers''), a book composed of two groups of short narratives written in different periods. That same year Rodoreda's entire work was awarded the Premi d'Honor de les Lletres Catalanes, the most prestigious award for a Catalan writer. She is the only woman to have received such a distinction. Rodoreda died in April 1983 from a heart attack. Her last work, *La mort i la primavera* (*La muerte y la primavera* 1986; "Death and Spring"), a novel she had been working on intermittently since 1961, was published unfinished in 1986.

MAJOR THEMES

While there are recurring themes throughout Rodoreda's total literary production, her works can be loosely grouped into three periods (prewar, exile, and postexile) that reflect her age, the circumstances surrounding her literary career, and Western literary currents in vogue at the time of the writing. At the risk of oversimplification, several generalizations can be drawn. First, there are two narrative currents that appear to have evolved simultaneously: a "realist" mode, in the sense that some works are tied to concrete spatial/temporal coordinates, and a fantastical or mythical current, which becomes more predominant in Rodoreda's postexile period. Furthermore, in the majority of her novels and short stories, the major themes are presented from a narrative perspective of innocence or naïveté. There is also a tendency to focus on the daily, ritual acts of characters and their subjective vision of reality, thus creating a schism between the external and internal worlds that results in a climate of "irreality." Finally, throughout her works there runs a thread of violence and/or cruelty that underscores the defenselessness and solitude of the characters.

The prewar and exile works merit special attention in this study because of their emphasis on women's issues. Although Rodoreda renounced her preexile "attempts" at writing and prohibited republication of her first four novels, the novels introduce two interrelated themes that remained a constant throughout her literary production: the frustrating condition of women, trapped in a gendered social environment that does not conform to their childhood dreams of happiness and self-fulfillment, and the mythification of childhood as a paradise lost through the process of socialization and maturation. With the exception of *Crim*, which is a parody of the detective novel, possibly influenced by C. A. Jordana of the Sabadell group, the novels of this early period present young female characters who fail in their attempt to escape bourgeois mores and morality. By focusing on the psychological state of the young and mostly female characters, who are in general passive victims of infelicitous love relations, the novels denounce the gendered social reality that results in a desolate and alienated adult life. The antagonism between external reality and the internal world (projected toward the future through dreams, toward the past through childhood memories, and nourished by romantic literary models) is developed more fully in *Aloma*, Rodoreda's 1938 award-winning novel that foreshadows her later treatment of female characters. Here the adolescent protagonist, Aloma, a solitary and introverted dreamer, is further marginalized as the result of a clandestine love affair that leaves her pregnant, alone, and suicidal.

In the novels and short stories published in the 1950s and 1960s, Rodoreda continued to focus on the interior worlds of her characters, whose social and/or economic marginality contributes to the overriding theme of individual alienation and self-estrangement. While most of these works are firmly grounded in concrete spatial/temporal realities (prewar and postwar Barcelona, the war zones, and exile ghettos of Europe), a fact that has led many critics to identify them with the "social realist" mode in vogue during this period, the predominant theme of the impossibility of meaningful and sustained love relationships places the emphasis on the subjective interior worlds of the protagonists, the majority of whom are female. In general, the stories in *Vint-i-dos contes* relate the characters' increasing sense of isolation and ostracism as they struggle to understand or articulate a newly perceived void. Jealousy, domestic entrapment, exile, lost youth, poverty, abandonment, cruelty, death, adultery, and deceit are but a few of the contributing factors that intensify the theme of individual solitude, alienation, and the struggle for self-knowledge.

It is important to note that not all of the stories focus on the inner worlds of women characters, yet there is little difference established between the female and male perspectives. Geraldine Nichols has pointed out that Rodoreda's fiction, in both structure and process, formulates two distinct experiences of alienation: the universal expulsion from the garden of childhood into the reality of adulthood and the more particular experience of exile. Nichols's observation that the exile theme is portrayed as a "female or feminizing experience of deprivation" ("Exile, Gender" 190) may be taken a step further, for throughout Rodoreda's works the interior psychological worlds of the protagonists, be they female or male, are shaped by similar "gendered" experiences of self-estrangement, dependency, and marginalization.

La plaça del Diamant, considered by many to be the best novel written in Catalan in the twentieth century, is representative of both Rodoreda's narrative techniques and her major themes. Natàlia, the protagonist, is a simple, working-class woman who recounts her life in Barcelona from shortly before the Second Republic into the post–Civil War period. She is typical of Rodoreda's characters: she speaks from a position of innocence, bewilderment, and marginality, struggling to understand and articulate the significant events of her bare and restricted existence, including her courtship, marriage, the birth of two children, widowhood, and remarriage. As with the vast majority of Rodoreda's narrators, Natàlia's first-person narrative gives the impression of oral communication, and the reader is struck by the blanks and gaps in her story.

La plaça begins with Natàlia's encounter with Quimet, her future husband, whose authoritarian and oppressive nature immediately begins to strip her of her sense of individuality and identity. One of Quimet's first acts, for example, is to impose on her a new name, Colometa (Little Dove). Natàlia/Colometa quickly becomes imprisoned in her apartment and marriage. Her process of self-estrangement, isolation, and loss of self is advanced by pregnancy and her tending to Quimet's doves. Doves figure prominently in the novel and are the visible symbol of Natàlia's oppression (Arnau, *Introducció* 248). Finally reaching a breaking point, Natàlia launches a silent rebellion by destroying the doves; the news of Quimet's death in the Civil War coincides with the demise of the last dove.

As her economic condition worsens, Natàlia desperately contemplates killing her children and herself. The contemplation of infanticide and suicide in this novel serves to underscore the schism between idealized valorizations of women's prescribed role as mother and the harsh socioeconomic realities and exploitation of working-class women. Natàlia's marriage to Antoni, a shopkeeper whose war wounds have left him impotent, saves her and her children from their desperate economic situation, although Natàlia remains imprisoned in her silent, internal world. Having now recuperated her original name, however, she returns to the Plaça del Diamant, the starting point of the novel, and lets out a rebellious scream that appears to signal an end to her silent passivity and the oppression of the past.

El carrer de les Camèlies is also an interiorized first-person narrative that has as its main theme the profound rupture between the female narrator and her external world. Cecilia's psychosocial alienation, aggravated by her orphaned state, poverty, and solitude, eventually leads her into prostitution, a situation that intensifies the theme of women's submission to and dependence upon men in an authoritarian and patriarchal society. As Janet Pérez has observed, the novel reflects a more exasperated vision of life and of female devaluation than its predecessor ("The Most Significant Writer" 82). Like previous Rodoredan heroines, most notably Aloma and Natàlia, Cecilia seeks refuge in an interior dream world, distancing herself further from the adverse external reality. Infanticide and suicide are once again posited as not only a consequence of, but perhaps also as a resolution to, the unhappy state of affairs: they are the means of recuperating the happiness of a lost or imagined paradise. Like Natàlia, Cecilia is saved by a sort of man different from the authoritarian and even sadistic types she has previously encountered—a man who offers her a degree of emotional and economic stability, symbolized by the garden that surrounds his house. Her new position of security enables her, like Natàlia, to initiate her search for her lost identity. While both *La plaça* and *El carrer* are female-centered texts denouncing the exploitation and devaluation of women, the protagonists' perseverance under such adverse circumstances offers a reading of their lives as a "metahistory" of the Catalan experience as well.

While the primary emphasis on the interior realities of marginalized, working-class women in concrete historical settings culminates with *El carrer*, alienation, solitude, and lack of communication continue to be central themes in Rodoreda's subsequent works, and are conditions that characterize male and female characters alike. The interrelated theme of metamorphosis, present in the early works as a desire for death and rebirth in the garden of childhood, becomes more visible after *El carrer* as Rodoreda moves increasingly into fantastical or mythical worlds generated by the imagination. This theme acquires primary visibility in the fantastical stories in *La meva Cristina* collection. As Joaquim Molas points out in his "Pròleg" to the collection (12), the majority of these stories were composed in 1960 and thus belong to the period in which Rodoreda's central theme is the oppression of women within the patriarchal value system.[2] While metamorphosis signifies the potential for liberation, it is not without violence; and often, as in "La Salamandra" ("The Salamander"), the change in form does not change one's fate. In this sense, metamorphosis functions as a "vehicle for protesting women's dependent condition," as Janet Pérez notes in her article on the theme ("Metamorphosis" 181). In Rodoreda's later works, particularly *Viatges i flors* and *Quanta, quanta guerra*, metamorphosis evolves into a carnivalesque device; that is, it is a means of breaking through "official" constructions of reality to lay bare repressed human impulses and desires.

The garden motif has appeared consistently in the works of Rodoreda, from *Jardí vora el mar* to *Viatges i flors*. It is frequently associated with her happy childhood in the Sant Gervasi district. Sometimes flowers and vegetation appear as a merely ornamental device in her works, but more often they are imbued with symbolic value; they evoke not only the lost pleasures and innocence of childhood, particularly for the female characters, but also the possibility of cosmic reabsorption and rebirth.

Although Rodoreda's postexile works are not specifically female-centered, they are nevertheless of interest to feminist scholars because they explore culturally taboo desires often linked to gender. As concrete sociohistorical settings disappear, they are replaced by primitive universes intimately related to dream, myth, and the unconscious. The journey as a means of attaining knowledge of the human condition, a condition predicated on Eve's temptation and the expulsion from paradise, is the thematic premise of *Quanta, quanta guerra* and the first group of narratives in *Viatges i flors*. Rodoreda's last work, *La mort i la primavera*, which presents a mythical universe governed by ritual death and violent desires, has as its central theme the repression and/or transgression of culturally taboo desires that result in guilt, self-alienation, enmity, and individual solitude. Although the narrators of these texts are not female, they speak from the same position of innocence, defenselessness, and marginality as their female predecessors.

SURVEY OF CRITICISM

Critical response to Rodoreda's early postwar works was generally limited to Catalan newspapers and journals, and consisted of book reviews, announcements of new publications, and short articles on major themes or stylistic aspects of her short stories and novels. The almost immediate translation of *La plaça del Diamant* into Castilian and other languages, however, brought Rodoreda into the national and international spotlight. Critical interest in her literary works continued to grow, both at home and abroad, throughout the late 1960s and 1970s.

Carme Arnau's *Introducció a la narrativa de Mercè Rodoreda: El mite de la infantesa* (1979) was the first book-length critical work to appear, providing biographical data, detailed plot summaries, and an overview of recurring themes in Rodoreda's 1932–1974 literary works. Arnau identifies the following as the major recurring and interrelated themes in Rodoreda's fictional universe: women's alienated condition, loneliness and lack of communication, the loss of innocence, the mythification of childhood as a paradise lost, death, and the development of mythical consciousness and rebirth through a process of metamorphosis. Arnau continues to be a leading Rodoredan scholar, having published several thematic analyses of Rodoreda's short stories and novels.

The late 1970s and the 1980s saw an abundance of wide-ranging articles representing a variety of critical approaches. The psychoanalytical approach from a Freudian perspective is best exemplified in Loreto Busquets's articles. Anna Murià, Montserrat Casals, and Mercè Ibarz have added additional biographical information to that provided by Arnau, and critics Joaquim Poch, Conxa Planas, Maria Lourdes Möller-Soler, and Angeles Encinar have drawn on the biographical data to probe historical and psychological relations between the author and her protagonists. Linguistic approaches are represented in articles by Josep Miquel Sobrer, J. W. Albrecht and Patricia Lunn, whose "A Note on the Language of *La plaça del Diamant*" documents the shift from a passive to an active role in Natàlia's self-presentation. Critics such as Joan Ramón Resina and Gonzalo Navajas, on the other hand, reemphasize the significance of Rodoreda's works within the Catalan cultural context.

Reappraisals of Rodoreda's works from a feminist perspective, pioneered by Frances Wyers and Kathleen McNerney, constitute important contributions not only to Rodoredan scholarship specifically but also to the larger fields of gender and exile studies. McNerney, Wyers, Kathleen Glenn, and Emilie Bergmann incorporate into their studies the Lacanian notion of woman as a culturally and linguistically constituted "Other," to clarify the thematic and narrative tensions in Rodoreda's works. Both Bergmann and Geraldine Nichols have made valuable contributions to the concept of double exile (gendered and geographical) and its symbolic representation in Rodoreda's works. Nichols has also explored issues such as the expression of female desire and cultural subversion in Rodoreda's fiction as a "return to the Mother." Janet Pérez's study of Rodoreda in *Contemporary Women Writers of Spain* (1988) combines introductory and biographical material, themes of interest to the feminist critic, and detailed textual analyses, as does Randolph Pope's chapter on Rodoreda in *Women Writers of Contemporary Spain: Exiles in the Homeland*.

The North American Catalan Society has been particularly instrumental in promoting study and debate of Rodoreda's works. It sponsored a special session at the 1987 Modern Language Association Conference, "New Feminist Perspectives on Mercè Rodoreda." The four papers presented at this session, along with many of the essays highlighted in the previous paragraph, were subsequently published in the Society's December 1987 *Catalan Review: Homage to Mercè*

Rodoreda. Both this collection and the 1993 McNerney and Vosburg anthology, *The Garden Across the Border: Mercè Rodoreda's Fiction*, are of major importance within the existing body of Rodoredan scholarship as they bring her works into the mainstream of current critical debates.

While much has been written of Rodoreda's "master" work, *La plaça del Diamant*, new directions, particularly in the areas of comparative feminist analyses and exile studies, are being mapped. In addition, we are just beginning to see more critical attention paid to her postexile works and her two unfinished novels, *La mort i la primavera* and *Isabel i Maria*. Rodoreda's recognition as the most important Catalan writer of the twentieth century has merited her inclusion in the canon of twentieth-century Spanish literature. As the recent trends in Rodoredan criticism indicate, her voice is emerging in the critical mainstream of world literature.

NOTES

1. Although previous published biographies of Rodoreda indicate that she was born in 1909, Montserrat Casals i Couturier, who published an updated biography of Rodoreda in 1991, maintains that 1908 is the correct date and attributes this confusion to a probable "dosis of feminine coquetry" ("El 'Rosebud' " 29). Her article in *Catalan Review* and Rodoreda's *Cartes a l'Anna Murià, 1939–1956* are the primary sources for the biographical information in this chapter.

2. Molas's findings about the date of the stories' composition also support the view that the fantastical/mythical tendency evolved simultaneously with the "realist" mode.

BIBLIOGRAPHY

Works by Mercè Rodoreda

Obres completes de Mercè Rodoreda. Ed. Carme Arnau. 3 vols. Barcelona: Edicions 62, 1976.

Novels

Sóc una dona honrada? Barcelona: Llibreria Catalònia, 1932.
Del que hom no pot fugir. Barcelona: Clarisme, 1934.
Un dia en la vida d'un home. Barcelona: Proa, 1934.
Aloma. Barcelona: Institució de les Lletres Catalanes, 1938.
Crim. Barcelona: La Rosa del Vents, 1938.
La plaça del Diamant. Barcelona: El Club dels Novel.listes, 1962.
El carrer de les Camèlies. Barcelona: El Club dels Novel.listes, 1966.
Jardí vora el mar. Barcelona: El Club dels Novel.listes, 1967.
Mirall trencat. Barcelona: El Club dels Novel.listes, 1974.
Quanta, quanta guerra. Barcelona: El Club dels Novel.listes, 1980.
La mort i la primavera. Barcelona: Institut d'Estudis Catalans, 1986.
Isabel i Maria. Valencia: Climent, 1991.

Short Stories

Vint-i-dos contes. Barcelona: Selecta, 1958.

"Rom Negrita." *Els set pecats capitals vistos per 21 contistes*. Barcelona: Selecta 292,
     1960. 113–35.

La meva Cristina i altres contes. Barcelona: Edicions 62, 1967.

"Flors de debò." *El Pont* 35 (1969): 33–35.

"Semblava de seda." *Els marges* 1 (May 1974): 75–80.

Tots els contes. Barcelona: Edicions 62, 1979.

Viatges i flors. Barcelona: Edicions 62, 1980.

Contes de guerra i revolució (1936–39). Ed. Maria Campillo. 2 vols. Barcelona: Editorial
     Laia, 1981. [Includes nine short stories]

Una campana de vidre. Barcelona: Destino, 1984.

Miscellaneous

Polèmica. Barcelona: Clarisme, 1934. [Essay written with Delfi Dalmau]

"La sala de nines." Performed in July 1979 in Barcelona. [Play]

"L'hostal de les tres camèlies." Performed in Oct. 1979 in Barcelona. [Play]

La plaça del Diamant. Figaro Films, 1982. [Film]

"Obra poètica." *Els Marges* 30 (1984): 55–71. [Poetry]

Cartes a l'Anna Murià. 1939–1956. Ed. Isabel Segura i Soriano. Barcelona: La Sal,
     1985. [Letters]

Translations

La plaza del Diamante. Trans. Enrique Sordo. Madrid: Edhasa, 1965.

The Pigeon Girl. Trans. Eda O'Shiel. London: Deutsch, 1967. [Trans. of *La plaça del
     Diamant*]

La calle de las Camelias. Trans. José Batlló. Barcelona: Planeta, 1970.

Aloma. Trans. J.F. Vidal. Madrid: Al-Borak, 1971. [Castilian translation]

Jardín junto al mar. Trans. J.F. Vidal. Barcelona: Planeta, 1975.

Espejo roto. Trans. Pere Gimferrer. Barcelona: Seix Barral, 1978. [Trans. of *Mirall
     trencat*]

Parecía de seda y otras narraciones. Trans. Clara Janés. Barcelona: Edhasa, 1981.

The Time of the Doves. Trans. David H. Rosenthal. New York: Taplinger, 1981. London:
     Arena, 1986. [Trans. of *La plaça del Diamant*]

Viajes y flores. Trans. Clara Janés. Barcelona: Edhasa, 1981.

Cuanta, cuanta guerra. Trans. Ana María Moix. Barcelona: Edhasa. 1982.

Mi Cristina y otros cuentos. Trans. José Batlló. Madrid: Alianza, 1982.

Two Tales. Trans. David H. Rosenthal. New York: Red Ozier, 1983. [Trans. of "La
     mainadera" and "La salamandra"]

My Christina and Other Stories. Trans. David H. Rosenthal. Port Townsend, WA:
     Graywolf Press, 1984. [Foreword by David Rosenthal]

La muerte y la primavera. Trans. Enrique Sordo. Barcelona: Seix Barral, 1986.

Veintidós cuentos. Trans. Ana María Moix. Madrid: Mondadori, 1988.

"Summer" and "That Wall, That Mimosa." Ed. and Trans. Josep Miquel Sobrer.
     Catalonia: A Self-Portrait. Bloomington: Indiana UP, 1992. 71–80. [Trans. of
     "Estiu" and "Aquella paret, aquella mimosa"]

Works about Mercè Rodoreda

The following is a selection from an exhaustive list of critical studies compiled by Nancy Vosburg.

Albrecht, J. W., and Patricia V. Lunn. "A Note on the Language of 'La plaça del Diamant'." *Catalan Review* 59–64.

Arnau, Carme. "L'àngel a les novel.les de Mercè Rodoreda." *Serra d'Or* 25.290 (1983): 678–81.

———. "Introducció a la narrativa de Mercè Rodoreda." Vol 1. *Obres completes* 5–46.

———. *Introducció a la narrativa de Mercè Rodoreda: El mite de la infantesa.* Barcelona: Edicions 62, 1976.

———. "Mercè Rodoreda o la força de l'escriptura." *Literatura de dones: una visió del món.* Barcelona: LaSal, 1988. N. pag.

———. *Miralls magics: Aproximació a l'última narrativa de Mercè Rodoreda.* Barcelona: Edicions 62, 1990.

———. "Mort et metamorphose: 'La meva Cristina i altes contes' de Mercè Rodoreda." *Revue des Langues Romanes* 93.1 (1989): 51–60.

———. "La obra de Mercè Rodoreda." *Cuadernos Hispanoamericanos* 383 (May 1982): 239–57.

———. "Vegetació i mort en la narrativa de Mercè Rodoreda." *Revista de Catalunya* 22 (Sept. 1988): 124–33.

———. "El viatge iniciàtic: 'Quanta, quanta guerra' de Mercè Rodoreda." *Catalan Review* 65–82.

Bergmann, Emilie. " 'Flowers at the North Pole': Mercè Rodoreda and the Female Imagination in Exile." *Catalan Review* 83–100.

———. "Mercè Rodoreda's Wartime Fiction." McNerney and Vosburg. [Forthcoming]

———. "Reshaping the Canon: Intertextuality in Spanish Novels of Female Development." *Anales de la Literatura Española Contemporánea* 12.1–2 (1987): 141–56.

Bieder, Maryellen. "Cataclysm and Rebirth: Journey to the Edge of the Maelstrom: Mercè Rodoreda's 'Quanta, quanta guerra.' " *Actes del Tercer Col.loqui d'Estudis Catalans a Nord Amèrica.* Ed. Patricia Boehne, Josep Massot i Muntaner, and Nathaniel B. Smith. Montserrat, Spain: l'Abadia, 1983. 227–37.

———. "The Woman in the Garden: The Problem of Identity in the Novels of Mercè Rodoreda." *Actes del Segon Col.loqui d'Estudis Catalans a Nord Amèrica.* Ed. Manuel Durán, Albert Porgueras-Mayo, and Josep Roca Pons. Montserrat, Spain: l'Abadia, 1982. 353–64.

Bou, Enric. "Exile in the City: Mercè Rodoreda's 'La plaça del Diamant.' " McNerney and Vosburg. [Forthcoming]

Busquets, Loreto. "El mito de la culpa en 'La plaça del Diamant.' " *Actes del Quart Col.loqui d'Estudis Catalans a Nord Amèrica.* Ed. Nathaniel B. Smith, Josep M. Solà-Solé, Mercè Vidal Tibbits, and Josep. M. Massot i Muntaner. Montserrat, Spain: l'Abadia, 1985. 303–10.

———. " 'La mort i la primavera' de Mercè Rodoreda." *Cuadernos Hispanoamericanos* 467 (May 1989): 117–22.

———. "The Unconscious in the Novels of Mercè Rodoreda." *Catalan Review* 101–18.

Callejo, Alfonso. "Corporeidad y escaparates en 'La plaça del Diamant' de Mercè Rodoreda." *Butlletí de la North American Catalan Society* 16 (1983): 14–17.

Campillo, María. "Mercè Rodoreda: la realitat i els miralls." *Els Marges* 21 (1981): 129–30.

Carbonell, Neus. "In the Name of the Mother and the Daughter: The Discourse of Love and Sorrow in Mercè Rodoreda's 'La plaça del Diamant.' " McNerney and Vosburg. [Forthcoming]

Casals i Couturier, Montserrat. *Mercè Rodoreda: contra la vida, la literatura. Biografía.* Barcelona: Edicions 62, 1991.

———. "El 'Rosebud' de Mercè Rodoreda." *Catalan Review* 27–48.

Castellet, J. M. "Mercè Rodoreda." *Els escenaris de la memòria.* Barcelona: Edicions 62, 1988. 29–52.

Catalan Review: Homage to Mercè Rodoreda. 2.2 (Dec. 1987). [Special issue]

Clarasó, Mercè. "The Angle of Vision in the Novels of Mercè Rodoreda." *Bulletin of Hispanic Studies* 57 (1980): 143–52.

Encinar, Ángeles. "Mercè Rodoreda: hacia una fantasía liberadora." *Revista Canadiense de Estudios Hispánicos* 11.1 (1986): 1–10.

Fayad, Mona. "The Process of Becoming: Engendering the Subject in Mercè Rodoreda and Virginia Woolf." *Catalan Review* 119–30.

Forcadas, A. M. " 'Time of the Doves' by Mercè Rodoreda." *World Literature Today* 55.3 (1981): 457–58.

Forrest, Gene Steven. "El diálogo circunstancial en 'La plaça del Diamant.' " *Revista de Estudios Hispánicos* 12 (1978): 15–24.

García Márquez, Gabriel. "Recuerdo de una mujer invisible: Mercè Rodoreda." *Clarín* 30 June 1983, Cultural Section: 6.

Glenn, Kathleen M. "The Autobiography of a Nobody: Mercè Rodoreda's 'El carrer de les camèlies.' " McNerney and Vosburg. [Forthcoming]

———. "Muted Voices in Mercè Rodoreda's 'La meva Cristina i altres contes.' " *Catalan Review* 131–42.

———. " 'La plaza del Diamante': The Other Side of the Story." *Letras Femininas* 12.1–2 (1986): 60–68.

Grilli, Giuseppe. "A partir d'Aloma." *Catalan Review* 143–58.

Hart, Patricia. "More Heaven and Less Mud: The Precedence of Catalan Unity over Feminism in Francesc Betriu's Filmic Version of Mercè Rodoreda's 'La plaça del Diamant.' " McNerney and Vosburg. [Forthcoming]

Ibarz, Mercè. *Mercè Rodoreda.* Barcelona: Empúries, 1991.

Lucio, Francisco. "La soledad, tema central en los últimos relatos de Mercè Rodoreda." *Cuadernos Hispanoamericanos* 242 (1970): 455–68.

Marco, J. "Humiliats i ofesos: 'El carrer de les Camèlies.' " *Sobre literatura catalana i altres assaigs.* Barcelona: Sinera, 1968. 149–54.

Martí-Olivella, Jaume, ed. Foreword. *Catalan Review* 9–15.

———. "Estructuras joyceanas en la narrativa catalana y latinoamericana contemporánea." *DAI* 49 (1989): 2650A U of Illinois at Urbana-Champaign.

———. "Rodoreda o la força bruixologica. *Actes del Cinque Col.loqui d'Estudis Catalans a Nord Amèrica.* Ed. Philip D. Rasico and Curt J. Wittlin. Montserrat, Spain: l'Abadia, 1988. 283–300.

———. "The Witches' Touch: Towards a Poetic of Double Articulation in Rodoreda." *Catalan Review* 159–70.

Martínez Rodríguez, María del Mar. "El lenguaje del auto-descubrimiento en la narrativa de Mercè Rodoreda y Carmen Martín Gaite." *DAI* 49 (1988): 1162A U of Wisconsin, Madison.

McGiboney, Donna. "Rituals and Sacrificial Rites in Mercè Rodoreda's 'La mort i la primavera.' " McNerney and Vosburg. [Forthcoming]

McNerney, Kathleen. "La identitat a 'La plaça del Diamant': supressió i recerca." *Actes del Quart Col.loqui d'Estudis Catalans a Nord Amèrica.* Ed. Nathaniel B. Smith, Josep M. Solà-Solé, Mercè Vidal Tibbits, and Josep M. Massot i Muntaner. Montserrat, Spain: l'Abadia, 1985. 295–302.

McNerney, Kathleen, and Nancy Vosburg, eds. *The Garden Across the Border: Mercè Rodoreda's Fiction.* Intro. Kathleen McNerney. Selinsgrove, PA.: Susquehanna UP, 1993.

Mees, Inge and Uta Windseimer. " 'Un roman: C'est un miroir qu'on promène le long du chemin': Rodoreda's 'Mirall trencat' und die 'gebrochene Spiegal'—perspektive." *Zeitschrift für Katalanistik* 1 (1988): 662–72.

Möller Soler, Maria-Lourdes. "El impacto de la guerra civil en la vida y obra de tres novelistas catalanas: Aurora Bertrana, Teresa Pàmies y Mercè Rodoreda." *Letras Femeninas* 12.1–2 (1986): 33–44.

Murià, Anna. "Mercè, o la vida dolorosa." *Catalan Review* 17–26.

Navajas, Gonzalo. "La microhistoria y Cataluna en 'El carrer de les Camèlies' de Mercè Rodoreda. *Hispania* 74.4 (1991): 848–49.

———. "Normative Order and the Catalan *Heimat* in Mercè Rodoreda's 'Mirall trencat.' " McNerney and Vosburg. [Forthcoming]

Navarro, Josep. "Ruptura i linealitat temporal als contes de Mercè Rodoreda." *Actes del Tercer Col.loqui Internacional de Llengua i Literatura Catalanes.* Ed. R B. Tate and Alan Yates. Oxford: Dolphin Books, 1976. 301–09.

Nichols, Geraldine Cleary. "Exile, Gender and Mercè Rodoreda." *Modern Language Notes* 101.2 (Mar. 1986): 405–417.

———. " 'Mitja poma, mitja taronja': Génesis y destino literarios de la catalana contemporánea." *Anthropos* 60–61 (1986): 118–25.

———. "Sex, the Single Girl, and Other Mésalliances in Rodoreda and Laforet." *Anales de la Literatura Española Contemporánea* 12.1–2 (1987): 123–40.

———. "Stranger Than Fiction: Fantasy in Short Stories by Matute, Rodoreda, Riera." *Monographic Review/Revista Monográfica* 4 (1988): 33–42.

———. "Writers, Wantons, Witches: Women and the Expression of Desire in Rodoreda." *Catalan Review* 171–80.

Ortega, José. "Mujer, guerra y neurosis en dos relatos de Mercè Rodoreda ('La plaza del Diamante' y 'La calle de las Camelias')" *Cuadernos Hispanoamericanos* 339 (1978): 503–12.

Pérez, Janet. "Gothic Spaces, Transgressions and Apparitions in 'Mirall trencat': Rodoreda's Adaption of the Paradigm." McNerney and Vosburg. [Forthcoming]

———. "Metamorphosis as a Protest Device in Catalan Feminist Writing: Rodoreda and Oliver." *Catalan Review* 181–98.

———. "The Most Significant Writer in Catalan." *Contemporary Women Writers of Spain.* Ed. Janet Pérez. Boston: Twayne, 1988. 74–89.

Poch i Bullich, Joaquim, and Conxa Planas. *Dona i psicoanàlisi a l'obra de Mercè Rodoreda.* Barcelona: Promociones y Publicaciones Universitarias, 1987.

————. "El fet femíní en els textos de Mercè Rodoreda (una refexió des de la psicoanàlisi)." *Catalan Review* 199–224.

Pope, Randolph D. "Aloma's Two Faces and the Character of Her True Nature." McNerney and Vosburg. [Forthcoming]

————. "Mercè Rodoreda's Subtle Greatness." *Women Writers of Contemporary Spain: Exiles in the Homeland*. Ed. Joan L. Brown. Newark, DE: U of Delaware P, 1991. 116–35.

Pujades, B. "Mercè Rodoreda trabaja y descansa en Romanya de la Selva." *Tele/eXpres* 19 Aug. 1975: n.pag.

Resina, Joan Ramón. "Detective Formula and Parodic Reflexity: 'Crim.' " McNerney and Vosburg. [Forthcoming]

————. "The Link in Consciousness: Time and Community in Rodoreda's 'La plaça del Diamant.' " *Catalan Review* 225–46.

Rhodes, Elizabeth. "The Salamander and the Butterfly." McNerney and Vosburg. [Forthcoming]

Roca Mussons, Maria A. "Aspectes del sistema simbòlic a 'La plaça del Diamant.' " *Catalan Review* 247–62.

Roig, Montserrat. "L'alè poètic de Mercè Rodoreda." *Retrats Paral.lels 2*. Montserrat Spain: l'Abadia, 1976.

Rueda, Ana. "Mercè Rodoreda: From Traditional Tales to Modern Fantasy." McNerney and Vosburg. [Forthcoming]

Scarlett, Elizabeth. "Vinculada a les flors': Flowers and the Body in 'Jardí vora el mar' and 'Mirall trencat.' " McNerney and Vosburg. [Forthcoming]

Sobrer, Josep Miquel. "L'artifici de 'La plaça del Diamant,' un estudi lingüistic." *In memoriam Carles Riba*. Ed. Antoni Comas. Barcelona: Ariel, 1973. 363–75. [Published originally under the name Sobré]

————. "Gender and Personality in Rodoreda's Short Fiction." McNerney and Vosburg. [Forthcoming]

Tavani, G. " 'Piazza del Diamante': Un romanzo catalano che 'cattura' il lettore." *Paese Sera* 25 May 1970: 363–75.

Triadú, J. "Una novel.la excepcional: 'La plaça del Diamant' de Mercè Rodoreda." *Llegir com viura*. Barcelona: Fontanella, 1963. 132–39.

Varderi, Alejandro. "Mercè Rodoreda: mès enllà del jardí." *Catalan Review* 263–72.

Vosburg, Nancy. "The Roots of Alienation: Rodoreda's 'Viatges i flors.' " McNerney and Vosburg. [Forthcoming]

Waldman, Gloria. "Vindicación feminista: Lidia Falcón, Esther Tusquets y Mercè Rodoreda." *La Torre, Revista General de la Universidad de Puerto Rico* 115 (Jan.–Mar. 1982): 10–25.

Wyers, Frances. "A Woman's Voices: Mercè Rodoreda's 'La plaça del Diamant.' " *Kentucky Romance Quarterly* 30.3 (1983): 301–09.

MONTSERRAT ROIG
(1946–1991)

Geraldine Cleary Nichols

BIOGRAPHY

Montserrat Roig was born June 13, 1946, in Barcelona to Albina Fransitorra and Tomàs Roig i Llop, whose family numbered six daughters and one son. She grew up in the graceful turn-of-the-century district of the city known as l'Eixample or el Ensanche (area of expansion), the invariable background for her fiction. Her father was a promising Catalan writer before the Civil War; like most of his generation, he had to abandon literature when the victorious Franco undertook to eradicate public use of Catalan. Her mother was a strong woman whom Roig credited with her first practical lessons in feminism. Fransitorra received a university degree after her family was raised, and has been active in the feminist project of reclaiming forgotten Catalan women writers. She also served as her daughter's business manager.

Montserrat attended a convent school, and she recalled that the nuns always thought of her as the "bad girl" (Graells and Pi de Cabanyes 1971, 27). Castilian was the only language permitted in the schools at that time, but at home she always spoke Catalan; her Catalanist parents took the unusual step of teaching her to read and write it as well (Nichols 147). A grandmother encouraged her to read the great European novels in Catalan translation. Roig believed this background prepared her, as few others in her Castilian-indoctrinated generation, to write in Catalan when interest in the language boomed after Franco's death in 1975.

At thirteen, Roig transferred to the Adrià Gual School for Dramatic Arts, where classes were taught in Catalan. One of her teachers was Maria Aurèlia Capmany, a prominent feminist who inspired Roig's affectionate portrait of Harmònia Carreras in *El temps de les cireres* (1977; *Tiempo de cerezas* 1980;

"Cherry Season"). Roig became active in politics while a student at the University of Barcelona; she participated in the 1966 anti-Franco student occupation of the Capuchin monastery (the Caputxinada), a collective action signaling the open resurgence of Catalan nationalism that was to mark her generation. She married an architect in 1966 and divorced him in 1969; he was the father of her first child, a son. She graduated from the University of Barcelona in 1968 with a degree in Spanish; she supplemented that eduction by attending clandestine seminars on Catalan literature led by Joaquim Molas. In 1977 Roig had a second son with her companion, Joaquim Sempere, from whom she subsequently separated. In 1977 she made an unsuccessful bid for a legislative seat as a member of the PSUC (United Socialist Party of Catalonia).

Roig's literary career began in 1966, when she won the prize for fiction at the traditional yearly celebration of Catalan letters called the Jocs Florals (Tourney of Flowers). In 1969 she won three more prizes: the Recull and the Sant Adrià for short stories, and the Serra d'Or for reporting. Her first book, *Molta roba i poc sabó . . . i tan neta que la volen* (1971; *Aprendizaje sentimental* 1980; "Lots of Clothes, Very Little Soap . . . and They Want It So Clean"), won the prestigious Victor Català Prize for fiction in 1970. The stories of *Molta roba* introduce many of the fictional denizens of the Eixample district who reappear in Roig's novelistic trilogy of the Catalan bourgeoisie, beginning with *Ramona, adéu* (1972; *Ramona, adiós* 1980; "Farewell, Ramona").

The trilogy follows the fortunes of the Miralpeix and Claret families from 1894 to 1979, concentrating particularly on the women, whose lives, thoughts, and perceptions of local and world history are privileged over those of their male relatives. The second novel of the trilogy, *El temps*, won the important San Jordi Prize for fiction and was a runaway best-seller. The trilogy concludes with *L'hora violeta* (1980; *La hora violeta* 1980; "The Violet Hour"). Roig's fourth novel, *L'òpera quotidiana* (*La ópera cotidiana* 1983; "The Everyday Opera"), was published in 1982. *L'òpera* and her fifth novel, *La veu melodiosa* (1987; *La voz melodiosa* 1987; "The Melodious Voice"), continue to explore the Eixample; a few characters from the earlier novels also reappear briefly. Her sixth work of fiction, a collection of stories entitled *El cant de la joventut* (1989; *El canto de la juventud* 1989; "The Song of Youth"), was an immediate best-seller.

Roig supported her family by working in a variety of print media, using both Castilian and Catalan: as an editor at a publishing house, as a journalist for newspapers and magazines, and as a writer of fiction and nonfiction. She began to work in television in 1977 as director and host of several series based on interviews of well-known personalities. She often said that she wrote journalistic articles and books in Castilian in order to finance her fiction writing in Catalan. Some of her books of reportage include *Rafael Vidiella, l'aventura de la revolució* (1974; "R. V., the Revolutionary Adventure"), *El catalans als camps nazis* (1977; *Noche y niebla* 1978; "Catalans in Nazi Concentration Camps"), *El feminismo* (1981; "Feminism"), *Mujeres en busca de un nuevo humanismo* (1981; "Women in Search of a New Humanism"), *Mi viaje al bloqueo* (1982;

"My Journey to the Siege" [of Leningrad]), *¿Tiempo de mujer?* (1980; "A Woman's World?"), and *L'agulla daurada* (1985; *La aguja dorada* 1985; "The Golden Spire"). Roig published numerous books of interviews, some drawn from her television programs and some from her newspaper and magazine work. She and Isabel-Clara Simó, a Valencian writer, are the joint subjects of book 5 in the series *Diàlegs a Barcelona* (1985; "Dialogues in Barcelona"), which transcribes a day-long conversation between them. *Diguis que m'estimes encara que sigui mentida* (1991; "Tell Me That You Love Me Even if It's a Lie") is a collection of essays that will greatly interest her critics. It is, as its subtitle explains, "about the solitary pleasure of writing and the shared vice of reading."

Roig was a well-known figure in Catalonia and in all of Spain, both because of her television programs and because her novels—which frequently appeared in Castilian within weeks of their publication in Catalan—were invariably best-sellers in both languages. She was early identified as a member of the Catalan literary generation of the 1970s. She has also become known outside of Spain; her works have been translated into Hungarian, Bulgarian, Russian, Greek, Hebrew, Dutch, German, Swedish, Italian, and English. She held two invited professorships: at the University of Strathclyde, in Glasgow (1983) and at Arizona State University, in Tempe (1990).

In November 1991, at the age of forty-five, Montserrat Roig died of breast cancer. A victim of misdiagnosis, she spent her last months educating women about the disease and its underdetection by the medical establishment. Her death was mourned throughout Spain, and thousands attended her burial. The early death of this vibrant and committed woman is a tragic loss for the Spanish/Catalan literary world, for feminists, and for all the marginalized.

MAJOR THEMES

Roig's feminism and Catalanism led her to be an active figure in political movements of the Left. Like many politicized students in Spain in the 1960s, she was drawn to the Communist Party, which provided the most organized—albeit still illegal—resistance to Franco. The bourgeoisie in which she and most of her classmates had been raised was a principal target of Marxist opprobrium in those years. From the beginning, Roig's writings reflected this critical stance toward her social class. Her choice of linguistic registers, her use of "unladylike" language, her "indelicate" mention of sexual practices and bodily functions, may be viewed in the context of her rebellion against her upbringing and the conventions it imposed, particularly on women. The title of her first work, *Molta roba*, may allude to "dirty linen," family secrets that she proposes to reveal as a way of shocking the bourgeoisie (Nichols 180–83).

In his prologue to the 1978 edition of *Molta roba*, Joan Fuster points out the salience of Roig's three allegiances: to her gender; to her nation, Catalonia; and to her political ideals. These allegiances conditioned all her writing, although she grew increasingly skeptical about the ability of politicians to change the world. Several recurrent themes and character types in her fiction reflect her sociopolitical convictions: women's seemingly irremediable subjection to the myth of love; postwar Catalonia as paradise lost; and the need to work toward a more equitable and less judgmental world. Roig's introduction to *Molta roba* in 1971 sets forth an artistic manifesto from which she did not swerve: "Since I saw myself as incapable of transforming the world—owing to possible defects inherent in my physiology or class origins, depending on how you look at it— I decided to write about it" (6). She posited the use of literature in the task of reforming the world; it was to be her response to a society that excluded people like herself from political protagonism.

Molta roba is not a collection of finished stories; she called them "pieces and sketches" (9–10). The first seems to be a draft of the section of *Ramona* dealing with the grandmother: "Una de les innombrables passejades que la Mundeta Claret féu, quan era jove, per Barcelona" ("One of the Innumerable Walks Around Barcelona Taken by Mundeta Claret When She Was Young"). It introduces Mundeta Claret, one of the three protagonists of *Ramona*, a figure partially inspired by Roig herself. The book's epigraph is from Cesar Pavese, and it introduces a recurrent theme in Roig's work: there are a million stories in the naked city. If for Pavese the city is inhabited by passersby who harbor their own secret cancer, for Roig the inhabitants of the Eixample are a continual source of wonderment and inspiration. In an article in *Barceldones*, a collection of essays on Barcelona by well-known women writers who visit or live there, Roig sums up this motivating principle of her fiction. As a child, she was endlessly fascinated by the ornate wrought iron balconies of the houses: "I thought that the originality of each piece of ironwork hid a life that was different from every other life beyond that balcony. Behind every portico, there was a story to be told" ("De finestres" 183). Women's lives, in particular, are hidden from passersby and from history. Roig attempted to make up for this silence in her fiction, creating a few imaginary women as a way of rescuing all women from oblivion.

In *Molta roba* we also meet Jordi Soteres, the prototype in Roig's fiction of the man consumed by politics. These men, who reappear in all of her novels, are amorously involved with the protagonists; in their university phase, they are often doctrinaire and supercilious with the women, mocking their bourgeois backgrounds and lecturing them constantly. In *L'hora violeta*, they have matured and married, but they are still absorbed in a clandestine political life, to the detriment of their marriages and work. They have taken lovers, but all of their women are secondary to politics.

Ramona, adéu follows the lives of three women: Ramona Jover, born in 1874; her daughter, Ramona Ventura, born in 1909; and the grandaughter, Ramona ("Mundeta") Claret, born in 1949. The novel's organization is rather rudimentary but effective: fragments of the grandmother's diary are interspersed with first- and third-person recollections of the daughter and an omniscient third-person description of the granddaughter's thoughts and activities. This juxtaposition shows how similar the problems faced by the three women are and how blind they are to these likenesses, in part because each has kept her problems— her dirty linen—secret. The difficulty of intergenerational communication was a frequent theme in Roig's fiction, related to her strong (Marxist?) sense of the weight of history on individual's lives. One is the product of a particular historical moment and social milieu, and communication with outsiders is always difficult.

The common problems faced by the three generations of women are the result of the limitations imposed on women in bourgeois society, a theme that suffuses the trilogy. Bourgeois women live unhappy lives because throughout history they have been allowed only one dream or avenue of expression: love. They are taught that finding a husband is the only important thing they will ever do; they read novels, go to movies, and listen to songs that encourage fantasies about romantic love. When they marry, they are inevitably disappointed, no matter how decent their mate; husbands are never lovers, and lovers are never husbands. Marriage has been a form of servitude for women, although Roig showed this to be changing somewhat for the women of her generation with professions of their own. But love continues to dominate the lives of the freer and less inhibited women of today, as shown in *L'hora* and *L'òpera*. Whether sanctified by bonds of marriage or not, great passionate loves do not last.

Ramona is not, however, solely a novel of interiority; it portrays three women who have lived through and been deeply affected by monumental political and historical changes in Catalonia. It shows them relatively ignorant of the causes or explanations for these events, but never indifferent to them, since they inevitably affect their lives and loved ones. In this portrayal of the women's-eye view of history, *Ramona* betrays its debt to Mercè Rodoreda's *Plaça del Diamant*, a novel Roig confessed to reading twelve times (Nichols 148).

El temps de les cireres reprises several favorite themes: the lack of communication between generations; the idea that everyone has enough secrets in his/ her past to inspire sympathy and perhaps a novel; and the concept that each generation has to suffer through the same sorts of sexual and family problems. New themes are introduced as well: the radical and unbreachable difference between the sexes; postwar Catalonia as a fallen and divided nation; the destructive synergy of sexual and political repression under Franco; and the relativity of all judgments and passions in the broad perspective of history.

The protagonist, Natàlia Miralpeix, returns to Barcelona after twelve years of self-imposed exile in England. The novel moves forward and backward around her, describing important present and past episodes of the relatives she reencounters, and interspersing this with flashbacks to events that led up to her abortion, which precipitated her break with her father and her decision to leave Barcelona. She returns in the last days of Franco's regime and finds the city noisier, more prosperous, and more superficial. Her brother, a highly successful architect, prides himself on his European life-style. Like many of Roig's male characters, he has drowned the voice of his conscience and adapted to life in a country he professes to despise: he feels it's easier not to get involved. His stay-at-home wife has fashioned her life around him, but their marriage is sterile and routine. She knows about his lovers but opts not to confront him; she, too, prefers peace to sincerity.

Natàlia remembers her father, Joan Miralpeix, whom she scorned for his perceived political cowardice after the war—he accepted the defeat of his side, and made no waves after he was released from prison—as well as for his shady construction practices during the 1960s, boom years on the Costa Brava. Subsequent flashbacks—to his troubled youth and his profound love for Judit, his young and sexually uninhibited wife, his dreams of building a better Catalonia, the loss of his friends to war or to exile—acquaint the reader with a man his daughter has never known, and allow us to perceive, as in *Ramona*, the deep similarities between the embattled generations. The women of the family can always point out some family resemblance unperceived by everyone else. Roig's interplay of recall and flashback, and her astute use of the omniscient narrator to reveal thoughts that the characters would never voice publicly, serve to relativize the harsh judgments any one character might have of another. Time, the great healer, also serves to mute earlier passions—romantic love, as well as hatred and bitterness.

L'hora violeta is a more complex work than the previous ones; it could be said to have three protagonists: Norma, a journalist and writer (like Roig); her friend Natàlia, a photographer; and Agnès, a politician's wife whose husband has left her for Natàlia. Intercalated between the musings of Natàlia, whose lover is about to leave her for yet another woman, and the ruminations of Norma, who has separated from her husband and is in the process of being left by her lover, is yet another story: "The Novel of the Violet Hour." This is Norma's imaginative re-creation of the wartime friendship between Kati and Judit (Natàlia's mother). Natàlia had urged Norma (author of the two previous novels of the trilogy, so in some ways a mask of Roig) to write the women's story, feeling it has something to say about their own friendship, or women's friendship in general.

This novel chronicles the "years of transition" between Franco and democracy in Spain. The women clearly find themselves between two worlds as well; the violet hour of the title, taken from T. S. Eliot's *The Waste Land*, refers to the border hour of twilight. Norma and Natàlia have been active in the feminist movement (often associated with the color violet in Spain), and while they are not in complete agreement with its more radical propositions, they cannot go back to an earlier stage of consciousness. They are still magnetized by the search for the great romantic love, even when they know that such loves come only inopportunely and cannot last. Their politicized male companions, on the other hand, seem to have lost the capacity to love specific individuals in their quest to legislate, in some future world, a love for all humanity.

By weaving in readings from *The Odyssey*, Roig suggests that men's fixation with abstract and long-term goals has always clashed with women's needs and that men are always willing to sacrifice the small everyday pleasures of love in pursuit of chimeras. Women can try to lure them away from their search, like Circe and Calypso, or sit home awaiting their return, like Penelope. In *L'hora*, Agnès's husband does return; the surprise is that she no longer wants him.

There is a great deal of reflection in *L'hora* on the relationship of life to literature and the arts in general. On the one hand, literature brings order, and thus aesthetic status, to life. It re-creates or prolongs the dead, and it resuscitates that which is materially lost to the passage of time. Roig is often described as an excessively "autobiographical" writer, a charge she felt to be unfounded and sexist; no one dismisses male writers for writing about their world, but in women writers it is considered a defect (Nichols 22–23, 179–80). If she chose to make the Eixample her mythic territory, as William Faulkner chose Yoknapatawpha, that did not necessarily mean she was writing about herself or her family.

In a related vein, Natàlia repeats several times in *L'hora* a sentiment that echoes Mercè Rodoreda and her obsession with privacy/secrecy. Natàlia states that she will never reveal herself totally to anyone; no matter how much she tells, part of her will always remain hidden. Roig's debt to Rodoreda becomes even more apparent when Norma interviews a "very famous writer" just returned from exile (62–63). This figure is indeed Mercè Rodoreda, and the advice she gives the young writer is clear: Men and women cannot live together happily; a creative woman must choose between being happy with her art or with her life.

L'òpera quotidiana, also set in the Eixample, has one of the Miralpeix women reappear in a secondary role, giving the work a satisfying sense of connection to the trilogy. But Roig ventures further afield in creating the other characters of *L'òpera*; several come from lower socioeconomic classes and non-Catalan regions. The novel's structure imitates that of an opera, with alternating voices. The principal singers are Horaci Duc, a retired butcher and widower who rents a room from Patricia Miralpeix, and Mari Cruz, a fatherless girl whose mother emigrated to Catalonia from Aragon in search of a better life. Mari Cruz cleans the Miralpeix apartment once a week. The third character is Senyora Altafulla, an eccentric older woman who rarely leaves her apartment. She has hired Mari Cruz to read to her, to listen to her reminiscences, and to put on plays with her. Both Duc and Altafulla live in the past, she embroidering a relationship that was never consummated and he lamenting a paradise lost because of his own "inner demons" (149 and passim). Mari Cruz is an ingenue who has no past to live in and, unlike all the Miralpeix and Clarets of the earlier novels, no family to fall back on. She is open to new experiences and eager to learn about life. She falls in love with Horaci Duc, but his "demons"—which turn out to be his rigid way of thinking and not jealousy, as he thought—destroy that relationship. The three protagonists end up mad.

Once again, the impossibility of communicating across generations is a major theme. This incommunication is exacerbated by two facts: the young people are not native Catalans, and they are products of the deplorable Francoist schools. So while they must be taught everything about their adopted nation—its language, its heroes, its cuisine, its history, its triumphs, and its shames—they have not been taught to learn or even to think. Raised in a historical period characterized by apathy, they have no ideals or dreams. The frenetic period of sexual liberation following Franco's death—*el destape*—eliminated another set of behavioral guidelines for these young people, who experiment with drugs and sex as unabashedly as they do with new words. Mari Cruz is portrayed as a fatherless innocent, with no defenses of her own: not verbal, not physical, not familial, not ideological. She is a lovable but pathetic tabula rasa.

The differences between men and women are clearly marked in *L'òpera*. History, for example, makes different demands on the two: Men are called upon to be heroes, although they may fail, whereas women are asked to adapt themselves to their man's choice. Women's sexuality is stronger and less complicated than men's, and they are more sensual and imaginative in their relationships. Roig depicts a world where family ties are fast unraveling, with older single women the first to pay the price of this invidious change. They live alone, in precarious economic straits, fearing the ultimate disgrace: a solitary death behind the locked doors of their empty flats. Catalonia's fate after the Civil War is compared to a woman's lot: silenced, relegated to the domestic sphere, placed on a pedestal, and declared useless. Like a woman, Catalonia has had to learn to be simultaneously open to change and closed to prying eyes; like a woman, she has had to know how to retreat when ill winds blow and emerge when they are fair.

La veu melodiosa represents an important departure from Roig's realist fiction, injecting allegorical elements into the concrete and by now well-known setting, the Eixample, from 1938 to the 1980s. The protagonist, a man whose real name we never learn but whose nom de guerre is Espardanya (Espadrille), was born during the waning days of the Civil War. He is a young man of monstrous appearance who has been brought up by his grandfather and a nanny in a carefully sealed apartment in the Eixample; he has been nurtured on their dreams and other collective illusions. When the young man decides to go to college, he falls in with the group of friends profiled in Mundeta's section of *Ramona, adéu*. Without briefing him about their political agenda, they let him participate in their May Day demonstration; as a result he is beaten and imprisoned. Under torture, he reveals the leaders' names, and is then ostracized by the other political prisoners. For months before this incident, he had been involved in a far more concrete form of healing the world: teaching the poor to read, an activity Roig herself carried out when she was eighteen (Candel 7). Like Horaci Duc, Espardanya was not cut out to be a hero under fire, but he could still contribute to the world's well-being through concrete acts of love to individuals and through his writing. The character attests to the fact that Montserrat Roig remained faithful to the artistic manifesto she expounded in her introduction to *Molta roba*.

Roig's fiction and nonfiction paint a world that is far from perfect, but whose salvation interested her passionately. Her characters are usually flawed or shortsighted beings enmeshed in, and often deformed by, difficult historical circumstances. Several of her men have triumphed materially, but most have been broken spiritually or are insufferable ideologues. Her women, less involved in the public arena and more centered on their affective life, often lead sad existences. They are, nonetheless, usually more imaginative, forgiving, sensual, and alive than the men. Roig's vision is not as Manichaean as it might sound, however. Her characters are not good or bad; they are all more or less adversely affected by personal, social, and historical circumstance, and thus not to blame for their shortcomings. Roig's vision of the world is rather pessimistic, but the fact that she continued to write—she submitted her last journalistic article, lamenting the victims claimed by ETA terrorism, only days before she died—proves that she did not despair.

SURVEY OF CRITICISM

In spite of her prominence in the world of Spanish and Catalan letters, Roig's work has not received extensive critical attention. Her uncompromising commitment to explore the world of women and the world's impact on them makes her an especially interesting subject for feminist analysis. Frequently mentioned in panoramic works on contemporary women's fiction, Roig's work is the exclusive focus of only five articles: Elizabeth Rogers's "Montserrat Roig's *Ramona, adiós*: A Novel of Suppression and Disclosure"; Akiko Tsuchiya's "Montserrat Roig's *La ópera cotidiana* as Historiographic Metafiction"; and Catherine Bellver's "Montserrat Roig and the Penelope Syndrome," "Montserrat Roig: A Feminine Perspective and a Journalistic Slant," and "Montserrat Roig and the Creation of a Gynocentric Reality."

Rogers sees *Ramona* as exploring whether a woman can develop her own identity or if she is "condemned to be a victim of . . . patriarchy" and "to continue to repeat the fall of Eve" (103). The novel also seeks to recover female history through the creation of the three protagonists. Techniques of "fragmentation, parallelism, and repetition complement and reinforce the content" (104), emphasizing the sameness of the women's lives and limning a more inclusive picture of the time chronicled. The text's gaps and misapprehensions underline "the lies, the immense silence, and the lack of communication—in short, the suppression" pervading the novel (105). Rogers's impeccable analysis of similarities in the women's experiences shows that all result from following the codes of bourgeois womanhood. Each woman modifies, silences, or erases overly painful memories, or those not "conform[ing] to what is perceived to be the role of the 'good wife' " (114). A central message in *Ramona* is "the need for honest, forthright communication, instead of silence, half-truths, and lies. Women must speak openly and gain a voice that is authentic and not trivial or masked" (118).

Tsuchiya's excellent article defines *La ópera* as "socially-committed metafiction" (145) in which the characters seek to forge new identities by rescripting old myths and creating new ones. When their fictions fail, they descend into madness. Their "literal madness becomes a metaphor of the textual process. Twentieth-century critics have equated madness and literature in their lack of a final signifier'' (155). The characters' and the novel's questioning of diverse signifying systems—''patriarchy, political centralism, or Francoism''—offers a challenge to history, showing it to be, much like an opera libretto, a textual construct.

Bellver's three essays are equally perceptive. ''A Feminine Perspective'' and ''A Gynocentric Reality'' together provide an excellent introduction to Roig's work. ''A Feminine Perspective'' notes how her fiction differs from that of her female contemporaries in style, since Roig's displays the ''simplicity, sturdiness, and unencumbered syntax common to a journalist's prose'' (154), and eschews the autobiographical mode. Her novels are not autobiographies, nor ''vehicles of self-revelation . . . nor are they instruments of psychological exorcism'' (154–55). Fiction is Roig's way of documenting the world she sees around her, particularly as that world impacts on women. Her titles, with their repetition of words denoting ''succession, change, history'' (155), draw attention to her novelistic project qua family saga. Bellver notes that Roig creates many more female than male characters, and that the few men invariably serve as obstacles to the women's self-fulfillment. She elaborates this further in ''Gynocentric Reality'': ''Roig stresses the divergence of male-female perspectives in order to question women's devaluation. She demythifies the patriarchal hero by revealing his deficiencies and stresses women's positive qualities'' (220). Her females are invariably absorbed by love; it is the central factor in their lives and, for Bellver, the major theme in Roig's work. ''Penelope Syndrome'' further explores the romantic thralldom of Roig's women, concluding that all of them assume Penelope's role as the woman ''patiently waiting'' (120).

Bellver asserts that Roig's journalistic background can be seen in her straightforward descriptions of sexual relationships and such topics as abortion, birth control, and gynecology, as well as in her prose style. She adduces convincing examples of media influence on Roig's style: her emphasis on the referential use of language, her preference for human portraiture, her montages, her compact reporting style, and her use of colloquial language. She observes that Roig ''increases the sense of female history by incorporating . . . a variety of female texts,'' including diaries (''Gynocentric Realities'' 221).

Roig's frank treatment of sexuality and other taboo topics, as well as her serious interest in historical and political issues, mark her as different from the majority of her female literary contemporaries. Her colloquialisms and monotonous language have yet to be explored in light of another influence: the relatively impoverished Catalan of present-day Barcelona (Nichols 106–10, 172–76).

BIBLIOGRAPHY

Works by Montserrat Roig

Fiction

Molta roba i poc sabó . . . i tan neta que la volen. Barcelona: Selecta, 1971. Rpt. Barcelona: Edicions 62, 1978. [Prologue by Joan Fuster]

Ramona, adéu. Barcelona: Edicions 62, 1972.
El temps de les cireres. Barcelona: Edicions 62, 1977.
L'hora violeta. Barcelona: Edicions 62, 1980.
L'òpera quotidiana. Barcelona: Planeta, 1982.
La veu melodiosa. Barcelona: Edicions 62, 1987.
El cant de la joventut. Barcelona: Edicions 62, 1989. [Collection of short stories]

Nonfiction

Rafael Vidiella, l'aventura de la revolució. Barcelona: Laia, 1974.
Los hechiceros de la palabra. Barcelona: Martínez Roca, 1975.
Retrats paral.lels: 1/2/3. Montserrat, Spain: Publicacions de l'Abadia de Montserrat. 1975–1978.
El catalans als camps nazis. Barcelona: Edicions 62, 1977.
Personatges. Barcelona: Pórtic, 1979.
Personatges. Segona sèrie. Barcelona: Pòrtic, 1980.
¿Tiempo de mujer? Barcelona: Plaza y Janés, 1980.
El feminismo. Barcelona: Salvat, 1981.
Mujeres en busca de un nuevo humanismo. Barcelona: Salvat, 1981.
Mi viaje al bloqueo. Moscow: Progreso, 1982.
L'agulla daurada. Barcelona: Edicions 62, 1985.
Barcelona a vol d'ocell. Barcelona: Edicions 62, 1987. [With Xavier Miserachs]
La beu melodiosa. Barcelona: Edicions 62, 1987.
"De finestres, balcons i galeries." *Barceldones.* Ed. Isabel Segura. Barcelona: Ediciones de l'Eixample, 1989. 159–87. Rpt. *Diguis que m'estimes encara que sigui mentida* 121–155.
Diguis que m'estimes encara que sigui mentida. Sobre el plaer solitari d'escriure i el vici compartit de llegir. Barcelona: Edicions 62, 1991.

Translations

Noche y niebla: Los catalanes en los campos nazis. Trans. C. Vilaginés. Barcelona: Península, 1978.
Aprendizaje sentimental. Trans. Mercedes Nogués. Barcelona: Argos Vergara, 1980. [Trans. of *Molta roba . . .*]
La hora violeta. Trans. Enrique Sordo. Barcelona: Argos Vergara, 1980.
Ramona, adiós. Trans. Joaquim Sempere. Barcelona: Argos Vergara, 1980.
Tiempo de cerezas. Trans. Enrique Sordo. Barcelona: Argos Vergara, 1980.
La ópera cotidiana. Trans. Enrique Sordo. Barcelona: Planeta, 1983.
La aguja dorada. Trans. Toni Picazo. Barcelona: Plaza y Janés, 1985.
La voz melodiosa. Trans. José Agustín Goytisolo. Barcelona: Plaza y Janés, 1987.
The Everyday Opera. Trans. Josep Miquel Sobrer. *On Our Own Behalf.* Ed. Kathleen McNerney. Lincoln: U of Nebraska P, 1988. 207–34. [Selections]
El canto de la juventud. Trans. Joaquim Sempere. Barcelona: Península, 1989.
"Catalans in Nazi Death Camps." *Catalonia: A Self-Portrait.* Ed. and trans. Josep Miquel Sobrer. Bloomington: Indiana UP, 1992. 129–45. [Chapter I]
Dime que me quieres aunque sea mentira. Sobre el placer solitario de escribir y el vicio compartido de leer. Trans. Antonia Picazo. Barcelona: Ediciones Península, 1992.

Works about Montserrat Roig

Bellver, Catherine G. "Montserrat Roig and the Creation of a Gynocentric Reality."
  Women Writers of Contemporary Spain. Ed. Joan L. Brown. Newark: U of
  Delaware P, 1991. 217–39.
———. "Montserrat Roig: A Feminine Perspective and a Journalistic Slant." *Feminine
  Concerns in Contemporary Spanish Fiction by Women.* Ed. Roberto C. Manteiga,
  Carolyn Galerstein, and Kathleen McNerney. Potomac, MD: Scripta Humanistica,
  1988. 152–68.
———. "Montserrat Roig and the Penelope Syndrome." *Anales de la Literatura Es-
  pañola Contemporánea* 12 (1987): 111–21.
Busquets i Grabulosa, Lluís. *Plomes catalanes contemporànies.* Barcelona: Ediciones del
  Mall, 1980. 177–84.
Candel, Francisco. "Montserrat Roig, del anonimato a la fama." *El Periódico* 28 June
  1990, sec. cultura: 7.
Diàlegs a Barcelona no. 5. Barcelona: Laia, 1985. [Transcription of a conversation
  between Montserrat Roig and Isabel-Clara Simó]
Graells, Guillem-Jordi and Oriol Pi de Cabanyes. "De la requesta que fou feta a Montserrat
  Roig." *Serra d'Or* 13.138 (1971): 27–29.
Nichols, Geraldine C. *Escribir, espacio propio: Laforet, Matute, Moix, Tusquets, Riera
  y Roig, por sí mismas.* Minneapolis: Institute for the Study of Ideologies and
  Literature, 1989. 147–85.
Rogers, Elizabeth. "Montserrat Roig's *Ramona, adiós.* A Novel of Suppression and
  Disclosure." *Revista de Estudios Hispánicos* 20 (1986): 103–21.
Tsuchiya, Akiko. "Montserrat Roig's *La ópera cotidiana* as Historiographic Metafic-
  tion." *Anales de la Literatura Española Contemporánea* 15 (1990): 145–59.

CONCHA ROMERO
(b. 1945)

John P. Gabriele

BIOGRAPHY

Concha Romero was born in Puebla del Río in Seville on January 1, 1945. During her youth she participated in a variety of activities sponsored by Seville's University Theater Group. She later attended the University of Salamanca, where she studied classical languages, and then went on to study acting at the Madrid School of Cinematography. She presently resides in Madrid with her husband, who is a physician, and her two teenage sons, and she teaches Latin in an *instituto*, the Spanish equivalent of a high school. In addition to writing for the stage, Romero has written for film and television, collaborating with film director Cecilia Bartolomé on several projects. Despite her lifelong interest in the theater, she did not begin writing plays until the 1980s. Writing for the theater is of personal importance to Romero. At a round table discussion at the International Institute in Madrid on April 11, 1991, she acknowledged that expressing herself through theater is a very gratifying experience.

Spain's transition to democracy breathed new life into artistic expression. Authors in the 1980s experimented freely with forms, techniques, and themes. Concha Romero's writing is pertinent to the literary, social, and political climate of her time. She is very much concerned with issues of gender, as she herself has intimated: "Men retain power and, what is more tragic still, women continue to accept this" ("Encuesta" 23). Her theater falls within the mainstream of Spain's sociocritical drama, whose primary objective since the years immediately preceding the Civil War and until the present, has been the creation of a consciousness of self. Among the women playwrights who have used the stage effectively to posit assertions about gender issues, Concha Romero is particularly adept at elaborating a historical perspective of the sexual and political oppression of Spanish women. She has succeeded in creating an awareness of the constructs that underpin Spanish political and social structures. Romero's theater addresses universal concerns of feminism. She combines a revisionist perspective and the use of metatheater to liberate feminist discourse from historical oppression. Her feminism works against dominant and essentialist views of gender.

Her first work, *Un olor a ámbar* (1983; "A Scent of Amber") was performed noncommercially by an independent theater group at the University of Madrid in 1985. In 1989 it was staged at the Ateneo of Madrid. Set in sixteenth-century Spain, the play re-creates, in a grotesque and exaggerated fashion reminiscent of Ramón del Valle-Inclán's *esperpento*, events surrounding the canonization of Santa Teresa de Jesús. In particular, it dramatizes the conflict that arose between the towns of Alba de Tormes and Ávila over possession of the Saint's mortal remains. Romero's first attempt at dramatic composition was highly successful, as observed by Patricia O'Connor ("Una nueva voz" 8) and Phyllis Zatlin (50). Noteworthy is Romero's capacity to elevate the image of Teresa's lifeless body to a heroic stature despite the covetous, self-serving, and manipulative efforts of the two towns to lay claim to her corpse. Through a skillful use of language and dialogue, Romero recounts the historic event with an unmistakably modern air, a technique that has become her trademark.

Following a five-year hiatus, Romero published three plays in rapid succession: *Las bodas de una princesa* (1988; "The Wedding of a Princess"), *Un maldito beso* (1989; "A Fatal Kiss"), and *Así aman los dioses* (1991; "When the Gods Make Love"). These works continue her exploration of gender ideology in Spanish society and utilize both historical and contemporary settings as the backdrop for the main action. Little is known about Romero's life and career as a playwright at this time. Two of her plays remain unpublished: "¿Tengo razón o no?" ("Am I Right or Not?") and "Juego de reinas" ("Queens' Game"), originally entitled "Razón de Estado" ("Reason of State"). "¿Tengo razón o no?" was staged in 1989. "Juego de reinas" was performed in Alcalá de Henares in February 1991, and in July it toured Spain. From what we know of her work, it is clear that Concha Romero has contributed positively to the literary tradition of her country and her gender.

MAJOR THEMES

Male and female characterization, coupled with the conflictive interaction that takes place between the sexes in Romero's plays, constitute the basis for a critical appraisal of her principal thematic concerns. We can deduce from her portrayal of female characters that Romero views women as the victims of a dominant social structure. By contrast, she represents her male characters as individuals who most often resort to subterfuge in order to exploit women and to deny them self-expression. Power (more specifically, the abuse of it) and the different ways it manifests itself in male–female relationships is central to Romero's ideological premise.

Certainly gender ideology is primary to the critique that Romero formulates in *Un olor a ámbar*. María del Pilar Pérez-Stansfield has succinctly summarized the concerns of Romero's first play: "The themes that stand out are repression; the abuse of power; the persecution of those who dare to rebel against an established order; the inequity of a society dominated by men in which women are alienated; the absurdity and uselessness of human behavior that is guided by egocentric ambitions; and the abuse suffered by the weak at the hands of the strong" (90). The result is a fascinating study of how men seek to thwart female independence.

When Teresa's corpse is disinterred two years after her death, it is discovered that her body is still intact. The immediate rumors of the nun's canonization lead to a power struggle between the towns of Alba de Tormes and Avila to lay claim to her mortal remains. Thus, from the outset, woman's body is symbolically reduced to nothing more than an object to be possessed or, as Candyce Leonard stated in 1987, "a trophy to be won." The first sign of the institutional abuse of power soon appears in the form of Father Gracián, who secretly cuts off the nun's left hand after he learns of the prospects of Teresa's sainthood and her transfer to Avila. His actions are, of course, a graphic display of men's objectification of women.

Romero further develops this thesis through the confrontation between the prioress of the convent where Teresa has died and Naciaceno, the church official who has been sent to reclaim the nun's remains for Avila. Naciaceno meets his most ardent opponent in the prioress, who is unyielding and obstinate in her refusal to allow him to leave with the nun's body. The conflict that unfolds provides Romero with an excellent pretext to make certain observations about codified gender behavior. Naciaceno, for example, when discussing the matter at hand with the prioress, tells her, "You reason well, for a woman" (61). The prioress on the other hand, demonstrates determination and fortitude, challenging Naciaceno's authority outright: "I will move heaven and earth, if necessary," she tells him. "With or without papers, her body will not leave this place" (63). In the course of their encounter, Naciaceno alludes continually to the double standard in Spanish society. At one point, he very clearly tells the prioress that she has no choice in the matter because "I am giving you orders that you must obey" (64). It is not until Naciaceno evokes the institutionalized power of the church and threatens the prioress with excommunication that she allows him to take the saint's body. The threat of excommunication not only serves to show how institutions abuse power but also reveals men's complicity and determination to silence outspoken women.

In a final attempt to impede Naciaceno's departure, the nuns of the convent, in an unprecedented display of solidarity and unity, band in a group to barricade the door. Again Naciaceno conveniently falls back on the dominant power structure within Spanish society that promotes servility and passivity in women: "Obedience, discipline, observance! That's what's needed! A heavy hand, a heavy hand and authority!" (67). Romero's criticism of such an attitude is

implicit. Still Naciaceno's reliance on institutionalized power provides him with
the upper hand and allows him, once again, to mask his personal insecurities.
Ultimately the prioress must acquiesce, but she bargains with Naciaceno to leave
a piece of the saint's body behind. He agrees, and cuts off Teresa's right arm
before leaving, heavily disguised and with Teresa's remains in a sack that he
irreverently throws over his back. Thus Naciaceno's denigrating view of women
is heightened and his cowardice is disclosed. At the same time, the play's ending
represents a small victory for the prioress. By resorting to the same grotesque
tactics employed by her opponent, she succeeds in claiming a portion of the
saint's body, which allows her to vow revenge: "My children, I promise you
that I will not rest until the body that is now being taken from us is rejoined
with this arm" (70).

Las bodas de una princesa further illustrates Romero's support for an egalitarian doctrine. In this play, as in *Un olor a ámbar*, the playwright reveals a
Spanish society steeped in historical bias against women and the concomitant
social expectations founded on this prejudice. The action of this play takes place
between 1465 and 1469, during the turbulent years of the reign of Enrique IV,
the last medieval monarch of the kingdom of Castile and León. The play focuses
on the events that led up to Isabel's coronation as queen of Castile and her
subsequent marriage to Fernando. Through the characterization of the young
Isabel as the incarnation of feminist ideals, Romero elaborates further on the
concepts of gender and patriarchy while refining her modernistic vision. As Peter
L. Podol has noted: "This play replaces Spain's traditional heroine with a dynamic and credible young woman who embodies modern feminist attitudes"
(28). *Las bodas de una princesa* centers on Isabel's individual struggle and
personal desire to choose freely whom she will marry. Consequently, Isabel
incarnates values that are inherent to feminism: self-realization, achievement of
self-worth, and defiant, even radical, action. The female protagonist of this play
picks up where the prioress of *Un olor a ámbar* left off. Isabel's liberal-minded
philosophy stands in direct contrast to her brother's weaker, less forceful nature;
he epitomizes the very traits that society has conditioned men to conceal or mask
in order to maintain a facade of supremacy such as that displayed by Naciaceno
in the previous play.

Isabel is quick to question the unjustness of contractual matrimony during the
general discussions about her marriage: "What a pity that princesses can't marry
freely. Others are always deciding whom and when we shall marry!" (23). Her
forthright nature is also revealed when she encourages her brother, Enrique, to
change his ways and be stronger: "I don't understand, Enrique. You are too
good, too soft and you don't make others respect you as they should!" (25).
Here, as in *Un olor a ámbar*, the male characters express themselves with
antifeminist rhetoric. In this case, it is women's involvement in politics that is
questioned: "Women don't understand anything about politics" (47).

Isabel's repression at the hands of a dominant culture is expressed in images
of enclosure, frequently found in feminist literature. At one point she explains,

"I'm beginning to feel imprisoned within these four walls" (51). As she prepares to inherit the Spanish throne, Isabel's will becomes stronger, her objective ever more focused: "From this moment on, I will do the impossible to be queen . . . I must concentrate and not be detoured and find a way to meet my destiny head on" (69). Her personal desires, however, are no less important. She continues to defy the state by refusing to marry the person chosen for her. Unable to understand Isabel's determination, the count of Villena feels the need to remind her "that princesses cannot choose and must proceed to their marriage just as men go to war, thereby complying with duties of the State" (67). The more Isabel is challenged, the more she resists, "scratching and biting" (67), despite the growing impatience of the Spanish people and the court officials. Ultimately, Isabel decides that she will marry Fernando, proclaiming the egalitarian principles that have moved her to action throughout the play: "In Castile and Aragón he and I will rule equally" (72).

Isabel's indomitable spirit, her personal decision to wed Fernando, and her determination to take an active political role in Spain's leadership are qualities of the princess that many historians have underscored, among them Fernando González-Doria (*Las reinas de España*) and Felipe Fernández-Armesto (*Ferdinand and Isabella*).[1] González-Doria also documents how Enrique and other state officials tried repeatedly but unsuccessfully to coerce Isabel to contract matrimony with men of their choice. Romero's play provides a faithful representation of Isabel's character and the historical events as they occurred, except for one minor detail. In Romero's play, Fernando and Isabel are married at a crossroads near an open field. In reality, the ceremony took place at Fuensaldaña Castle in Valladolid.

Un maldito beso is a fanciful mixture of reality and illusion, and by far Romero's most elaborate dramatization of a feminist critique to date. This "multi-layered text," as Candyce Leonard has appropriately called it ("Women Writers and Their Characters" 248), deals with a husband's infidelity and his wife's need to understand the motives behind his actions. *Un maldito beso* is an intriguing display of a play within a play in which reality and illusion intersect at varying levels. The text bears testimony to Romero's adeptness at combining both a dramatic technique—metatheater, which concerns itself with humanity's existential dilemma—and a gender-related theme to focus on the concept of self. The concept of metatheater permeates the play. In many ways, this play coalesces themes and characterizations of previous works. María, for example, combines the resourcefulness and determination of the prioress and Isabel. Male apprehension in the face of women who display self-assurance, such as that clearly witnessed in Naciaceno, Enrique, and Villena, is further reiterated in the naive, insecure, and even squeamish Manolo, whose inflated ego does not allow him to understand the need for equality among men and women.

The plot is sufficiently complex to warrant summary. The play begins with María rehearsing a part for the opening of a play that her husband, Manolo, is directing. Manolo's entire fortune and career hinge on the play's success. When

María interrupts her rehearsal to attend a funeral, an aspiring young actress, Sabrina, comes to Manolo's home to ask if she can try out for him. He suggests they do a kissing scene. During the audition María returns. Witnessing this scene brings about a dramatic change in her personality. She no longer remembers the lines of the play, nor does she acknowledge her husband's existence. Instead, she speaks of the funeral she has just attended as if it had been Manolo's, illustrating Candyce Leonard's observation that María "metaphorically kills her husband, displacing him in her memory" ("Women Writers and Their Characters" 248). Manolo's future—in fact, his identity—hangs in the balance. He calls in Jorge, a psychiatrist, who decides that reenacting the kiss will bring María back to reality. It is of course no coincidence that Jorge mentions Freudian hysteria in diagnosing María's condition. What follows is a fascinating series of role reversals and an intricate convergence of reality and illusion.

Reproducing the kissing scene serves as a device for Romero to explore María's crucial search for personal identity and to disclose Manolo's self-centered, egotistical outlook on life. When Manolo admits to María that he has been unfaithful for ten of their twelve years of marriage, he resorts to shallow, sexist reasoning to justify his actions: "Infidelity is not the same for women as for men. Being unfaithful to women is natural; it's a given, while women's infidelity is a motive for mockery" (142). This allows Romero to adopt a critical perspective vis-à-vis the personal and social expectations of the institution of marriage that accords certain liberties to men but not to women. For Manolo, seduction and infidelity are a source of power and self-esteem. When María asks him why he has deceived her, he sheepishly replies: "I don't know, maybe because I'm Spanish, maybe because I'm a man, maybe it's because I'm a bit of a Don Juan . . . I don't know. Infidelity is attractive to me, it gives me a sense of reaffirmation, it gives me security" (142).

Throughout their discussion Manolo insists that he loves María and is devoted to her. He vows to do anything she wants to prove it. This provides an opportunity for María to take the initiative and test her husband's word. She asks him to bring her a man to kiss. Her request constitutes at once a challenge to patriarchy, an attempt to proclaim her autonomy, and a defense of parity among the sexes. Furthermore, it shows that she can play a man's game with a man's rules. As might be expected, Manolo finds his wife's request absurd and swears to be faithful from then on. María insists. In her determination, she decides to kiss Jorge, claiming, "I must demonstrate to myself that I am capable and that I will be capable from now on" (141). Manolo seeks to dissuade her and calls her act an "infidelity of vengeance" (141). In response, María espouses a feminist perspective: "If there is to be infidelity, infidelity for all. In my opinion, honor is not dominant, it relies on equality. And I will fight for it even if it is difficult, even though it is contrary to what I believe" (143). When Manolo accompanies the actress Sabrina to the door, María takes the initiative and kisses the psychiatrist Jorge, thus completing the circle of the first kiss. We may assume that María is now an actress in a play that she, not her husband, directs. Romero shows convincingly that we must deconstruct gender roles in order to reconstruct them anew.

The feminist notion that women must reclaim their bodies in order to be independent and free from male dominance is at the center of Romero's most recent play, *Así aman los dioses*. Here the exploration of gender differentiation takes place within a mythohistorical context. Jupiter, the principal male character, espouses a male supremacist view of women. He believes that women are sex objects whose responsibility is to satisfy men sexually, with no consideration whatsoever for their own feelings. For Jupiter, gender categories are categories of polarity and difference. The other male characters, such as Vulcan, Mars, and Cupid, share this view.

Self-interest and national political interests motivate Jupiter's actions. In an interchange with his wife, Juno, for example, Jupiter claims that if she really loved him, she would not criticize his sexual involvement with other goddesses but would assist him in his conquests of women. Juno criticizes her husband for appreciating "maturity," "intelligence," and "valor" only in men, while expecting women to be "submissive" and "humble" (34–35). Although initially adamant in her criticism of her husband's sexist views, Juno succumbs to his position of authority. Jupiter's relationships with other female characters follows a similar pattern. When Jupiter insists that Venus marry Vulcan because it is a matter of extreme national importance, Venus objects vehemently, refusing to obey, but ultimately acquiesces. The paradigm is repeated in the play whenever women confront men about their views on male-female relationships.

The female characters in *Así aman los dioses* lack the fundamental endurance and tenacity necessary to promote change. What is interesting about this play is Romero's use of the genealogy of the gods to illustrate the evolution of gender categories as opposites. More important still, the binary opposition is as much the result of men's determination to oppress women as of women's ineffectiveness in subverting patriarchy. Romero implies that words alone are not enough; action is necessary in order to effect change. Her directive is clear: Women must unite in order to confront men's abuse of them. In many ways, Romero depicts in this play the foundation of the traditional ideology against which the protagonists of her earlier plays react. Isabel, the prioress, and María, for example, conform to the tactics of their respective male opponents to realize their objectives.

Romero's theater reflects her consciousness of writing as a woman. Nowhere is this more evident than in the scene of *Un olor a ámbar* where the nuns of the convent reenact the canonization of Saint Coloma to celebrate the prioress's birthday. When the prioress comments on the exceptional direction of the play by Sister Catalina, she says, "If God had not called you to his service and women were not prohibited from taking part in the theater of our times, you would have been a success in the world of theater" (56–57).

Though the present discussion has been limited to Romero's published work, it is equally applicable to her unpublished texts. Her work has evolved within the general context of feminist drama, and there is every reason to believe that it will continue to do so.

SURVEY OF CRITICISM

Much of what has appeared in print to date discusses Romero's theater in relationship to the work of other female playwrights of her generation. In essence, this criticism does more to acknowledge her status as a relative newcomer to the Spanish theater than to evaluate her individual accomplishments. The studies of Lourdes Ortiz, María Victoria Cansinos and Patricia O'Connor are typical of this approach.

María del Pilar Pérez-Stansfield's study of *Un olor a ámbar* and Peter L. Podol's analysis of *Las bodas de una princesa* are by far the most sustained treatments of individual plays by Romero to date. There is no doubt, according to Pérez-Stansfield, that Romero champions the feminist cause in *Un olor a ámbar*. She illustrates how Romero uses national history and myth in order to satirize men's abuse of power and simultaneously disclose the gender constructs of Spanish society. The play, in Pérez-Stansfield's own words, invites us to "reflect on the confrontation between man's repressive use of power and woman's intimidated and powerless state" (95). Podol also provides insight into Romero's feminist orientation, her use of historical themes, and the demythologizing objective of her work. His study compares Romero's characterization of Isabel and her "profound understanding of the female psyche" (30) with that of two male playwrights, Manuel Martínez Mediero and Alberto Miralles, who also focus on the Spanish queen as the consummate embodiment of liberal thinking at a time in Spanish history when women were denied an active part in any realm of society. According to Podol, Romero's work centers on examining and challenging gender stereotypes. He views Romero's Isabel as a "mythic young heroine, liberated, astute, determined, and courageous," willing to confront and overcome "the corrupt and sexist politics that surround her" (30).

Very little in print applies current feminist literary theory to Romero's work. Worthy of mention in this regard is the feminist scholarship of Carolyn J. Harris and Candyce Leonard, whose treatment of Romero's theater up to now has mainly taken the form of papers delivered at professional conferences. Harris's work is distinctive in that it analyzes Romero's revisionist perspective in light of fundamental feminist literary theories such as those developed by Elaine Showalter, Adrienne Rich, and Phyllis Chesler ("The Portrayal"; "La protagonista"). Similarly, Candyce Leonard's efforts have focused on the basic feminist issues present in Romero's work and that of other women playwrights of her generation. Leonard is primarily concerned with Romero's dramatic technique. Her one published study, "Women Writers and Their Characters in Spanish Drama in the 1980s," is a perceptive analysis of how patriarchy and female repression are couched in the subtext of *Un olor a ámbar* and *Un maldito beso*.

Collectively, the criticism published to date contends that Concha Romero's contribution to the Spanish theater is noteworthy and that her exploration of gender is incisive. Furthermore, there is a sense that Romero will not compromise her commitment to explore the theoretical as well as practical tenets of feminism in her future work.

NOTE

1. Fernando González-Doria, *Las reinas de España* (Madrid: Alce, 1979); Felipe Fernández-Armesto, *Ferdinand and Isabella* (London: Weidenfeld and Nicholson, 1975).

BIBLIOGRAPHY

Works by Concha Romero

Un olor a ámbar. Madrid: La Avispa, 1983.
Las bodas de una princesa. Madrid: Lucerna, 1988.
"Juego de reinas." MS. 12903. Biblioteca Fundación Juan March, Madrid. [Unpublished play, 1989. Previously titled "Razón de Estado"]
Un maldito beso. *Gestos* 8 (1989): 109–44.
Así aman los dioses. Madrid: Ediciones Clásicas, 1991.
"¿Tengo razón o no?" [Unpublished play]

Works about Concha Romero

Cansinos, María Victoria. "Las dramaturgas españolas también existen." *La Caja* 16.64 (1986): 8–11.
"Encuesta: ¿Por qué no estrenan las mujeres en España?" *Estreno* 10.2 (1984): 13–25.
Faraldos, Gloria. Introduction. *Las bodas de una princesa*. By Concha Romero. Madrid: Lucerna, 1988. 5–9.
García Gual, Carlos. "Prólogo." *Así aman los dioses*. By Concha Romero. Madrid: Ediciones Clásicas, 1991. ix–xiii.
Harris, Carolyn J. "El discurso femenino y la desacralización del mito en la obra de Concha Romero." 38th Annual Mountain Interstate Foreign Language Conference. Knoxville, 7 Oct. 1988.
———. "The Portrayal of Feminine Consciousness in Two Plays by Concha Romero: 'Razón de estado' and *Un maldito beso*." Wichita State University Conference on Foreign Literatures. Wichita, 7 Apr. 1990.
———. "La protagonista histórica en el teatro de Concha Romero." Meeting of the American Association of Teachers of Spanish and Portuguese. Chicago, 9 Aug. 1991.
———. "La 're-lectura' de la historia en el teatro de Concha Romero: *Un olor a ámbar* y *Las bodas de una princesa*." 40th Annual Mountain Interstate Foreign Language Conference. Radford, VA: 11 Oct. 1990.
———. "La 're-visión' de la experiencia femenina en la obra teatral de Carmen Resino y Concha Romero." 39th Annual Mountain Interstate Foreign Language Conference. Clemson, SC: 29 Sept. 1989.

Leonard, Candyce. "The Feminine Image in Female-Authored Spanish Drama in the 1980s." Twentieth-Century Literature Conference. Louisville, 21 Feb. 1991.

———. "Feminism or Vocation: The Emergence of 'Dramaturgas' in Spain." Second Northeast Biennial Meeting of the American Association of Teachers of Spanish and Portuguese. Amherst, 26 Sept. 1986.

———. "Spanish Playwrights in the 1980s." Agora Japanese Feminist Meeting. Fukuoka, Japan, 17 Dec. 1988.

———. "Women Writers and Their Characters in Spanish Drama in the 1980s." *Anales de la Literatura Española Contemporánea* 17.1-3 (1992): 243–56.

———. "Women Writers in Post-Franco Theatre: A Tentative Feminism." 7th Annual Cincinnati Conference on Romance Languages and Literatures." Cincinnati, 15 May 1987.

O'Connor, Patricia W., ed. *Dramaturgas españolas de hoy*. Madrid: Fundamentos, 1988. 46.

———. "Una nueva voz femenina para el teatro." *Un olor a ámbar*. By Concha Romero. Madrid: La Avispa, 1983. 7–13.

———. "¿Quiénes son las dramaturgas españolas contemporáneas, y qué han escrito?" *Estreno* 10.2 (1984): 9–12.

———. "Six 'Dramaturgas' in Search of a Stage." *Gestos* 5 (1988): 116–20.

Ortiz, Lourdes. "Nuevas autoras españolas." *Primer Acto* 220 (1987): 10–21.

Pérez-Stansfield, María del Pilar. "La desacralización del mito y de la historia: Texto y subtexto en dos nuevas dramaturgas españolas." *Gestos* 4 (1987): 83–99.

Podol, Peter L. "Three Stages in the Life of Isabel: Plays by Alberto Miralles, Manuel Martínez Mediero and Concha Romero." *Estreno* 16.1 (1990): 28–31.

Zatlin, Phyllis. "*Un olor a ámbar*." *Estreno* 10.2 (1984): 50. [Review]

ANA ROSSETTI
(b. 1950)

Nancy L. Bundy

BIOGRAPHY

Born in San Fernando, Cádiz, on May 5, 1950, Ana Rossetti first gained public notice with three plays: "El saltamontes" (1974; "The Grasshopper"), "Sueño en tres actos" (1975; "Dream in Three Acts"), and "La casa de los espirales" (1977; "The House of Spirals"). However, she has established herself as a literary figure of the 1980s, along with Amparo Amorós and Blanca Andreu, primarily as a poet.

Rossetti credits her early years in a small town with her development as an independent female writer; it was there that she was given considerable physical, social, and intellectual freedom. She spent most of her unfettered youth living with her grandparents, and when they died she stayed with her siblings in a house adjacent to that of her parents. Although she reveled in the sensuous pleasures of Andalusian gardens and orchards (Bundy, Interview 135), she also enjoyed the solitary hours spent in her room, reading the lives of saints and stories of martyrs that would appear, radically changed, years later in her book of poetry *Devocionario* (1986; "Prayer Book"). The children's house saw a steady stream of visitors who joined Ana and her two brothers and sister in imaginative letter exchanges, art projects, and theatrical performances. Rossetti claims that it was during this period that she started to learn the technique of writing, for every activity was in some way transcribed in literary code (Bundy, Interview 136). She was also influenced by her parents and by her parochial school experiences, and she absorbed the rituals and images of the Catholic Church, which she eventually integrated into her work.

Rossetti moved to Madrid at age eighteen for a brief stint at the university. However, loath to fulfill the mathematics requirement and uninterested in education for the sake of a degree, she spent more time as a student activist than she did in the classroom. Through this involvement, she became a part of the independent vanguard theater in Madrid, often serving as dresser for the actors. During this time Rossetti wrote her three plays. The range of her theater experiences is reflected most notably in her novel *Plumas de España* (1988; "Plumes of Spain") and in her book-length essay *Prendas íntimas. El tejido de la seducción* (1989; "Intimate Apparel. The Weaving of Seduction"), both of which deal with (re)presentations of the body and with the idea that costume often becomes custom, a preoccupation in many of Rossetti's works. Not coincidentally, in her first year in Madrid, Rossetti entered the School of Decorative Arts, where she pursued her interests in art and art history.

Although Rossetti began her literary career in earnest in 1980 with a book of poetry, *Los devaneos de Erato* ("Erato's Diversions"), she has maintained the theater ties that led to the 1989 presentation of "Devocionario," a ballet that gave dramatic visual proof of her attention to woman as subject and as erotic being. She has published five books of poetry: *Devaneos*, which won the second Premio Gules de Poesía; *Dióscuros* (1982; "Children of Zeus"); *Indicios vehementes* (1985; "Passionate Signs"), her collected poetry; *Devocionario*, which won the third Premio Juan Carlos I; and *Yesterday* (1988), which includes five poems each from *Devaneos*, *Indicios*, and *Devocionario*, as well as fifteen new poems. In addition to the volumes of prose already mentioned, Rossetti has written some vignettes, *Aquellos duros antiguos* (1988; "Those Old Coins"), and three short stories: "La sortija y el sortilegio" (1988; "The Ring and the Spell"), "Hasta mañana, Elena" (1989; "Until Tomorrow, Elena"), and "El soberbio celeste" (1990; "The Heavenly Snob"). As of 1991, Rossetti was working on a novel about the seventeenth century. Besides her prolific writing, she devotes time to travel, radio and television performances, participation in seminars and conferences, and fashion design for movies and publicity.

MAJOR THEMES

Since the publication of *Devaneos*, Rossetti has attracted attention for the boldly erotic nature of her work, for which she offers no disclaimer. She has stated that her main purpose is not to disturb her readers but, rather, to seduce them, to provoke a reaction (Núñez 12). Rossetti appeals to the reader in a variety of styles, and he or she quickly realizes that the writer's close focus on eroticism does not necessarily imply a narrowness of expression. Her prose and poetry are filled with classical, baroque, romantic, and contemporary images, from the exquisite decadence of *Devaneos* to the dreams of martyrdom in *Devocionario*, and from the "leather boy" of *Indicios* to the motorcycle jacket in *Prendas íntimas*. Rossetti has described herself as "very pre-Raphaelite and very Rossetti" (*Indicios vehementes* 14), identifying herself with the group of nineteenth-century poets and painters, including Christina and Dante Gabriel Rossetti, whose work is characterized by its realism, sensuousness, and attention to detail (Preminger 661–62). It is likely that the "very Rossetti" also suggests the author's sense of individuality and creative strength.

The erotic, a leitmotif of Rossetti's work, is not just an echo of earlier authors and movements. It may assume protean forms in her writing, but the unifying element is the persistence of a strong female voice. Her eroticism is surprising, aggressive, and direct, both in its content and in its expression. Although Rossetti has not openly called herself a feminist, she is certain of her identity as a woman entitled to rights and privileges equal to those of men. Her poetic persona, especially, is a dominant one in the sexual fantasies and relationships she portrays, and she clearly demands both due respect and immediate satisfaction. Her eroticism is therefore both corporeal and intellectual, and is manifested in two kinds of seduction. For her, the seduction of words is as important as the words of seduction, and she delights in destroying virginity, physically as well as metaphorically (Núñez 12). In doing so, she attempts to break away from the patriarchal tradition that mandates that women not write and that only implicitly sanctions their writing about quotidian matters. Rossetti's confidence with regard to her ability to seduce through writing reflects the seductive power that words have over her. Rossetti herself was seduced at an early age by the images and words of the Catholic Church at its most grandiose and theatrical. In *Devocionario*, for instance, the poet continually merges sexual and intellectual concerns and offers a sort of panegyric to the flesh couched in liturgical terms. This is but one example of the sense of liberation from the traditional that appears throughout her work.

As Rossetti begins to record her childhood and adolescent adventures, she also learns that the craft of writing demands more than wonderful experiences; there is a need for laws and codes and the formulation of one's own style (Bundy, Interview 136). There are strong metapoetic elements in her penetrating verse, and she communicates a sense of revelation in describing the process of writing as well as the process of erotic attraction. This dual code of desire is evident in "Festividad del dulcísimo nombre" ("Celebration of the Sweetest Name"), the first poem of *Devocionario*, and demonstrates Rossetti's use of the church as a point of departure. In her search for a female identity, she rejects the traditional underpinnings of that patriarchal institution and offers a feminist and contemporary response to the liturgy. Unlike St. John of the Cross and St. Teresa, who used secular images to convey spiritual messages, Rossetti puts the religious at the service of the erotic, as seen in *Devocionario*. In "Festividad," the poet addresses the Christ of her childhood as master in "tan terrible amor" (13; so terrible a love) and expresses her awe of the ritual of the Eucharist as well as the physical longing it arouses in her:

Y anulada, enamorada yo
entreabría mi boca, mientras mi cuerpo todo
tu cuerpo recibía. (13)

And unconscious, enamored I
half-opened my mouth, while my body received
your body whole.

This literary-erotic-liturgical strain is a constant in Rossetti's work. In the novel *Plumas de España*, for example, the narrator mirrors Rossetti's fascination with being an erstwhile voyeur. A writer from the provinces who recounts the life of one of her tenants—a female impersonator turned church devotee turned soldier—the narrator seems particularly enchanted with the ambiguity inherent in the "travestí." Although the novel is ostensibly about the shaping of alternative life-styles, it also deals with the formation of a writer on the verge of erotic discovery, and it is interesting to note the parallel with Rossetti's own life. She began *Plumas* in 1982, when she was just becoming aware of her potential as a writer and of her ability to express her own point of view. The fact that she chooses a male, and a transvestite, as her subject is a revealing metaphor for her own fluctuating identity as a writer at the time.

Rossetti seduces the reader with words and with her use of the erotic as theme. As previously mentioned, her first publication, *Los devaneos de Erato*, introduces libidinal elements that persist in later works dealing with the poet's search for sexual identity. Both the classical and the religious are infused with the erotic in such poems as "Triunfo de Artemis sobre Volupta" ("Triumph of Artemis over Volupta"), which suggests lesbianism as it describes the frustrated yearnings of schoolgirls for a "goddess" engrossed in her own ablutions:

No bebistéis tampoco en las sabrosas fuentes
que anegaban los turbios laberintos
que una maligna virginidad clausuró. (53)

You did not drink from the delicious fountains
which flooded the shady labyrinths
that a guarded virginity forbade.

The same elements appear in "El gladiolo blanco de mi primera comunión se vuelve púrpura" ("The White Gladiolus of My First Communion Turns Purple"), which hints at masturbation in its allusion to the pure but sensually budding flower:

Nunca más, oh no, nunca más
me prenderá la primavera con sus claras argucias.
Desconfío del tumescente
gladiolo blanco . . .
su apariencia es tan pura
que, sin malicia, lo exponemos
a la vista de muchachas seráficas.
Y sin embargo, qué hermoso señuelo,
jamás encontró Himeneo instructor más propicio. (25)

Nevermore, oh no, nevermore,
will spring capture me with her bright deceits.
I distrust the burgeoning
white gladiolus . . .
its appearance is so pure
that, without malice, we expose it
to the view of seraphic girls.
And yet, what a beautiful lure,
Hymen never found a better guide.

Her use of the words and images of the church is but one striking manifestation of Rossetti's skill in depicting the erotic. In *Devaneos*, she offers two more poems with whimsical titles but serious content: "Un señor casi amante de mi marido, creo, se empeña en ser joven" ("A Man Almost a Lover of My Husband, I Think, Insists on Being Young") and "De cómo resistí las seducciones de mi compañera de cuarto, no sé para bien o para mal" ("How I Resisted My Roommate's Seduction, for Better or Worse"). In them, Rossetti addresses the subject of homosexuality and lesbianism, not in complicity, perhaps, but certainly in sympathy. In the first poem, she seems almost to mourn the man's loss of his "esplenderosa juventud" (22; splendorous youth). In the second poem, Rossetti views lesbianism as a sexual option in general, though one she rejects for herself:

[Si no] hago por ti ofrenda a Eros,
es porque mis vigías
me impiden avivarte en tu hoguera. (39)

[If I don't] make an offering to Eros for you,
it is because my sentinels
won't let me inflame you in your fire.

In addition to her eroticization of Catholic liturgy and her suggestive exploration of homosexuality and lesbianism, Rossetti's apology for desire is directly related to women's attitude toward men. She rejects the common male view of woman as object to be seduced and conquered. *Devaneos* offers at least two clear examples of her claim to her own identity. In "Inconfesiones de Gilles de Rais" (" 'Un-confessions' of Gilles de Rais"), she reverses the traditional gender roles by portraying the female as seducer: "Es adorable pervertir a un muchacho" (32; It is delightful to pervert a boy). In the same vein, she asserts elsewhere that "that value, so dear to machista culture, of being the first in the life of a woman, could also be coveted by a woman who aspires to be the first in the sexual life of a man" (Núñez 12). The title of "Cierta secta feminista se da consejos patrimoniales" ("A Certain Feminist Sect Gives Itself Some Patrimonial Advice") offers both humor and irony, for it is actually aimed at patriarchy:

Y besémonos, bellas vírgenes, besémonos.
Rasgando el azahar, gocémonos, gocémonos
del premio que celaban nuestros muslos.
El falo, presto a traspasarnos
encontrará, donde creyó virtud, burdel. (37)

And let us kiss, beautiful virgins, let us kiss.
Shredding the orange blossom, let us enjoy, enjoy
the reward that our thighs conceal.
The phallus, ready to pierce us
will find a brothel instead of virtue.

Rossetti calls this poem a warning to the macho who seeks virginity in a woman; women, as well as men, can be intimate and deceptive at the same time (Núñez 12).

Rossetti's poetry and prose are most obviously informed by her use of a complicated eroticism based on early training and habit. She learned creative writing and church ritual at the same time, and, profoundly affected by the spiritual and physical possibilities of both, she has ever since dramatically connected the word with the Word and the body with both. The religious experience serves only as backdrop, however; Rossetti has converted childhood and adolescent images into ones of her own making. Rather than allowing the church to shape her thought, she has used this experience as a springboard for freeing herself and creating her own identity as writer and erotic being. She takes command of both roles, asserting herself beyond literary tradition and beyond the submissive female role in a relationship. Her eroticism permits her to explore both paths of liberation.

SURVEY OF CRITICISM

Rossetti's writings have generally received praise from the critics, although even in these less restrictive post-Franco years several male critics have looked askance at her work. Few have questioned her literary capability, but some have misunderstood her proudly defiant role as a woman who openly and graphically celebrates her own erotic nature.

A prime example of this dualistic criticism is offered by Florencio Martínez Ruiz in his article on *Indicios vehementes*. Affirming that Rossetti has mastered the art of seduction and crafted a refined literature of eroticism, he nonetheless claims that her "savage feminism" introduces a distorted eroticism (9).

Antonio Núñez has called Rossetti's literary production "monothematic" in its insistence on sex and eroticism but, in an interview with the poet, he insists upon talking about these themes rather than the art that embellishes them. The quotes included in this chapter from the Núñez interview reveal the critic's desire to engage Rossetti in a dialogue centered on the erotic.

Other critics have seen greater richness in Rossetti's work. María Grazia

Profeti, in her study of *Plumas de España*, describes the poet's work as written against a background of baroque opulence, in a universe of brocades, silks, and blood (23), and calls her a rebel for her subversion of the traditional baroque. In *Devocionario*, for instance, she claims that Rossetti uses the language of the Golden Age to express her own female desire daringly, and that she portrays the martyrdom of saints and the mysteries of physical passion in an ornate and dynamic fashion.

John C. Wilcox defends Rossetti's work against other male critics and portrays her as much more than a hedonist poet. In his analysis of Rossetti's four muses, who revolve around love, death, religion, and historical-literary models, he gives evidence of Rossetti's pleasure in defining the limits of the androcentric vision of traditional reality (18). For her, eroticism is one more weapon or technique for confronting that reality, and her feminism and eroticism are by design (525–40).

Feminist critic Sharon Ugalde furnishes perhaps the most lucid explanation of Rossetti's intention as writer and female: "The force and beauty of her poetic expression reside in a delicate play between accepting and rejecting the patriarchal tradition that had deformed or excluded woman's authentic identity" (28). Taking advantage of the established language of post-Franco literature, Rossetti has created a remarkably original and daring voice.

BIBLIOGRAPHY

Works by Ana Rossetti

Poetry

Los devaneos de Erato. Valencia, Spain: Prometeo, 1980.
Dióscuros. Málaga, Spain: Jarazmin, 1982.
Misterios de pasión. Málaga, Spain: Diputación Provincial, 1985.
Devocionario. Madrid: Visor, 1986.
Indicios vehementes. (Poesía 1979–1984). 3rd ed. Madrid: Hiperión, 1987.
Yesterday. Madrid: Torremozas, 1988.

Prose

Aquellos duros antiguos. Almería, Spain: Aula de Poesía, 1988. [Vignettes]
Plumas de España. Barcelona: Seix Barral, 1988. [Novel]
Prendas íntimas. El tejido de la seducción. Madrid: Ediciones Temas de Hoy, 1989. [Essay]
Apuntes de ciudades. Málaga, Spain: Plaza de la Marina, 1990.

Short Stories

"La sortija y el sortilegio." *Cuentos eróticos*. Ed. Laura Freixas. Madrid: Grijalbo, 1988. 153–68.
"Hasta mañana, Elena." *Diario 16* 30 Aug. 1989: 20.

"El soberbio celeste." *Los pecados capitales*. Ed. Laura Freixas. Madrid: Grijalbo, 1990. 159–74.

"La sortija y el sortilegio." *Relatos eróticos*. Ed. Carmen Estévez. Madrid: Editorial Castalia, 1990. 109–23.

Alevosías. Barcelona: Tusquets, 1991.

Theater

"El saltamontes." Premiered on International Theater Day, 1974. [Monologue]

"Sueño en tres actos." Premiered in Madrid in the Certamen of the University Theater, 1975.

"La casa de los espirales." Premiered at the International Theater Festival in Cuenca, 1977.

Articles

"Vox populi." *ABC* 5 May 1989: 84.

"En torno al abandono." *ABC* 12 May 1989: 89.

"Usted tiene ojos de mujer fatal." *ABC* 19 May 1989: 88.

"Muerte de un soldado." *ABC* 26 May 1989: 97.

"En pie de danza." *ABC* 2 June 1989: 96.

"La comedia sin título." *ABC* 23 June 1989: 84.

"Veranos de la Villa." *ABC* 7 July 1989: 88.

"Dichas y desdichas." *ABC* 21 July 1989: 69.

"Guarecerse de Argos." *ABC* 28 July 1989: 67.

"Festival de otoño." *ABC* 22 Sept. 1989: 60.

"Advertencia." *ABC* 29 Sept. 1989: 20.

"Isadora." *ABC* 6 Oct. 1989: 85.

"Don Perlimpín." *ABC* 13 Oct. 1989: 78.

" . . . that's the question." *ABC* 21 Oct. 1989: 97.

Works about Ana Rossetti

Azancot, Leopoldo. "Plumas de España." *El País* 20 Mar. 1988: 17.

Bundy, Nancy L. "Entrevista con Ana Rossetti." *Letras Femeninas* 16:1–2 (Spring–Fall 1990): 135–38.

Coco, Emilio. "La verdadera Ana Rossetti. Entrevista con la autora de *Devocionario*." *Zarza Rosa: Revista de Poesía* 7 (1986): 49–73.

Fernández Palacios, Jesús. "Entrevista a Ana Rossetti." *Fin de Siglo. Revista de Literatura* 6–7 (1983): n. pag.

Jiménez Faro, Luzmaría, ed. "Ana Rossetti." *Panorama antológico de poetisas españolas (siglo XV al XX)*. Madrid: Torremozas, 1987. 293–99.

Legaza, J. L. "Devocionario. Una cosa rara." *Ya* 1 July 1989: n. pag.

Martín, Julia. "Poesía bailada." *El País* 8 June 1989: 44.

Martínez Ruiz, Florencio. "*Indicios vehementes (Poesía 1979–1984)*. Ana Rossetti." *Insula* 418 (1981): 9.

Miró, Emilio. "Dos premios para dos nuevas voces: Blanca Andreu y Ana Rossetti." *Insula* 418 (1981): 6.

Núñez, Antonio. "Encuentro con Ana Rossetti." *Insula* 474 (1986): 1, 12.

Palomero, María Pepa, ed. "Ana Rossetti." *Poetas de los 80*. Madrid: Hiperión, 1981. 211–24.

Preminger, Alex, ed. *Princeton Encyclopedia of Poetry and Poetics*. Princeton: Princeton UP, 1965. 661–62.

Profeti, María Grazia. "Plumas de España de Ana Rossetti." *Insula* 505 (Jan. 1989): 23.

Rico, Mercedes. "El difícil movimiento de la poesía." *El País* 12 June 1989: 46.

Ugalde, Sharon Keefe. "Erotismo y revisionismo en la poesía de Ana Rossetti." *Siglo XX/20th Century* 7 (1989–90): 24–29.

Wilcox, John C. "Ana Rossetti y sus cuatro musas poéticas." *Revista Canadiense de Estudios Hispánicos* 14.3 (1990): 525–40.

———. "Observaciones sobre el *Devocionario* de Ana Rossetti." Tenth Louisiana Conference on Hispanic Languages and Literatures. *La Chispa '89: Selected Proceedings*. Ed. Gilbert Paolini. New Orleans: Tulane U, 1989: 335–44.

FAUSTINA SÁEZ DE MELGAR (1833?–1895)

Cristina Enríquez de Salamanca

BIOGRAPHY

Faustina Sáez de Melgar was born in 1833 or 1834 in Villamanrique de Tajo, a small town located near the provinces of Cuenca and Toledo. Born into a family of rural landowners, Faustina was the daughter of Silverio Sáez and Tomasa Toro, a woman of aristocratic lineage. Most of what is known about her childhood and adolescence comes from two short biographies by Sáez's contemporaries. The first, by María del Pilar Sinués, is included in Sáez's popular story *La higuera de Villaverde* (1860; "The Fig Tree of Villaverde"). The second, by Juan Eugenio Hartzenbusch, is a partial reproduction of the first, and appears as the introduction to Sáez's novel *Aniana o la quinta de Peralta* (1866; "Aniana or the Peralta Manor"). Both portraits mention that Faustina lacked any formal education, that she learned to write on her own when she was nine years old, and that she educated herself by reading her brothers' schoolbooks. In the face of opposition from "loving" but traditional parents, she began writing poems, novels, and popular stories, activities that caused her family to criticize and taunt her, even after she had published the poem "La paloma torcaz" (1852; "The Ringdove") in the magazine *Album de Señoritas* (Simón Palmer, *Escritoras* 613). Despite her family's opposition, Faustina continued contributing to many magazines, among them *El Trono y la Nobleza*, *El Occidente*, *La Discusión*, and *La Época* (Sinués 84).

In 1851, after her marriage to Valentín Melgar, the couple settled in Madrid, where they remained for some thirty years. Four children were born—Hernán, Lucas, Gloria, and Virginia—but only the two daughters survived. In 1858, Hernán died while still an infant, and Faustina mourned the loss of her son in her first published collection of poetry, *La lira del Tajo* (1859; "The Lyre from the Tajo River"). Lucas died around 1864, as indicated in Ángela Grassi's poem "En la muerte del malogrado niño Lucas Melgar y Sáez," published in the magazine *La Violeta*.

Between 1851 and 1880 Faustina was extremely active. Arthur Corwin states that she joined the women's committee of the Spanish Abolitionist Society (159), and according to María del Carmen Simón Palmer (*Escritoras* 607) she published books, contributed to magazines, participated in collective works, and edited two magazines for women: *La Violeta* (Madrid, 1862–66) and *La Mujer* (Madrid, 1871–?). *La Violeta* launched Sáez de Melgar as a public literary figure and enabled her to publish and distribute her own novels as well as to establish contacts with the fashion world. Queen Isabel's authorization of this magazine as an official text for elementary schools and women's teacher training schools gave Sáez de Melgar prominence in the emerging field of female education.

Simultaneously, *La Violeta* became an important literary outlet for many women who, encouraged by the editors Ángela Grassi, María del Pilar Sinués, and Sáez del Melgar, published their works in this journal. Further, as Alda Blanco notes, the editors of *La Violeta* assumed a leading role among literary women, as Carolina Coronado had done years before with her "lyrical sisterhood" (Kirkpatrick, *Las Románticas* 79–87), and "continued the tradition, forged by romantic women writers . . . of writing prefaces for each other's books and lauding each other's literary production" ("Domesticity" 373). Unfortunately, *La Violeta* disappeared in 1866, for still unknown reasons, but shortly afterwards, in the effervescent atmosphere of the 1868 Revolution, Sáez campaigned for the promotion of women's education in the pages of the liberal newspaper *La Iberia* (*Memoria del Ateneo* 16–21). In 1869, she founded the Ateneo Artístico y Literario de Señoras, which, according to Geraldine Scanlon, was the origin of the Asociación para la Enseñanza de la Mujer, a leading institution in the organization of women's education (33; Concha Fagoaga 55–60).

A turning point occurred in Sáez's life during the 1880s. Valentín Melgar seems to have gone through professional difficulties, as can be deduced from the letters she wrote to Víctor Balaguer, in which she asked for a position for her husband. Her request was granted (whether by Balaguer or someone else is not known), and Valentín Melgar moved to the Philippines in the 1880s, leaving his wife and two daughters in Spain. According to her descendants, Sáez then sold her remaining land and moved to Paris in order to begin an international career as a writer. Very little is known about her life in Paris apart from what can be found in her reports, "Crónicas del extranjero," in the Barcelona magazine *La Ilustración de la mujer* (1883–1887). Simón Palmer (*Escritoras* 608) and Juan Criado y Domínguez (145–146) document that she edited two magazines in France, *La Canastilla Infantil* and *París Charmant Artistique*. The French publishing house Bouret issued one of Sáez's last books, *La semana de los niños*. *Lecturas instructivas para la infancia* (1882; "Children's Week. Instructive Readings for Childhood").

Simultaneously, Sáez del Melgar became one of the major contributors to the *folletines* (serialized novels) of *La Iberia*. Between 1875 and 1887 she published several long novels: *Ayer y hoy* (1875–76; "Yesterday and Today"), *Amar después de la muerte* (1876; "Love After Death"), *Blanca la extranjera* (1878; "Blanca the Foreigner"), *Irene. Memorias de una religiosa* (1886; "Irene. Memoirs of a Nun"), and *Los dos maridos de Tula* (1886–87; "Tula's Two Husbands"). Curiously, two of these novels had been published before in book form under different titles: *Blanca la extranjera* as *Los miserables de España* (1862–63; "The Wretched of Spain") and *Los dos maridos de Tula* as *Rosa la cigarrera de Madrid* (1872; "Rosa, the Cigarmaker from Madrid").

It is not known whether Sáez de Melgar ever returned to Spain. Her death certificate, however, states that Faustina Sáez Toro died in Madrid on March 19, 1895. As the study of her works will reveal, neither marriage nor maternity stopped the intellectual and political work of this "domestic" woman, for Sáez legitimated her political, intellectual, and artistic career through her espousal of woman's "natural" roles as daughter, wife, and mother.

MAJOR THEMES

Sáez del Melgar is one of several writers recently classified as *literatas*, producers of a corpus of fiction that appeared in Spain between 1850 and 1880 with remarkable success. They were, however, excluded from the Spanish literary canon, and they placed themselves—or were placed—in a "feminine" or secondary position with respect to canonical authors. Like so many other writers, she began publishing poetry and later cultivated novels, didactic works, children's literature, and essays. Her writings reveal her as an ideologue with a strong political agenda. Her fictional work and the numerous essays published in periodicals contain both a design for the political sphere and a set of rules for private individuals according to a middle-class worldview: domesticity. As such, her works interrelate three themes: a political definition of the Spanish nation in which she stands for a liberal constitutional monarchy and rails against the absolutist system of the Old Regime; a solution to the conflicts between classes through domesticity; and a view of the middle-class woman as the "angel in the house." As an author of domestic fiction, however, Sáez de Melgar differs from her English counterpart, Mrs. Sarah Ellis, and from her Spanish counterpart, Pilar Sinués, in that she does not provide practical advice but designs an individual, the "angel" who embodies middle-class values and behavior.

The analysis of her fiction alone reveals Sáez's world view, since there is a unity of thought in both her novelistic and her didactic writings. Two major trends can be discerned in her narrative. In the first, the author resorts to a melodramatic mode in order to illustrate the conflict between the worldviews of different social classes that were prevalent in nineteenth-century Spain. In the second, she utilizes a realist mode as a framework for her analysis of women's place in a middle-class milieu. Many of the elements proper to the nineteenth-century popular novel are visible in such works as *La pastora de Guadiela* (1860; "The Shepherdess from the Guadiela River"), *Los miserables de España*, and *Matilde o el ángel de Valde Real* (1862; "Matilde or the Angel from Valde Real"): a sinusoidal narrative structure based on tension, resolution, renewed tension, further resolution,[1] and coups de theatre consisting of a multiplicity of time, place, and action, good and wicked characters, and deus ex machina devices.

Sáez's works within the first trend can perhaps be defined as popular novels, or *folletines*, whose central conflict revolves around the fight between good and evil female aristocratic characters for the title and wealth of the family. Usually the latter usurps the place of the former by violence and deceit, only to be defeated after a long and complicated story by the legitimate heir, who finally recovers her place. A sizable number of artisans, as well as popular and rural secondary characters, are the protagonists of several plots woven into the central story, thus highlighting the relationship between Spanish class structure and the affairs of the central characters. The conflicts within aristocratic families are caused by events directly or tangentially related to the Carlist Wars between the Liberals, who favored a constitutional liberal monarchy, and the Carlists, who supported the absolutist pretender to the Spanish crown, Don Carlos. This political confrontation brings about the misfortune of the lawful heirs of aristocratic but liberal families, whose adversities are caused by the usurping Carlists.

Sáez de Melgar deals with the reorganization of class structure in Spain through love stories in which lovers of different social classes face family opposition. Usually, but not always, it is the female character who belongs to a lower class. In most cases, and always in the case of the protagonists, this impediment is surmounted when by chance or coincidence the lower-class woman is revealed to be an aristocrat by birth, lost in childhood and subsequently raised in poverty. This theme, found in many folk and literary stories, including Cervantes's *La gitanilla*, provides an opportunity for a detailed description of the opposition and individual reactions that intermarriage raised in families, conflicts that Sáez's family could have experienced firsthand.

Adding new complexity to the topic of the lost noble child, Sáez explores a major issue of the nineteenth century, the problem of individual identity—or, rather, inquires into what type of person should become the model in contemporary society. The development of her thesis encompasses two aspects of her novels. On the one hand, the poor lost child always reveals some special quality that causes her to stand out in her common surroundings. That specialness leads the reader to suspect the heroine's aristocratic heritage, a suspicion later confirmed by the narrative. On the other hand, the marks of distinction are actually not aristocratic traits but those personality traits that are valued and promoted by the middle class: honesty, sincerity, hardwork, frugality. Moreover, Sáez embodies these middle-class values in the woman, the "angel in the house."

Although Sáez herself does not use this term, a "domestic angel" is the powerful female figure around which her fictional world is built and a symbol that can be found in most major nineteenth-century European cultures. Like those of her European counterparts, her "angel" bears the marks of an older Marianism that found new impulse during the nineteenth century, while her personality and behavior are the expression of secularized Christian values. Furthermore, the "angel," who is endowed with aesthetic qualities, carries the ability to poeticize everything that she touches, to the point that she incarnates *buen gusto*, art in daily life. In other words, the "angel" is an appropriation by the middle classes of an aesthetic sensibility that was until then the patrimony of the aristocracy. All of her good female aristocratic protagonists are "angels," but so are the good female characters of the lower class. Although Sáez promotes middle-class values, she ultimately wants us to believe that her "angels" do not belong to a specific social class: They are general "feminine" types.

The power of the "angel" is carried to its extreme in *Los miserables de España*, in which the protagonist, Blanca, is a noble child whose place is usurped by evil relatives. Taken by a priest to Brazil, she inherits a huge fortune and later returns to Spain, where she executes a complicated strategy to recover her name and title. Blanca's power to direct everyone's life converts her into a kind of earthly Providence. No less great, however, is the power of the evil female protagonist, who characteristically represents the aristocracy with all its negative traits: superficiality, vanity, self-interest, selfishness, moral corruption, and decadence. The plea for middle-class values is thus presented as a cosmic struggle— a battle between good and evil, between the middle-class "angel" and the aristocratic female "demon." The final victory of the "angels" can therefore be understood as a quest for the domestication of the aristocracy: Only by accepting those middle-class values, Sáez seems to argue, will the aristocracy keep its legitimacy.

Coexisting with Sáez's *folletín* mode, another trend reveals itself in such novels as *Ángela o el ramillete de jazmines* (1863–65; "Angela or the Bouquet of Jasmine"), *Ayer y hoy*, and *Irene. Memorias de una religiosa*. Following a linear narrative, these novels use a language, setting, and style that may be called realist. The author's attention now focuses on the bourgeoisie: rich rural landowners, businessmen, high officials, politicians, and professionals. The angel of her previous works is endowed with another dimension, that of the educated woman.

This emphasis is clearly a product of Sáez's campaign to promote the education of women, and her novels subtly weave together the relationships between women's psychological development and their access to learning and professional training. Implying that "education is another form of wealth" (*Ayer y hoy*), her novels dramatize the contradictory fates of her feminist protagonists with regard to education and the incompatibility between love and an artistic profession. Neither love nor marriage allows the protagonist of *Ángela* to harmonize her professional and emotional life. Only as a mother can Ángela keep her career as an internationally acclaimed singer and maintain a family. This proposal is in itself an acceptance of "woman's difference," a position from which Sáez argues for the access of women to education and a professional life. Similarly, although accepting woman's "different nature," Sáez advocates equality between men and women within family life. *Aniana o la quinta de Peralta*, for example, argues against the "double standard" and pleads for the legal right of women to separate in cases of marital infidelity.

Just as a link between domesticity and the aristocracy was established through the *folletín*, so a connection between the bourgeoisie and domesticity can be seen in the realist mode. Finally, the same relationship is developed in a working-class context in *Rosa la cigarrera de Madrid*. This work mingles Spanish history (the first Carlist War in the 1830s and the Liberal Revolution of 1854) with the life of Rosa, a woman of the lower classes. Seduced by the aristocrat Jaime when she is an adolescent, Rosa becomes the leader of a group of bandits; moves to Madrid, where she works in a tobacco factory; and participates in the Madrid riots of 1854 before finally marrying a repentant Jaime.

Jaime's seduction of Rosa represents a sexual relationship between master and subject: Ignoring marriage as a sacrosanct institution, Jaime perpetrates on Rosa's body a privilege conferred by his status. Rosa responds to this seduction and subsequent abandonment by rejecting a "feminine" identity that objectifies her. Instead she adopts a "masculine" identity, and in this role becomes a bandit, a factory worker, and a revolutionary agent. The narrative closure marked by Rosa and Jaime's marriage symbolically unifies and resolves class conflicts and gender ideology. Jaime's marriage to a working-class woman also signals his rejection of the kinship norms of his class. Rosa, in turn, renounces all "masculine" activity and adopts the role of a domestic woman. Class conflicts are thus displaced to the private sphere, and are resolved in a politically "neutral" space. This conclusion of *Rosa la cigarrera* affirms domesticity as a key for the harmony between social classes and suggests the possibility of social elevation for those working-class women who accept domestic ideology.

While the analysis of her fictional work allows us to characterize Sáez de Melgar as a female ideologue, the author herself claimed that her ideas derived from an apolitical position. Sáez explicitly and repeatedly denied any political intentions in her writing, reserving that realm for men and insisting that she was writing, publishing, and editing magazines only as a "woman" and only for "women." Her paradoxical position—similar to that of many *literatas*—implies that her domestic discourse carried an internal contradiction. It operated simultaneously in favor of and against the interests of its own social class: in favor, since she propagated domestic ideology as a way of life that could be shared by all social sectors, from the aristocracy to the working class; in opposition, because she thus assumed an active political role that contradicted the domestic ideal, and opened new fields of action for women.

One may argue that Sáez paradoxically contributed to providing women with a political language by claiming to speak about an apolitical matter, the "woman question." From this "feminine sphere," the *literatas*, including Sáez del Melgar, created and addressed a female audience. In many of her works her readers were renamed *las lectoras* (women readers), an epithet that signaled a "difference." Speaking as a woman and addressing women, she pointed out a distinction between male and female readers unique in that era. The wide diffusion of her work, as well as her presence in literary, social, political, and economic activities, exposed Sáez to society's gaze, and in this way, by bringing *las lectoras* into the public eye, she made visible the social group of middle-class women that she herself epitomized. Her writing also established an intimate relationship among women who were interested in self-knowledge, in knowing what it was like to be a woman. This communication, or "domestic sisterhood," can be identified through their editorials, their letters to magazines, and their introductions and dedications to one another's books.

The suffragist movement began in Spain in 1877 (Fagoaga, *La voz y el voto de la mujeres*). Its beginnings overlap with the last years of the production of domestic writers such as Ángela Grassi, María del Pilar Sinués, and Faustina Sáez de Melgar. A link between those two social phenomena—the emergence of middle-class women into the public sphere and the political organization of women—has a logic as compelling as the relationship that Alda Blanco defined in the literary sphere between the protofeminist legacy of the romantic writers and the feminist authors of the latter part of the century ("Domesticity, Education and the Woman Writer" 391).

SURVEY OF CRITICISM

No major study exists of either Faustina Sáez de Melgar or any of her sister writers, since literary criticism has basically ignored the existence of any women's writing produced between 1850 and 1880. For a long time Sáez's name appeared only in general works. Juan P. Criado y Domínguez included her among four-hundred other women in his 1889 *Literatas españolas del siglo XIX*. Three histories of Spanish literature list Sáez de Melgar among the female producers of the "lesser" *folletín*: Ernest Mérimée's *Précis d'Histoire de la Littérature Espagnole*, Francisco Blanco García's *La literatura española en el siglo XIX*, and Julio Cejador y Frauca's *Historia de la lengua y literatura castellana*. José María de Cossío, in contrast, wrote an affectionate account of *La Violeta's* "lyrical sisterhood," and Carmen Bravo-Villasante devoted a few not very enthusiastic remarks to Sáez de Melgar's production of children's literature (*Historia de la literatura infantil española*).

Some literary and biographical details can be found in *Veinticuatro diarios de Madrid* (Seminario de Bibliografía) and in José Luis Pécker's "Faustina Sáez de Melgar," in his *Colmenar de Oreja (1881–1991)*. Other bibliographical accounts are Juan Ignacio Ferreras's *Catálogo de novelas y novelistas del siglo XIX*, Carolyn Galerstein's *Women Writers of Spain*, and Maria del Carmen Simón Palmer's *Escritoras españolas del siglo XIX*. The latter has an exhaustive bibliography that includes many of Sáez's contributions to magazines. In addition,

Concha Fagoaga dedicates a few pages to the Ateneo Artístico y Literario in *La voz y el voto de las mujeres españolas*.

The only monographic studies of Sáez de Melgar's writings deal with the relationship between her particular form of narrative and realist/naturalist fiction. Alicia G. Andreu proposed the heroine of *La cruz del olivar* as a literary model for *La desheredada* by Benito Pérez Galdós. To that purpose Andreu first reprinted *La cruz del olivar* in *Anales Galdosianos* with an introduction that was later expanded in *Galdós y la literatura popular*. Cristina Enríquez de Salamanca developed the relationship between Emilia Pardo Bazán and the Spanish female literary tradition in her article about Sáez's *Rosa la cigarrera de Madrid* as a literary model for Pardo Bazán's *La tribuna*.

Other aspects of Sáez's production have been considered in general studies of nineteenth-century women writers. Maryellen Bieder has recovered the term *literatas* for critical discussions in her unpublished manuscripts focusing on Emilia Pardo Bazán and nineteenth-century women writers. Juan Ignacio Ferreras acknowledges the existence of many authors of that period (*Catálogo*) as well as what he considers the machismo of most female authors ("La novela decimonónica"). Simón Palmer and Enríquez de Salamanca have studied the position of women as writers in nineteenth-century Spanish society. Simón Palmer explains the conservatism shown by most women writers as an apology for their devotion to literary tasks in "Escritoras españolas del siglo XIX o el miedo a la marginación." Enríquez de Salamanca, through a sampling of writers who contributed to the magazine *La Ilustración de la Mujer* (Barcelona 1883–87), draws a prototype of the nineteeth-century woman writer and points out the contradiction between their alleged conservatism and their actual lives ("¿Quién era la escritora del siglo XIX?").

The exclusion of nineteenth-century women writers from the canon of Spanish literature has been studied by Blanco and Enríquez de Salamanca. For Blanco, the exclusion of the *literatas* from the history of Spanish literature is connected to the rise of realist and naturalist fiction as the best exponents of Spanish national concerns. Enríquez de Salamanca analyzes three histories of Spanish literature that list Sáez de Melgar among the female producers of the *folletín*. Her study elucidates how domestic writers could have been considered politically subversive by historians of literature ("Angélicas o subversivas"). In "Gender and the Literary Canon," Enríquez de Salamanca carries out a deconstruction study of a broad sample of histories of literature. She further argues that such histories are grounded in a "masculine" notion of literary authority that gives way to a distinction between *escritoras* and *literatas*, that is, canonical and noncanonical women writers, justifying the inclusion of the former and the exclusion of the latter from literary criticism.

Domesticity, as the ideological ground of the *literatas*, is the concern of such publications as Bridget Aldaraca's "El Ángel del Hogar: The Cult of Domesticity in Nineteenth-Century Spain," Susan Kirkpatrick's *Las Románticas*, and Alicia Andreu's *Galdós y la literatura popular*. Each criticizes a different aspect of the *literatas* writings: Aldaraca, their sentimentalism; Kirkpatrick, their antifeminism; and Andreu, their conservatism. Kirkpatrick has modified her position in "The Female Tradition in Nineteenth-Century Spanish Literature" and has found women writers to be exceptions to the "apparently conformist appropriation of the authority of the domestic angel" (354). Lou Charnon-Deutsch proposes a psychoanalytical interpretation of Spanish domestic fiction through a reading of the novels of Pilar Sinués. Christine Stopp studies the midcentury construction of womanhood, and Catherine Jagoe unravels Galdós's ambiguities in relation to the domestic ideal popularized by such authors as María del Pilar Sinués, Ángela Grassi, and Faustina Sáez de Melgar. Alda Blanco's appreciation of a dialogue between "femininity" and "feminism" in the *literatas*, revealing the contradictory forces at work in the midcentury construction of womanhood ("Domesticity"), is further developed in *The Good Woman As Writer*, where she argues for the importance of Spanish female writers in the development of the realist and naturalist novel.

There is a growing interest in the literary production of Spanish women in the 1850s and, among them, Sáez de Melgar. She played a major role in the consolidation of nineteenth-century Spanish middle-class values and culture. Through her diffusion of domestic ideology, middle-class women acquired a political language and social subjectivity that paved the way for the rise of the suffragist movement in Spain.

NOTE

1. Umberto Eco, "Sue's 'Les Mystéres de Paris,' " *The Role of the Reader. Explorations in the Semiotics of Texts* (Bloomington: Indiana UP, 1984) 132.

BIBLIOGRAPHY

Works by Faustina Sáez de Melgar

In this chapter, only first registered editions and bibliographical information on novels published in the periodical press and studied within the texts are listed. For a comprehensive bibliography see Simón Palmer, *Escritoras españolas*, and Seminario de Bibliografía, *Veinticuatro diarios*.

África y España. Cantos poéticos escritos con motivo de la guerra de Marruecos. Madrid: Imprenta de Bernabé Fernández, 1859.

La lira del Tajo. Poesías de la Señora Doña Faustina Sáez de Melgar dedicadas a Isabel II. Madrid: Imprenta de Bernabé Fernández, 1859.

La higuera de Villaverde. Leyenda tradicional. Madrid: Imprenta de Bernabé Fernández, 1860.

La pastora de Guadiela. Novela original. 2nd ed. Madrid: Imprenta de Bernabé Fernández, 1860.

La marquesa de Pinares. Novela original. Madrid: Imprenta de Bernabé Fernández, 1861.

Matilde o el ángel de Valde Real. Episodio histórico de la guerra civil. Madrid: Imprenta de Manuel de Rojas, 1862. *La Iberia* [Madrid] 4 July 1865: n. pag.

Los miserables de España o secretos de la Corte. Novela de costumbres. 2 vols. Barcelona: Imprenta Hispana de Vicente Castaños, 1862–63. Rpt. *Blanca la extranjera. Novela original. La Iberia* [Madrid] 1 Jan.–30 June 1878: n. pag.

Ángela o el ramillete de jazmines. Novela original. 3 vols. Madrid: Establecimiento Tipográfico de R. Vicente, 1863–65. *La Iberia* [Madrid] 3 Jan.–12 Apr. 1868: n. pag.

Ecos de gloria. Leyendas históricas en verso por la Señora Doña Faustina Sáez de Melgar. Madrid: Antonio Pérez Dubrull, 1863.

La abuelita o cuentos de la aldea. La Violeta [Madrid] 3 Jan. 1864: n. pag.

María. Novela original. La Violeta [Madrid] 28 May–25 June 1865: n. pag.

Aniana o la quinta de Peralta. Novela original. 2nd ed. Madrid: Imprenta de La Iberia, 1866. [Prologue by Fernán Caballero. Preface by Juan Eugenio Hartzenbusch]. (*Aniana* y *Amar después de la muerte. La Iberia* [Madrid] 23 July–26 Sept. 1876; 26 Sept.–21 Dec. 1876; 1 Jan.–7 Mar. 1877: n. pag.

Deberes de la mujer. Colección de artículos sobre la educación. 2nd ed. Madrid: R. Vicente, 1866.

Amar después de la muerte. Novela original. Barcelona: Imprenta Verdaguer, 1867. [Second part of *Aniana o la quinta de Peralta*]. *La Iberia* [Madrid] 26 Sept.–21 Dec. 1876; 1 Jan.–7 Mar. 1877: n. pag.

La cruz del olivar. Novela original. Correo de la Moda [Madrid] 15 Mar.–31 May 1867. Madrid: F. Peña, 1868. Rpt. in *Anales Galdosianos* Suplementos 14 (1980): 1–68.

La loca del encinar. Novela original. Biblioteca del Viajero III. Madrid: J. A. García, 1867.

Memoria del Ateneo de Señoras. Leída en junta general celebrada el día 27 de junio de 1869 por la presidenta y fundadora Doña Faustina Sáez de Melgar. Madrid: Imprenta de los Señores Rojas, 1869.

Rosa la cigarrera de Madrid. Gran novela original de la señora Doña Faustina Sáez de Melgar. 2 vols. Barcelona: Biblioteca Hispano-Americana, 1872.

Ayer y hoy. Novela original. La Iberia. [Madrid] 4–6 Nov. 1875; 1 Jan.–25 Feb. 1876: n. pag.

Contra indiferencia, celos. Juguete cómico en un acto y en prosa. Madrid: Imprenta de J. Rodríguez, 1875. [Premiered at Teatro Eslava, Madrid, 1 Dec. 1875.]

La abuelita. Cuentos de la aldea. Barcelona: Bastinos, 1877. *La abuelita o cuentos de la aldea.* 2nd ed. Barcelona: Bastinos, 1879.

Epistolario moral literario. Barcelona: Librería de Juan y Antonio Bastinos, 1877. [With Joaquina Balmaseda, Ángela Grassi, María de la Peña, and María del Pilar Sinués]

Un libro para mis hijas. Educación cristiana y social de la mujer. Barcelona: Librería de Juan y Antonio Bastinos, 1877. [Prologue by Rev. Dr. D. José Ildefonso Gatel]

Blanca la extranjera. Novela original. La Iberia [Madrid] 1 Jan.–30 June 1878: n. pag.

Inés o la hija de la caridad. Novela original. 2 vols. Madrid: Imprenta de los Señores Rojas, 1878.

Sendas opuestas y La bendición paterna. Novelas originales. Madrid: Imprenta de los Señores Rojas, 1878.

Aurora y Felicidad. Novela de costumbres. Barcelona: Salvador Manera, 1879. Partially rpt. in José Luis Pécker, *Colmenar de Oreja (1881–1911)*. Colmenar, Madrid: Ayuntamiento de Colmenar de Oreja, 1991. 392–404.

La cadena rota. Drama en tres actos. Madrid: Imprenta de F. Macías, 1879.

El collar de esmeraldas. Novela. Madrid: Imprenta de P. Núñez, 1879.

El deber cumplido. Novela original. Madrid: Imprenta de P. Núñez, 1879.

Páginas para las niñas. Ejercicios de lectura en prosa y verso. Barcelona: Juan y Antonio Bastinos, 1881.

La semana de los niños. Lecturas instructivas para la infancia. Paris: Ch. Bouret, 1882.

Las mujeres españolas, americanas y lusitanas pintadas por sí mismas. Obra dedicada a la mujer por la mujer . . . bajo la dirección de Faustina Sáez de Melgar. Barcelona: n.p., 1885.

Irene. Memorias de una religiosa. La Iberia [Madrid] 14–23 Mar. 1886: n. pag.

Works about Faustina Sáez de Melgar

Aldaraca, Bridget. "El ángel del hogar: The Cult of Domesticity in Nineteenth-Century Spain." *Theory and Practice of Feminist Literary Criticism.* Ed. Gabriela Mora and Karen S. Van Hooft. Ypsilanti, MI: Bilingual Press/Editorial Bilingüe, 1982. 62–87.

Andreu, Alicia G., ed. & intro. "*La cruz del Olivar* por Faustina Sáez de Melgar: Un modelo literario en la vida de Isidora Rufete." *Anales galdosianos* Suplementos 14 (1980): 7–16. [Introduction]

———. *Galdós y la literatura popular.* Madrid: Sociedad General Española de Librería, 1982. 111–30.

Bieder, Maryellen. "Emilia Pardo Bazán and *Las literatas*: Women Writers in Spain (1870–1921)." [Unpublished MS]

———. "Emilia Pardo Bazán y *Las literatas*: Las escritoras del XIX y su literatura." [Unpublished MS]

Blanco, Alda. "Domesticity, Education and the Woman Writer: Spain 1850–1880." *Cultural and Historical Grounding for Hispanic and Luso-Brazilian Feminist Literary Criticism.* Ed. Hernán Vidal. Minneapolis: Institute for the Study of Ideologies and Literature, 1989. 373–94.

———. "Gender and National Identity: The Novel in Nineteeth-Century Spanish Literary History." MLA Annual Meeting. Minneapolis, 1–4 Nov. 1989.

———. *The Good Woman as Writer: Fiction in Mid-Nineteenth Century Spain.* Madrid: Siglo XXI. [Forthcoming]

Blanco García, Francisco. *La literatura española en el s. XIX.* 3rd ed. Madrid: Sáenz de Jubera, 1909.

Bravo-Villasante, Carmen. *Historia de la literatura infantil española.* Madrid: Editorial Escuela Española, 1985. 110, 341.

Cejador y Frauca, Julio. *Historia de la lengua y literatura castellana.* Vol 8. Madrid: Tipología de Archivos, 1915–22. 14 Vols.

Charnon-Deutsch, Lou. "On Desire and Domesticity in Nineteenth-Century Women's Novels." *Revista Canadiense de Estudios Hispánicos* 14. 3 (Spring 1990): 395–414.

Corwin, Arthur F. *Spain and the Abolition of Slavery in Cuba 1817–1886.* Austin: U of Texas P, 1967. 167.

Cossío, José María de. *Cincuenta años de poesía española (1850–1900).* Vol. 1. Madrid: Espasa-Calpe, 1960. 65–66. 2 Vols.

Criado y Domínguez, Juan P. *Literatas españolas del siglo XIX*. Madrid: Antonio Pérez Dubrull, 1889. 143–46.

Enríquez de Salamanca, Cristina. "Angélicas o subversivas: el problema de las escritoras decimonónicas ante el canon historiográfico español." MLA Annual Convention. Minneapolis, 1–4 Nov. 1989.

———. "Gender and the Literary Canon: The Case of Nineteenth-Century Spanish Women Writers." M.A. Diss. U of Minnesota, 1990.

———. "¿Quién era la escritora del siglo XIX?" *Letras Peninsulares* 4 (1989): 81–108.

———. "*Rosa la cigarrera de Madrid* como modelo literario de *La tribuna*." *Continental, Latin-American and Francophone Women Writers. Vol.3. Selected Papers from the Sixth Annual Wichita State University Conference on Foreign Literatures. April 13–16, 1989*. Ed. Ginette Adamson and Eunice Myers. Lanham, MD: UP of America, 1993.

Fagoaga, Concha. *La voz y el voto de las mujeres españolas. El sufragismo en España 1877–1931*. Barcelona: Icaria, 1985.

Ferreras, Juan Ignacio. *Catálogo de novelas y novelistas españoles del siglo XIX*. Madrid: Cátedra, 1979.

———. "La novela decimonónica escrita por mujeres." *Escritoras románticas españolas*. Ed. Marina Mayoral. Madrid: Fundación Banco Exterior, 1990. 17–24.

———. *La novela por entregas 1840–1900. (Concentración obrera y economía editorial)*. Madrid: Taurus Ediciones, 1972.

Hartzenbusch, Juan Eugenio. "Doña Faustina Sáez de Melgar." *La Violeta* (Madrid) 16 Oct. 1886: 296–99.

———. "Doña Faustina Sáez de Melgar." *Aniana o la quinta de Peralta*. By Faustina Sáez de Melgar. 2nd ed. Madrid: Imprenta de La Iberia, 1866. 3–15. [Preface]

Jagoe, Catherine Anne. "Ambivalent Angels: Gender-Roles and the Ideology of Domesticity in the Novels of Galdós." Diss. Girton College, Cambridge, 1988.

Kirkpatrick, Susan. "The Female Tradition in Nineteenth-Century Spanish Literature." *Cultural and Historical Grounding for Hispanic and Luso-Brazilian Feminist Literary Criticism*. Ed. Hernán Vidal. Minneapolis: Institute for the Study of Ideologies and Literature, 1989. 344–70.

———. *Las Románticas. Women Writers and Subjectivity in Spain 1835–1850*. Berkeley: U of California P, 1989.

Mérimée, Ernest. *Précis d'Histoire de la Littérature Espagnole*. Paris: Garnier Frères, Libraires-Editeurs, 1908.

Pécker, José Luis. "Faustina Sáez de Melgar." *Colmenar de Oreja (1881–1991)*. Colmenar, Madrid: Ayuntamiento de Colmenar de Oreja, 1991.

Rey, Arsenio. "Faustina Sáez de Melgar." *Women Writers of Spain: An Annotated Bio-Bibliographical Guide*. Ed. Carolyn Galerstein. Westport, CT: Greenwood Press, 1986. 285–86.

Scanlon, Geraldine. *La polémica feminista en la España contemporánea. 1868–1974*. 2nd ed. Madrid: Ediciones Akal, 1986.

Seminario de Bibliografía de la Facultad de Filosofía y Letras de Madrid. *Veinticuatro diarios (Madrid 1830–1900). Artículos y noticias de escritores españoles del siglo XIX*. 4 vols. Madrid: C.S.I.C., Instituto "Miguel de Cervantes," 1968.

Simón Palmer, María del Carmen. *Escritoras españolas del siglo XIX. Manual bio-bibliográfico*. Madrid: Castalia, 1991. 607–18.

————. "Escritoras españolas del siglo XIX o el miedo a la marginación." *Anales de Literatura Española de la Universidad de Alicante* 2 (1985): 477–90.

Stopp, Christine. "Women as Represented and Discussed in the Popular and Periodical Literature of Spain in the Period 1860–1900." Diss. Oxford U, 1984.

Sinués de Marco, María del Pilar. "Biografía de la Señora Doña Faustina Sáez de Melgar." *La higuera de Villaverde. Leyenda tradicional.* By Faustina Sáez de Melgar. Madrid: Imprenta de D. Bernabé Fernández, 1860. 76–88.

MARÍA DEL PILAR SINUÉS DE MARCO (1835–1893)

Catherine Jagoe

BIOGRAPHY

Born in Zaragoza in 1835 as María del Pilar Sinués y Navarro, she had a lifelong passion for writing that manifested itself, according to her own account, at the age of eight, when she wrote her first novel, "Rosa." By the 1850s she had risen to literary fame, which she continued to enjoy for the next forty years. Although Sinués was one of the most prolific and highly acclaimed authors of the nineteenth century, and probably the first woman in Spain to become an independent professional writer (Pérez 39), there is very little reliable information about her life. Her earliest surviving works are books of poetry and historical legends from the early 1850s. Around 1855 she was married by proxy to the playwright José Marco on the strength of a brief correspondence; he proposed to her in verse. Although Marco (who had a reputation as a womanizer) acted on a whim, the marriage lasted for many years.

A move from the provinces to Madrid, where Sinués spent the rest of her life, proved to be an advantageous one for the aspiring young author. In 1857, the women's journal *La Moda de Cádiz* began serializing the work that was to become the touchstone of Sinués's literary fame, *El ángel del hogar* (1859; "The Angel of the House"), a compendium of moral homilies for young ladies interspersed with fictional illustrations that promoted the ideal of the virtuous wife-mother. This work was published in book form in 1859 and reprinted throughout the century. The daily newspaper *La Iberia* reported on March 20, 1864, that Sinués received a gold medal from the French empress in recognition of *El ángel del hogar* and *La ley de Dios: Leyendas morales* (1858; "The Law of God: Moral Tales"). Sinués went on to found two highly successful journals for women, *El Ángel del Hogar* (1864–69) and *Flores y Perlas* ("Flowers and Pearls"), which she edited in 1883 and 1884.

She was a prodigious worker, producing over one hundred book-length works in a variety of genres: novels, collections of short stories and essays, domestic conduct manuals, and biographies of famous women. She also published innumerable articles on the domestic mission of women in society, and was described in the prefatory note to one of the English translations of her works as ''an assiduous contributor to all the best reviews in Spain and America'' (*The Outcasts of a King*). She translated many French and English romantic novels into Spanish; some of these were published in her own magazines.

Julio Nombela, an acquaintance of Sinués and José Marco, recorded that Sinués and her husband eventually separated. He throws out the tantalizing hint that this happened because Sinués had become involved in an affair of her own (2:336). The date of their separation is not known, but it appears to have been in the mid-1870s, since by 1877 Sinués had stopped signing her work with her married name ''de Marco'' and had reverted to ''María del Pilar Sinués.'' She supported herself thereafter by her writing.

All her life Sinués was painfully conscious of the stigma attached to being a woman writer in a patriarchal culture. Despite her great literary fame, she took pains to avoid being a public figure. Both her own writing and contemporary reports suggest that she was uneasy about the dichotomy between the culture's feminine ideal and her status as an author, especially since after the separation she was neither a wife nor a mother. Nombela recalls that when visitors arrived, she was always dutifully sewing; however, this was evidently a camouflage, for he notes that it was the same piece all her life (4:430).

Sinués died on November 20, 1893, in Madrid, of a heart attack. Her contemporaries made much of the fact that the title of her last novel was *Morir sola* (1890; ''She Died Alone''), attributing to it autobiographical significance. It is hard to know how much to credit the myths of suffering, isolation, and financial hardship surrounding Sinués, which are reflected in the verse of the satirist Ángel Segovia: ''She writes in order to forget / her unhappy life'' (144). It is possible that they are the product of a patriarchal mentality that assumed single women were by definition lonely and unfulfilled.

MAJOR THEMES

Unfortunately, the dates and even the form in which many of Sinués's works first appeared are as hazy as her life. It is probable that many of her works were serialized in journals or delivered in installments to the homes of subscribers prior to their publication in book form. Sinués made a name for herself as the indefatigable spokeswoman for bourgeois domestic ideology. She firmly believed in the concept of separate masculine and feminine spheres—the public versus the domestic—and in the idea of innate mental and emotional differences between men and women. She addressed all her work to women, constantly advocating the model of feminine behavior known as the ''angel of the house.'' This ideal of womanhood was defined in a subordinate relation to men as "daughter, wife, and mother." Women, wrote Sinués, should be chaste, pious, meek, loving, attentive, patient, and cheerful; they should value and enjoy their domestic duties and strive to turn their homes into the cozy sanctuary so cherished by the Victorian imagination. If they did so, they would be rewarded with respect, love, happiness, peace of mind, and material security.

Sinués, like her English counterpart Mrs. Sarah Ellis, aimed to provide practical and psychological advice for young middle-class women, as specifically seen in her nonfiction: journal articles and conduct books. The latter fall into two types: practical manuals such as *La dama elegante* (1880; "The Elegant Lady"), full of hints on running a middle-class household—how to choose servants, preserve clothes and furs, make home remedies, remove stains, and plan dinner parties. The other variety consisted of collections of essays or homilies such as the series *Un libro para las damas* (1875; "A Book for Ladies"), *Un libro para las madres* (1877; "A Book for Mothers"), *Un libro para las jóvenes* (1879; "A Book for Young Women"), and *Verdades dulces y amargas* (1882; "Sweet and Bitter Truths"). The theme of these works is sentimental education. The author's message to young women is not to set their expectations too high. She depicts marriage as full of tribulations and emotional pitfalls that women must learn to bear with resignation and humility. Sinués portrays suffering—often at the hands of men, other times at the hands of evil women—as the good woman's ineluctable lot in life: "We are born to sacrifice and self-denial" (*Hija, esposa y madre* 82 [1863; "Daughter, Wife and Mother"]). She advocates domesticity and submission not merely as a duty but because they provide women with emotional and economic stability.

Ever conscious of the advances of feminism in Spain and elsewhere, Sinués is careful to disassociate herself from the women's rights movement. Almost every work contains an ostentatious disclaimer, such as the following from *Un libro para las damas*: "I am not one of those who advocate women's emancipation, nor do I belong to those who believe that it is a possibility . . . woman constantly requires the protection of a father, a husband, a son, a brother" (9–10). Yet at the same time, she deplores women's limited education, commenting bitterly in the same work on "the great difference between the intellectual level attained today in men's education, and the well-nigh total lack of learning which is usually seen in our sex" (7).

Directed specifically at the middle classes, Sinués's work strongly supports the bourgeois ethic of thrift, order, duty, and industriousness. She contrasts these values to the consumer-oriented mentality promoted by nineteenth-century capitalism, which had made it possible for people to acquire large amounts of goods on credit, thereby risking financial embarrassment and even ruin. Sinués stresses not only the difficulty but also the importance of accepting one's middle-class status, and not trying to keep up an aristocratic appearance at ruinous expense. She reflects a current theme by representing women as one of the main dangers to the bourgeois enterprise, thanks to their supposed propensity for the peculiarly nineteenth-century vice of *el lujo* (luxury), a compulsive need to acquire luxury goods such as clothes and jewels.

In addition to her nonfiction, Sinués wrote a considerable amount of fiction. As she advertises in the prologues to her many novels, her aim here, too, is to promote the cult of the domestic woman, and there is, indeed, no shortage of virtuous, long-suffering heroines redeeming evil antiheroines and errant husbands alike. Yet there is a pervasive and intriguing subtext to her novels, which have, at points, curiously feminist overtones despite her own antifeminist intentions. In her own life, Sinués patently did not live up to her own prescriptions for women to put up with unfaithful husbands, stay chaste, and find fulfillment in family life. The blurring of genres in *El ángel del hogar*—the conduct manual that bursts into fiction with its three intercalated novellas—is significant. While cultivating a demure facade as domestic moralist, Sinués actually wrote racy, even sensationalist, adventure novels that subvert the feminine ideal on a number of different levels.

In the first place, Sinués studiously cultivates the notion of feminine solidarity and superiority, a tactic that Elaine Showalter sees as creating a kind of "covert solidarity that sometimes amounted to a genteel conspiracy."[1] The titles, subtitles, and modes of address in Sinués's novels show that they were explicitly "woman-to-woman" literature; as she says in the preface to *La mujer en nuestros días* (1878; "Woman in Our Day"), "since the beginning of my literary life I have always written for my own sex." Sinués creates a strong sense of a women's tradition in literature by her frequent references to and quotations from other women writers. In her fiction, she portrays a woman-centered world dominated by heroines, where men are shadowy, subsidiary, weak, and often despicable. Everything takes place within the domestic interiors of upper-middle-class households. Most important, Sinués is concerned with women as a special group with their own specific interests and talents. Her plots allow her women readers to indulge in fantasies of centrality and significance.

The central drama of Sinués's fiction is the pitting of two types against one another: the virtuous woman and the corrupt woman. *Fausta Sorel* (1861), *El alma enferma* (1864; "The Sick Soul"), and *Morir sola* are among the many illustrations of this formula. The good woman (Lía, Modesta, Cecilia) suffers at the hands of the scheming and aggressive bad woman (Fausta Sorel, Dolores Herrera, Alicia Valenzuela), who usually manipulates men to carry out her evil plans. Eventually the good woman wins out through patience and fortitude, cures the men of their bewitchment, and redeems her opponent, who then dies. Although this compulsive rewarding of the patient Griselda type is exasperating to a modern reader, we should note that Sinués attributes enormous power to women. It lies in their hands to make or break not only their families but also the whole fabric of bourgeois society. Her evil women squander vast fortunes and ruin men financially and psychologically, while her good women can work miracles in the most hardened of hearts and the most desperate of situations.

A further part of the feminization of Sinués's fictional world can be seen in the treatment of male characters. There are many attacks on men as cruel, shallow, and fickle. Men tend to be typecast as rakes, cold, and heartless beings of science, or the Sinués masculine ideal: the tender, poetic, nurturing, emotional man such as Héctor (*Fausta Sorel*) or Tomás Barrientos (*Morir sola*). Even the best of men, such as Teodoro (*Fausta Sorel*), are helpless before the seductive wiles of the evil femme fatale. Under emotional pressure, men, unlike women, always crack; many go insane and some die, such as Enrique (*Fausta Sorel*).

Viewed as a whole, Sinués's fiction problematizes the very ideology it was designed to convey, for it in fact denaturalizes the role of the *ángel del hogar*. Although women were supposed to be innately chaste, virtuous, submissive, and motherly, Sinués never ceases to stress that these qualities are in fact the result of nurture and not nature. Over and over again, she presents child-parent, and particularly mother–daughter, relationships as illustrations of this theme. For her, there is an absolute and unwavering connection between environment and human product; good mothering will produce an angelic daughter, bad or inadequate mothering will produce a monster. This is the central theme of *El alma enferma*; Amparo's treatment of her little daughter, Dolores, inevitably results in a hard, cruel, egotistical woman who proceeds to wreak havoc in the families around her until she is redeemed by the angelic Margarita Warner. Sinués posits the absolute centrality of motherhood to the continued well-being of society. Although her portraits of mother–daughter relationships are highly stylized, they are not idealized: there is a remarkably high proportion of bad or absent mothers.

Perhaps the most subversive aspect of Sinués's writing is her treatment of the image of the woman writer. In almost every one of her works there is a major or a minor woman character who is either a professional or an amateur writer. Sinués reverses the patriarchal trope of the *literata* (literary lady) as selfish, ugly, slatternly, and neglectful of her husband and children. All her women authors are angels of the house who manage to combine writing with being beautiful, saintly, loving mothers. She depicts writing as a purely womanly activity, through fictional mothers who write poetry and memoirs for their daughters. In times of necessity her authors support their families by their writing, such as María Mendoza, Sinués's fictional character in *Fausta Sorel*, whose name was borrowed from the Catalan novelist and poet. Frequently, Sinués intervenes through asides defending women writers, or she allows sentiments such as the following to be uttered by virtuous characters: "I don't understand why we women should be condemned with such animosity for our writing" (*Fausta Sorel* 2:472).

In a biographical essay on Faustina Sáez de Melgar, a well-known author who was her contemporary, Sinués records with great feeling the resistance of Faustina's parents to their daughter's desire to write, their refusal to allow her access to books, and their destruction of everything she wrote: "They would denounce her for loving literature as if it were a crime: they mortified her constantly with cruel ridicule" (*Biografía* 83). She comments bitterly on the scant financial rewards of writing and on the educational limitations placed in the path of the woman who becomes a writer:

> Since she is not given books, since she is not taught to do anything but sew, and knit stockings for the family, only a great effort of will on her part, only a vocation so strong that one cannot doubt but that it was sent by God, is what guides her and sustains her on her painful path. (79)

Creative women are the central subject of novels such as *El ángel de las tristezas* (1865; "The Angel of Sadness"), *Las alas de Ícaro* (1872; "Icarus's Wings"), and *La senda de la gloria* (1863; "The Road to Glory"). The latter is a brave and utopian work centered on the friendship between Julia, a painter, and Clemencia, a writer. Both are sublime models of womanhood who are highly successful and gifted in their respective fields. Julia is unhappily married to a fellow artist, Diego, who is deeply jealous of her success, and who, after being cruel and unfaithful to her, goes raving mad. Clemencia makes a happy marriage to a kindly old man who approves of her writing. Both reach the heights of fame, but it is the woman writer who survives and flourishes at the end. The title of the novel neatly conveys Sinués's message that writing is part of women's mission, filled with the ambiguity of the word "gloria," which means both "fame" and "heaven."

Interestingly, the portrayal of evil women (ostensibly as a moral lesson to her readers) functions in the Sinués novel as a means of exploring the repressed underside of bourgeois femininity. The sensational and gothic current in Sinués's work is most clearly illustrated in *Fausta Sorel*. Fausta is a poor, beautiful, motherless girl who is secretly dedicated to seeking revenge on men and the aristocracy for the sufferings of her childhood. A heartless vamp, she coolly seduces numerous men for her evil ends, defies all perils, and rises to the top of the social scale with a spotless reputation, effortlessly concealing her demonic interior. Finally confronted by her outraged husband and the police, she deftly jumps out a window and escapes into the slums, where she encounters one of her former lovers, Mauricio, who is so embittered that he throws acid in her face. Horribly disfigured, she takes to a mask and masculine disguise, and continues undeterred, setting fire to the palace of her rival, Lía. After a miraculous escape from the burning ruins, she is redeemed by a motherly nun and becomes a nun herself. Finally, stricken with consumption, she dedicates the remaining months of her life to repairing the emotional damage she has done. Through characters like these, Sinués portrays taboo themes: illegitimacy, sexuality, incest, violence, and rejection of the feminine role. The presence of the vamps also permits the angels to go into heroic action: in *Fausta Sorel* the angelic Lía has to take on a masculine disguise and send her child away in order to restore the sanity of her husband, which has been destroyed by Fausta.

Sinués's reputation as a "romantic" novelist deserves closer examination. The typical romance structure, which centers on a single heroine followed through courtship to marriage, is not seen in her work. Relationships with men are perfunctory—courtships are often dispensed with in one paragraph, whereas relationships between women form the very stuff of her fiction. The typical Sinués novel has not one heroine but several, all interrelated by friendship or family ties. In *Fausta Sorel*, for example, there are three heroines: Fausta, Lía, and Laurencia. Often, Sinués's books are family sagas, following the progress of groups of women over the course of two or three generations. Her plots are long, complicated, and full of unexpected twists, violence, seduction, betrayal, orphans, and madmen. Yet for all their sentimental melodrama, they never create the sense that marriage is the end of a woman's story; rather, it is the beginning of a life of trial. They do contain doses of domestic realism—unpleasant in-laws, sexually and temperamentally mismatched couples, disillusioned wives— as well as flashes of psychological insight. Sinués's novels present to their young women readers the possibility that marriage will be followed by the infidelity of one or both partners, illness, incompatibility, hardship, and the death of family members.

Although Sinués continued to use the same highly successful subject matter and formulas all her life, there is a telling shift toward a more favorable representation of single or working women in her later work, as well as evidence of a heightened awareness of the legal and political situation of women.

SURVEY OF CRITICISM

During her lifetime, Sinués's work was acclaimed for its instructive moral value and its powerful expression of feelings. She figured prominently in nineteenth-century literary histories, all of which described her as the most productive woman author of the time. In his prologue to *Fausta Sorel*, Miguel de Losada compared her to Balzac, and forecast a great future: "It is from young people like Mrs. Sinués de Marco that great writers are made" (20–21). Yet only a few years into the twentieth century, Sinués's name—like that of many of her female contemporaries—had almost entirely disappeared from the literary canon, displaced as "high art" by the male authors of the realist novel, which had flowered after 1868. We cannot attribute this purely to a shift in literary taste, since the men who wrote nonrealist novels at the same time as Sinués—especially Enrique Pérez Escrich, Wenceslao Ayguals de Izco, and Manuel Fernández y González—continue to be acknowledged in the history of the Spanish novel.

No critical biography of Sinués exists, but there is a useful biobibliographical piece by Alda Blanco in the *Encyclopedia of Continental Women Writers*, published by Garland. The feminist critics who first rediscovered Sinués were primarily seeking to reconstruct the image of the *ángel del hogar*, which she was so influential in promoting. As a result, they have tended to concentrate exclusively on her antifeminist, moralizing message, and their attitude has been highly condemnatory. Bridget Aldaraca calls her one of the "sentimental hacks" (63), and Estrella de Diego categorizes her as one of Spain's most antifeminist writers

(*La mujer y la pintura* 149–51; ''Prototipos y antiprototipos'' 248), as does Janet W. Pérez in ''Spanish Women Narrators of the Nineteenth Century.'' Alicia Andreu, who devotes half of her fascinating and informative *Galdós y la literatura popular* to the ideology of domesticity, shares this view and holds, furthermore, that writers such as Sinués were not only antifeminist but classist, promoting a bourgeois-aristocratic alliance at the expense of the lower classes.

Some more recent articles seek to revise this condemnatory stance. María del Carmen Simón Palmer, in ''Escritoras españolas . . . o el miedo a la marginación,'' and Cristina Enríquez de Salamanca, in ''¿Quién era la escritora del siglo XIX?,'' offer a more sympathetic reading of Sinués's work. They share the premise that Spanish women writers of her generation became the self-appointed spokeswomen for domesticity in order to atone for the ''crime'' of writing. This theory helps to explain the ambivalence present in Sinués's work and the contradiction between her advertised beliefs about women's duty to remain in the home and the way she lived her own life in public as a professional writer.

An interesting new approach to Sinués is offered by Lou Charnon-Deutsch in ''On Desire and Domesticity in Nineteenth-Century Women's Novels.'' She writes that it is time to move beyond the fruitless search for subversion in nineteenth-century women's writing. Instead, she uses psychoanalytical concepts of female desire and intersubjectivity in order to examine the domestic novel's role in the evolution of nineteenth-century feminine subjectivity, arguing that domesticity and the ''angel in the house'' were, for women, empowering concepts that opened up a space for female desire.

A comprehensive and illuminating critique of Sinués appears in Alda Blanco's forthcoming book, *The Good Woman as Writer*. Blanco documents the process whereby major female figures of the nineteenth-century literary scene, such as Sinués, were successively edged out of literary histories and critical esteem by a male establishment. She argues that the attack on the women writers of the 1850s to 1880s was framed in terms of nationalism as well as gender, and she shows how Hispanic critics, from the late nineteenth century on, repeatedly accused women's writing of being ''un-Spanish,'' ''impure,'' and ''adulterated'' by foreign (particularly French) influences. Having exposed the ideology that has so successfully contributed to the disappearance of a whole generation of women writers in Spain, Blanco goes on to argue that Sinués and her sister writers in fact played a crucial role in determining the future history both of the novel and of women in Spanish society.

NOTE

1. Elaine Showalter, *A Literature of Their Own* (Princeton: Princeton UP, 1977) 15–16.

BIBLIOGRAPHY

Works by Pilar Sinués

Mis vigilias: Poesías. Zaragoza, Spain: Imprenta de Cristóbal Juste y Olona, 1854.
Amor y llanto. Colección de leyendas históricas. Madrid: Imprenta de T. Núñez Amor, 1857.
Cantos de mi lira: Colección de leyendas en verso. Madrid: Imprenta de T. Núñez Amor, 1857.
La diadema de perlas: Novela histórica original. 2nd ed. N.p.: Imprenta de la Península, 1857.
Margarita: Novela original. 2nd ed. Madrid: Imprenta de J. Peña, 1857.
Rosa. 3rd ed. Madrid: Imprenta de J. Minuesa, 1857.
La ley de Dios: Leyendas morales. Madrid: Rivadeneyra, 1858.
El ángel del hogar: Obra moral y recreativa dedicada a la mujer. 2nd ed. Madrid: Imprenta y Esteriotipia Española de los Señores Nieto, 1859.
"Biografía de la señora Doña Faustina Sáez de Melgar." *La higuera de Villaverde*. By Faustina Sáez de Melgar. Madrid: Imprenta de D. Bernabé Fernández Barco, 1860. 77–88.
Flores del alma: Poesías. Barcelona: Establecimiento Tipográfico de N. Ramírez, 1860.
A la sombra de un tilo. Madrid: n.p., 1861.
Fausta Sorel. 2 vols. Madrid: n.p., 1861.
Un nido de palomas. Madrid: La Correspondencia de España, 1861.
A la luz de una lámpara: Colección de cuentos morales. Madrid: Imprenta Española, 1862.
Dos venganzas: Novela histórico-original. Madrid: Imprenta Española, 1862.
El lazo de flores. Madrid: n.p., 1862.
Memorias de una joven de la clase media. 2 vols. Madrid: n.p., 1862.
Narraciones del hogar. Madrid: n.p., 1862.
La rama de sándalo. 2nd ed. Madrid: n.p., 1862.
Celeste. Madrid: n.p., 1863.
Hija, esposa y madre: Cartas dedicadas a la mujer acerca de sus deberes para con la familia y la sociedad. Madrid: Imprenta Hijos de García, 1863.
La senda de la gloria. Madrid: n.p., 1863.
El sol de invierno. 2 vols. Madrid: n.p., 1863.
La virgen de las lilas. Madrid: n.p., 1863.
El alma enferma. 3 vols. Madrid: n.p., 1864.
El almohadón de rosas. Madrid: Imprenta Española, 1864.
Galería de mujeres célebres. 15 vols. Madrid: n.p., 1864–69.
No hay culpa sin pena. Madrid: n.p., 1864.
El ángel de las tristezas. Madrid: n.p., 1865.
El cetro de flores: Colección de leyendas. Madrid: Imprenta de M. Tello, 1865.
Querer es poder. Madrid: n.p., 1865.
Sueños y realidades: Memorias de una madre para su hija. Madrid: Imprenta Española, 1865.
A río revuelto. 2 vols. Madrid: n.p., 1866.

Veladas de invierno en torno de una mesa de labor. 2 vols. Barcelona: Manero, 1866.

Cuentos de color de cielo. Madrid: Leocadio López, 1867.

El camino de la dicha: Cartas a dos hermanos sobre la educación. Madrid: n.p., 1868.

La familia cristiana. Madrid: A. Pérez Dubrull, 1871.

Las alas de Ícaro. Valencia: Imprenta Católica de Piles, 1872.

El último amor. Mexico City: Tipografía de J. M. Aguilar Ortiz, 1872.

Volver bien por mal. Manila: Ramírez y Giraudier, 1872.

Una hija del siglo. Madrid: Imprenta de El Correo de las Antillas, 1873.

El becerro de oro. Barcelona: Manero, 1875.

Un libro para las damas: Estudios acerca de la educación de la mujer. Madrid: Imprenta
  de Aribau, 1875.

Combates de la vida: Dos novelas originales. Madrid: M. Minuesa, 1876.

La vida íntima: Correspondencia de dos familias del gran mundo. Madrid: Imprenta de
  Aribau, 1876.

Un libro para las madres. Madrid: Imprenta de Aribau, 1877.

Plácida. Barcelona: Manero, 1877.

La abuela. Madrid: Oficinas de la Ilustración Española y Americana, 1878.

La amiga íntima. Barcelona: Manero, 1878.

Cortesanas ilustres. Madrid: Saturnino Calleja, 1878.

Damas galantes: Historietas de amor. Madrid: Leocacio López, 1878.

Las esclavas del deber. Madrid: Saturnino Calleja, 1878.

La gitana. Madrid: Salvador Manero, 1878.

Glorias de la mujer. Madrid: Saturnino Calleja, 1878.

Las mártires del amor: Leyendas originales. Madrid: Saturnino Calleja, 1878.

La mujer en nuestros días. Madrid: Agustín Jubera, 1878.

Palmas y flores: Leyendas del hogar. Madrid: Saturnino Calleja, 1878.

Reinas mártires. Madrid: Saturnino Calleja, 1878.

Cuentos de niñas. Barcelona: n.p., 1879.

Un libro para las jóvenes: Estudio social. Madrid: n.p., 1879.

Luz y sombra: Leyendas originales. Madrid: Saturnino Calleja, 1879.

La primera falta. Barcelona, Manero, 1879.

Tres genios femeninos. Madrid: Saturnino Calleja, 1879.

*La dama elegante: Manual práctico y completísimo del buen tono y del buen orden
  doméstico.* 3rd ed. Madrid: Librería de A. de San Martín, 1880.

Una herencia trágica. 2nd ed. Madrid: Viuda e Hijos de J. A. García, 1882.

Verdades dulces y amargas: Páginas para la mujer. Madrid: Viuda e Hijos de J. A.
  García, 1882.

Dramas de familia. 2 vols. Madrid: Viuda e Hijos de J. A. García, 1883–85.

Leyendas morales. Paris: C. Bouret, 1884.

Mujeres ilustres. 3 vols. Madrid: n.p., 1884.

La vida real: Estudio social. Madrid: Imprenta y Fundación de los Hijos de J. A. García,
  1884.

La expiación. Barcelona: Manero, 1886.

Una historia sencilla. Barcelona: Manero, 1886.

La misión de la mujer. Barcelona: Manero, 1886.

Páginas del corazón. Madrid: Victoriano Suárez, 1887.

Isabel: Estudio del natural. Madrid: Imprenta de los Hijos de J. A. García, 1888.

Cómo aman las mujeres. Madrid: Administración J. Roldán [1889?].

Morir sola. Madrid: Administración B. N. Giménez, 1890.
Novelas cortas. Madrid: Victoriano Suárez, 1890.
Los ángeles de la tierra. Madrid: Hijos de J. A. García, 1891.
Cuentos de niños. 5th ed. Barcelona: Bastinos, 1898.

Translations

Doña Uraca, Queen of Leon and Castile. Trans. Reginald Huth. Bath, UK: privately printed, 1890.
The Outcasts of a King. Trans. unknown. London: Odhams, 1909.

Works about Pilar Sinués

Aldaraca, Bridget. " 'El ángel del hogar': The Cult of Domesticity in Nineteenth-Century Spain." *Theory and Practice of Feminist Literary Criticism*. Ed. Gabriela Mora and Karen S. Van Hooft. Ypsilanti; MI: Bilingual Press, 1982. 62–87.

Andreu, Alicia. *Galdós y la literatura popular*. Madrid: SGEL, 1982.

Blanco, Alda. *The Good Woman as Writer: Fiction in Mid-Nineteenth Century Spain*. Madrid: Siglo XXI. [Forthcoming]

———. "Pilar Sinués de Marco." *Encyclopedia of Continental Women Writers*. Ed. Katharina Wilson. New York: Garland Press, 1991. 1157–58.

Charnon-Deutsch, Lou. "On Desire and Domesticity in Nineteenth-Century Women's Novels." *Revista Canadiense de Estudios Hispánicos* 14.3 (1990): 395–414.

Diego, Estrella de. *La mujer y la pintura del XIX español: cuatrocientas olvidadas y algunas más*. Madrid: Cátedra, 1987.

———. "Prototipos y antiprototipos de comportamiento femenino a través de las escritoras españolas del último tercio del siglo XIX." *Literatura y vida cotidiana: Actas de las Cuartas Jornadas de Investigación Interdisciplinaria*. Ed. María Angeles Durán. Madrid: Seminario de Estudios de la Mujer, 1987. 233–50.

Enríquez de Salamanca, Cristina. "¿Quién era la escritora del siglo XIX?" *Letras Peninsulares* 2.1 (1989): 81–107.

García Llanso, Antonio, Ramón Pomés, La Baronesa de Wilson, and Alfredo Opisso. *Historia de la mujer contemporánea*. Barcelona: Libería de Antonio J. Bastinos, 1899.

Losada, Miguel de. Prologue. *Fausta Sorel*. By María de Pilar Sinués. Madrid: n.p., 1861. 20–21.

Nombela, Julio. *Impresiones y recuerdos*. 4 vols. Madrid: Casa Editorial de "La Ultima Moda," 1909.

Parada, Diego Ignacio. *Escritoras y eruditas españolas*. Madrid: Establecimiento Tipográfico de M. Minuesa, 1881.

Peña, Concha. "Pilar Sinués." *Mujeres Españolas* 56 (1930): 6–7.

Pérez, Janet W. "Spanish Women Narrators of the Nineteenth Century: Establishing a Feminist Canon." *Letras Peninsulares* 1.1 (1988): 34–50.

Segovia, Ángel. *Melonar de Madrid*. Madrid: n.p., 1876.

Simón Palmer, María del Carmen. "Escritoras españolas del siglo XIX o el miedo a la marginación." *Anales de Literatura Española* [University of Alicante] 2 (1983): 477–90.

TERESA DE JESÚS
(1515–1582)

Alison Weber

BIOGRAPHY

For centuries biographers of Teresa de Jesús, the celebrated mystic of Ávila, propagated the pious legend of her noble birth. In fact, documents first published in the 1940s revealed she was a *conversa*, or descendant of converted Jews. In an autodafé celebrated in Toledo in 1485, her paternal grandfather, Juan Sánchez de Cepeda, accused of secret Judaizing, had been "reconciled" to the Church; his ignominious sanbenito was then displayed in the parish church. Juan Sánchez moved his family to Ávila where he prospered in the silk and wool trade. By 1500 he was able to purchase a patent of *hidalguía* that proclaimed his status as a gentleman of "pure blood." His son, Alonso de Cepeda, married into an Old Christian family when he took Beatriz de Ahumada as his second wife. Teresa, born in Ávila on March 28, 1515, was the first child of this marriage.

By Teresa's own account in *Libro de la vida* (1562–65; *The Book of Her Life* 1946, 1976) she was the favorite of her father's twelve children. A gregarious and attractive girl, she delighted in reading romances of chivalry and tales of Christian martyrs. Teresa confesses that, when left motherless as an adolescent, she indulged in frivolous pastimes and other "vanities." She also alludes obliquely to a minor scandal that occurred when she was about sixteen—apparently a broken engagement with a cousin prompted her father to place her as a lay boarder in the convent of Our Lady of Grace. After eighteen months, she returned to live with her father. In 1534 Teresa ran away from home and, against her father's wishes, entered the Carmelite convent of the Incarnation in Ávila. A year after her profession in 1537, she became seriously ill and was brought to a local healer, who subjected her to a series of devastating purges that left her paralyzed and near death.

In 1538 Teresa became acquainted with a handbook on *recogimiento* (recollection) written by Francisco de Osuna. As opposed to the vocal chanting of the rosary and prayers for the souls of the dead, this form of mental prayer involved a negation of the self and passive receptivity to God's will. Though drawn to *recogimiento*, Teresa was beset by feelings of unworthiness and experienced episodes of spiritual aridity for nearly twenty years. A reading of Saint Augustine's *Confessions* in 1554 inspired a second "conversion" to mental prayer, after which Teresa began to experience frequent and powerful visions, voices, and other "quiet" or interior manifestations of the divine. As she writes in *Libro de la vida*, "Since at that time other women had fallen into serious illusions and deceptions caused by the devil, I began to be afraid" (126; ch. 23, sec. 2).[1] Her alarm was magnified by her confessors and religious advisers, who initially determined that she suffered from a demonic delusion and recommended exorcism. In time, Teresa assuaged her own doubts and won over her confessors.

In 1561 Teresa was inspired with the missionary ideal of reforming the Carmelite order. She envisioned a small, unendowed convent that would provide a safe haven for nuns who wished to devote themselves to mental prayer, free from worldly distractions and ritual obligations to patrons. Her project met with enormous opposition. As Jodi Bilinkoff has shown, Teresa's reform challenged Ávila's class and racial prejudices as well as the traditional dependence of monastic institutions on the aristocracy. Teresa was nonetheless able to marshal sufficient financial and ecclesiastical support to dedicate the convent of San José in 1562. Shortly thereafter, she began to write her first version of *Camino de perfección* (ca. 1562; *Way of Perfection* 1946, 1980) a spiritual handbook for the nuns of the new convent.

In 1567 the general of the Carmelite order granted Teresa permission to extend her reform. In the same year she met the young Carmelite monk who was to become the great poet and mystic Saint John of the Cross. Teresa won him over to her cause, entrusting him with the task of extending her reforms to the Carmelite monasteries. Over the following years until her death, this frail but indefatigable woman traversed the impossible roads of Castile and Andalusia, establishing sixteen additional Discalced religious houses. While the governance of the new convents was far from democratic, Teresa abolished distinctions based on social rank and insisted on the nuns' rights to elect their own prioress and choose their own confessors. The history of the reform is recorded in *Libro de las fundaciones* (*Book of the Foundations* 1946, 1980) begun in 1573, and expanded in 1576 and 1582.

Teresa suffered from a variety of ailments throughout her life, with symptoms that included nausea, headaches, ringing in the ears, and neuralgia. She continued to experience mystical raptures, although as she grew older she found that they were less violent and painful. In spite of poor health, she was enormously active in the administrative affairs of the order. From the evidence of her letters, she was a gregarious woman with a wide circle of friends, both religious and lay. She remained close to her large family, offering them advice and solace during their periodic economic and domestic crises. When possible, she kept her favorite niece, Teresita, at her side. In 1575 she met Jerónimo Gracián, a Carmelite priest many years her junior, who became her confessor and closest collaborator in the reform. Teresa's characteristic astuteness apparently did not extend to this ambitious confidant, whose misjudgment led the Discalced into internecine struggles with the unreformed or Calced branch of the order. In 1577 Teresa began *Moradas del castillo interior* (*The Interior Castle* 1946, 1980), a mystical treatise on the life of prayer.

In 1582 Teresa founded her last convent, in the Castilian city of Burgos, and died later that year in Alba de Tormes. She was beatified in 1614 and canonized in 1622. In 1970, in the wake of the reforms of Vatican II, Teresa was declared a doctor of the church, the first woman to be accorded this honor. Although Teresa is revered as a canonized saint and doctor of the church today, during her lifetime her orthodoxy was continually scrutinized. Her problematic standing can be analyzed in terms of three interrelated factors: her *converso* lineage, her dedication to mental prayer, and her gender.

Although Teresa was evidently aware of her Jewish ancestry, there seems to be no clear evidence of direct Judaic influence on her religious beliefs. Nonetheless, most historians concur that her *converso* background had a profound if indirect influence on her social attitudes and spiritual affiliation. In Counter-Reformation Spain, converted Jews and their descendants were subjected to wide-ranging forms of legal and social discrimination; proof of "purity of blood" was a qualification for most public offices and entry into many religious orders. Teresa's social marginality undoubtedly contributed to her disdain for "wretched honor," as she referred to her society's obsession with wealth, status, and lineage. Her dedication to mental prayer may also reflect the attraction many *conversos* shared for pietistic forms of interior Christianity. Historian Américo Castro has further speculated that Teresa's mystical longings reflect a desire to compensate for the stigma of her social origins (27–28).

Teresa's status was precarious, moreover, because her spirituality had its roots in a form of religious devotion that was the subject of intense debate in Counter-Reformation Spain. Mental prayer, many theologians warned, could lead to a neglect, if not a total rejection, of vocal prayer. Furthermore, contemplative spirituality, and the mystical raptures that sometimes resulted from it, appeared to deny the indispensable mediating role of the priest. Even those who defended the orthodoxy of mental prayer felt that it was a highly dangerous practice for those untrained in theology, especially women.

Finally, it must be remembered that Teresa lived during a period of heightened ecclesiastical misogyny. Although the pre-Reformation Catholic Church had granted women wider and more active roles, the spiritual atmosphere changed dramatically as the Spanish church armed itself to meet the threat of Protestantism. The fact that women figured prominently as leaders in a variety of pietistic movements embracing humanist, Protestant, and Illuminist tendencies further raised apprehensions that they had forgotten the biblical mandate to "wait in silence." To ensure the church's control over religious instruction and scriptural interpretation, Inquisitor Juan de Valdés in 1559 issued an Index of Prohibited Books that suppressed translations of Scripture and nearly all religious literature in the vernacular. Many families preferred to keep their daughters illiterate rather than expose them to the dangers of heresy. Although we can point to individuals, like San Pedro de Alcántara, who defended the ideal of spiritual equality of the sexes, ecclesiastical "profeminists" clearly were on the defensive in Counter-Reformation Spain. The dominant view was that women should "stick to their distaff and rosary."

The sixteenth century witnessed, furthermore, a heightened preoccupation with the power of the devil; the great witch-hunts of the period testify to the devastating consequences of this obsession. Confessors were therefore increasingly vigilant for signs of demonic possession in their spiritual daughters, since women were believed to be morally and intellectually inferior, exquisitely susceptible to the devil's seductions. As the century progressed, the Inquisition also manifested greater hostility to other, more traditional forms of female religiosity, while preachers like Pedro de Rivadeneira bewailed the plagues of "women who with their ecstasies, revelations and stigmata have upset and fooled many people."[2]

Teresa was well aware that she lived in "tiempos recios"—that the times were dangerous for women whose religious experiences surpassed routine observance. She was cognizant, too, that the Spanish church zealously guarded the priestly magisterial privilege. She continually sought guidance from *letrados* (learned theologians) and declared her obedience to the church hierarchy. As Janice Mary Luti has demonstrated, however, her obedience was "often characterized by tension, ambiguity and a high degree of strategic manipulation" ("Maestra espiritual" 218). She could not avoid several harrowing brushes with the Inquisition. In 1574 *Libro de la vida* was denounced to the Inquisition. Approved by censors in 1577, copies of the manuscript were retained in the Inquisition's archives until 1588, six years after Teresa's death. Disgruntled nuns twice appeared before the tribunal of Seville, accusing Teresa of immoral conduct and sacramental irregularities. The charges were dropped, but not before Teresa and her followers had been subjected to a rigorous investigation. Shortly after her death, a zealous Inquisitorial examiner declared Teresa an Illuminist heretic and urged that all her works be burned. Again, the Inquisition chose not to act on these denunciations.

Despite such multifarious opposition, Teresa managed to break the Pauline mandate that enjoined women to silence. Her success must be attributed not only to her skill in winning influential friends, disarming opponents, and circumventing institutional obstacles but also to her extraordinary rhetorical and magisterial gifts.

MAJOR THEMES

Teresa wrote and rewrote the text that would become known as *Libro de la vida* to defend the authenticity of her mystical experiences before a shifting circle of skeptical confessors and advisers. Following Augustine's literary as well as spiritual model, she structures her spiritual autobiography as a conversion narrative, delineating a trajectory of sin, repentance, and salvation. In a striking and subversive modification of the Augustinian model, however, Teresa suggests that her most serious transgressions were not specific "sins" but those earlier occasions when she had been tempted to abandon mental prayer and reject the mystical experiences that her confessors were now calling into question.

Another narrative thread might be described as Teresa's battle with the devil. Her antagonist is not the seductive, sexualized devil who deceives frail women by transforming himself into "the angel of light," however; he is, rather, a demon who tempts timid souls to despair of God's love and renounce their spiritual goals. With these and other subversive strategies, Teresa succeeds in transforming a written confession (with legalistic ramifications) into a psychological as well as a theological apologia.

Teresa's second work was composed at the behest of the nuns of the fledgling convent of San José. Ostensibly a gloss on the Lord's Prayer, *Camino de perfección* is in fact a guidebook to mental prayer and an impassioned defense of the rights of women to pursue the mystical path. In a censored passage from the first version of this text, Teresa boldly proclaims women's equality in God's compassionate eyes: "Lord of my soul, you did not hate women when You walked in the world; rather, you favored them always with much pity and found in them as much love and more faith than in men."[3] Teresa takes up the pen not only to transmit her knowledge of mental prayer but also to inculcate the values essential for the success of the reform: asceticism, strict poverty, and egalitarianism. She warns against exclusive friendships that might destroy the convent with factionalism and decries the preoccupation with family "honor": "[The sister] who is from the nobler lineage should be the one to speak least about her father. All the sisters must be equals" (*Camino de perfección*, Escorial Codex 348; ch. 45, sec. 2).

In *Libro de las fundaciones* Teresa records for her spiritual daughters the adventures and trials she experienced in founding the sixteen Discalced convents after San José. This is no dry-as-dust chronicle, however, but a captivating and often humorous narrative. Teresa alternates picaresque anecdotes of her triumph over petty bureaucrats and obstinate ecclesiastical authorities with dramatic tales of rebel daughters who find refuge behind the veil. The account of Beatriz de Chávez, who was cruelly abused by her parents, is particularly arresting. Though Beatriz eventually proved to be one of the unstable nuns who denounced Teresa and her prioress to the Inquisition, Teresa narrates her story with great compassion. *Libro de las fundaciones* is also a pastoral letter, a shared meditation on the inevitable conflicts between obedience and spiritual autonomy that could arise within the convent walls. Here we find a more cautious Teresa. If previously she had encouraged nuns to be resolute in their mystical vocation, she now warns of the dangers of *abobamiento* (false raptures) precipitated by excessive asceticism and melancholy humors.

Moradas del castillo interior, Teresa's description of the soul's progress toward the mystical union with the divine, is regarded as her masterpiece. She begins by comparing the soul to a castle "all of diamond or very clear crystal where there are many rooms, just as in heaven there are many mansions" (472; 1st *Morada*, ch. 1). The castle is of a crystalline rather than linear configuration, with rooms above, below, and on all sides; the central room "is where the most secret things happen between God and the soul" (473; 1st *Morada*, ch. 1). Though allegorical in its overall design, the coherence of *Moradas* is sometimes elusive, for Teresa intertwines shifting and contradictory metaphors in a way that defies linear thinking. Composed hurriedly during a period of ill health and political uncertainty, it nevertheless contains Teresa's most lyrical imagery. The soul is compared variously to a silkworm metamorphosed through God's love, to an exhausted soldier on the battlements, and to a suckling child who will perish if taken from its mother's breast. Water imagery expresses the involuntary nature of the spiritual consolations that flow into the soul effortlessly as it progresses toward higher stages of prayer. In the final chapters, the mystical marriage, in the tradition of the Song of Songs, emerges as the dominant allegorical motif. Here, the soul as bride finally surrenders to the Bridegroom's embrace.

Other works by Teresa include over 450 letters addressed to her family, friends, disciples, superiors, and the king himself; *Cuentas de conciencia* (1560–81; *Spiritual Testimonies* 1976), accounts of divine favors written over a period of years for the scrutiny of her spiritual directors; *Meditaciones sobre los Cantares* (ca. 1566; *Meditations on the Song of Songs* 1946, 1980), an exegesis inspired by verses from the Song of Songs; *Exclamaciones* (ca. 1569; *Soliloquies* 1946, 1976), a collection of brief, fervent prayers; miscellaneous writings on convent administration; and a small corpus of religious poetry.

SURVEY OF CRITICISM

Much of what has been written on Teresa over the centuries has been hagiographic in the worst sense—ahistorical, apologetic, sentimental, or chauvinistic. (In Franco's Spain, Teresa was hailed as *la santa de la raza*, "the saint of the Spanish race.") Now that once-suppressed information pertaining to Teresa's lineage (Egido Martínez, "La familia") and Inquisitorial proceedings (Llamas Martínez) is in print, the historical reassessment of Teresa is progressing apace. Advances in social and religious history, and in particular studies on contemporary heterodox movements by Francisco Márquez, Álvaro Huerga, and others, have done much to illuminate the sociotheological preconditions for Teresa's writing. Examples of revisionist Teresian historiography include Otger Steggink and Teófanes Egido Martínez's contributions to an understanding of the contentious theological climate; Bilinkoff's study of the socioeconomic context of Teresa's reform; Luti's analysis of Teresa's magisterial vocation; and Alison Weber's discussion of her dissident demonological attitudes ("Demonologist").

The best biography available in English on Teresa is by Stephen Clissold. Highly recommended is Rosa Rossi's *Teresa de Ávila. Biografía de una escritora*, the first biography to place the impact of Teresa's gender on her writing within a historical context. The volume edited by Alberto Barrientos and others offers an excellent essay on Teresa's life and times by Teófanes Egido Martínez, as well as an introduction to Teresa's individual works with an extensive bibliography on editions, and literary, historical, and doctrinal studies.

Literary criticism on Teresa can be said to begin with the comments of her first editor, the Augustinian Luis de León, who wrote in 1588: "[I]n the form of her writing, in the purity and ease of her style, in the gracefulness and skillful arrangement of the words and in an unaffected elegance which is delightful in the extreme, I doubt if there has been any writing of equal merit in our language" (qtd. in translation by Peers, *Complete Works* 3:371–72). Most subsequent criticism has continued to wrestle with the paradox of Teresa's natural artistry. For example, the great Spanish philologist Ramón Menéndez Pidal describes Teresa as, above all, a spontaneous, colloquial writer who "speaks in writing" (125). However, he also formulated the hypothesis of deliberate stylistic "debasement." Noting such substandard or "rustic" expressions as "relisión" for "religión," he wrote, "In cases such as these, deviation from correct forms undoubtedly was more difficult for her than following them; it was an act of ascetic mortification" (124). In a similar vein, Peers analyzes the colloquial disorder of Teresa's syntax, with its ellipses, convoluted parentheses, and strings of dependent clauses; yet he also finds evidence of such rhetorical figures as alliteration, antithesis, catalog, and etymological repetition ("Saint Teresa's Style").

Francisco Márquez's "Santa Teresa y el linaje" marks a significant advance in the contextualization of Teresian criticism. This 1968 essay succeeded in integrating Castro's insights on Teresa's marginality with unexplored documentary evidence on contemporary heterodox movements, and prejudices against *conversos* and *espirituales* (adherents of mental prayer). Márquez concludes that "Saint Teresa's style is a musical fugue in which the tremendous problem of expressing the ineffable is intertwined with the need to anticipate hostile interpretations at every turn (203–4). With notable results, other critics have continued to explore the pragmatics of Teresa's discourse, analyzing her response to the conflicting demands of her historical addressees (Concha, Carreño, A. Egido, Davis).

Most recent criticism has tended to qualify or reject the idea of Teresa as an "unlettered" or naive writer. Joel Sangnieux and Germán Vega García have elucidated Teresa's rich intellectual formation in terms of the print and oral cultures of her day; and Victor de la Concha shows how Teresa was influenced by contemporary sermon rhetoric as well as the new ideal of naturalness in written language advocated by Renaissance humanists. Scholars such as Márquez Villanueva, Rossi, and Luti have gone on to challenge the notion that Teresa was a reluctant writer who took up the quill only in response to her confessor's mandate. As Márquez observes, "She is ready to defy the powers of this world every time she takes her pen in hand, and 'writing from obedience' forms part of a broad alibi that informs her work, like her repeated claims of ignorance, and her recourse to a debased vocabulary'' (''Vocación'' 362). The emerging critical consensus sees Teresa's stylistic debasement as a strategic response to constraints placed on her as a woman, *conversa*, and mystic, and not simply or primarily as an act of ascetic mortification.

Attempts to achieve an overarching definition of Teresa's style, in terms of either artistry or spontaneity, have proved to be frustrating, however. Some texts were obviously written hurriedly, whereas others—notably *Camino de perfección*—were extensively revised. In significant ways, Teresa's style deviates from accepted literary norms, yet stylistic analyses (such as those of Lázaro Carreter, Lapesa, and Chorpenning) reveal a brilliant range of highly ''literary'' tropes, motifs, and narrative strategies. Again, the critical picture emerging today is that Teresa was above all a pragmatic writer, and that each work must be examined with an eye to its particular configuration of addressees and potential censors.

Much criticism written in the first half of the twentieth century reflects a tendency to define Teresa in terms of patronizing sexual stereotypes, rendering homage to her ''delicious femininity,'' ''charm,'' and ''coquetry.'' While rejecting Freudian theories of hysteria, critics like Castro and Rodolphe Hoornaert nonetheless saw in Teresa's style, as well as in her mysticism, indications of excessive feminine affectivity. Recent feminist criticism has resisted the essentialism of this tradition and has attempted to examine the implications of Teresa's gender from a sociohistorical perspective. Weber argues that Teresa paradoxically gained access to the male realm of public discourse by deliberately adopting a subversive ''rhetoric of femininity.'' That is, by exploiting stereotypes about women's language and character, Teresa was able to defend and propagate her ideas without appearing to usurp the priestly magisterial prerogative. In an article on *Meditaciones sobre los Cantares*, Carole Slade explores how Teresa disguised an audacious exegetical project and succeeded in delineating ''a uniquely feminine principle of [biblical] interpretation'' (30). From a very different viewpoint, post-Lacanian feminist theories have inspired a reconsideration of the erotic and charismatic qualities of Teresa's writing. Paul Julian Smith and Catherine Swietlicki (''Writing 'Femystic' Space''), for example, have suggested that the logical and syntactic ruptures in Teresa's prose are manifestations of *écriture féminine*, the prelogical phase of linguistic development associated with the female body.

In spite of the intense and fruitful scholarly activity of the 1970s and 1980s, it seems clear that Teresa will remain central to future interrogations of women's roles and women's writing in early modern Spain. Electa Arenal and Stacey Schlau have called attention to Teresa's significance as a literary and apostolic model for other women; this Teresian legacy is in much need of further study. Teresa's ambivalent response to the medieval tradition of female spirituality, and her place within the ecclesiastical pro- and antifeminist debates of the period, are other promising and largely unexplored topics. So, too, her success in subverting structures of authority has much to reveal about the possibilities and mechanisms of resistance within a repressive society. Finally, a study of Teresa's literary and theological reception—already initiated independently by Luti and by Weber—and her various metamorphoses as "silly woman," "manly woman," "hysteric," "coquette," and *mysterique*, could prove to be an invaluable source of information about the history of Western gender ideology since the sixteenth century.

NOTES

1. All references to Teresa de Jesús's works are to standard chapter and section divisions. Page numbers refer to the 1986 edition of *Obras completas*.
2. S. J. Pedro de Rivadeneira, "Tratado de la tribulación," *Obras escogidas*, vol. 60 of Biblioteca de Autores Españoles (Madrid: BAC, 1899) 439.
3. This passage was heavily scored with crosshatches in the first manuscript version, known as the Escorial Codex, but has been deciphered by modern editors.

BIBLIOGRAPHY

Selected Editions of Works by Teresa de Jesús

Obras completas. Ed. Efrén de la Madre de Dios and Otger Steggink. Madrid: Católica, 1986. This convenient one-volume edition includes, along with Teresa's letters, poetry, and occasional writings, the following works mentioned in this essay:

Cuentos de conciencia (1560–81)
Libro de la vida (1562–65)
Camino de perfección (ca. 1562; ca. 1566–69)
Meditaciones sobre los Cantares (ca. 1566)
Exclamaciones (ca. 1569)
Libro de las fundaciones (1573–82)
Moradas del castillo interior (1577)

Libro de la vida. Ed. Otger Steggink. Madrid: Castalia, 1986. This paperback edition of Teresa's autobiography includes an excellent introductory essay and copious notes.

Selected Translations

Peers, E. Allison, trans. *The Complete Works of St. Teresa of Jesus*. 3 vols. London: Sheed and Ward, 1946:

Vol. 1: *The Book of Her Life*
Vol. 2: *Conceptions of the Love of God (Meditations on the Song of Songs)*
         Exclamations of the Soul to God (Soliloquies)
         The Interior Castle
         The Way of Perfection
Vol. 3: *Book of the Foundations*

————. *The Letters of Saint Teresa of Jesus*. 2 vols. London: Burns and Oates, 1951. Rpt. London: Sheed and Ward, 1981.

Kavanaugh, Kieran, and Otilio Rodríguez, trans. *The Collected Works of St. Teresa of Ávila*. 3 vols. Washington, D.C.: Institute of Carmelite Studies, 1976–85.

Vol. 1 (1976): *The Book of Her Life*
Soliloquies
Spiritual Testimonies
Vol. 2 (1980): *The Interior Castle*
Meditations on the Song of Songs
The Way of Perfection
Vol. 3 (1985): *The Book of Her Foundations*
Minor works and poetry

Selected Works about Teresa de Jesús

Arenal, Electa, and Stacey Schlau. *Untold Sisters: Hispanic Nuns in Their Own Works*. With translations by Amanda Powell. Albuquerque: U of New Mexico P, 1989.

Barrientos, Alberto, et al., eds. *Introducción a la lectura de Santa Teresa*. Madrid: Espiritualidad, 1978.

Bilinkoff, Jodi. *The Avila of Saint Teresa: Religious Reform in a Sixteenth-Century City*. Ithaca; NY: Cornell UP, 1989.

Carreño, Antonio. "Las paradojas del 'Yo' autobiográfico." Criado de Val 255–64.

Castro, Américo. *Teresa la Santa y otros ensayos*. Madrid: Alfaguara, 1972.

Chorpenning, Joseph F. *The Divine Romance: Teresa of Avila's Narrative Theology*. Chicago: Loyola UP, 1993.

————. "The Monastery, Paradise and the Castle: Literary Images and Spiritual Development in St. Teresa of Avila." *Bulletin of Hispanic Studies* 62 (1985): 245–57.

Clissold, Stephen. *St. Teresa of Avila*. London: Sheldon, 1979.

Concha, Víctor G. de la. *El arte literario de Santa Teresa*. Barcelona: Ariel, 1978.

Criado de Val, Manuel, ed. *Santa Teresa y la literatura mística hispánica*. Actas del I Congreso Internacional sobre Santa Teresa y la mística hispánica. Madrid: EDI-6, 1984.

Davis, Elizabeth. "De nuevo, sobre la 'literariedad' de Teresa de Jesús." *Anuario de letras* 28 (1990): 159–80.

Egido, Aurora. "Los prólogos teresianos y la 'santa ignorancia'." Egido Martínez, *Actas del Congreso* 2: 581–607.

————. "Santa Teresa contra los letrados. Los interlocutores en su obra." *Criticón* 20 (1982): 85–121.

Egido Martínez, Teófanes. "El ambiente histórico de Santa Teresa." Barrientos 43–102.

————. "La familia judía de Santa Teresa. (Ensayo de erudición histórica)." *Studia Zamorensia* 3 (1982): 449–79.

————. "The Historical Setting of Saint Teresa." Trans. Steven Payne and Michael Dodd. *Carmelite Studies* 1 (1980): 122–80. [An abbreviated version of "El ambiente histórico"]

————. "Santa Teresa y las tendencias de la historiografía actual." *Ephemerides Carmeliticae* 33 (1982): 159–80.

———. "El tratamiento historiográfico de Santa Teresa. Inercias y revisiones." *Revista de Espiritualidad* 40 (1981): 171–89.

Egido Martínez, Teófanes, et al., eds. *Actas del Congreso Internacional Tersiano 4–7 octubre, 1982.* 2 vols. Salamanca: Universidad de Salamanca, 1983.

Hoornaert, Rodolphe. *Sainte Thérèse, écrivain, son milieu, ses facultés, son oeuvre.* Paris: Desclée de Brouwer, 1922.

Lapesa, Rafael. "Estilo y lenguaje de Santa Teresa en las 'Exclamaciones del alma a su Dios.'" *Aerum Saeculum Hispanum. Festschrift für Hans Flasche zum 70 Geburtstag.* Ed. Karl-Hermann Korner and Dietrich Briesemeister. Wiesbaden: Franz Steiner Verlag, 1983. 125–40. Rpt. in *De Ayala a Ayala: Estudios literarios y estilísticos.* Madrid: Istmo, 1988. 151–68.

Lázaro Carreter, Fernando. "Santa Teresa de Jesús, escritora." Egido Martínez, *Actas del Congreso* 1:11–27.

Llamas Martínez, Enrique. *Santa Teresa de Jesús y la Inquisición española.* Madrid: CSIC, 1972.

Luti, Janice Mary. "Teresa of Avila, maestra espiritual." Diss., Boston College, 1988. Ann Arbor: U of Michigan, 1989. 8904027.

———. *Teresa of Avila's Way.* Collegeville, MN: Liturgical Press, 1991.

Márquez Villanueva, Francisco. "Santa Teresa y el linaje." *Espiritualidad y literatura en el siglo XVI.* Madrid: Alfaguara, 1968. 141–205.

———. "La vocación literaria de Santa Teresa." *Nueva Revista de Filología Hispánica* 32 (1983): 355–74.

Menéndez Pidal, Ramón. "El estilo de Santa Teresa." *La lengua de Cristóbal Colón y otros estudios sobre el siglo XVI.* 4th ed. Madrid: Espasa-Calpe, 1958. 119–42.

Peers, E. Allison. "Saint Teresa's Style: A Tentative Appraisal." *Saint Teresa of Jesus and Other Essays and Addresses.* London: Faber and Faber, 1953. 81–135.

Rossi, Rosa. *Teresa de Avila. Biografía de una escritora.* Trans. Marieta Gargatagli. Barcelona: Icaria, 1984. [From *Teresa d'Avila. Biografia di una scrittrice.* Rome: Editori Riuniti, 1983]

Sangnieux, Joel. "Santa Teresa y los libros." Egido Martínez, *Actas del Congreso* 2: 747–64.

Slade, Carole. "Saint Teresa's *Meditaciones sobre los Cantares*: The Hermeneutics of Humility and Enjoyment." *Religion and Literature* 18 (1986): 27–44.

Smith, Paul Julian. "Writing Women in Golden Age Spain: Saint Teresa and María de Zayas." *Modern Language Notes* 102 (1987): 220–40.

Steggink, Otger. "Teresa de Jesús, mujer y mística ante la teología y los teólogos." *Carmelus* (Rome) 29 (1982): 111–29.

Swietlicki, Catherine. *Spanish Christian Cabala: The Works of Luis de León, Santa Teresa de Jesús, and San Juan de la Cruz.* Columbia: U of Missouri P, 1986.

———. "Writing 'Femystic' Space: In the Margins of Saint Teresa's 'Castillo interior.' " *Journal of Hispanic Philology* 13 (1989): 273–93.

Vega García, Germán. "La dimensión literaria de Santa Teresa." *Teresa de Jesús. Mujer. Cristiana, Maestra.* Ed. in collaboration. Madrid: Espiritualidad, 1982. 29–62.

Weber, Alison. "Saint Teresa, Demonologist." *Culture and Control in Counter-Reformation Spain.* Ed. Anne J. Cruz and Elizabeth Perry. Hispanic Issues. Minneapolis: U of Minnesota P, 1992. 171–95.

———. *Teresa of Avila and the Rhetoric of Femininity.* Princeton: Princeton UP, 1990.

ESTHER TUSQUETS
(b. 1936)

Mirella Servodidio

BIOGRAPHY

Born on August 30, 1936, to an upper-middle-class family, the Catalan writer Esther Tusquets received her primary and secondary education at the Colegio Alemán in her native Barcelona. Books and films were the reliable and cherished companions of a childhood marked by painful shyness and inflected by a strained mother–daughter relationship. By her own account, Tusquets's literary vocation had its roots in the desultory solitude of these early years, gladdened only by tales told, heard, dreamed, or imagined. Her active experimentation with poetry and prose also began early on, but came to an abrupt halt when she entered her twenties. Having specialized in history at the universities of Barcelona and Madrid, Tusquets taught for several years at the Academia Carillo, where she gave courses in literature and history. In the early 1960s, following in the footsteps of her father, Tusquets assumed the directorship of the Barcelona publishing house Editorial Lumen, a position she holds to this day. She takes special pride in having launched the Lumen series on children's literature, which she personally oversees. When she was in her mid-thirties, Tusquets gave birth, a year apart, to a daughter and a son, whom she credits with bringing balance and harmony to her life. A frequent contributor to Spanish newspapers and journals, she has been an energetic and prominent participant in Spanish cultural life.

Tusquets was forty-two when her first novel, *El mismo mar de todos los veranos* (*The Same Sea as Every Summer* 1989), appeared in 1978. In the throes of depression and marital discord, she began a vertiginous writing streak that produced four novels in as many years. Despite a gestation period of two years, laced with false starts and the author's struggle to find an authentic voice, *El mismo mar* took the world by storm by virtue of its explicit lesbian eroticism and its striking verbal prowess and stylistic assurance. Following easily and in rapid succession were the novels *El amor es un juego solitario* (1979; "Love Is a Solitary Game"), awarded the Ciudad de Barcelona Prize, and *Varada tras el último naufragio* (1980; *Stranded* 1992), which completed the trilogy initiated by *El mismo mar*. A collection of thematically related stories, *Siete miradas en un mismo paisaje* (1981; "Seven Glances at the Same Landscape"), and a children's tale, *La conejita Marcela* (1979; "Marcela the Little Rabbit"), appeared during the same period. In 1985, a four-year hiatus was broken with the publication of a fourth novel, *Para no volver* ("Never to Return").

Esther Tusquets's literary tastes and preferences run from the nineteenth-century Spanish Restoration novel to Marcel Proust, Virginia Woolf, and the writers of the Latin American Boom, with a special nod to Alejo Carpentier. Her own style is clearly linked to that of Juan Benet, however, and she readily accedes to the placement of her fiction within the broad parameters of the "new novel," a genre that since the 1970s has veered from the mimetic accuracy characterizing the social realism of the 1950s toward greater self-referentiality and formal innovation.

The metacritical inflection of Tusquets's work is unmistakable, for it is acutely conscious of its signifying practices and offers a running commentary on its condition of intertextuality. The writer engages in what she has characterized as a "perverse relationship" with language, with the ludic, sensual, phonemic allure of words—alliteration, assonance, meter, and rhyme—all that allows the eye, ear, and mind to make conscious or unconscious connections. Yet despite its self-reflexive scaffolding, Tusquets's fiction never strays far from the specific sociopolitical and existential circumstances of her biography. By her own account, Tusquets's painful self-questioning and disconformity to her social milieu have been the primary agents of her creativity, for the pen—wielded defensively or aggressively—becomes a transfigurative instrument of reparation or reform. The crucial act of the mind, then, is an act of interiorization, transforming the world into itself.

MAJOR THEMES

Tusquets's fiction is not end-determined, and plots are used in almost a residual way. Her novels instigate an obsessive viewing and reviewing of the text of life in which the literal and the figurative engage in a process of continuous and fluid exchange. Although the constituent components of all five works remain constant, they arrange themselves differently in each, much like the rotating angular facets of a single stone. With repetition as their shaping energy, they absorb, amplify, and extend each other synergetically, upholding a principle of fusion and indifferentiation that points to a single and unchanging order.

Although they locate themselves in the post-Franco era, the novels engage in a review and assessment of the crucially formative Franco years, which also are the framework of the stories of *Siete miradas*. All five of these works gesture toward a common referential reality, that of the Catalan upper bourgeoisie, which, while never explicitly foregrounded, remains a constant target of the author's barbs. This hegemonic, consumer class is portrayed as complacent and spiritually dwarfed. Surrendering to an empty aesthetic of good taste, its members have suffered a failure of vision, nerve, and leadership in setting an agenda for the post-Franco period.

Tusquets brings a feminist consciousness to bear on this insular, patriarchal world, inscribing it through the shaping sensibility of alienated female characters. Because the similarities of the female heroes exceed their differences, they coalesce as a composite character who typifies the fit between individual psychic structure and the social, economic, and sexual arrangements that prevail in post–Civil War Spain. Literate, leisured women of class and of fine-grained sensibility, Tusquets's protagonists define themselves exclusively in relationships of dependency, for they are the heirs of a cultural discourse (promulgated with special vehemence by the Sección Femenina—"Female Section"—of the Falange) that equates female virtue with passivity and self-abnegation. As members of the intellectual elite, their avid assimilation and interpretation of literature, and their constant textualization of the world and life, dramatize the powerful influence of literary codes on the psychosocial development of women. As incipient writers, they define themselves in self-trivializing terms and invariably fall short of any measurable professional achievement. Absolved of the economic terrors of self-making, they are free to indulge in immovable self-absorption. They succumb to asphyxiating lethargy and drift, periodically transcended by rounds of barbiturates and games of sex and trivial pursuit.

If the psychic pain of these privileged women springs, in part, from a socially constructed betrayal of the self, it is also frequently tied to the betrayal of the "other," the faithless partner whose desertion sparks self-scrutiny and self-doubt. Myths of love, happy endings, and "forever afters" come crashing down with a desolate thud. The illusion of female narrative autonomy is also largely shattered, for while the organizing consciousness of these works remains that of a female subject, masculinity is not relegated to parentheses. In truth, the male is still the nexus of continued authority and validation because it is his abandonment that condemns his partner to silence or provokes her to express her solitary pain. The humiliation of rejection, heightened by feelings of transience and dwindling mortality, propels the female heroes to return to the substratum of the past in search of origins and authentic selfhood. What their existential odysseys uncover are the deficits of childhood that give the lie to myths of Eden or of maternal altruism and unconditional love. Thus, in Tusquets's opus, female self-possession, subjective agency, and the right to self-determination are explicitly problematized as precarious operations that—in going against the grain of prevailing norms—are susceptible to failure. Her double-voiced narrative, in which female selfhood is both elided and affirmed, is the site of political contention, a literary space constructed from the conflicting materials of political, cultural, and sexual bias and from which the writer maintains a vigilant, disruptive stance.

The codes and characteristics of Tusquets's artistic universe are delineated in her masterful first novel, *El mismo mar de todos los veranos*. The most lavishly baroque of her works, it is written with a torrential flow of words that arrange themselves periphrastically or associatively in elongated clauses of daunting syntactic complexity. The first-person confessional narrative, suffused with tonalities of irony, parody, and cynicism, is that of a fifty-year-old professor of literature and writer manqué, newly betrayed by Julio, her movie-director husband, who has gone off with a young starlet. The narrator returns to the two homes of her childhood—that of her mother and of her grandmother—to recuperate the pastiche of texts, both read and self-invented, in which her authentic self is buried. Her story unfolds as a pre-Oedipal narrative that locates its source of movement and conflict in the figure of a mother who encodes absence and rejection and who drives the child to a compensatory reliance on the myths and fairy tales of her childhood books. In her distorted readings, designed to mirror her own existential dilemmas and lacks, all happy endings have been proscribed.

The well of solitary pain and self-depreciation is deepened by a second tale of betrayal, that of Jorge, inscribed in her university years. As the revolutionary and iconoclastic outsider, Jorge effaces the stultifying bourgeois reality and the unresolved pre-Oedipal longings that enfold her. Yet his unexplained suicide on the eve of their elopement nullifies all promises of liberation, validation, and requited love. Mentally casting herself as Ariadne abandoned by Theseus on the island of Naxos, the narrator again textualizes her life as a fiction with an unhappy end. Her subsequent marriage to Julio, the result of maternal pressure, registers a zombielike acquiescence to a conformist, bourgeois script. The daughter who is the issue of this union reenacts the cold rejection associated with the narrator's mother.

The novel's central story, however, is that of the narrator and Clara, a young Colombian student with whom—on the dare of a decadent friend—she initiates a relationship as no more than a cynical game designed to relieve her solitary tedium. However, Clara stirs the narrator's self-recognition and residual pre-Oedipal longings, for the young girl wears the vulnerability of a motherless child. With Clara as her interlocutor, she reweaves the desolate strands of her past history. Their lovemaking, which explicitly formulates a discourse of female passion and desire, and spills over into the long-awaited culmination of symbiotic fusion, subverts narrative orthodoxy as well as sociocultural norms, for it inscribes a cyclic, spatialized time. A "normal" order, however, is restored at the book's conclusion when the abulic narrator, proving incapable of shrugging off old habits or scripting new tales, is reclaimed by her husband. Like a discredited, domesticated Sappho, she is "naturalized" and returned to society's basic language of gender and a sexuality that is phallically defined.

El amor es un juego solitario, Tusquets's prize-winning second novel, overlaps metonymically with *El mismo mar* yet offers significant differences of character and intonation. Locating itself solipsistically in the interior, constricted landscapes of the mind, the novel's historic reference is weaker than that of its predecessor, for it focuses narrowly on a love triangle formed by Elia, Ricardo, and Clara. A rigorously symmetrical narrative design, governed by a third-person authorial voice, magnifies the deliberately programmed decadence of the novel.

Elia, the listless central character of *El amor*, is a younger version of her precursor and, like her, is a member of the decadent, upper bourgeoisie. Her husband and children are conspicuously absent from the space of the novel, and Elia is free to give full reign to a neurasthenic self-indulgence. Materially privileged yet spiritually deprived, she has habitually relieved the numbing inutility of her life with serial adulteries that have patterned themselves on a remembered, oft-cited childhood text: an innocent book of adventures abruptly contaminated by an obscenely graphic description of primates mating in springtime. This literary referent becomes the framing text of the novel's game of love, which is also set in spring.

Reenacting the ritualistic behavior of the female primate in heat, Elia is momentarily amused and aroused by the novelty and variance of a game of sexual initiation that first involves Ricardo, a university student and aspiring poet, who is both sexually and socially insecure. It extends to include Clara, his classmate, who mirrors the Clara of *El mismo mar* in her vulnerability and selfless homosexual devotion. All three characters are marked by failures of mother–child bonding that condition the values and attitudes each brings to love. Their frenetic and unorthodox couplings, which subvert accepted social boundaries and conventions, also undermine the expectations created by the linguistic signs of the novel's title. Fed by narcissistic self-affirmation, ''love'' is but a charade masking the power struggle of clashing wills, especially as Ricardo strives to gain mastery over his partners and draws a reluctant Clara into a lurid game of three-way sex.

The stylized gestures of play or self-conscious humor cannot camouflage an unsettling sense of cynicism and moral decay. Even more, the correlation of psychosexual codes and the game codes of society, so clearly heralded in the title, acts as a decoy and deflects attention from the real referent of the novel, which is literature itself and which transforms the codes of love and play into literary artifice and illusion. Fired by the prior readings that fertilized their own powers of invention, Elia, Clara, and Ricardo are bent on living their common adventure according to aesthetic requirements and convention. The body of *El amor* is, in fact, composed of a web of disparate texts, those already read by the three principals and those they actively write, alone or together. If love is but a game, then it is a game of the imagination, a literary act intent on staging and testing its own illusion.

Completing Tusquets's trilogy, *Varada tras el último naufragio* rereads and reconfigures the previous works as if to offer an obsessive reminder that any forward movement is predicated on an understanding and integration of the past. The novel's kinship with *El mismo mar* is especially striking, for it is grounded in the same referential and existential landscapes and, again, takes as its point of departure the depression and radical loss of self of a middle-aged female character, Elia, that is triggered by the abandonment of her husband, Jorge. A professional writer, Elia is literally silenced by her partner's defection, for she can no longer place reliance on the arsenal of words with which she has fictionalized her reality and thus been able to blunt the edge of a lifelong insecurity and a persistent obsession with death.

Jorge, a direct spin-off of the Jorge of *El mismo mar*, has been mythified by Elia as a romantic savior rescuing her from a stultifying bourgeoise reality, the Abelard to her Héloïse and the very wellspring of her creativity. Her dependency on this relationship ill prepares her for an unwanted freedom, and she uses the barbiturates prescribed by her psychiatrist to eradicate all traces of her past. However, Elia's incremental recovery of voice and self-esteem is found, in fact, to depend on a tireless looking back, the working through of the repressed and unresolved in a play of repetition. Her growing awareness of the fusions and fissures of reality and imagination, and her final resolve to use her knowledge constructively, make her one of Tusquets's more positive heroes. At the novel's conclusion, Elia's principled resistance to reconciliation with Jorge and her renewed connectedness to her son are the tangible signs of greater self-possession.

Elia's experience is also mirrored in the marital crisis of her close friend, Eva, to whose seaside home she has repaired. A feminist labor lawyer, Eva's liberalism is challenged by the discovery that Pablo, her progressive husband who has been supportive of her career, is having an ego-building affair with a girl half his age. Trapped in the roles that have been etched by biographical circumstance or failures of nerve, Eva and Pablo pull back from the self-scrutiny this crisis invites, yielding instead to pragmatic compromise and willful myopia.

The Clara of *Varada*, like the two Claras before her, is locked in a pre-Oedipal love fantasy now centered on the socially enlightened Eva, who is bent on rehabilitating her. Like the Clara of *El amor*, she mentally places herself against the backdrop of a fanciful bestiary and cosmography that recasts her childhood reading. The hero and victim of her own delusional fictions, she is less successful than Elia in breaking from the literary codes that entrap her. *Varada* thus shapes itself around a set of binary oppositions: denial/acceptance, stasis/progression, silence/enunciation, reality/imagination. A rotating point of view allows an assessment of every character by each of the others.

The stories of *Siete miradas en un mismo paisaje*, set in the period 1945–57, are, by the author's own admission, the most explicitly autobiographical of her works. Foregrounding the sociology of family life of the Catalan upper bourgeoisie, they view the development of a female protagonist, Sara, through the prism of the emblematic rites of passage that occur from the time she is nine until she turns eighteen. While the biographical circumstances and details vary for each, and no chronological order is upheld, the thematic interdependence of the seven stories and the psychic oneness of the central character create the equivalent of a fourth novel that might appropriately be seen as a prelude to Tusquets's trilogy depicting the initiatory stages of the mature hero's life.

The dramatic impressions and crucial milestones of Sara's "sentimental education" are found to be controlled by a social construction of gender freighted with an ideological content that is historically specific. The paraphernalia of culture—the values, customs, education, and habits of play of the upper bourgeoisie—are brought into bold relief, and dualities of male/female, winners/losers, adults/children, masters/servants figure the social facts of history that undergird Sara's youthful idealism. She expresses her social conscience and her opposition to the vacuous consumer society to which she belongs through the rush to artistic self-expression, a solidarity with the "losers" in the Francoist "text," and her romantic crushes and sexual experimentation with lovers, male and female, who are social and ideological outsiders. While Tusquets captures the adolescent mind in all its intensity and insecurity, the stories engage in the point and counterpoint of a double vision, for they are recounted retrospectively by a mature and jaundiced narrator. Thus, Sara's passionate enunciations and her idealistic faith in love as the reliable agency of social equality are cruelly subverted and invalidated by the desultory skepticism of authorial hindsight.

Despite an interval of four years, *Para no volver* (1985) coalesces effortlessly with the novels of Tusquets's trilogy in its extension of a principle of identity that shapes a single gender-marked tale. The case history of Elena, the menopausal protagonist, rereads both chapter and verse of the symptomologies and circumstances of her fictional sisters. Like them, Elena slips into a depression marked by feelings of uselessness and abandonment. This midlife crisis is framed by two situational concomitants: Julio, her movie-director husband, has embarked on a promotional tour with a nubile mistress firmly in tow, and her grown sons have left the nest and are leading distantly independent lives. Elena's abrupt solitude, and the tearing asunder of the domestic fabric of her life, leave her vulnerable, naked, unsure. An unpublished writer, her talent is untested, for Elena has drawn her identity exclusively from the socially abetted role of "angel in the house"—mother, mistress, and muse all in one.

Unlike Tusquets's other protagonists, Elena eventually moves beyond pharmacological solutions for her woes and enters into psychoanalysis to root out the originating causes of her psychic pain. Using a feminist perspective, Tusquets strengthens the links her earlier works established between psychosexual development and the sociocultural realm. Through Elena's relationship with her male analyst, Tusquets poses important questions regarding power, psychoanalytic discourse, and women. She also challenges the dominant concepts of a Freudian master text that theorizes psychosexual development around the experience of a male child. The novel traces Elena's resistance to analytic discourse and her wary struggle with the protocol of the patient–analyst relationship. Ironic posturing, banalization, and parody are the rhetorical manifestations of her entrenched resistance to self-knowledge. Yet at the novel's conclusion, Elena's pledge to "initiate" analysis functions as the "yes" after the final "no" and establishes her kinship with the Elia of *Varada*.

Like the stories of *Siete miradas*, the novel privileges the sociocultural text that acts as its determining point of reference. Elena is the product of clashing ideological and cultural codes created by the "unnatural marriage" of Francoism and existentialism that occurred in the 1950s and 1960s. Along with the other members of the Catalan intellectual elite, Elena's vision of a changing order was largely shaped by excursions to Paris and Perpignan, where she avidly assimilated the films, Marxist texts, and erotic magazines that were censored at home. Elena's analysis entails coming to terms with the forfeiture of youthful dreams of change and unmuzzled creativity that the members of her circle shared, and that have fallen victim to compromise, inertia, and mediocrity.

SURVEY OF CRITICISM

Despite the recentness of her fiction, Esther Tusquets has already carved out a prominent niche in the pantheon of Spanish letters. Her reputation has been helped along by the favorable reviews appearing in Spanish periodicals that have kept pace with each of her publications. They range tonally from unvarnished hyperbole—Ricardo Rico hails *El mismo mar* as a "splendid miracle" (n. pag.)— to carefully considered praise. Yet all the reviewers share a common belief in the seriousness and importance of Tusquets's fiction.

Tusquets's reputation has extended beyond the reaches of her native Spain, and her works have been translated into French, Italian, German, and English. She has been especially fortunate in capturing the attention and allegiance of a sizable contingent of North American Hispanists who have been instrumental in bringing her to American campuses for lectures and in having her elected honorary fellow of the Society of Spanish and Spanish-American Studies, in tribute to her contribution to Hispanism and to the humanities.

Tusquets's North American exegetes have produced the most meticulous and probing Tusquets scholarship to date, the lion's share of which is composed of comparative studies organized around specific thematic and formal concerns (Catherine Bellver's "The Language of Eroticism in the Novels of Esther Tusquets," Mary Vásquez's "Actor and Spectator in the Fiction of Esther Tusquets"). Of her individual works, *El mismo mar* has generated both the greatest volume and the most sustained scholarly attention, with critical essays appearing regularly from 1983 to the present. *El amor es un juego solitario*, *Para no volver*, and *Siete miradas en un mismo paisaje* have stirred a roughly equivalent share of scholarly interest. Only *Varada tras el último naufragio*, one of Tusquets's most fully realized and hopeful novels, has failed to draw exclusive critical attention, a curious inequity that even the excellent monographic volume, *The Sea of Becoming: Approaches to the Fiction of Esther Tusquets*, edited by Mary S. Vásquez, fails to redress. Nonetheless, the Vásquez tome, which contains an overview of Tusquets's fiction by the editor, ten essays, and a fully annotated bibliography by Elizabeth Espadas, offers the most comprehensive and richly varied collection of essays on Tusquets to date.

The published scholarship on Tusquets provides an interesting compendium of critical methodologies and perspectives. Numerous feminist readings have yielded provocative explorations of the problematic relationship of writing to gender. Critics like Catherine Bellver, Luis Costa, Stacey Dolgin, Linda Gould Levine, Elizabeth Ordóñez, and Mirella Servodidio have focused on the cultural and psychological aspects of gender identity, the inscription of difference in language and text, the specificity of female psychology and its symbolic realizations, theories of archetypal criticism that structure the female psyche and its quest, and the sociocultural conditioning of women in Franco Spain.

Essays dealing with intertextual and metatextual elements of Tusquets's fiction also abound. Bellver, Kathleen Glenn, Levine, Gonzalo Navajas, Geraldine Nichols, Ordóñez, and Mercedes de Rodríguez read her works against established literary canons, epistemological systems, and ideologies of power. The semiological and narratological structures of Tusquets's prose—its discursive systems and codes, its use of rhetoric, dialogue, defamiliarization, parody, and ironic rereading—have been examined by Janet Gold, Nichols, Navajas, Servodidio, Robert Spires, and Vásquez. Specific themes, symbols, and motifs have been studied by Roberta Johnson, Janet Pérez, and Carlota Marval.

The critical following Tusquets has earned seems to expand exponentially with the appearance of each new work. At this writing, new studies are being readied for publication, and scholars are poised in anticipation of the future harvests of a writer still in her creative prime.

BIBLIOGRAPHY

Works by Esther Tusquets

Novels

El mismo mar de todos los veranos. Barcelona: Lumen, 1978.
El amor es un juego solitario. Barcelona: Lumen, 1979.
Varada tras el último naufragio. Barcelona, Lumen, 1980.
Para no volver. Barcelona: Lumen, 1985.

Short Stories

La conejita Marcela. Barcelona: Lumen, 1979. [Children's story]
"Juego o el hombre que pintaba mariposas." *Cuadernos Hispanoamericanos* 347 (1979): 319–27.
Siete miradas en un mismo paisaje. Barcelona: Lumen, 1981.
"Las inútiles leyes de la simetría." *Doce relatos de mujeres*. Ed. Ymelda Navajo. Madrid: Alianza, 1982. 203–16.
"Recuerdo de Safo." *Los Cuadernos del Norte*. (Nov.–Dec. 1982): n. pag.
"Olivia." *Litoral Femenino: Literatura Escrita Por Mujeres en la España Contemporánea* 169–70 (1986): 365–71.

"La niña lunática." *Relatos eróticos*. Ed. Carmen Estévez. Madrid: Castalia, 1990. 125–46.

Translations

Lo stesso mare di ogni estate. Trans. unknown. Milan: La Tartaruga, 1979.
La mer toujours recommencée. Trans. unknown. Paris: R. Laffont, 1981.
Die Liebe ein einsames Spiel. Trans. unknown. Hamburg: Rowholt, 1982.
Arenata dopo l'ultimo naufragio. Trans. G. Masotto. Milan: Feltrinelli, 1983.
Love Is a Solitary Game. Trans. Bruce Penman. New York: Riverrun Press; London: J. Calder, 1985.
The Same Sea as Every Summer. Trans. Margaret E. W. Jones. Lincoln: U of Nebraska P, 1989.
Stranded. Trans. Susan E. Clarke. Normal, IL: Dalkey Archive Press, 1992.

Works about Esther Tusquets

Bellver, Catherine G. "Intertextuality in *Para no volver*." Vásquez 103–22.
———. "The Language of Eroticism in the Novels of Esther Tusquets." *Anales de la Literatura Contemporánea* 9.1–3 (1984): 13–27.
Costa, Luis. "*Para no volver*: Women in Franco's Spain." Vásquez 11–28.
Dolgin, Stacey L. "The Aesthetic of Eroticism in *El amor es un juego solitario*." Vásquez 79–92.
———. "Conversación con Esther Tusquets: Para salir de tanta miseria." *Anales de la Literatura Española Contemporánea* 12.3 (1988): 397–407.
———. "Esther Tusquets: proyección novelística de la psique femenina." *Los Cuadernos de Literatura* 8.44 (1987): 80–86.
Gascón Vera, Elena. "El naufragio del deseo: Esther Tusquets y Sylvia Molloy." *Plaza* 11 (1987): 20–24.
Gil Casado, Pablo. *La novela deshumanizada española, 1958–1988*. Barcelona: Anthropos, 1990. 432–52, 475–82.
Glenn, Kathleen M. "*El mismo mar de todos los veranos* and the Prism of Art." Vásquez 29–43.
Gold, Janet N. "Reading the Love Myth: Tusquets with the Help of Barthes." *Hispanic Review* 55 (1987): 337–46.
Johnson, Roberta. "On the Wave of Time: Memory in *El mismo mar de todos los veranos*." Vásquez 65–77.
Levine, Linda Gould. "Reading, Rereading, Misreading and Rewriting the Male Canon: The Narrative Web of Esther Tusquets' Trilogy." *Anales de la Literatura Española Contemporánea* 12 (1987): 203–16.
Manteiga, Robert. "El triunfo del Minotauro: Ambigüedad y razón en *El mismo mar de todos los veranos* de Esther Tusquets." *Letras Femeninas* 14.1–2 (1988): 22–31.
Marval, Carlota. "El universo erótico de Esther Tusquets." *Nueva Estafeta* 28 (1981): 72–74.
Molinaro, Nina L. *Foucault, Feminism and Power: Reading Esther Tusquets*. Lewisburg: Bucknell UP, 1991.
Murphy, Marie. "Metafictional and Erotic Games: *El amor es un juego solitario*." *La escritora hispánica: Actas de la decimotercera conferencia anual de literatura*

hispánica. Ed. Nora Erro-Orthmann and Juan Cruz Mendizábal. Miami: Indiana U of PA, Ediciones Universal, 1990. 251–59.

Navajas, Gonzalo. "Civilization and Fictions of Love in *Para no volver*." Vásquez 123–36.

———. "Repetition and the Rhetoric of Love in Esther Tusquets' *El mismo mar de todos los veranos*." *Nuevos y novísimos: Algunas perspectivas críticas sobre la narrativa española desde la década de los sesenta*. Ed. Ricardo Landeira and Luis T. González-del-Valle. Boulder, CO: Society of Spanish and Spanish-American Studies, 1987. 113–29.

———. "Retórica de la novela postmodernista española." *Siglo XX/Twentieth Century* 4 (1986–87): 16–26.

Nichols, Geraldine Cleary. "The Prison-House (and Beyond): *El mismo mar de todos los veranos*." *Romanic Review* 75.3 (1984): 366–85.

Ordóñez, Elizabeth J. "The Barcelona Group: The Fiction of Alós, Moix and Tusquets." *Letras Femeninas* 6.1 (1980): 38–50.

———. "*Para no volver*: Through the Mirror and Over the Threshold of Desire." Vásquez 137–55.

———. "A Quest for Matrilineal Roots and Mythopoesis: Esther Tusquets' *El mismo mar de todos los veranos*." *Crítica Hispánica* 6.1 (1984): 37–46.

Pérez, Janet. "Representation, Epiphany, and Passage in *Siete miradas en un mismo paisaje*." Vásquez 45–63.

Rico, Ricardo E. "Esther y el mismo mar." *La Vanguardia* 3 Aug. 1978: n. pag.

Rodríguez, Mercedes M. de. "Motivos mitológicos y del folklore en *El mismo mar de todos los veranos* de Esther Tusquets." Selected Proceedings of the Mid-America Conference on Hispanic Literature. Ed. Luis T. González-del-Valle and Catherine T. Nickel. Boulder, CO: Society of Spanish and Spanish-American Studies, 1986. 129–36.

———. "Talking with Esther Tusquets." Vásquez 173–88.

Servodidio, Mirella d'Ambrosio. "A Case of Pre-Oedipal and Narrative Fixation: Tusquets' *El mismo mar de todos los veranos*." *Anales de la Literatura Española Contemporánea* 12.2 (1987): 157–75.

———. "Esther Tusquets' Fiction: The Spinning of a Narrative Web." *Contemporary Women Authors*. Ed. Joan L. Brown. Newark, DE: U of Delaware P, 1991. 159–78.

———. "Perverse Pairings and Corrupted Codes: *El amor es un juego solitario*." *Anales de la Literatura Española Contemporánea* 11.3 (1986): 237–54.

Spires, Robert. "The Dialogic Structure of *Para no volver*." Vásquez 93–102.

Vásquez, Mary S. "Actor and Spectator in the Fiction of Esther Tusquets." *The Sea of Becoming: Approaches to the Fiction of Esther Tusquets*. Ed. Mary S. Vásquez. Westport: Greenwood Press, 1991. 157–72.

———. "Esther Tusquets and the Trilogy Which Isn't." *La Chispa 1986*. Ed. Alfredo Lozada. Baton Rouge: Louisiana State U, 1987. 243–50.

———. "Image and the Linear Progression Toward Defeat in Esther Tusquets' *El mismo mar de todos los veranos*." *La Chispa 1983*. Ed. Gilbert Paolini. New Orleans: Tulane U, 1983. 307–13.

———. "Mito y desmitificación en *Siete miradas en un mismo paisaje*." *Hacia la rehumanización del arte: Discurso femenino actual*. Ed. Adelaida López de Martínez. Madrid: Orígenes. [Forthcoming]

————. "*The Sea of Becoming*: An Introduction to the Fiction of Esther Tusquets."
    Vásquez 1–10.
————. "Tusquets, Fitzgerald and the Redemptive Power of Love." *Letras Femeninas*
    14.1–2 (1988): 10–21.

MARÍA DE ZAYAS Y SOTOMAYOR (1590?–1661?/1669?)

Marcia L. Welles and Mary S. Gossy

BIOGRAPHY

María de Zayas's life is shrouded in mystery. With the exception of a few minor corrections, very little information has been added to the findings of Manuel Serrano y Sanz in his ground-breaking *Apuntes para una biblioteca de escritoras españolas desde el año 1401 al 1833*, published in 1903. A probable baptismal document records her birth in 1590, in the parish of Saint Sebastian in Madrid, to Doña María de Barasa and Don Fernando de Zayas y Sotomayor, an infantry captain who was granted knighthood in the prestigious military order of Santiago. Her father served the seventh count of Lemos during his viceroyalty in Naples from 1610 to 1616, and indications of a special relationship to this distinguished family make plausible the assumption that María accompanied her family to Italy. Between 1621 and 1639 María de Zayas published occasional verses as prefatory material to publications by others, and panegyric verses upon the deaths of Lope de Vega and Pérez de Montalbán; evidently active in the literary academies of Madrid, she merited the praises of Alonso de Castillo Solórzano, Pérez de Montalbán, and the great Lope de Vega.

Until recently her post-1639 whereabouts remained unknown. Though some have suggested a move to Zaragoza, the fact of publication there of both first editions of her collections (1637 and 1647) does not necessarily prove residence. Kenneth Brown's edition of a *Vexamen* (academic satire in verse) by the Catalan author Francesc Fontanella, dated March 15, 1643, indicates the presence of María de Zayas in Barcelona at this time, during Catalonia's war of secession (1641–59). Her virtual disappearance after the date of the second volume of tales (1647) has led many to conjecture that she entered a convent (perhaps the oft-mentioned Conceptionist order), thus imitating the action of so many of her protagonists. It is also possible, considering her age (fifty-eight), and the lack of editorial meticulousness of this final work, that the author died shortly thereafter (Yllera 15). While there are two extant death certificates (1661, 1669) of Madrid widows bearing her name, neither seems authentic: María de Zayas was a very common name.

In an attempt to supplement the scanty and unsatisfying biographical data, one can turn to the texts to glean further information. The exclusively aristocratic environment and value system of the tales, their obvious stylistic sophistication, and the evidence of a knowledge of literary source materials, point to a writer with a privileged, though probably not formal, education. This is particularly noteworthy in the case of a woman writer.

There are no documents that indicate whether Zayas was married; it is known, however, that she was close to the poet/playwright Ana Caro de Mallén, with whom she shared a home in Madrid for a period of time. The eulogies by the famous male authors tend to ''unsex'' her by turning her into a rara avis (they refer to her as the ''Tenth Muse'' or the ''Sybil of Madrid,'' for example). In the verses of the *Laurel de Apolo* relevant to María de Zayas, Lope de Vega refers to the specifically female poetic tradition of Sappho of Lesbos, and Fontanella's satire derides the author's physical appearance as manly (*varonil*) though lacking the requisite ''equipment''—there is no ''sword'' under her skirts, conveniently called *sayas* in Spanish to allow for wordplay with the name Zayas (''Semblava a algun cavaller, / mes jas' vindrà a descubrir / que una espasa mal se amaga / baix las 'sayas' feminils'' [vv. 729–32; qtd. in Brown, *Vexamen* 231]; She looked like a gentleman, / but it will be discovered eventually / that it is hard to hide a sword / under feminine petticoats).

MAJOR THEMES

In addition to the occasional verses, María de Zayas's extant works include one play (others may have been lost), *La traición en la amistad* (mid-1600s; ''The Betrayal of Friendship''), and two collections of short stories: *Novelas amorosas y ejemplares (primera parte)* (1640s; *The Enchantments of Love. Amorous and Exemplary Novels* 1990) and *Desengaños amorosos. Parte segunda del sarao y entretenimiento honesto* (1647; ''The Disenchantments of Love'').[1] It is for these so-called *novelas cortesanas* (courtly novels) that she is justly famous. They were an instant success, and although in the second part the author refers to only three editions of the first volume (Yllera 258), there were five (or six) by 1646 (Yllera 69). The two parts were published together in 1659, and twice in 1664; their popularity continued unabated throughout the eighteenth century, during which time there were eleven editions, but declined thereafter. There were only two editions in the nineteenth century, followed by a hiatus of almost one hundred years before the appearance of Amezúa's two volumes in 1948–50, still considered the standard edition of the complete works (Alicia

Yllera's excellent 1983 critical edition for Cátedra restricts itself to *Desengaños amorosos*).

After the initial impetus of the publication of Cervantes's *Novelas ejemplares* in 1613, and the continuing influence and circulation of the Italian *novellieri* (short story writers), there was a proliferation of collections of tales. With the possible exception of Marguerite de Navarre's collection of short stories, the *Heptameron* (1559), which she would have had to read in French, María de Zayas had no known literary foremothers. The title of her first volume is undoubtedly inspired by Cervantes's and, like his, is designed to mitigate the negative association with the Italianate *novella* (short story, tale), considered lascivious in the stern moral climate of post-Tridentine Spain. Within the collection itself, the tales are consistently referred to as *maravillas* (marvels), in keeping with the aesthetic of *admiratio*, which is meant to produce wonder and surprise in the audience, thus heightening the impact of both the pleasure of the text and its instructional value. The title of the second volume has a very specific meaning. *Desengaño* (disillusionment, disenchantment) is a widespread and generalized concept in Golden Age literature, obsessed with the ascetic recognition of the difference between illusion and reality; in Zayas's work it refers exclusively to relations between the sexes, to the deceits perpetrated by men upon women.

The tales are organized within a narrative frame of clear *Decameron* provenance. In the *Novelas amorosas* ten friends (five women, five men) meet at Christmas time in the home of the convalescent Lisis and take turns telling tales of love over a five-night period. Within the frame itself an "exemplary" tale unfolds that is related to the "marvels" being told: At the beginning, Don Juan is courting Lisis but is increasingly attracted to Lisarda, whereupon Lisis accepts Don Diego as her suitor. This frame plot provides the motivation for the continuation. The group reconvenes at Carnival time, on the final day of which Lisis and Diego plan to marry. The temporal disposition of the second volume is different (three nights instead of five), as is the intent: Only the women narrate, the subject specified is not the "enchantments" but the "disenchantments" of love, and the stories must be true. The female usurpation of the narrator's role is a radical departure from the equilibrium sought between gender perspectives in the first volume (Williamsen) and prepares us for another subversion at the end. A living testament to the transformative power of fiction, Lisis, duly instructed by these tales of woe, announces her intention to renounce marriage and instead enter a convent. Her decision, which her guests greet with wonder and her suitor with despair, curiously anticipates that of the princess in Madame de Lafayette's *La Princesse de Clèves* (1678).

The success of the collections of María de Zayas was not based on the novelty of the plot, in spite of commonplace protestations to the contrary. Nor did the main themes of fate, love, honor, and death provide any innovation. What accounts, then, for the readers' pleasure in the text, then and now? To understand this, we must move beyond the customary practices governing subject matter and style, repeated and reproduced in these texts, and perceive the transgressions of the moral and aesthetic norms of received paradigms.

Of the three primary functions assigned to baroque literature—*delectare* (to delight), *prodesse* (to instruct), *movere* (to move)—only the first receives conventional treatment. Zayas declares herself a partisan of the school of her much-admired Lope de Vega, espousing the cause of a natural, accessible style and repudiating the affectations and exaggerations of the *culto* school of Gongorine fame (or notoriety). This stance indicates her involvement in the (male) literary battle of the day; it also bespeaks her concern with the clarity required to deliver a moral message, the impact of which ambiguity and difficulty would impede. Lisis states her intention to reach both *el culto y el lego* (Yllera 469–70; the tutored and the untutored), thus echoing Zayas's intention. And, because her audience was primarily female (Montesa Peydro 307–08), it was largely a *lego* group, assuming the characteristics typical of a ''popular culture''—''lowbrow'' as opposed to ''highbrow'' in its literary tastes and preferences (Montesa Peydro ch. 9).

The novelty of Zayas's didacticism is its gender-specific target audience. Her cause is a defense of women, whom she considers universally and unjustifiably maligned. In one of the frequent conflations of authorial and narrative voices, Laura in *La fuerza del amor* (''The Power of Love'') bemoans the fate of women in a society that leaves them so defenseless, debilitated physically and intellectually castrated: ''for a sword you give us the distaff, and instead of books, a sewing cushion'' (175). Female powerlessness—enunciated in propagandistic terms as a political concern within both the tales and the prefatory material— engenders many of the plot sequences and their significance: a warning to women against the deceits of men.

This is not to say that negative female portraits do not exist. Characteristically, in the tales of María de Zayas the archetypal negative feminine is manifested in the figure of a sorceress, a seductress, or a wicked older woman—a polarization that corresponds to the opposition established in Christian mythology between the temptress Eve and the chaste Mary. Does the presentation of negative examples of womanhood mitigate the impact of Zayas's feminism, converting it into a rhetorical topos with a long literary tradition (Griswold)? It is admittedly dangerous to identify authorial intention in texts. But the uniqueness of Zayas's voice, the insistence of her message, not only reiterated but also reinforced in the second collection, and the subversions of expected plot resolutions in her works warrant another interpretation. Rhetoric is, after all, not only a literary tool: It is a political one as well. Zayas's call for change, which is pervasive, is compelling in its authenticity. The ''wicked'' women do not serve to balance— in the interests of fair representation, as it were—the portrayal of the male/female dichotomy, countering misandry with misogyny. Their sex is female, but they are co-opted into the dominant system in which ''it is always the men who preside over everything'' (Yllera 118); they act in collusion with the male against other females. Adversaries instead of allies, they serve to accentuate the perilousness of a female's journey through a hostile land fraught with enemies.

To move her audience, María de Zayas makes use of such recognized sources of *admiratio* as *peripety* (unexpected reversal) and *anagnorisis* (sudden discovery or recognition), which abound in these tales of amorous intrigue where plot development is externally motivated by the vicissitudes of fortune. In addition, she does not hesitate to create more extraordinary effects. The use of magic in *La inocencia castigada* ("Innocence Punished") or witchcraft in *El desengaño amando y premio de la virtud* ("Disillusionment in Love and Virtue Rewarded"), for example, are in keeping with popular belief. Occurrences that defy empirical possibility—the appearance of the devil in *El jardín engañoso* ("The Magic Garden"), the wondrous resurrection in *El imposible vencido* ("Triumph over the Impossible"), the intervention of the Virgin Mary in *La perseguida triunfante* ("Triumph over Persecution") and *El verdugo de su esposa* ("His Wife's Executioner"), to cite some instances—are justified because they fall within the realm of what the literary theorists referred to as the "Christian marvelous."

These are not uncommon strategies in Counter-Reformation literature, however. What is unusual is Zayas's incorporation of sensationalistic effects, variously labeled "pregothic" or "pre-Romantic." In the first volume there are instances of wife-beating (Laura in *La fuerza del amor*) and lover-beating (Violante in *El prevenido engañado* ["Forewarned but Not Forearmed"] and Hipólita in *Al fin se paga todo* ["Just Deserts"]). In *El juez de su causa*, the frustrated abductor Amete hits Estela in the face and threatens her with death if she does not give in to him. The use of grotesque elements is intensified in the second volume, the *Desengaños*, and focuses on descriptions of bodily disintegration or dismemberment. Macabre decapitations occur in *Tarde llega el desengaño* ("Too Late Undeceived") and in *El traidor contra su sangre* ("Traitor to His Own Blood"), and morbid details of physical putrefaction are at their most horrific in *La inocencia castigada* ("Innocence Punished"), where, as a result of being immured, the once golden locks of Inés are filled with vermin, and her wasted body covered in excrement.

How does one assess the intent and effect of this cruelty to women? Audience expectation is certainly one factor to consider: the theater presented outrageous cases of vengeance, including, of course, such famous wife-murder plays as those of Calderón de la Barca; hagiographic materials provided examples of female martyrdom, and the bloody art of the Spanish baroque offered visual representations of violent (male) suffering (Grieve). At the aesthetic level, the intent was the elevation of the spirit through amazement and terror. At the psychological level, such chilling details, which prefigure the effect sought in the eighteenth-century gothic novel, provided for the description of intense bodily sensations without transgressing the rigid moral codes, and can thus be seen as a form of sublimation of the inherent eroticism of these tales where the search for love and concomitant avoidance of lust are the prime motivations for the action. At the political level, one could argue, the violence done to women reproduces the essential social relations between men and women in patriarchy, with its structures of dominance and submission.

An episode key to the understanding of the function of those structures appears in *La inocencia castigada*. A Moorish necromancer fashions a doll-like image of Inés, so true to life that her desperate suitor, Don Diego, verges on falling in love with it. The difference between the woman and the doll is, in fact, not great: In a trance, the enchanted Inés is deprived of the last reserve of subjecthood—discourse—and during copulation she remains consistently mute to Don Diego's solipsistic prattle. In a dreadful mirroring or inversion, the doll moves Inés against her will and she loses her consciousness; then, having regained consciousness, she loses her mobility when her husband, brother, and sister-in-law enclose her in a chimney hole for six years. This time she retains her ability to speak, however; her prayers save her when they are overheard by a neighboring young widow, who calls for help. Inés escapes the oppressions and deceits of love and matrimony by entering a convent.

In the frame tale, which provides the denouement for the collection, Lisis, accompanied by two friends and her mother, refuses marriage and enters a convent. At this point the narrative necessarily ends. When the system of exchange of women based on wealth and beauty comes to an end, the violence and cruelty that are the handmaidens of marriage also cease. Thus is resolved the unifying theme of Zayas's works: the distortion of the obsessive preoccupation with love and marriage of the prototypical *novela cortesana*.

SURVEY OF CRITICISM

A review of the secondary materials concerning María de Zayas reveals that different periods have tended to problematize different aspects of her work. In the early twentieth century, source studies predominated (E. B. Place [1923]; Bourland [1927]), followed by specific refinements in more recent commentaries, such as those by Edwin Morby (1948), Ricardo Senabre (1963), Sandra Foa (1976), Maxime Chevalier (1982). One aspect of this focus impacted upon a controversial feature of Zayas's work: the unusual sensuality evidenced in her tales, which literary historians such as George Ticknor (1849) and Ludwig Pfandl (1933) assailed as inappropriate and immodest (especially for a woman writer), as well as morally reprehensible. To account for this distinctive characteristic, Place and Senabre stress the impact of the *Decameron* on Zayas's work.

In part to counterbalance the negative assessments of Ticknor and Pfandl, in part as a natural by-product of the realist school of criticism that views literature as mimesis, in his introductory study Amezúa (1948) insists upon Zayas's fidelity to contemporary reality. He thus justifies the content on the basis of its being an accurate reflection of the life and mores of the time, unmediated by literary considerations. Juan Goytisolo has brilliantly and decisively argued against such a claim of naive realism, showing the conventionality of plots and themes and the stylized artificiality of the generic encoding of the *novela cortesana*. According to Goytisolo, the uniqueness of Zayas's novels lies exclusively in their eroticism. In fact, Zayas describes an explicit homosexual relationship between men in *Mal presagio casar lejos* ("Marrying Abroad") and a manifestly lesbian attraction in *La burlada Aminta y venganza del honor* ("Aminta Deceived and Honor's Revenge") and *Amar solo por vencer* ("Love for the Sake of Conquest").

Goytisolo is also of the opinion that, with the exception of her staunch defense of the rights of women—to education, to greater self-determination, and freedom from calumny—Zayas's ideological position is basically conservative (nostalgically traditionalist and aristocratic), an apparent contradiction further discussed by Salvador Montesa Peydro and William Clamurro. Early critics, influenced by the emerging feminist movement (Sylvania in the 1920s in the United States; Nelken and Lara in the Spain of the Second Republic in the 1930s), noted this instrumental level of feminism in Zayas's work; more recently Foa (*Feminismo*) has traced its intellectual sources in the *querelle des femmes* (debate about women) theme, the influence of Neoplatonism, and the impact of Erasmus's Christian humanism. Its political use value, which Hans Felten subsumes into the larger embrace of the contemporary moral literature of *desengaño*, is akin to that of a document such as John Stuart Mill's "The Subjection of Women," where nothing less than "the moral regeneration of mankind" is dependent on the amelioration of this most basic of relationships—between men and women. According to Lisis's summary statements at the end of the *Desengaños amorosos*, a reversal of Spain's declining political fortunes requires a radical change in men's view and treatment of women. In other words, the private, domestic world is a microcosm of the larger world, and the spheres are connected intimately.

Another approach to Zayas's feminism concerns the level of textual practice. The focus is not on the ideology expressed by authorial or narrative voices within the text but on the text itself as ideologically significant. Reading for difference, Foa ("Visión conflictiva"; *Feminismo* 86–88) compares Zayas's work with other contemporary texts, and emphasizes her rejection of the apotheosis of marriage. Montesa Peydro, in turn, moving from genre to gender, makes an ad feminam judgment, attributing this difference to what he perceives as "a phobia of men" (129) and "antimale chauvinist resentment" (125–37). Patricia Grieve convincingly outlines Zayas's revisionary treatment of Cervantine and hagiographic canons. Elizabeth Ordóñez sees Zayas's use of the convent in the resolution of the plot as an affirmation of female bonding without regard to men, and "a metonymic synonym for the women-authored text located beyond the erotic executioner's plot" (9). She links the convent with a writing space outside of conventional narrative or discourse.

This may seem similar to the "gaps and discontinuities" that Paul Julian Smith analyzes. For him, the anacolutha and ellipses that surface in Zayas's writing are evidence that ''woman's experience cannot be spoken in a man-made language without gaps and discontinuities; and that the utopia of a purely female space must be a break or threshold in a dominant male order'' (38).

Smith is trying to find a way to describe what he thinks is Zayas's *écriture féminine* (speaking or writing as a woman), as articulated by Luce Irigaray and Hélène Cixous. But, the ''syntactic disruption'' (41) that surfaces in the two women writers is also amply present in Cervantes and Góngora. Thus the question becomes why readers seize upon these traits in writing attributed to women, and try to use them as a point of entry into a feminized text object, in a way that they do not with texts written by men.

The problem may be with the conception of a ''utopia of a purely female space,'' and the reader's position in relation to that space. The space created by gaps, like the space of a convent, is not a utopia, a no-place; it is, however, a space inaccessible to the reader. The unreadable aspects of a text are, precisely, impossible to penetrate. Thus, the convent that Lisis and her friends enter is not utopia. It is a place where neither menacing marriage arrangements, nor the scopophilia (male voyeurism) that precedes it, pertain. It is simply a place for which the desiring mechanisms and interpretations of phallologocentrism are irrelevant. It exists independently of patriarchal determinations and sign systems. It is not, of necessity, ''a break or threshold in a dominant male order''—it is, rather, a place that relegates a ''male order'' to the realm of nonbeing, and makes the convent a no-place. The discomfiture produced by gaps, convents, and other supposedly ''purely female spaces'' is not that they are utopias but that they fill the reader in the male order with the dread of being a dead letter whose own address is no place. The gap, here metaphorized as the convent space, is not a ''threshold'' or a boundary/passage for some heroic reader to traverse. It is a meaning space but not to be inscribed, interpreted, or excised.

Until the end of the *Desengaños*, the characters of Zayas's stories constantly have commerce with the economies of love and marriage. The preoccupation with these themes throughout the collection shows that Zayas is aware that it is impossible to write outside patriarchy while living within it. Her usefulness for feminists in the late twentieth century is that despite epistemological limitations, her work hints at a way for women to be in the world but not of it. And that is the beginning of feminist theory.

NOTE

1. Page citations from the *Novelas amorosas y ejemplares* are to the Amezúa edition; page citations from the *Desengaños amorosos* are to the Yllera edition. English translations of novel titles of both volumes, and of the text of the first collection, are from H. Patsy Boyer, whom we thank for her generous help.

BIBLIOGRAPHY

Works by María de Zayas y Sotomayor

Plays

La traición de la amistad. MS mid-1600s. Ed. Manuel Serrano y Sanz. *Apuntes para una biblioteca de escritoras españolas desde el año 1401 al 1833.* Biblioteca de Autores Españoles. Vol. 271. Madrid: Atlas, 1975. 590–620. Rpt. of 1903 ed. Madrid: Sucesores de Rivadeneyra.

Complete Editions of Novels

For editions before the twentieth century, consult Alicia Yllera's introduction in the edition of the *Desengaños amorosos.*
Novelas amorosas y ejemplares and *Desengaños amorosos. Parte segunda del sarao y entretenimiento honesto.* Mid-1640s. Ed. Agustín G. de Amezúa. Vols. 7 and 8. Real Academia Española, Biblioteca Selecta de Clásicos Españoles, ser. 2. Madrid: Aldus, 1948–50.
Novelas completas. Ed. María Martínez del Portal. Barcelona: Bruguera, 1973. [This popular paperback edition does not include preliminary materials of the first volume: the approbations; laudatory poems; introductory note by the author, "Al que leyere" ("To the Reader"); "Prólogo de un desapasionado" ("Prologue by an Objective Reader")]
Desengaños amorosos. Ed. Alicia Yllera. Madrid: Cátedra, 1983. [This is a thorough, scholarly, and accessible edition. To the serious scholar of Zayas's work, we recommend the utilization of Amezúa's edition of the first collection and Yllera's of the second volume]

Selected Partial Editions of Novels

For further information, consult Yllera's introduction.
Novelas. La burlada Aminta y Venganza del honor. El prevenido engañado. Ed. José Hesse. Madrid: Taurus, 1965.
María de Zayas y Sotomayor. Novelas amorosas y ejemplares o Decamerón español. Ed. Eduardo Rincón. Madrid: Alianza, 1968.
Tres novelas amorosas y tres desengaños. Madrid: Castalia, Instituto de la Mujer, 1989.

Translations (Partial listing)

For full details and publication information, see Yllera's introduction.

Selected Adaptations into French

The Spanish *novela* achieved great popularity in seventeenth-century France. There were adaptations of Zayas's novels by Paul Scarron, Abbé François de Boisrobert, and M. D'Ussieux, as well as two actual translations. Of special importance are the Scarron adaptations, for the diffusion of Zayas's works was primarily through his translations—into English, German, Dutch, Russian, Italian. In addition, there are German translations of the first eight novels of volume 1, a Dutch translation (from the French) of six novels from volume 1, and an Italian translation (also from the French).

Les nouvelles tragi-comiques. Trans. Paul Scarron. Paris: Antoine de Sommaville, 1655–57. [Includes adaptions of *El prevenido engañado* and *Al fin se paga todo.* Vol. 1 of *Dernières oeuvres,* Paris 1663 also includes an adaptation of *El castigo de la miseria*]

Le Roman comique. Trans. Paul Scarron. Second Part. Paris: G. De Luyne, 1757. [Includes an adaption of *El juez de su causa*]

Selected Translations into English

Most translations into English are based on Scarron's adaptations.

The Miser Chastised. Trans. Thomas Roscoe. *The Spanish Novelists.* Vol. 2. London, 1832. 302–41. In 1880 ed., 334–52. [Trans. of *El castigo de la miseria*]

A Shameful Revenge and Other Stories. Trans. John Sturrock. London: The Folio Society, 1963. [Contains two tales from the *Novelas amorosas* and six from the *Desengaños*]

The Enchantments of Love. Amorous and Exemplary Novels. Trans. H. Patsy Boyer. Berkeley: U of California P, 1990. [This is a complete translation of the first volume of tales. Its sequel, the forthcoming "The Disenchantments of Love," has been translated by H. Patsy Boyer]

Works about María de Zayas y Sotomayor

Amezúa y Mayo, Agustín González de. *Formación y elementos de la novela cortesana.* Madrid: Tipología de Archivos, 1929.

Azorín (José Martínez Ruiz). "Doña María de Zayas." *Los clásicos redivivos. Los clásicos futuros.* 3rd ed. Madrid: Austral, 1958. 69–73.

Barbero, Teresa. "María de Zayas y Sotomayor, o la picaresca cortesana." *La Estafeta Literaria* 527 (1973): 24, 25.

Bourland, Caroline B. "Boccaccio and the *Decameron* in Castilian and Catalan Literature." *Revue Hispanique* 12 (1905): 1–232.

———. *The Short Story in Spain in the Seventeeenth Century.* Northampton, MA: Smith College, 1927. Rpt. New York: Burt Franklin, 1973.

Boyer, H. Patsy. "María de Zayas." *Women Writers of Spain: An Annotated Bio-Bibliographical Guide.* Ed. Carolyn L. Galerstein. Westport, CT: Greenwood Press, 1986. 338–39.

———. "La visión artística de María de Zayas." *Estudios sobre el Siglo de Oro en homenaje a Raymond R. MacCurdy.* Ed. Angel González, Tamara Holzapfel, and Alfred Rodríguez. Madrid: Cátedra, 1983. 253–63.

Brown, Kenneth. "Context i text del *Vexamen* d'academia de Francesc Fontanella." *Llengua i Literatura* 2 (1987): 173–252.

———. "María de Zayas y Sotomayor: Writing Poetry in Barcelona Under Siege (1643)." [In circulation]

Chevalier, Maxime. "Un cuento, una comedia, cuatro novelas (Lope de Rueda, Juan Timoneda, Cristóbal de Tamariz, Lope de Vega, María de Zayas)." *Essays on Narrative Fiction in the Iberian Peninsula in Honour of Frank Pierce.* Ed. R. B. Tate. Oxford: Dolphin, 1982. 26–38.

Clamurro, William H. "Ideological Contradiction and Imperial Decline: Towards a Reading of Zayas's *Desengaños amorosos.*" *South Central Review* 5.2 (1988): 43–50.

de Armas, Frederick A. *The Invisible Mistress: Aspects of Feminism and Fantasy in the Golden Age.* Charlottesville, VA: Biblioteca Siglo de Oro, 1976.

Diez Borque, José María. "El feminismo de doña María de Zayas." *La mujer en el teatro y la novela del siglo XVII: Actas del 11° Coloquio del Grupo de Estudios sobre Teatro Español.* Toulouse-Le Mirail: U of Toulouse-LeMirail, 1979. 61–83.

Dolz-Blackburn, Inés. "María de Zayas y Sotomayor y sus *Novelas ejemplares y amorosas.*" *Explicación de Textos Literarios* 14.2 (1985–86): 73–82.

Felten, Hans. *María de Zayas y Sotomayor. Zum Zusammenhang zwischen moralistischen Texten und Novellenliteratur.* Frankfurt am Main: V. Klostermann, 1978.

———. "La mujer disfrazada: un tópico literario y su función. Tres ejemplos de Calderón, María de Zayas y Lope de Vega." *Hacia Calderón.* Stuttgart: Franz Steiner, 1988. 77–82.

Foa, Sandra M. *Feminismo y forma narrativa. Estudio del tema y las técnicas de María de Zayas.* Valencia: Albatros, 1979.

———. "Humor and Suicide in Zayas and Cervantes." *Anales Cervantinos* 16 (1977): 71–83.

———. "María de Zayas: Visión conflictiva y renuncia del mundo." *Cuadernos hispanoamericanos* 331 (1978): 128–35.

———. "María de Zayas y Sotomayor: Sibyl of Madrid (Spanish, 1590?–1661?)." *Female Scholars: A Tradition of Learned Women Before 1600.* Ed. J. R. Brink. Montreal: Eden Press Women's Publications, 1980. 54–67.

———. "Zayas y Timoneda: elaboración de una patraña." *Revista de archivos, Bibliotecas y Museos* 79 (1976): 835–49.

Fox Lockert, Lucia. "María de Zayas." *Women Novelists in Spain and Latin America.* Metuchen, NJ: Scarecrow Press, 1979. 25–35.

Goytisolo, Juan. "El mundo erótico de María de Zayas." *Cuadernos de Ruedo Ibérico* 39–40 (1972). Rpt. in *Disidencias.* Barcelona: Seix-Barral, 1977. 63–115.

Grieve, Patricia E. "Embroidering with Saintly Threads: María de Zayas Challenges Cervantes and the Church." *Renaissance Quarterly* 44. 120–1 (1991): 86–106.

Griswold, Susan C. "Topoi and Rhetorical Distance: The 'Feminism' of María de Zayas." *Revista de Estudios Hispánicos* 14.2 (1980): 97–116.

Kaminsky, Amy Katz. "Dress and Redress: Clothing in the *Desengaños amorosos* of María de Zayas y Sotomayor." *Romanic Review* 79.2 (1988): 377–91.

King, Willard F. *Prosa novelística y academias literarias en el siglo XVII.* Madrid: Anejos del Boletín de la Real Academia Española 10, 1963.

Lara, María Victoria de. "De escritoras españolas–II. María de Zayas y Sotomayor." *Bulletin of Spanish Studies* 9 (1932): 31–37.

Levisi, Margarita. "La crueldad en los *Desengaños amorosos* de María de Zayas." *Estudios literarios de hispanistas norteamericanos dedicados a Helmut Hatzfeld con motivo de su 80 aniversario.* Ed. Josep M. Solá-Solé, Alessandro Crisafulli, and Bruno Damiani. Barcelona: Hispam, 1974. 447–56.

Maldonado, Felipe C. R. "Otra María de Zayas, . . . y van cuatro." *La Estafeta Literaria* 501 (1972): 10–13.

Martín Gaite, Carmen. "Mirando a través de la ventana." *Desde la ventana: enfoque femenino de la literatura española*. Madrid: Espasa-Calpe. 1978. 21–39.

McKay, Carol. "María de Zayas: Feminist Awareness in Seventeenth-Century Spain." *Studies in Language and Literature*. Proceedings of the 23rd Mountain Interstate Foreign Language Conference. Ed. Charles Nelson. Richmond, KY: Eastern Kentucky UP, 1976. 377–81.

McKendrick, Melveena. *Women and Society in the Spanish Drama of the Golden Age: A Study of the "Mujer varonil."* London: Cambridge UP, 1974.

Melloni, Alessandra. *Il sistema narrativo de María de Zayas*. Turin: Quaderni Ibero-Americani, 1976.

Moll, Jaime. "La primera edición de las *Novelas amorosas y exemplares* de María de Zayas y Sotomayor." *Dicenda. Cuadernos de Filología Hispánica* 1 (1982): 177–79.

Montesa Peydro, Salvador. *Texto y contexto en la narrativa de María de Zayas*. Madrid: Dirección General de la Juventud y Promoción Sociocultural, 1981.

Morby, Edwin S. "The *Difunta pleitada* Theme in María de Zayas." *Hispanic Review* 16 (1948): 238–42.

Nelken, Margarita. "Las *Novelas amorosas y exemplares* de doña María de Zayas y Sotomayor, y la escuela cínica." *Las escritoras españolas*. Barcelona: Labor, 1930. 151–55.

Oltra, José Miguel. "Zelima o el arte narrativo de María de Zayas." *Formas breves del relato*. Ed. Yves-René Fonquerne and Aurora Egido. Zaragoza, Spain: Secretariado de Publicaciones de la Universidad de Zaragoza; Madrid: Casa de Velázquez, 1986. 177–90.

Ordóñez, Elizabeth J. "Woman and Her Text in the Works of María de Zayas and Ana Caro." *Revista de Estudios Hispánicos* 19.1 (1985): 3–15.

Pabst, Walter. *La novela corta en la teoría y en la creación literaria. Notas para la historia de su antinomia en las literaturas románicas*. Trans. P. de la Vega. Madrid: Gredos, 1972.

Palomo, María del Pilar. *La novela cortesana (forma y estructura)*. Barcelona: Planeta, 1976.

Pardo Bazán, Emilia. "Breve noticia sobre doña María de Zayas y Sotomayor." *Novelas de María de Zayas y Sotomayor*. Biblioteca de la Mujer 3. Madrid, 1892. 13–14.

Pérez-Erdelyi, Mireya. *La pícara y la dama. La imagen de las mujeres en las novelas picaresco-cortesanas de María de Zayas y Sotomayor y Alonso de Castillo Solórzano*. Miami, FL: Ediciones Universal, 1979.

Pfandl, Ludwig. *Historia de la literatura nacional española en la Edad de Oro*. Trans. Jorge Rubió Balaguer. Barcelona: Sucesores de Juan Gili, 1933.

Place, Edwin B. *Manual elemental de novelística española. Bosquejo histórico de la novela corta y el cuento durante el Siglo de Oro*. Madrid: V. Suárez, 1926.

———. "María de Zayas, an Outstanding Woman Short-Story Writer of Seventeenth-Century Spain." *University of Colorado Studies* 13 (1923): 1–57.

Riera, Carmen, and Luisa Cotoner. "Los personajes femeninos de Doña María de Zayas, una aproximación." *Literatura y vida cotidiana*. Ed. M. A. Durán and J. A. Rey. Actas de las Cuartas Jornadas de Investigación Interdisciplinaria: Seminario de Estudios de la Mujer. Zaragoza: Universidad de Zaragoza; Madrid: Universidad Autónoma de Madrid, 1987. 145–59.

Rudat, Kahiluoto Eva M. "Ilusión y desengaño: el feminismo barroco de María de Zayas." *Letras Femeninas* 1 (1975): 27–43.

Sánchez, Alberto. "Un tema picaresco en Cervantes y María de Zayas." *La Picaresca: Orígenes, textos y estructuras.* Actas del I Congreso Internacional sobre la Picaresca. Ed. Manuel Criado de Val. Madrid: Fundación Universidad Española, 1979. 563–75.

Senabre Sempere, Ricardo. "La fuente de una novela de Doña María de Zayas." *Revista de Filología Española* 46 (1963): 163–72.

Serrano Poncela, Segundo. "Casamientos engañosos (Doña María de Zayas, Scarron y un proceso de creación literaria)." *Bulletin Hispanique* 44 (1962): 248–59.

Serrano y Sanz, Manuel. "Doña María de Zayas y Sotomayor." *Apuntes para una biblioteca de escritoras españolas desde el año 1401 al 1833.* Madrid: Atlas, 1975. Biblioteca de Autores Españoles. Vol. 271. 583–620. Rpt. of 1903 ed. Madrid: Sucesores de Rivadeneyra.

Simón Díaz, José. "María de Zayas y Sotomayor." *Cien escritores madrileños del Siglo de Oro (Notas bibliográficas).* Madrid: Instituto de Estudios Madrileños, 1975. 143–47.

Smith, Paul Julian. "Writing Women in the Golden Age." *The Body Hispanic.* Oxford: Clarendon P, 1990. 11–43.

―――. "Writing Women in Golden Age Spain: Saint Teresa and María de Zayas." *Modern Language Notes* 102.2 (1987): 220–40.

Spieker, Joseph B. "El feminismo como clave estructural en las novelas de doña María de Zayas." *Explicación de Textos Literarios* 6.2 (1978): 153–60.

Stackhouse, Kenneth A. "Verisimilitude, Magic and the Supernatural in the *Novelas* of María de Zayas y Sotomayor." *Hispanófila* 62 (1978): 65–76.

Stroud, Matthew D. "Love, Friendship, and Deceit in *La traición en la amistad* by María de Zayas." *Neophilologus* 69 (1985): 539–47.

Sylvania, Lena E. V. *Doña María de Zayas y Sotomayor. A Contribution to the Study of Her Works.* New York: Columbia UP, 1922. Rpt. New York: AMA Press, 1966.

Ticknor, George. *History of Spanish Literature.* Vol. 3. New York: Harper & Brothers, 1849. 143. 3 vols.

Val, Joaquín del. "La novela española en el siglo XVII." *Historia general de las literaturas hispánicas.* Ed. Guillermo Díaz-Plaja. Vol. 3. Barcelona: Barna, 1949–58. xlv–lxxx. 5 vols.

Van Praag, J. A. "Sobre las novelas de María de Zayas." *Clavileño* 15 (1952): 42–43.

Vasileski, Irma V. *María de Zayas y Sotomayor: Su época y su obra.* New York: Plaza Mayor, 1972.

Welles, Marcia L. "María de Zayas y Sotomayor and her *novela cortesana*: A re-evaluation." *Bulletin of Hispanic Studies* 55 (1978): 301–10.

Williamsen, Amy R. "Engendering Interpretation: Irony as Comic Challenge in María de Zayas." *Romance Languages Annual* 3 (1992): 643–48.

Yllera, Alicia, ed. *Desengaños amorosos.* Madrid: Cátedra, 1983. 11–110. [Critical introduction]

SELECTED BIBLIOGRAPHY

Alcalde, Carmen. *La mujer en la guerra civil española*. Madrid: Editorial Cambio 16, 1976.

Aldaraca, Bridget. "El ángel del hogar: The Cult of Domesticity in Nineteenth-Century Spain." *Theory and Practice of Feminist Literary Criticism*. Ed. Gabriela Mora and Karen S. Van Hooft. Ypsilanti, MI: Bilingual Press/Editorial Bilingüe, 1982. 62–87.

———. "The Medieval Construction of the Feminine Subject in Nineteenth-Century Spain." Vidal 395–413.

Araújo, Helena. "¿Escritura femenina?" *Escandalar* 4 (1981): 32–36.

Arenal, Electa, and Stacey Schlau. *Untold Sisters: Hispanic Nuns in Their Own Works*. Albuquerque: U of New Mexico P, 1988.

Barbeito Carneiro, María Isabel. *Escritoras madrileñas del siglo XVI (Estudio biblio-gráfico-crítico)*. Madrid: Universidad Complutense, 1986.

Bergmann, Emilie. "Reshaping the Canon: Intertextuality in Spanish Novels of Female Development." Servodidio 141–56.

Blanco, Alda. "Domesticity, Education and the Woman Writer: Spain 1850–1880." Vidal 371–94.

Brown, Joan L. *Women Writers of Contemporary Spain: Exiles in the Homeland*. Newark: U of Delaware P, 1991. [Introduction, "Women Writers of Spain: An Historical Perspective" 13–25]

Calvo de Aguilar, Isabel. *Antología biográfica de escritoras españolas*. Madrid: Biblioteca Nueva, 1954.

Campo Alange, María. *La mujer en España: Cien años de su historia*. Madrid: Aguilar, 1964.

Capel Martínez, Rosa María, ed. *Mujer y sociedad en España (1700–1975)*. Madrid: Dirección General de Juventud y Promoción Socio-Cultural, 1982.

Charnon-Deutsch, Lou. *Gender and Representation: Women in Spanish Realist Fiction*. West Lafayette, IN: Purdue U Monographs, 1990.

————. "On Desire and Domesticity in Nineteenth-Century Women's Novels." *Revista Canadiense de Estudios Hispánicos* 14.3 (Spring 1990): 395–414.

Chown, Linda E. "American Critics and Spanish Women Novelists, 1942–1980." *Signs* 9 (1983): 91–107.

Ciplijauskaité, Biruté. "El narrador, la ironía, la mujer: Perspectivas del XIX y del XX." *Homenaje a Juan López-Morillas*. Ed. José Amor y Vázquez and A. David Kossoff. Madrid: Castalia, 1982. 129–42.

————. La novela femenina contemporánea (1970–1985). *Hacia una tipología de la narración en primera persona*. Barcelona: Anthropos, 1988.

Conde, Carmen. *Poesía femenina española (1939–1950)*. Barcelona: Bruguera, 1967.

————. *Poesía femenina española (1950–1960)*. Barcelona: Bruguera, 1971.

Criado y Domínguez, Juan Pedro. *Literatas Españolas del siglo XIX: Apuntes bibliográficos*. Madrid: Imprenta de Antonio Pérez Dubrull, 1889.

Cruz, Anne J. "Studying Gender in the Spanish Golden Age." Vidal 193–222.

de Armas, Frederick A. *The Invisible Mistress: Aspects of Feminism and Fantasy in the Golden Age*. Charlottesville, VA: Biblioteca Siglo de Oro, 1976.

Deyermond, Alan. "Spain's First Women Writers." Miller 27–52.

di Febo, Giuliana. *Resistencia y movimiento de mujeres en España. 1936–1976*. Barcelona: Icaria, 1979.

Dupláa, Cristina. "Imagen femenina, hegemonía y discurso literario." Vidal 497–516.

Durán, María Angeles, and José Antonio Rey, comps. *Literatura y vida cotidiana*. Actas de las Cuartas Jornadas de Investigación Interdisciplinaria. Zaragoza: Seminario de Estudios de la Mujer, Universidad Autónoma de Madrid, 1987.

Enríquez de Salamanca, Cristina. "¿Quién era la escritora del siglo XIX?" *Letras Peninsulares* 4 (1989): 81–108.

Estreno 10.2 (Fall 1984). [Special issue devoted to Spain's women dramatists]

Fagundo, Ana María. "Twentieth-Century Spanish Poetry by Women." *Alaluz* 19.1–2 (1987), 20.1–2 (1988): 14–22.

Fernández-Quintanilla, Paloma. *La mujer ilustrada en la España del siglo XVIII*. Madrid: Ministerio de Cultura, 1981.

Ferreras, Juan Ignacio. "La novela decimonónica escrita por mujeres." *Escritoras románticas españolas*. Comp. Marina Mayoral. Madrid: Fundación Banco Exterior, 1990. 17–24.

Foa, Sandra. "Women in the Literature of Medieval and Golden Age Spain." *Conversations in the Disciplines*. Syracuse, NY: Onondaga Community College, 1979.

Fox-Lockert, Lucía. *Women Novelists in Spain and Spanish-America*. Metuchen, NJ: Scarecrow Press, 1979.

Galerstein, Carolyn L., ed. *Women Writers of Spain: An Annotated Bio-Bibliographical Guide*. Westport: Greenwood Press, 1986. [Non-Castilian materials edited by Kathleen McNerney]

Gallego Méndez, María Teresa. *Mujer, Falange y franquismo*. Madrid: Taurus, 1983.

Gómez-Ferrer, Guadalupe. "Mentalidad, vida cotidiana y literatura. Las actitudes femeninas socializadas en la novela española de la restauración." Vidal 435–72.

González, Anabel, Amalia López, Ana Mendoza, and Isabel Ureña. *Los orígenes del feminismo en España*. Madrid: Zero, S.A., 1980.

Gossy, Mary S. *The Untold Story: Women and Theory in Golden Age Texts*. Ann Arbor: U of Michigan P, 1989.

Irizarry, Estelle. "Echoes of the Amazon Myth in Medieval Spanish Literature." Miller 53–66.

Kaminsky, Amy. *Flores del agua/Water Lilies: Spanish Women Writers*. Minnesota: U of Minnesota P. [Forthcoming]

Kirkpatrick, Susan. "The Female Tradition in Nineteenth-Century Spanish Literature." Vidal 343–70.

———. *Las Románticas: Women Writers and Subjectivity in Spain, 1835–1850*. Berkeley: U of California P, 1989.

Kish, Kathleen. "A School for Wives: Women in Eighteenth-Century Spanish Theater." Miller 184–200.

Leonard, Candyce. "Women Writers and Their Characters in Spanish Drama in the 1980s." *Anales de la Literatura Española Contemporánea* 17.1–3 (1992): 243–56.

Letras Femeninas 12: 1–2 (Spring-Fall 1986). [Special issue devoted to Spanish women writers and the Civil War]

Levine, Linda Gould. "Woman as Author and Character in Franco's Spain." Miller 289–315.

———, and Gloria Feiman Waldman. *Feminismo ante el franquismo: Entrevistas con feministas de España*. Miami: Ediciones Universal, 1980.

Lindstrom, Naomi. "Feminist Criticism of Hispanic and Lusophone Literatures. Bibliographic Notes and Considerations." Vidal 19–51.

López Anglada, Luis. "La mujer en la poesía española contemporánea." *Panorama poético español (Historia y antología: 1939–64)*. Madrid: Editora Nacional, 1965.

Manteiga, Roberto, Carolyn Galerstein, and Kathleen McNerney, comps. *Feminine Concerns in Contemporary Spanish Fiction by Women*. Potomac, MD: Scripta Humanistica, 1988.

McKendrick, Melveena. "The 'Mujer Esquiva'—A Measure of the Feminist Sympathies of Seventeenth-Century Spanish Dramatists." *Hispanic Review* 40 (Spring 1972): 162–97.

———. "Women Against Wedlock: The Reluctant Brides of Golden Age Drama." Miller 115–46.

———. *Woman and Society in the Spanish Drama of the Golden Age: A Study of the "Mujer Varonil."* London: Cambridge UP, 1974.

McNerney, Kathleen, and Cristina Enríquez de Salamanca. *Double Minorities of Spain: A Bio-Bibliographical Guide to Women Writers of Catalonia, Galicia, and the Basque Country*. New York: MLA, 1993.

Miller, Beth, ed. *Women in Hispanic Literature: Icons and Fallen Idols*. Berkeley: U of California P, 1983. [Introduction, "Some Theoretical Considerations" 1–25]

Moreno, Amparo. *Mujeres en lucha: El movimiento feminista en España*. Barcelona: Editorial Anagrama, 1977.

La mujer en el teatro y la novela del siglo XVII: Actas del 11 Coloquio del Grupo de Estudios Sobre Teatro Español. Toulouse-Le Mirail: U of Toulouse-Le Mirail, 1979.

Myers, Eunice, and Ginette Adamson, eds. *Continental, Latin-American and Francophone Women Writers. Selected Papers from the Wichita State University Conference on Foreign Literatures, 1984–1985*. Lanham, MD: UP of America, 1987.

Nash, Mary. *Mujer, familia y trabajo en España (1875–1936)*. Barcelona: Anthropos, 1983.

Nichols, Geraldine C. *Des/cifrar la diferencia. Narrativa femenina de la España contemporánea.* Madrid: Siglo XXI, 1992.

———. *Escribir, espacio propio: Laforet, Matute, Moix, Tusquets, Riera y Roig por sí mismas.* Minneapolis: Institute for the Study of Ideologies and Literature, 1989.

———. "Limits Unlimited: The Strategic Use of Fantasy in Contemporary Women's Fiction of Spain." Vidal 107—28.

O'Connor, Patricia W. *Dramaturgas españolas de hoy: una introducción.* Madrid: Editorial Fundamentos, 1988.

———. "Six Dramaturgas in Search of a Stage." *Gestos* 5 (1988): 116–20.

———. "Women Dramatists in Contemporary Spain and the Male-Dominated Canon." *Signs* 15.2 (Winter 1990): 376—90.

Oñate, María del Pilar. *El feminismo en la literatura española.* Madrid: Espasa-Calpe, 1938.

Ordóñez, Elizabeth J. "Inscribing Difference: 'L'Ecriture Féminine' and New Narrative by Women." Servodidio 45–58.

———. "The Problematical Permutations of Feminist Theory." Vidal 79–94.

———. *Voices of Their Own. Contemporary Spanish Narrative by Women.* Lewisburg, PA: Bucknell UP, 1991.

Pérez, Janet, ed. *Contemporary Women Writers of Spain.* Boston: Twayne, 1988.

———. *Novelistas femeninas de la postguerra española.* Madrid: José Porrúa, 1983.

———. "Spanish Women Narrators of the Nineteenth Century: Establishing a Feminist Canon." *Letras Peninsulares* 1.1 (1988): 34–50.

Perry, Mary Elizabeth. *Gender and Disorder in Early Modern Seville.* Princeton: Princeton UP, 1990.

Resnick, Margery, and Isabelle de Courtivron, eds. *Women Writers in Translation. An Annotated Bibliography, 1945–1982.* New York: Garland, 1984.

Rodrigo, Antonina. *Mujeres de España.* Barcelona: Plaza y Janés, 1977.

Romero, Isabel, Isabel Alberdi, Isabel Martínez, and Ruth Zauner. "Feminismo y literatura: la narrativa de los años setenta." Durán and Rey 337–57.

Rovira, Rosalina R. "La función de la mujer en la literatura contemporánea española." *Explicación de Textos Literarios* 3.1 (1974): 21–24.

Rudat, Eva Kahiluoto. "La mujer ilustrada." *Letras Femeninas* 2.1 (1976): 2–32.

Salstad, Louise. *The Presentation of Women in Spanish Golden Age Literature.* Boston: G.K. Hall, 1980.

Scanlon, Geraldine. *La polémica feminista en la España contemporánea (1868–1974).* Madrid: Siglo XXI, 1976.

Serrano y Sanz, Manuel. *Antología de poetisas líricas.* Madrid: Real Academia, 1915.

———. *Apuntes para una biblioteca de escritoras españolas desde el año 1401 al 1833.* Madrid: Atlas. 1975. Biblioteca de Autores Españoles. 4 vols. Rpt. of 1903 ed. Madrid: Sucesores de Rivadeneyra.

Servodidio, Mirella, ed. *Reading for Difference: Feminist Perspectives on Women Novelists of Contemporary Spain. Anales de la Literatura Española Contemporánea* 12. 1–2 (1987). [Introduction, "Demeter or the Joyful Finding" 11–16]

Simms, Edna. "Notes on the Negative Image of Women in Spanish Literature." *CLA Journal* 19 (1976): 468–83.

Simón Palmer, María del Carmen. *Escritoras españolas del siglo XIX. Manual bio-bibliográfico.* Madrid: Castalia, 1991.

————. "Escritoras españolas del siglo XIX o el miedo a la marginación." *Anales de Literatura Española de la Universidad de Alicante* 2 (1983): 477–90.

Smith, Paul Julian. *The Body Hispanic: Gender and Sexuality in Spanish and Spanish American Literature.* New York: Oxford UP, 1989.

Sponsler, Lucy. *Women in the Medieval Spanish Epoch and Lyric Traditions.* Lexington: UP of Kentucky, 1975.

Stoll, Anita K. and Dawn L. Smith, eds. *The Perception of Women in Spanish Theater of the Golden Age.* Lewisburg, PA: Bucknell UP, 1991.

Sullivan, Constance A. "Re-reading the Hispanic Literary Canon." *Ideologies and Literature: A Journal of Hispanic and Luso-Brazilian Studies* 4 (1983): 93–101.

Traba, Marta. "Hipótesis sobre una escritura diferente." *Quimera* 13 (Nov. 1981): 9–11.

Ugalde, Sharon Keefe. *Conversaciones y poemas. La nueva poesía femenina española.* Madrid: Siglo XXI, 1991.

Valis, Noël, and Carol Maier, eds. *In the Feminine Mode: Essays on Hispanic Women Writers.* Lewisburg, PA: Bucknell UP, 1990.

Vance, Birgitta. "The Great Clash: Feminist Literary Criticism Meets up with Spanish Reality." *Journal of Spanish Studies: Twentieth Century* 2.2 (1974): 109–14.

Vidal, Hernán, ed. *Cultural and Hispanic Grounding for Hispanic and Luso-Brazilian Feminist Literary Criticism.* Minneapolis: Institute for the Study of Ideologies and Literature, 1989.

Weber, Alison, ed. Special issue of *Feminist Topics. Journal of Hispanic Philology* (Spring 1989).

Zatlin, Phyllis. "Women Novelists in Democratic Spain: Freedom to Express the Female Perspective." Servodidio 29–44.

APPENDIX A:
LIST OF AUTHORS BY DATE OF BIRTH

late fourteenth–early fifteenth century	Leonor López de Córdova
1420/25?–after 1460?	Teresa de Cartagena
1515–1582	Teresa de Jesús (Saint Teresa)
1548–1603	María de San José (María de Salazar)
1590?–1661?/1669?	María de Zayas y Sotomayor
1605–1687	Marcela de San Félix (Sor Marcela)
seventeenth century	Ana Caro Mallén de Soto
first half of seventeenth century	Leonor de la Cueva y Silva
1749–1833	Josefa Amar y Borbón
1796–1877	Cecilia Böhl de Faber y Larrea (Fernán Caballero)
1820–1893	Concepción Arenal
1823–1911	Carolina Coronado
1833?–1895	Faustina Sáez de Melgar
1835–1893	María del Pilar Sinués de Marco
1837–1885	Rosalía de Castro
1851–1921	Emilia Pardo Bazán
1851–1923	Rosario de Acuña
1852?–1919	Concepción Gimeno de Flaquer
1867–1932	Carmen de Burgos (''Colombine'')
1869–1966	Caterina Albert i Paradís (''Víctor Català'')
1874–1974	María Martínez Sierra (''Gregorio Martínez Sierra'')
1896–1968	Margarita Nelken y Mausberger

b. 1898	Rosa Chacel
1902–1984	Ángela Figuera Aymerich
1904–1988	María Teresa León
b. 1905	Ernestina de Champourcin
1906–1971	Julia Maura
1908–1983	Mercè Rodoreda
1918–1991	Maria Aurèlia Capmany
b. 1918	Gloria Fuertes
b. 1919	Teresa Pàmies
b. 1921	Carmen Laforet
b. 1922	Concha Alós
b. 1925	Carmen Martín Gaite
b. 1926	Ana María Matute
b. 1931	María Victoria Atencia
b. 1935	Lidia Falcón O'Neill
b. 1936	Esther Tusquets
b. 1938	Ana Diosdado
b. 1940	Clara Janés
b. 1942	Marina Mayoral
b. 1945	Concha Romero
1946–1991	Montserrat Roig
b. 1947	Ana María Moix
b. 1947	Soledad Puértolas
b. 1948	Carme Riera
b. 194?	Adelaida García Morales
b. 1950	Ana Rossetti
b. 1951	Rosa Montero
b. 1957	Paloma Pedrero

APPENDIX B:
WORKS AVAILABLE IN ENGLISH
TRANSLATION

Albert i Paradís, Caterina ("Víctor Català")

Solitude. (Trans. David H. Rosenthal)

Alós, Concha

"Armor." (Trans. Doris Rolfe)

Amar y Borbón, Josefa

"*Discurso sobre la educación física y moral de las mugeres* by Josefa Amar y Borbón: A Translation with Introduction and Notes." (Trans. Carmen Chaves McClendon)

Arenal, Concepción

"Spain." (Trans. Theodore Stanton)

Atencia, María Victoria

Selected Poems. (Trans. Louis Bourne)

Böhl de Faber y Larrea, Cecilia (Fernán Caballero)

Air Built Castles: Stories from the Spanish of F. Caballero. (Trans. Mrs. Pauli)
The Alvareda Family. (Trans. Viscount Pollington)
The Bird of Truth and Other Fairy Tales. (Trans. John H. Ingram)
The Castle and the Cottage in Spain. (Trans. Lady Wallace)
Elia; or, Spain Fifty Years Ago. (Trans. unknown)
"The Old and the New; or Three Souls Too Good for This World." (Trans. Helen Zimmern and Alice Zimmern)
The Sea Gull. (Trans. Augusta Bethell)
The Sea Gull. (Trans. Joan Maclean)
The Sea Gull. (Trans. J. Leander Starr)
Silence in Life and Forgiveness in Death. (Trans. J. J. Kelly)

Caro Mallén de Soto, Ana

"Valor, Affront, and Woman." (Trans. Amy Kaminsky and Donna Lazarus)

Castro, Rosalía de

Beside the River Sar. (Trans. Griswold S. Morley)

Selected poems in *The Defiant Muse: Hispanic Feminist Poems from the Middle Ages to the Present. A Bilingual Anthology.* ("Feeling Her End Would Come with Summer's End." [Trans. Kate Flores]; "From the Cadenced Roar of the Waves." [Trans. Kate Flores]; "Justice of Men! I Look for You." [Trans. Kate Flores]; "Lieder." [Trans. Angel Flores and Kate Flores]; "This One Goes and That One Goes." [Trans. Kate Flores]; "Today Black Hair." [Trans. Kate Flores])

Poems. (Trans. Anna-Marie Aldaz, Barbara N. Gantt, and Anne C. Bromley)

Poems. (Trans. Charles David Ley)

Chacel, Rosa

"Alarm!" (Trans. Rolfe Humphries)

The Maravillas District. (Trans. d. a. démers)

Teresa. Selection. (Trans. Angel Flores)

"Twilight in Extremadura." (Trans. Beatrice P. Patt)

Diosdado, Ana

"The Okapi." (Trans. Marion Peter Holt)

Figuera Aymerich, Ángela

"Accusative Case." (Trans. Diana L. Vélez)

Selected poems in *Antología bilingüe (español-inglés) de la poesía española moderna.* (Trans. Helen Wohl Patterson: "Giving," "Only Before the Man," "Without a Key")

Selected poems in *The Defiant Muse. Hispanic Feminist Poems From the Middle Ages to the Present. A Bilingual Anthology.* (Trans. Kate Flores: "Destiny," "Market Women," "Mothers")

Selected poems in *Recent Poetry of Spain. A Bilingual Anthology.* (Trans. Louis Hammer and Sara Schyfter: "If You Haven't Died for an Instant," "Insomnia," "The Jail," "My Lover's Flesh," "Symbol," "When My Father Painted," "Women of the Market")

"Unity." (Trans. Noël Valis)

Fuertes, Gloria

Selected poems in *The Defiant Muse. Hispanic Feminist Poems from the Middle Ages to the Present. A Bilingual Anthology.* ("The Bird's Nest in My Arms." [Trans. Kate Flores]; "I Don't Know." [Trans. Kate Flores]; "I Make Poems, Gentlemen!" [Trans. Kate Flores]; "Not Allowed to Write." [Trans. Robert L. Smith and Judith Candullo]; "To Have a Child These Days." [Trans. Kate Flores])

Off the Map. Selected Poems by Gloria Fuertes. (Trans. Philip Levine and Ada Long)

"Prayer." (Trans. unknown)

Selected poems in *Recent Poetry of Spain. A Bilingual Anthology.* (Trans. Louis Hammer and Sara Schyfter: "Biographical Note," "Don't Run Away from Pain," "Homage to Rubén Darío," "Hospital-old-age Asylum for the Poor," "I Fell,"

"The Lady-Termite," "Let's Not Waste Time," "Look at Me Here," "The Man's Departure," "Nighttime Tears," "The Truth Inside the Lie")

García Morales, Adelaida

The Silence of the Sirens. (Trans. Concilia Hayter)

Laforet, Carmen

Andrea. (Trans. Charles F. Payne)
Nada. (Trans. Inez Muñoz)

López de Córdova, Leonor

"To Restore Honor and Fortune: 'The Autobiography of Leonor López de Córdoba'." (Trans. Amy Katz Kaminsky and Elaine Dorough Johnson)

Marcela de San Félix (Sor Marcela)

Selected translations in *Untold Sisters: Hispanic Nuns in Their Own Works.* (Trans. Amanda Powell: "An Account of the Life of the Mother Soror Catalina de Sant Joseph, a Nun of the Order of Discalced Trinitarians," "A Spiritual Drama, Entitled *The Death of Desire*," "To a Solitude")

María de San José (María de Salazar)

Selected translations in *Untold Sisters: Hispanic Nuns in Their Own Works.* (Trans. Amanda Powell: "Book of Recreations," "Elegy," "Letter from a Poor, Imprisoned Discalced Nun")

Martín Gaite, Carmen

The Back Room. (Trans. Helen R. Lane)
Behind the Curtains. (Trans. Frances M. López-Morillas)

Martínez Sierra, María ("Gregorio Martínez Sierra")

Ana María. (Trans. Mrs. Emmon Crocker)
The Cradle Song. (Trans. John Garrett Underhill)
The Cradle Song and Other Plays. (Trans. John Garrett Underhill)
Holy Night: A Miracle Play in Three Scenes. (Trans. Philip Hereford)
Idyll. (Trans. Charlotte Marie Lorenz)
The Kingdom of God: A Play in Three Acts. (Trans. Helen Granville-Barker and Harley Granville-Barker)
Let Us Be Happy. (Trans. T. S. Richter)
A Lily Among Thorns. (Trans. Helen Granville-Barker and Harley Granville-Barker)
Love Magic. (Trans. John Garrett Underhill)
The Lover. (Trans. John Garrett Underhill)
Plays of Gregorio Martínez Sierra. (Trans. John Garrett Underhill)
Poor John. (Trans. John Garrett Underhill)
Reborn. (Trans. Nena Belmonte)
The Romantic Young Lady. (Trans. Helen Granville-Barker and Harley Granville-Barker)
Take Two from One. (Trans. Helen Granville-Barker and Harley Granville-Barker)
The Two Shepherds. (Trans. Helen Granville-Barker and Harley Granville-Barker)

Matute, Ana María

Awakening. (Trans. James H. Mason)
The Heliotrope Wall and Other Stories. (Trans. Michael S. Doyle: "Do Not Touch,"
"The Heliotrope Wall," "The King of the Zennos," "News of Young K.," "Math
Notebook," "A Star on the Skin," "Very Happy")
The Lost Children. (Trans. Joan MacLean)
School of the Sun. (Trans. Elaine Kerrigan)

Montero, Rosa

Absent Love: A Chronicle. (Trans. Cristina de la Torre and Diana Glad)
The Delta Function. (Trans. Kari Easton and Yolanda Molina Gavilán)

Pardo Bazán, Emilia

The Angular Stone. (Trans. Mary J. Serrano)
A Christian Woman. (Trans. Mary Springer)
A Galician Girl's Romance. (Trans. Mary J. Serrano)
Homesickness. (Trans. Mary J. Serrano)
The House of Ulloa. (Trans. Roser Caminals-Heath)
The House of Ulloa. (Trans. Paul O'Prey and Lucia Graves)
Midsummer Madness. (Trans. Amparo Loring)
The Mystery of the Lost Dauphin. (Trans. Annabel Hord Seeger)
The Son of the Bondswoman. (Trans. Ethel Harriet Hearn)
The Swan of Vilamorta. (Trans. Mary J. Serrano)
A Wedding Trip. (Trans. Mary J. Serrano)

Pedrero, Paloma

"The Color of August." (Trans. Phyllis Zatlin)
"Lauren's Call." (Trans. Nancy L. Rogers)
"A Night Divided." (Trans. Phyllis Zatlin)
"The Voucher." (Trans. Phyllis Zatlin)

Riera, Carme

Selected short stories in *On Our Own Behalf. Women's Tales from Catalonia*. ("A
Cool Breeze for Wanda." [Trans. Eulalia Benejam Cobb]; "I Leave You, My Love,
the Sea as a Token." [Trans. Alberto Moreiras]; "The Knot, the Void." [Trans.
Alberto Moreiras]; "Miss Angels Ruscadell Investigates the Horrible Death of Mar-
ianna Servera." [Trans. Eulalia Benejam Cobb]; "Some Flowers." [Trans. Alberto
Moreiras])

Rodoreda, Mercè

My Christina and Other Stories. (Trans. David H. Rosenthal)
The Pigeon Girl. (Trans. Eda O'Shiel)
"Summer" and "That Wall, That Mimosa." (Trans. Josep Miquel Sobrer)
The Time of the Doves. (Trans. David H. Rosenthal)
Two Tales. (Trans. David H. Rosenthal)

Roig, Montserrat

"Catalans in Nazi Death Camps." (Trans. Josep Miquel Sobrer)
The Everyday Opera. Selections. (Trans. Josep Miquel Sobrer)

Sinués de Marco, María del Pilar

Doña Uraca, Queen of Leon and Castile. (Trans. Reginald Huth)
The Outcasts of a King. (Trans. unknown)

Teresa de Jesús, Saint

The Collected Works of St. Teresa of Avila. (Trans. Kieran Kavanaugh and Otilio Rodríguez: *The Book of Her Foundations, The Book of Her Life, The Interior Castle, Meditations on the Song of Songs*, minor works and poetry, *Soliloquies, Spiritual Testimonies, The Way of Perfection*)
The Complete Works of St. Teresa de Jesús. (Trans. E. Allison Peers: *The Book of Her Life, Book of the Foundations, Conceptions of the Love of God, Exclamations of the Soul to God, The Interior Castle, The Way of Perfection*)
The Letters of Saint Teresa of Jesus. (Trans. E. Allison Peers)

Tusquets, Esther

Love is a Solitary Game. (Trans. Bruce Penman)
The Same Sea as Every Summer. (Trans. Margaret E. W. Jones)
Stranded. (Trans. Susan E. Clark)

Zayas y Sotomayor, María de

"The Disenchantments of Love." (Trans. H. Patsy Boyer)
The Enchantments of Love. Amorous and Exemplary Novels. (Trans. H. Patsy Boyer)
The Miser Chastised. (Trans. Thomas Roscoe)
A Shameful Revenge and Other Stories. (Trans. John Sturrock)

TITLE INDEX

"Canción de las locas" (Gloria Fuertes), 199

Canciones (Federico García Lorca), 184

Canciones para todo el año (Ángela Figuera Aymerich), 183

Cándida otra vez (Marina Mayoral), 331, 334

Cangura para todo (Gloria Fuertes), 197

"Cantad, hermosas" (Carolina Coronado), 120

Cantares Gallegos (Rosalía de Castro), 104, 105, 107, 108

El cant de la joventut (Montserrat Roig), 430

El cant dels messos (Víctor Català), 13, 14

Cántico, 54

Cántico inútil (Ernestna de Champourcin), 142, 144

El canto de la juventud (Montserrat Roig), 430

"Los cantos de Safo" (Carolina Coronado), 119

Caperucita en Manhattan (Carmen Martín Gaite), 291

Caracola, 54

"La cárcel" (Ángela Figuera Aymerich), 187

Cárcel de los sentidos (Ernestina de Champourcin), 143

Carmen de Burgos, defensora de la mujer (Elizabeth Starčević), 153

"Carnestoltes" (Víctor Català), 16

Carolina Coronado y su época (Adolfo de Sandoval), 122

El carrer de les Camèlies (Mercè Rodoreda), 417, 420

Carta abierta al macho ibérico (Maria Aurèlia Capmany), 79

"Carta a Eduarda" (Rosalía de Castro), xxvii

Cartas a Adriana (Clara Janés), 231

"Cartas a Juan Eugenio Hartzenbusch" (Carolina Coronado), 116

Cartas a los delincuentes (Concepción Arenal), 46, 47, 49

Cartas a mujeres de España (María Martínez Sierra), 300

Cartas a una idiota española (Lidia Falcón O'Neill), 170, 175

Cartas a un obrero (Concepción Arenal), 46

Cartas cerradas (Ernestina de Champourcin), 143

Cartas sin destinatario (Carmen de Burgos), 151

Les cartes (Víctor Català), 13

Cartes a l'Anna Murià (Mercè Rodoreda), 423

Cartes al fill recluta (Teresa Pàmies), 372

Cartes impertinents (Maria Aurèlia Capmany), 79, 81

"Casa de Blanca" (María Victoria Atencia), 57

La casa de enfrente (Ernestina de Champourcin), 142

"La casa de los espirales" (Ana Rossetti), 451

El castillo de las tres murallas (Carmen Martín Gaite), 291

Catalan, 14

Catalan Review: Homage to Mercè Rodoreda, 422, 423

El catalans als camps nazis (Montserrat Roig), 430

Catálogo bibliográfico y biográfico del teatro antiguo español (Cayetano Alberto de la Barrera y Leirado), 129

Catálogo de novelas y novelistas del siglo XIX (Juan Ignacio Ferreras), 466, 467

Catalunya. Tres generacions (J. M. Serviá), 375

Una celebridad desconocida (S. J. Julio Alarcón y Meléndez), 45

La Celestina (Fernando de Rojas), xxii

"El cel no és transparent" (Maria Aurèlia Campany), 78

Els cementiris de Barcelona (Carme Riera), 411

Chamábase Lluís (Marina Mayoral), 331, 334

"La Chanza de la Universidad" (Luis Bonafoux), 4

"Chinina Migone"(Rosa Chacel), 132

SUBJECT INDEX

Note: Pages in **boldface** indicate dictionary entries.

125, 128, 240, 457

Golden Age of Spain, *comedia*, Caro and, 89, 90, 92, 94

Golden Age of Spain, literary conventions of, xxxi; Cueva and, 126, 129; Zayas and, 509, 510

Gómez de Avellaneda, Gertrudis, 5, 6, 121, 224, 227

Gómez de la Serna, Ramón, 122, 131, 148, 150, 153, 154

Gómez-Santos, Marino, 327

Gómez Uriel, Miguel de, 38

Goncourt brothers, 381

Góngora, Luis de, 126, 510, 514

González, Ángel, 198

González, Felipe, xxviii

González-Arias, Francisca, 402

González Blanco, Andrés, 150

González Blanco, Edmundo, 150

González de Eslava, Fernán, 275

González-del-Valle, Luis, 344

González-Doria, Fernando, 445, 449

González Martín, J. P., 181, 184, 190, 204

González-Muela, Joaquín, 203, 204

González Rodas, Pablo, 201, 204, 205

Good vs. evil, as theme, xxiv; Diosdado and, 160, 161; Figuera and, 189; Maura and, 322; Sáez and, 463, 464; Sinués and, 476, 478

Gorki, Maxim, 254, 260

Gothic novel, Zayas and, 511

Gothic romance, Sinués and, 478

Gottwald, Klement, 373

Gouges, Olympe de, 39

Goya, Francisco, 30, 60

Goyri, María, 254

Goytisolo, José Agustín, 411

Goytisolo, Juan, xxv, xxxii, 310, 342, 512, 513

Gracián, Fray Jerónimo, 280, 283, 284, 486

Gracia Vicente, Alfredo, 181

Graells, Guillem-Jordi, 429

Gramsci, Antonio, 342

Granada, Fray Luis de, 280

Grassi, Ángela, xxvii, 117, 121, 461, 466, 468

Greco, El, 255

Greek mythology, xxxiii; Alós and, 28, 30; Caro and, 91; Chacel and, 134; Gimeno and, 225; Janés and, 235; León and, 257, 261; Roig and, 435, 438; Rossetti and, 454; Tusquets and, 498

"Green world" archetype, in the writings of: Alós, 28; Fuertes, 200

Grieve, Patricia E., 511, 513

Griffin, Susan, 205

Griselini, Francesco, 33, 35, 38

Griswold, Susan C., 510

Gubar, Susan, xxiii, xxvii, xxix, 305, 312, 317, 328

Guerrero, Teodoro, 227

Guerrillas de Teatro, 255, 257, 261

Guillén, Jorge, xix, 54

Guizot, François, 51

Gullón, Germán, 333, 334

Gullón, Ricardo, 292, 302, 303

Gutiérrez Abascal, José, 4

Gutiérrez de Finestrosa, Ruy, 264, 265

Hafter, Monroe Z., 123

Halevy, Salomon, 98

Haro Tecglen, Eduardo, 164

Harris, Carolyn J., 448

Hartzenbusch, Juan Eugenio, 117, 122, 123, 460

Heilbrun, Carolyn, xvi, 296, 305

Heine, Heinrich, 112

Heinerman, Theodore, 68

Hemingway, Mauricio, 385

Hennessy, Alistair, 360

Hernández, María Cruz, 175

Hernández, Miguel, xix

Hernández de Larrea, Juan Antonio, 33

Hernes, Helga María, 176

Herrera Maldonado, don Francisco de, 270

Herrero, Javier, 67, 68, 72

Hespelt, Herman, 67, 71, 72

Heterosexuality, as theme: Capmany and, 81, 83; Caro and, 91; Moix and, 342; Riera and, 406

Higgenbotham, Virginia, 249

Híjar, Marisa, 175

Love/hate relationship, as theme:
Montero and, 354; Pedrero and, 393
Love relationships and women, failed:
Cueva and, 127; Mayoral and, 333;
Rodoreda and, 418; Rossetti and, 457;
Tusquets and, 497
Love relationships and women,
impossible: Chacel and, 136; Mayoral
and, 334; Pardo Bazán and, 382; Riera
and, 407; Rodoreda and, 419
Love relationships and women,
unrequited: Cueva and, 127, 128;
Fuertes and, 201
Luis, Leopoldo de, 181, 190, 204
Luján, Micaela de, 271
Luke, 100, 102
Luna, Álvaro de, 126
Luna, Pedro de, 103
Luna-Enríquez, Doña Leonor de
(Countess of Salvatierra), 89
Lunn, Patricia V., 422
Luti, Janice Mary, 487, 489, 490, 492
Luxemburg, Rosa, 342
Lyceum Club Femenino, 258, 297
Lytton, Edward George Bulwer, 6

MacDonald, Sharman, 351
McClendon, Carmen, 39, 40
McKendrick, Melveena, 93, 94
McNerney, Kathleen, xxiii, 422, 423
Machado, Antonio, xix, 142, 171, 185, 254
Machado da Rosa, Alberto, 112
Machismo. *See* Patriarchy
Madness and women, 260, 412; Castro
and, 108, 111; Fuertes and, 199; León
and, 258, 260; Riera and, 406, 407,
412; Roig and, 435, 437
Madrazo, Enrique D., 9
Madrid Economic Society, 33, 34, 36
Maetzu, María de, xxvii, 258, 297
Magic, as theme: Caro and, 90, 91, 92;
Janés and, 239; Zayas and, 511, 512
Maillol, Aristides, 61
Male disguise and women, xxi, xxiii;
Arenal and, 44; Català and, 16, 17;
Chacel and, 135–36; Sinués and, 478.
See also Subversion, strategies of

Mallorcan dialect, Riera and, 407, 412
Mañach, Francisco, 46, 50
Mancha, Teresa de la, 133
Mandlove, Nancy, 190, 205
Mangini, Shirley, 135, 136, 138, 260
Manrique, Gómez, 99
Manrique de Lara, José Gerardo, 190
Mansfield, Katherine, 339, 426
Manteiga, Roberto, 355
Mantero, Manuel, 190
Manuel, don Juan, 264
Maragall, Joan, 13, 17, 18
Marañón, Gregorio, 152
Marcela de San Félix (Sor Marcela), xvi,
xvii, xxi, xxxii, **270–78**
March, Kathleen N., 108, 112
Marco, Joaquín, 181, 190, 260, 261
Marco, José, 473, 474
Marcos, Julián, 183, 190
Margination and women: Falcón and,
174; Fuertes and, 198; Pardo Bazán
and, 384; Rodoreda and, 418, 419,
420; Teresa de Jesús and, 486, 490
María de San José (María de Salazar),
xvii, xix, xxi, xxv, xxvii, xxix, **279–
85**
Marías, Julián, 181
Marichal, Juan, 102
Mariscal, Julio, 196
Marqués, Josep-Vicent, 176
Márquez Villanueva, Francisco, 489, 490
Marriage, as theme, xxiv, xxxi; Acuña
and, 7; Alós and, 25, 26; Amar and,
36, 37, 39; Caro and, 89, 90, 91, 92,
93, 94; Cueva and, 128; de Burgos
and, 153; Diosdado and, 159, 164;
Fuertes and, 202; Gimeno and, 225,
226; Martínez Sierra and, 299, 300;
Matute and, 313; Maura and, 323,
325; Mayoral and, 333; Nelken and,
359, 362; Pardo Bazán and, 382;
Puértolas and, 400, 401; Rodoreda
and, 419; Roig and, 433; Romero and,
444, 445; Sáez and, 463, 465; Sinués
and, 475, 479; Tusquets and, 498;
Zayas and, 92, 512, 513, 514
Marson, Ellen Engelson, 346
Martí, José, 8

452; Sáez and, 462, 464, 465, 466,
468; Sinués and, 479; Zayas and, 512–
13
Reception aesthetics, 374
Reconquest, the, 87
Regis, Celsia, 81
Religion, as theme: Arenal and, 47;
  Cartagena and, 99, 100, 101, 102;
  Champourcin and, 143, 144, 145; de
  Burgos and, 153; Laforet and, 244,
  247, 248; Marcela de San Félix and,
  275, 276; María de San José and, 281,
  282; Rossetti and, 457
Religious orders, Calced Carmelite, 486
Religious orders, Carmelite, 280; María
  de San José and, 279, 283, 284;
  Teresa de Jesús and, 279, 485
Religious orders, Conceptionist, Zayas
  and, 507
Religious orders, Discalced Carmelite,
  xxii, 486; María de San José and, 280,
  281, 282, 284; Teresa de Jesús and,
  283, 485, 488
Religious orders, Mercedarian, 274
Religious orders, Order of Guadalajara,
  López de Córdova and, 265
Religious orders, Trinitarian, Marcela de
  San Félix and, 270, 274
Religious writing: *auto sacramental*, Caro
  and, 86; *auto sacramental*, Marcela de
  San Félix and, 275; *coloquio
  espiritual*, Marcela de San Félix and,
  272, 274, 275; *loa sacramental*, Caro
  and, 88; Mariology poetry, Atencia
  and, 62; Nativity pieces, Marcela de
  San Félix and, 275–76
Renaissance, the, xvi, xxii, 130; Amar
  and, 37, 40; Coronado and, 119;
  Cueva and, 125; López de Córdova
  and, 266; Riera and, 409; Teresa de
  Jesús and, 490
Reproduction, Falcón and, 172
Resina, Joan Ramón, 422
Restoration novel, Tusquets and, 496
Restoration of 1874, 105, 109
"Revisionist mythmaking," 346; Janés
  and, 235; Moix and, 345

"Revolutionary" literature, León and,
  260
Revolution of 1868, 105, 461
Reyes, Alfonso, 143
Rhys, Jean, 339
Riba, Carles, 14
Rich, Adrienne, 63, 204, 448
Rico, Ricardo, 502
Riddel, María Carmen, 316
Riera, Carme, xxviii, xxx, 374, **404–14**
Riera, Miguel, 398, 401
Riestra, Gloria, 205
Riffatere, Michael, 204
Ríos, Blanca de la, 150
Rites of initiation, Laforet and, 249
Rites of passage, xvii; Laforet and, 245;
  Moix and, 344; Tusquets and, 500
Rivadeneira, Pedro de, 487, 492
Roca de Togores, María Teresa, 141
Rodin, Auguste, 56
Rodoreda, Mercè, xvi, xvii, xviii, xix,
  xxi, xxvi, xxix, 374, 411, **415–28**;
  Moix and, 338, 339; Roig and, 433,
  435
Rodrigo, Antonina, 253, 254, 255, 256,
  259
Rodríguez, Ana, 138
Rodríguez, Claudio, 198
Rodríguez, Fermín, 24, 29
Rodríguez Luis, Julio, 70
Rodríguez, Mario B., 327
Rodríguez, Mercedes de, 503
Rodríguez Sánchez, Francisco, 104, 105,
  106, 112
Rof Carballo, J., 105
Roger, Isabel, 293
Rogers, Elizabeth, 437
Rogers, Timothy, 204
Roig, Montserrat, xii, xvi, xviii, xxvi,
  xxviii, xxix, 374, **429–40**
Roig i Llop, Tomàs, 429
Rojas, Fernando de, xxii, xxxii
Roldán, Concha, 397, 398
Roman Mythology, xxiv; Romero and,
  447
Romanticism: Acuña and, 2; Caballero
  and, 72; Coronado and, 119; Pardo
  Bazán and, 381; Rossetti and, 452;

Rossetti and, 456; Teresa de Jesús and, 492; Zayas and, 508, 512

Women and writing, defense of, xxvii; Alós and, 29–30; Caro and, 87, 93; Cartagena and, 99, 101; Coronado and, 117; Gimeno and, 224, 225; León and, 258; María de San José and, 283; Martínez Sierra and, 302, 304; Roig and, 435; Romero and, 447; Rossetti and, 453, 457; Sáez and, 467; Sinués and, 477, 478, 480; Teresa de Jesús and, 490–91

Women and writing, image of woman as writer, xxix-xxx; Acuña and, 6, 8; Caballero and, 69; Castro and, 106, 110; Chacel and, 132; Figuera and, 185, 187, 188, 189; Fuertes and, 199, 201–2; Laforet and, 247; López de Córdova and, 268; Marcela de San Félix and, 275; Martínez Sierra and, 302; Martín Gaite and, 290, 291, 292; Matute and, 314, 315; Maura and, 321–22, 323, 326; Moix and, 342, 343, 344; Pardo Bazán and, 380; Puértolas and, 398; Rodoreda and, 418; Roig and, 431, 432, 434; Rodoreda and, 435; Rossetti and, 452, 456; Sáez and, 465; Sinués and, 474, 477; Teresa de Jesús, 490; Tusquets and, 500, 501

Women and writing, neglect of: Acuña and, 9; Amar and, 38; Arenal and, 50; Atencia and, 62; Caballero and, 71, 72; Caro and, 93, 94–95, 363; Castro and, 106, 110; Chacel and, 132, 134, 138; Champourcin and, 146; Coronado and, 122; de Burgos and, 150, 153; Diosdado and, 164; Falcón and, 174; Fuertes and, 199; León and, 261; Marcela de San Félix and, 276; Martínez Sierra and, 302, 303, 304; Maura and, 327, 328; Pàmies and, 375, 376; Pardo Bazán and, 385; Pedrero and, 393–94; Puértolas and, 402; Riera and, 411, 412; Sáez and, 466; Sinués and, 479

Women and writing, obstacles to, xvi, xviii, xix, xxvii, xxxi, 5, 312;

Champourcin and, 145; Coronado and, 116; Fuertes and, 198; Laforet and, 244, 247; Maura and, 327; Moix and, 339; Rodoreda and, 416; Sáez and, 460, 477–78

Women and writing, poeta/poetisa, xxxii; Castro and, 112; Coronado and, 122; Figuera and, 186, 190; Fuertes and, 203

Women and writing, private/public self, xxii, xxiii, xxiv, 467; Caballero and, 69; Català and, 17; Maura and, 322; Sinués and, 474, 480

Women and writing, silences, xxiv; Acuña and, 1; Amar and, 35; Atencia and, 55, 61; Castro and, 106; Català and, 14, 18; Champourcin and, 143; Laforet and, 244–45; Martínez Sierra and, 297, 302; Maura and, 327; Moix and, 338, 339, 343, 344, 346

Women and writing, societal criticism of, xxvii, 126; Acuña and, 2; Caro and, 87; Pardo Bazán and, 380

Women's periodicals, xx, xxvi, xxvii, 81; Acuña and, 6; Falcón and, 169, 170; Gimeno and, 220; Moix and, 338–39; Pardo Bazán and, 220, 380; Sáez and, 220, 461, 465; Sinués and, 473

Women's rights, xx, 66, 169; Acuña and, 2, 7, 9; Arenal and, 48, 49, 51; Castro and, 108; Falcón and, 168, 170, 171–72, 174, 175; Gimeno and, 223, 225; Martínez Sierra and, 297; Teresa de Jesús and, 488; Zayas and, 513

Women's suffrage, xx, 466; de Burgos and, 149, 153; Gimeno and, 222; Martínez Sierra and, 298; Nelken and, 360, 363; Sáez and, 468

Woolf, Virginia, 58, 80, 82, 135, 244, 339, 496

World Conference to Appraise the United Nations Decade for Women (1985, Nairobi), 170

World War I, 137

World War II, 186, 243, 247, 361

Wright, Eleanor, 181, 182, 183, 190

ABOUT THE EDITORS, CONTRIBUTORS, AND TRANSLATOR

LINDA GOULD LEVINE is Professor of Spanish at Montclair State College where she also teaches Women's Studies and has served as the Acting Director of the program. She is the author of *Juan Goytisolo: La destrucción creadora* (1976) and a critical edition of his *Reivindicación del Conde don Julián* (1985). She has written, with Gloria F. Waldman, *Feminismo ante el franquismo: Entrevistas con feministas de España* (1980), and she has published feminist criticism on contemporary women writers, among them Ana María Moix, Esther Tusquets, Carmen Martín Gaite, and Isabel Allende. She was visiting professor at Dartmouth College and serves on the editorial board of *Siglo XX/20th Century* and on the organizing committee for the Annual Conference on Spanish Women held at Madrid's International Institute.

ELLEN ENGELSON MARSON has taught at the State University of New York at Stony Brook and is Associate Professor of Spanish at John Jay College of Criminal Justice, at the City University of New York (CUNY). She was invited to serve on the Professional Staff Congress of CUNY Award Committee. She has published articles on contemporary Spanish poets, among them José Ángel Valente, Ana María Moix, and the "novísimos," and is the author of *Poesía y poética de José Ángel Valente* (1978). Her current work explores the relationship between gender consciousness and poetic expression in contemporary women poets from Spain.

GLORIA FEIMAN WALDMAN is Chair of the Foreign Languages department and Professor of Spanish at York College, at the City University of New York (CUNY), where she teaches Women's Studies and Latin American Studies. She is the author of *Luis Rafael Sánchez: Pasión teatral* (1988); coauthor with Linda

Gould Levine of *Feminismo ante el franquismo* (1980); coauthor with Elena Paz and Dolores Santos of *Teatro contemporáneo* (1983); and cotranslator with Ronald Christ of *Borges in/and/on Film* (1989). She is a Fulbright, NDEA, and NEH Grant Recipient. She was visiting professor at the University of Puerto Rico. She has completed an anthology on the presence of the Jew in the Argentine theater with Nora Glickman and is compiling a volume of the complete works of José (Papo) Márquez for the Institute of Puerto Rican Culture.

CONCHA ALBORG, Associate Professor at Saint Joseph's University in Philadelphia, was a Katharine E. McBride Visiting Scholar at Bryn Mawr College, 1989–90. She is the author of *Temas y técnicas en la narrativa de Jesús Fernández Santos* and has published articles on the contemporary Spanish novelists Rosa Montero, Elena Soriano, Eulalia Galvarriato, and José Luis Castillo-Puche. She is currently completing a book on five female novelists from Spain's postwar generation. Her short story "Al Club Náutico" appeared in *Letras Femeninas* (1991). She also edited *Caza menor* by Elena Soriano for the Biblioteca de Escritoras Españolas (1992).

ELECTA ARENAL, writer, playwright, and translator, teaches Spanish Literature and Feminist Critical Studies at the Graduate Center of City University of New York and at the College of Staten Island (CUNY). With Georgina Sabat-Rivers, she has written *Literatura conventual femenina: Sor Marcela de San Félix, hija de Lope de Vega* (1988), and with Stacey Schlau, *Untold Sisters: Hispanic Nuns in Their Own Works* (1989). With Amanda Powell, she has annotated, introduced, and edited an English language version of Sor Juana Inés de la Cruz's "Answer to Sister Philotea."

BETH WIETELMANN BAUER is currently Adjunct Assistant Professor of Hispanic Studies at Brown University. She has published articles on major nineteenth-century Spanish writers in journals such as *Hispanic Review*, *Bulletin of Hispanic Studies*, *Revista de Estudios Hispánicos*, *Modern Language Notes*, and *Anales Galdosianos*, and is now at work on a number of projects devoted to Spanish women writers and the literary representation of women.

MARYELLEN BIEDER is Associate Professor of Spanish at Indiana University. She is the author of articles on Emilia Pardo Bazán, Concepción Gimeno de Flaquer, and the Catalan writer Mercé Rodoreda. She studies narrative strategies, gender and genre boundaries, and the forging of a female literary tradition in Spain. Her current work explores the literary relations between Pardo Bazán and coetaneous women writers.

ALDA BLANCO teaches at the University of Wisconsin–Madison. She has published articles on women's autobiographical writing in early-twentieth-century Spain. Her critical edition of María Martínez Sierra's *Una mujer por caminos de España* (1989) has been published in Spain. She is the author of *The Good Woman as Writer: Fiction in Mid-Nineteenth Century Spain*.

JOAN LIPMAN BROWN is Professor of Spanish at the University of Delaware. She is the author of *Secrets from the Back Room: The Fiction of Carmen Martín Gaite* (1987) and the editor of *Women Writers of Contemporary Spain: Exiles in the Homeland* (1991).

NANCY L. BUNDY, Associate Professor of Spanish and French at Simpson College in Iowa, has published critical work on contemporary Spanish and Catalan women poets. She has also translated Ana Rossetti's poetry and has completed studies of the novelist Miguel Delibes and the poet Claudio Rodríguez.

ELEANORE MAXWELL DIAL is Associate Professor of Spanish in the Department of Foreign Languages and Literatures at Iowa State University. She has published articles on a number of Spanish exiles, including Carlota O'Neill, Isabel de Palencia, Constancia de la Mora, Alvaro Custodio, León Felipe, and Rafael Alberti, and has written on theater in Spain, Mexico, and Chile. Her articles and book reviews have appeared in *Celestinesca*, *Hispanófila*, *Hispania*, *Latin American Theatre Review*, *Romance Notes*, and other journals.

RUTH EL SAFFAR is a Research Professor of the Humanities at the University of Illinois–Chicago. Author of four books on Cervantes and editor of three collections of studies on Spanish literature of the Golden Age, she has also written widely on other areas of Spanish literature. Currently she is working on a study of cultural changes in Spain over the course of its ascension to a position of world power, taking particular note of the role of women as the empire grew in importance.

CRISTINA ENRÍQUEZ DE SALAMANCA is a doctoral candidate at the University of Minnesota, Minneapolis. With Kathleeen McNerney, she has edited *Double Minorities: A Bio-Bibliographical Guide to Women Writers from Catalunya, Galicia and the Basque Country* (1993) and is a member of the editorial board of Biblioteca de Escritoras Españolas. She has published on nineteenth-century women writers as a group as well as on individual authors: Faustina Sáez de Melgar, Cèlia Sunyol, and María de Zayas. Her doctoral thesis relates nineteenth-century female writing to the problematics of the private/public sphere.

JOHN P. GABRIELE, Associate Professor of Spanish and Comparative Literature at The College of Wooster, has published articles on Ramón del Valle-Inclán, Federico García Lorca, Pedro Salinas, Antonio Buero Vallejo, Manuel Martínez Mediero, Juan Rulfo, and others. He is also the editor of three collections of essays on Valle-Inclán, Antonio Machado, and the Generation of 1898.

KATHLEEN M. GLENN is Professor of Spanish at Wake Forest University. She is the author of two books on Azorín and has published articles on a number of contemporary Spanish novelists, including Carmen Laforet, Ana María Matute, Carmen Martín Gaite, Marina Mayoral, Mercè Rodoreda, and Esther Tusquets. She is coeditor of *Anales de la Literatura Española Contemporánea* and a member of the editorial board of *Letras Peninsulares*.

MARY S. GOSSY is Assistant Professor of Spanish and Comparative Literature at Rutgers University. She has written *The Untold Story: Women and Theory in Golden Age Texts* (1989) and is continuing research in theories of representation, pornography, and reader response.

ESTELLE IRIZARRY, Professor of Spanish at Georgetown University, has published more than twenty books and editions, among them *La broma literaria*, *Escritores-pintores españoles del siglo XX*, and critical studies of Francisco Ayala, Rafael Dieste, Enrique A. Laguerre, and E. F. Granell. She is the editor of *Hispania*, the journal of the Association of Teachers of Spanish and Portuguese, and has contributed to many journals and collections of criticism.

CATHERINE JAGOE, Assistant Professor of Spanish at Northern Illinois University, moved to the United States from England in 1988. She is the author of *Gender in the Novels of Galdós. 1870–1915*, as well as of various essays of feminist criticism, including ''The Subversive Angel in *Fortunata y Jacinta*'' (*Anales Galdosianos*), ''Krausism and the Pygmalion Motif in Galdós's *La familia de León Roch*'' (*Romance Quarterly*), and ''*Gloria*: A Revision'' (*Crítica Hispánica*). She is currently coediting a documentary account of nineteenth-century ideas about women in Spain.

YVONNE JEHENSON is Associate Professor of Foreign Languages and English at the State University of New York at Oswego. Among her publications are a book on the pastoral in the English, French, and Spanish Renaissance and articles on feminist and contemporary literary theory. She is currently completing a book on Latin American women authors.

ROBERTA JOHNSON, Professor of Spanish and department chairperson at the University of Kansas, has published books on Carmen Laforet and Gabriel Miró and articles on twentieth-century Spanish fiction in numerous professional journals. Her most recent book is *Crossfire: Philosophy and the Novel in Spain (1900–1934)* (1993). She has been a Fulbright Professor in Spain, a member of the MLA Twentieth-Century Spanish Division Committee and the MLA Delegate

Assembly, and currently serves on the PMLA Advisory Committee. She also sits on the editorial boards of *Letras Femeninas* and *Siglo XX/Twentieth Century*.

AMY KAMINSKY is Associate Professor of Women's Studies at the University of Minnesota and Archivist of Feministas Unidas. She is a feminist critic who has written many articles on Spanish and Latin American literature. Her most recent project is *Flores del Agua/Waterlilies: Anthology of Spanish Women Writers (1400–1900)*, a bilingual anthology of Spanish women writers before the twentieth century.

SUSAN KIRKPATRICK, currently Professor of Spanish and Comparative Literature at the University of California, San Diego, has published *Larra: El laberinto inextricable de un romántico liberal* (1977) and *Las Románticas: Women Writers and Subjectivity in Spain, 1835–1850* (1989) as well as articles on Mariano Larra, Ramón del Valle-Inclán, Fernán Caballero, Benito Pérez Galdós, and Rosalía de Castro.

IRIDE LAMARTINA-LENS teaches language, literature, and film courses in Spanish and Italian at Pace University in New York. She has published several articles on contemporary theater, focusing on theater written by women.

JOY B. LANDEIRA teaches in the Department of Spanish and Portuguese at the University of Colorado, Boulder. A personal friend of Ernestina de Champourcin, she has interviewed her on several occasions and is currently writing a book on Champourcin's life and works. Among her other interests, Landeira writes poetry in Spanish: Her first book, *Poex* is in press.

MYRSA LANDRÓN won the Samuel R. Quiñones Award from the Academia Puertorriqueña de la Lengua Española for her part in the Spanish translation of Gloria F. Waldman's *Luis Rafael Sánchez: Pasión teatral* (1988). She has translated literary, scientific, and legal documents for major Puerto Rican newspapers (*El Nuevo Día*), journals (*Cuadernos*), and organizations (the Caribbean Project for Justice and Peace). She was Associate Editor of the literary magazine *Sargasso* (University of Puerto Rico).

SHIRLEY MANGINI is Chair and Professor of Spanish and Associate Dean of Humanities at California State University, Long Branch. Author of *Rojos y rebeldes. La cultura de la disidencia durante el franquismo*, she has also published extensively on Jaime Gil de Biedma, Rosa Chacel, and other contemporary authors. At present she is completing a book on the autobiographies and testimonies of female activists from the Spanish Civil War.

MARTHA J. MANIER, Associate Professor of Spanish at Humboldt State University in California, has published on Fernán Caballero and is currently completing two manuscripts on the same author.

KATHLEEN N. MARCH, Professor of Spanish at the University of Maine, founded the Galician Studies Association in 1985. She edited *Festa da palabra: An Anthology of Contemporary Galician Women Poets* (1989) and *Homenaxe a Ramón Martínez López* (1990). She is the translator of *Así vai o conto: A Bilingual Anthology of Contemporary Galician Short Stories* (1991). She has written articles on Latin American, Spanish, and Galician authors and has published *De musa a literata: El feminismo en la prosa de Rosalía de Castro* (1993). She is working on English translations of Castro's novels and a book on the avant-garde movements in Galicia.

BARBARA DALE MAY is Associate Professor of Romance Languages at the University of Oregon and an affiliate of the Center for the Study of Women in Society. She has published articles in *Cuadernos Hispanoamericanos*, *Estudios Ibero-Americanos*, *Letras Femeninas*, *Hispania*, and other journals, and she is the author of *El dilema de la nostalgia en la poesía de Rafael Alberti* (1978).

GERALDINE CLEARY NICHOLS is Professor of Spanish at the University of Florida. Her book *Escribir, espacio propio* . . . contains interviews of six Spanish women writers. Her most recent publication, a book of essays, is *Des/cifrar la diferencia: Narrativa femenina de la España contemporánea* (1992). Increasingly interested in the theoretical implications for narrative of the intersection of gender and ethnic identity, she has undertaken a long-term research project on women's fiction in Catalonia, studying authors who write in Castilian as well as those who write in Catalan.

PATRICIA W. O'CONNOR, Professor of Spanish at the University of Cincinnati, is editor of *Estreno*, a scholarly journal devoted to twentieth-century Spanish theater. She has contributed numerous articles to journals, anthologies, and literary reference works. She also has written several books and edited others on contemporary Spanish theater, among them *Dramaturgas españolas de hoy*. In 1982 she won the Rieveschl Award for Scholarly Work. In 1990 she was elected to the Royal Spanish Academy (foreign division) and named Distinguished Research Professor at the University of Cincinnati.

ADA ORTÚZAR-YOUNG is Professor of Spanish and Chair of the Spanish Department at Drew University. She is the author of *Tres representaciones literarias de la vida política cubana* and is currently working on a book about Hispanics in the United States. She publishes and presents papers at conferences on contemporary women from the Hispanic world.

ANNE M. PASERO is Associate Professor of Spanish at Marquette University in Milwaukee. Her fields of research include Golden Age poetry and theater and twentieth-century Spanish poetry. Her recent projects include work on contemporary Spanish women poets and translations of contemporary Latin American women poets. During a three-year stay in Madrid (1982–85) as Resident Director of Marquette's program, she interviewed numerous women poets.

JANET PÉREZ is Associate Dean of the Graduate School at Texas Tech University. Her seven books include three on women: *Ana María Matute* (1971), *Novelistas femeninas de la postguerra española* (ed., 1983) and *Women Writers of Contemporary Spain* (1988). She has edited or coedited some one hundred volumes in the Twayne World Authors Series, and is the author of more than one hundred articles and chapters in books.

MARGERY RESNICK taught for six years at Yale University, then went to MIT as Chair of Foreign Languages and Literatures and is currently teaching there. She was active in establishing Women's Studies programs at both institutions and continues to divide her teaching and research between Spanish and Women's Studies. Her most recent book, edited with Isabelle de Courtivron, is *Women Writers in Translation: An Annotated Bibliography*. She chairs an annual colloquium on Spanish women at the International Institute in Madrid.

MARÍA CARMEN RIDDEL, Associate Professor of Spanish Language and Literature at Marshall University in Huntington, West Virginia, researches and writes on feminine fiction in Spain, and has presented papers at national conferences on the works of Elena Fortún, Carmen Martín Gaite, Ana María Matute, and Elena Quiroga.

STACEY SCHLAU directs the Women's Studies Program and teaches Women's Studies, Spanish, and Hispanic literatures at West Chester University in Pennsylvania. She has published articles on Hispanic women narratists from the seventeenth through the twentieth centuries, and with Electa Arenal she wrote *Untold Sisters: Hispanic Nuns in Their Own Works* (1989). She has served as president of Feministas Unidas (MLA).

THERESA ANN SEARS, Associate Professor of Spanish in the Department of Foreign Languages and Classics at the University of Maine, Orono, has published articles on *El Caballero Cifar*, *Tirante el Blanco*, and the *Cárcel de amor*, as well as on nineteenth- and twentieth-century Spanish and Spanish American literature.

MIRELLA SERVODIDIO is Professor of Spanish at Barnard College. She is the author of *Azorín, escritor de cuentos* and *The Quest for Harmony: The Dialects of Communication in the Poetry of Eugenio Florit* and editor with Marcia Welles of *From Fiction to Metafiction: Essays in Honor of Carmen Martín Gaite* (1983). She is also the editor of four other volumes, among them *Reading for Difference: Feminist Perspectives on Women Novelists of Contemporary Spain*. She has published articles on Pío Baroja, Ramón del Valle-Inclán, Azorín, Julio

Cortázar, Carmen Laforet, Carmen Martín Gaite, and Esther Tusquets and serves on the editorial board of *Siglo XX/20th Century*, *ALEC*, and *Revista Hispánica Moderna*.

MARÍA DEL CARMEN SIMÓN PALMER is a researcher for the Consejo Superior de Investigaciones Científicas in Madrid. She presently directs the "Información Bibliográfica" section of the *Revista de Literatura*. She is the author of several books, the latest of which is *Escritoras españolas del siglo XIX. Manual bio-bibliográfico* (1991).

TERESA S. SOUFAS is Associate Professor of Spanish at Tulane University. In addition to her book *Melancholy and the Secular Mind in Spanish Golden Age Literature* (1990), she has written numerous articles on seventeenth-century Spanish drama, poetry, and prose, including studies of works by women authors such as Ana Caro, María de Zayas, and Leonor de la Cueva.

ELIZABETH STARČEVIĆ is Professor of Spanish at City College at the City University of New York (CUNY). She has published articles on women writers from Spain, Latin America, and the Caribbean, and is the author of *Carmen de Burgos, defensora de la mujer* (1976). She was president of Feministas Unidas, an allied organization of the Modern Language Association. She also served as president of the CUNY Council on Foreign Language Study. Her current focus is on Latina women writers in the United States.

CONSTANCE A. SULLIVAN is Associate Professor of Spanish Literature and Culture at the University of Minnesota (Twin Cities). She has published articles on contemporary Spanish literature, traditional Spanish proverbs, Spanish literary historiography, feminist criticism, and eighteenth-century women writers of Spain. She is preparing a book-length biography of Josefa Amar y Borbón and an English translation of that author's "Defensa del talento de las mugeres."

RONALD E. SURTZ is Professor of Spanish at Princeton University. He is the author of *Teatro medieval castellano* (1983), an anthology of medieval Castilian plays, and *The Guitar of God: Gender, Power, and Authority in the Visionary World of Mother Juana de la Cruz* (1990), a study of the visions of a sixteenth-century Spanish nun. He is currently writing a book on early Spanish female writers and visionaries, "The Mothers of Saint Teresa of Avila."

MARY JANE TREACY, Associate Professor of Spanish at Simmons College in Massachusetts, is interested in contemporary women's writing, particularly that of Latin American and U.S. Hispanic authors. She is currently studying how Latin American women writers conceptualize the place of women in national political struggles. She has written on Isabel Allende, Marta Traba, Alicia Partnoy, and the many guerrillas whose lives have been recorded in interviews, biographies, and memory.

SHARON KEEFE UGALDE, Professor of Spanish at Southwest Texas State University, is the author of *Gabriel Celaya* (1978), *Conversaciones y poemas. La nueva poesía femenina española* (1991), and numerous articles on postwar Spanish poetry and on Latin American dictator novels. She spent 1988 in Madrid with a U.S.–Spain Joint Committee Fellowship studying contemporary women poets of Spain.

TERESA M. VILARÓS is Assistant Professor of Spanish at the University of Wisconsin–Madison. Interested in feminist criticism and psychoanalysis, she has published articles on twentieth-century Spanish women writers, including Rosa Chacel, Clementina Arderiu, and María Jaén. At present she is working on a study of erotic literature written by women in Spain. She is also completing a book on three of Benito Pérez Galdós's novels from a feminist psychoanalytic perspective.

NANCY VOSBURG, Assistant Professor of Spanish at Stetson University in Florida, is at present working on a book-length manuscript exploring multiple states of exile in relation to Spanish women writers of the post–Civil War period, and is coediting a collection of new critical essays on Rodoreda's works.

ALISON WEBER, Associate Professor of Spanish at the University of Virginia, is the author of *Teresa of Avila and the Rhetoric of Femininity* (1990). She is also the editor of *Feminist Topics*, a special number of the *Journal of Hispanic Philology* (Spring 1989). A specialist in Spanish Golden Age literature, she is currently at work on a book on women and religion in sixteenth-century Spain.

MARCIA L. WELLES is Professor of Spanish at Barnard College. She is author of *Style and Structure in Gracián's "El Criticón"* (1976) and *Arachne's Tapestry: The Transformation of Myth in Seventeenth-Century Spain* (1986). With Mirella Servodidio she has edited a volume of essays on Carmen Martín Gaite, *From Fiction to Metafiction: Essays in Honor of Carmen Martín Gaite* (1983).

JOHN C. WILCOX is Associate Professor of Spanish and acting chair of the department of Spanish, Italian, and Portuguese at the University of Illinois at Urbana-Champaign. He has published *Self and Image in Juan Ramón Jiménez (Modern and Postmodern readings)* (1987), and with Salvador J. Fajardo he has edited *At Home and Beyond: New Essays on Spanish Poets of the Twenties* (1983) and *After the War: Essays on Recent Spanish Poetry* (1988). The author of numerous articles on twentieth-century Spanish poets, he is now at work on a study of Spain's women poets.

PHYLLIS ZATLIN is Professor of Spanish at Rutgers University. Her areas of specialization are contemporary Spanish theater, contemporary Spanish writers, and translation studies. Her publications include three books in the Twayne World Authors Series, several editions of Spanish plays, and numerous scholarly articles. She is the associate editor of *Estreno*.